CompTIA® Security+

Guide to Network Security Fundamentals

Mark Ciampa, Ph.D.

Eighth Edition

Information Security

Australia • Brazil • Canada • Mexico • Singapore • United Kingdom • United States

CompTIA Security+ Guide to Network Security Fundamentals, **Eighth Edition**
Mark Ciampa

SVP, Product: Cheryl Costantini

VP, Product: Thais Alencar

Senior Product Director, Portfolio Product Management: Mark Santee

Director, Product Management: Rita Lombard

Portfolio Product Manager: Natalie Onderdonk

Product Assistant: Anh Nguyen

Learning Designer: Carolyn Mako

Senior Content Manager: Brooke Greenhouse

Digital Project Manager: Jim Vaughey

Technical Editor: Danielle Shaw

Developmental Editor: Lisa Ruffolo

VP, Product Marketing: Jason Sakos

Director, Product Marketing: Danae April

Product Marketing Manager: Mackenzie Paine

Portfolio Specialist: Matt Schiesl

Content Acquisition Analyst: Callum Panno

Production Service: Straive

Senior Designer: Erin Griffin

Cover Image Source: shuoshu/DigitalVision Vectors/Getty Images

For product information and technology assistance, contact us at **Cengage Customer & Sales Support, 1-800-354-9706 or support.cengage.com.**

For permission to use material from this text or product, submit all requests online at **www.copyright.com.**

Library of Congress Control Number: 2023916394

ISBN: 979-8-21-400063-3
Looseleaf: ISBN: 979-8-21-400064-0

Cengage
5191 Natorp Boulevard
Mason, OH 45040
USA

Cengage is a leading provider of customized learning solutions. Our employees reside in nearly 40 different countries and serve digital learners in 165 countries around the world. Find your local representative at **www.cengage.com.**

To learn more about Cengage platforms and services, register or access your online learning solution, or purchase materials for your course, visit **www.cengage.com.**

Notice to the Reader

Publisher does not warrant or guarantee any of the products described herein or perform any independent analysis in connection with any of the product information contained herein. Publisher does not assume, and expressly disclaims, any obligation to obtain and include information other than that provided to it by the manufacturer. The reader is expressly warned to consider and adopt all safety precautions that might be indicated by the activities described herein and to avoid all potential hazards. By following the instructions contained herein, the reader willingly assumes all risks in connection with such instructions. The publisher makes no representations or warranties of any kind, including but not limited to, the warranties of fitness for particular purpose or merchantability, nor are any such representations implied with respect to the material set forth herein, and the publisher takes no responsibility with respect to such material. The publisher shall not be liable for any special, consequential, or exemplary damages resulting, in whole or part, from the readers' use of, or reliance upon, this material.

Printed at CLDPC, USA, 08-24

Brief Contents

Table of Contents

Part 2

Cryptography 67

Module 3

Fundamentals of Cryptography 68

Module 4

Advanced Cryptography 102

Part 3

Device Security 139

Module 5

Endpoint Vulnerabilities, Attacks, and Defenses 140

Module 10

Wireless Network Attacks and Defenses 325

Module 11

Cloud and Virtualization Security 363

Part 5

Operations and Management 395

Module 12

Vulnerability Management 396

Introduction

Astronomical, enormous, humongous—these are all words to describe the impact and scope of cyberattacks today. A security operations center at a port authority reports that they receive 40 million attempted cyberattacks each *month*. The total number of instances of malware has grown from 182 million in 2013 to over 1.34 billion today. Cybercrime has been called the "greatest transfer of economic wealth in history," and it is estimated that it could reach $10.5 trillion *annually* by 2025. And the recent introduction of artificial intelligence (AI) tools has only heightened cybersecurity attacks. A 135 percent increase in phishing and spam emails has been directly linked to AI. Two security researchers used an AI tool to win a "hack-a-thon" contest, earning them a prize of $123,000. The extent to which AI tools will assist attackers to launch hard-to-detect attacks is frightening.

The need to identify and defend against around-the-clock cyberattacks that target all businesses large and small has created an essential workforce that is now at the very core of the information technology (IT) industry. Known as information security, these professionals are focused on protecting electronic information. The demand for these certified professionals in information security has never been higher. However, a large gap remains. Although the global cybersecurity workforce grew to 4.7 million workers in 2021, reaching its highest-ever levels, there is still a need for more than *3.4 million* security professionals, an increase of over 26 percent from the prior year.

When filling cybersecurity positions, an overwhelming majority of enterprises use the Computing Technology Industry Association (CompTIA) Security+ certification to verify security competency. Of the hundreds of security certifications currently available, Security+ is one of the most widely acclaimed security certifications. Because it is internationally recognized as validating a foundation level of security skills and knowledge, the Security+ certification has become the foundation for today's IT security professionals. The value for an IT professional who holds a CompTIA security certification is significant. On average, an employee with a CompTIA certification commands a salary between 5 and 15 percent higher than their counterparts with similar qualifications but lacking a certification.

The CompTIA Security+ certification is a vendor-neutral credential that requires passing the current certification exam SY0-701. A successful candidate has the knowledge and skills required to identify attacks, threats, and vulnerabilities; design a strong security architecture; implement security controls; be knowledgeable of security operations and incident response; and be well versed in governance, risk, and compliance requirements.

Certification provides job applicants with more than just a competitive edge over their noncertified counterparts competing for the same IT positions. Some institutions of higher education grant college credit to students who successfully pass certification exams, moving them further along in their degree programs. For those already employed, achieving a new certification increases job effectiveness, which opens doors for advancement and job security. Certification also gives individuals who are interested in careers in the military the ability to move into higher positions more quickly.

CompTIA® Security+ Guide to Network Security Fundamentals, Eighth Edition, is intended to equip learners with the knowledge and skills needed to be information security IT professionals. Yet it is more than an "exam prep" book. While teaching the fundamentals of information security by using the CompTIA Security+ exam objectives as its framework, the book takes a comprehensive view of security by examining in depth today's attacks against networks and endpoints and what is needed to defend against these attacks. This book is a valuable tool for those who want to learn about information security and enter the field. It also provides the foundation that will help prepare for the CompTIA Security+ certification exam. For more information on CompTIA Security+ certification, visit CompTIA's website at comptia.org.

Intended Audience

This book is designed to meet the needs of students and professionals who want to master basic information security. A fundamental knowledge of computers and networks is all that is required to use this book. Those seeking to pass the CompTIA Security+ certification exam will find the text's approach and content especially helpful; all Security+ SY0-71 exam objectives are covered in the text (see Appendix A). *Security+ Guide to Network Security Fundamentals, Eighth Edition*, covers all aspects of network and computer security while satisfying the Security+ objectives.

The book's pedagogical features are designed to provide a truly interactive learning experience to help prepare you for the challenges of network and computer security. In addition to the information presented in the text, each module includes Hands-On Projects that guide you through implementing practical hardware, software, network, and Internet security configurations step by step. Each module also contains case studies that place you in the role of problem solver, requiring you to apply concepts presented in the module to achieve successful solutions.

Module Descriptions

The following list summarizes the topics covered in each module of this course:

Module 1: Introduction to Information Security introduces the cybersecurity fundamentals that form the basis of the Security+ certification. The module begins by defining information security and identifying attackers. It also looks at how attacks occur and various information security resources.

Module 2: Pervasive Attack Surfaces and Controls looks at three topics—social engineering, physical security, and data controls—considered as "pervasive" since they apply universally across IT security.

Module 3: Fundamentals of Cryptography explores what cryptography is and how it is used along with cryptographic limitations and attacks on cryptography.

Module 4: Advanced Cryptography looks at the advanced features of cryptography, such as authentication and distribution of public keys through digital certificates, the management of keys through public key infrastructure, and different secure communication and transport protocols.

Module 5: Endpoint Vulnerabilities, Attacks, and Defenses examines vulnerabilities in applications and malware attacks on endpoints along with the defense measures that can be taken to mitigate these attacks.

Module 6: Mobile and Embedded Device Security explores mobile, embedded, and specialized device security by looking at securing mobile devices and Internet of Things devices along with how application software that runs on these and other devices can be securely designed and coded.

Module 7: Identity and Access Management (IAM) looks at how devices can be accessed by authorized users and restricting what users can do on the devices. It examines the different types of authentication credentials that can be used to verify a user's identity, best practices for authentication, and how to limit privileges through access controls.

Module 8: Infrastructure Threats and Security Monitoring begins a study of attacks and defenses of enterprise-level infrastructures and architectures by exploring common attacks that are launched against networks and tools for monitoring network security, and raising alerts when that security is compromised.

Module 9: Infrastructure Security investigates how to build a secure infrastructure through network security appliances and security software, network design, and access technologies.

Module 10: Wireless Network Attacks and Defenses explores wireless network security. It examines the attacks on wireless devices that are common today, then explores vulnerabilities in wireless security, and finally examines several secure wireless protections.

Module 11: Cloud and Virtualization Security looks at cloud computing and virtualization: what these technologies are, how they function, and how they can be secured.

Module 12: Vulnerability Management examines the security vulnerability management process by looking at running a vulnerability scan and how to address the results along with different types of audits and assessments, particularly penetration testing.

Module 13: Incident Preparation and Investigation focuses on the plans that must be made for when a cyber incident occurs. These plans cover incident preparation, building resilience through redundancy, and follow-up investigations as to how an incident occurred and how similar future events can be mitigated.

Module 14: Oversight and Operations explores administration principles such as governance and compliance and also looks at security operations: automation, orchestration, and threat hunting. It also examines the impact of AI on information security.

Module 15: Information Security Management examines five key information security management processes: asset management, risk management, third-party risk management, change management, and awareness management.

Appendix A: CompTIA SY0-701 Certification Examination Objectives provides a complete listing of the latest CompTIA Security+ certification exam objectives and shows the modules and headings in the modules that cover material associated with each objective, as well as the Bloom's Taxonomy level of that coverage.

Features

The course's pedagogical features are designed to provide a truly interactive learning experience and prepare you to face the challenges of cybersecurity. To aid you in fully understanding computer and network security, this course includes many features designed to enhance your learning experience.

- **Maps to CompTIA Objectives.** The material in this text covers all the CompTIA Security+ SY0-701 exam objectives.
- **Module Objectives.** Each module lists the concepts to master within that module. This list serves as a quick reference to the module's contents and as a useful study aid.
- **#TrendingCyber.** This section opens each module and provides an explanation and analysis of some of the latest attacks and defenses related to topics that are covered in the module. The sections establish a real-world context for understanding information security.
- **Illustrations, Tables, and Bulleted Lists.** Numerous full-color diagrams illustrating abstract ideas and screenshots of cybersecurity tools help learners better visualize the concepts of cybersecurity. In addition, the many tables and bulleted lists provide details and comparisons of both practical and theoretical information that can be easily reviewed and referenced in the future.
- **Summary.** Each module reading concludes with a summary of the concepts introduced in that module. These summaries revisit the ideas covered in each module.
- **Key Terms.** All of the terms in each module that were introduced with blue text are gathered in a Key Terms list, providing additional review and highlighting key concepts. Key term definitions are included in the Glossary at the end of the text.
- **Review Questions.** The end-of-module assessment begins with a set of review questions that reinforce the ideas introduced in each module. These questions help you evaluate and apply the material you have learned. Answering these questions will ensure that you have mastered the important concepts and provide valuable practice for taking CompTIA's Security+ exam.
- **Hands-On Projects.** Projects at the end of each module give you the opportunity to apply in practice what you have just learned. These projects include detailed step-by-step instructions to walk you through endpoint security configuration settings and demonstrate actual security defenses using websites or software downloaded from the Internet. In addition, instructions are provided regarding how to perform these projects in a protected sandbox environment so that the underlying computer is not impacted.
- **Case Projects.** Although it is important to understand the theory behind information security technology, nothing beats real-world experience. To this end, each module includes several case projects aimed at providing practical implementation experience as well as practice in applying critical thinking skills to reinforce the concepts learned throughout the module.

New to This Edition

- Maps fully to the latest CompTIA Security+ exam SY0-701
- Completely revised and updated with expanded coverage on attacks and defenses
- New module units: Security Foundations, Cryptography, Device Security, Infrastructure and Architectures, and Operations and Management
- All new "#TrendingCyber" opener in each module

- All new Two Rights & a Wrong self-assessments that give you opportunities to quickly assess your understanding of the topics
- All new live virtual machine labs that help you refine the hands-on skills needed to master today's cybersecurity toolset
- New and updated Hands-On Projects cover some of the latest security software
- Expanded and new Case Projects that provide opportunities to explore topics in greater depth
- All new introductions to the Hands-On Projects and Case Projects provide time estimates, objectives, and project descriptions
- New cybersecurity consultant and assurance service scenarios in which you serve as an intern and gain practical experience regarding what you might encounter on the job
- All SY0-701 exam topics fully defined
- Linking of each exam subdomain to Bloom's Taxonomy (see Appendix A)

Text and Graphic Conventions

Wherever appropriate, additional information and exercises have been added to this book to help you better understand the topic at hand. Icons throughout the text alert you to additional materials. The following icons and elements are used in this textbook:

Note 1

Numbered Note elements draw your attention to additional helpful material related to the subject being described.

Caution !

The Caution icons warn you about potential mistakes or problems and explain how to avoid them.

Two Rights & A Wrong

The "Two Rights & a Wrong" elements let you quickly assess your understanding of the topics. The answers to these assessments appear at the end of each module.

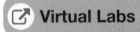 **Virtual Labs**   The VM Lab icons alert you to live, virtual machine labs that reinforce the material in each module.

Certification

Certification icons indicate CompTIA Security+ objectives covered under major module headings.

Instructor's Materials

Instructors, please visit cengage.com and sign in to access instructor-specific resources, which include the Instructor's Manual, Solution and Answer Guide, Instructor Test Banks, and PowerPoint presentations.

- **Instructor's Manual.** The Instructor's Manual that accompanies this text provides additional instructional material to assist in class preparation, including suggestions for discussion topics and additional projects.
- **Solution and Answer Guide.** The instructor's resources include solutions to all end-of-module material, including review questions, hands-on projects, and case projects.
- **Cengage Testing Powered by Cognero.** This flexible, online system allows you to do the following:
  - Author, edit, and manage test bank content from multiple Cengage solutions.
  - Create multiple test versions in an instant.
  - Deliver tests from your learning management system, your classroom, or wherever you want.
- **PowerPoint Presentations.** This course comes with Microsoft PowerPoint slides for each module. These slides are meant to be used as a teaching aid for classroom presentations, to make available to students on the network for module review, or to be printed for classroom distribution. Instructors can add their own slides for additional topics introduced to the class.

MindTap

MindTap for *Security+ Guide to Network Security Fundamentals, Eighth Edition*, is an online learning solution designed to help you master the skills needed in today's workforce. Research shows that employers need critical thinkers, troubleshooters, and creative problem-solvers to stay relevant in our fast-paced, technology-driven world. MindTap helps you achieve this with assignments and activities that provide hands-on practice, real-life relevance, and proficiency in difficult concepts. Students are guided through assignments that progress from basic knowledge and understanding to more challenging problems. MindTap activities and assignments are tied to learning objectives. MindTap features include the following:

Live Virtual Machine Labs allow you to practice, explore, and try different solutions in a safe sandbox environment. Each module provides you with an opportunity to complete an in-depth project hosted in a live virtual machine environment. You implement the skills and knowledge gained in the module through real design and configuration scenarios.

Simulations allow you to apply concepts covered in the module in a step-by-step virtual environment. The simulations provide immediate feedback.

Security for Life assignments encourage you to stay current with what is happening in the field of cybersecurity.

Reflection activities encourage classroom and online discussion of key topics covered in the modules.

Pre- and Post-Assessments assess your understanding of key concepts at the beginning and end of the course and emulate the text.

Lab Manual contains hands-on exercises that use fundamental networking security concepts as they are applied in the real world. Each module lab manual offers review questions to reinforce your proficiency in network security topics and to sharpen your critical thinking and problem-solving skills.

For instructors, MindTap is designed around learning objectives and provides analytics and reporting so you can easily see where the class stands in terms of progress, engagement, and completion rates. Use the content and learning path as is or pick and choose how your materials will integrate with the learning path. You control what the students see and when they see it. Learn more at www.cengage.com/mindtap/.

Instant Access Code: (9798214000664)

Printed Access Code: (9798214000671)

Figure A   Bloom's taxonomy

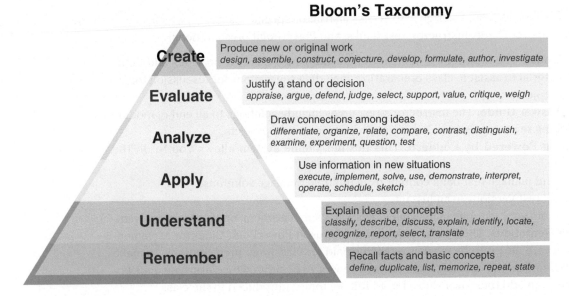

What's New with CompTIA Security+ Certification

The CompTIA Security+ SY0-701 exam was updated in November 2023. Several significant changes have been made to the exam objectives. The exam objectives have been expanded to reflect current security issues and knowledge requirements more accurately. These exam objectives place importance on knowing "how to" rather than just knowing or recognizing security concepts.

Here are the domains covered on the new Security+ exam:

Domain	% of Examination
1.0 General Security Concepts	12%
2.0 Threats, Vulnerabilities, and Mitigations	22%
3.0 Security Architecture	18%
4.0 Security Operations	28%
5.0 Security Program Management and Oversight	20%
Total	100%

CompTIA.

Your Next Move Starts Here!

Get CompTIA certified to help achieve your career goals and gain a powerful, vendor-neutral credential that is trusted by employers.

Why get CompTIA certified?

Increase your confidence
91% of certification earners show increased confidence.*

Earn more money
77% of IT pros got a raise within six months of earning their certification.*

Stand out to employers
64% of IT decision makers say certified employers add additional value.**

Join a global community
92% of IT professionals hold at least one certification.**

Get ready for exam day.

• **Download the exam objectives:** Visit CompTIA.org to find the exam objectives for your IT certification and print them out. This is your roadmap!

• **Create your study plan:** Decide how many hours each week you are going to dedicate to studying, choose your preferred study tools and get to work. Studying is a unique experience. Download a study plan worksheet on CompTIA.org.

• **Get certified:** If you haven't already, use the coupon on this page when you purchase your exam voucher and schedule your exam. CompTIA offers flexible testing options to fit your busy life.

Choose your testing option.

Online testing
Earn a CompTIA certification online, from your home – or any quiet, distraction-free, secure location – at a time that's convenient for you.

In-person testing
Test at any of the Pearson VUE test centers around the world, where you can use their equipment under the supervision of a proctor.

To purchase your exam voucher and learn how to prepare for exam day, visit CompTIA.org.

*Pearson VUE 2021 Value of IT Certifications
**2021 Global Knowledge IT Skills and Salary Report

About the Author

Dr. Mark Ciampa is Professor of Analytics and Information Systems and Program Director of the graduate Cyberse-curity Data Analytics program in the Gordon Ford College of Business at Western Kentucky University in Bowling Green, Kentucky. Prior to this, he was an associate professor and served as the Director of Academic Computing at Volunteer State Community College in Gallatin, Tennessee, for 20 years. Dr. Ciampa has worked in the IT industry as a computer consultant for businesses, government agencies, and educational institutions. He has published over 25 articles in peer-reviewed journals and books. He is also the author of over 30 technology textbooks from Cengage, including *CompTIA CySA+ Guide to Cybersecurity Analyst, Second Edition, CWNA Guide to Wireless LANs, Third Edition, Guide to Wireless Communications, Security Awareness: Applying Practical Cybersecurity in Your World, Sixth Edition,* and *Networking BASICS.* Dr. Ciampa holds a PhD in technology management with a specialization in digital communication systems from Indiana State University and has certifications in security and healthcare.

Acknowledgments

A large team of dedicated professionals all contributed to this project, and I am honored to be part of such an outstanding group. First, thanks go to Cengage Portfolio Product Manager Natalie Onderdonk for providing me with the opportunity to work on this project and for providing continual support. Thanks also to Senior Content Manager Brooke Greenhouse for answering all my questions, to Learning Designer Carolyn Mako for her helpful suggestions, and to Danielle Shaw for her technical reviews. And special recognition goes to developmental editor Lisa Ruffolo. From beginning to end Lisa was there to manage the details, provide me with innumerable helpful suggestions, and coordinate all the different activities so that I could focus on my work. It is truly a great pleasure to work with Lisa. I also appreciated the significant contributions of the reviewers for this edition: Bess Ann Gonyea, Ivy Tech Commu-nity College; Willis Holmes, Hopkins County Schools; and Dr. Seon A. Levius, State University of New York at Potsdam. To everyone on this team and at Cengage Learning, I extend my sincere thanks.

Finally, I want to thank my wonderful wife, Susan. Her continual patience, support, and love were always a great encouragement to me. I could not have done this project without her.

Dedication

To Braden, Mia, Abby, Gabe, Cora, Will, and Rowan

Before You Begin

This book should be read in sequence, from beginning to end. Each module builds on those that precede it to provide a solid understanding of networking security fundamentals. The book may also be used to prepare for CompTIA's Security+ certification exam. Appendix A pinpoints the modules and sections in which specific Security+ exam objectives are covered.

Hardware and Software Requirements

Following are the hardware and software requirements needed to perform the end-of-module Hands-On Projects.

- Microsoft Windows 11
- An Internet connection and web browser
- Microsoft Office

Free, Downloadable Software Requirements

Free, downloadable software is required for the Hands-On Projects in the following modules.

Module 3:
- OpenPuff Steganography
- 7-Zip

Module 4:
- Microsoft Root Certificates

Module 5:
- Microsoft Safety Scanner
- Refog Keylogger

Module 6:
- NoxPlayer

Module 7:
- KeePass

Module 8:
- Technitium MAC address changer

Module 9:
- GlassWire
- ProtonVPN

Module 10:
- WifiInfoView
- Vistumbler

Module 11:
- VirtualBox

Module 13:
- Directory Snoop

Module 14:
- Browzar

Part 1
Security Foundations

Unrelenting, unyielding, and *unstoppable* are the three words that may best describe today's cyberattacks. Everyone, ranging from a single user with a simple handheld device to massive multinational corporations with millions of employees, are all targets of attacks—and these attacks show no end in sight. The modules in Part 1 lay the foundations of information security by explaining what information security is, who is responsible for these attacks, and how they are being carried out.

Module 1
Introduction to Information Security

Module 2
Pervasive Attack Surfaces and Controls

Introduction to Information Security

Module Objectives

After completing this module, you should be able to do the following:

1   Define information security and explain its principles

2   Identify threat actors and their motivations

3   Describe how attacks occur and the impact of attacks

4   List various information security resources

#TrendingCyber

A commonly held perception is that successful "hackers" will rarely face lengthy jail time or financial penalties if caught. Instead, they are offered lucrative careers in cybersecurity to protect the very systems that they once breached. However, this perception is false. As more attackers are caught and complete their prison sentences, they are finding it very difficult to land a job in cybersecurity or other technology fields.

Individuals convicted of certain crimes cannot always have the same privileges they once enjoyed prior to their arrest. In many states, convicted felons are not immediately eligible to vote in elections. Most states have other restrictions that impact people's employment once they are paroled from prison. For example, a former inmate who becomes a journalist may need additional approvals to ride along with police while researching a story, or they may not qualify for expedited screening like other journalists to enter a courthouse to cover a trial.

In a similar way, convicted cyberattackers in the United States and many European countries usually face restrictions on their use of computers and access to the Internet once they have served their sentence. The stated purpose of these restrictions is to prevent them from being in a position in which they would be tempted to reoffend. Restrictions for those convicted of a cybercrime typically require that their computers and technology devices must be registered with the court system, and they are prohibited from using any web applications or technologies that could mask their online behavior, such as virtual private networks. These restrictions can last up to 10 years after their release from prison.

Many former cybercriminals have reported that these restrictions on using technology have made it virtually impossible to find any job that uses technology at any level. One attacker was arrested and convicted for breaking into a telecom's system and exposing the personal data of 156,000 customers, costing the telecom $48 million. The attacker was only 18 years old when he committed the crime. After serving two years of a four-year sentence, he then faced three years of restrictions, which included a requirement to register any technology device he used and limited his access to apps and online services. Every few months authorities—without prior notice—seized his devices for inspection and made a copy of all his data. Another convicted cyberattacker applied for multiple tech jobs after being released from prison, but the restrictions made it impossible to find a job. He was forced to work in construction and restaurants for several years until his probationary period expired.

A common step for entering the corporate workforce in information security is to earn a certificate in the field from a respected cyber organization. However, for most convicted cyberattackers, this too is a path that is unavailable to them. Many high-level certificates require the applicants to go through ethics and background checks before being certified. These certifications typically have ethics codes that require applicants to have acted "honorably, honestly, justly, responsibly, and legally." As the chief executive of one certification organization said, "It would be very unlikely we would allow them to hold our certification because of how closely tied that is to the violation of our ethical canons."[1] Another certification body said that they had received just 10 applications over the past decade from those with a cybercrime charge or conviction.

So, instead of attackers being generously rewarded for their exploits with a well-paying job in cybersecurity, the reality is just the opposite: they are severely restricted from virtually any job that uses technology.

Did you hear that one of the leading online password managers reported that attackers had stolen backups of customer password data as well as personal information (billing address, email addresses, telephone numbers, and IP addresses), and this was after the company had denied for over four months that any customer data was stolen? And that government researchers had discovered that suspected Russian attackers had infected and were lurking inside a U.S. satellite network? That a settlement based on a five-year-old data breach affecting hundreds of millions of U.S. citizens—with some states reporting almost 60 percent of its population as victims—was finally reached but only provides credit monitoring and identity restoration services to all victims? That a data breach of 427 gigabytes (GB) of data occurred on third-party software used by restaurants and hotels around the world? And that information security companies have been laying off hundreds of cyber workers in recent months due to an unsure economy?

And all of this happened in just over *one day*?

You may not have heard of any of these incidents. While in the past, just one of these cyber events would have made newsworthy headlines that immediately went viral across the Internet, today they barely register a blip on the radar screen. It's not because they are unimportant; rather, it's simply because cybersecurity attacks have become so commonplace that we hardly notice them any longer. *Oh, there was another data breach today? So, what else is new?*

The sheer volume of attacks has reached astronomical proportions. The AV-TEST Institute receives instances of over 450,000 new malicious programs (malware) and potentially unwanted applications (PUAs) each day. The total number of instances of malware has grown from 182 million in 2013 to over 1.34 billion today.[2] Cybercrime has been called the "greatest transfer of economic wealth in history." It is estimated that it could reach *$10.5 trillion annually* by 2025.[3] And the dismal numbers go on and on.

The need to identify and defend against these continual attacks has created a domain that is now at the very core of the information technology (IT) industry. Known as **information security**, this domain is concerned with protecting the secrecy of information, ensuring that it has not been altered and that it can be reliably accessed. Elements of information security include mitigating threats and vulnerabilities, applying security architectures, and managing and overseeing security operations.

The workforce that manages information security in an enterprise is usually divided into two broad categories. Information security **managerial personnel** administer and manage plans, policies, and people, while information security **technical personnel** are concerned with designing, configuring, installing, and maintaining technical security equipment. Within these two broad categories are four generally recognized types of security positions:

- **Chief information security officer (CISO).** This person reports directly to the CIO. (Large enterprises may have more layers of management between this person and the CIO.) This person is responsible for assessing, managing, and implementing security.
- **Security manager.** The security manager reports to the CISO and supervises technicians, administrators, and security staff. Typically, a security manager works on tasks identified by the CISO and resolves issues identified by technicians. This position requires an understanding of configuration and operation but not necessarily technical mastery.

- **Security administrator**. The security administrator has both technical knowledge and managerial skills. A security administrator manages daily operations of security technology and may analyze and design security solutions within a specific entity as well as identify users' needs.
- **Security technician**. This is generally an entry-level position for a person who has the necessary technical skills. Technicians provide technical support to configure security hardware, implement security software, and diagnose and troubleshoot problems.

There is a desperate demand for these qualified security personnel. Despite the fact that the worldwide information security workforce has reached an all-time high of 4.7 million professionals and just under half a million new workers are added annually, there is still a global shortage of *3.4 million* workers in this field. The United States alone has more than 700,000 unfilled security jobs.[4]

When hiring workers for cybersecurity positions, an overwhelming majority of enterprises use the Computing Technology Industry Association (CompTIA) Security+ certification to verify security competency. Of the hundreds of security certifications currently available, Security+ is one of the most widely acclaimed security certifications. Because it is internationally recognized as validating a foundation level of security skills and knowledge, the Security+ certification has become the security baseline for today's IT security professionals.

Note 1

The value of a security certification for an IT professional is significant. Along with years of experience, sector employed, and geographic location, holding a security certification is considered one of the primary drivers to merit a higher salary. And over 60 percent of information technology workers continue to seek additional security certifications for growing their skills and staying current with security trends.[5]

The CompTIA Security+ certification is a vendor-neutral credential that requires passing the current certification exam SY0-701. A successful candidate has the knowledge and skills required to identify attacks, threats, and vulnerabilities; design a strong security architecture; implement security controls; be knowledgeable of security operations and incident response; and be well versed in governance, risk, and compliance requirements.

Note 2

The CompTIA Security+ certification meets the ISO 17024 standard and is approved by the U.S. Department of Defense (DoD) to fulfill multiple levels of the DoD 8140/8570.01-M directive. This directive outlines which cybersecurity certifications are approved to validate the skills for certain job roles.

This module introduces the foundations of information security that form the basis of the Security+ certification. It begins by defining information security and looks at attackers and their motivations. The module also investigates how attacks occur and the impacts of those attacks. It concludes by examining various resources of information security.

What Is Information Security?

Certification

1.1 Compare and contrast various types of security controls.

1.2 Summarize fundamental security concepts.

The first step in a study of information security is to define exactly what it is. This involves understanding security and knowing its basic principles. It also includes comparing information security to cybersecurity.

Understanding Security

The word *security* comes from the Latin, meaning "free from care." Sometimes security is defined as "the state of being free from danger," which is the **goal** of security. It is also defined as the "measures taken to ensure safety," which is the **process** of security. Since complete security can never be fully achieved, the focus of security is more often on the process instead of the goal. In this light, security can be defined as "the necessary steps to protect from harm."

It is important to understand the relationship between **security** and **convenience**. The relationship between these two is not **directly proportional** (*as security is increased, convenience is increased*) but, instead, it is completely the opposite, known as **inversely proportional** (*as security is increased, convenience is decreased*). As illustrated in Figure 1-1, inversely proportional means that when security increases (from *low* to *high* on the horizontal *x*-axis), convenience decreases (from *high* to *low* on the vertical *y*-axis).

Figure 1-1   Relationship of security to convenience

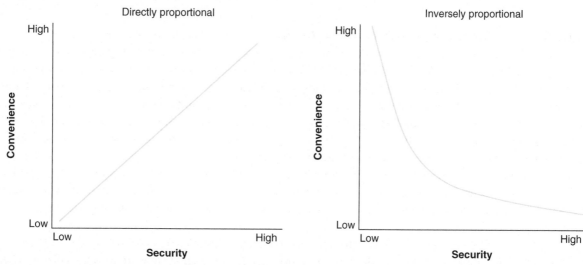

Note 3

In addition, as convenience is increased, usually security is decreased.

Consider a user who changes the screen timeout setting on their Apple iPhone from *Never* to *30 seconds* to minimize the risk of a thief stealing and using their phone. Although the security is increased, the convenience is decreased because they must now log in after 30 seconds of inactivity. Thus, the *more* secure something is, the *less* convenient it may be to use. Security is often described as sacrificing convenience for safety.

Principles of Security

There are several basic principles of security. These include security concepts and security controls.

Security Concepts

There are two fundamental security concepts. These are confidentiality, integrity, and availability and authentication, authorization, and accounting.

Confidentiality, Integrity, and Availability (CIA)   Today security is usually focused on protecting information that provides value to people and enterprises. Three basic security protections must be extended over the information: confidentiality, integrity, and availability (CIA). These may be defined as follows:

- **Confidentiality**. It is important that only approved individuals can access sensitive information. For example, the credit card number used to make an online purchase must be kept secure and not made available to other parties. Confidentiality ensures that only authorized parties can view the information. Providing confidentiality can involve several different security tools, ranging from software to encrypt the credit card number stored on the web server to door locks to prevent access to those servers.

- **Integrity**. Integrity ensures that the information is correct and no unauthorized person or malicious software has altered the data. In the example of the online purchase, an attacker who could change the amount of a purchase from $10,000.00 to $1.00 would violate the integrity of the information.
- **Availability**. Information has value if the authorized parties who are assured of its integrity can access the information. Availability ensures that data is accessible to only authorized users and not to unapproved individuals. In this example, the total number of items ordered as the result of an online purchase must be available to an employee in a warehouse so that the correct items can be shipped to the customer but not made available to a competitor.

Authentication, Authorization, and Accounting (AAA)   The second basic security principle, authentication, authorization, and accounting (AAA; sometimes called "triple-A"), involves controlling access to information. Consider this scenario. Suppose that Gabe is babysitting his sister Mia one afternoon. Before leaving the house, his mother tells Gabe that a package delivery service is coming to pick up a box, which is inside the front door. Soon there is a knock at the door, and as Gabe looks out, he sees the delivery person standing on the porch. Gabe asks them to display their employee credentials, which the delivery person is pleased to do, and then he opens the door to allow them inside—but only to the area by the front door to pick up the box. Gabe then signs the delivery person's tablet device so there is a confirmation record that the package was picked up.

This illustrates controlling access to information. The package delivery person first presents their ID to Gabe to be reviewed. A user accessing a computer system would likewise present credentials or **identification**, such as a username, when logging on to the system. Identification is the process of recognizing and distinguishing the user from any other user.

Checking the delivery person's credentials to be sure that they are authentic and not fabricated is authentication. Computer users, likewise, must have their credentials authenticated to ensure that they are who they claim to be. This is often done by entering a password, fingerprint scan, or other type of approved credentials.

Authorization, granting permission to take an action, is the next step. Gabe allowed the package delivery person to enter the house because their credentials were authentic. Likewise, once users have presented their identification and been authenticated, they can log in to a computer system. But what can they do once they have logged in? Gabe only allowed the package delivery person access to the area by the front door to retrieve the box; he did not allow them to go upstairs or into the kitchen. Likewise, computer users are granted access only to the specific services, devices, applications, and files needed to perform their job duties.

Gabe signing on the tablet is akin to accounting. Accounting creates a record that is preserved of who accessed the enterprise network, what resources they accessed, and when they disconnected from the network.

Note 4

Accounting data can be used not only to provide an audit trail but also for billing, determining trends, identifying resource usage, and future capacity planning.

AAA provides a framework for controlling access to computer resources. The basic steps in this access control process are summarized in Table 1-1.

Security Controls

A security control is a safeguard (sometimes called a **countermeasure**) that is employed within an enterprise to protect the CIA of information. A control attempts to limit the exposure of an asset to a danger. The four broad categories of controls are listed in Table 1-2.

Table 1-1   Basic steps in controlling access

Action	Description	Scenario example	Computer process
Identification	Review of credentials	Delivery person shows employee badge	User enters username
Authentication	Validate credentials as genuine	Gabe reads badge to determine it is real	User provides password
Authorization	Permission granted for admittance	Gabe opens door to allow delivery person in	User allowed to access only specific data
Accounting	Record of user actions	Gabe signs to confirm he picked up the package	Information recorded in log file

Table 1-2   Categories of controls

Control category	Description	Example
Managerial	Controls that use administrative methods	Acceptable use policy that specifies users should not visit malicious websites
Operational	Controls implemented and executed by people	Conducting workshops to help train users to identify and delete suspicious messages
Technical	Controls incorporated as part of hardware, software, or firmware	Hardware that blocks malicious content from entering the network
Physical	Controls that implement security in a defined structure and location	Installing a fence to prevent an unauthorized person from entering a building

Specific types of controls are found within these four broad categories:

- **Deterrent controls**. A deterrent control attempts to discourage security violations before they occur.
- **Preventive controls**. A preventive control works to prevent the threat from coming in contact with the vulnerability.
- **Detective controls**. A detective control identifies any threat that has reached the system.
- **Compensating controls**. A compensating control provides an alternative to normal controls that for some reason cannot be used.
- **Corrective controls**. A corrective control mitigates or lessens the damage caused by the incident.
- **Directive controls**. A directive control ensures that a particular outcome is achieved.

Note 5

One type of directive control is **incentive**, which is the "carrot" instead of the "stick." Incentives are often overlooked as a control, but they can be very powerful. One recent study looked at how incentive programs affected gym attendance. It found that gym goers who missed a workout but then received an extra incentive (in this case, bonus points that could be converted to cash) if they returned after a missed workout increased their gym visits by 27 percent compared with those who did not receive the incentive.[6]

These control types are summarized along with examples in Table 1-3.

Table 1-3   Control types

Control type	Description	When it occurs	Example
Deterrent control	Discourage attack	Before attack	Signs indicating that the area is under video surveillance
Preventive control	Prevent attack	Before attack	Security awareness training for all users
Directive control	Prevent attack	Before attack	An incentive to employees who pass a training course
Detective control	Identify attack	During attack	Installing motion detection sensors
Compensating control	Alternative to normal control	During attack	An infected computer is isolated on a different network
Corrective control	Lessen damage from attack	After attack	A virus is cleaned from an infected server

Caution

Security professionals do not universally agree on the nomenclature and classification of control types. Some researchers divide control types into only managerial, operational, and technical, while others divide them into administrative, logical, and physical. Some security researchers specify up to18 different control types.

Cybersecurity versus Information Security

Different terms are sometimes used when describing security protections in an enterprise: **information security**, **computer security**, **IT security**, **cybersecurity**, and **information assurance**, to name just a few. Currently the two most used terms are *cybersecurity* and *information security*. Although they are often used as synonyms, strictly speaking, they are different.

Cybersecurity usually involves a range of practices, processes, and technologies intended to protect devices, networks, and programs that process and store data in an electronic form. Information security, on the other hand, protects "processed data" (information) that is essential in an enterprise business environment (more so than "raw data"). In addition, in a business, this information may be in any format, from electronic files to paper documents. Because business enterprises most often deal with information and that information is in a variety of formats, *information security* is often considered the most appropriate term used in this setting.

Note 6

Although there is no universal agreement on these definitions, generally speaking, *cybersecurity* is considered an overall umbrella term under which information security is found.

Defining Information Security

Information security describes the tasks of securing enterprise information often found in a digital format, whether it be manipulated by a microprocessor (such as on a laptop or file server), preserved on a storage device (like a hard drive or USB flash drive), or transmitted over a network (such as a local area network or the Internet). Yet information security cannot completely prevent successful attacks or guarantee that a system is totally secure, just as the security measures used in a house can never guarantee complete safety from a burglar. The goal of information security is to ensure that protective measures are properly implemented to ward off attacks, prevent the total collapse of the system when a successful attack does occur, and recover as quickly as possible. Thus, information security is, first and foremost, **protection**.

Second, information security is intended to protect **information** that provides value to people and enterprises. CIA makes up the three basic protections that must be extended over information.

Because this information is often stored on computer hardware, manipulated by software, and transmitted by communications, each of these areas must be protected. The third objective of information security is to protect the CIA of information *on the devices that store, manipulate, and transmit the information.*

This protection is achieved through a process that is a combination of three entities. As shown in Figure 1-2, information and hardware, software, and communications are protected in three layers: **products**, **people**, and **policies and procedures**. The procedures enable people to understand how to use products to protect information.

Figure 1-2   Information security layers

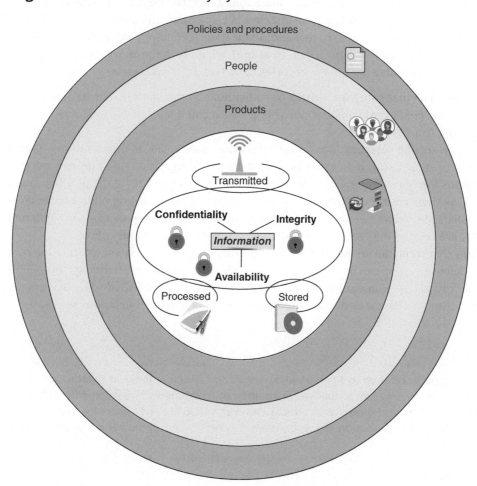

Thus, information security may be defined as *that which protects the integrity, confidentiality, and availability of information through products, people, and procedures on the devices that store, manipulate, and transmit the information.*

Two Rights & A Wrong

1. Integrity ensures that only authorized parties can view information.
2. The relationship between security and convenience is inversely proportional: as security is increased, convenience is decreased.
3. A deterrent control is designed to discourage an attack from taking place.

See the answers at the end of the module.

Threat Actors and Their Motivations

Certification

2.1 Compare and contrast common threat actors and motivations.

In information security a threat actor (also called a **malicious actor**) is a term used to describe individuals or entities who are responsible for attacks (the generic term **attacker** is also commonly used). The very first cyberattacks were mainly for threat actors to show off and earn recognition for their technology skills (**fame**). However, that soon gave way to threat actors with the goal of financial gain (**fortune**), which is the primary focus today. This financial cyber-crime can be divided into the following three categories based on different targets:

- **Individual users**. The first category focuses on individuals as the victims. Threat actors steal and use stolen data, credit card numbers, online financial account information, or Social Security numbers to profit from its victims.
- **Enterprises**. The second category focuses on enterprises and business organizations. Threat actors attempt to steal research on a new product from an enterprise so that they can sell it to an unscrupulous foreign supplier who will then build an imitation model of the product to sell worldwide. This deprives the legitimate business of profits after investing often hundreds of millions of dollars in product development and, because these foreign suppliers are in a different country, they are beyond the reach of domestic enforcement agencies and courts.
- **Governments**. Governments are also the targets of threat actors. If the latest information on a new missile defense system can be stolen, it can be sold—at a high price—to that government's enemies. In addition, government information is often stolen and published to embarrass the government before its citizens and force it to stop what is considered a nefarious action.

Note 7

In the past, the term **hacker** referred to a person who used advanced computer skills to attack computers. Yet this term was not always accurate, so it was then qualified in an attempt to distinguish between different types of hackers. For example, a **white hat hacker**, also known as an **ethical attacker**, would probe a system for weaknesses and then provide that information back to the organization. However, today "hacker" is considered pejorative and instead more accurate terms should be used.

The attributes of actors, or characteristic features, of the different groups of threat actors vary widely. Some groups have a high level of power and complexity (called level of sophistication/capability) and a massive network of resources, while others are "lone wolves" with minimal skills and no resources. In addition, some groups have deep resources/funding while others have none. Whereas some groups of threat actors may originate from within the enterprise, others are strictly outside (internal/external).

Today, threat actors are classified in distinct categories, such as unskilled attackers, shadow IT, organized crime, insiders, hacktivists, nation-state actors, and others. Each group has varying motivations, or the reason why it attacks.

Note 8

This listing of threat actors is in ascending sequence of least sophisticated to most sophisticated.

Unskilled Attackers

To the surprise of many users, high technical skills and knowledge are not a prerequisite to attack a system. Instead, easy-to-use attack tools are freely available or can be purchased at a low cost to perform sophisticated attacks. Figure 1-3 illustrates a current, widely available software package that allows for a sophisticated attack to be launched by simply making selections from a menu. Individuals who want to perform attacks yet lack the technical knowledge to carry them out are sometimes called unskilled attackers.

Figure 1-3   Menu of attack tools

Source: Kali Linux

> **Note 9**
>
> In the early days of information security, the term "script kiddies" was used to describe unskilled attackers since they downloaded freely available automated attack software called **scripts** to perform malicious acts.

Unskilled attackers use these types of tools to carry out their attacks. They can often be successful in penetrating defenses, particularly if the defenses are weak. Their motivation is usually data exfiltration (unauthorized copying of data) or service disruption (obstructing normal business electronic processes).

> **Note 10**
>
> In early 2023, security researchers discovered that just a few weeks after the open-source artificial intelligence tool ChatGPT was released, participants in underground cybercrime forums, some with little or no coding experience, were using it to create malicious software code and craft emails to use for attacks. The researchers themselves used this tool to create an email with an attached Excel document that contained harmful Visual Basic for Applications (VBA) code, and then used it to mount a successful attack. The researchers noted that ChatGPT did the hard work of creating the attack and all that was left to do was to execute the attack.

Shadow IT

It is not uncommon for employees to become frustrated with the slow pace of acquiring technology at their workplace. Arcane forms must be completed, multiple levels of signatures must be secured, and unending back-and-forth emails with the IT Department negotiating what can be purchased causes even the most patient employee to throw up their hands and scream!

A cumbersome purchasing process that may take months before a single item of hardware or software can be acquired has pushed some employees to order the item online and pay for it with their own credit card, circumventing the enterprise's approval process. However well-intentioned the employee might be, they may actually purchase software that contains malware or connect their hardware to the corporate network that creates a security vulnerability. The process of bypassing corporate approval for technology purchases is known as shadow IT. The employee's motivation is often ethical (it has sound moral principles) but nevertheless weakens security.

> **Note 11**
>
> It is estimated that one-third of all successful thefts of corporate data by threat actors are from data stored on unapproved hardware or accessed through unapproved software purchased via shadow IT.[7] And 52 percent of survey respondents said that individual employees are purchasing software apps without IT's knowledge or consent while 69 percent of tech executives reported that shadow IT is their top security concern.[8]

Organized Crime

Organized crime is a close-knit group of highly centralized enterprises set up for the purpose of engaging in illegal activities. Organized crime is usually run by a small number of experienced criminal networks who do not commit crimes themselves but act as entrepreneurs. Historically, these organizations have engaged in crimes such as the theft of cargo, fraud, robbery, kidnapping for ransom, and demanding "protection" payments. The income from these activities have enabled organized crime to supply goods and services that are illegal but for which there is demand, such as gambling, drugs, prostitution, and loansharking.

In recent years, evidence indicates that organized crime has moved into cyberattacks, which they consider to be less risky and more rewarding than traditional crimes. The motivation by organized crime is generally financial gain (earning revenue).

Insider Threats

Another serious threat to an enterprise actually comes from its own employees, contractors, and business partners, called **insiders**, who pose an insider threat from the position of a trusted entity. For example, a healthcare worker disgruntled about being passed over for a promotion (with the motivation of revenge or avenge by retaliation) might illegally gather health records on celebrities and sell them to the media. Another example is an employee who is pressured by someone threatening them with blackmail (extortion or coercion by using threats) unless they cooperate by stealing research and development data.

Attacks from an insider threat are hard to recognize. This is because the threat actor is already trusted to use the computer system and because they come from within the enterprise, whose focus is watching for outsiders. In recent years, government insiders have stolen large volumes of sensitive information and then published it to alert its citizens of clandestine governmental actions.

> **Note 12**
>
> Because most intellectual property (IP) thefts occur within 30 days of an employee resigning, it is thought that these insiders believe that either the IP belongs to them instead of the enterprise or that they were not properly compensated for their work behind the IP.

Hacktivists

A group that is strongly motivated by philosophical/political beliefs (ideology for the sake of principles) is hacktivists (a combination of the words *hack* and *activism*). Most hacktivists do not explicitly call themselves "hacktivists," but the term is commonly used by security researchers and journalists to distinguish them from other types of threat actors.

Attacks by hacktivists are often used to "make a statement." For example, they may break into a website and change the contents on the site. (One hacktivist group changed the website of the U.S. Department of Justice to read "Department of Injustice.") Other attacks were retaliatory: Hacktivists have disabled the website belonging to a bank because that bank stopped accepting online payments deposited into accounts belonging to groups supported by hacktivists. Today many hacktivists work through disinformation campaigns by spreading fake news and supporting conspiracy theories, making their motivation disruption/chaos (extreme confusion).

> **Note 13**
>
> Hacktivists were particularly active during the coronavirus disease (COVID-19) pandemic of 2020. One large group of what were considered far-right neo-Nazi hacktivists embarked on a months-long disinformation campaign designed to weaponize the pandemic by questioning scientific evidence and research. In another instance, thousands of breached email addresses and passwords from U.S. and global health organizations, including the National Institutes of Health, Centers for Disease Control and Prevention, and the World Health Organization, were distributed on Twitter by these groups to harass and distract these health organizations.

Nation-State Actors

Instead of using an army to march across the battlefield to strike an adversary, governments are increasingly employing their own state-sponsored attackers for launching cyberattacks against their foes. These are known as nation-state actors. Their foes may be foreign governments or even citizens of its own nation that are considered hostile or threatening. The motivation for nation-state actors is espionage (spying) or even to create war (armed hostile combat).

> **Note 14**
>
> A growing number of attacks from nation-state actors are directed toward businesses in other countries with the goal of causing financial harm or damage to the enterprise's reputation.

Many security researchers believe that nation-state actors might be the deadliest of any threat actors. When fortune motivates a threat actor but the target's defenses are too strong, the attacker simply moves onto another promising target with less effective defenses. With nation-state actors, however, the target is very specific, and the attackers keep working until they are successful. This is because state-sponsored attackers are highly skilled and have enough government resources to breach almost any security defense.

Nation-state actors are often involved in multiyear intrusion campaigns targeting highly sensitive economic, proprietary, or national security information. This has created a new class of attacks called **Advanced Persistent Threats (APTs)**. These attacks use innovative attack tools (**advanced**) and once a system is infected, it silently extracts data over an extended period of time (**persistent**). APTs are most commonly associated with nation-state actors.

Other Threat Actors

In addition, there are other categories of threat actors. These are summarized in Table 1-4.

Table 1-4   Descriptions of other threat actors

Threat actor	Description	Explanation
Competitors	Launch attack against an opponent's system to steal classified information.	Competitors may steal new product research or a list of current customers to gain a competitive advantage.
Brokers	Sell their knowledge of a weakness to other attackers or governments.	Individuals who uncover weaknesses do not report them to the software vendor but instead sell them to the highest bidder, who are willing to pay a high price for the unknown weakness.
Cyberterrorists	Attack a nation's network and computer infrastructure to cause disruption and panic among citizens.	Targets may include a small group of computers or networks that can affect the largest number of users, such as the computers that control the electrical power grid of a state or region.

Caution !

Often the perception of an attacker by the general public is a "hacker in a hoodie," a disgruntled teenager looking for an easy target. Nothing could be further from the truth. Threat actors today generally have excellent technology skills, are tenacious, and have strong financial backing. Attackers have even modeled their work after modern economic theories (such as finding the optimum "price point" at which victims will pay a ransom) and software development (attack tools that threat actors sell are often software suites that receive regular updates). It is a serious mistake to underestimate modern threat actors.

Two Rights & A Wrong

1. Nation-state actors are responsible for the class of attacks called Advanced Persistent Threats.
2. A usual motivation for organized crime is service disruption.
3. Hacktivists are motivated by philosophical/political beliefs.

See the answers at the end of the module.

How Attacks Occur

Certification

2.2 Explain common threat vectors and attack surfaces.

2.3 Explain various types of vulnerabilities.

How do attacks occur? Threat actors target different digital platforms to exploit their weaknesses so that these platforms in the eyes of the threat actors are merely threat vectors and attack surfaces. The vulnerabilities found in these platforms are so numerous they can be broken into categories of vulnerabilities. There are several impacts of successful attacks.

Threat Vectors and Attack Surfaces

An attack surface, also called a threat vector, is a digital platform that threat actors target for their exploits. These can be divided into mainstream attack surfaces and specialized threat vectors.

Mainstream Attack Surfaces

Some attack surfaces can be considered **mainstream** for several reasons. First, they have been the primary targets of threat actors since the beginning of cyberattacks. Second, these attack surfaces are found in all technology settings. Third, they continue to bear the brunt of attacks today.

The categories of mainstream attack surfaces are software, hardware, and networks. Table 1-5 describes these different attack surfaces.

Table 1-5 Mainstream attack surfaces

Category	Attack surface	Explanation
Software	Vulnerable software	Vulnerable software contains one or more security vulnerabilities; this software can be either client-based software (software applications installed on a computer connected to a network) or agentless software (no additional processes are required to run in the background).
Software	File-based	Many attacks focus on infecting individual files on a computer.
Software	Image-based	An image is a copy of all the computer's contents, and a vulnerability would permit an attack on the image.
Hardware	Unsupported systems and applications	Computer systems and applications no longer supported by the organization are often ignored and do not receive security updates.
Hardware	Removable devices	A removable media device, like a USB flash drive, can be connected to an unsecure computer and become infected with malware and, when inserted into a "clean" computer, it can infect that device.
Network	Unsecure networks	Unsecured wired and wireless networks are a vulnerability since an attacker who can breach the network could have access to hundreds of connected devices.
Network	Open service ports	Unnecessary ports that are not disabled can allow attackers access to devices and networks.
Network	Default credentials	Networks may have default (preselected options) administrator accounts with a well-known password that attackers could target.

Specialized Threat Vectors

Other threat vectors eyed by threat actors as potential targets are more specialized. These categories include communications and supply chain.

Communications   Humans are creatures who depend on communication with others, in both written and oral forms. Today these forms have been enhanced through technology communication tools, and these tools have become ubiquitous. Yet a weakness of some of these tools is that the other person may not always be validated: it is *assumed* that the person with whom a written conversation is taking place is *actually* that person and not an imposter.

Due to their popularity and widespread usage, coupled with the fact that the other person's true identity can be easily masked, these communication tools are popular threat vectors by attackers. The most common communication tools are message-based, including the following:

- **Email**. Almost 94 percent of all malware is delivered through email to an unsuspecting user.[9] The goal is to trick the user to open an attachment that contains malware or click a hyperlink that takes the user to an imposter website that looks legitimate but belongs to the threat actor.

> ## Caution !
>
> Threat actors often reference current events when sending email messages, taking advantage of distracted and unsuspecting users. For example, using a natural disaster like a blizzard, hurricane, or flood, unscrupulous attackers will send out email messages with tempting subject lines such as "Click Here to Contribute to Disaster Relief Efforts" or "These Flood Pictures Are Unbelievable!" But these are intended to trick a user to open an email attachment that contains malware or click a hyperlink that redirects them to a malicious website. Users should always be cautious of opening and responding to these types of email messages.

- **Texts**. Texts are short, typed narratives that use a cellular network and are typically sent by a cell phone. Mobile devices use a messaging service called the Short Message Service (SMS) that has a limit of 160 characters. A similar service, Multimedia Messaging Service (MMS), allows for the text to be accompanied with an attached file such as a picture, video, emoji, or website link. Threat actors may send a text containing a link that installs malware and then persuade the victim to click the link.
- **Instant messages**. Instant messaging (IM) is a technology that allows users to send real-time messages through a software application over the Internet and is not restricted to a cell phone. Like texts, instant messages from threat actors pretend to be from a reliable source but can contain malicious links.

> ## Note 15
>
> Popular instant message applications are Facebook Messenger, WhatsApp, WeChat, and iMessage.

- **Voice calls**. Voice calls from threat actors are often directed to older users, who have relied on the telephone more than younger users and thus tend to trust a helpful voice on the other end. Attackers may call pretending to be from a credit card company with news that the user's account has been breached and that the victim should immediately give their password over the phone to stop the attack.

Supply Chain   A supply chain is a network that moves a product from its creation to the end-user. This chain is typically made up of suppliers (the first step in the chain) that provide the raw materials, manufacturers who convert the material into products, vendors who purchase the products to resell them, warehouses that store products, distribution centers that deliver products to the retailers, and retailers who sell the product ultimately to the consumer. Today's supply chains are global in scope, as shown in Figure 1-4. This makes each link in the chain potentially

Figure 1-4 Supply chain

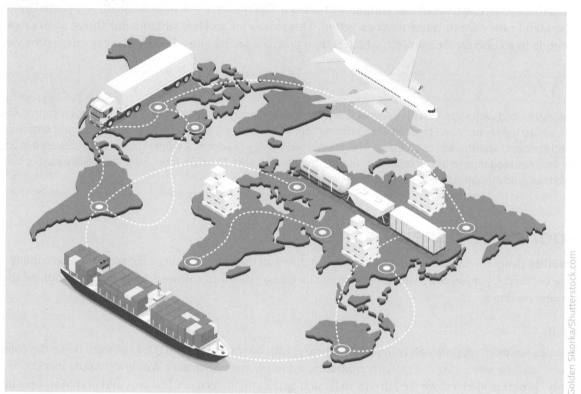

Golden Sikorka/Shutterstock.com

thousands of miles away overseas and cannot be under any direct and coordinated supervision and monitoring. Thus, each link in a supply chain can be a potential threat vector.

Products like computer hardware sold by a hardware provider move through many steps in the supply chain, which has opened the door for malware to be injected into the product during its manufacturing, storage, and distribution. These are called **supply chain infections**.

Note 16

Hardware supply chain infections are considered especially dangerous. Users receiving infected devices at the point of purchase are completely unaware that a brand-new computer or network appliance may be infected. Also, there is rarely any means by which the user can be contacted to inform them of an infected device. Because it is virtually impossible to closely monitor every step in the global supply chain, these infections cannot be easily prevented.

More recently, software supply chains, which sources software from a software provider (the software developer and supplier) for delivery to an end-user, have been the target of attackers. In one well-publicized attack, threat actors targeted a company that sold network and computer management software tools to enterprises. One tool had over 33,000 clients. Threat actors were able to access the provider's software development and distribution pipeline. They inserted malicious code into the software so that it would then be distributed to the software provider's clients as a software update. This single infection then spread exponentially to tens of thousands of clients, who then passed it on to their customers, too.

Instead of targeting the originating software provider (supplier), other software supply chain infections have focused on the downstream "middlemen" service providers (businesses that furnish solutions or services to users and organizations). IT service providers who manage networks, computers, cloud resources, and information security typically for small-to-medium enterprises (SMEs) are called managed service providers (MSPs). An infected MSP can distribute malicious software to its many SME clients.

A particularly alarming type of supply chain infection targets **open-source software**, software for which the source code is available for anyone to freely use without restrictions. Open-source software is usually supported by volunteer contributors, and rarely are the contributions vetted. This makes for an ideal situation for threat actors to add their malicious code to an open-source project, which is then downloaded and installed by many unsuspecting victims.

> ### Note 17
>
> The risks associated with supply chain vulnerabilities can be seen in an incident in late 2021. The open-source software Log4j is used to log security and performance information. It is found in a wide variety of consumer and enterprise services, websites, and applications as well as in operational technology products. A vulnerability was discovered in Log4j on a Friday that resulted in over 100 attacks per minute. By Monday, just 72 hours later, over *1.2 million* attacks had been launched taking advantage of this single vulnerability.[10]

Categories of Vulnerabilities

A **vulnerability** (from the Latin meaning "wound") is defined as the state of being exposed to the possibility of being attacked or harmed. Cybersecurity vulnerabilities can be categorized into software, hardware, misconfigurations, and zero-day vulnerabilities.

Software

Vulnerabilities are most predominately found in software, with operating system (OS) software being the chief culprit (known as OS-based vulnerabilities). Early operating systems, such Microsoft Windows, Apple macOS, and Linux, were simply "program loaders" whose job was to launch applications. As more features and graphical user interfaces (GUIs) were added, OSs became more complex.

> ### Note 18
>
> Today's Windows 11 is estimated to have over 50 million lines of code, Linux Debian has 68 million lines, and Apple macOS may have upward of 86 million lines of code. In contrast, Microsoft's first OS, MS-DOS v1.0, had only 4,000 lines of code.

Due to the increased complexity of OSs, unintentional vulnerabilities were introduced that could be exploited by attackers. In addition, new attack tools made what were once considered secure functions and services on OSs now vulnerable.

> ### Note 19
>
> Despite the best intentions to create secure OSs, it is still a challenge for software developers. For example, when Apple released its latest version of macOS Ventura 13.0 in October 2022, two weeks later it was forced to release an update (13.0.1) that addressed two major security vulnerabilities. Six weeks later it released another update (13.1) that fixed at least 39 security vulnerabilities. Microsoft Windows 11 was released in October 2021, and 88 vulnerabilities had to be fixed by the end of the year. The following year (2022) 501 security vulnerabilities had to be addressed.

In addition to OS software containing vulnerabilities, applications (software programs) can also have vulnerabilities. One attack uses a malicious update, in which a threat actor uses deceptive methods to cause a user to download and install code that is believed to be a valid update to the application. However, in reality, this update originates from a source that is controlled by the attacker and is malicious, infecting the application.

Hardware

Several hardware vulnerabilities can lead to a successful attack. These include difficulty patching firmware, legacy platforms, and end-of-life hardware.

Difficulty Patching Firmware   Firmware is software that is embedded into hardware. It provides low-level controls and instructions for the hardware. Updating firmware to address a vulnerability contained in its code can be difficult and requires specialized steps. Not all firmware can be patched with security updates. As a result, firmware with a vulnerability can be a target for attackers.

Legacy Platforms   One type of platform that is well known for its vulnerabilities is a legacy platform. A legacy platform is an older hardware platform for which a more modern version is available but for a variety of reasons has not been updated or replaced. These reasons may include limited hardware capacity, an application that only operates on an outdated OS version, or even neglect. The result is that the hardware legacy platform has been deprived of the most recent security fixes. This creates hardware that is just asking to be attacked.

End-of-Life (EOL) Hardware   While some things seem to last forever, the same cannot be said for technology devices. Improved models regularly supersede these devices. As a result, hardware eventually reaches its end-of-life (EOL), or the end of its manufacturing lifespan. By this point—preferably sooner—the device should be retired and a new model installed.

> **Caution** !
>
> EOL does not mean that the device will no longer function, but rather that it is no longer manufactured and supported.

At the EOL point, support provided by vendors is no longer available, which includes tech support, hardware repairs, or firmware updates. To ignore EOL can lead to the issues outlined in Table 1-6.

Table 1-6   EOL risks

EOL risk	Explanation
Lack of security updates	The primary risk of EOL hardware is that any vulnerability will not be patched and will remain until the device is replaced; it may also be difficult to identify that a vulnerability in EOL hardware is the culprit for a successful attack.
High cost of maintenance	In addition to no security updates, EOL hardware receives no firmware upgrades or new functionality, and hardware replacement parts or accessories are not available, thus dramatically increasing the cost of maintenance.
Loss of comprehensive security	In addition to creating employee downtime, aging hardware is often unreliable and fails more frequently, making it likely to result in an unexpected security "hole" in the network that threat actors can exploit.
Legal implications	Using EOL hardware can be considered a failure to comply with regulatory standards that could result in fines and legal consequences.

Misconfigurations

Modern hardware and software platforms provide a wide array of features and security settings. Each of these must be properly configured to repel attacks. However, often the configuration settings are not properly implemented, resulting in misconfigurations. Table 1-7 lists several misconfigurations that can result in vulnerabilities.

Zero-Day Vulnerabilities

Security updates are created and distributed when the software developer learns of a vulnerability and corrects it. But what happens if it is not the developer who uncovers the vulnerability but instead is a threat actor who finds it first? In this case, attackers can exploit the vulnerability before anyone else even knows it exists. This situation is called a zero-day vulnerability because there are zero days of warning. Zero-day vulnerabilities are considered extremely serious because systems are open to attack with no security fixes available.

Table 1-7 Misconfigurations

Configuration	Explanation	Example
Default settings	Default settings are predetermined by the vendor for usability and ease of use (and not security) so the user can immediately begin using the product.	A router comes with a default password that is widely known.
Open ports and services	Devices and services are often configured to allow the most access so that the user can then close those that are specific to that organization.	A firewall comes with FTP ports 20 and 21 open.
Unsecured root accounts	A root account can give a user unfettered access to all resources.	A misconfigured cloud storage repository could give any user access to all data.
Open permissions	Open permissions are user access over files that should have been restricted.	A user could be given Read, Write, and Execute privileges when they should have only been given Read privileges.
Unsecure protocols	Also called *insecure protocols*, it is using protocols for telecommunications that do not provide adequate protections.	Using devices that run services with unsecure protocols like Telnet or SNMPv1.
Weak encryption	Choosing a known vulnerable encryption mechanism.	Selecting an encryption scheme that has a known weakness or a key value that is too short.
Errors	Human mistakes in selecting one setting over another without considering the security implications.	Using deprecated settings instead of current configurations.

Note 20

How widespread are zero-day attacks? Google's Project Zero, which tracks these vulnerabilities, has reported a sharp increase. In 2014, the year records were first kept by Project Zero, there were only 14 vulnerabilities, but in 2021 there were 68 zero-day vulnerabilities used by attackers. To date, attackers have taken advantage of 244 previously unknown vulnerabilities to launch attacks.

Impacts of Attacks

When vulnerabilities in attack surfaces are exploited, the result is almost always a successful attack. And a successful attack always results in several negative impacts. These impacts can be classified as data impacts and overall effects on the organization.

Data Impacts

Whereas the goal of some attacks may be harm to a system, such as manipulating an industrial control system to shut down a water filtration facility, most attacks focus on data as the primary target. The consequences of a successful attack on data are listed in Table 1-8.

Overall Effects

A successful attack can also have grave consequences for an enterprise. First, systems may be inaccessible and cannot be accessed (**availability loss**). This results in lost productivity, which can impact the normal tasks for generating income (**financial loss**).

One of the most devastating effects is the impact upon the public perception of the enterprise (**reputation**). An organization that is the victim of an attack in which customer data is stolen faces a serious negative impression in the eyes of the public. Many current customers will become disgruntled at the lack of perceived security in the organization and will move their business to a competitor.

Table 1-8 Consequences of data attack

Impact	Description	Example
Data loss	The destruction of data so that it cannot be recovered	Maliciously erasing patient data used for cancer research
Data exfiltration	Stealing data to distribute it to other parties	Taking a list of current customers and selling it to a competitor
Data breach	Stealing data to disclose it in an unauthorized fashion	Theft of credit card numbers to sell to other threat actors
Identity theft	Taking personally identifiable information to impersonate someone	Stealing a Social Security number to secure a bank loan in the victim's name

Note 21

Another impact of an attack is for IT cyber professionals to be put in prison! Prosecutors in Albania recently asked for the house arrest of five IT officials of the Public Administration Department whom they blame for not protecting the country from a cyberattack by alleged Iranian nation-state actors. These prosecutors said the IT officials had failed to check the security of the system that was compromised and had not kept it updated with the most recent antivirus software. They are accused of "abuse of post," which can result in a prison sentence of up to seven years.

Two Rights & A Wrong

1. An attack surface is also called a threat vector.
2. A particularly alarming type of supply chain infection targets open-source software.
3. End-of-life means that a device will no longer function.

See the answers at the end of the module.

Information Security Resources

It would be a sobering task for an organization all by itself to attempt to mount a defense against threat actors. Fortunately, that is not the case. Defenders have a variety of external cybersecurity resources at their disposal to help ward off attacks. These resources include frameworks, regulations, legislation, standards, benchmarks/secure configuration guides, and information sources.

Frameworks

An information security **framework** is a series of documented processes used to define policies and procedures for implementation and management of security controls in an enterprise environment. About 84 percent of U.S. organizations use a security framework, and 44 percent use multiple frameworks.[11]

One of the most popular frameworks comes from the National Institute of Standards and Technology (NIST), operating under the U.S. Commerce Department. The NIST cybersecurity frameworks are a set of guidelines for helping private companies identify, detect, and respond to attacks. These frameworks also include guidelines for how to prevent and recover from an attack.

The NIST frameworks are divided into three basic parts. The first part is the **framework core** that defines the activities needed to attain different cybersecurity results. The framework core is further subdivided into four different elements, which are listed in Table 1-9.

The second part of the NIST frameworks is the **implementation tiers**. The NIST framework specifies four implementation tiers that help organizations identify their level of compliance; the higher the tier, the more compliant the organization is.

Table 1-9   NIST framework core elements

Element name	Description	Example
Functions	The most basic information security tasks	Identify, protect, detect, respond, and recover.
Categories	Tasks to be carried out for each of the five functions	To protect a function, organizations must implement software updates, install antivirus and anti-malware programs, and have access control policies in place.
Subcategories	Tasks or challenges associated with each category	To implement software updates (a category), organizations must be sure that Windows computers have auto-updates turned on.
Information sources	The documents or manuals that detail specific tasks for users and explain how to accomplish the tasks	A document is required that details how auto-updates are enabled on Windows computers.

The third and final part is **profiles**. Profiles relate both to the status of the organization's cybersecurity measures and the "roadmaps" toward compliance with the NIST cybersecurity framework. Profiles are like an executive summary of everything an organization has done for the NIST cybersecurity framework and can help demonstrate how each function, category, or subcategory can increase security. These profiles allow organizations to see their vulnerabilities at each step; once the vulnerabilities are mitigated, the organization can move up to higher implementation tiers.

There are two widely used NIST frameworks:

- **Risk Management Framework**. The **NIST Risk Management Framework (RMF)** is considered a guidance document designed to help organizations assess and manage risks to their information and systems. It is viewed as a comprehensive roadmap that organizations can use to seamlessly integrate their cybersecurity, privacy, and supply chain risk management processes.
- **Cybersecurity Framework**. The **NIST Cybersecurity Framework (CSF)** is used as a measuring stick against which companies can compare their cybersecurity practices relative to the threats they face. The elements of the CSF are shown in Figure 1-5.

Figure 1-5   NIST Cybersecurity Framework (CSF) functions

Source: National Institute of Standards and Technology

Note 22

Other common frameworks are from the International Organization for Standardization (ISO), American Institute of Certified Public Accountants (AICPA), Center for Internet Security (CIS), and Cloud Security Alliance.

speaking, they are different. Cybersecurity usually involves a range of practices, processes, and technologies intended to protect devices, networks, and programs that process and store data in an electronic form. Information security protects information essential in an enterprise business environment that may be in virtually any format, from electronic files to paper documents. Because business enterprises most often deal with information and that information is in a variety of formats, information security is often considered the most appropriate term used in this setting.

- Information security is that which protects the integrity, confidentiality, and availability of information through products, people, and procedures on the devices that store, manipulate, and transmit the information.

- The threat actors behind attacks fall into several categories and exhibit different motivations. Some actors have a high level of power and complexity and have a massive network of resources, while others work alone and have minimal skills and no resources. Some groups have deep resources and funding while others have none. Certain threat actors are internal and work within the enterprise while others work strictly outside the organization. The intent and motivation, or the reasons "why" for the attacks, vary widely.

- Unskilled attackers do their work by downloading automated attack software from websites and then using it to break into computers. The process of bypassing corporate approval for technology purchases is known as shadow IT. Employees who purchase unapproved software or hardware can create a security vulnerability. Organized crime is a close-knit group of highly centralized enterprises set up for the purpose of engaging in illegal activities and recently has been moving into cyberattacks. Insiders can pose an insider threat from the position of a trusted entity. Hacktivists are strongly motivated by their ideology and often attack to make a political statement. Nation-state actors are employed by governments as state-sponsored attackers for launching computer attacks against foes. Other threat actors include competitors, brokers, and cyberterrorists.

- An attack surface (threat vector) is a digital platform that threat actors target for their exploits. Several general attack surfaces relate to software, hardware, and networks: vulnerable software, file-based and image-based vulnerabilities, unsupported systems and applications, removable devices, unsecure networks, open service ports, and default credentials. Specialized threat vectors are message-based (email, texts, instant messages, and voice calls) and supply chain attack surfaces. Supply chain surfaces include hardware, software, and managed service providers (MSPs).

- Several vulnerabilities are the result of the platform being used. Software vulnerabilities include OS-based and applications. Updating firmware to address a vulnerability contained in its code can be difficult and requires specialized steps. Legacy platforms have not been updated and are prime targets for attacks. Hardware eventually reaches its end-of-life (EOL) or the end of its manufacturing lifespan and can create a vulnerability. Modern hardware and software platforms provide a wide array of features and security settings, and if the configuration settings are not properly implemented, they can result in misconfigurations. A zero-day vulnerability is one for which there is no advanced warning because there previously has been no knowledge of the vulnerability.

- A successful attack always results in several negative impacts. Most attacks focus on data as the primary target. The consequences of a successful attack on data are data loss, data exfiltration, data breach, and identity theft. A successful attack can also have significant consequences for an enterprise. Systems may be inaccessible and cannot be accessed, which results in lost productivity and impacts the normal tasks for generating income. One of the most devastating effects is the impact on the public perception of the enterprise, or its reputation. An organization that is the victim of an attack in which customer data is stolen faces a serious negative impression in the eyes of the public.

- Defenders have a variety of external cybersecurity resources at their disposal to help ward off attacks. These resources include frameworks, regulations, legislation, standards, benchmarks/secure configuration guides, and information sources.

Key Terms

accounting
agentless software
applications
attack surface (threat vector)
attributes of actors
authentication
authentication, authorization, and
   accounting (AAA)
authorization
availability
blackmail
client-based software
compensating controls
confidentiality
confidentiality, integrity, and
   availability (CIA)
control
corrective controls
data exfiltration
default credentials
detective controls
deterrent controls
directive controls
disruption/chaos

end-of-life (EOL)
espionage
ethical
file-based
financial gain
firmware
hacktivists
hardware provider
image-based
insider threat
Instant messaging (IM)
integrity
internal/external
legacy platform
level of sophistication/capability
malicious update
managed service providers (MSPs)
managerial controls
message-based
misconfigurations
nation-state actors
open service ports
operational controls
organized crime

OS-based vulnerabilities
philosophical/political beliefs
physical controls
preventive controls
removable devices
resources/funding
revenge
service disruption
service providers
shadow IT
Short Message Service (SMS)
software provider
suppliers
supply chain
technical controls
threat actor
unsecure networks
unskilled attackers
unsupported systems and
   applications
vendors
vulnerable software
war
zero-day

Review Questions

1. Vittoria is working on her computer information systems degree at a local college and has started researching information security positions. Because she has no prior experience, which of the following positions would Vittoria most likely be offered?

   a. Security administrator
   b. Security technician
   c. Security officer
   d. Security manager

2. Which of the following is false about the CompTIA Security+ certification?

   a. Security+ is one of the most widely acclaimed security certifications.
   b. Security+ is internationally recognized as validating a foundation level of security skills and knowledge.
   c. The Security+ certification is a vendor-neutral credential.
   d. Professionals who hold the Security+ certification earn about the same or slightly less than security professionals who have not achieved this certification.

3. Ginevra is explaining to her roommate the relationship between security and convenience. Which statement most accurately indicates this relationship?

   a. Security and convenience are directly proportional.
   b. Security and convenience have no relationship.
   c. Any proportions between security and convenience depends on the type of attack.
   d. Security and convenience are inversely proportional.

4. Serafina is studying to take the Security+ certification exam. Which of the following of the CIA elements ensures that only authorized parties can view protected information?

   a. Confidentiality
   b. Integrity
   c. Availability
   d. Credentiality

5. Which of the following AAA elements is applied immediately after a user has logged into a computer with their username and password?

   a. Authentication
   b. Authorization
   c. Identification
   d. Recording

6. Gia has been asked to enhance the security awareness training workshop for new hires. Which category of security control would Gia be using?

   a. Managerial
   b. Technical
   c. Operational
   d. Physical

7. Which specific type of control is intended to mitigate (lessen) damage caused by an attack?

   a. Corrective control
   b. Compensating control
   c. Preventive control
   d. Restrictive control

8. Which control is designed to ensure that a particular outcome is achieved by providing incentives?

   a. Deterrent control
   b. Incentive control
   c. Detective control
   d. Directive control

9. Which of the following controls is NOT implemented before an attack occurs?

   a. Detective control
   b. Deterrent control
   c. Preventive control
   d. Directive control

10. Complete this definition of information security: That which protects the integrity, confidentiality, and availability of information _____.

    a. on electronic digital devices and limited analog devices that can connect via the Internet or through a local area network
    b. through a long-term process that results in ultimate security
    c. using both open-sourced as well as supplier-sourced hardware and software that interacts appropriately with limited resources
    d. through products, people, and procedures on the devices that store, manipulate, and transmit the information

11. Which of the following groups have the lowest level of technical knowledge for carrying out cyberattacks?

    a. Unskilled attackers
    b. Hacktivists
    c. Nation-state actors
    d. Organized crime

12. Ilaria is explaining to her parents why *information security* is the preferred term when talking about security in the enterprise. Which of the following would Ilaria NOT say?

    a. Cybersecurity usually involves a range of practices, processes, and technologies intended to protect devices, networks, and programs that process and store data in an electronic form.
    b. In a business, information may be in any format, from electronic files to paper documents.
    c. Cybersecurity is a subset of information security.
    d. Information security protects "processed data" or information.

13. Which of the following is NOT considered an attribute of threat actors?

    a. Level of sophistication/capability
    b. Educated/uneducated
    c. Resources/funding
    d. Internal/external

14. What is considered the motivation of an employee who practices shadow IT?

    a. Deception
    b. Ignorance
    c. Ethical
    d. Malicious

15. Which tool is most commonly associated with nation-state actors?

    a. Closed-Source Resistant and Recurrent Malware (CSRRM)
    b. Advanced Persistent Threat (APT)
    c. Unlimited Harvest and Secure Attack (UHSA)
    d. Network Spider and Worm Threat (NSAWT)

16. Flavia is reading about insider threats. Which of the following is NOT true about insider threats?

    a. Attacks from an insider threat are hard to recognize.
    b. Insider threats are usually dismissed as not being a serious risk.
    c. Insider threats often occur because the enterprise is watching for outsiders.
    d. Government insiders have stolen large volumes of sensitive information.

17. What is the primary motivation of hacktivists?

    a. Disruption/chaos

    b. Financial gain

    c. Data exfiltration

    d. War

18. What is another name for "attack surface"?

    a. Vulnerability exposure

    b. Threat vector

    c. Legacy platform

    d. Attack floor

19. Which of the following is NOT a message-based attack surface?

    a. Voice calls

    b. Instant messages

    c. Texts

    d. Network protocols

20. Which of the following is NOT true about supply chains?

    a. A supply chain is a network that moves a product from its creation to the end-user.

    b. Vendors are the first step in a supply chain.

    c. Each link in a supply chain can be a potential attack surface.

    d. Hardware providers and software providers are types of supply chains.

Hands-On Projects

Project 1-1: Examine Data Breaches – Visual

Estimated Time: 20 minutes

Objective: Research the biggest data breaches.

Description: In this project, you use a visual format to view the biggest data breaches resulting in stolen information.

1. Open your web browser and enter the URL **http://www.informationisbeautiful.net/visualizations /worlds-biggest-data-breaches-hacks**. (If you are no longer able to access the site through this web address, use a search engine to search for "Information Is Beautiful World's Biggest Data Breaches.")

2. This site will display a visual graphic of the data breaches, similar to Figure 1-6.

3. Scroll down the page to view the data breaches by year. Note that the size of the breach is indicated by the size of the bubble.

4. Scroll back up to the top.

5. Hover over several bubbles to read a quick story of the breach.

6. Note the color of the bubbles that have an "Interesting Story." Click one of the bubbles and read the story. When finished, close only this tab in your browser.

7. Click **filter** to display the filter menu.

8. Under sector, click **retail** to view those breaches related to the retail industry.

9. Click one of the bubbles and read the story.

10. Click **RESET** in the filter menu.

11. Select the sector **finance**.

12. Select the method **poor security**.

13. Click one of the bubbles and read the story.

14. Create your own filters to view different types of breaches. Does this graphic convey a compelling story of data breaches?

15. How does this visualization help you with the understanding of threats?

16. Close all windows.

Figure 1-6   World's biggest data breaches & hacks webpage

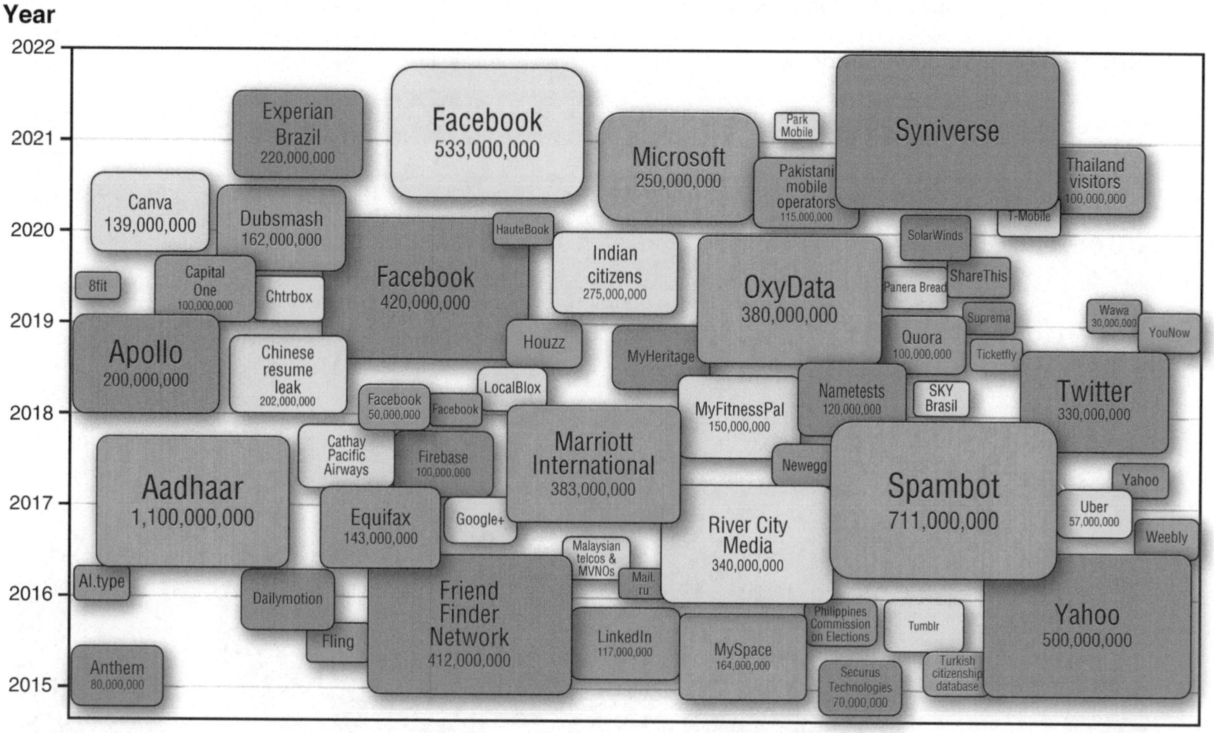

Year

Project 1-2: Configure Microsoft Windows Sandbox

Estimated Time: 15 minutes

Objective: Given a scenario, implement host or application security solutions.

Description: A **sandbox** is an isolated "virtual" computer (called a "virtual machine") within a "physical" computer. Anything done within a sandbox will impact only this virtual machine and not the underlying computer. Once you close the sandbox, nothing remains on your computer; when you launch the sandbox again it is just like starting over again. A sandbox is an ideal tool for downloading software and testing it to be sure that it contains no malware without impacting the physical computer. In this project, you will configure the Microsoft Windows 11 Sandbox.

> **Note 23**
>
> After configuring the Windows Sandbox, you can use it for the projects in this book if you do not want to download and install software on your physical computer.

1. First check if your system has virtualization turned on. Right-click the **Start** icon in the taskbar and select **Task Manager**.

2. Click the **Performance** tab.

3. If necessary, click **CPU** in the left pane.

4. Under "Virtualization" it must say "Enabled." If it says "Disabled" you will need to reboot and enter your computer's BIOS or UEFI and turn on virtualization. Close Task Manager.

5. Now enable Windows Sandbox. Click the magnifying glass icon in the taskbar.

6. In the Windows search box, enter **Windows Features** and press **Enter**.

7. Click **Turn Windows features on or off**.

8. Click the **Windows Sandbox** check box to turn on this feature.

9. To launch Windows Sandbox, click **Start**, type **Windows Sandbox**, and then press **Enter**. A protected virtual machine sandbox that looks like another Windows instance will start, as shown in Figure 1-7.

Figure 1-7   Windows Sandbox

Source: Microsoft Corporation

10. Explore the settings and default applications that come with the Windows Sandbox.

11. You can download a program through the Microsoft Edge application in Windows Sandbox. (Edge is included within Windows Sandbox along with a handful of other Windows applications, including access to OneDrive.) Open Edge and go to **www.google.com** to download and install the Google Chrome browser in the Windows Sandbox.

Note 24

You can also copy an executable file from your normal Windows environment and then paste it to the Windows Sandbox desktop to launch it.

12. After the installation is complete, close the Windows Sandbox.

13. Now relaunch the Windows Sandbox. What happened to Google Chrome? Why?

14. Close all windows.

Note 25

There are several advantages to using the Windows Sandbox. It relies on the Microsoft hypervisor to run a separate kernel that isolates the Windows Sandbox from the host so that this makes it more efficient since it can take advantage of the Windows integrated kernel scheduler, smart memory management, and a virtual graphics processing unit. Once you close the Windows Sandbox, nothing remains on your computer; when you launch Windows Sandbox again it is as clean as new. As an alternative to configuring the Windows Sandbox, you may create a virtual machine using Oracle VirtualBox software, which is a free application (www.virtualbox.org). However, you will need to acquire a licensed copy of Windows 11 to use in VirtualBox.

Project 1-3: Are You a Victim?

Estimated Time: 20 minutes
Objective: Assess the personal impact of cyberattacks.
Description: Even though all states require some type of notification sent to victims of a data breach, there are several loopholes in the requirements and not all users pay strict attention to these notification emails. In this activity, you will test your email addresses to determine if they are contained in a database of known breaches.

Caution !

This website is considered highly reputable. However, other websites may actually capture your email address that you enter and then sell it to marketers as a valid email address. You should be cautious about entering your email address in a site that does not have a strong reputation.

1. Open a web browser and enter the URL **https://haveibeenpwned.com/**. (If you are no longer able to access the site through this web address, open a search engine and enter "Have I been pwned.")
2. Scroll down and note the **Largest breaches**. Also, note the total number of **pwned accounts**.
3. Enter one of your email addresses in the box and click **pwned?**.
4. If this email address has been stolen and listed in the database, you will receive a **Oh no – pwned!** message. If this email address has not been stolen, enter another of your email addresses.
5. Scroll down to **Breaches you were pwned in**.
6. Read the information about the breach, noting in particular the **Compromised data** of each breach. Do you remember being alerted to these data breaches with a notification letter?
7. For any breaches that list **Passwords** in the **Compromised data**, this serves as a red flag that your password for this account was also stolen. Although the stolen password should be "scrambled" in such a way that an attacker would not be able to view it, that may not always be the case. You should stop immediately and change your password at once for that website.

Note 26

Other information listed as compromised data, while important, may be difficult or impossible to change, such as a phone number or physical address. The most critical item that can be changed and should be changed are any passwords.

8. Enter another email address and look for **Compromised data** that shows any exposed passwords. Change the passwords for those accounts as well.
9. What are your feelings now that you know about your compromised data? Does this inspire you to take even greater security protections?
10. Close all windows.

Case Projects

Case Project 1-1: #TrendingCyber

Estimated Time: 20 minutes

Objective: Summarize your thoughts on the #TrendingCyber opener.

Description: Read again the opening #TrendingCyber in this module. What are your thoughts? Should convicted attackers be restricted from using technology because it could tempt them to reoffend? Is it reasonable today to prevent someone who is trying to integrate back into society to restrict their access to technology? Or would the knowledge that this is a result of a conviction become a deterrent to cyberattackers? Are there other deterrents that would be better? Write a one-page paper about restricting convicted attackers from technology.

Case Project 1-2: Personal Attack Experiences

Estimated Time: 20 minutes

Objective: Describe personal experiences of a cyberattack.

Description: What type of computer attack have you (or a friend or another student) experienced? When did it happen? What type of computer or device was involved? What type of damage did it inflict? What type of threat actor do you think was behind it, and what was their motivation? What had to be done to clean up following the attack? How was the computer fixed after the attack? What data did you lose, or how much did it cost you to have your device restored? What could have prevented it? List the reason or reasons you think that the attack was successful. Write a one-page paper about these experiences.

Case Project 1-3: Security Podcasts or Video Series

Estimated Time: 45 minutes

Objective: Identify audio or video sources of information security information.

Description: Many different security vendors and security researchers now post weekly audio podcasts or video series on YouTube on security topics. Locate two different podcasts and two different video series about computer security. Listen and view one episode of each. Then, write a summary of what was discussed and a critique of the podcasts and videos. Were they beneficial to you? Were they accurate? Would you recommend them to someone else? Write a one-page paper on your research.

Case Project 1-4: Sources of Security Information

Estimated Time: 30 minutes

Objective: Determine the relative value of different sources of information.

Description: The following is a partial overall list of some of the sources for security information:

- Security content (online or printed articles that deal specifically with unbiased security content)
- Consumer content (general consumer-based magazines or broadcasts not devoted to security but occasionally carry end-user security tips)
- Vendor content (material from security vendors who sell security services, hardware, or software)
- Security experts (IT staff recommendations or newsletters)
- Direct instruction (college classes or a workshop conducted by a local computer vendor)
- Friends and family
- Personal experience

Create a table with each of these sources and columns listing Advantages, Disadvantages, Example, and Rating. Use the Internet to complete the entire table. The Rating column is a listing from 1 to 7 (with 1 being the highest) of how useful each of these sources is in your opinion. Compare your table with other learners.

Case Project 1-5: Career in Information Security

Estimated Time: 20 minutes

Objective: Research information security careers.

Description: Write a one-page paper on the pros and cons of pursuing a career in information security. Use the Internet to research topics such as information security employment in your area, salary ranges for specific cyber jobs, prospects for advancement, etc. Include a "pathway" that you would recommend for someone who wants to make this a career choice. Then research any negative concerns about a career in this area. Finally, write a short paragraph of why you would or would not pursue this career.

Case Project 1-6: Bay Point Ridge Security

Estimated Time: 45 minutes

Objective: Gather information on threat actors and CIA, AAA, and controls.

Description: Bay Point Ridge Security (BPRS) is an MSP that manages networks, computers, cloud resources, and information security for SMEs in the region. Their work in information security has gained a very positive reputation and they are now gaining large enterprises as clients. BPRS provides internships to students who are in their final year of the security degree program at the local college.

BPRS often holds lunch-and-learn workshops and invites SMEs to learn more about information security and the services that BPRS provides. Next week, BPRS is holding a workshop and you have been asked to create a presentation at area community centers and libraries about threat actors and their motivations. (BPRS has discovered that SMEs often do not have a clear understanding of who these adversaries are.)

1. Create a PowerPoint presentation that lists the different types of threat actors, what their motivations are, and typically who they may target. Your presentation should be seven to ten slides in length.

2. As a follow-up to your presentation, create a Frequently Asked Questions (FAQ) sheet that outlines CIA, AAA, and security controls. Write a one-page FAQ about these topics.

Two Rights & A Wrong: Answers

What Is Information Security?

1. Integrity ensures that only authorized parties can view information.

2. The relationship between security and convenience is inversely proportional: as security is increased, convenience is decreased.

3. A deterrent control is designed to discourage an attack from taking place.

Answer: The wrong statement is #1.

Explanation: Confidentiality ensures that only authorized parties can view information.

Threat Actors and Their Motivations

1. Nation-state actors are responsible for the class of attacks called Advanced Persistent Threats.

2. A usual motivation for organized crime is service disruption.

3. Hacktivists are motivated by philosophical/political beliefs.

Answer: The wrong statement is #2.

Explanation: A usual motivation for organized crime is financial gain.

How Attacks Occur

1. An attack surface is also called a threat vector.
2. A particularly alarming type of supply chain infection targets open-source software.
3. End-of-life means that a device will no longer function.

Answer: The wrong statement is #3.

Explanation: EOL does not mean that the device will no longer function, but rather that it is no longer manufactured and supported.

Information Security Resources

1. The two NIST frameworks are the NIST Risk Management Framework (RMF) and NIST Cybersecurity Framework (CSF).
2. An information security standard is considered mandatory.
3. Requests for comments (RFCs) are document "white papers" that are authored by technology bodies employing specialists, engineers, and scientists who are experts in those areas.

Answer: The wrong statement is #2.

Explanation: Strictly speaking, compliance to a standard is not mandatory, but there may be restrictions for those organizations that do not.

References

1. Stupp, Catherine, "After prison, hackers face tech restrictions, limited job prospects," *Wall Street Journal*, Sep. 21, 2022, accessed Dec. 26, 2022, https://www.wsj.com/articles/after-prison-hackers-face-tech-restrictions-limited-job-prospects-11663788389.
2. "Malware," *AV-Test*, accessed Apr. 8, 2022, https://www.av-test.org/en/statistics/malware/.
3. Kress, Robert, "How to develop a cyber-competent boardroom," *Accenture*, Jan. 5, 2022, accessed Apr 8, 2022, https://www.accenture.com/us-en/blogs/security/cyber-competent-boardroom.
4. "(ISC)² Cybersecurity Workforce Study," *(ISC)²*, accessed Dec. 26, 2022, https://www.isc2.org/Research/Workforce-Study#.
5. Lake, Sydney, "The cybersecurity industry is short 3.4 million workers—that's good news for cyber wages," *Fortune*, Oct. 20, 2022, accessed Dec 26, 2022, https://fortune.com/education/articles/the-cybersecurity-industry-is-short-3-4-million-workers-thats-good-news-for-cyber-wages/.
6. Milkman, Katherine, et al., "Megastudies improve the impact of applied behavioural science," *Nature*, Dec. 8, 2021, accessed Dec. 28, 2022, https://www.nature.com/articles/s41586-021-04128-4.
7. Goasduff, Laurence, "Protect your organization from cyber and ransomware attacks," *Gartner*, Feb. 14, 2018, accessed Dec. 27, 2022, https://www.gartner.com/smarterwithgartner/protect-your-organization-from-cyber-and-ransomware-attacks.
8. "Nor Torii study reveals 69% of tech executives say shadow IT is top security concern," *Business Wire*, Apr. 20, 2022, accessed Dec. 27, 2022, https://www.businesswire.com/news/home/20220420005191/en/New-Torii-Study-Reveals-69-of-Tech-Executives-Say-Shadow-IT-is-Top-Security-Concern.
9. Carlson, Brian, "Top cybersecurity statistics, trends, and facts," *CSO*, Oct. 7, 2021, accessed Dec. 27, 2022, https://www.csoonline.com/article/3153707/top-cybersecurity-facts-figures-and-statistics.html.
10. Murphy, Hannah, "Hackers launch more than 1.2m attacks through Log4J flaw," *Financial Times*, Dec. 14, 2021, accessed Dec. 29, 2022, https://www.ft.com/content/d3c244f2-eaba-4c46-9a51-b28fc13d9551.
11. Watson, Melanie, "What are the top 4 cybersecurity frameworks?" *IT Governance*, Jan. 17, 2019, accessed Jan. 19, 2023, https://www.itgovernanceusa.com/blog/top-4-cybersecurity-frameworks.

Pervasive Attack Surfaces and Controls

Module Objectives

After completing this module, you should be able to do the following:

1   Define social engineering and list types of attacks
2   List different types of physical defenses
3   Describe controls for protecting data

#TrendingCyber

One of the most effective types of attacks is social engineering. It involves tricking the user into taking an action or giving information that will benefit the attacker. While social engineering is often associated with cyberattacks and technology, in reality deceiving a victim for gain has been around for thousands of years. Some social engineering schemes are highly complicated and involve multiple participants working over long periods of time, whereas others are less involved. However, one successful social engineering attack stands out as being perhaps the very simplest of all.

In the 1970s, a small group of activists (eight men and women) wanted to find evidence that the U.S. government was operating outside the boundaries of established laws. These activists were people with ordinary jobs leading ordinary lives and were not considered to be experts or professionals. This group decided to break into a low-security FBI building in a small town west of Philadelphia to steal classified documents. They took great pains to consider every possible step so as to be successful and not get caught, since the jail sentence for breaking into a government office and stealing documents was significant. The group "cased" the office for several weeks to learn who used the building, when it was vacant, and what time employees arrived each morning. Most importantly, they looked at the type of door lock they would have to defeat to break into the office.

They chose to break in the same night as an event that was billed as "The Fight of the Century," a nationally televised heavyweight boxing match. One fighter was a strong supporter of the current president and his policies while the other had resisted entering the draft for the Vietnam War. The activists thought that the building superintendent, who lived right below the FBI office, would be watching the heavyweight fight on TV and might pay little attention to the security of the building. They also thought that if the boxer who was the presidential supporter lost the fight, it would make a strong political statement in support of their robbery. (As it turned out, the fighter supporting the president won in 15 rounds by unanimous decision.)

However, the activists' interest in the building aroused suspicion by the FBI. Wanting to take no chances, the FBI had the owner of the building change the door lock shortly before the planned break-in. This thwarted the activists' initial plans to pick the lock, so they had to come up with an alternative plan.

The night of the break-in, the burglars used a crowbar and a jack to break in through a seldom-used back door that had a deadbolt lock. Fortunately for the activists, the superintendent was watching the fight and evidently paid no attention to any sounds.

But after the burglars broke the lock, they discovered that a heavy filing cabinet had been placed in front of the door and was blocking their access. However, the room had been carpeted, so they were able to slide the filing cabinet far enough to slip in. The activists rummaged through the office, found what they were looking for, and quietly left without being detected.

Their success emboldened the group to search for their next target, which were the offices of area draft boards. One office in Philadelphia had a padlock on the door. The group was able to break off the padlock, ransack the office, and then replace the padlock so as not to cause any immediate attention by a broken lock hanging on the door.

However, their next target, a draft board in Delaware, proved to be much more difficult. There was no padlock on the door and the lock could not be picked. The only other means of access was through another office that had an interior door leading into the draft board office, but the door between the two offices was always locked.

After exhausting all of their various options for entrance, the activists finally came up with one last idea. A few hours before their planned burglary, one of the members of the group wrote a note and tacked it to the interior door that was always locked. The note simply said, "Please don't lock this door tonight."

Sure enough, when the group arrived later that evening, someone had obediently left the door unlocked. The activists entered the office, stole the records, and left.

Before leaving, one of the burglars even suggested that a thank-you note be tacked on the door as a demonstration of their good manners. They ultimately decided against it.

Pervasive is defined as "existing in or spreading through every part of something." For example, a *pervasive smell of a Thanksgiving dinner* can warmly welcome guests as they enter the kitchen.

The three topics in this module—social engineering, physical security, and data controls—are considered pervasive since they apply universally across information technology (IT) security. Unlike some IT topics that are closely linked to, for example, computer networking or mobile devices, these topics "run the gamut" across information security. Defeating attempts to trick users into making the wrong decisions, the need for strong physical security to protect assets, and controls necessary to ensure the confidentiality, integrity, and availability of data are universally important.

In this module, you explore these three pervasive elements of social engineering, physical security, and data controls. These are considered fundamental to securing information.

Social Engineering Attacks

> **Certification**
>
> 2.2 Explain common threat vectors and attack surfaces.

Not all attacks rely on technology vulnerabilities; in fact, most cyberattacks today rarely exploit a technology weakness as the initial first step. Instead, they start with social engineering. Social engineering is a means of eliciting information or convincing a user to take action that weakens security. Social engineering is almost always performed through deception and manipulation of the user. Because social engineering occurs through the exploitation of a person, it is sometimes said to be accomplished using human vectors as the attack surface.

> **Note 1**
>
> One reason why most cybersecurity attacks are successful today is because they start with highly successful social engineering attacks, which then open the door for the next steps in the attack. It is estimated that cybercriminals use social engineering in 98 percent of their attacks.[1]

There are different ways in which threat actors attempt to manipulate users to their advantage. This results in several types of social engineering attacks.

Examples of Human Manipulation

Social engineering begins with the threat actor first selecting a human target. Next, they create a believable scenario that is usually specific to the target. It often involves inventing a false story or creating a seemingly plausible situation in hopes of obtaining information or gaining leverage to breach a system.

Note 2

Threat actors using social engineering have been called "masters of the art of deception."

Social engineering relies heavily on human psychology (a person's conscious and unconscious feelings and thoughts). Threat actors' clever manipulation of human nature can persuade the target to provide information or take action—without even realizing that they are being taken advantage of. There are several basic principles of psychology that attackers use in their favor. These are listed in Table 2-1 with the example of an attacker pretending to be the chief executive officer (CEO) calling the organization's help desk to reset a password.

Table 2-1 Human manipulation for social engineering

Principle	Description	Example
Authority	Directed by someone impersonating authority figure or falsely citing their authority	"I'm the CEO calling."
Intimidation	To frighten and coerce by threat	"If you don't reset my password, I will call your supervisor."
Consensus	Influenced by what others do	"I called last week, and your colleague reset my password."
Scarcity	Something is in short supply	"I can't waste time here."
Urgency	Immediate action is needed	"My meeting with the board starts in 5 minutes."
Familiarity	Victim is well known and well received	"I remember reading a good evaluation on you."
Trust	Confidence	"You know who I am."

Note 3

Another technique is called prepending, which is influencing the subject before the event occurs. A common general example is a preview of a soon-to-be-released movie that begins with the statement, "The best film you will see this year!" By starting with the desired outcome ("The best film") it influences the listener to think that way. Threat actors use prepending with social engineering attacks, such as including it with an urgency principle of "You need to reset my password immediately because my meeting with the board starts in 5 minutes."

Some social engineering involves person-to-person contact. When it involves direct contact with the target, attackers use a variety of personal techniques to gain their trust. For example:

- **Provide a reason.** Many social engineering threat actors are careful to add a reason along with their request. By giving a rationalization and using the word *because*, it is much more likely for the target to provide the information. For example, "I was asked to call you because the director's office manager is out sick today."

- **Project confidence.** A threat agent is unlikely to generate suspicion if they enter a restricted area but calmly walks through the building as if they know exactly where they are going (without looking at signs, down hallways, or reading door labels) and even greets people they see with a friendly, "Hi, how are you doing?"
- **Use evasion and diversion.** When challenged, a threat actor might evade a question by giving a vague or irrelevant answer. They could also feign innocence or confusion, or just keep denying any allegations, until the target eventually believes their suspicions are wrong. Sometimes a threat actor can resort to anger and cause the target to drop the challenge. "Who are you to ask that? Connect me with your supervisor immediately!"
- **Make them laugh.** Humor is an excellent tool to put people at ease and to develop a sense of trust. "I can't believe I left my badge in my office again! You know, some mistakes are too much fun to only make once!"

Types of Social Engineering Attacks

There are several types of social engineering attacks. These include phishing, impersonation, redirection, misinformation and disinformation, watering hole attacks, and data reconnaissance.

Phishing

One of the most common forms of social engineering is phishing. Phishing is sending an email or displaying a web announcement that falsely claims to be from a legitimate source in an attempt to trick the user into taking an action.

> **Note 4**
>
> The word *phishing* is a variation on the word "fishing," with the idea being that bait is thrown out knowing that while most will ignore it, some will "bite."

In a typical phishing attack, users are asked to respond to an email or are directed to a website where they are requested to update personal information, such as passwords, credit card numbers, Social Security numbers, bank account numbers, or other information. However, the email or website is actually an imposter and is set up to steal the entered information.

> **Caution !**
>
> Phishing is also used to validate email addresses. A phishing email can display an image retrieved from a website that is requested when the user opens the email message. A unique code is used to link the image to the recipient's email address, which then tells the phisher that the email address is active and valid. This is the reason most email today does not automatically display images in emails.

Several variations on phishing attacks are:

- **Spear phishing.** Whereas phishing usually sends generic email messages to millions of users, **spear phishing** targets specific users. The emails used in spear phishing are customized to the recipient, often including their names and detailed personal information, in order to make the message appear legitimate.
- **Whaling.** One type of spear phishing is **whaling**. Instead of going after "little fish" or average users, whaling targets the "big fish," namely, wealthy individuals or senior executives within a business who typically would have larger sums of money in a bank account that an attacker could access. By focusing on this smaller but more lucrative group, the attacker can invest more time in the attack and finely tune the message to achieve the highest likelihood of success.
- **Vishing.** Instead of using email to contact the potential victim, a telephone call can be used instead. Known as vishing (*voice* ph*ishing*), an attacker calls a target who, upon answering,

hears a recorded message that pretends to be from the user's bank stating that a large charge is being made on their credit card or that their bank account has had an unusual activity. The target is instructed to call a specific phone number immediately (which has been set up by the attacker). When the target calls, it is answered by automated instructions telling them to enter their credit card number, bank account number, Social Security number, or other information on the telephone's keypad—all of which is then captured by the threat actor.

- **Smishing.** Another avenue for spreading social engineering attacks uses the short message service (SMS) to send fraudulent text messages. This is known as smishing and can be combined with callback recorded phone messages. Threat actors first send a text message to a user's cell phone that pretends to come from their bank saying that a large withdrawal from their account has just occurred and asks the user if this is legitimate. Along with the text message is a callback telephone number the customer is instructed to call immediately. That phone number plays a recording telling the customer to first enter their credit card number for verification. The attackers then simply capture the information that is entered.

One particular type of phishing attack that is increasing in popularity is a business email compromise (BEC). A BEC takes advantage of the common practice today by businesses and organizations of electronically making payments or transferring funds. Attackers take advantage of the size and complexity of large enterprises to request funds from what appears to be a legitimate source, knowing that the target will often comply without investigating if the request is legitimate. Table 2-2 lists common BEC attacks.

Table 2-2 Common BEC attacks

BEC attack	Description
Bogus invoice	Pretending to be a legitimate supplier, an attacker sends a fake invoice for goods or services demanding immediate payment on an overdue account.
Executive fraud	Posing as a company executive, a threat actor sends an email to employees in the Finance Department telling them to immediately transfer funds for an unpublicized new company initiative but not to tell anyone about it.
Account compromise	A Finance Department employee's email account is compromised and then each vendor in the contact list is sent an email demanding immediate payment for a fictitious service.

BECs are not limited to businesses: Users can also be victims of these attacks demanding immediate payment for goods or services. For example, a threat actor can pose as a distant relative on vacation overseas who has just had their wallet stolen, and immediately needs money wired to them. Other times these attacks may have a different goal than asking for money. In Figure 2-1, an email says that it is a receipt for an automatic withdrawal payment, and users wishing to stop the payment and request a refund are instructed to call the phone number listed in the email. However, this telephone number is a direct line to the attackers, who will then use the telephone to extract information such as the credit card number from the target.

Note 5

Phishing should not be confused with *spamming*, which is sending unsolicited email advertising. Sending spam is very lucrative because it costs spammers little to send millions of spam email messages, and even if they receive only a small percentage of responses, they still make a large profit. For example, if a spammer sent spam to 6 million users for a product with a sale price of $50 that cost only $5 to make, and if only 0.001 percent of the recipients responded and bought the product (a typical response rate), the spammer would still make more than $270,000 in profit.

Phishing is considered to be one of the largest and most consequential cyber threats facing both enterprises and consumers. During the third quarter of 2022, there were over 1.2 million phishing attacks, which was a new record for the worst quarter ever observed. Attacks against the financial sector represented 23 percent of all phishing attacks. BEC attacks increased by 59 percent.[2]

Figure 2-1   BEC phishing email message

INVOICE NUMBER

Product Details

NOR04142022GB

NORTON 360 PROTECTION

Order Summary

INVOICE NO.:   NOR04142022GB
Start Date: 2022-04-14
End Date: 1 year from Start Date
Payment Mode: Auto debit from account
Status: Completed

--

Product Title	Quantity	Total
NORTON 360 PROTECTION (NOR04142022GB)	1	$566.00 USD
	Sub-total	$566.00 USD
	Discount	00.00
	Total	$566.00 USD

If you wish to stop subscription and ask for a **REFUND** then please feel free to call our Billing Department as soon as possible!

You can Reach us on : **+1   – (877) – (209) – 2392**

Regards,
Refund & Settlement Dept.

Caution

Whereas at one time phishing messages were easy to spot with misspelled words and obvious counterfeit images, that is no longer the case. In fact, one of the reasons that phishing is so successful today is that the emails and the fake websites are difficult to distinguish from those that are legitimate: logos, color schemes, and wording seem to be almost identical. It is considered risky to attempt to determine if an email message is phishing just by how it looks. And although most web browsers automatically block known phishing websites, because so many sites are appearing so rapidly, it is difficult for the browsers to stay up to date. Users should remain constantly vigilant to guard against phishing attacks.

Impersonation

Social engineering impersonation is masquerading as a real or fictitious character and then playing out the role of that person on a target. For example, an attacker could impersonate a help desk support technician who calls the target, pretends that there is a problem with the network, and asks them for their username and password to reset their account. Sometimes the goal of the impersonation is to obtain private information, called pretexting.

Caution !

Common roles that are often impersonated include a repairperson, IT support, a manager, or a trusted third party. Often attackers will impersonate individuals whose roles are authoritative because users generally resist saying "no" to anyone in power. Users should exercise caution when receiving a phone call or email from these types of individuals asking for something suspicious.

One type of impersonation is brand impersonation. As its name implies, a threat actor uses brand impersonation to pretend to be a highly recognizable and well-known brand of a product or service (such as the name of a large bank) in an attempt to build immediate recognition and trust. By posing as a recognizable brand that is familiar to the target, attackers can trick them into a dangerous action, such as clicking a link or opening an attachment in an email.

Redirection

If a threat actor cannot trick a user to visit a malicious website through phishing or impersonation, there are other tactics that can be used instead.

What happens when a user makes a typing error when entering a uniform resource locator (URL) address in a web browser, such as typing *goggle.com* (a misspelling) or *google.net* (incorrect domain) instead of the correct *google.com*? In the past, an error message like *HTTP Error 404 Not Found* would appear. However, today most often the user will be directed to a fake look-alike site. These sites may pretend to be the legitimate site or just be filled with ads for which the attacker receives money for traffic generated to the site. These fake sites exist because attackers purchase and register the domain names of sites that are spelled similarly to actual sites. This is called typo squatting. A well-known site like google.com may have to deal with thousands of typo-squatting domains.

Note 6

One squatting detector system discovered 13,857 typo-squatting domains that mimic actual websites were registered in a single month, or an average of 450 each day.[3]

"Squatters" prefer to mimic two categories of sites. The first are mainstream search engines and social media sites. This is because these sites generate a large amount of traffic and typically will have a high number of redirections through misspellings. The second category are financial, online shopping, and banking websites. When visiting these sites, users are often expecting to enter sensitive information and it is easier to trick them into giving that information.

Note 7

The most popular sites to mimic using typo squatting are Paypal.com, Apple.com, Royalbank.com, Netflix.com, Linkedin.com, and Amazon.com.

Enterprises have tried to preempt typo squatting by registering themselves the domain names of close spellings of their website. At one time, top-level domains (TLDs) were limited to .com, .org, .net, .int, .edu, .gov, and .mil, so it was easy to register close-sounding domain names. However, today there are over 1,239 generic TLDs (gTLDs), such as .museum, .office, .global, and .school. Organizations must now attempt to register a very large number of sites that are a variation of their registered domain name.

Note 8

Typo squatting should not be confused with *cybersquatting*. Cybersquatting involves registering an Internet domain name that contains trademarks for the sole purpose of selling that domain name to the trademark owner. The Anti-Cybersquatting Consumer Protection Act of 1999 outlaws this practice.

In addition to registering names that are similar to the actual names (like *goggle.com* for *google.com*), threat actors are now registering domain names that are *one bit* different. This is because the billions of devices that are part of the Internet have multiple instances of a domain name in domain name system (DNS) memory at any time, so the likelihood increases of a RAM memory error of a bit being "flipped." Figure 2-2 illustrates that the change of one bit in the letter *g* (0110011*1*) results in the change of the entire character from *g* to *f*. In this example, a threat agent would register the domain *foo.gl* as a variation of the actual *goo.gl*.

Figure 2-2   Character change by bit flipping

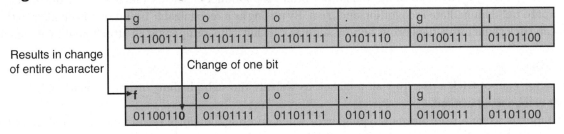

Another redirection technique is **pharming**. Pharming attempts to exploit how a URL such as www.cengage.com is converted into its corresponding Internet Protocol address, 69.32.308.75. A threat actor may install malware on a user's computer that performs the redirection when the user enters the URL in a web browser. A variation is to infect a DNS that would then direct large numbers of users to the fake site.

Misinformation and Disinformation

Although definitions vary, misinformation is false or inaccurate information, regardless of the intent to mislead. Because misinformation does not consider the intent, it can be used as a term for almost any type of information that is not true. Disinformation is false or inaccurate misinformation that comes from a malicious intent. Disinformation is knowingly false and intentionally spread. There are many nefarious motivations behind the creation and spread of disinformation.

One example of cyber disinformation is a **hoax** or a false warning. These are often contained in an email message sent by a threat actor falsely claiming to come from the IT Department. The hoax purports that a "deadly virus" is circulating through the Internet and that the recipient should erase specific files or change security configurations, and then forward the message to other users. However, changing configurations allows an attacker to compromise the system. Or, erasing files may make the computer unstable, prompting the victim to call the telephone number in the hoax email message for help, which is actually the phone number of the attacker.

Note 10

Hacktivists and nation-state actors often are responsible for spreading disinformation that is not part of a cyberattack.

Watering Hole Attack

In the natural world, similar types of animals are known to congregate around a pool of water for refreshment. In a similar manner, a watering hole attack is directed toward a smaller group of specific individuals, such as the major executives working for a manufacturing company. These executives all tend to visit a common website, such as that of a parts supplier to the manufacturer. An attacker who wants to target this group of executives will attempt to determine the common website that they frequent and then infect it with malware that will make its way onto the group's computers.

Data Reconnaissance

In addition to these types of social engineering attacks, there are other means by which a threat actor can gather valuable information. These can even be done without any interaction with the target and include the following:

- **Dumpster diving. Dumpster diving** involves digging through trash receptacles to find information that can be useful in an attack. Items that may have valuable information include calendars, memos, organizational charts, phone directories, and policy manuals. Similar to dumpster diving is purchasing used technology equipment that originates from a business. Often sensitive information has not been "scrubbed" from this equipment and can still be retrieved.
- **Google dorking.** An electronic variation of dumpster diving is to use Google's search engine to look for documents and data posted online that can be used in an attack. This is called **Google dorking** and it uses advanced Google search techniques to look for information that unsuspecting victims have carelessly posted on the web.

Note 11

Google dorking is from a slang term that originally was used to refer to someone who is not considered intelligent (a *dork*) and later came to refer to uncovering security vulnerabilities that are the result of the actions of such a person.

- **Shoulder surfing.** If a relatively small amount of data is needed, such as the access code for a door, a threat actor can simply watch an individual entering the security code on a keypad. Known as **shoulder surfing**, it can be used in any setting in which a user casually observes someone entering secret information without drawing attention to themselves. Attackers are also using hidden webcams and smartphone cameras to shoulder-surf unsuspecting victims.

Caution !

College students and other young adults are considered as tempting targets for threat actors using social engineering. Emails and text messages offering free scholarships, high-paying part-time jobs, low-cost car loans, and low-interest credit cards are directed toward their current life settings and may be too tempting to pass up. Users should be particularly wary of these types of offers.

Two Rights & A Wrong

1. A threat actor who threatens to contact a superior of the target if the actor's demands are not met is an example of authority.
2. Spear phishing targets specific users.
3. Pretexting is designed to obtain private information.

See the answers at the end of the module.

Physical Security Controls

A security control is a countermeasure that attempts to limit the exposure of an asset to a danger. Of the four broad categories of controls—managerial, operational, technical, and physical—the most often overlooked are physical controls. Preventing a threat actor from physically accessing a web server can be as important as preventing the attacker from accessing it remotely through the Internet. Physical security controls include perimeter defenses, preventing data leakage, and computer hardware security.

> **Note 12**
>
> Controls and categories of controls are found in Module 1.

Perimeter Defenses

Some organizations have used "industrial camouflage" in an attempt to make the physical presence of a building as nondescript as possible so that it does not draw attention. However, this is rarely effective. Instead, perimeter defenses must be used to restrict access. This type of defense includes barriers, security guards, sensors, security buffers, and locks.

Barriers

Different types of passive barriers can be used to restrict unwanted individuals or vehicles from entering a secure area. Fencing is usually a tall, permanent structure to keep out unauthorized personnel. It is accompanied with signage that explains the area is restricted along with proper lighting so the area can be monitored after dark. However, standard chain-link fencing offers limited security because it can easily be circumvented by climbing over it or cutting the links. Most modern perimeter security consists of a fence equipped with other deterrents such as those listed in Table 2-3.

Table 2-3   Fencing deterrents

Technology	Description	Comments
Anticlimb paint	A nontoxic petroleum gel-based paint that is thickly applied and does not harden, making any coated surface difficult to climb.	Typically used on poles, downpipes, wall tops, and railings above head height (8 feet or 2.4 meters).
Anticlimb collar	Spiked collar that extends horizontally for up to 3 feet (1 meter) from the pole to prevent anyone from climbing it; serves as both a practical and visual deterrent.	Used for protecting equipment mounted on poles like cameras or in areas where climbing a pole can be an easy point of access over a security fence.
Roller barrier	Independently rotating large cups (diameter of 5 inches or 115 millimeters) affixed to the top of a fence prevent the hands of intruders from gripping the top of a fence to climb over it.	Often found around public grounds and schools where a nonaggressive barrier is important.
Rotating spikes	Installed at the top of walls, gates, or fences; the tri-wing spike collars rotate around a central spindle.	Designed for high-security areas; can be painted to blend into fencing.

Like fencing, a barricade is designed to block the passage of traffic. However, barricades are most often used for directing large crowds and are generally not designed to keep out individuals. This is because barricades are usually not as tall as fences and can more easily be circumvented by climbing over them. A bollard is a short but sturdy vertical post that is used as a vehicular traffic barricade to prevent a car from "ramming" into a secure area. A pair of bollards is pictured in Figure 2-3.

Figure 2-3   Bollards

MartineDF/Shutterstock.com

Security Guards

Whereas barriers function as passive devices to restrict access, human security guards who patrol and monitor restricted areas are an active security defense. Unlike passive devices, security guards can differentiate between an intruder and someone looking for a lost pet and then make split-second decisions about a need to take appropriate action.

In settings that require a higher level of protection, multiple security guards may be required. This prevents one security guard who has been compromised (through bribery, threats, or other coercion) from participating in an attack, such as allowing malicious actors to enter through a locked door. Using two security guards is called **two-person integrity/control**.

Note 13

Most of the major heists involving the theft of large amounts of cash or precious jewels have been the result of an inside employee of a bank, airport warehouse, or other facility participating in the theft.

Often guards are responsible for monitoring activity captured by video surveillance cameras that transmit a signal to a specific and limited set of receivers (called closed-circuit television or CCTV). Some video surveillance cameras are fixed in a single position pointed at a door or a hallway; other cameras resemble a small dome and allow guards to move the camera 360 degrees for a full panoramic view. High-end video surveillance cameras send alerts and begin recording when they detect movement or identify a suspicious object, such as a backpack left in a chair. Increasingly drones, called unmanned aerial vehicles (UAVs), are being used for monitoring activity.

Note 14

When security guards actively monitor video surveillance it is a preventive measure: Any unauthorized activity seen on video surveillance results in the guard taking immediate action by either going to the scene or calling for assistance. When a guard does not actively monitor a camera, the video is recorded and, if a security event occurs, the recording is examined later to identify the culprit. A new technology combines these two features. Artificial intelligence can be used to immediately identify an object in a live video feed, such as a gun on a school campus, and then sound an alert and lock the doors.

Sensors

When using human personnel for security, an incident may occur during a lapse of attention by a security guard. To supplement the work of a security guard, sensors (devices that detect or measure a physical property and respond to it) can be placed in strategic locations to alert guards by generating an alarm of an unexpected or unusual action. There are four basic types of sensors: infrared, microwave, ultrasonic, and pressure.

Infrared   All the different types of light that travel from the sun to the earth make up what is called the light spectrum. Visible light is just a small part of that entire spectrum. Some of the other energies of the spectrum, such as x-rays, ultraviolet rays, and microwaves, are invisible to the human eye. Infrared (IR) light is another invisible energy.

IR is used in a wide variety of applications. For example, IR can be used for data transmissions. Data can be sent by the intensity of the IR light wave instead of "on-off" signals of, for example, a flashlight. To transmit a "1," an emitter (a device that transmits a signal) increases the intensity of the current and sends a "pulse" using infrared light. On the receiving end, a detector (a device that receives a signal) senses the higher-intensity pulse of light and produces a proportional electrical current. Most television remote control devices use IR.

Note 15

The original wireless local area network (Wi-Fi) standard known as IEEE 802.11 specified that wireless transmissions could take place in either one of two different ways: through IR or by sending radio signals through the radio frequency spectrum. Due to the limitations of IR for data transmissions, it was never widely used for Wi-Fi.

In addition to sending signals, IR can be used as a detector. An infrared (IR) sensor is an electronic device that can measure and detect IR in the surrounding area. There are two types of IR sensors: active and passive. Active IR sensors both emit and detect infrared radiation using a light-emitting diode (LED) and a receiver. When an object comes close to the sensor, the IR light from the LED reflects off of the object and is detected by the receiver. Active IR sensors act as proximity sensors to determine how close an objective is.

Passive IR sensors do not rely on IR reflection. They instead can only detect IR radiation from an object. Passive IR sensors take advantage of the fact that all living beings emit heat that gives off IR radiation. When a moving object that generates IR radiation enters the sensing range of the passive IR sensor, the increase in IR level can be detected and an alarm sounded. This makes passive IR ideal for motion-based detection to determine if an unauthorized person has entered an area.

Note 16

A passive IR sensor can measure anything that has a temperature above 5 degrees Kelvin, which is equivalent to −450 degrees Fahrenheit.

Microwave   A limitation of IR sensors is that they can only monitor a limited space. A technology that can be used to monitor a large area is a microwave sensor, which uses high-frequency radio waves and functions similarly to radar. Radio waves, projected in 360 degrees, can detect changes in the reflected radio waves that are returned. Microwave sensors are especially effective in monitoring large areas such as a warehouse to determine if an intruder has entered a restricted area.

Note 17

Another advantage of a microwave sensor is that it can also sense levels of daylight and can dim interior lights accordingly to save energy.

Ultrasonic   Sound is a pressure wave caused when something vibrates, making particles bump into each other and then apart. The distance between one wave and the next produces a wavelength. High-frequency (high-pitched) sounds have waves very close together, whereas low-frequency sounds have a greater distance between each wave. Frequency is measured in hertz (Hz).

Note 18

The volume or loudness relates to the maximum pressure produced as particles are squeezed together as they are made to vibrate and is measured in decibels (dB). This is a measure of intensity, which relates to how much energy the pressure wave has.

Not all creatures can hear the same sounds. Humans can hear sounds between 16 and 20,000 Hz (**audible frequencies**), while some animals can hear sounds below or above the normal range for humans. Figure 2-4 illustrates that cats can hear sounds below the normal human range (**infrasound**) and bats use sounds above the normal range (**ultrasound**).

Figure 2-4   Sound frequencies

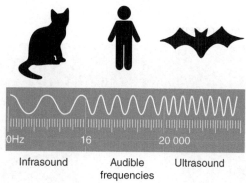

Using ultrasound, ultrasonic sensors can measure how far away a target object is located. Ultrasonic waves are transmitted to bounce off the target back to the receiver, in which the waves are converted into an electrical signal that can be measured. The measurement formula is Distance = ½ Time × 343 (343 is the speed of the sound in meters per second).

Note 19

Ultrasonic technology has enabled the medical profession to produce images of internal organs, identify tumors, and ensure the health of babies in the womb.

Compared to IR sensors, ultrasonic sensors are not as susceptible to interference by smoke, gas, and other airborne particles. Like active IR sensors, ultrasonic sensors are used primarily as proximity sensors. For physical security applications, an ultrasonic sensor could be used to allow an individual to be present in an area but sound an alarm if the person moves too close to a door.

Note 20

Ultrasonic technology can also be used in cyberattacks. Researchers have used ultrasonic waves transmitted through solid materials like a desk to send inaudible voice commands to a smartphone resting on the desk. They are able to intercept SMS text messages and place phone calls without the owner's knowledge.

Pressure   Pressure is an expression of force exerted on a surface per unit area. A pressure sensor can be used in physical security to detect if a person has entered a restricted area. However, pressure sensors can do more than just indicate if someone has stepped into a room. Modern pressure sensors can differentiate between what has entered and where they are headed.

Note 21

The scientific unit for pressure is the Pascal, which is equivalent to one Newton per meter squared. In the United States, the common standard is pounds per square inch (PSI); nations using the metric system use kilograms per square centimeter (kg/cm²).

Underground pressure sensors usually consist of a controller box with two plastic tubes extended on two sides. The controller and tubes are buried about 4–6 inches (10–15 centimeters) deep and the tubes on each side are parallel to each other and form a *U* shape. The pressure sensor in the controller converts the change in pressure to an electric signal that is then analyzed by a microprocessor. The pressure sensor can automatically detect as well as identify targets (pedestrian, car, truck, etc.) and, for vehicles, determine the direction of travel. A pressure sensor is shown in Figure 2-5.

Figure 2-5   Pressure sensor

Security Buffers

A **buffer** serves as a protective barrier. In a building or office, buffers are used to help provide an additional layer of security to keep intruders from entering areas but still allow approved personnel. The common security buffers depend on the level of security necessary. These include high-, medium-, and low-security areas.

High Security: Access Control Vestibule

In high-security areas before electronic security was available, vestibules (small rooms) with two locked doors were used to control access to sensitive areas. Individuals would give their credentials (usually an access badge or other token that indicates they have been preapproved) to a security officer, who would then open the first door to the vestibule and ask the individuals to enter and wait while their credentials were being checked. If the credentials were approved, the second door would be unlocked; if the credentials were fraudulent, the person would be trapped in the vestibule. This was sometimes called a **mantrap**.

Today, an automated access control vestibule is used instead to create a buffer to separate a nonsecure area from a secure area. A device monitors and controls two interlocking doors to a vestibule, as shown in Figure 2-6. When in operation, only one door can be open at any time. Access control vestibules are used in high-security areas where only authorized persons can enter, such as cash handling areas and research laboratories.

Medium Security: Reception Area

In areas in which medium security is needed, a **reception area** can be used. Users are allowed to enter the area (and are not restricted as with an access control vestibule) in which a receptionist can check credentials. Anyone not approved could not be allowed to pass through the inner door to the next area.

Figure 2-6   Access control vestibule

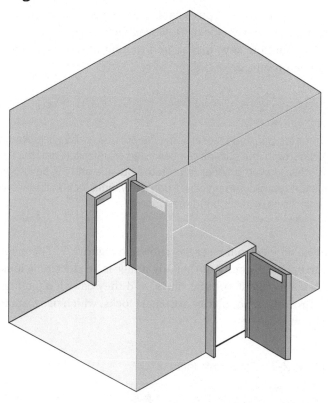

However, reception areas can be a risk. Once visitors are in the reception area, they are already inside the facility beyond external barriers and are one step closer to the secure area. There should be additional precautions taken in a reception area.

One precaution regards the receptionist. The receptionist's duty should be to observe and interact appropriately with the public so that a potential malicious actor feels that they are always being observed. This means a receptionist should not have additional clerical duties beyond maintaining a visitor log of those individuals; otherwise, the receptionist will be distracted from their primary duty. In this way, the receptionist can provide a higher level of active security.

Note 22

A receptionist should not always be expected to physically intercept or impede a real or perceived threat, but instead should call for help.

Other precautions include anchoring furnishings and wall hangings so they cannot be picked up and thrown or used as weapons; the reception room should not be used for mail deliveries, as an employee entrance, or a designated escape route; and receptionists should be able to observe visitors before they enter the reception room and electrically lock out suspicious persons.

Low Security: Waiting Room   In areas of low security, a generic **waiting room** can be used instead. Although this room still serves as an important buffer with two doors as with an access control vestibule, it is more friendly to the public. A reception area is typically used to control traffic flow. Usually, a check-in window is used to ensure individuals have the proper credentials or identification before they are approved to pass on to the next area. This type of setting is commonly seen in doctors' offices in which patients check in with a receptionist behind a window before a nurse or assistant opens the inner door at the time for the appointment.

Locks

A variety of types of locks can be used to restrict physical access. Locks that require a key or other device to open doors or cabinets are the most common types of locks. However, locks that use keys can be compromised if the keys are lost, stolen, or duplicated. And multiple keys distributed to multiple users to access a single locked door only increases the risk of a key being compromised.

Note 23

The categories of commercial door locks include storeroom (the outside is always locked, entry is by key only, and the inside lever is always unlocked), classroom (the outside can be locked or unlocked, and the inside lever is always unlocked), store entry double cylinder (includes a keyed cylinder in both the outside and inside knobs so that a key in either knob locks or unlocks both at the same time), and communicating double cylinder lock (includes a keyed cylinder in both outside and inside knobs, and the key unlocks its own knob independently).

A more secure option is to use an electronic lock, as shown in Figure 2-7. These locks use buttons that must be pushed in the proper sequence to open the door. Another advantage is an electronic lock can be programmed to allow a certain individual's code to be valid only at specific times, and they can also maintain a record of when the door was opened and by which code. Growing in popularity are smart locks, which use a smartphone that sends a code via wireless Bluetooth to open the door.

Figure 2-7   Electronic lock

myboys.me/Shutterstock.com

Note 24

One of the problems with an electronic lock is that someone can watch a user enter the code on a physical keypad by shoulder surfing or even detect fingerprint "smudges" on keys to uncover the code. One brand of electronic lock mitigates this by using a virtual screen that substitutes physical buttons with four circles. Each of the circles displays the numbers associated with that circle (for example, Circle A may display the digits 1, 2 and 3, and Circle B displays the digits 4, 5 and 6) and the digits are randomly assigned to different circles: Circle A now may be 4, 7, and 0; later, it may be 2, 5, and 9. This prevents a shoulder surfer from pressing the same circles to unlock the door.

Preventing Data Leakage

Another means of physical security applies to preventing important data from escaping (leakage). Two physical controls can be applied. These include a Faraday cage and protected cable distribution systems.

Faraday Cage

Computer systems, printers, and similar digital electronic devices all emit electromagnetic fields, and often these can result in interference, called **electromagnetic interference (EMI)**. In addition to interference, unauthorized persons could detect and read these electromagnetic signals.

One means of protecting against this eavesdropping is to use a **Faraday cage**, which is a metallic enclosure that prevents the entry or escape of an electromagnetic field. A Faraday cage, consisting of grounded, fine-mesh copper screening, as shown in Figure 2-8, is often used for testing in electronic labs. In addition, lightweight and portable **Faraday bags** made of special materials can be used to shield portable devices.

Figure 2-8   Faraday cage

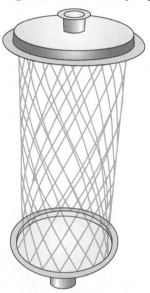

Note 25

Faraday bags are often used in crime scene investigations. Phones, tablets, or laptops found on-scene are placed in Faraday bags, thus eliminating inbound and outbound signals and preventing the devices from being remotely wiped of evidence.

Protected Distribution System

Cable conduits are hollow tubes that carry copper wire or fiber-optic cables, as shown in Figure 2-9. A **protected distribution system (PDS)** is a system of cable conduits used to protect classified information transmitted between two secure areas. PDS is a standard created by the U.S. Department of Defense (DoD).

Figure 2-9   Cable conduits

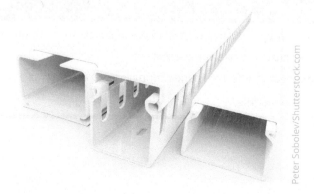

Peter Sobolev/Shutterstock.com

Two types of PDSs are commonly used. In a **hardened carrier PDS**, the data cables are installed in a conduit that is constructed of special electrical metallic tubing or similar material. All the connections between the different segments are permanently sealed with welds or special sealants. If the hardened carrier PDS is buried underground, such as running between buildings, the carrier containing the cables must be encased in concrete, and any maintenance hole covers that give access to the PDS must be locked down. A hardened carrier PDS must be visually inspected on a regular basis.

An alternative to a hardened carrier PDS is an **alarmed carrier PDS**. In this type of PDS, the carrier system is deployed with specialized optical fibers in the conduit that can sense acoustic vibrations that occur when an intruder attempts to gain access to the cables, which triggers an alarm. The advantages of an alarmed carrier PDS are that it provides continuous monitoring, eliminates the need for periodic visual inspections, allows the carrier to be hidden above the ceiling or below the floor, and eliminates the need for welding or sealing connections.

Computer Hardware Security

Computer hardware security is the physical security that specifically involves protecting some types of mobile hardware, such as laptops, that can easily be stolen. Most portable devices (as well as many expensive computer monitors) have a special steel bracket security slot built into the case. A **cable lock** can be inserted into the security slot of a portable device and rotated so that the cable lock is secured to the device, as illustrated in Figure 2-10. The cable can then be connected to an immovable object.

Figure 2-10   Cable lock

O. Bellini/Shutterstock.com

When storing a laptop, it can be placed in a safe or a vault, which is a ruggedized steel box with a lock. Some offices have safes in employee cubicles for the users to lock up important papers when away from their desks, even for a short period of time. The sizes typically range from small (to accommodate one laptop) to large (for multiple devices). Safes and cabinets can also be prewired for electrical power as well as wired network connections. This allows the laptops stored in the locking cabinet to charge their batteries and receive software updates while not in use.

Two Rights & A Wrong

1. A barricade is a short but sturdy vertical post used to prevent a car from "ramming" into a secure area.

2. There are two types of IR sensors: active and passive.

3. Microwave sensors are especially effective in monitoring large areas such as a warehouse.

See the answers at the end of the module.

Data Controls

Certification

3.3 Compare and contrast concepts and strategies to protect data.

4.2 Explain the security implications of proper hardware, software, and data asset management.

Data is the lifeblood of technology: without data, there would be little need for computers, smartphones, and technology devices. Thus, it is imperative to have adequate controls in place to protect this data. Protecting data involves knowing the different classifications and types of data, the consequences of a data breach, and controls for protecting data.

Data Classifications

Consider the data that can be accessed from a smartphone: SMS texts, emails, digital photos, credit card numbers, fitness tracking data, driver's license numbers, the latest news headlines, tweets, and much more. Is all this data of equal value? The answer is clearly no. Some data, such as digital photos, may be virtually priceless, whereas other data, such as yesterday's news headlines, generally have little value. And the value of the data can be one consideration in how secure protections should be for that data. Some data requires a high level (like credit card numbers) while other data needs little, if any, protections (like tweets).

How can it be determined what data needs what level of protection? One means is to categorize data into distinct classifications, and then protect these classifications accordingly. Instead of grouping data into broad categories such as customer data, financial data, and human resources data—which may have varying levels of importance and thus need different levels of control—it is far more beneficial to use data classifications to group like data that needs similar protections. Table 2-4 lists the different data classifications and the recommended steps for handling this data.

Table 2-4   Data classifications

Data type	Description	Recommended handling
Confidential	Highest level of data sensitivity	Should only be made available to users with the highest level of preapproved authentication
Private	Restricted data with a medium level of confidentiality	For users who have a need-to-know basis of the contents
Sensitive	Data that could cause catastrophic harm to the company if disclosed, such as technical specifications for a new product	Restricted to employees who have a business need to access the data and have been approved
Critical	Data classified according to availability needs; if critical data are not available, the function and mission would be severely impacted	Critical data must be rigorously protected
Public	No risk of release	For all public consumption; data is assumed to be public if no other data label is attached
Restricted	Data that is not available to the public	Caution should be exercised before using this kind of information in emails

Note 26

When considering which classification, a data element should be assigned and the confidentiality of the data should be considered along with its integrity and availability.

> **Caution** !
>
> There is no universal agreement on data classifications or definitions. Some entities use three types (confidential, internal, and public), some use four (controlled unclassified information, restricted, controlled, and public), and others use five (top secret, secret, confidential, sensitive, and unclassified) or even more.

Government data classifications use different data types and have continued to evolve. At one time the classification levels were *top secret*, *secret*, *confidential*, *sensitive but unclassified (SBU)*, and *unclassified*, but now only the first three levels are used (*top secret*, *secret*, and *confidential*). The level of sensitivity is based on a calculation of the damage to national security that the information's disclosure would cause.

Types of Data

There are various data types. These are not to be confused with a data classification; similar data types would be categorized into a single data classification. The different data types include the following:

- **Regulated.** Regulated data is that which external stipulations are placed on it regarding who can see and use the data and in what contexts. Examples of regulated data include *Protected Health Information (PHI)*, which is data about a person's health status, provision of healthcare, or payment for healthcare, and is regulated by the Health Insurance Portability and Accountability Act of 1996 (HIPAA).
- **Intellectual property.** Intellectual property (IP) data is an invention or a work that is the result of creativity. The owner of IP can apply for protection from others who attempt to duplicate it; these protections over IP or its expression are patent, trademark, copyright, or trade secret.

> **Note** 27
>
> Threat actors actively seek to steal IP research on a new product from an enterprise so that they can sell it to an unscrupulous foreign supplier who will then build an imitation model of the product to sell worldwide. This deprives the legitimate business of profits after investing hundreds of millions of dollars in product development and, because these foreign suppliers are in a different country, they are beyond the reach of domestic enforcement agencies and courts.

- **Trade secret.** Trade secret data is enterprise data that is undisclosed. A trade secret has three elements: it is information that has either actual or potential independent economic value by virtue of not being generally known, it has value to others who cannot legitimately obtain the information, and it is subject to reasonable efforts to maintain its secrecy. All three of these elements are required and, if any one of them ceases to exist, then the trade secret will also cease to exist. Otherwise, there is no limit on the amount of time a trade secret is protected.

> **Note** 28
>
> Trade secret protection is considered a complement to patent protection. Patents require the inventor to provide a detailed disclosure about the invention in exchange for the right to exclude others from practicing the invention for a limited period of time. When a patent expires that information is no longer protected. Patent protection also eliminates the need to maintain secrecy.

- **Enterprise information.** There are various types of information in an enterprise that can be used as a type of data. Legal information is general factual information about the law and the legal process. Legal information is different from legal advice, which involves giving guidance regarding an individual's legal rights and obligations in light of their particular facts and circumstances. Legal information is considered as being neutral. Financial information is data about the monetary transactions of the enterprise. Examples of financial information are credit card numbers, credit ratings by third-party credit analysis firms, financial statements, and payment histories.

- **Human- and non-human-readable.** As its name suggests, human-readable data is that which a person can read and interpret, while non-human-readable data (also called **machine-readable**) is data that a device can "interpret" and in its native state is not readily understood by a person. An example of non-human-readable data is JavaScript object notation (JSON), which is derived from the JavaScript language and a "lightweight" format for storing and transporting data from one device to another. Figure 2-11 shows a segment of JSON. Another non-human-readable example is Extensible Markup Language (XML).

Figure 2-11 JSON segment

```
"rules": {
  "align": [false,
    "parameters",
    "arguments",
    "statements"],
  "ban": [true,
    ["angular", "forEach"]
  ],
  "class-name": true,
  "comment-format": [false,
    "check-space",
    "check-lowercase"
  ],
```

Data Breach Consequences

Enforcing strong data controls is critical for enterprises today. The consequences to an organization that has suffered a data breach are significant. These consequences include the following:

- **Reputation damage.** The bad publicity that surrounds an organization that has been the victim of a data breach usually results in a tarnished reputation. This has been evidenced by the loss of customers and a drop in the stock price of publicly traded organizations following a breach. In addition, organizations that experience a data breach are usually required by regulatory agencies or by state or local law to send out a data breach letter to all users alerting them to the breach, thus magnifying the reputational damage.
- **IP theft.** Another consequence of a data breach is the theft of IP that the organization or its customers may own.
- **Fines.** A financial penalty may be assessed against the organization following a data breach. Several federal and state laws have been enacted to protect the privacy of electronic data, and businesses that fail to protect data they possess may face serious financial penalties. Some of these laws include HIPAA, the Sarbanes-Oxley Act of 2002 (Sarbox), the Gramm-Leach-Bliley Act (GLBA), the Payment Card Industry Data Security Standard (PCI DSS), and various state notification and security laws. Organizations in nations who belong to the European Union (EU) face two tiers of fines due to a data breach based on the General Data Protection Regulation (GDPR). The first tier is a fine up to 10 million euros or 2 percent of the firm's worldwide annual revenue from the preceding year, whichever amount is higher. The second tier is 20 million euros or 4 percent of worldwide annual revenue.

Note 29

Many users are surprised to learn that the rules regarding a breach of a smaller number of medical records is not strong. The HIPAA Breach Notification Rule requires that data breaches of 500 or more records must be reported to the Secretary of the Department of Health and Human Services (DHHS) no later than 60 days after the discovery of a breach. But breaches of less than 500 records can be reported to the Secretary at any time, but no later than 60 days from the end of the calendar year in which the data breach was experienced. That means a breach of 450 records that occurred in January 2025 would not have to be reported until March 2026.

Protecting Data

Establishing strong data controls involves general considerations about data. It also includes methods to secure data.

General Data Considerations

Several general considerations about data should be taken into account prior to creating data controls. The first consideration is the data state or its condition. Not all data is in the same state all the time. The three states in which it may reside are:

- **Data in processing.** Data in use (also called **data in processing**) is data on which actions are being performed by devices, such as printing a report from a device.
- **Data in transit.** Actions that transmit the data across a network, like an email sent across the Internet, are called data in transit (sometimes called **data in motion**).
- **Data at rest.** Data at rest is data that is stored on electronic media.

Another consideration is where the data is located. This is actually a misnomer, since data is not in a tangible format. Instead, it involves where the device on which the data is stored or being processed is located. Geolocation is a term encompassing all techniques that identify the data's location. Geolocation is designated in terms of latitude and longitude coordinates, which can be obtained using different sources. While geolocation uses different information sources to reveal data's location, geolocation by Internet Protocol (GeoIP) relies specifically on the Internet Protocol address of the device on which the data resides.

Note 30

There is also a difference in the information natively revealed from geolocation and GeoIP: geolocation produces longitude and latitude coordinates while GeoIP does not have that local information because it only uses the Internet Protocol address information. However, most Internet service providers (ISPs) combine the address with customer details to reveal specific information such as city and state.

A final consideration is to know the country-specific government regulations that apply to protecting data. However, these regulations are not necessarily those where the organization is headquartered. Data sovereignty is the country-specific requirements that apply to data. Generally, data is subject to the laws of the country in which it is collected or processed. And in many instances the data must remain within its borders. Countries like Russia, China, Germany, France, Indonesia, and Vietnam all require that their citizens' data be stored on physical servers within the country's borders, arguing that it is in the citizens' (and government's) best interest to protect private data against any misuse from foreign governments, and this is not possible if the data is outside of that country's jurisdiction.

Note 31

Many countries have had laws on the books for decades that data of its citizens must be stored within its borders, but it was less of an issue and was not always enforced. However, new privacy laws such as the GDPR are now making the requirement more prominent. And with the rising popularity of cloud computing, data sovereignty issues have taken on even greater importance.

Data Security Methods

Different techniques and technologies can be used to enhance the protection of data. These include the following:

- **Data minimization. Data minimization** is limiting the collection of personal information to that which is directly relevant and necessary to accomplish a specific task. In other words, the collection of privacy data should be adequate, relevant, and not excessive in relation to the designated purpose. Organizations should periodically review their privacy data collection to ensure that the collection is following the principle of data minimization.

- **Data masking.** Data masking involves creating a copy of the original data but using obfuscation (making unintelligible) any sensitive elements such as a user's name or Social Security number. Data masking should replace all actual information that is not absolutely required. Proper data masking provides no means to reverse the process to restore the data back to its original state. Data masking is one means of performing data sanitization, which is the process of cleaning data to provide privacy protection.
- **Tokenization.** Similar to masking, tokenization obfuscates sensitive data elements, such as an account number, into a random string of characters (token). The original sensitive data element and the corresponding token are then stored in a database called a token vault so that if the actual data element is needed, it can be retrieved as needed. When it is possible to restore the original data tokenization, it is called **pseudo-anonymization**.
- **Restrictions.** Restrictions on the data can also be imposed. Permission restrictions limit individuals and devices to only those that have a legitimate business need to access the data; restrictions on accessing the data are then placed on all other users and devices. Geographic restrictions limit access to data to specific locations. For example, HIPAA data in a hospital may only be accessible on the hospital campus itself and nowhere else.
- **Segmentation.** Data segmentation involves first identifying the classification of data elements, then tagging those data elements with that classification, and finally separating the most sensitive data from the rest of the data. That most sensitive data is then defined as the "protect surface" and additional security measures are applied around all protect surfaces that have been identified. When a breach occurs the most sensitive data is now protected by extra layers of data security controls.

Two Rights & A Wrong

1. Sensitive data is that which could cause catastrophic harm to the company if it were disclosed.
2. JSON is an example of human-readable data.
3. Data sovereignty is the country-specific requirements that apply to data.

See the answers at the end of the module.

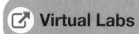 **Virtual Labs**   You're now ready to complete the simulations and live virtual machine labs for this module. The labs can be found in each module in MindTap.

Summary

- Not all attacks rely on technology vulnerabilities. Social engineering is a means of eliciting information or convincing a user to take action that weakens security. Social engineering begins with the threat actor first selecting a human target. Next, they create a believable scenario that is usually specific to the target. Often it involves inventing a false story or creating a seemingly plausible situation in hopes of obtaining information or gaining leverage to breach a system.

- Social engineering relies heavily on human psychology. Threat actors' manipulation of human nature can persuade the victim to provide information or take actions without even realizing it. There are several basic principles of psychology that attackers use to their favor. These include authority, intimidation, consensus, scarcity, urgency, familiarity, and trust. Because some social engineering involves person-to-person contact, attackers use a variety of personal techniques to gain their trust.

- There are several types of social engineering attacks. Phishing is sending an email or displaying a web announcement that falsely claims to be from a legitimate source in an attempt to trick the user into taking an action. One particular type of phishing attack that is increasing in popularity is a business email compromise (BEC). A BEC takes advantage of the common practice today by businesses and organizations of electronically making payments or transferring funds. Social engineering impersonation is masquerading as a real or fictitious character and then playing out the role of that person on a victim. One type of impersonation is brand impersonation. By posing as a recognizable brand that is familiar to the targets, attackers can trick them into a dangerous action.

- Attackers purchase and register the domain names of sites that are spelled similarly to actual sites to capture users who make typing errors when entering a URL. This is called typo squatting. In addition to registering names that are similar to the actual names, threat actors are now registering domain names that are one bit different. This is because the billions of devices that are part of the Internet have multiple instances of a domain name in DNS memory at any time, so the likelihood increases of a RAM memory error of a bit being "flipped." Misinformation is false or inaccurate information, regardless of the intent to mislead, while disinformation is false or inaccurate misinformation that comes from a malicious intent. One example of cyber disinformation is a hoax or a false warning.

- A watering hole attack is directed toward a small group of specific individuals. There are other means by which a threat actor can gather valuable information that can be done without any interaction with the target. These include dumpster diving, Google dorking, and shoulder surfing.

- Physical controls are an important yet overlooked control. Preventing a threat actor from physically accessing a web server can be as important as preventing the attacker from

accessing it remotely through the Internet. Different types of passive barriers can be used to restrict unwanted individuals or vehicles from entering a secure area. Fencing is usually a tall, permanent structure to keep out unauthorized personnel and is accompanied with proper lighting so the area can be monitored after dark. A bollard is a short but sturdy vertical post that is used as a vehicular traffic barricade.

- Human security guards patrol and monitor restricted areas and are an active security defense. Unlike passive devices, security guards can make decisions about situations. Often guards are responsible for monitoring activity captured by video surveillance cameras that transmit a signal to a specific and limited set of receivers. Some video surveillance cameras are fixed in a single position pointed at a door or a hallway while other cameras can move for a full panoramic view. High-end video surveillance cameras send alerts and begin recording when they detect movement or identify a suspicious object.

- To supplement the work of a security guard, sensors can be placed in strategic locations to alert guards by generating an alarm of an unexpected or unusual action. An infrared (IR) sensor is an electronic device that can measure and detect IR in the surrounding area. There are two types of IR sensors: active and passive. Passive IR is used for motion-based detection. A microwave sensor uses high-frequency radio waves and functions similarly to radar. Microwave sensors are especially effective in monitoring large areas. Ultrasonic sensors can measure how far away a target object is located. Ultrasonic waves are transmitted to bounce off the target back to the receiver, in which the waves are converted into an electrical signal that can be measured. A pressure sensor can detect if an object like a person or car has entered a restricted area.

- An automated access control vestibule is used to create a buffer to separate a nonsecure area from a secure area. A device monitors and controls two interlocking doors to a vestibule, and only one door can be open at any given time. In areas in which medium security is needed, a reception area can be used. Users are allowed to enter the area in which a receptionist can check credentials. In areas of low security, a generic waiting room can be used instead. Although this room still serves as an important buffer with two doors as with an access control vestibule, it is more friendly to the public. A variety of types of locks can be used to restrict physical access. Locks that use keys can be compromised if the keys are lost, stolen, or duplicated. A more secure option is to use an electronic lock.

- Another means of physical security applies to prevent data leakage. A Faraday cage is a metallic enclosure that prevents the entry or escape of an electromagnetic field. A protected cable distribution is a system of cable conduits used to protect classified information that is being transmitted between two secure areas.

- Computer hardware security is the physical security that specifically involves protecting some types of mobile hardware, such as laptops, that can easily be stolen. Most portable devices have a special steel bracket security slot built into the case. When storing a laptop, it can be placed in a safe or a vault, which is a ruggedized steel box with a lock. Some offices have safes in employee cubicles for the users to lock up important papers when away from their desks, even for a short period of time.

- It is important to have adequate controls in place to protect data. Instead of grouping data into categories that may have varying levels of importance and thus need different levels of control, it is far more beneficial to use data classifications to group like data that needs similar protections. The classifications are confidential, private, sensitive, critical, public, and restricted. There are various data types: regulated data, IP data, trade secret data, legal information, financial information, human-readable data and non-human-readable data. There are significant consequences to an organization that has suffered a data breach.

- Several general considerations about data should be taken into account prior to creating data controls. The first consideration is the data state or its condition. The states are data in use, data in transit, and data at rest. Geolocation is a term encompassing all techniques that identify the data's location. Data sovereignty is the country-specific requirements that apply to data. Generally, data is subject to the laws of the country in which it is collected or processed. Some of the different technologies and techniques to enhance data protection include data minimization, data masking, tokenization, restrictions, and segmentation.

Key Terms

access badge
access control vestibule
bollard
brand impersonation
business email compromise (BEC)
confidential
critical
data at rest
data classifications
data in transit
data in use
data sanitization
data sovereignty
data state
disinformation
fencing
financial information
geographic restrictions

geolocation
human-readable data
human vectors
impersonation
infrared (IR) sensor
intellectual property (IP) data
legal information
lighting
masking
microwave sensor
misinformation
non-human-readable data
obfuscation
permission restrictions
phishing
pressure sensor
pretexting
private

public
regulated data
restricted
security guards
segmentation
sensitive
sensor
smishing
social engineering
tokenization
trade secret data
typo squatting
ultrasonic sensor
video surveillance
vishing
watering hole attack

Review Questions

1. What is the attack surface of social engineering?

   a. Manipulation
   b. Human vectors
   c. Persuasion
   d. Deception

2. Bjorn just received a phone call in which the person claimed to be a senior vice president demanding that his password be reset, or else Bjorn's supervisor would be contacted about his lack of cooperation. Bjorn was convinced that this was a social engineering attack. Which principle of human manipulation did the attacker attempt on Bjorn?

   a. Authority
   b. Fright
   c. Intimidation
   d. Urgency

3. Which of the following is NOT a personal technique used by social engineering attackers to gain the trust of the target?

   a. Provide a reason.
   b. Project confidence.
   c. Demand compliance.
   d. Use evasion and diversion.

4. Albrecht received a call from a senior vice president of finance who had received a phishing email and had deleted it. What type of phishing attack was this?

   a. Dolphining
   b. Harpooning
   c. Phishing spear
   d. Whaling

5. Tobias received an SMS text message that falsely said his bank account was overdrawn and, to avoid a $45 fee, he should contact the bank immediately with an explanation. What type of social engineering attack is this?

   a. Texting attack
   b. SMS phishing
   c. Smishing
   d. IM vectoring

6. Which of the following is NOT true about BEC?

   a. It is decreasing in popularity among threat actors.
   b. It takes advantage of electronically making payments or transferring funds.
   c. It takes advantage of the size and complexity of large enterprises.
   d. It is not limited to businesses.

7. Which social engineering attack is masquerading as a real or fictitious character and then playing out the role of that person on a target?

   a. Pretending
   b. Pretexting
   c. Impersonation
   d. Acting

8. Wolfgang-Cashman is a new intern at the online company WebHighSchoolStore.com. He has been assigned the task of researching all the similar domain names to theirs in order to counteract attacks. What is Wolfgang-Cashman combating?

   a. Mistranslations
   b. Spimming
   c. Typo squatting
   d. Redactioning

9. What is false or inaccurate information that comes from a malicious intent?

   a. Misinformation
   b. Half-truths
   c. Disinformation
   d. Varication

10. Which of the following is NOT a type of data reconnaissance?

    a. Purchasing used technology equipment
    b. Excel dorking
    c. Dumpster diving
    d. Shoulder surfing

11. Which type of sensor is most appropriate for monitoring a large warehouse for intruders?

    a. Microwave sensor
    b. IR sensor
    c. XG sensor
    d. Passive RGP sensor

12. Which of the following statements is NOT true about a pressure sensor?

    a. A pressure sensor can differentiate between a car and a person.
    b. Modern pressure sensors can differentiate between what has entered and where they are headed.
    c. A pressure sensor is a type of management control.
    d. A pressure sensor can be used to detect if a person has entered a restricted area.

13. Arndt is on a team that is increasing the security in an office. They want to allow anyone to pass by a

door but have an alarm sound whenever someone gets too close to the door. Which sensor would Arndt recommend using?

a. IR sensor
b. Microwave sensor
c. Ultrasonic sensor
d. Pressure sensor

14. Which type of buffer is automated and has two interlocking doors, only one of which can be opened at a time?

a. Access control vestibule
b. Reception area
c. Waiting room
d. Vestibule office

15. Milan is on a design team that needs to run a hardened carrier PDS underground between two buildings. What requirement would Milan add to the specifications?

a. It must be buried at least 25 feet below surface level.
b. It can only be used for fiber-optic cables.
c. It must be visually inspected on a weekly basis.
d. It must be encased in concrete.

16. Which data classification has the highest level of data sensitivity?

a. "Eyes-only"
b. Sensitive
c. Private
d. Confidential

17. Jan is working on classifying data. Some data has been identified that if compromised, the function and mission of the enterprise would be severely impacted. Which data classification should Jan give this data?

a. Secret
b. Top secret
c. Critical
d. Classified

18. Which type of data is hospital patient information protected by HIPAA?

a. Restricted data
b. Regulated data
c. Secure data
d. Private data

19. JSON and XML would be classified as which type of data?

a. Compiled data
b. Lightweight data
c. Schematic data
d. Non-human-readable data

20. Which of the following data security methods creates a copy of the original data but uses obfuscation on any sensitive elements?

a. Data masking
b. Data protecting
c. Data tokening
d. Data covering

Hands-On Projects

Project 2-1: Comparing Data Breach Notification Letters

Estimated Time: 20 minutes

Objective: Compare and contrast data breach notifications.

Description: All states have their own laws requiring that users be notified if their personal information has been stolen. However, these notifications have come under criticism for not containing useful information for targets. Many businesses are wary of bad press and legal liability and are reluctant to provide more information than is required. Also, breach notification requirements vary from industry to industry and state to state. Finally, new privacy laws are setting shorter and shorter deadlines for breach notification, and sometimes new information comes to light weeks or even months after a breach is first discovered. In this project, you will compare several California data breach notifications.

1. Open a web browser and enter the URL **https://oag.ca.gov/privacy/databreach/list** (if you are no longer able to access the site through this web address, open a search engine and enter "California search database security breaches").

2. Scroll down to see a listing of the most recent California data breaches. Does the number surprise you?

3. Select one of the first listings by clicking it.

4. In the **Submitted Brief Notification Sample**, click the **Sample of Notice** entry.

5. Download this PDF to your computer and read through it.

6. Click your browser's Back button twice to return to the **Search Database Security Breaches** page.

7. Select a different listing by clicking it.

8. In the **Submitted Brief Notification Sample**, click the **Sample of Notice** entry.

9. Download this PDF to your computer and read through it.

10. Click your browser's Back button twice to return to the **Search Database Security Breaches** page.

11. Select one more listing, download the PDF, read through it, and finally return to the **Search Database Security Breaches** page.

12. If necessary, open all three PDFs. Create a table of the same elements that are found in each document. Also create a table that lists the different elements in each document.

13. Which elements are most useful if you were the target of this breach? What additional information would be helpful?

14. Now create your own sample notification letter. Include those elements that you find useful and add elements that you think a target would benefit from.

15. Close all windows.

Project 2-2: Online Phishing Training

Estimated Time: 25 minutes
Objective: Identify phishing attacks.
Description: In this project, you will use an online phishing training tool. Also note the user awareness training features in this simulation as you proceed.

1. Use your web browser to go to **https://public.cyber.mil/training/phishing-awareness/**. (If you are no longer able to access the program through this URL, use a search engine and search for "phishing awareness.")

2. Click **Launch Training**.

3. If necessary, adjust your web browser settings, and then click **Start/Continue Phishing and Social Engineering: Virtual Communication Awareness**.

4. Watch the brief video on accessibility features. Click the right arrow button.

5. Read the information. Click either the URL or **Continue** depending on your needs.

6. Listen to the video message about your choice. Is this a good learning technique? Why? Click the right arrow button.

7. Continue through the phishing training. Slides 16–18 ask you for answers to questions about what you have learned.

8. How effective was this training? What did you learn? Would you recommend this to others to learn about phishing?

9. Close all windows.

Project 2-3: Viewing Your Annual Credit Report

Estimated Time: 20 minutes
Objective: Review a credit report.
Description: Security experts recommend that one means to reduce personal risk for consumers is to receive a copy of their credit report at least once per year and check its accuracy to protect their identity. In this project, you access your free credit report online.

1. Use your web browser to go to **www.annualcreditreport.com**. Although you could send a request individually to one of the three credit agencies, this website acts as a central source for ordering free credit reports.

2. Click **Request your free credit reports**.

3. Read through the three steps and click **Request your credit reports**.

4. Enter the requested information, click **Continue**, and then click **Next**.

5. Click **TransUnion**. Click **Next**.

6. After the brief processing completes, click **Continue**.

7. You may then be asked personal information about your transaction history to verify your identity. Answer the requested questions and click **Next**.

8. Follow the instructions to print your report.

9. Review it carefully, particularly the sections of "Potentially negative items" and "Requests for your credit history." If you see anything that might be incorrect, follow the instructions on that website to enter a dispute.

10. Follow the instructions to exit from the website.

11. Close all windows.

Project 2-4: Generating and Viewing JSON

Estimated Time: 20 minutes
Objective: Examine JSON code statements.
Description: Non-human-readable data, also called machine-readable data, is data that a device can read and interpret. An example of non-human-readable data is JSON, which is derived from the JavaScript language and is a "lightweight" format for storing and transporting data from one device to another. Another non-human-readable example is XML. Although JSON, XML, and other non-human-readable data is primarily to be read by a technology device, that does not mean that it is completely unintelligible to humans. One of the advantages of JSON and XML is that with some training, humans can interpret this code. In this project, you will generate and view JSON code.

1. Open your web browser and enter the URL **https://www.objgen.com/**. (If you are no longer able to access the site through this web address, use a search engine to look for "ObjGen.")

2. Click **JSON Generator**.

3. Two windows will appear: the **Model Definition** on the left and the **JSON** window on the right.

4. In the **Model Definition** window, click **Demo**.

5. The Model Definition code will generate along with the corresponding JSON code. Watch as the code creates JSON and compare the two windows. Click the **Stop** button to pause the generation and the **Play** button to resume the generation.

6. When the Model Definition is completed, attempt to read the JSON code without referring to the Model Definition window.

7. Now read the Model Definition code and compare it line-by-line with the JSON code. How difficult is it to read and interpret this code?

8. Sometimes JSON and XML are called both human-readable and non-human-readable data. Would this be an accurate description? Why?

9. Close all windows.

Case Project 2-1: #TrendingCyber

Estimated Time: 20 minutes
Objective: Determine effective security procedures.
Description: Read again the opening #TrendingCyber in this module. For each of the three break-ins described, list the three physical and three operational security procedures that you would have implemented to prevent these types of attacks. Write a one-page paper about these experiences.

Case Project 2-2: Phishing Simulators

Estimated Time: 30 minutes
Objective: Identify phishing attacks.
Description: Search the Internet for three different phishing simulators. Take the phishing challenge on each simulator to determine if you can identify the phishing attacks. Then create a table that lists the different features of the phishing simulators, their ease of use, and how accurate you think they were. Would these simulators be helpful in training users about phishing? Write a one-paragraph summary along with your table.

Case Project 2-3: CCTV Technologies

Estimated Time: 20 minutes
Objective: Research CCTV Technologies.
Description: Research new technologies for CCTV, including motion recognition and object detection. How accurate are they? What are the advantages? What are the disadvantages? How do they train these devices to recognize some objects but ignore others? Write a one-page paper on your research.

Case Project 2-4: Comparing Sensors

Estimated Time: 25 minutes
Objective: Compare and contrast sensors.
Description: Use the Internet to research four types of sensors (IR, microwave, ultrasonic, and pressure). Create a table that lists each sensor and their features, advantages, disadvantages, how they would be used for physical security, and cost. Include a brief description of the technology behind the sensor, Write a one-page paper on your research.

Case Project 2-5: Data Sovereignty

Estimated Time: 30 minutes
Objective: Research data sovereignty.
Description: Many different nations are creating laws regarding data sovereignty, and often these laws conflict with those laws of other nations. Research the latest news on data sovereignty. Select three nations that have enacted data sovereignty laws and compare them. Where do they mandate that citizen data be stored? What are the penalties for those companies that fail to comply? In your opinion, are these laws reasonable? What happens if there is a conflict between two nations on the storage of data? Write a one-page paper of your research.

Case Project 2-6: Bay Point Ridge Security

Estimated Time: 35 minutes

Objective: Outline data security methods.

Description: Bay Point Ridge Security (BPRS) is a managed service provider (MSP) that manages networks, computers, cloud resources, and information security for small-to-medium enterprises (SMEs) in the region. BPRS provides internships to students who are in their final year of the security degree program at the local college and has recently hired you.

A prospective new client is Stellarson Construction. BPRS is giving a presentation to their senior-level executives regarding how to protect their data.

1. Create a PowerPoint presentation that lists the different types of data security methods: data minimization, data masking, tokenization, restrictions, and segmentation. Define each method, its level of protection, how complex it is to implement, and the advantages and disadvantages. Your presentation should be 7–10 slides in length.

2. As a follow-up to your presentation, Stellarson has asked for more information on tokenization. Use the Internet to research how this procedure works and create a one-page explanation with an appropriate figure.

Two Rights & A Wrong: Answers

Social Engineering Attacks

1. A threat actor who threatens to contact a superior of the target if the actor's demands are not met is an example of authority.

2. Spear phishing targets specific users.

3. Pretexting is designed to obtain private information.

Answer: The wrong statement is #1.

Explanation: A threat actor who threatens to contact a superior of the target if the actor's demands are not met is an example of intimidation.

Physical Security Controls

1. A barricade is a short but sturdy vertical post used to prevent a car from "ramming" into a secure area.

2. There are two types of IR sensors: active and passive.

3. Microwave sensors are especially effective in monitoring large areas such as a warehouse.

Answer: The wrong statement is #1.

Explanation: A bollard is a short but sturdy vertical post that is used as a vehicular traffic barricade to prevent a car from "ramming" into a secure area.

Data Controls

1. Sensitive data is that which could cause catastrophic harm to the company if it were disclosed.

2. JSON is an example of human-readable data.

3. Data sovereignty is the country-specific requirements that apply to data.

Answer: The wrong statement is #2.

Explanation: JSON is an example of non-human-readable data.

References

1. Galov, Nick, "17+ sinister social engineering statistics for 2022," *Web Tribunal*, Oct. 15, 2022, accessed Jan. 3, 2023, https://webtribunal.net/blog/social-engineering-statistics/#gref.
2. Antiphishing Working Group, "Phishing activity trends report," accessed Jan. 5, 2023, https://apwg.org/trendsreports/.
3. Chem, Zhanhoa, and Szurdi, Janos, "Cybersquatting: Attackers mimicking domains of major brands including Facebook, Apple, Amazon and Netflix to scam consumers," *Unit 42*, Sep. 1, 2020, accessed Jan. 5, 2023, https://unit42.paloaltonetworks.com/cybersquatting/.
4. Domabirg, Artem, "Bitsquatting: DNS hijacking without exploitation," *Diaburg.org*, accessed Jan. 20, 2023, http://dinaburg.org/bitsquatting.html.

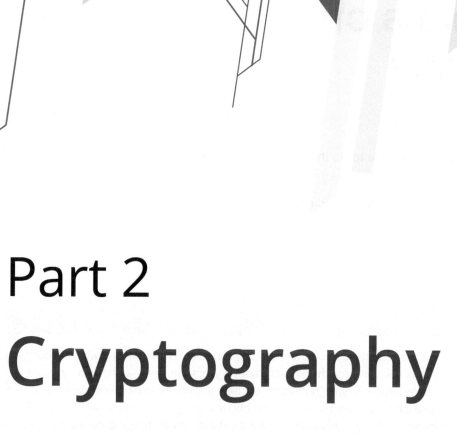

Part 2
Cryptography

This part introduces you to an essential element of modern information security, that of cryptography. Cryptography provides an additional layer in securing data. Module 3 defines cryptography, explains different cryptographic algorithms, shows how cryptography is implemented, and looks at attacks and weaknesses of cryptography. Module 4 continues with more advanced cryptography topics such as digital certificates, public key infrastructure (PKI), and secure communication and transport protocols.

Module 3
Fundamentals of Cryptography

Module 4
Advanced Cryptography

Fundamentals of Cryptography

Module Objectives

After completing this module, you should be able to do the following:

1 Define cryptography

2 Describe hash, symmetric, and asymmetric cryptographic algorithms

3 List the various ways in which cryptography is used

4 Explain different cryptographic limitations and attacks

#TrendingCyber

If you were to pick up virtually any book on cybersecurity, you would undoubtedly come across the names of what has been called the world's most famous "cryptographic couple." Since their introduction 45 years ago, they—along with a growing cryptographic family—have not only graced the pages of cryptography texts but have also moved into other disciplines, too.

In late 1976, a seminal paper that dramatically changed the thinking about cryptography was published. It proposed a new theory for encrypting communication over insecure channels without first exchanging the secret keys needed to unlock the messages. In this paper, the authors referred to the communicating parties as simply the sender "A" and the recipient "B." This was considered standard practice at the time.

The following year, three researchers from the Massachusetts Institute of Technology (MIT) started working on a way to implement this new theory. In 1978, they published a paper explaining possible complex secure communication scenarios. To simplify their explanations, they wrote, "For our scenarios we suppose that A and B (also known as Alice and Bob) are two users . . . ."

And Alice and Bob were born.

One of the researchers later wrote that Alice and Bob were invented to maintain the traditional use of "A" and "B" but also make it easier for users to follow the complex logic in their paper. In addition, they chose a traditional female and male name so that they could also use the pronouns *she* and *he* in the paper without the need to keep repeating their proper names.

Over the next several years, Alice and Bob started to appear in other academic research about cryptography. One research paper began with the sentence, "Bob and Alice each have a secret . . . " while another paper started with, "Alice and Bob want to flip a coin by telephone. . . . " Soon virtually every cryptographic paper had adopted the use of these names, although on occasion, researchers would hedge their usage by saying, "The goal is that A(lice) becomes able to securely send a message to B(ob)."

Because Alice and Bob were used to represent two individuals who needed to communicate but were separated by a long distance, soon other researchers began to paint Alice and Bob's background. In 1981, another researcher included in a paper about Alice and Bob, "They have just divorced, live in different cities, and want to decide who gets the car." Other researchers soon added their own take on the backgrounds of Alice and Bob.

In the ensuing years since Alice and Bob were first introduced, other characters have joined their cryptographic family. Carol is a generic third character, Eve is an eavesdropper, Mallory is a malicious attacker, Trudy is an intruder, and Wendy is a whistleblower. To date, there are 26 named members of the cryptographic family.

Over time, Alice and Bob also became common characters in economics, physics, and other engineering research. Recently they have been referenced in domains well outside of science and technology.

The legacy of Alice and Bob continues to live on today and shows no signs of slowing down. And sometimes this fictitious cryptographic couple even overshadows the cryptography that they were meant to help explain. As one researcher laments, "Today, nobody remembers I invented Strong Primes (a key element in cryptography), but everyone knows me as the guy who wrote the story of Alice and Bob."

Since the dawn of human communication, there have been efforts to hide private communications from outsiders. This likely started with whispering in a friend's ear or using hand gestures. These were fine when the sender and receiver were standing in the same cave but could not be used if they were far apart. And when written communication was developed, it was likewise challenging to hide these messages from outsiders.

This led to many different techniques being created and used throughout the centuries to hide written messages. But invariably the outsiders were able to "reverse-engineer" the technique to read the hidden message, so new techniques had to be developed. With the introduction of mechanical devices over 100 years ago, it was possible to increase hiding to a new level so that it was virtually impossible for humans by themselves to uncover the original message. However, outsiders then turned to using mechanical devices to unmask the messages. The same became true when computers were developed almost 60 years ago: electronic technology raised the bar even higher, but outsiders could also use computers to read the messages.

Using technology to hide a message or mask data is a foundational element today. For example, just using a web browser to perform a simple online search or purchase a product online uses this hiding technology extensively. And it has become the cornerstone of information security: a threat actor may be able to defeat protections to reach the data, but if that data is in a form that cannot be read, then the attacker faces an even higher obstacle to uncover it.

In this module, you learn about the fundamentals of cryptography. You first look at what cryptography is and how it is used. Then you examine cryptographic limitations and attacks on cryptography.

Note 1

Cryptography has become so foundational to information security that the latest CompTIA Security+ exam objectives SY0-701 have moved cryptography from being its own domain as in previous years to now being included under "General Security Concepts."

Defining Cryptography

Certification

1.2 Summarize fundamental security concepts.

1.4 Explain the importance of using appropriate cryptographic solutions.

2.4 Given a scenario, analyze indicators of malicious activity.

2.5 Explain the purpose of mitigation techniques used to secure the enterprise.

3.3 Compare and contrast concepts and strategies to protect data.

Defining cryptography involves comparing it with steganography to understand what it is and how it works. It also involves knowing the benefits of cryptography.

Steganography: Hiding the Message

As early as 600 BC, the ancient Greeks wrestled with how to keep messages sent by couriers from falling into enemy hands. One early method was to tell the message to the courier so they could later repeat it when they arrived at their destination. However, the disadvantage to this approach was that the courier would often paraphrase the message in their own words, which would result in omissions or variations due to forgetfulness. In some cases, the courier might even intentionally alter the message if they had been bribed or blackmailed by the enemy.

Written dispatches, on the other hand, would accurately convey the message and enable it to be sent without the courier knowing its contents, thus reducing the risk of a security breach. But written messages could be found by the enemy if the courier were searched, so the Greeks contrived ingenious ways of disguising and concealing documents. News of an imminent Persian invasion early in the fifth century BC was sent by writing the message in ink on wooden tablets and then covering them with wax, the substance in which messages were normally written. An innocuous message was then written on the wax, which hid the underlying secret message. Other techniques included messages disguised in the form of a wound dressing, hidden in an earring, written as a tattoo, or concealed in a sandal or a mule's hoof.

> ## Note 2
>
> The award for the all-time most creative method for hiding a message certainly goes to Histaniaeus, who wanted to encourage Aristagora of Miletus to revolt against the Persian king Xerxes in 500 BC. Histaniaeus did not dare write down his message of sedition to Aristagora for fear of it being intercepted. So, Histaniaeus shaved the head of a messenger and wrote the message on their bald scalp. After the messenger's hair had regrown, they were able to freely travel to Miletus without carrying anything suspicious. When the messenger arrived in Miletus, they promptly shaved their head and showed the message to Aristagora!

By hiding the message on tablets covered with wax or as a tattoo, the Greeks were performing **steganography**, a word from Greek meaning "covered writing." Steganography attempts to hide the very existence of the message or information. Today, steganography often hides data in a harmless image file, audio file, or even video file. It typically takes the data, divides it into small pieces, and hides these among invisible portions of the file. A common scheme is to hide data in the file header fields that describe the file, between sections of the **metadata** (data that is used to describe the content or structure of the actual data), or in the areas of a file that contain the content itself. An example of steganography is shown in Figure 3-1.

Figure 3-1   Data hidden by steganography

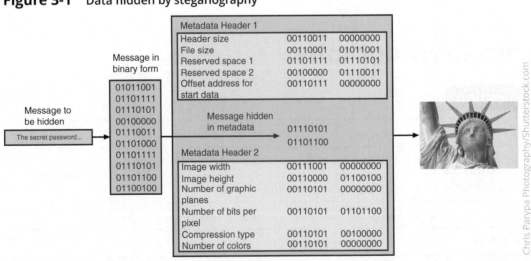

Chris Parypa Photography/Shutterstock.com

Steganography is one form of obfuscation (from Latin meaning "to darken"), or the action of making something obscure. Other forms of obfuscation include **data masking**, which involves creating a copy of the original data and making it unintelligible, and **tokenization**, which obfuscates sensitive data elements, such as an account number, into a random string of characters (token).

> **Note 3**
>
> Obfuscation, data masking, and tokenization are covered in Module 2.

Cryptography: Hiding the Meaning

Although the ancient Greeks used steganography to attempt to hide the **existence** of the message, what happened if it were to be discovered? Obviously once the message was found it could be easily read by interceptors. Simply trying to hide the message was not a good solution.

But what if it was possible instead to hide the **meaning** of the message? Anyone who intercepted the message could then not determine its contents. Due to the problems with steganography, the ancient Greeks turned to making their messages intelligible only to the desired recipient.

The Greeks used two different methods to hide the meaning of a message, and these methods are still used today. One method is **transposition**, in which each letter of the message is rearranged (for example, the word *ran* could be rearranged to become *arn*). The problem with transposition is that it can be difficult for the recipient to unscramble the message. In addition, for short messages that use few words, the message could easily be "broken" by an interceptor (for example, there are only six different ways to reorder *ran*). However, if the message is longer and the number of letters increases, it is much more difficult for the outsider to uncover the message—but more difficult for the recipient, too.

> **Note 4**
>
> It has been estimated that if transposition was used on the famous sentence *The quick brown fox jumps over the lazy dog*, which contains 36 letters, it would result in over 50,000,000,000,000,000,000,000,000,000,000,000 different arrangements.

A second method is **substitution**. Using this technique, one letter is substituted for another letter. One type of substitution (called **ROT13**) rotates the entire alphabet 13 steps ($A = N$, $B = O$, $C = P$, etc.) so that the word *security* becomes *frphevgl*. Another method is substituting numbers for letters ($A = 1$, $B = 2$, $C = 3$, etc.) so the word *security* becomes *1804022017081924*. However, these are relatively easy to break by an interceptor. A more involved substitution is the **XOR cipher**, which is based on the binary operation e*X*clusive *OR* to compare two bits: If the bits are different, a *1* is returned, but if they are identical, then a *0* is returned. For example, to encrypt the word *security* using the word *flapjack* with the XOR cipher, the result is *00010101 00001001 00000010 00000101 00011000 00001000 00010111 00010010*.

> **Note 5**
>
> The ancient Greeks went to great lengths to hide their messages. They marked letters of an ordinary text with tiny dots to indicate which letters, when combined, revealed the secret message. At other times, they would substitute letters from one language for another language. The Greeks even wrote poems in which the first letter of each line of the poetry could be extracted to spell out a message.[1]

By hiding the meaning of the message instead of hiding the message itself, the ancient Greeks were also performing one of the early forms of cryptography (from Greek meaning "hidden writing"). Cryptography is the practice of transforming ("scrambling") information so that its meaning cannot be understood by unauthorized parties but can only be understood by approved recipients.

When using cryptography, the process of changing the original text into a scrambled message is known as encryption. The reverse process is decryption or changing the message back to its original form. In addition, the following terminology applies to cryptography:

- **Plaintext.** Unencrypted data that is input for encryption or is the output of decryption is called **plaintext**.
- **Ciphertext. Ciphertext** is the scrambled and unreadable output of encryption.
- **Cleartext.** Unencrypted data that is not intended to be encrypted is **cleartext** (it is "in the clear").

Note 6

Steganography is sometimes used together with encryption so that the information is doubly protected. First encrypting the data and then hiding it requires someone seeking the information to first find the data and then decrypt it.

Plaintext data to be encrypted is input into a cryptographic algorithm (also called a **cipher**), which consists of procedures based on a mathematical formula. A **key** is a mathematical value entered into the algorithm to produce the ciphertext. Just as a key is inserted into a door lock to lock the door, in cryptography a unique mathematical key is input into the encryption algorithm to "lock" the data by creating the ciphertext. Once the ciphertext needs to be returned to plaintext so the recipient can view it, the reverse process occurs with the decryption algorithm and key to "unlock" it. The cryptographic process is illustrated in Figure 3-2.

Figure 3-2   Cryptographic process

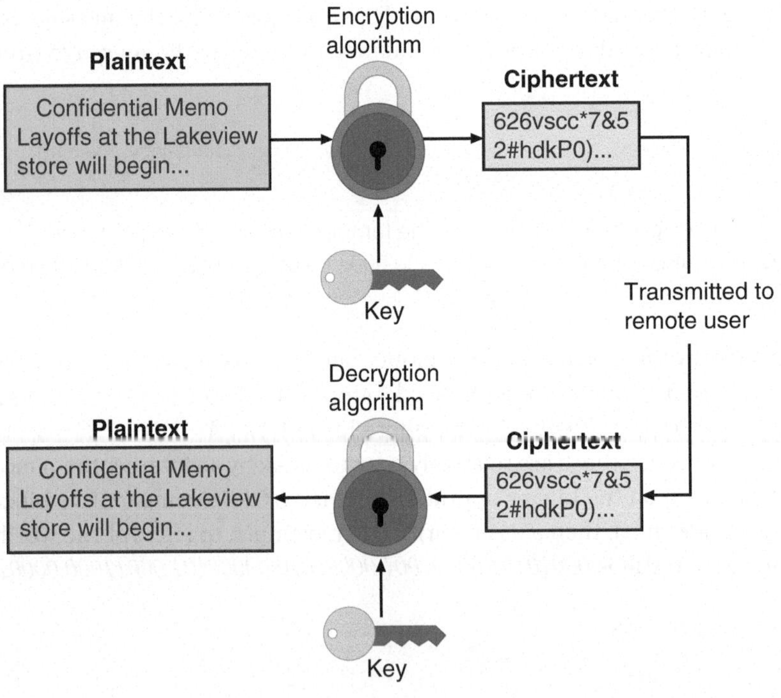

The critical factor in cryptography is that one or more elements must be kept secret at all costs. Cryptographic algorithms are designed to be public and well known, and how they function is no secret. However, the individualized key for the algorithm that a user possesses must *always* be kept secret.

Benefits of Cryptography

Why use cryptography? Hiding information through encryption so that threat actors cannot view it is considered one of several different **mitigation** techniques (mitigation is reducing the vulnerability or severity) that enterprises can use to protect information. It is also considered a **hardening** technique that makes a system more resilient to attacks.

Cryptography is also unique in that it can provide protections to data in each of its three states: data at rest, data in use, and data in transit.

Note 7

Data states are covered in Module 2.

There are several common use cases (situations) for which cryptography can provide security protections. These protections include:

- **Confidentiality.** Cryptography can protect the confidentiality of information by ensuring that only authorized parties can view it. When private information, such as a list of employees to be laid off, is transmitted across the network or stored on a file server, its contents can be encrypted, which allows only authorized individuals who have the key to read it.
- **Integrity.** Cryptography can protect the integrity of information. Integrity ensures that the information is correct and no unauthorized person or malicious software has altered that data. Because ciphertext requires that a key must be used to open the data before it can be changed, cryptography can ensure its integrity. The list of employees to be laid off, for example, can be protected so that no names can be added or deleted by unauthorized personnel.
- **Authentication.** The authentication of the sender can be verified through cryptography. Specific types of cryptography, for example, can prevent a situation such as circulation of a list of employees to be laid off that appears to come from a manager but, in reality, it was sent by an imposter.
- **Nonrepudiation.** Cryptography can enforce nonrepudiation. Repudiation is defined as denial; nonrepudiation is the inability to deny. In information technology (IT), nonrepudiation is the process of proving that a user performed an action, such as sending an email message. Nonrepudiation prevents an individual from fraudulently reneging on an action. The nonrepudiation features of cryptography can prevent a manager from claiming they never sent the list of employees to be laid off to an unauthorized third party.

Note 8

A practical example of nonrepudiation is Astrid taking her car into a repair shop for service and signing an estimate form of the cost of repairs and authorizing the work. If Astrid later returns and claims she never approved a specific repair, the signed form can be used as non-repudiation.

- **Obfuscation.** Obfuscation is making something obscure or unclear. Cryptography can provide a degree of obfuscation by encrypting a list of employees to be laid off so that an unauthorized user cannot read it.

The security protections afforded by cryptography are summarized in Table 3-1.

Obfuscation is frequently misunderstood and often misapplied. By definition, encryption obfuscates data—but its protection is still based on a secret key. However, in other areas of information security, obfuscation is often erroneously applied in an attempt to hide something from outsiders ("If the bad guys don't know about it, that makes it secure"). This approach (called **security through obscurity**) is flawed since the only element that makes it secure is the fact that it is unknown. Because it is essentially impossible to keep something completely hidden from everyone all the time, eventually it will be discovered, and the security compromised. Thus, obfuscation cannot by itself be used as a general information security protection.

Some software developers have created their own proprietary cryptographic algorithms (often touted as "military-grade" cryptography) and suggest that because their algorithm is "secret" it is more secure. However, proprietary algorithms are weak. Modern cryptographic algorithms are instead based on known mathematical proofs and the

Table 3-1 Information protections by cryptography

Characteristic	Description	Protection
Confidentiality	Ensures that only authorized parties can view the information	Encrypted information can only be viewed by those who have been provided the key.
Integrity	Ensures that the information is correct and no unauthorized person or malicious software has altered the data	Encrypted information cannot be changed except by authorized users who have the key.
Authentication	Provides proof of the genuineness of the user	Proof that the sender was legitimate and not an imposter can be obtained.
Nonrepudiation	Proves that a user performed an action	Individuals are prevented from fraudulently denying that they were involved in a transaction.
Obfuscation	Makes something obscure or unclear	By making it obscure, the original information cannot be determined.

algorithms are selected by competition after having been thoroughly vetted by the cryptographic community. The algorithms have proven their value over time by their wide adoption and use. Proprietary algorithms, on the other hand, have not been properly analyzed (and cannot be since they are kept secret) and will likely contain flaws. Proprietary cryptographic algorithms should not be used.

Two Rights & A Wrong

1. Transposition and substitution are two methods to hide the meaning of a message.
2. Repudiation is the process of proving that a user performed an action.
3. A key is a mathematical value entered into an algorithm to produce a ciphertext.

See the answers at the end of the module.

Cryptographic Algorithms

Certification

1.4 Explain the importance of using appropriate cryptographic solutions.

3.3 Compare and contrast concepts and strategies to protect data.

A cryptographic algorithm consists of procedures based on a mathematical formula. Different variations of cryptographic algorithms exist. The three broad categories of cryptographic algorithms are hash algorithms, symmetric cryptographic algorithms, and asymmetric cryptographic algorithms.

Variations of Algorithms

While algorithms have many different variations, two of the most common are cipher machines versus computers and stream versus block.

Cipher Machines versus Computers

Today computing devices are used almost exclusively to encrypt data. However, that has not always been the case. Prior to the age of electronic digital computers, various mechanical machines were used. Known as "cipher machines," one of the first was a cipher disk, developed in 1470 by an Italian architect and author. A cipher disk is an encrypting and decrypting tool consisting of two concentric circular plates mounted on top of each other. The larger plate is stationary while the smaller is moveable; the alphabet (in order) is inscribed on the outer edge of each plate. Turning the smaller plate to align with the larger plate provides for a fast and easy method to encrypt and decrypt messages. Due to their ease of use, cipher disks were used for almost 500 years and were a mainstay in the U.S. Civil War. A cipher disk is seen in Figure 3-3.

Figure 3-3   Cipher disk

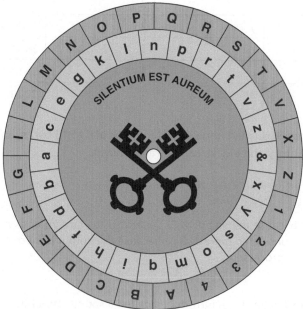

One of the most famous cipher machines was essentially a mechanical replacement of the cipher disk but with many enhancements. Known as the Enigma, this device had three separate elements connected by wires: a keyboard for entering each letter of plaintext, a scrambling unit composed of a series of disks (instead of a single disk like on a cipher disk) for creating the ciphertext, and a display board with lights that indicated the ciphertext to be transmitted or had been received via Morse code. The Enigma machine was the primary cryptography device used by Germany during World War II. This device was so sophisticated that some security professionals have speculated that had it been properly used, it never would have been broken by the Allies.

However, strong encryption does not require using a computer. One secure cryptographic algorithm is entirely hand-calculated. A **one-time pad (OTP)** combines plaintext with a random key. A **pad** is a long sequence of random letters. These letters are combined with the plaintext message to produce the ciphertext. To decipher the message, the recipient must have a copy of the pad to reverse the process.

To encipher a message, the position in the alphabet of the first letter in the plaintext message is added to the position in the alphabet of the first random letter from the pad. For example, if *secret* is to be encrypted using the pad *cbyfea*, the first letter *s* (#19 of the alphabet) is added to the first letter of the pad *c* (#3 of the alphabet) and then 1 is subtracted (19 + 3 − 1 = 21). This results in *u* (#21 of the alphabet). Each letter is similarly encrypted (any number larger than 26 is wrapped around to the start of the alphabet). To decipher a message, the recipient takes the first letter of the ciphertext and subtracts the first random letter from the pad (any negative numbers are wrapped around to the end of the alphabet). An OTP is illustrated in Table 3-2.

As its name implies, the one-time pad should be used only one time and then destroyed. Because OTP is hand-calculated and is the only known encryption method that cannot be broken mathematically, OTPs were used by special operations teams and resistance groups during World War II as well as by intelligence agencies and spies during the Cold War.

Stream Versus Block

Another variation in cryptographic algorithms is the amount of data that is processed at a time. Some algorithms use a **stream cipher** that takes one character and replaces it with one character. Other algorithms make use of a **block cipher**. Whereas a stream cipher works on one character at a time, a block cipher manipulates an entire block of plaintext

Table 3-2   One-time pad

Plaintext	Position in alphabet	Pad	Position in alphabet	Calculation	Result
s	19	c	3	19+3−1=21	u
e	5	b	2	5+2−1=6	f
c	3	y	25	3+25−1=1	a
r	18	f	6	18+6−1=23	w
e	5	e	5	5+5−1=9	i
t	20	a	1	20+1−1=20	T

at one time. The plaintext message is divided into separate blocks of 8 to 16 bytes, and then each block is encrypted independently. For additional security, the blocks can be randomized.

> **Caution** !
>
> Stream ciphers are less secure because the engine that generates the stream does not vary; the only change is the plaintext itself. Block ciphers are considered more secure because the output is more random, as the cipher is reset to its original state after each block is processed.

Recently a third type of algorithm has been introduced called a **sponge function**. A sponge function takes as input a string of any length and returns a string of any requested variable length. This function repeatedly applies a process on the input that has been padded with additional characters until all characters are used ("absorbed in the sponge").

Hash Algorithms

One type of cryptographic algorithm is a one-way algorithm. Its purpose is not to create ciphertext that can later be decrypted back into plaintext; in fact, it is designed so that it *cannot* be reversed to reveal the original set of data.

A **hash** algorithm creates a unique "digital fingerprint" of a set of data. This process is called hashing, and the resulting fingerprint is a **digest** (sometimes called a **message digest** or simply a **hash**) that represents the contents. Hashing protects the integrity of data, proving that no one has altered it, and is used primarily for comparison purposes.

> **Note** 9
>
> The protections of confidentiality, integrity, and availability (CIA) are covered in Module 1.

To illustrate how a hash algorithm functions, consider when 12 is multiplied by 34, the result is 408. If a user were asked to determine the two numbers used to create the number 408, it would not be possible to work backward and derive the original numbers with absolute certainty because there are too many mathematical possibilities $(1 \times 408, 2 \times 204, 3 \times 136, 4 \times 102, \text{etc.})$. Hashing is similar in that it is not possible to determine the plaintext from the digest.

> **Note** 10
>
> Although hashing and checksums are similar in that they both create a value based on the contents of a file, hashing is not the same as creating a checksum. A checksum is intended to verify ("check") the integrity of data and identify data-transmission errors, while a hash is designed to create a unique digital fingerprint of the data.

A hashing algorithm is considered secure if it has these characteristics:

- **Fixed size.** A digest of a short set of data should produce the same size as a digest of a long set of data. For example, a digest of the single letter *a* is 86be7afa339d0fc7cfc785e72f578d33, while a digest of 1 million occurrences of the letter *a* is 4a7f5723f954eba1216c9d8f6320431f, the same length.
- **Unique.** Two different sets of data cannot produce the same digest. Changing a single letter in one data set should produce an entirely different digest. For example, a digest of *Sunday* is 0d716e73a2a7910bd4ae63407056d79b while a digest of *sunday* (lowercase *s*) is 3464eb71bd7a4 377967a30da798a1b54.
- **Original.** It should not be possible to produce a data set that has a desired or predefined hash.
- **Secure.** The resulting hash cannot be reversed to determine the original plaintext.

There are several common hash algorithms. One of the earliest hash algorithms is a "family" of algorithms known as Message Digest (MD). Different versions of MD hashes were introduced over almost 20 years, and the most widely used of these algorithms is MD5. However, serious weaknesses have been identified in MD5 and it is no longer considered suitable for use. Other secure hash algorithms include:

- **Secure Hash Algorithm (SHA).** Another family of hashes is the Secure Hash Algorithm (SHA). SHA-1 was developed in 1993 but is no longer considered suitable for use. SHA-2 has six variations, the most common are SHA-256, SHA-384, and SHA-512 (the last number indicates the length in bits of the digest that is generated) and is currently considered to be a secure hash. In 2015, after eight years of competition between 51 original entries, SHA-3 was announced as a new standard. One of the design goals of SHA-3 was for it to be dissimilar to previous hash algorithms to prevent threat actors from building upon any earlier work of compromising these algorithms.
- **RipeMD.** RipeMD stands for RACE Integrity Primitives Evaluation Message Digest. The primary design feature of RipeMD is two different and independent parallel chains of computation, the results of which are then combined at the end of the process. There are several versions of RipeMD, all based on the length of the digest created, including RipeMD-160, RipeMD-256, and RipeMD-320.
- **Whirlpool.** Another strong hash algorithm is Whirlpool. Whirlpool uses a block cipher and takes a message of any length less than 2256 bits and returns a 512-bit message digest. The authors of Whirlpool have stated that it is not and will never be patented and may be used free of charge for any purpose.

Table 3-3 illustrates the digests generated from several one-way hash algorithms of the word *Cengage*.

Table 3-3 Digests generated from one-time hash algorithms

Hash	Digest
RipeMD160	dd52a79bce64a1d145b51ce639e0dadda976516d
SHA-256	f6c8a86bf6a5128cbaf2ad251b0beaa3604c11c51587de518737537800098d76
SHA3-512	3a82d58e17f3991413c5f4e9811930b69513bba02a860eed82070f892ab381f9fd926a88cf68745565f51a93 b97a1317ae8b84e2dfb798e4a2aa331187dc9e34
Whirlpool	1428cacf499fce9ef439f95a27f0efdc518e97edf9714e234cfffe0c22dcb0e2c4bd3f22a975670f4a229452062 b8bd0c6c9244e4c986f22c61ce951de31c505

Hashing is often used as a check to verify that the original contents of an item have not been changed. For example, digests are often calculated and then posted on websites for files that can be downloaded, as seen in Figure 3-4. After downloading the file, a user can create their own digest on the file and then compare it with the digest value posted on the website; a match indicates that there has been no change to the original file while being downloaded.

Figure 3-4 Verify downloads with digests

Hashes

KeePass 2.53

KeePass-2.53.zip:

SHA-1:   092CC353 1A46B600 968636B5 6851E23F FEE5505F
SHA-256:   DCA1B970 9A87BA67 ECEF8905 80C0B2AD 6E3ACF38 546A642C AFE36D70 62E40AD4
Size: 3225609 B
Sig.:   [OpenPGP ASC]

Symmetric Cryptographic Algorithms

The original cryptographic algorithms for encrypting and decrypting data are symmetric cryptographic algorithms. Symmetric cryptographic algorithms use the same key to encrypt and decrypt the data. Data encrypted by Bob with a key can only be decrypted by Alice using that same key. Thus, it is essential that the key be kept private (secret) so, for this reason, symmetric encryption is also called **private key cryptography**. Symmetric encryption, which protects the confidentiality of data, is illustrated in Figure 3-5, where identical keys are used to encrypt and decrypt a document.

Figure 3-5   Symmetric (private key) cryptography

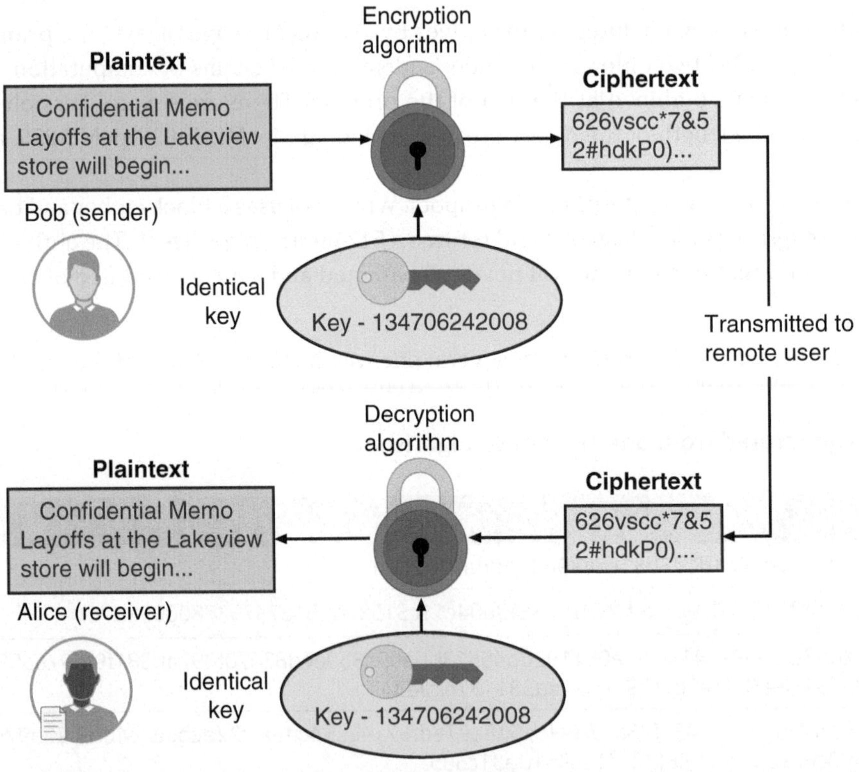

Caution !

The element that must be kept secret in symmetric cryptography is the key.

Symmetric cryptography can provide strong encryption—if the key is kept secure between the sender and all the recipients. There are several strong symmetric cryptographic algorithms. These include:

- **Advanced Encryption Standard (AES).** The Advanced Encryption Standard (AES) is a symmetric algorithm that performs three steps on every block (128 bits) of plaintext. Within step 2, multiple rounds are performed depending on the key size: a 128-bit key performs 9 rounds, a 192-bit key performs 11 rounds, and a 256-bit key, known as AES-256, uses 13 rounds. Within each round, bytes are substituted and rearranged, and then special multiplication is performed based on the new arrangement. To date, no attacks have been successful against AES.
- **Blowfish and Twofish.** Blowfish is a block cipher algorithm that operates on 64-bit blocks and can have a key length from 32 to 448 bits. To date, no significant weaknesses have been identified. A later derivation of Blowfish known as Twofish is also considered to be a strong algorithm, although it has not been used as widely as Blowfish.

Caution !

Like hash algorithms, several symmetric cryptography algorithms have been deprecated and should no longer be used. These include Data Encryption Standard (DES), Triple Data Encryption Standard (3DES), and Rivest Cipher (RC).

Asymmetric Cryptographic Algorithms

If Bob wants to send an encrypted message to Alice using symmetric encryption, he must be sure that she has the key to decrypt the message. Yet how should Bob get the key to Alice? He cannot send it electronically as an email attachment because that would make it vulnerable to interception by attackers. Nor can he encrypt the key and send it because Alice would not have a way to decrypt the encrypted key. This illustrates the primary weakness of symmetric encryption algorithms: distributing and maintaining a secure single key among multiple users, who are often scattered geographically, poses significant challenges.

A completely different approach is asymmetric cryptographic algorithms, also known as **public key cryptography**. Asymmetric encryption, which protects the confidentiality of data, uses two keys instead of only one. These keys are mathematically related and are known as the public key and the private key. The public key is known to everyone and can be freely distributed, while the private key is known only to the individual to whom it belongs. When Bob wants to send a secure message to Alice, he uses Alice's public key to encrypt the message. Alice then uses her private key to decrypt it. Asymmetric cryptography is illustrated in Figure 3-6.

Caution !

The element that must be kept secret in asymmetric cryptography is the private key.

Several important principles regarding asymmetric cryptography are:

- **Key pairs.** Unlike symmetric cryptography that uses only one key, asymmetric cryptography requires a pair of keys.
- **Public key.** Public keys by their nature are designed to be public and do not need to be protected. They can be freely given to anyone or even posted on the Internet.
- **Private key.** The private key should be kept confidential and never shared.
- **Both directions.** Asymmetric cryptography keys can work in both directions. A document encrypted with a public key can be decrypted with the corresponding private key. In the same way, a document encrypted with a private key can be decrypted with its public key.

There are different asymmetric algorithms and variations, discussed next. Also, there are issues surrounding key management.

Figure 3-6   Asymmetric (public key) cryptography

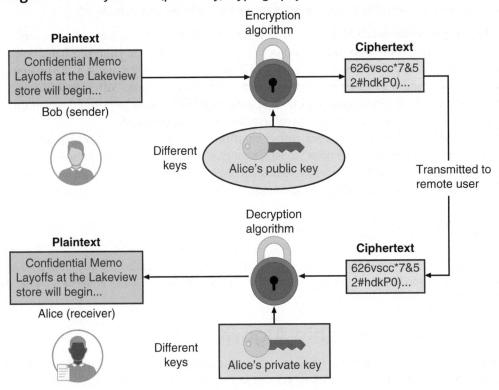

RSA

The asymmetric algorithm RSA was published in 1977 and became the basis for several products. The RSA algorithm multiplies two large prime numbers (a prime number is a number divisible only by itself and 1), p and q, to compute their product ($n = pq$). Next, a number e is chosen that is less than n and a prime factor to $(p-1)(q-1)$. Another number d is determined, so that $(ed-1)$ is divisible by $(p-1)(q-1)$. The values of e and d are the public and private exponents. The public key is the pair (n, e) while the private key is (n, d). The numbers p and q can be discarded.

An illustration of the RSA algorithm using very small numbers is as follows:

1. Select two prime numbers, p and q (in this example, $p = 7$ and $q = 19$).
2. Multiply p and q together to create n ($7 * 19 = 133$).
3. Calculate m as $p - 1 * q - 1$ ($[7-1]*[19-1]$ or $6 * 18 = 108$).
4. Find a number e so that it and m have no common positive divisor other than 1 ($e = 5$).
5. Find a number d so that $d = (1 + n * m) / e$ or ($[1 + 133 * 108] / 5$ or $14,364 / 5 = 2875$).

For this example, the public key n is 133 and e is 5, while the private key n is 133 and d is 2873.

Elliptic Curve Cryptography (ECC)

The basis of RSA asymmetric encryption security is factoring, or the prime numbers that make up a value. As computers become faster and more powerful, the ability to "crack" RSA asymmetric encryption by computing the factoring has grown. Instead of using factoring as the basis, other research looked at an obscure (and esoteric) branch of mathematics called elliptic curves. In short, an elliptic curve is a set of points that satisfy a specific mathematical equation. This paved the way for a different form of asymmetric encryption not based on factoring.

Instead of using large prime numbers as with RSA, elliptic curve cryptography (ECC) uses sloping curves. An elliptic curve is a function drawn on an x- or y-axis as a gently curved line. By adding the values of two points on the curve, a third point on the curve can be derived, of which the inverse is used, as illustrated in Figure 3-7. With ECC, users share one elliptic curve and one point on the curve. One user chooses a secret random number and computes a public key based on a point on the curve; the other user does the same. They can now exchange messages because the shared public keys can generate a private key on an elliptic curve.

Figure 3-7 Elliptic curve cryptography

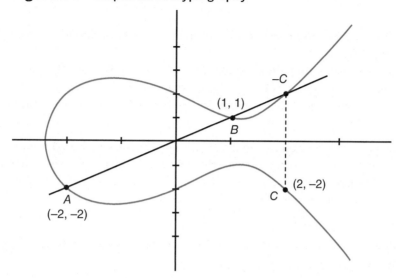

The difference in size necessary to produce the same level of security between RSA and ECC keys is significant. Table 3-4 compares the key length (in bits) of RSA and ECC keys that have the same level of security. Despite a slow start, ECC has gained wide popularity. It is used by the U.S. government to protect internal communications, by the Tor project to help ensure anonymity, and as the mechanism to prove ownership of bitcoins. All modern operating systems (OSs) and web browsers rely on ECC. Because mobile devices are limited in terms of computing power due to their smaller size, ECC offers security that is comparable to other asymmetric cryptography algorithms but with smaller key sizes, resulting in faster computations and lower power consumption.

Table 3-4 RSA versus ECC key length for same security level

RSA key length	ECC key length
1024	160
2048	224
3072	256
7680	384
15360	521

Note 11

According to one study, to break a 228-bit RSA key, the amount of energy needed would take less energy than what is required to boil a teaspoon of water. However, breaking a 228-bit ECC key would require more energy than it would take to boil all the water on Earth.[2]

Digital Signature Algorithm (DSA)

Asymmetric cryptography can also be used to provide proofs. Suppose Alice receives an encrypted document that says it came from Bob. Although Alice can be sure that the encrypted message was not viewed or altered by someone else while being transmitted, how can she know for certain that Bob was the sender? Because Alice's public key is widely available, anyone could use it to encrypt the document. Another individual could have created a fictitious document, encrypted it with Alice's public key, and then sent it to Alice while pretending to be Bob. Alice's key can verify that no one read or changed the document in transport, but it cannot verify the sender.

Proof can be provided with asymmetric cryptography, however, by creating a digital signature, which is an electronic verification of the sender. A handwritten signature on a paper document serves as proof that the signer has read and agreed to the document. A digital signature is much the same but can provide additional benefits. A digital signature can:

- **Verify the sender.** A digital signature serves to confirm the identity of the person from whom the electronic message originated.
- **Prevent the sender from disowning the message.** The signer cannot later attempt to disown the message by claiming the signature was forged (nonrepudiation).
- **Prove the integrity of the message.** A digital signature can prove that the message has not been altered since it was signed.

The basis for a digital signature rests on the ability of asymmetric keys to work in both directions (a public key can encrypt a document that can be decrypted with a private key, and the private key can encrypt a document that can be decrypted by the public key).

The steps for Bob to send a digitally signed message to Alice are:

1. After creating a memo, Bob generates a digest on it.
2. Bob then encrypts the digest with his private key. This encrypted digest is the digital signature for the memo.
3. Bob sends both the memo and the digital signature to Alice.
4. When Alice receives them, she decrypts the digital signature using Bob's public key, revealing the digest. If she cannot decrypt the digital signature, then she knows that it did not come from Bob (because only Bob's public key can decrypt the digest generated with his private key).
5. Alice then hashes the memo with the same hash algorithm Bob used and compares the result to the digest she received from Bob. If they are equal, Alice can be confident that the message has not changed since he signed it. If the digests are not equal, Alice will know the message has changed since it was signed.

These steps are illustrated in Figure 3-8.

Figure 3-8   Digital signature

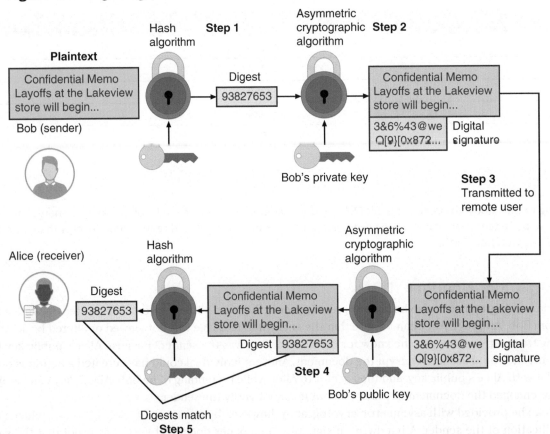

> **Caution** !
>
> Using a digital signature does not encrypt the message itself. In the example, if Bob wanted to ensure the privacy of the message, he also would have to encrypt it using Alice's public key.

The Digital Signature Algorithm (DSA) is a U.S. government standard for digital signatures. DSA was proposed by the National Institute of Standards and Technology (NIST) in 1991 for use in their Digital Signature Standard (DSS). Although patented, NIST has made this patent available worldwide royalty-free. The standard continues to be revised and updated periodically by NIST.

Key Exchange

Public and private keys may result in confusion regarding whose key to use and which key should be used. Table 3-5 lists the practices to follow when using asymmetric cryptography.

Table 3-5 Asymmetric cryptography practices

Action	Whose key to use	Which key to use	Explanation
Bob wants to send Alice an encrypted message.	Alice's key	Public key	When an encrypted message is to be sent, the recipient's, and not the sender's, key is used.
Alice wants to read an encrypted message sent by Bob.	Alice's key	Private key	An encrypted message can be read only by using the recipient's private key.
Bob wants to send a copy to himself of the encrypted message that he sent to Alice.	Bob's key	Public key to encrypt Private key to decrypt	An encrypted message can be read only by the recipient's private key. Bob would need to encrypt it with his public key and then use his private key to decrypt it.
Bob receives an encrypted reply message from Alice.	Bob's key	Private key	The recipient's private key is used to decrypt received messages.
Bob wants Susan to read Alice's reply message that he received.	Susan's key	Public key	The message should be encrypted with Susan's key for her to decrypt and read with her private key.
Bob wants to send Alice a message with a digital signature.	Bob's key	Private key	Bob's private key is used to encrypt the hash.
Alice wants to see Bob's digital signature.	Bob's key	Public key	Because Bob's public and private keys work in both directions, Alice can use his public key to decrypt the hash.

In addition to confusion regarding which key to use, there are also issues with sending and receiving keys (**key exchange**) such as exchanging a symmetric private key. One solution is to make the exchange outside of the normal communication channels (for example, Alice could hire Carol to deliver a USB flash drive containing the key directly to Bob).

There are different solutions for a key exchange that occurs within the normal communications channel of cryptography, including:

- **Diffie-Hellman (DH).** The DH key exchange requires Alice and Bob to each agree upon a large prime number and related integer. Those two numbers can be made public, yet Alice and Bob, through mathematical computations and exchanges of intermediate values, can separately create the same key.

- **Diffie-Hellman Ephemeral (DHE).** Whereas DH uses the same keys each time, DHE uses different keys. Ephemeral keys are temporary keys that are used only once and then discarded.
- **Elliptic Curve Diffie–Hellman (ECDH).** ECDH uses elliptic curve cryptography instead of prime numbers in its computation.
- **Perfect forward secrecy.** Public key systems that generate random public keys that are different for each session are called perfect forward secrecy. The value of this is that if the secret key is compromised, it cannot reveal the contents of more than one message.

Two Rights & A Wrong

1. A stream cipher is more secure than a block cipher.
2. Hashing is used primarily for comparison purposes.
3. Asymmetric cryptography keys can work in both directions.

See the answers at the end of the module.

Using Cryptography

Certification

1.4 Explain the importance of using appropriate cryptographic solutions.

Cryptography can be applied through either software or hardware. Also, a relatively new technology known as blockchain uses cryptography as its basis.

Encryption through Software

Software-based cryptography can be implemented at the file level or disk level. It can also be implemented across an entire database using software.

File and File System Cryptography

Cryptographic software can be used to encrypt or decrypt files one by one (file-level encryption). However, this can be a cumbersome process. Instead, protecting groups of files, such as all files in a specific folder, can take advantage of the operating system's (OS's) file system. A **file system** is a method used by OSs to store, retrieve, and organize files. Protecting individual files or multiple files through file system cryptography can be performed using third-party software or native OS cryptographic features.

Third-Party Software   A wide variety of third-party software tools are available for performing encryption. This encryption is essentially file-level encryption. These tools include GNU Privacy Guard (which is abbreviated GnuPG), AxCrypt, Folder Lock, and VeraCrypt, which is seen in Figure 3-9.

Operating System Encryption   Modern OSs provide encryption support natively. Microsoft's Encrypting File System (EFS) is a cryptography system for the Windows operating systems that use the Windows NTFS file system, while Apple's FileVault performs a similar function. Because these are tightly integrated with the file system, file encryption and decryption are transparent to the user. Any file created in an encrypted folder or added to an encrypted folder is automatically encrypted. When an authorized user opens a file, it is decrypted as data is read from a disk; when a file is saved, the OS encrypts the data as it is written to the disk.

Figure 3-9 VeraCrypt

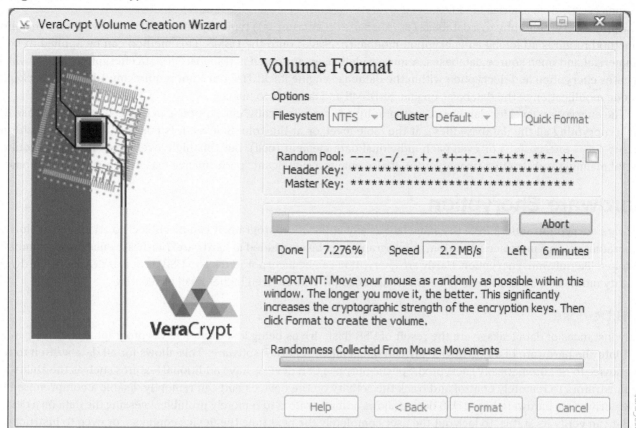

VeraCrypt

Disk Encryption

Instead of protecting individual files or groups of files, cryptography can also be applied to entire disks as well, either in part or in full. The different types of a disk encryption include:

- **Disk-level encryption.** Protecting the entire drive using cryptography is known as full-disk encryption (FDE) and protects all data on a drive, including the installed OS. One example of FDE software is included in Microsoft Windows and is known as BitLocker drive encryption software. BitLocker encrypts the entire disk, including the Windows Registry and any temporary files that might hold confidential information. BitLocker prevents attackers from accessing data by booting from another OS or placing the drive in another computer.

- **Volume-level encryption.** A **volume** is a section of a drive that is accessible by a user and has a file system associated with it. That is, a volume is a single accessible storage area with a single file system. A **partition** is not the same as a volume. A partition is a logical division of a hard drive and is essentially a "chunk" of a disk that does not necessarily contain a file system or is even formatted to store data. Software can apply cryptography to a volume, known as volume-level encryption. Partition-level encryption may be applied depending on if the partition is formatted and contains a file system.

Database Encryption

A database is an organized collection of structured information stored electronically on a computer. A database has an engine that stores and retrieves the data, and that engine is manipulated by a user through a database management system (DBMS) or a programming language. (Most databases use the Structured Query Language [SQL] to interact with a database.) A relational database, the most common type of database, is organized into rows (horizontal) and columns (vertical) in a series of tables.

Applying cryptography to a database (database-level encryption) typically occurs in one of two ways. The plug-in method requires attaching an encryption module (package) onto the DBMS. This method can be applied to both commercial and open-source databases. A more widely used approach is transparent data encryption (TDE), which executes encryption and decryption within the database engine itself. TDE does not require any additional packages or code modification of the database, engine, or DBMS and is easier to manage.

The encryption level for database cryptography can vary. Typically, encryption is performed at the database file level (encrypting all the database files), at the table level, or at the column level. It is possible to encrypt each row (record-level encryption) or even each individual data element (cell), but this high level of "granularity" requires careful planning and strict key management. It also enacts a significant "performance tax" when using the database.

Hardware Encryption

Software encryption suffers from the same fate as any application program: it can be subject to attacks to exploit its vulnerabilities. As a more secure option, cryptography can be embedded in hardware. Hardware encryption cannot be exploited like software encryption. Hardware encryption can be incorporated into a USB device or drive. The hardware security model and trusted execution environment can provide an even higher level of security.

USB Devices

Many instances of data leakage are the result of USB flash drives being lost or stolen. Cryptographic features can be built into the hardware of a USB device instead of installing separate software. This allows for all data written to the USB device to be automatically encrypted. Special-purpose USB devices have additional features such as the ability for administrators to remotely control and track the activity on the devices and can remotely disable a compromised or stolen drive. One hardware-based USB device allows administrators to remotely prohibit accessing the data on a device until it can verify its status, to lock out the user completely the next time the device connects, or even to instruct the drive to initiate a self-destruct sequence to destroy all data.

Self-Encrypting Drives (SEDs)

Just as a cryptographic hardware-based USB device can automatically encrypt any data stored on it, **self-encrypting drives (SEDs)** are drives that can protect all the data written to them. When the computer or other device with an SED is initially powered up, the drive and the host device perform an authentication process. If the authentication process fails, the drive can be configured to deny any access to the drive or even perform a cryptographic erase on specified blocks of data, deleting even the decryption keys so that no data can be recovered. This also makes it impossible to install the drive on another computer to read its contents.

Hardware Security Module (HSM)

A hardware security module (HSM) is a removable external cryptographic device. An HSM can be a USB device, an expansion card, a device that connects directly to a computer through a port, or a secure network server. It includes an onboard random number generator and key storage facility, as well as accelerated symmetric and asymmetric encryption, and can even back up sensitive material in encrypted form. Because all of this is done in hardware and not through software, it cannot be compromised by malware.

Some financial banking software comes with a specialized USB HSM hardware key, also called a "security dongle." This device is paired with a specific financial account and cannot be cloned or compromised. Figure 3-10 shows a USB HSM.

Trusted Execution Environment (TEE)

Instead of relying on vulnerable software or an external device to be connected to a computer, a **trusted execution environment (TEE)** is a secure cryptoprocessor (a motherboard chip) that is internal to the computer itself. Because it is hardware that cannot be tampered with, its contents are secure. A TEE protects the confidentiality and integrity of the code and data stored on it.

The Trusted Platform Module (TPM) is an international standard for a cryptoprocessors that provides cryptographic services. A TPM includes a random number generator and full support for asymmetric encryption and can

Figure 3-10   USB HSM

also generate public and private keys. In addition, a TPM can measure and test key components as the computer is starting up to prevent the computer from booting if system files or data have been altered. Personal computers (PCs) typically have a TPM, while Apple and Android devices have a similar technology known as a secure enclave.

Note 12

TPM v2.0 is required for any computer running Microsoft Windows 11.

Blockchain

Consider the company JetGo, which manufactures self-balancing hoverboards. Several suppliers sell raw materials to JetGo: tires, metal, plastic, seats, nuts, and washers, just to name a few. JetGo sells its hoverboards to many retailers and then deposits the proceeds into its bank so that JetGo can pay its suppliers, employees, and others. In the Accounting Department, a ledger is maintained of all transactions of raw materials that are bought and hoverboards that are sold. This ledger serves as the central repository of the accounting information for JetGo.

But JetGo is not the only entity to keep a ledger: all of its suppliers, all of the retailers who buy from JetGo, the banks, and everyone else also keep ledgers of their transactions with JetGo as well as other customers. This is seen in Figure 3-11

For each entity to maintain their own ledger is very inefficient. Because there is duplication among many different suppliers, retailers, and banks, what happens if one supplier to JetGo records a transaction in error? It may take a long time to correct the error because the supplier must contact JetGo, who may need to contact its bank, and even its retailers, to track down the error.

Instead, what if there was a single, shared, tamper-evident ledger that JetGo and everyone else shared? It would eliminate or reduce paper processes, speeding up transaction times and increasing efficiencies. With a shared ledger, any transactions would be recorded only once and could not be altered. All parties must also give consensus before a new transaction is added to the network. Having a single shared ledger is seen in Figure 3-12.

This is essentially the definition of a blockchain. A blockchain is a shared, immutable ledger that facilitates the process of recording transactions and tracking assets in a business network. At a high level, blockchain technology allows a network of computers to agree at regular intervals on the true state of a distributed ledger. It is a system in which a record of transactions made are maintained across several computers that are linked in a peer-to-peer network.

Note 13

Blockchain relies heavily on cryptographic hash algorithms, most notably the SHA-256, to record its transactions. This makes it computationally infeasible to try to replace a block or insert a new block of information without the approval of all entities involved.

Figure 3-11 Multiple organizations with ledgers

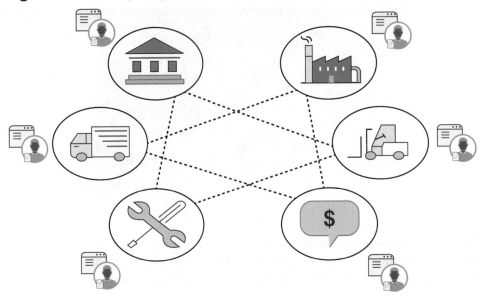

Figure 3-12 Multiple organizations using single ledger

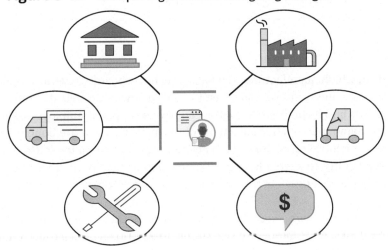

There are different types of blockchains. A **public blockchain**, also called an open public ledger, is a blockchain network that anyone can join and become part of it. A common use of public blockchains is for exchanging cryptocurrencies and crypto mining. A **private blockchain** operates in a closed network and is best suited for enterprises and businesses that implement a blockchain only for internal uses. A **federated blockchain**, also called a consortium blockchain, is typically used when organizations need both a public and private blockchain. In this type, there is more than one organization involved who provides access to preselected nodes for reading, writing, and auditing.

Despite the initial excitement over blockchain as a way for enterprises to track their assets through complex supply chains, to date they have not been widely implemented. For example, a global shipping container company started work in 2018 to use blockchain to track its containers, cutting down on paperwork to clear customs and offering the owners of the cargo in the containers more visibility during transit. However, this required the collaboration of many different companies and nations, which never materialized, and the project was abandoned five years later. During the COVID-19 pandemic, a major drug chain considered blockchain for vaccine distribution but decided to pursue other options that were faster to implement. In 2018, a major grocery chain started tracking one item of produce, leafy greens, through blockchain. Over the next four years, they only added one more item to the blockchain, green bell peppers.

Two Rights & A Wrong

1. FDE protects all data on a hard drive except the installed OS.
2. Transparent data encryption (TDE) executes encryption and decryption within the database engine itself.
3. An HSM is a removable external cryptographic device.

See the answers at the end of the module.

Cryptographic Limitations and Attacks

Certification

1.4 Explain the importance of using appropriate cryptographic solutions.

2.3 Explain various types of vulnerabilities.

2.4 Given a scenario, analyze indicators of malicious activity.

As with all information security defenses, cryptography is not an absolute protection. There are limitations to cryptography, and it continually faces attacks.

Limitations of Cryptography

Despite providing widespread protections, cryptography faces constraints (limitations) that can impact its effectiveness. In recent years, the number of small electronic devices that consume very small amounts of power (low-power devices) has grown significantly. These devices range from tiny sensors that control office heating and lighting to consumer devices such as thermostats and lightbulbs. These devices need to be protected from threat actors who could accumulate their data and use it in nefarious ways.

Note 14

Compared with the average energy requirements of a laptop computer (60 watts), the typical wireless sensor draws only .001 watt.

In addition, many applications require extremely fast response times, most notably communication applications (like collecting car toll road payments), high-speed optical networking links, and secure storage devices such as solid-state disks. Cryptography is viewed as a necessary feature to add to protect low-power devices and applications with fast response times to make them secure.

However, adding cryptography to low-power devices or those that have near instantaneous response times can be difficult. To perform their computations, cryptographic algorithms require both time and energy, each of which are typically in short supply for low-power devices and applications needing ultra-fast response times. This results in a resource versus security constraint, or a limitation in providing strong cryptography due to the tug-of-war between the available resources (time and energy) and the security provided by cryptography. Table 3-6 lists additional cryptographic constraints.

Attacks on Cryptography

There are several different types of attacks on cryptography. Two of the most common include algorithm attacks and collision attacks. In addition, a new type of computing, called quantum computing, may have a profound impact on cryptography.

Table 3-6 Cryptographic Constraints

Limitation	Explanation
Speed	The speed at which data can be encrypted or decrypted depends on several hardware and software factors and, in some instances, a slower speed is unacceptable.
Size	The resulting size of an encrypted file can be as much as one-third larger than the plaintext version.
Weak keys	Some ciphers can produce a weak key that causes the cipher to behave in unpredictable ways or may compromise overall security.
Key length	Some ciphers have a short key length, or the number of bits in a key, that results in weaker security.
Longevity	As computers continue to become more powerful and can "crack" keys, the longevity or useful lifetime of service of ciphers may diminish.
Predictability	A weak random number generator of the cipher may create predictable output.
Reuse	If someone reuses the same key for each encryption, then it provides a larger data footprint for an attacker to use in attempting to break the encryption.
Entropy	Entropy is the measure of randomness of a data-generating function, and ciphers with low entropy give the ability to predict future-generated values.
Computational overhead	Sensors and Internet of Things (IoT) devices often lack the capacity to accommodate the computational overhead for cryptography.

Algorithm Attacks

Modern cryptographic algorithms are reviewed, tested, and vetted by specialists in cryptography over several years before they are released to the public for use. Very few threat actors have the advanced skills needed to even attempt to break an algorithm. However, there are other methods by which attackers can focus on circumventing strong algorithms. These include known ciphertext attacks, downgrade attacks, and taking advantage of misconfigurations.

Known Ciphertext Attacks   When properly implemented, cryptography prevents the threat actor from knowing the plaintext or the key; the only item they can see is the ciphertext itself. Yet there are sophisticated statistical tools that can be used to perform an analysis of the ciphertext in an attempt to discover a pattern in the ciphertexts, which then may be useful in revealing the plaintext or key. This is called a known ciphertext attack or ciphertext-only attack because all that is known is the ciphertext—but it can still reveal clues that may be mined.

> **Note 15**
>
> Wireless data networks are particularly susceptible to known ciphertext attacks. This is because threat actors can capture large sets of ciphertexts to be analyzed, and the attackers may be able to inject their own frames into the wireless transmissions.

Downgrade Attacks   Because of the frequent introduction of new hardware and software, often they include backward compatibility so that a newer version can still function with the older version. However, in most instances, this means that the newer version must revert to the older and less secure version. In a downgrade attack, an attacker forces the system to abandon the current higher security mode of operation and instead "fall back" to implementing an older and less secure mode. This then allows the threat actor to attack the weaker mode.

Attacks Based on Misconfigurations   Most breaches of cryptography are the result of incorrect choices or misconfigurations of the cryptography options, known as misconfiguration implementation. Selecting weak algorithms, like DES or SHA-1, should be avoided since these are no longer secure. Many cryptographic algorithms have several configuration options and, unless careful consideration is given to these options, the cryptography may be improperly implemented. Also, careless users can weaken cryptography if they choose SHA-256 when a much stronger algorithm like SHA3-512 is available through a simple menu choice, for example.

Collision Attacks

One of the foundations of a hash algorithm is that each digest must be unique. If it were not unique, then a threat actor could trick users into performing an action that was assumed to be safe but in reality was not. For example, digests are calculated and then posted on websites for files that can be downloaded. Suppose an attacker could infiltrate a website and post their own malicious file for download, but when the digest was generated for this malicious file, it created the same as that posted for the legitimate file. Two files having the same digest is known as a collision. A **collision attack** is an attempt to find two input strings of a hash function that produce the same hash result.

Note 16

While hash algorithms that produce long digests, like SHA3-512, have very low odds of such a collision, for hash algorithms that produce shorter digests, such as MD5, the odds increase. Table 3-4 compares the length of various digests.

Typically, a threat actor would be forced to try all possible combinations until a collision was found. However, a statistical phenomenon called the birthday attack makes it easier. It is based on the **birthday paradox**, which says that for there to be a 50 percent chance that someone in a given room shares your birthday, 253 people would need to be in the room. If, however, you are looking for a greater than 50 percent chance that any two people in the room have the same birthday, you only need 23 people. That's because the matches are based on pairs. If you choose yourself as one side of the pair, then you will need 253 people to have 253 pairs (in other words, it is you combined with 253 other people to make up all 253 sets). But if you are only concerned with matches and not concerned with matching someone with you specifically, then you only need 23 people in the room because it only takes 23 people to form 253 pairs when cross-matched with each other. This applies to hashing collisions in that it is much harder to find something that collides with a specific hash than it is to find any two inputs that hash to the same value.

Note 17

With the birthday paradox, the question is whether each person must link with every other person. If so, only 23 people are needed; if not, when comparing only your single birthday to everyone else's, 253 people are needed.

Quantum Computing

The foundation of modern technology is the bit (binary digit) that can either be off (0) or on (1). However, the development of a revolutionary different type of computer has been underway for several years called a quantum computer. **Quantum computing** relies on quantum physics using atomic-scale units (**qubits**) that can be both 0 and 1 at the same time. As a result, it is possible for one qubit to carry out two separate streams of calculations simultaneously, so that quantum computers will be much faster and more efficient than today's computers.

However, quantum computing poses a risk for cryptography. Asymmetric cryptography begins by multiplying two prime numbers, and what makes this method strong is that it is difficult for today's computers to determine the prime numbers that make up the value (factoring). A single quantum computer could perform factoring by using hundreds of atoms in parallel to quickly factor huge numbers. This would result in virtually all current asymmetric cryptographic algorithms being rendered useless.

While some researchers think that quantum computers will create a "cryptographic apocalypse" very soon (10 years from now), other security professionals think it is farther out in the future, perhaps even 30 years or more. Currently, new encryption proposals are being developed that are "quantum-safe" and that could not be broken by quantum computers. This is called **post-quantum cryptography**, or cryptographic algorithms that are secure against an attack by a quantum computer.

Two Rights & A Wrong

1. In a downgrade attack, an attacker forces the system to abandon the current higher security mode of operation and instead "fall back" to implementing an older and less secure mode.

2. A collision attack is an attempt to find two input strings of a hash function that produce the same hash result.

3. The basis of a quantum computer is a bit.

See the answers at the end of the module.

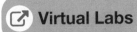 **Virtual Labs** You're now ready to complete the simulations and live virtual machine labs for this module. The labs can be found in each module in MindTap.

Summary

- Steganography hides the existence of information, while cryptography hides the meaning of the information. Cryptography masks information so that it cannot be read. There are two basic methods that are often used in cryptography dating back to ancient times. One method is transposition, in which each letter of the message is rearranged. Another method is substitution, in which one letter is substituted for another letter.

- When using cryptography, the original data, called plaintext, is input into a cryptographic encryption algorithm that has a mathematical value (a key) used to create ciphertext. Cryptographic algorithms are designed to be public, while the individualized key for the algorithm that a user possesses must always be kept secret. Cryptography can provide confidentiality, integrity, authentication, nonrepudiation, and obfuscation. It can also protect data as it resides in any of three states: data in use, data in transit, and data at rest.

- There are different variations of cryptographic algorithms. One variation is based on the device (if any) that is used in the cryptographic process. Another variation is the amount of data that is processed at a time. A stream cipher takes one character and replaces it with one character, while a block cipher manipulates an entire block of plaintext at one time. A sponge function takes as input a string of any length and returns a string

of any requested variable length. This function repeatedly applies a process on the input that has been padded with additional characters until all characters are used.

- Hashing creates a unique digital fingerprint called a digest, which represents the contents of the original material. Hashing is not designed for encrypting material that will be later decrypted. Instead, it protects the integrity of data, proving that no one has altered it, and is used primarily for comparison purposes. If a hash algorithm produces a unique fixed-size hash and the original contents of the material cannot be determined from the hash, the hash is considered secure. Common hashing algorithms are the Secure Hash Algorithm, RACE Integrity Primitives Evaluation Message Digest, and Whirlpool.

- Symmetric cryptography, also called private key cryptography, uses a single key to encrypt and decrypt a message. Symmetric cryptography can provide strong protections against attacks if the key is kept secure. Common symmetric cryptographic algorithms include Advanced Encryption Standard, Blowfish, and Twofish.

- Asymmetric cryptography, also known as public key cryptography, uses two keys instead of one. These keys are mathematically related and are known as the public key and the private key. The public key is widely available and can be freely distributed, while the private key is known only to the recipient of the message and must be kept secure. Common asymmetric cryptographic algorithms include RSA, Elliptic Curve Cryptography, and Digital Signature Algorithm. There are also algorithms relating to key exchange.

- Cryptography can be applied through either software or hardware. Software-based cryptography can protect large numbers of files on a system or an entire disk. There are several third-party software tools and modern OSs provide encryption support natively. Cryptography can also be applied to entire disks, known as full-disk encryption (FDE), as well as to volumes and partitions if the partition is properly structured. Applying cryptography to a database (database-level encryption) typically occurs using transparent data encryption (TDE) that executes encryption and decryption within the database engine itself.

- Hardware encryption cannot be exploited like software cryptography. Hardware encryption devices can protect USB devices and standard hard drives. More sophisticated hardware encryption options include self-encrypting drives (SEDs), the hardware security model (HSM), and the Trusted Platform Module (TPM) and secure enclave.

- A blockchain is a shared, immutable ledger that facilitates the process of recording transactions and tracking assets in a business network. At a high level, blockchain technology allows a network of computers to agree at regular intervals on the true state of a distributed ledger, and it is a system in which a record of transactions made are maintained across several computers that are linked in a peer-to-peer network.

- Despite providing these protections, cryptography faces constraints that can impact its effectiveness. Adding cryptography

to low-power devices or those that have near instantaneous response times can be a problem because the algorithms require both time and energy, which are typically in short supply for low-power devices and applications needing ultra-fast response times. This results in a resource versus security constraint. Other constraints are speed, size, weak keys, key length, longevity, predictability, reuse, entropy, and computational overhead. Due to the importance of incorporating cryptography in low-power devices, a new subfield of cryptography is being developed called lightweight cryptography.

- There are several types of attacks on cryptography. A known ciphertext attack uses statistical tools to attempt to discover a pattern in the ciphertexts, which then may be useful in revealing the plaintext or key. In a downgrade attack, a threat actor forces the system to abandon the current higher security mode of operation and instead fall back to implementing an older and less secure mode. Many breaches of cryptography are the result not of weak algorithms but instead of misconfigurations. When two files have the same digest this is known as a collision. A collision attack is an attempt to find two input strings of a hash function that produce the same hash result.

- Quantum computing relies on quantum physics using atomic-scale units that can be both 0 and 1 at the same time. As a result, it is possible for one qubit to carry out two separate streams of calculations simultaneously, so that quantum computers will be much faster and more efficient than today's computers. However, quantum computing poses a risk for cryptography. Due to its speed and efficiency, quantum computing may be able to break the foundations of cryptography.

Key Terms

algorithm	digital signature	nonrepudiation
asymmetric cryptographic algorithm	downgrade attack	open public ledger
	encryption	partition-level encryption
birthday attack	file-level encryption	record-level encryption
blockchain	full-disk encryption (FDE)	secure enclave
collision	hardware security module (HSM)	steganography
cryptography	hashing	symmetric cryptographic algorithm
database-level encryption	key exchange	Trusted Platform Module (TPM)
decryption	key length	volume-level encryption

Review Questions

1. Aaliyah wants to send a message to a friend, but she does not want anyone else to know that she is communicating with them. Which technique would she use?

   a. Cryptography
   b. Steganography
   c. Encryption
   d. Ciphering

2. Zeinab has been asked by her supervisor to speak with an angry customer who claims that they never received notification of a change in the terms of service agreement. Zeinab learned that an automated "read receipt" was received, showing that the customer opened the email with the new terms of service outlined. What action will Zeinab now take regarding this customer?

   a. Repudiation
   b. Obfuscation
   c. Integrity
   d. Nonrepudiation

3. Which of the following is NOT a form of obfuscation?

   a. Tokenization
   b. Ciphering
   c. Steganography
   d. Data masking

4. Which of the following is NOT correct about "security through obscurity"?

   a. It attempts to hide its existence from outsiders.
   b. Proprietary cryptographic algorithms are a common example.
   c. It is essentially impossible to achieve.
   d. It should only be used as a general information security protection in extreme circumstances.

5. Layla has encrypted a document so that it can only be viewed by those who have been provided the key. What protection has she given to this document?

   a. Confidentiality
   b. Integrity
   c. Authentication
   d. Obfuscation

6. Which of the following is NOT correct about an OTP?

   a. It combines plaintext with a random key.
   b. The recipient must have a copy of the pad to decrypt the message.
   c. It was used during the Cold War.
   d. It requires a cipher disk.

7. What is data called that is to be encrypted by inputting it into a cryptographic algorithm?

   a. Plaintext
   b. Byte-text
   c. Cleartext
   d. Ciphertext

8. Which of the following creates the most secure ciphertext?

   a. Redundant function
   b. Stream cipher
   c. Block cipher
   d. Sponge function

9. Karyme needs to select a hash algorithm that will produce the longest and most secure digest. Which would she choose?

   a. RipeMD160
   b. SHA-256
   c. XRA3-512
   d. Whirlpool

10. Which algorithm uses the same key to both encrypt and decrypt data?

    a. Asymmetric cryptographic algorithm
    b. Hashing algorithm
    c. Pairwise keypair algorithm
    d. Symmetric cryptographic algorithm

11. Which of the following is NOT to be decrypted but is only used for comparison purposes?

    a. Digest
    b. Key
    c. Stream
    d. Algorithm

12. Which of these is NOT a characteristic of a secure hash algorithm?

    a. Collisions may occur, but they are rare.
    b. A message cannot be produced from a predefined hash.
    c. The hash should always be the same fixed size.
    d. The results of a hash function should not be reversed.

13. Which of the following is a weakness of RSA?

    a. RSA weaknesses are based on ECC.
    b. RSA has no known weaknesses.
    c. As computers become more powerful, the ability to compute factoring has increased.
    d. The digest produced by the RSA algorithm is too short to be secure.

14. Which of these is NOT true about ECC?

  a. ECC has gained wide popularity.
  b. All modern OSs and web browsers use ECC.
  c. ECC security is comparable to other asymmetric cryptography but has smaller key sizes.
  d. It uses both sloping curves and prime numbers.

15. If Bob wants to send a secure message to Alice using an asymmetric cryptographic algorithm, which key does he use to encrypt the message?

  a. Alice's private key
  b. Alice's public key
  c. Bob's public key
  d. Bob's private key

16. Farah needs to encrypt only a few files and does not want the entire disk contents to be encrypted. What type of encryption would she use?

  a. File-level encryption
  b. Byte-level encryption
  c. Folder-level encryption
  d. Device-level encryption

17. Which type of encryption would protect all data on a hard drive, including the installed OS?

  a. FDE
  b. SSED
  c. TXPM
  d. HRHS

18. What is a collision?

  a. Two files that produce the same digest.
  b. Two ciphertexts that have the same length.
  c. Two algorithms that have the same key.
  d. Two keys that are the same length.

19. Nahla has been asked to make a recommendation about the most secure TEE. Which of the following would she choose?

  a. SED
  b. HSM
  c. TPM
  d. ARC

20. Which type of blockchain can anyone join?

  a. Federated blockchain
  b. Private blockchain
  c. Hybrid blockchain
  d. Public blockchain

Hands-On Projects

Note 18

If you are concerned about installing any of the software in these projects on your regular computer, you can instead install the software using the Windows Sandbox created in the Module 1 Hands-On Projects. Software installed within the sandbox will not impact the host computer.

Project 3-1: Using OpenPuff Steganography

Estimated Time: 30 minutes
Objective: Explore steganography.
Description: Unlike cryptography, which scrambles a message so that it cannot be viewed, steganography hides the existence of the data. In this project, you will use OpenPuff to create a hidden message.

   1. Use your web browser to go to **embeddedsw.net/OpenPuff_Steganography_Home.html**. (It is not unusual for websites to change the location of where files are stored. If the URL above no longer works, open a search engine and search for "OpenPuff.")

   2. Click **Manual** to open the OpenPuff manual. Save this file to your computer. Read through the manual to see the different features available. Return to the home page when finished.

3. Click **Download binary for Windows/Linux** to download the program. A page will appear asking for payments; however, click the **.ZIP** link to download the program for evaluation without submitting a payment.

4. Click **Screenshot** to view a screen capture of OpenPuff. Right-click this image and save it as **OpenPuff_Screenshot.jpg** on your computer. This will be the carrier file that will contain the secret message.

Note 19

For added security, OpenPuff allows a message to be spread across several carrier files.

5. Navigate to the location of the download and uncompress the OpenPuff zip file on your computer.

6. Now create the secret message to be hidden. Open Notepad and enter **This is a secret message**.

7. Save this file as **Message.txt** and close Notepad.

8. Create a zip file from the **Message** file. Navigate to the location of this file through File Explorer and right-click it.

9. Click **Compress to ZIP file** (Windows 11) or click **Send to** and select **Compressed (zipped) folder** (Windows 10) to create the zip file.

10. Navigate to the OpenPuff folder and double-click **OpenPuff.exe**.

11. Click **Hide**.

Note 20

Under Bit selection options, note the wide variety of file types that can be used to hide a message.

12. Under **(1)**, create three unrelated passwords and enter them into **Cryptography (A)**, **(B)**, and **(C)**. Be sure that the **Scrambing (C)** password is long enough to turn the **Password check** bar from red to green.

13. Under **(2)**, locate the message to be hidden. Click **Browse** and navigate to the file **Message.zip**. Click **Open**.

14. Under **(3)**, select the carrier file. Click **Add** and navigate to **OpenPuff_Screenshot.jpg**.

15. Click **Hide Data!**.

16. Navigate to a different location from that of the carrier files and click **OK**.

17. After the processing has completed, navigate to the location of the carrier file that contains the message and open the file. Can you detect anything different with the file now that it contains the message?

18. Now uncover the message. Close the OpenPuff Data Hiding screen to return to the main menu.

19. Click **Unhide!**.

20. Enter the three passwords.

21. Click **Add Carriers** and navigate to the location of **Carrier1** that contains the hidden message.

22. Click **Unhide!** and navigate to a location to deposit the hidden message. When it has finished processing, click **OK**.

23. Click **Done** after reading the report.

24. Go to the location of the hidden message and you will see **Message.zip**.

25. Close OpenPuff and close all windows.

Project 3-2: Running an RSA Cipher Demonstration

Estimated Time: 20 minutes

Objective: Observe how RSA creates public and private keys.

Description: The steps for encryption using RSA can be illustrated in a Java applet on a website. In this project, you will observe how RSA encrypts and decrypts.

> ### Note 21
>
> It is recommended that you review the section earlier in this chapter regarding the steps in the RSA function.

1. Use your web browser to go to **people.cs.pitt.edu/~kirk/cs1501/notes/rsademo**. (It is not unusual for websites to change the location of where files are stored. If the URL above no longer works, open a search engine and search for "RSA Cipher Demonstration.")
2. Read the information about the demonstration.
3. Click **key generation page**.
4. Change the first prime number (P) to **7**.
5. Change the second prime number (Q) to **5**.
6. Click **Proceed**.
7. Read the information in the pop-up screen and record the necessary numbers. Close the screen when finished.
8. Click **Encryption Page**.
9. Next to **Enter Alice's Exponent key, E:** enter **5** as the key value from the previous screen.
10. Next to **Enter Alice's N Value:** enter **35**.
11. Click **Encrypt**. Read the message and record the values. Close the screen when finished.
12. Click **Decryption Page**.
13. Next to **Enter the encrypted message:** enter **1**.
14. Next to **Enter your N value:** enter **35**.
15. Next to **Enter your private key, D:** enter **5**.
16. Click **Proceed**. Note that **1** has been decrypted to **A**.
17. Close all windows.

Project 3-3: Using Microsoft's Encrypting File System

Estimate Time: 20 minutes

Objective: Demonstrate how to use EFS.

Description: Microsoft's Encrypting File System (EFS) is a cryptography system for Windows operating systems that uses the Windows NTFS file system. Because EFS is tightly integrated with the file system, file encryption and decryption are transparent to the user. In this project, you will turn on and use EFS.

1. Create a Word document with the contents of the first two paragraphs following **#TrendingCyber**.
2. Save the document as **Encrypted.docx**.
3. Save the document again as **Not Encrypted.docx**.
4. Right-click the **Start** button and then click **File Explorer**.
5. Navigate to the location of **Encrypted.docx**.
6. Right-click **Encrypted.docx**.

7. Click **Properties**.

8. Click the **Advanced** button.

9. Check the box **Encrypt contents to secure data**. This document is now protected with EFS. All actions regarding encrypting and decrypting the file are transparent to the user and should not noticeably affect any computer operations. Click **OK**.

10. Click **OK** to close the Encrypted Properties dialog box.

11. Launch Microsoft Word and then open **Encrypted.docx**. Was there any delay in the operation?

12. Now open **Not Encrypted.docx**. Was it any faster or slower?

13. Close all windows.

Project 3-4: Using 7-Zip Cryptography

Estimated Time: 15 minutes
Objective: Use file level cryptography.
Description: There are a wide variety of third-party software tools available for performing file-level encryption and decryption. In this project, you will download and use 7-Zip.

1. Use your web browser to go to **www.7-zip.org/index.html**. (If you are no longer able to access the site through the web address, use a search engine and search for "7-zip.")

2. Click the appropriate version and click **Download**.

3. Follow the instructions to install the program.

4. Locate a file or a folder on the computer to use to create an encrypted archive file.

5. Right-click the file. Note that there is now a **7-Zip** option. (In Windows 11, click **Show more options** on the shortcut menu to display the 7-Zip option.)

6. Click **7-Zip**.

7. Click **Add to Archive**.

8. The **Add to Archive** dialog box appears. Be sure the **Archive format:** is **7z**.

9. Under **Encryption**, enter a strong password.

10. Enter the password again under **Reenter password**.

11. Click **OK**.

12. A new encrypted file is created with the extension 7z. Now open this encrypted file by right-clicking it and then clicking **7-Zip**. (In Windows 11, click **Show more options** on the shortcut menu to display the 7-Zip option.)

13. Click **Extract files**.

14. Under **Password**, enter the password and then click **OK**. The encrypted file will be extracted and available for use.

15. Close all windows.

Case Projects

Case Project 3-1: #TrendingCyber

Estimated Time: 15 minutes

Objective: Summarize your thoughts on the #TrendingCyber opener.

Description: Read again the opening #TrendingCyber in this module. Some individuals have said that it is time to retire the names "Alice" and "Bob" and go with more modern and diverse names. Others have said that these names represent a long tradition in cybersecurity research. What do you think? Should they be retired or retained? Write a one-paragraph summary of your thoughts.

Case Project 3-2: Broken SHA-1

Estimate Time: 30 minutes

Objective: Research how SHA-1 was broken.

Description: Since 2004, security researchers theorized that SHA-1 would be vulnerable to a collision attack, in which the same digest from two different plaintexts could be created. In early 2017, security researchers decisively demonstrated that SHA-1 could create a collision from two separate documents. However, this attack was limited and it was estimated it would cost attackers from $110,000 to $560,000 on Amazon's Web Services (AWS) to carry it out. In early 2020, researchers unveiled a new attack on SHA-1 that was even more powerful. The new collision attack gives attackers more options and flexibility to produce the same digest for two or more data sets simply by appending data to each of the sets. This attack cost as little as $45,000 to carry out. This compromise of SHA-1 has rendered it no longer suitable for use. How did the researchers do it? Visit the website Shattered (shattered.io) to find information about how SHA-1 was breached in 2017. Read the Q&A section and view the infographic. Try dragging one of your files to the File tester to see if it is part of the collision attack. What did you learn? How serious is the collision? What is the impact? Now conduct research on the 2020 SHA-1 attack. How was it carried out? Write a one-page paper on what you learned.

Case Project 3-3: Compare Ciphers

Estimated Time: 20 minutes

Objective: Explore different ciphers.

Description: A variety of online cipher tools demonstrate different cryptographic algorithms. Visit the website Ciphers and Codes (rumkin.com/tools/cipher/) and explore the different tools. Select the tools "Caesar" and "One Time Pad," each of which were referenced in this module (ROT13 is part of "Caesar"). Experiment with these two tools. Then select one more tool and experiment with it. Which is easy to use? Which is more difficult? Which tool would you justify as more secure than the others? Why? Write a one-page paper on your analysis of the tools.

Case Project 3-4: Twofish and Blowfish

Estimate Time: 30 minutes

Objective: Research symmetric encryption algorithms.

Description: Twofish and Blowfish are considered strong symmetric cryptographic algorithms. For example, Blowfish can accommodate key lengths of up to 448 bits (56 bytes). Use the Internet to research both Twofish and Blowfish. How secure are they? What are their features? What are their strengths and weaknesses? How are they currently being used? How would you compare them? Write a one-page paper on your findings.

Case Project 3-5: SHA-3

Estimated Time: 30 minutes

Objective: Explore how algorithms are vetted.

Description: The hash algorithms SHA-1 and SHA-2 were not created by publicly sourced contests but instead were created by the National Security Agency (NSA) and then released as public-use patents. Although they are not identical, they share some of the same underlying mathematics, which has been proven to contain some cryptographic flaws. SHA-2 is a safer hash largely because of its increased digest length. SHA-3 is a completely different type of hash algorithm. Research SHA-3. What were its design goals? How is it different from SHA-1 and SHA-2? What are its advantages? How does its performance in hardware and software compare? When will it be widely implemented? Write a one-page paper on your research.

Case Project 3-6: One-Time Pad (OTP) Research

Estimated Time: 20 minutes

Objective: Explore OTPs.

Description: Use the Internet to research one-time pads (OTPs): who was behind the initial idea, when they were first used, in what applications they were found, how they are used today, and other relevant information. Then visit an online OTP creation site such as www.braingle.com/brainteasers/codes/onetimepad.php and practice creating your own ciphertext with OTP. If possible, exchange your OTPs with other students to see how you might try to break them. Would it be practical to use OTPs? Why or why not? Write a one-page paper on your findings.

Case Project 3-7: Compare Hashing Algorithms

Estimated Time: 15 minutes

Objective: Compare hash algorithms.

Description: Go to the All Hash Generator website (www.browserling.com/tools/all-hashes) to compare hashes. First, enter the sentence **The quick brown fox jumped over the lazy dog** in the input box (do not include an ending period). Click **Calculate Hashes** to see the different digests that are generated using different hash algorithms. Now add a period at the end of the sentence and calculate the hashes again. What changed? Why? Now replace the period with an exclamation point and recalculate the hashes. Which digests changed? Why? Which of the hash algorithms would be the most secure? Why? Write a one-page paper on your research.

Case Project 3-8: Bay Point Ridge Security

Estimated Time: 45 minutes

Objective: Gather information on software cryptographic tools.

Description: Bay Point Ridge Security (BPRS) is a managed service provider (MSP) that manages networks, computers, cloud resources, and information security for small-to-medium enterprises (SMEs) in the region. BPRS provides internships to students who are in their final year of the security degree program at the local college and has recently hired you.

A new client wants to provide encryption for any data that leaves their premises. You are asked to provide an overview of the different ways in which encryption can be used.

1. Create a PowerPoint presentation about encryption through software (third-party software and OS), FDE, SED, HSM, and TPM. Include the advantages and disadvantages of each. Your presentation should contain at least 10 slides.

2. After the presentation, the client asks for your recommendation regarding meeting their needs for encryption when taking data off-site. Create a memo communicating the actions you believe would be best for the company to take.

Two Rights & A Wrong: Answers

Defining Cryptography

1. Transposition and substitution are two methods to hide the meaning of a message.
2. Repudiation is the process of proving that a user performed an action.
3. A key is a mathematical value entered into an algorithm to produce a ciphertext.

Answer: The wrong statement is #2.

Explanation: Nonrepudiation is the process of proving that a user performed an action

Cryptographic Algorithms

1. A stream cipher is more secure than a block cipher.
2. Hashing is used primarily for comparison purposes.
3. Asymmetric cryptography keys can work in both directions.

Answer: The wrong statement is #1.

Explanation: A block cipher is more secure than a stream cipher.

Using Cryptography

1. FDE protects all data on a hard drive except the installed OS.
2. Transparent data encryption (TDE) executes encryption and decryption within the database engine itself.
3. An HSM a removable external cryptographic device.

Answer: The wrong statement is #1.

Explanation: Full-disk encryption (FDE) also protects the installed operating system.

Cryptographic Limitations and Attacks

1. In a downgrade attack, an attacker forces the system to abandon the current higher security mode of operation and instead "fall back" to implementing an older and less secure mode.
2. A collision attack is an attempt to find two input strings of a hash function that produce the same hash result.
3. The basis of a quantum computer is a bit.

Answer: The wrong statement is #3.

Explanation: The basis of a quantum computer is a qubit.

References

1. Russell, Frank. *Information gathering in classical Greece.* Ann Arbor: University of Michigan Press, 1999.
2. Lenstra, Arjen, et al. "Universal security from bits and mips to pools, lakes—and beyond," accessed Jan. 30, 2023, https://eprint.iacr.org/2013/635.pdf.

Module 4

Advanced Cryptography

Module Objectives

After completing this module, you should be able to do the following:

1 Define digital certificates
2 Describe the components of Public Key Infrastructure (PKI)
3 List the secure communication and transport protocols
4 Explain how to implement cryptography

#TrendingCyber

When was the last time you locked yourself out of your house because you forget to take your keys? And you finally had to call a locksmith because you simply could not get in by yourself? Sometimes our security is so strong that it defeats even us, and professionals must be called in to help. That is what happened recently with a user who encrypted the key to their cryptocurrency wallet and locked themselves out: he was forced to turn to an information security professional for help to break the encryption.

Mike S., after completing his PhD and working on Google's applied security team, became the chief technology officer (CTO) of a blockchain software development firm. One day Mike received a message on LinkedIn from someone Mike simply called "The Guy" (TG). TG had purchased $10,000 worth of bitcoin four years earlier, well before the cryptocurrency boom. With the escalation in price, the bitcoin was now worth over $300,000. However, TG had a problem: he had forgotten his keys to access his Bitcoin wallet. TG wanted to know if Mike could help.

Mike knew that he could not break into TG's Bitcoin wallet; it is too well protected by cryptography. However, that was not the problem. TG had stored the password to his Bitcoin wallet in a zip file that was password protected (zip is a file format that supports compressing one or more files or directories together into a single file, and for security a zip file can be password protected). TG had put his Bitcoin wallet password into a zip file and then password protected the zip file but had forgotten the zip password. He needed help breaking the zip file encryption. TG had found information online that Mike had written a paper 20 years earlier about a technique for cracking zip encryption. TG wanted to know if Mike would help him. And TG offered to pay Mike up to one-third of the value of his Bitcoins, or $100,000. Mike agreed to help, and they settled on a contract.

There were several things working in Mike's favor. First, TG used zip's proprietary encryption algorithm instead of Advanced Encryption Standard (AES), which is commonly used today. Also, TG still had the laptop he used to encrypt the zip file, so Mike could narrow down which version of zip was used. And the laptop contained the time stamp of when the file was created, which the zip program used as one part of the encryption key. That information would help reduce the number of possible passwords from 10 sextillion (a 1 followed by 21 zeros) down to "only" 10 quintillion (a 1 followed by 18 zeros), according to Mike. However, what Mike did not have was the entire zip file: TG likely did not trust Mike and was afraid that he would crack the file and then use the information to steal his Bitcoins. What Mike did have was the encrypted header metadata.

Mike worked with his colleague Nash to write cryptanalysis code (using the programming language C) to crack the encryption of the zip file. Mike and Nash originally estimated that it would take several months to engineer the attack and then several more months to run the code to test all possible combinations to crack the zip encryption. However, they ended up spending more time engineering the attack so that running the code would be shortened to several days.

About four months after Mike was first contacted by TG, he launched the attack on the zip file. He used a network of personal computers with video cards that had graphics processing units (GPUs), a specialized processor originally designed to accelerate graphics rendering but can also be used for cracking encryption. After running for 10 straight days, they were unable to crack the zip encryption. Mike said he was "heartbroken." And by this time the value of Bitcoins was starting to fall, so Mike was under increasing pressure from TG to finish as quickly as possible.

Mike started looking for an obscure or incorrect assumption he might have made, or even a hidden bug in the zip encryption code. TG was also working on the problem, and he noticed that an error occurred if the GPU did not process the guess correctly on the first attempt. This error was corrected, and Mike tried again. This time the correct key was found within one day. TG was so happy he gave Mike and Nash a "large bonus" for finding the key so quickly.

Since that time Mike has received numerous requests for help unlocking Bitcoin wallets. One person had about $4 million in Bitcoins locked up that he could not retrieve because he too had forgotten the password and was willing to pay $1 million for someone to break into his wallet. Mike said that although it is exceedingly difficult to break a Bitcoin wallet, he could conduct a code review—but he would need to be paid for his time.

Despite the clear benefits of cryptography in protecting data, most end-users do not implement it other than what occurs by default. Yet for enterprises, the encrypting and decrypting of data is not only considered essential but in many instances is required by regulations.

However, when cryptography is utilized in the enterprise, a much higher degree of complexity is involved, particularly regarding keys. What happens if the employee Alice has encrypted an important proposal but suddenly falls ill and cannot return to work? Does only she know the key? Or is there a copy of her key that could be retrieved? Where is this copy of her key stored? Can Bob acquire access to Alice's key? And what happens if Bob is away at a conference? Should multiple employees have key access, or will this weaken security? And how can the keys of hundreds or even thousands of employees be managed?

These and other advanced cryptography issues, particularly in the enterprise, are the topics of this module. First you learn about the authentication and distribution of public keys through digital certificates. Next, you study the management of keys through public key infrastructure. Finally, you look at different secure communication and transport protocols to see the role of cryptography on data in transit and how to implement cryptography.

Digital Certificates

Certification

1.4 Explain the importance of using appropriate cryptographic solutions.

4.1 Given a scenario, apply common security techniques to computing resources.

One of the common applications of public key cryptography is digital certificates. Using digital certificates involves understanding their purpose, knowing how they are managed, and determining which type of digital certificate is appropriate for different situations.

Defining Digital Certificates

Asymmetric cryptography uses a pair of related keys. Also known as public key cryptography, the public key can be distributed and shared with anyone, while the corresponding private key must be kept confidential by the owner. Asymmetric cryptography protects the confidentiality of data to ensure that only authorized parties can view it.

Note 1

Asymmetric cryptography is covered in Module 3.

Suppose that Alice receives an encrypted document that claims it is from Bob. Because it is encrypted, Alice knows that the document was not viewed by someone else. But how can she know for *certain* that Bob was the sender? Because Alice's public key is widely available, anyone could use it to encrypt a document. Suppose that Mallory created a fictitious document, encrypted it with Alice's public key, and then sent it to Alice while pretending it came from Bob. Alice can use her private key to decrypt the document to read it, but she does not know with absolute certainty who sent it.

A degree of proof can be provided with asymmetric cryptography by creating a digital signature, which is an electronic verification of the sender. After creating a document, Bob generates a digest (hash) on it and then encrypts the digest with his private key, which serves as the digital signature. Bob sends both the encrypted document and the digital signature to Alice, who decrypts the digital signature using Bob's public key, revealing the digest. If she cannot decrypt the digital signature, then she knows that it did not come from Bob (because only Bob's public key can decrypt the digest generated with his private key).

Note 2

Digital signatures and hash algorithms are covered in Module 3.

However, there is a weakness with a digital signature: it can only prove the *owner* of the private key. But that owner could pretend to be someone else (Mallory could pretend to be Bob). It does not necessarily confirm the *true identity* of the sender because it cannot definitively prove who was the sender of that key. If Alice receives a message with a digital signature claiming to be from Bob, she cannot know for certain that it is the "real" Bob.

For example, suppose Bob created a message along with a digital signature and sent it to Alice. However, Mallory intercepted the message. Mallory then created her own set of public and private keys using Bob's identity. Mallory could create a new message and digital signature (with the imposter private key) and send them to Alice. Upon receiving the message and digital signature, Alice would unknowingly retrieve Mallory's imposter public key (thinking it belonged to Bob) and decrypt it. Alice would be tricked into thinking Bob had sent it when it came from Mallory. This interception and imposter public key are illustrated in Figure 4-1.

Figure 4-1   Imposter public key

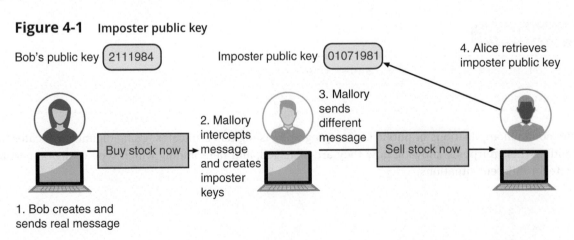

Suppose that Bob wants to ensure that Alice receives his real public key and not an imposter public key. He could travel to Alice's city, knock on her front door, and say, "I'm Bob and here's my key."

Yet how would Alice even know *this* was the real Bob and not Mallory in disguise? For verification, she could ask to see Bob's passport. A passport is a document that is provided by a trusted third party who is different from either the sender or receiver. Although Alice may not initially trust Bob because she does not know him, she will trust the government agency that required Bob to provide proof of his identity when he applied for the passport. Using a trusted third party who has verified Bob—and who Alice also trusts—would solve the problem.

This is the concept behind a digital certificate. A digital certificate is a technology used to associate a user's identity to a public key and has been digitally signed by a trusted third party. This third party verifies the owner and that the public key belongs to that owner.

A digital certificate is basically a verified container for a public key. Typically, a digital certificate contains information such as the owner's name or alias, the owner's public key, the name of the issuer, the digital signature of the issuer, the serial number of the digital certificate, and the expiration date of the public key that has been digitally signed. It can contain other user-supplied information, such as an email address, postal address, and basic registration information.

Note 3

Digital certificates can be used to identify more than just users; they can authenticate the identity of a website, organization, device, server, email, and application.

When Bob sends a message to Alice, he does not ask her to retrieve his public key from a central site. Instead, Bob attaches the digital certificate to the message. When Alice receives the message with the digital certificate, she can check the signature of the trusted third party on the certificate. If the signature was signed by a party that she trusts, then Alice can safely assume that the public key—contained in the digital certificate—is actually from Bob. Digital certificates make it possible for Alice to verify Bob's claim that the key belongs to him and prevent an attack by Mallory who impersonates the owner of the public key.

Managing Digital Certificates

Several entities and technologies are used to manage digital certificates. These include the certificate authorities and tools for managing certificates.

Certificate Authorities

Suppose that Alice purchases a new car and visits the local county courthouse to fill out the car title application paperwork to register her car. After signing the application and verifying her identity, the information is forwarded to the state capital, where the state's department of motor vehicles (DMV) issues an official car title that is sent to her as the new owner.

This scenario illustrates some of the entities involved with digital certificates. If a user wants a digital certificate, they must, after creating the public and private keys to be used, complete a request with information such as name, address, and email address. The user electronically signs it by affixing their public key and then sends it to a **registration authority** that is responsible for verifying the credentials of the applicant. Once verified, it is transferred to an **intermediate certificate authority** (intermediate CA). The intermediate CA, of which there are many, processes the request and issues the digital certificates. These intermediate CAs perform functions on behalf of a certificate authority (CA) that is responsible for digital certificates. This entire process is known as certificate signing request (CSR) generation. A comparison between the earlier car title scenario and the elements of a digital certificate are shown in Table 4-1.

Note 4

Just as there are many county courthouses across a state, there are many intermediate CAs.

Table 4-1   Digital certificate elements

Car title scenario	Digital certificate element	Explanation
Car title application	Certificate signing request (CSR) generation	Formal request for digital certificate
Sign car title application	Create and affix public key to certificate	Added to digital certificate for security
Visit county courthouse	Intermediate certificate authority	Party that can process CSR on behalf of CA
Title sent from state DMV	Certificate authority (CA)	Party responsible for digital certificates

Intermediate CAs are subordinate entities designed to handle specific CA tasks such as processing certificate requests and verifying the identity of the individual. Depending on the type of digital certificate, the person requesting a digital certificate can be authenticated by the following:

- **Email.** In the simplest form, the owner might be identified only by an email address. Although this type of digital certificate might be sufficient for basic email communication, it is insufficient for other verifications.
- **Documents.** A registration authority can confirm the authenticity of the person requesting the digital certificate by requiring specific documentation such as a birth certificate or a copy of an employee badge that contains a photograph.
- **In person.** In some instances, the registration authority might require the applicant to apply in person to prove their existence and identity by providing a government-issued passport or driver's license.

Note 5

Although the registration function could be implemented directly with the CA, there are advantages to using separate intermediate CAs. If many entities require a digital certificate, or if these are spread out across geographical areas, using a single centralized CA could create bottlenecks or inconveniences. Using multiple intermediate CAs, who can "off-load" these registration functions, can create an improved workflow. This process functions because the CAs trust the intermediate CAs.

Certificate Management

Multiple entities make up strong certificate management. These include a certificate repository and a means for certificate revocation.

Certificate Repository (CR)   A **certificate repository (CR)** is a publicly accessible centralized directory of digital certificates that can be used to view the status of a digital certificate. This directory can be managed locally by setting it up as a storage area that is connected to the CA server.

Certificate Revocation   Digital certificates normally have an expiration date. However, some circumstances might cause the certificate to be revoked before it expires. Some reasons might be benign, such as when the certificate is no longer used or the details of the certificate, such as the user's address, have changed. Other circumstances could be more dangerous. For example, if Mallory were to steal Alice's private key, she could impersonate Alice through using digital certificates without Alice being aware of it. In addition, what would happen if digital certificates were stolen from a CA? The thieves could then issue certificates to themselves that would be trusted by unsuspecting users. It is important that the CA publishes lists of approved certificates as well as revoked certificates in a timely fashion; otherwise, it could lead to a situation in which security may be compromised.

Caution !

There have been several incidences of digital certificates being stolen from CAs or intermediate CAs. The thieves can then trick unsuspecting users into connecting with an imposter site, thinking it is a legitimate site. There have also been charges that nation-state actors have stolen digital certificates to trick their own citizens into connecting with fraudulent sites. This allows the actors to monitor the citizen's activities so as to locate dissidents.

There are two means by which the status of a certificate can be checked to see if it has been revoked. The first is to use a certificate revocation list (CRL), which is a list of certificate serial numbers that have been revoked. Many CAs maintain an online CRL that can be queried by entering the certificate's serial number. In addition, a local device receives updates to the operating system (OS) or web browser software on the status of certificates and maintains a local CRL.

The second method is the Online Certificate Status Protocol (OCSP), which performs a real-time lookup of a certificate's status. OCSP is called a "request-response" protocol. The web browser sends the certificate's information to a trusted entity like the CA, known as an OCSP Responder. The OCSP Responder then provides revocation information on that one specific certificate.

A variation of OCSP is called OCSP **stapling**. OCSP requires the OCSP Responder to provide responses to every web client of a certificate in real time, which may create a high volume of traffic. With OCSP stapling, web servers send queries to the Responder OCSP server at regular intervals to receive a signed, time-stamped OCSP response. When a client's web browser attempts to connect to the web server, the server can include (staple) in the handshake with the web browser the previously received OCSP response. The browser then can evaluate the OCSP response to determine if it is trustworthy. OCSP stapling is illustrated in Figure 4-2.

Figure 4-2   OCSP stapling

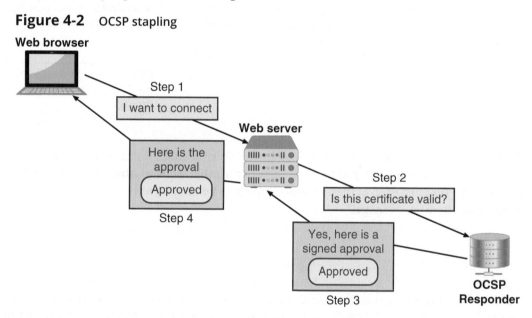

Determining the revocation status of certificates presented by websites is an ongoing problem in web security. Initially, web browsers (Chrome, Firefox, Internet Explorer, Safari, and Opera) used OCSP. However, if the web browser cannot reach the OCSP Responder server, such as when the server is down, then the browser receives the message that there is a network error (called a "soft-fail") and the revocation check is simply ignored. Also, online revocation checking by web browsers can be slow. For these reasons, modern web browsers have implemented a range of solutions to reduce or eliminate the need for online revocation checking by instead "harvesting" lists of revoked certificates from CAs and then pushing them to the user's browser. Table 4-2 lists the solutions used by selected web browsers for determining the revocation status of certificates.

Types of Digital Certificates

There are several types of digital certificates. These can be grouped into the broad categories of root certificates, domain certificates, and hardware and software certificates. In addition, there are standardized certificate formats and attributes.

Root Digital Certificates

Suppose that Alice is making a purchase at an online ecommerce site and needs to enter her credit card number. How can she be certain that she is at the authentic website of the retailer and not an imposter's look-alike site that will steal her credit card number? The solution is a digital certificate. The online retailer's web server issues to Alice's web browser a digital certificate that has been signed by a trusted third party. In this way, Alice can rest assured that she is at the authentic online retailer's site.

Table 4-2   Web browser certificate revocation procedures

Browser	Procedure name	Description	Resources
Google Chrome	CRLSet	CRLSet is a list of revoked certificates determined by searching CRLs published by CAs that is pushed to the browser as a software update.	Users can view the CRLSet version and manually check for updates at chrome://components.
Mozilla Firefox	OneCRL	OneCRL is list of intermediate certificates that have been revoked by CAs and then pushed to Firefox in application updates; the browser can also be configured to query OCSP responders.	Lists of OneCRL can be viewed as webpages at https://crt.sh /mozilla-onecrl.
Apple Safari	No name	Apple collects revoked certificates from CAs that are then periodically retrieved by Apple devices; when a revoked certificate request occurs, Safari performs an OCSP check to confirm.	Users can view blocked certificates at https://support.apple.com/en-us /HT209144#blocked.
Microsoft Edge	CRLSet	Windows OS checks for server certificate revocation and Edge relies on this listing.	Can be viewed through Windows or in the Edge browser at edge://settings /privacy.

However, by some estimates, there are 24 million ecommerce sites.[1] In addition, there are websites for banks, credit card companies, schools, and workplaces, just to name a few of the other websites that need to provide protection to its customers and clients. How can each of these digital certificates be verified as being authentic and not expired or revoked, and how should they be organized?

> **Note 6**
>
> In 2016, the nonprofit Internet Security Research Group (ISRG) created "Let's Encrypt," which is advertised as a free, auto-mated, and open CA run for the public's benefit. Their goal is to provide free digital certificates to any website with the stated reason "because we want to create a more secure and privacy-respecting web." Of the over 309 million domains protected by Let's Encrypt, the "daily issuance" (how many digital certificates are sent to users) averages 2.5 million with over 3 billion total digital certificates sent since it started.

Grouping and verifying digital certificates relies on **certificate chaining**. Certificate chaining creates a path between the trusted "root" CAs (of which there are a few) and the intermediate CAs (of which there are many) with the digital certificates that have been issued. Every certificate is signed by the entity that is identified by the next higher certified entity in the chain. In this way, the trust of a certificate can be traced back to the highest level of CA. This is known as the root of trust.

The beginning point of the chain is a specific type of digital certificate known as a **root digital certificate**. A root digital certificate is created and verified by a CA. Because there is no higher-level authority than a CA, root digital certificates are self-signed and do not depend on any higher-level authority for authentication. The next level down from the root digital certificate is one or more **intermediate certificates** that have been issued by intermediate CAs. The root digital certificate (verified by a CA) trusts the intermediate certificate (verified by an intermediate CA), which may in turn validate more lower-level intermediate CAs until it reaches the end of the chain. The endpoint of the chain is the **user digital certificate** itself. The path of certificate chaining is illustrated in Figure 4-3. An example of certificate chaining is shown in Figure 4-4.

Figure 4-3   Path of certificate chaining

Figure 4-4   Example of certificate chaining

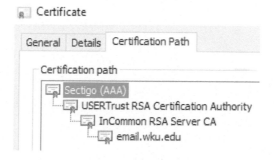

Approved root digital certificates and intermediate certificates are distributed in one of three ways. First, they can be distributed through updates to the OS. Trusted root CAs, intermediate CAs, and untrusted certificates can be viewed through the OS. Figure 4-5 illustrates these certificates in Microsoft Windows 11, which includes trusted root CAs, intermediate CAs, CRLs, and untrusted certificates.

Figure 4-5 Microsoft Windows certificates

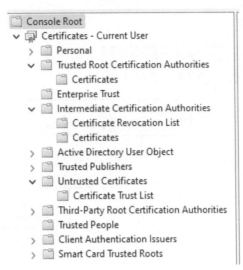

A second means is that certificates can be distributed through updates to the web browser. At one time, browsers relied on the underlying OS-approved list, but today many rely on their own browser updates. Information pertaining to a digital certificate can be seen in the browsers and is illustrated in Figure 4-6.

Figure 4-6 Web browser digital certificate information

Certificate Viewer: www.digicert.com   ✕

General   Details

Issued To

Common Name (CN)	www.digicert.com
Organization (O)	DigiCert, Inc.
Organizational Unit (OU)	<Not Part Of Certificate>

Issued By

Common Name (CN)	DigiCert SHA2 Extended Validation Server CA
Organization (O)	DigiCert Inc
Organizational Unit (OU)	www.digicert.com

Validity Period

Issued On	Sunday, April 17, 2022 at 7:00:00 PM
Expires On	Thursday, May 4, 2023 at 6:59:59 PM

Fingerprints

SHA-256 Fingerprint	A2 26 BC F5 13 62 20 5E AD 89 7B 8D 36 F8 F6 F8 55 90 F4 9E E8 70 1C 4E 99 DB 84 10 21 7B 66 ED
SHA-1 Fingerprint	2B EB D6 FE AE C1 C2 EF 43 6C EB 66 5A 4C 31 72 93 74 48 82

A third option is **pinning**, in which a digital certificate is hard-coded (pinned) within the app or program that is using the certificate. Pinning is common for securing mobile messaging apps and for certain web-based services and browsers.

Note 9

The consequences of a compromised root CA are very significant because a breach could likewise taint all its intermediate CAs along with all the digital certificates that they issued. This makes it essential that all CAs must be kept safe from unauthorized access. A common method to ensure the security and integrity of a root CA is to keep it in an offline state from the network (offline CA) and even "powered down." It is only brought online when needed for specific and infrequent tasks, typically limited to the issuance or re-issuance of certificates authorizing intermediate CAs.

Domain Digital Certificates

Most digital certificates are web server digital certificates that are issued from a web server to a device. These web server digital certificates perform two primary functions: they ensure the authenticity of the web server to the client and the authenticity of the cryptographic connection to the web server. Web servers can set up secure cryptographic connections by providing the server's public key with a digital certificate to the client. This handshake setup between web browser and web server, also called a key exchange, is illustrated in Figure 4-7:

1. The web browser sends a message ("ClientHello") to the server that contains information including the list of cryptographic algorithms that the client supports.
2. The web server responds ("ServerHello") by indicating which cryptographic algorithm will be used. It then sends the server digital certificate to the browser.
3. The web browser verifies the server certificate (such as making sure it has not expired) and extracts the server's public key. The browser generates a random value (called the *pre-master secret*), encrypts it with the server's public key, and sends it back to the server ("ClientKeyExchange").
4. The server decrypts the message and obtains the browser's pre-master secret. Because both the browser and server now have the same pre-master secret, they can each create the same *master secret*. The master secret is used to create *session keys*, which are symmetric keys to encrypt and decrypt information exchanged during the session and to verify its integrity.

Figure 4-7   Key exchange

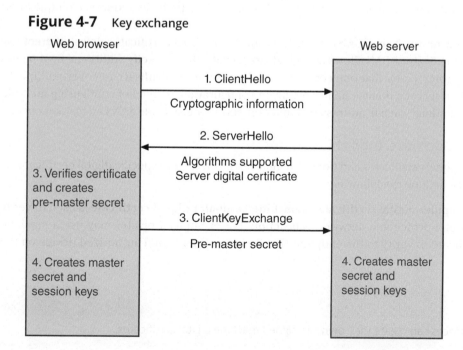

Several types of domain digital certificates address the security of web server digital certificates. These include domain validation digital certificates, extended validation digital certificates, wildcard digital certificates, and subject alternative names digital certificates.

Domain Validation   Some entry-level certificates provide domain-only validation to authenticate that only a specific organization has the right to use a particular domain name. A **domain validation digital certificate** verifies the identity of the entity that has control over the domain name. These certificates indicate nothing regarding the trustworthiness of the individuals behind the site; they simply verify who has control of that domain.

> **Note 10**
>
> Because domain validation digital certificates are not verifying the identity of a person but only the control over a site, they often can be generated automatically and are very inexpensive or even free.

Extended Validation (EV)   An enhanced type of domain digital certificate is the **Extended Validation (EV) certificate**. This type of certificate requires more extensive verification of the legitimacy of the business. Requirements include:

- The intermediate CA must pass an independent audit verifying that it follows the EV standards.
- The existence and identity of the website owner, including its legal existence, physical address, and operational presence, must be verified by the intermediate CA.
- The intermediate CA must verify that the website is the registered holder and has exclusive control of the domain name.
- The authorization of the individual(s) applying for the certificate must be verified by the intermediate CA, and a valid signature from an officer of the company must accompany the application.

Wildcard   A wildcard digital certificate is used to validate a main domain along with all subdomains. For example, a domain validation digital certificate for *www.example.com* would only cover that specific site. A wildcard digital certificate for **.example.com* would cover *www.example.com*, *mail.example.com*, *ftp.example.com*, and any other subdomains.

Subject Alternative Name (SAN)   A limitation of wildcard digital certificates is that while they can protect all first-level subdomains on an entire domain, they cannot apply to different domains, such as *www.example.com* and *www.example.org*. And hosting multiple websites on a single server typically requires a unique Internet Protocol (IP) address per site.

The **Subject Alternative Name (SAN)** solves these problems. This certificate allows different values to be associated with a single certificate. A SAN allows a single digital certificate to specify additional host names (sites, common names, etc.) to be protected by that one certificate. It also permits a certificate to cover multiple IP addresses. This can greatly simplify a server's domain name certificate configuration: instead of configuring multiple IP addresses on a server and then "binding" each IP address to a different certificate, a single SAN can instead cover all the addresses.

Hardware and Software Digital Certificates

In addition to root digital certificates and domain digital certificates, more specific digital certificates relate to hardware and software. These include the following:

- **Machine/computer digital certificate.** A **machine/computer digital certificate** is used to verify the identity of a device in a network transaction. For example, a printer may use a machine digital certificate to verify to the endpoint that it is an authentic and authorized device on the network.

> **Note 11**
>
> Many network devices can create their own self-signed machine digital certificates.

- **Code signing digital certificate.** Digital certificates are used by software developers to digitally sign a program to prove that the software comes from the entity that signed it and no unauthorized third party has altered or compromised it. This is known as code signing, and it produces a **code signing digital certificate**. When the installation program is launched that contains a code signed digital certificate, a pop-up window appears. Clicking the **Show more details** link will display **Verified publisher** as seen in Figure 4-8. An installation program that lacks a code digital certificate will display a window with the warning **Publisher: Unknown**.

Figure 4-8   Verified publisher message

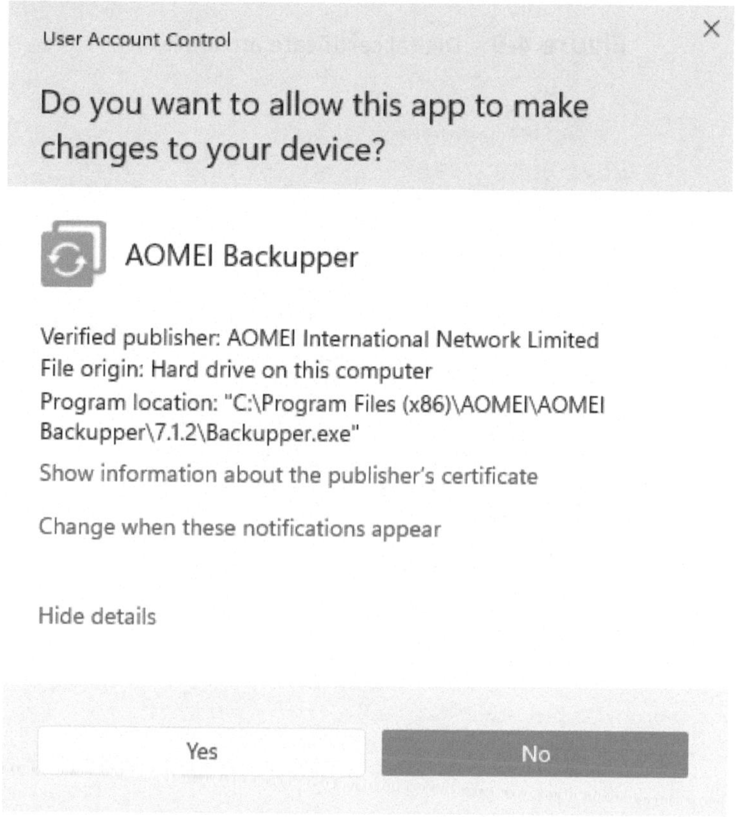

- **Email digital certificate.** An **email digital certificate** allows a user to digitally sign and encrypt mail messages. Typically, only the user's name and email address are required to receive this certificate.

Note 12

In addition to email messages, digital certificates can also be used to authenticate the authors of documents. For example, a user can create a Microsoft Word or Adobe Portable Document Format (PDF) document and then use a digital certificate to create a digital signature.

Digital Certificate Attributes and Formats

Hardware devices require that digital certificates contain specific attributes (fields) and are presented in a specific format. This allows the device to read and process the digital certificate. The standard format for digital certificates is X.509 Version 3. Digital certificates following this standard can be read or written by any hardware device or application that follows the X.509 format.

Several certificate attributes make up an X.509 digital certificate. These attributes are used when the parties negotiate a secure connection. Attributes that must be included are the certificate validity period, end-host identity information, encryption keys that will be used for secure communications, the signature of the issuing CA, and the common name (CN). CN is the name of the device protected by the digital certificate. The CN can reference a single device (*www.example.com*) or multiple devices with a wildcard certificate (**.example.com*) but is not the URL (*https://example.com*). Other optional attributes may also be included. Figure 4-9 illustrates several attributes in a digital certificate.

Figure 4-9 Digital certificate attributes

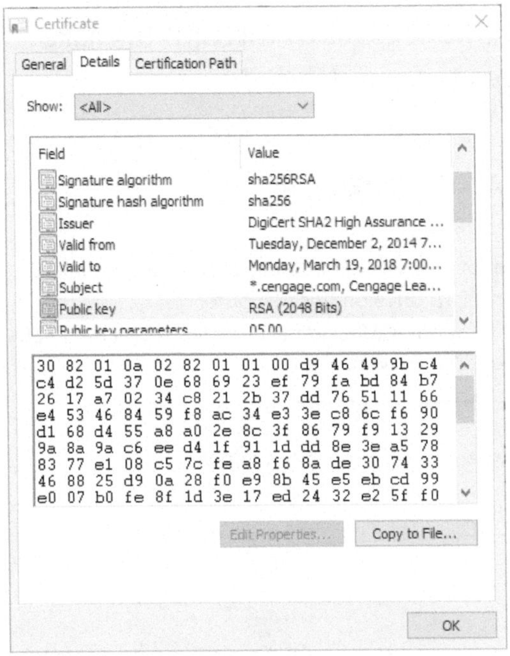

Note 13

X.509 certificates can either be contained in a binary file with a .cer extension or in a Base64 file, which is a binary-to-text encoding scheme that presents binary data in ASCII string format.

Two Rights & A Wrong

1. A digital certificate is a technology used to associate a user's identity to a public key and that has been digitally signed by the owner of the private key.
2. The Online Certificate Status Protocol (OCSP) performs a real-time lookup of a certificate's status.
3. Root digital certificates are self-signed.

See the answers at the end of the module.

Public Key Infrastructure (PKI)

Certification

1.4 Explain the importance of using appropriate cryptographic solutions.

One of the important management tools for the use of digital certificates and asymmetric cryptography is public key infrastructure. This involves defining public key infrastructure, and knowing its trust models, how it is managed, and the features of key management.

What Is Public Key Infrastructure (PKI)?

Suppose that Alice wants to obtain a digital certificate for her personal use. She must go through the entire CSR generation process that involves multiple steps and interacting with multiple entities. She must use asymmetric cryptography to create her public and private keys, a registration authority must verify the request, an intermediate CA must process the request, the digital certificate must be placed in a CR, and then the CR finally moved to a CRL when it expires. For one user creating a digital certificate through the CSR generation process, this involves multiple steps interacting with multiple entities.

Now consider the CSR generation process on a large scale ("at scale"), such as in a typical enterprise with hundreds, thousands, or tens of thousands of users. Multiple users have digital certificates, and sometimes a user may have multiple digital certificates. When going through the CSR generation process, the number of steps and number of entities grows exponentially to the point that it can quickly become overwhelming. And a single missed step or error could result in a digital certificate not being generated or even having a vulnerability. There needs to be a consistent means to manage digital certificates.

Public key infrastructure (PKI) is what you might expect from its name: it is the underlying infrastructure that serves as a key management system for controlling public keys, private keys, and digital certificates. Strictly speaking, PKI is the set of software, hardware, processes, procedures, and policies that are needed to create, manage, distribute, use, store, and revoke digital certificates across large user populations. The goal of a PKI is to establish the identity of people, devices, and services in order to control access to resources, protect data, and provide accountability. In short, PKI is *digital certificate management at scale*.

Trust Models

Trust is defined as confidence in or reliance on another person or entity. One of the principal foundations of PKI is that of trust: Alice must trust that the public key in Bob's digital certificate belongs to him.

A **trust model** refers to the type of trust relationship that can exist between individuals or entities. In one type of trust model, **direct trust**, a relationship exists between two individuals because one person knows the other person. Because Alice knows Bob—she has seen him, she can recognize him in a crowd, she has spoken with him—she can trust that the digital certificate that Bob personally gives her contains his public key.

A **third-party trust** refers to a situation in which two individuals trust each other because each trusts a common third party. An example of a third-party trust is a courtroom. Although the defendant and prosecutor may not trust one another, they both can trust the judge (a third party) to be fair and impartial. In that case, they implicitly trust each other because they share a common relationship with the judge. In terms of PKI, if Alice does not know Bob, this does not mean that she can never trust his digital certificate. Instead, if she trusts a third-party entity who knows Bob, then she can trust that the digital certificate with the public key is Bob's.

A less secure trust model that uses no third party is called the **web of trust** model and is based on direct trust. Each user signs a digital certificate and then exchanges certificates with all other users. Because all users trust each other, each user can sign the certificate of all other users.

Essentially three PKI trust models use a CA. These are the hierarchical trust model, the distributed trust model, and the bridge trust model.

Hierarchical Trust Model

The **hierarchical trust model** assigns a single hierarchy with one master CA called the root. This root signs all digital certificate authorities with a single key. A hierarchical trust model is illustrated in Figure 4-10.

Figure 4-10   Hierarchical trust model

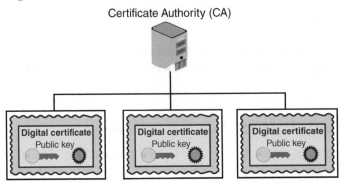

A hierarchical trust model can be used in an organization where one CA is responsible for only the digital certificates for that organization. However, on a larger scale, a hierarchical trust model has several limitations. First, if the CA's single private key were to be compromised, then all digital certificates would be worthless. Also, having a single CA that must verify and sign all digital certificates may create a significant backlog.

Distributed Trust Model

Instead of having a single CA, as in the hierarchical trust model, the **distributed trust model** has multiple CAs that sign digital certificates. This essentially eliminates the limitations of a hierarchical trust model. The loss of a CA's private key would compromise only those digital certificates it had signed, and the workload of verifying and signing digital certificates can be distributed. In addition, these CAs can delegate authority to other intermediate CAs to sign digital certificates. The distributed trust model is the basis for most digital certificates used on the Internet. A distributed trust model is illustrated in Figure 4-11.

Figure 4-11   Distributed trust model

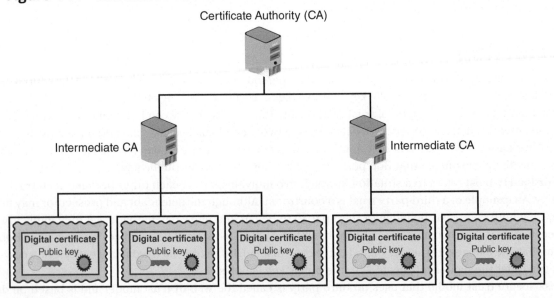

Bridge Trust Model

The **bridge trust model** is similar to the distributed trust model in that no single CA signs digital certificates. However, with the bridge trust model, one CA acts as a facilitator to interconnect all other CAs. This facilitator CA does not issue digital certificates; instead, it acts as the hub between hierarchical trust models and distributed trust models. This allows the different models to be linked together. The bridge trust model is shown in Figure 4-12.

Figure 4-12   Bridge trust model

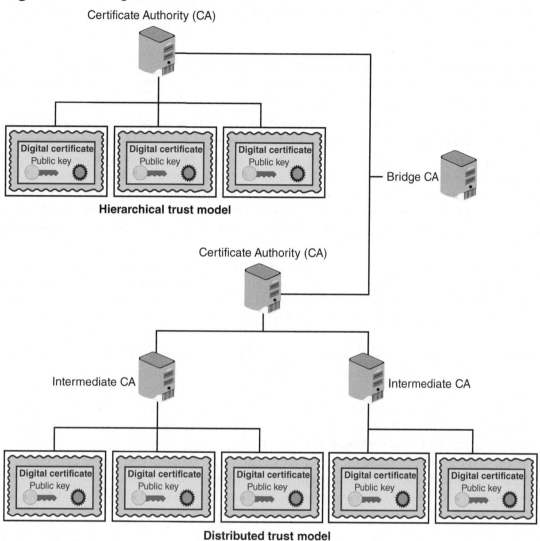

Managing PKI

An organization that uses multiple digital certificates on a regular basis will need to properly manage those digital certificates. This includes establishing policies and practices and determining the life cycle of a digital certificate.

Certificate Policy (CP)

A **certificate policy** (**CP**) is a published set of rules that govern the operation of a PKI. The CP provides recommended baseline security requirements for the use and operation of CA, intermediate CA, and other PKI components. A CP should cover such topics as CA or intermediate CA obligations, user obligations, confidentiality, operational requirements, and training.

Certificate Practice Statement (CPS)

A **certificate practice statement (CPS)** is a more technical document than a CP. A CPS describes in detail how the CA uses and manages certificates. Additional topics for a CPS include how end-users register for a digital certificate, how to issue digital certificates, when to revoke digital certificates, procedural controls, key pair generation and installation, and private key protection.

An X.509 certificate contains a specific field that can link to the associated CP. In addition, extensions may be added to X.509 certificates that indicate how the certificate should be used. One such field, the Extended Key Usage field, can contain an object identifier (OID), which names an object or entity. OIDs are made up of a series of numbers separated with a dot, such as 1.2.840.113585, and correspond to a node in a hierarchy tree structure. OIDs can name every object type in an X.509 certificate, including the CPS. A large, standardized set of OIDs exists, or an enterprise can have a root OID assigned to it and then create its own sub-OIDs, much like creating subdomains beneath a domain.

Certificate Life Cycle

Digital certificates do not last forever: employees leave, new hardware is installed, applications are updated, and cryptographic standards evolve. Each of these changes affects the usefulness of a digital certificate. The life cycle of a certificate is typically divided into four parts:

1. **Creation.** At this stage, the certificate is created and issued to the user. Before the digital certificate is generated, the user must be positively identified. The extent to which the user's identification must be confirmed can vary, depending on the type of certificate and any existing security policies. Once the user's identification has been verified, the request is sent to the CA for a digital certificate. The CA can then apply its appropriate signing key to the certificate, effectively signing the public key. The relevant fields can be updated by the CA, and the certificate is then forwarded to the registration authority. The CA can also keep a local copy of the certificate it generated. A certificate, once issued, can be published to a public directory, if necessary.

2. **Suspension.** This stage could occur once or multiple times throughout the life of a digital certificate if the certificate's validity must be temporarily suspended. This may occur, for example, when an employee is on a leave of absence. During this time, it may be important that the user's digital certificate not be used for any reason until they return. Upon the user's return, the suspension can be withdrawn or the certificate can be revoked.

3. **Revocation.** At this stage, the certificate is no longer valid. Under certain situations a certificate may be revoked before its normal expiration date, such as when a user's private key is lost or compromised. When a digital certificate is revoked, the CA updates its internal records and any CRL with the required certificate information and timestamp (a revoked certificate is identified in a CRL by its certificate serial number). The CA signs the CRL and places it in a public repository so that other applications using certificates can access this repository to determine the status of a certificate.

4. **Expiration.** At the expiration stage, the certificate can no longer be used. Every certificate issued by a CA must have an expiration date. Once it has expired, the certificate may not be used any longer for any type of authentication and the user will be required to follow a process to be issued a new certificate with a new expiration date.

Key Management

One common vulnerability that allows threat actors to compromise a PKI is improper certificate and key management. Because keys form the foundation of PKI systems, they must be carefully managed. Proper key management includes key storage, key usage, and key handling procedures.

Key Storage

The means of storing keys in a PKI system is important. Public keys can be stored by embedding them within digital certificates, while private keys can be stored on the user's local system. The drawback to software-based storage is that it can leave keys open to attacks; vulnerabilities in the client operating system, for example, can expose keys to attackers.

Storing keys in hardware is an alternative to software-based storage. For storing public keys, special CA root and intermediate CA hardware devices can be used. Private keys can be stored on smart cards or in tokens.

Caution !

Whether private keys are stored in hardware or software, they must be adequately protected. To ensure basic protection, never share the key in plaintext, always store keys in files or folders that are themselves password protected or encrypted, do not make copies of keys, and destroy expired keys.

Key Usage

If more security is needed than a single set of public and private keys, multiple pairs of dual keys can be created. One pair of keys may be used to encrypt information, and the public key can be backed up to another location. The second pair would be used only for digital signatures, and the public key in that pair would never be backed up.

Key Handling Procedures

Certain procedures can help ensure that keys are properly handled. These procedures include:

- **Escrow.** Key escrow refers to a process in which keys are managed by a third party, such as a trusted CA. In key escrow, the private key is split and each half is encrypted. The two halves are registered and sent to the third party, which stores each half in a separate location. A user can then retrieve the two halves, combine them, and use this new copy of the private key for decryption. Key escrow relieves the end-user from the worry of losing their private key. The drawback to this system is that after the user has retrieved the two halves of the key and combined them to create a copy of the key, that copy of the key can be vulnerable to attacks.

- **Expiration.** Keys have an expiration date after which they cease to function. This prevents an attacker who may have stolen a private key from being able to decrypt messages for an indefinite period. Some systems set keys to expire after a set period by default.

- **Renewal.** Instead of letting a key expire and then creating a new key, an existing key can be renewed. With renewal, the original public and private keys can continue to be used and new keys do not have to be generated. However, continually renewing keys makes them more vulnerable to theft or misuse.

- **Revocation.** Whereas all keys should expire after a set period, a key may need to be revoked prior to its expiration date. For example, the need for revoking a key may be the result of an employee being terminated from their position. Revoked keys cannot be reinstated. The CA should be immediately notified when a key is revoked and then the status of that key should be entered on the CRL.

- **Recovery.** What happens if an employee is hospitalized, yet their organization needs to transact business using their keys? Different techniques may be used. Some CA systems have an embedded key recovery system in which a key recovery agent (KRA) is designated, a highly trusted person responsible for recovering lost or damaged digital certificates. Digital certificates can then be archived along with the user's private key. If the user is unavailable or if the certificate is lost, the certificate with the private key can be recovered. Another technique is known as **M-of-N control**. A user's private key is encrypted and divided into a specific number of parts, such as three. The parts are distributed to other individuals, with an overlap so that multiple individuals have the same part. For example, the three parts could be distributed to six people, with two people each having the same part. This is known as the N group. If it is necessary to recover the key, a smaller subset of the N group, known as the M group, must meet and agree that the key should be recovered. If a majority of the M group can agree, they can then piece the key together. M-of-N control is illustrated in Figure 4-13.

Note 14

The reason for distributing parts of the key to multiple users is that the absence of one member would not prevent the key from being recovered.

- **Suspension.** The revocation of a key is permanent; key suspension is for a set period. For example, if an employee is on an extended medical leave, it may be necessary to suspend the use of their key for security reasons. A suspended key can be later reinstated. As with revocation, the CA should be immediately notified when a key is suspended, and the status of that key should be checked on the CRL to verify that it is no longer valid.

Figure 4-13   M-of-N control

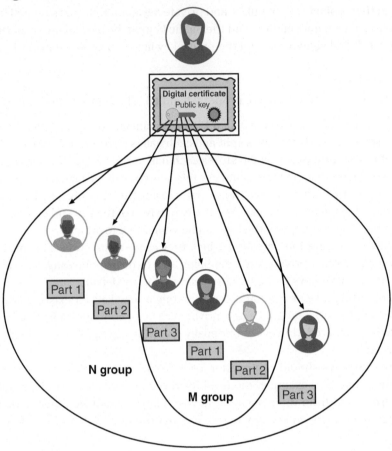

- **Destruction.** Key destruction removes all private and public keys along with the user's identification information in the CA. When a key is revoked or expires, the user's information remains on the CA for audit purposes.

Two Rights & A Wrong

1. The goal of a PKI is to establish the identity of people, devices, and services in order to control access to resources, protect data, and provide accountability.

2. A key management system is used for controlling only public keys.

3. Key escrow refers to a process in which keys are managed by a third party, such as a trusted CA.

See the answers at the end of the module.

Secure Communication and Transport Protocols

Certification

1.4 Explain the importance of using appropriate cryptographic solutions.

3.2 Given a scenario, apply security principles to secure enterprise infrastructure.

In addition to protecting data in use and data at rest, cryptographic algorithms are used to protect data in transit (transport/communication encryption). There are different secure communication and transport protocols based on cryptographic algorithms for protecting data in transit. These protocols typically rely on "encapsulating" or enveloping the data to be transmitted inside something else.

Consider a road that must be built between two cities. However, a tall mountain separates the cities, and it is not practical or economically feasible to build the road over the mountain. As an alternative, a tunnel can be bored through the mountain to create a road, as seen in Figure 4-14.

Figure 4-14 Tunnel through a mountain

FOTOGRIN/Shutterstock.com

In a similar fashion, private data can be sent through a public network in which it normally could be visible to prying eyes. A private tunnel can "bore through" a public network to hide its contents. Conceptually, first the data is encrypted and then it is encapsulated. Encapsulation is the process of enclosing the encrypted data with an additional header so that the data can be directed to its destination. If the data were to be completely encrypted, including its header, then network routers would not be able to forward the packet to its destination since they do not have the decryption key to view the header. By encapsulating the encrypted information with unencrypted information, the data can be protected and travel across the networks as normal. This technique for transporting data securely across a network is called tunneling.

Note 15

Tunneling refers to the entire process of encapsulation, transmission, and "de-encapsulation." Encapsulation itself is only a single step within the entire process. However, sometimes the terms are improperly used synonymously.

Two primary secure communication and transport protocols use tunneling. These are Transport Layer Security (TLS) and IP Security (IPSec). In addition, other secure protocols can provide protection.

Transport Layer Security (TLS)

One of the early and most widespread secure communication and transport protocols was **Secure Sockets Layer (SSL)**. This protocol was developed by Netscape in 1994 in response to the growing concern over Internet security. The design goal of SSL was to create an encrypted data path between a client and a server that could be used on any platform or operating system. However, the way SSL functioned left it vulnerable to attack.

As a replacement for SSL, the Transport Layer Security (TLS) provides a higher degree of protection. The current version of TLS, v1.3, is considered a significant upgrade over TLS v1.2. It removes support for MD5 and SHA-224, requires use of Perfect Forward Secrecy for public key–based key exchange, and encrypts handshake messages after the ServerHello exchange.

Caution !

Although the algorithms SSL and TLS are sometimes listed as being interchangeable or even in conjunction with each other ("TLS/SSL"), this is not correct. They are different, and SSL is deprecated and is being replaced by TLS.

A **cipher suite** is a named combination of the encryption, authentication, and message authentication code (MAC) algorithms that is used with TLS. These are negotiated between the web browser and web server during the initial connection handshake. Cipher suites typically use descriptive names to indicate their components. For example, *TLS_ECDHE_ECDSA_WITH_AES_128_GCM_SHA256* specifies that TLS is the protocol, during the handshake keys will be exchanged via the ephemeral Elliptic Curve Diffie Hellman (ECDHE), AES running the Galois Counter Mode with 128-bit key size is the encryption algorithm, and SHA-256 is the hashing algorithm.

IP Security (IPSec)

A more comprehensive communication and transport security protocol is IP Security. It is important to know what IP Security is and how it can be implemented.

Definition

Internet Protocol Security (IPSec) is a group or suite of protocols for securing Internet Protocol (IP) communications. IPSec encrypts and authenticates each IP packet of a session between devices.

Note 16

IPSec is not a single protocol but a framework of multiple protocols, encryption methods, authentication processes, and cryptographic algorithms.

IPSec is considered to be a transparent security protocol. It is transparent to the following entities:

- **Applications.** Programs do not have to be modified to run under IPSec.
- **Users.** Unlike some security tools, users do not need to be trained on specific security procedures, such as encrypting with a specific application.
- **Software.** Using IPSec does not require that software changes to an application must be made on the local device.

IPSec provides three areas of protection that correspond to three IPSec protocols:

- **Authentication.** IPSec authenticates that packets received were sent from the source. This is identified in the header of the packet to ensure that no specific attacks took place to alter the contents of the packet. This is accomplished by the **Authentication Header (AH)** protocol.

- **Confidentiality.** By encrypting the packets, IPSec ensures that no other parties could view the contents. Confidentiality is achieved through the **Encapsulating Security Payload (ESP)** protocol. ESP supports authentication of the sender and encryption of data.
- **Key management.** IPSec manages the keys to ensure that they are not intercepted or used by unauthorized parties. For IPSec to work, the sending and receiving devices must share a key. This is accomplished through a protocol known as Internet Security Association and Key Management Protocol/Oakley (ISAKMP/Oakley), which generates the key and authenticates the user using techniques such as digital certificates.

IPSec supports two encryption modes: transport and tunnel. **Transport mode** encrypts only the data portion (payload) of each packet yet leaves the header unencrypted. The more secure **tunnel mode** encrypts both the header and the data portion. IPSec accomplishes transport and tunnel modes by adding new headers to the IP packet. The entire original packet (header and payload) is then treated as the data portion of the new packet.

Note 17

Because tunnel mode protects the entire packet, it is generally used in a network-to-network communication, while transport mode is used when a device must see the source and destination addresses to route the packet.

IPSec is considered a more robust protocol than TLS. This is because it provides security to IP, which is the basis for all other TCP/IP protocols. In protecting IP, IPSec is essentially protecting everything else in TCP/IP as well. Table 4-3 lists some of the differences between IPSec and TLS.

Table 4-3   IPSec versus TLS

	IPSec	TLS
Definition	A set of protocols that provide security for all IP traffic by directly encrypting IP packets	A secure protocol developed for protecting specific information over the Internet
OSI layer	Layer 3	Layers 4–7
Installation	Generic and requires full client installed on device	Vendor specific and capabilities incorporated within all web browsers, so no separate client needed
Configuration	Complex	Basic
Changes to protocol	Depends on implementation but no need to change application	Must change application but not OS
Protections	All IP-based applications	Web-enabled applications, file sharing, and email

Note 18

There is debate over which OSI layer SSL operates. Because it runs "on top" of TCP, which is Layer 4, some say that it runs on Layer 5 or Layers 5 and 6. Others say that it only operates at Layer 6, while still others say that because it's an application it runs on Layer 7.

Architectures and Implementation

How exactly can IPSec be integrated into IP? The following are different methods for deploying IPSec:

- **Devices.** Installing IPSec into all devices provides the highest security because it provides "end-to-end" security between all devices on the network. However, installing it on a network with a large number of devices requires more work. Another option is to install it only on routers through which network data passes. While this gives protection only for the portion of the route that the data takes outside the enterprise and may be sufficient for certain applications, the connections between routers and local devices would not be secured.
- **Integration into TCP/IP.** Ideally IPSec would be infused directly into IP itself so that all IPSec security modes and capabilities would be transparently provided and no additional hardware or software is needed. IPv6 has integrated the features of IPSec, making it the best option. With IPv4, however, integration requires making changes to the IP implementation on each device.
- **Architectures.** Using a bump in the stack (BITS) architecture, IPSec is made a separate architectural layer between IP and the OSI Data Link layer: IPSec intercepts IP data as it is passed down the protocol stack, processes the data to provide security, and then passes it on to the Data Link layer. The advantage of BITS is that IPSec can be applied to any IP device, while the disadvantage is a duplication of effort to manage all devices. BITS is generally used for IPv4 devices. Instead of adding software to the IP stack using BITS, a bump in the wire (BITW) adds a hardware device that provides IPSec services. These devices intercept outgoing data and add IPSec protection while removing it from incoming data.

Note 19

BITS adds IPSec to legacy hosts while BITW adds it to legacy network equipment.

Other Protocols

There are other secure communication and transport protocols. These include Hypertext Transport Protocol Secure (HTTPS), Secure Shell (SSH), Secure/Multipurpose Internet Mail Extensions (S/MIME), and Secure Real-time Transport Protocol (SRTP).

Hypertext Transport Protocol Secure (HTTPS)

One common use of TLS is to secure Hypertext Transport Protocol (HTTP) communications between a browser and a web server. This secure version is "plain" HTTP sent over TLS or SSL and is called **Hypertext Transport Protocol Secure (HTTPS)**. HTTPS uses port 443 instead of HTTP's port 80 and is indicated by *https://* instead of *http://* in the URL.

Note 20

Another cryptographic protocol for HTTP was Secure Hypertext Transport Protocol (SHTTP). However, it was not as secure as HTTPS and is now obsolete.

At one time, web browsers prominently displayed a colored visual indicator to alert users that the connection between the browser and the web server was using HTTPS. Most browsers displayed a green padlock to indicate the connection was encrypted and secure. However, as more websites transitioned to HTTPS, web browsers changed from displaying a color indicator that the connection *was* secure to only a warning that the connection was *not* secure. Today most browsers display a padlock, but it is gray in color.

Note 21

The change away from the green padlock is much like the lights on a car dashboard. There are lights to warn drivers of low tire air pressure, low oil pressure, and low gasoline, among others. These lights are designed to turn on only when there is a problem, such as when the tire air pressure falls below a certain point. This approach of keeping the lights off when "All is OK" but only turn on the warning light when something demands attention is the reason for migrating away from web browser indicators when there is no problem.

Secure Shell (SSH)

Secure Shell (SSH) is an encrypted alternative to the Telnet protocol used to access remote computers. SSH is a Linux/UNIX-based command interface and protocol for securely accessing a remote computer. Both the client and server ends of the connection are authenticated using a digital certificate, and passwords are protected by being encrypted. SSH can even be used as a tool for secure network backups.

Secure/Multipurpose Internet Mail Extensions (S/MIME)

Secure/Multipurpose Internet Mail Extensions (S/MIME) is a protocol for securing email messages. MIME is a standard for how an electronic message will be organized, so S/MIME describes how encryption information and a digital certificate can be included as part of the message body. It allows users to send encrypted messages that are also digitally signed.

Secure Real-time Transport Protocol (SRTP)

The **Secure Real-time Transport Protocol (SRTP)** has several similarities to S/MIME. Just as S/MIME is intended to protect MIME communications, SRTP is a secure extension protecting transmissions using the Real-Time Transport Protocol (RTP). Also, as S/MIME is designed to protect only email communications, SRTP provides protection for Voice over IP (VoIP) communications. SRTP adds security features, such as message authentication and confidentiality, for VoIP communications.

Two Rights & A Wrong

1. SSL is a replacement cryptographic protocol for TLS.
2. A cipher suite is a named combination of the encryption, authentication, and message authentication code (MAC) algorithms that are used with TLS.
3. IPSec can provide protection to a much wider range of applications than TLS.

See the answers at the end of the module.

Implementing Cryptography

Cryptography that is improperly applied can lead to vulnerabilities that threat actors will exploit. There are different options and configurations that relate to cryptography that must be implemented correctly. Implementing cryptography includes understanding key strength, secret algorithms, and block cipher modes of operation.

Key Strength

A cryptographic key is a value that serves as input to an algorithm, which then transforms plaintext into ciphertext (and vice versa for decryption). A key, which is essentially a random string of bits, serves as an input parameter for hash, symmetric encryption, and asymmetric cryptographic algorithms.

> **Caution** !
>
> A key is different from a password. Passwords are designed to be created and remembered by humans so that the passwords can be reproduced when necessary. A key is used by hardware or software that is running the cryptographic algorithm; as such, human readability is not required.

The following three primary characteristics determine the resiliency of the key to attacks (called key strength):

- **Randomness.** For a key to be considered strong, it must be random with no predictable pattern. This thwarts an attacker from attempting to uncover the key.
- **Cryptoperiod.** Another characteristic that determines key strength is its **cryptoperiod**, or the length of time for which a key is authorized for use. Having a limited cryptoperiod helps protect the ciphertext from extended cryptanalysis and limits the exposure time if a key is compromised. Different cryptoperiods are recommended for different types of keys.
- **Key length.** The final characteristic is the length of the key. Shorter keys can be more easily broken than longer keys. All the possible values for a specific key make up its **key space**. The formula for determining a given key space for symmetric algorithms is $character\text{-}set^{key\text{-}length}$. For example, suppose a key has a length of 3 and is using a 26-character alphabet. The list of possible keys (*aaa, aab, aac,* etc.) would be 26^3 or 17,576 possible outcomes. Thus, the key length in this example is 3 and the key space is 17,576.

> **Note 22**
>
> On average, half the key space must be searched to uncover the key. A key with a length of only 3 that has a key space of 17,576 requires only 8,788 keys to be searched (on average) until the correct key is discovered. However, if the key length was increased by just one character to 4, the key space increases to 456,976 requiring on average 228,488 attempts. Just increasing the key length can have a significant impact on security.

Secret Algorithms

Although keys need to be kept secret (except for public keys), does the same apply to algorithms? That is, should an enterprise invest in hiring a cryptographer to create a new cryptographic algorithm and then hide the existence of that algorithm from everyone? Wouldn't such a secret algorithm enhance security in the same way as keeping a key or password secret?

The answer is no. In the past, cryptographers have often attempted to keep their algorithms or the workings of devices that encrypted and decrypted documents a secret. However, this approach has always failed. One reason is because for cryptography to be useful, it needs to be widespread: a military force that uses cryptography must by nature allow many users to know of its existence to use it. The more users who know about it, the more difficult it is to keep it a secret. In contrast, a password only requires one person—the user—to keep it confidential.

> **Note 23**
>
> In 1883, Auguste Kerckhoffs, a Dutch linguist and cryptographer, published what is known as the *Kerckhoffs's Principles*, which were six design standards for military ciphers. One of his principles stated that systems should not require secrecy so that it should not be a problem if it falls into enemy hands. This principle is still applied today by splitting algorithms from keys: algorithms are public while keys are private.

Block Cipher Modes of Operation

One variation in cryptographic algorithms is the amount of data that is processed at a time. Some algorithms use a stream cipher, while other algorithms make use of a block cipher. Whereas a stream cipher works on one character at a time, a block cipher manipulates an entire block of plaintext at one time. Because the size of the plaintext is usually larger than the block size itself, the plaintext is divided into separate blocks of specific lengths, and then each block is encrypted independently.

Note 24

Stream and block ciphers are covered in Module 3.

A **block cipher mode of operation** specifies how block ciphers should handle these blocks. It uses a symmetric key block cipher algorithm to provide an information service. This service could be **authentication mode of operation** that provides a credentialing service or **unauthentication mode of operation** that provides a service such as confidentiality. Some of the most common modes are:

- **Electronic Code Book (ECB).** The ECB mode is the most basic approach: the plaintext is divided into blocks, and each block is then encrypted separately. However, this can result in two identical plaintext blocks being encrypted into two identical ciphertext blocks. Attackers can use this repetition to their advantage. They could modify the encrypted message by modifying a block or even reshuffle the order of the blocks of ciphertext. ECB is not considered suitable for use.

Note 25

Using ECB is like assigning code words from a codebook to create an encrypted message and was the basis for naming this process Electronic Code Book.

- **Cipher Block Chaining (CBC).** CBC is a common cipher mode. After being encrypted, each ciphertext block gets "fed back" into the encryption process to encrypt the next plaintext block. Using CBC, each block of plaintext is XORed with the previous block of ciphertext before being encrypted. Unlike ECB in which the ciphertext depends only on the plaintext and the key, CBC is also dependent on the previous ciphertext block, making it much more difficult to break.

Note 26

XOR ciphers are covered in Module 3.

- **Counter (CTR).** CTR mode requires that both the message sender and receiver access a counter, which computes a new value each time a ciphertext block is exchanged. The weakness of CTR is that it requires a synchronous counter for both the sender and receiver.
- **Galois/Counter (GCM).** GCM mode both encrypts plaintext and computes a message authentication code (MAC) to ensure that the message was created by the sender and that it was not tampered with during transmission. Like CTR, GCM uses a counter. It adds a plaintext string called additional authentication data (AAD) to the transmission. The AAD may contain the addresses and parameters of a network protocol that is being used.

Note 27

There are a variety of block cipher modes, with specific modes specializing in encryption, data integrity, privacy and integrity, and hard drive encryption. There are even specialized modes that gracefully recover from errors in transmission while other modes are designed to stop upon encountering transmission errors.

Two Rights & A Wrong

1. The cryptoperiod is the length of time for which a key is authorized for use.
2. All the possible values for a specific key make up its key space.
3. A block cipher mode of operation specifies how stream ciphers should handle streams.

See the answers at the end of the module.

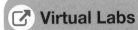 **Virtual Labs**   You're now ready to complete the simulations and live virtual machine labs for this module. The labs can be found in each module in MindTap.

Summary

- A digital certificate is the user's public key that has been digitally signed by a trusted third party who verifies the owner and that the public key belongs to that owner. It also binds the public key to the certificate. A user who wants a digital certificate must generate the public and private keys to be used and then complete a process known as a certificate signing request (CSR) generation. The user electronically signs the CSR by affixing their public key and then sending it to a registration authority, who verifies the authenticity of the user. The CSR is then sent to an intermediate certificate authority (CA), who processes the CSR. The intermediate CAs perform functions on behalf of a certificate authority (CA) that is responsible for digital certificates.

- A Certificate Repository (CR) is a list of approved digital certificates. Revoked digital certificates are listed in a Certificate Revocation List (CRL), which can be accessed to check the certificate status of other users. The status can also be checked through the Online Certificate Status Protocol (OCSP). When using OCSP stapling, web servers send queries to the Responder OCSP server at regular intervals to receive a signed, time-stamped OCSP response. Because digital certificates are used extensively on the Internet, modern web browsers are configured with a default list of CAs and the ability to automatically update certificate information.

- The process of verifying that a digital certificate is genuine depends on certificate chaining, or linking several certificates together to establish trust between all the certificates involved. The beginning point of the chain is a specific type of digital certificate known as a root digital certificate, which is created and verified by a CA and also self-signed. Between the root digital certificate and the user certificate can be one or more intermediate certificates that have been issued by intermediate CAs. Approved root digital certificates and intermediate certificates are distributed in one of three ways: through updates to the OS, through updates to the web browser, or by pinning (hard-coding within the program). The endpoint of the chain is the user digital certificate itself.

- Domain validation digital certificates verify the identity of the entity that has control over the domain name but indicate nothing regarding the trustworthiness of the individuals behind the site. Extended Validation (EV) certificates require more extensive verification of the legitimacy of the business. A wildcard digital certificate is used to validate a main domain along with all subdomains. The limitation of wildcard digital certificates is addressed by the Subject Alternative Name (SAN), which allows different values to be associated with a single certificate and also permits a certificate to cover multiple IP addresses.

- A machine/computer digital certificate is used to verify the identity of a device in a network transaction. Digital certificates are used by software developers to digitally sign a program to prove that the software comes from the entity that signed it and no unauthorized third party has altered or compromised it are called code signing digital certificates. The most widely accepted format for digital certificates is the X.509 standard. There are several different certificate attributes that make up an X.509 digital certificate.

- Public key infrastructure (PKI) is the underlying foundation that serves as a key management system for controlling public keys, private keys, and digital certificates. PKI is the set of software, hardware, processes, procedures, and policies that are needed to create, manage, distribute, use, store, and revoke digital certificates across large user populations. The goal of a PKI is to establish the identity of people, devices, and services to control access to resources, protect data, and provide accountability. PKI can be considered as digital certificate management at scale.

- One of the principal foundations of PKI is that of trust. Three basic PKI trust models use a CA. The hierarchical trust model assigns a single hierarchy with one master CA called the root, who signs all digital certificate authorities with a single key. The bridge trust model is similar to the distributed trust model. No single CA signs digital certificates, and yet the CA acts as a facilitator to interconnect all other CAs. The distributed trust model has multiple CAs that sign digital certificates.

- An organization that uses multiple digital certificates on a regular basis needs to properly manage those digital certificates. Such management includes establishing policies and practices and determining the life cycle of a digital certificate. Because keys form the very foundation of PKI systems, they must be carefully stored and handled. Handling keys includes key escrow, setting expirations, generating renewals, revoking keys, recovering keys, suspending keys, and finally key destruction.

- Cryptographic algorithms are used to protect data in transit, called transport/communication encryption. There are different secure communication and transport protocols based on cryptographic algorithms for protecting data in transit. These protocols typically rely on encapsulating the data to be transmitted through tunneling. Secure Sockets Layer (SSL) was an early cryptographic transport protocol but is replaced with the more secure Transport Layer Security (TLS). Internet Protocol Security (IPSec) is a group or suite of protocols for securing IP communications. IPSec encrypts and authenticates each IP packet of a session between devices. IPSec is considered a more robust protocol than TLS. This is because it provides security to IP, which is the basis for all other TCP/IP protocols. There are different methods for deploying IPSec.

- There are other secure communication and transport protocols. Hypertext Transport Protocol Secure (HTTPS), a secure version for web communications, is HTTP sent over TLS. Secure Shell (SSH) is a Linux/UNIX-based command interface and protocol for securely accessing a remote computer communicating over the Internet. Secure/Multipurpose Internet Mail Extensions (S/MIME) is a protocol for securing email messages. The Secure Real-time Transport Protocol (SRTP) provides protection for Voice over IP (VoIP) communications.

- Cryptography that is improperly applied can lead to vulnerabilities that will be exploited; thus, it is necessary to understand the different options that relate to cryptography so that it can be implemented correctly. A key must be strong to resist attacks. A strong key must be random with no predictable pattern. Keys should also be long and the length of time for which a key is authorized for use should be limited. Any attempt to keep an algorithm secret will not result in strong security. A block cipher mode of operation specifies how block ciphers should handle blocks of plaintext.

Key Terms

certificate authority (CA)
certificate revocation list (CRL)
certificate signing request (CSR)
  generation
code signing
digital certificate
Internet Protocol Security (IPSec)

key escrow
key management system
Online Certificate Status Protocol
  (OCSP)
public key infrastructure (PKI)
root of trust
self-signed

third party
transport/communication
  encryption
Transport Layer Security (TLS)
tunneling
wildcard digital certificate

Review Questions

1. Alarik is explaining to a colleague about digital certificates. Which of the following statements would he use to correctly describe the need for digital certificates?

   a. It can speed up processing time when using a web browser.
   b. It can hide the public key so that it cannot be abused.
   c. It can confirm the true identity of the sender of an encrypted message.
   d. It can replace digital signatures with a more robust technology.

2. What is a technology used to associate a user's identity to a public key and has been digitally signed by a trusted third party?

   a. Digital signature
   b. Digital certificate
   c. Digital codebook
   d. Digital signing repository (DSR)

3. Ville has been asked by his supervisor to review the contents of a questionable digital certificate. Which of the following would Ville NOT find in it?

   a. Owner's private key
   b. Serial number of the digital certificate
   c. Name of the issuer
   d. Owner's name or alias

4. Who is responsible for verifying the credentials of an applicant for a digital certificate?

   a. CA
   b. Registration authority
   c. CSR
   d. Intermediate CSR

5. Which of the following is NOT a means by which a person requesting a digital certificate can be authenticated?

   a. Birth certificate
   b. Employee badge
   c. Email
   d. Telephone number

6. What is the strongest technology that would assure Alice that Bob is the sender of a message?

   a. Digital signature
   b. Encrypted signature
   c. Digest
   d. Digital certificate

7. What is a publicly accessible centralized directory of digital certificates that can be used to view the status of a digital certificate?

   a. CA
   b. CR
   c. CB
   d. CX

8. Ansgar is studying how digital certificates can be used. Which of the following is NOT a use of a digital certificate?

   a. To encrypt messages for secure email communications
   b. To encrypt channels to provide secure communication between clients and servers
   c. To verify the authenticity of the CA
   d. To verify the identity of clients and servers on the web

9. Which of the following performs a real-time lookup of a certificate's status?

   a. Pinning
   b. OCSP
   c. Clipping
   d. Remote lookup protocol (RLP)

10. Which of the following is NOT true about a root digital certificate?

   a. The next level down is one or more intermediate certificates.
   b. It is self-signed.
   c. It is created and verified by a CA.
   d. It is the endpoint of the chain.

11. Tordis has been asked to acquire a digital certificate that will cover all the subdomains of a new site. Which type of certificate would he acquire?

   a. Omnibus digital certificate
   b. Subname digital certificate
   c. Wildcard digital certificate
   d. NAXX

12. Bengt is setting up a new web server that will have several IP addresses. He only wants to acquire a single digital certificate. Which type of certificate will he acquire?

   a. SAN
   b. Asterisk digital certificate (ADC)
   c. Domain digital certificate
   d. EV

13. What is the standard format for digital certificates?

   a. CN
   b. RCN
   c. CER x9
   d. X.509 Version 3

14. Which of the following is false about PKI?

   a. It is the underlying infrastructure that serves as a key management system for controlling public keys, private keys, and digital certificates.
   b. It is the set of software, hardware, processes, procedures, and policies that are needed to create, manage, distribute, use, store, and revoke digital certificates across large user populations.
   c. It is digital certificate management at scale.
   d. It must be used by all enterprises with over 1,000 employees.

15. Which is the first step in a key exchange?

   a. The browser generates a random value ("pre-master secret").
   b. The web server sends a message ("ServerHello") to the client.
   c. The web browser verifies the server certificate.
   d. The web browser sends a message ("ClientHello") to the server.

16. Dag wants to set up a trust model in which he only will serve as a CA. Which trust model will he choose?

   a. Bridge trust model
   b. Distributed trust model
   c. Hierarchical trust model
   d. Sole trust model

17. Einar has been asked to create a new policy that outlines the process in which keys are managed by a third party and the private key is split with each half encrypted. What policy is Einar creating?

   a. Key recovery policy
   b. Key expiration policy
   c. Extended validation policy
   d. Key escrow policy

18. Which of the following is the most comprehensive secure communication and transport protocol?

   a. SSL
   b. TLS
   c. IPSec
   d. HSS

19. Gjord has been assigned to design an implementation of IPSec at an old manufacturing plant that has legacy network equipment and many devices. Which implementation will he choose?

   a. SRSR
   b. AR Stack
   c. BITW
   d. BITS

20. Which of the following is NOT a primary characteristic for determining the resiliency of a key to attacks?

   a. Randomness
   b. Key derivation
   c. Cryptoperiod
   d. Key length

Hands-On Projects

Note 28

If you are concerned about installing any of the software in these projects on your regular computer, you can instead install the software in the Windows virtual machine created in the Module 1 Hands-On Projects. Software installed within a sandbox or the virtual machine will not impact the host computer.

Project 4-1: SSL Server and Browser Tests

Estimated Time: 30 minutes
Objective: Test servers and web browsers for security.
Description: In this project, you will use online tests to determine the security of web servers and your local web browser.

1. Go to **www.ssllabs.com**. (It is not unusual for websites to change the location of where files are stored. If this URL no longer functions, open a search engine and search for "Qualys SSL Server Test.")

2. Click **Test your server**.

3. Click the first website listed under **Recent Best**.

4. Note the grade given for this site. Under **Summary**, note the **Overall Rating** along with the scores for **Certificate**, **Protocol Support**, **Key Exchange**, and **Cipher Strength**, which make up the cipher suite.

5. If this site did not receive an Overall Rating of *A* or better under **Summary**, you will see the reasons listed. Read through these. Would you agree? Why?

6. Scroll down through the document and read through the **Certificate #1** information. Note the information supplied regarding the digital certificates. Under **Certification Paths**, click **Click here to expand** if necessary to view the certificate chaining. What can you tell about it?

7. Scroll down to **Configuration**. Note the list of protocols supported and not supported. If this site were to increase its security, which protocols should it no longer support? Why?

8. Under **Cipher Suites**, interpret the suites listed. Notice that they are given in server-preferred order. To increase its security, which cipher suite should be listed first? Why?

9. Under **Handshake Simulation**, select the web browser and operating system that you are using or is similar to what you are using. Read through the capabilities of this client interacting with this web server. Note particularly the order of preference of the cipher suites. Click the browser's Back button when finished.

10. Scroll to the top of the page. This time select one of the **Recent Worst** sites. As with the previous excellent example, now review the **Summary**, **Authentication**, **Configuration**, **Cipher Suites**, and **Handshake Simulation**. Would you agree with this site's score?

11. If necessary, return to the **SSL Report** page and enter the name of your school or work URL and generate a report. What score did it receive?

12. Review the **Summary**, **Authentication**, **Configuration**, **Cipher Suites**, and **Handshake Simulation**. Would you agree with this site's score?

13. Make a list of the top five vulnerabilities that you believe should be addressed in order of priority. If possible, share this with any IT personnel who may be able to take action.

14. Click **Home** on the navigation menu.

15. Now test the capabilities of your web browser. Click **Test your browser**. Review the capabilities of your web browser. Print or take a screen capture of this page.

16. Close this web browser.

17. Now open a different web browser on this computer or on another computer.

18. Return to the **www.ssllabs.com** home page and then click **Test your browser** to compare the two scores. From a security perspective, which browser is better? Why?

19. Close all windows.

Project 4-2: Viewing Digital Certificates

Estimated Time: 20 minutes
Objective: View details of digital certificates.
Description: In this project, you will view digital certificate information using the Google Chrome web browser.

1. Use the Google Chrome web browser to go to **www.google.com**.

2. Note the padlock in the address bar. Although you did not enter *https://*, nevertheless Google created a secure HTTPS connection. Why would it do that?

3. Click the three vertical buttons at the far edge of the address bar.

4. Click **More tools**.

5. Click **Developer tools**.

6. Click the **Security** tab, if necessary. (If the Security tab does not appear, click the **More tabs** (>>) button to display more tabs.)

7. Read the information under **Security overview**.

8. Click **View certificate**.

9. Note the general information displayed on the **General** tab.

10. Now click the **Details** tab.

11. Note the root of trust under **Certificate Hierarchy**.

12. Under **Certificate Fields**, click **Serial Number** to view the unique number associated with this digital certificate in the **Field Value** box.

13. If necessary, scroll down to **Validity** and then click **Not After**. What is the expiration date of this certificate?

14. Locate **Subject Public Key Info** and click **Subject Public Key Algorithm**. What type of encryption is used?

15. Locate **Certificate Signature Algorithm** and click it. What hash and encryption are used for this certificate?

16. Click **Subject's Public Key** to view the public key associated with this digital certificate. Why is this site not concerned with distributing this key? How does embedding the public key in a digital certificate protect it from impersonators?

17. Close all windows.

Project 4-3: Viewing Digital Certificate Revocation Lists (CRLs) and Untrusted Certificates

Estimated Time: 25 minutes
Objective: Examine certificates.
Description: Revoked digital certificates are listed in a certificate revocation list (CRL), which can be accessed to check the certificate status of other users. In this project, you will view the CRL and any untrusted certificates on your Microsoft Windows computer.

1. Press the **Windows+R** keys.

2. Type **mmc.exe** and then press **Enter** to launch the Microsoft Management Console.

3. Click **File**.

4. Click **Add/Remove Snap-in**.

5. Click **Certificates** and then click **Add**.

6. Select **Computer account**, click **Next**, and then click **Finish**.

7. Click **OK**.

8. In the left pane, expand **Certificates – Current User**.

9. Expand **Trusted Root Certification Authorities**. These are the CAs approved for this computer. Scroll through this list. How many of these have you heard of before?

10. In the left pane, expand **Intermediate Certification Authorities**.

11. Click **Certificates** to view the intermediate CAs. Scroll through this list.

12. In the left pane, click **Certificate Revocation List**.

13. All revoked certificates will be displayed. Select a revoked certificate and double-click it.

14. Read the information about it and click fields for more detail, if necessary. Why do you think this certificate has been revoked? Close the Certificate Revocation List by clicking the **OK** button.

15. In the left pane, expand **Untrusted Certificates**.

16. Click **Certificate Trust List**. The certificates that are no longer trusted are listed.

17. Double-click one of the untrusted certificates. Read the information about it and click fields for more detail, if necessary. Why do you think this certificate is no longer trusted?

18. Click **OK** to close the Certificate dialog box.

19. Close all windows.

Project 4-4: Downloading and Installing Trusted Root Certificates

Estimated Time: 25 minutes
Objective: Install certificates.
Description: By default Windows 11 updates its root certificate over the Internet through Windows Update at least once per week through a Trusted Root Certificate List (CTL). However, if a device is not connected to the Internet, then certificates will expire over time. This could prevent scripts and applications from functioning properly. The latest root certificates can be downloaded directly from Microsoft and installed. These are stored in a Serialized Certificate Store (SST) format. In this project, you will use Windows PowerShell to download and install root certificates.

1. Press the **Windows+R** keys.

2. Type **powershell** and then press **CTRL+SHIFT+ENTER** to launch PowerShell in administrator mode.

3. PowerShell can be used to view the details on all root certificates. Type **Get-Childitem cert:\ LocalMachine\root |format-list** and press **Enter**. Scroll up to view the details on the root certificates.

4. To view the expired certificates, type **Get-ChildItem cert:\LocalMachine\root | Where {$_.NotAfter -lt (Get-Date).AddDays(40)}** and press **Enter**.

5. In PowerShell, navigate to a drive or location from which you can easily retrieve a file; for example, enter **F:** and then press **Enter**.

6. Download the latest certificates in an SST file by typing **certutil.exe -generateSSTFromWU roots.sst** and press **Enter**.

7. Type **dir** to confirm that the **roots.sst** file was downloaded.

8. Run the following command while replacing **CertPath** with the complete path to the downloaded SST file, for example, **$sstStore = (Get-ChildItem -Path F:\roots.sst)**, and press **Enter**.

9. Now import all the certificates by typing **$sstStore | Import-Certificate -CertStoreLocation Cert:\ LocalMachine\Root** and press **Enter**.

10. All the certificates have now been imported. Type **Get-Childitem cert:\LocalMachine\root |format-list** and press **Enter**.

11. Close all windows.

Project 4-5: Downloading and Installing a Digital Certificate

Estimated time: 25 minutes

Objective: Install a certificate.

Description: In this project, you will download and install a digital certificate within the Adobe Acrobat Reader DC.

1. Check to determine if you already have Adobe Acrobat Reader DC or Adobe Acrobat Professional installed on your computer. If so, you may skip these download and installation steps and go directly to Step 5.

2. Go to **get.adobe.com/reader/**. (It is not unusual for websites to change the location of where files are stored. If this URL no longer functions, open a search engine and search for "Adobe Acrobat Reader DC Download.")

3. Click **Download Acrobat Reader**.

4. Follow the instructions to install Acrobat Reader.

5. Launch Acrobat Reader.

6. Click **Edit**.

7. Click **Preferences**.

8. Click **Signatures**.

9. Under **Identities & Trusted Certificates**, click **More**.

10. In the left pane, if necessary, click **Digital IDs** to display the menu choices.

11. On the menu at the top of the main pane, click the **Add ID** icon (it is the first icon and has a plus sign).

12. Click **A new digital ID I want to create now**. Click **Next**.

13. If necessary, click **New PKCS#12 digital ID file**. Click **Next**.

14. Enter the requested information. Under **Key Algorithm**, click the down arrow to see the two options. The default is **2048-bit RSA**, which provides more security, while 1024-bit RSA provides less security but is more universally compatible. Accept the 2048-bit RSA.

15. Under **Use digital ID for**, click the down arrow to see the three options. Select the default **Digital Signatures and Data Encryption**. Click **Next**.

16. Create and enter a strong password and then confirm that password. Click **Finish**.

17. Your file is now created. Click **Export**.

18. If necessary, click **Save the data to a file** and click **Next**.

19. Save the file to your computer.

20. Close the windows associated with configuring your certificate.

21. You can use this certificate by sending it to anyone who needs to validate your identity. Close all windows.

Case Project 4-1: #TrendingCyber

Estimated Time: 15 minutes
Objective: Summarize your thoughts on the #TrendingCyber opener.
Description: Read again the opening #TrendingCyber in this module. What precautions should TG have taken? What are the risks of using another means to remember a password other than memory? Should there be a "back door" into encrypted documents that only the owner could access? How would the owner prove their authenticity? Write a one-paragraph summary of your thoughts.

Case Project 4-2: IPSec

Estimated Time: 30 minutes
Objective: Research IPSec.
Description: Use the Internet to research IPSec. Who was responsible for developing it? When was the first version released? What protections does it provide? What are its strengths and weaknesses? How does IPv6 incorporate IPSec? Write a one-page paper on your research.

Case Project 4-3: Recommended Cryptoperiods

Estimated Time: 30 minutes
Objective: Learn about cryptoperiods.
Description: How long should a key be used before it is replaced? Search the Internet for information regarding cryptoperiods for hash, symmetric, and asymmetric algorithms. Find at least three sources for each of the algorithms. Create a table that lists the algorithms and the recommended time, and then calculate the average for each. Do you agree or disagree? What would be your recommendation on cryptoperiods for each? Why?

Case Project 4-4: Research Certificate Authorities

Estimated Time: 30 minutes
Objective: Research CAs.
Description: Web browsers contain digital certificates from many certificate authorities (CAs). Use Table 4-2 and the Internet to view the CAs for the web browser you commonly use. How many of these CAs are you familiar with? How many are unknown? Are there too many CAs? Does this create a greater potential for abuse by threat actors instead of having only a few CAs? Select three of the CAs and research their organizations on the Internet. Write a one-paragraph summary of each CA.

Case Project 4-5: Root and Intermediate Certificate Breaches

Estimated Time: 30 minutes
Objective: Explain the implications of root certificate breaches.
Description: Use the Internet to research breaches of CAs. What CAs were involved? Were they root or intermediate CAs? Who was behind the theft? How did the thefts occur? How were the stolen certificates then used? Are certificates from these CAs still accepted? Write a one-page paper of your research.

Case Project 4-6: Protecting PKIs

Estimated Time: 35 minutes

Objective: Determine how to protect PKIs.

Description: A compromised PKI has enormous consequences, and thus it must be protected. Research different ways an enterprise can protect its PKI. What are the implications if it is compromised? What are the recommendations regarding how to keep it secure? What steps should be taken if an intermediate CA is compromised? What should be done if a root CA is compromised? What recommendations would you have for protecting a root CA? Write a one-page paper of your research.

Case Project 4-7: Monitoring a PKI Environment

Estimated Time: 35 minutes

Objective: Monitor a PKI environment.

Description: Due to the critical nature of a PKI, it is important to monitor the environment. Use the Internet to research how to monitor a PKI environment. What are the signs that may indicate a compromise? How should these be addressed? How frequently should the PKI be reviewed and by whom? Write a one-page paper on your research.

Case Project 4-8: Bay Point Ridge Security

Estimated Time: 45 minutes

Objective: Research digital certificates.

Description: Bay Point Ridge Security (BPRS) is a managed service provider (MSP) that manages networks, computers, cloud resources, and information security for small-to-medium enterprises (SMEs) in the region. BPRS provides internships to students who are in their final year of the security degree program at the local college and has recently hired you.

The vice president of a new client has recently discovered digital certificates for the first time and now wants all employees to have and use digital certificates for every function related to their job responsibilities. They want each employee to have multiple digital certificates. You are asked to provide information about digital certificates to help the client create and use digital certificates in the most meaningful way.

1. Create a PowerPoint presentation about digital certificates, including what they are, what they can protect, how they should be used, and the various types of certificates. Include the advantages and disadvantages of each. Your presentation should contain at least 10 slides.

2. After the presentation, the vice president asks which certificates they should use and how they should be managed. Create a memo communicating the actions you believe would be best for the company to take.

Two Rights & A Wrong: Answers

Digital Certificates

1. A digital certificate is a technology used to associate a user's identity to a public key and that has been digitally signed by the owner of the private key.

2. The Online Certificate Status Protocol (OCSP) performs a real-time lookup of a certificate's status.

3. Root digital certificates are self-signed.

Answer: The wrong statement is #1.

Explanation: A digital certificate is a technology used to associate a user's identity to a public key that has been digitally signed by a trusted third party.

Public Key Infrastructure

1. The goal of a PKI is to establish the identity of people, devices, and services in order to control access to resources, protect data, and provide accountability.
2. A key management system is used for controlling only public keys.
3. Key escrow refers to a process in which keys are managed by a third party, such as a trusted CA.

Answer: The wrong statement is #2.

Explanation: A key management system is used for controlling public keys, private keys, and digital certificates.

Secure Communication and Transport Protocols

1. SSL is a replacement cryptographic protocol for TLS.
2. A cipher suite is a named combination of the encryption, authentication, and message authentication code (MAC) algorithms that are used with TLS.
3. IPSec can provide protection to a much wider range of applications than TLS.

Answer: The wrong statement is #1.

Explanation: TLS is a replacement for SSL.

Implementing Cryptography

1. The cryptoperiod is the length of time for which a key is authorized for use.
2. All the possible values for a specific key make up its key space.
3. A block cipher mode of operation specifies how stream ciphers should handle streams.

Answer: The wrong statement is #3.

Explanation: A block cipher mode of operation specifies how block ciphers should handle blocks.

Reference

1.   Gennaro, Lisa, "68 useful ecommerce statistics you must know in 2023," *Wpforms*, Jan. 3, 2023, accessed Jan. 25, 2023, https://wpforms.com/ecommerce-statistics/.

Part 3

Device Security

Today virtually any hardware device is a target for threat actors. This includes stationary devices (desktop computers and printers), mobile devices (laptops, smartphones, and tablets), and specialized hardware (Internet of Things [IoT] devices). The modules in this third part identify the threats and attacks directed at these devices and the security that can protect them.

Module 5
Endpoint Vulnerabilities, Attacks, and Defenses

Module 6
Mobile and Embedded Device Security

Module 7
Identity and Access Management (IAM)

Endpoint Vulnerabilities, Attacks, and Defenses

Module Objectives

After completing this module, you should be able to do the following:

1 Identify the different types of attacks using malware

2 Describe attacks based on application vulnerabilities

3 Explain the steps of securing endpoint devices

#TrendingCyber

A federal trial of a highly respected figure in information security has raised serious concerns among security professionals. This incident challenges the very definition of an attack and how victims may react.

Joseph S. was the chief security officer of Cloudflare, a web performance and security company. He was a former federal prosecutor who had worked at several high-profile tech firms including Facebook, eBay, and Uber. While at Uber, threat actors breached the company's security and downloaded about 57 million records, many of them containing private data, and then demanded a $100,000 payment. But this demand was not the typical ransomware demand that threat actors usually make. Instead, they contacted Uber saying that they had discovered a vulnerability in the company's website that allowed them to steal the data. They demanded that Uber provide "high compensation" for finding this flaw.

These attackers were defining themselves as old-fashioned "white hat hackers." In the past, the term "hacker" referred to a person who used advanced computer skills to attack computers. Yet because that title often carried a negative connotation, it was qualified in an attempt to distinguish between different types of attackers. "Black hat hackers" were those attackers who violated computer security for personal gain (such as to steal credit card numbers) or to inflict malicious damage (corrupt a hard drive). However, "white hat hackers" were described as "ethical attackers": they would probe a system for weaknesses and then privately provide information back to that organization about any uncovered vulnerabilities. And that was the role these attackers against Uber claimed to be taking.

This attack and the corresponding demand resulted in more than 30 other Uber employees, including the company's chief executive and the entire legal team, becoming involved. After much deliberation, an Uber attorney advising the team told them that the matter could be treated not as an attack but as a request for a "bug bounty."

A common practice of large corporations is to pay security researchers who uncover security bugs in their products and then privately report them so that the bugs can be patched before threat actors find them. This is called a bug bounty. Google, who started its program back in 2010, pays from $100 to $31,337 per reported bug. In 2022, Google paid out over $29 million in bounties (compared to 2017 when it only paid $2.8 million). Zerodium, on the other hand, pays up to $2.5 million for information on a single vulnerability. Google even maintains a bug bounty "Leaderboard" hall of fame listing those who have revealed the most bugs.

With Uber's support, Joseph decided to follow the advice of the legal counsel and treat this event as white hat hackers asking for a bug bounty instead of an attack that exposed customer data. The attackers were required to enroll in the company's bug bounty program and were paid $100,000 in Bitcoin. Before they were paid, the threat actors were required to sign both a nondisclosure agreement (NDA) attesting that they had destroyed all stolen data and a confidentiality agreement stating they would not talk about the incident.

However, federal prosecutors, who were investigating Uber for a different security incident, found out about what occurred. They charged Joseph with criminal obstruction. The prosecutors alleged that Joseph helped orchestrate a cover-up of the security breach and then sought to conceal it to avoid required disclosures to the Federal Trade Commission (FTC) and different states (all states now have required breach notification laws). "This is a case about cover-up, about payoff, and about lies," said a Justice Department attorney. Joseph was later fired by Uber.

Many security professionals said they viewed this as a test case of the potential criminal penalties that they also could face over security lapses. These professionals said that it is not always as clear as the federal prosecutors claimed. Decisions on how to respond to a cyber incident are almost always made by consensus with the senior leadership of the company and not unilaterally by the chief security officer. Many top security officers said that Joseph did nothing wrong, and the criminalization of the reporting decisions that were made will make future decisions for them more difficult. Such charges, it was said, only muddy the definition of an attack and how it should be handled.

In late 2022, Joseph was convicted of obstruction of justice. He is currently appealing his case.

Throughout the years, different words have been used to describe network-connected hardware devices. Forty years ago, when the TCP/IP protocol was becoming popular, the word *host* referred to any communicating device on the network (networks were made up of hosts). Thirty years ago, as servers became more popular, the word *client* was used (clients made requests to servers). Twenty years ago, the term workstation described a special computer designed for scientific or highly technical applications.

Today, a different word is commonly used when referring to network-connected hardware devices: *endpoints*. This change reflects the fact that today computing devices are far more than a desktop computer with a keyboard and monitor. Instead, devices ranging from mobile smartphones and tablets to wearable fitness trackers, industrial control system sensors, automotive telematics units, and even personal drones are all network-connected hardware devices. The word "endpoint" has become a more accurate description of today's technology devices.

This change in terminology also reflects the fact that increased risks have multiplied—exponentially—with the increasing number of these devices. They have become a prime target for attackers. And because the endpoints are connected to some type of network, a vulnerability on a single endpoint can result in an attack that penetrates the network and infects all other connected endpoints. Every endpoint can be a potential entry point for attackers.

This module examines vulnerabilities and attacks on endpoints. It also looks at defense measures that can be taken to mitigate these attacks.

Malware Attacks

Certification

2.4 Given a scenario, analyze indicators of malicious activity.

Mal comes from an Old French word dating back to the ninth century meaning "evil." And that is an accurate prefix to describe a set of computer instructions that can do evil or harm to an endpoint. Malware (*mal*icious soft*ware*) is a word coined in the early 1990s that describes software designed to interfere with a computer's normal functions and can be used to commit an unwanted and harmful action. Today, malware is the general term that refers to a wide variety of "evil" software.

Malware is continuing to grow at an exponential pace. It is estimated that 560,000 new instances of malware are detected *daily*. Yet despite this large number, no standard has yet been established for the classification of the different types of malware.

One attempt at classifying the diverse types of malware can be to examine the primary action that the malware performs and then group it together with other malware that performs similar primary actions. These malware actions used for groupings, using common vernacular, are kidnap, eavesdrop, masquerade, launch, and sidestep. And there are different indicators of an attack.

Note 1

Some malware performs more than one of these actions. However, in terms of classification, the primary action of the malware is used here.

Kidnap

Kidnapping is a crime that involves capturing a person and then holding them as a captive until a ransom is paid for their release. In a similar fashion, attackers perform a "kidnapping" of a user's device and hold it "hostage" until a ransom is paid. **Ransomware** is the malicious software designed to extort money from victims in exchange for their endpoint device to be restored to its normal working state.

Note 2

Although sometimes used interchangeably, there is a difference between kidnapping, abduction, and holding hostage. Kidnapping is seizing and imprisoning a person against their will for the purpose of receiving a ransom for their release. Abducting occurs when a person has been taken away from their original location by persuasion, fraud, force, or even violence but there is no intent to exchange the person for money. Holding hostage involves a person held by a captor for the purpose of forcing the government to meet certain conditions, such as the release of prisoners.

Ransomware prevents a user's device from properly functioning or accessing data until a fee is paid. The ransomware embeds itself into the device in such a way that it cannot be bypassed, and even performing a "power cycle" (turning the device off and on) does not clear the ransomware.

Ransomware dates back over a dozen years. As it has evolved over time, this has resulted in two general categories of ransomwares: legacy blocking ransomware and modern locking ransomware.

Blocking Ransomware

Ransomware first became widespread around 2010. This earliest form of ransomware prevents or blocks the user from using their computer in a normal fashion and is sometimes called **blocking ransomware**. This occurs by the ransomware infecting the computer and then manipulating its operating system (OS) in such a way as to block all normal access to the device.

Typically, once blocking ransomware infects a computer, then the computer is restricted by the malware from performing its normal functions. For example, an attempt to launch a web browser or open a file is thwarted. Instead, a message on the user's screen appears pretending to be from a reputable third party and provides a "valid" reason for blocking the user's access to the device. One typical example is a message that purports to come from a law enforcement agency. Using official-looking imagery, the message states that the user has performed an illegal action such as downloading pirated software and must now immediately pay a fine online by entering a credit card number. Once the fine is paid, the message says, the computer will be restored to its normal function. However, both the payment and the credit card number are sent to the threat actors. Figure 5-1 shows a blocking ransomware message.

Some blocking ransomware pretends to come from a reputable software vendor. It displays a fictitious warning that a software license has expired or there is a problem with the computer such as imminent hard drive failure or—in a touch of irony—a malware infection. This message tells users that they must immediately renew their license or purchase additional software online to fix a nonexistent problem. The ransomware example in Figure 5-2 uses color schemes and icons like those found on legitimate software.

Figure 5-1   Blocking ransomware message

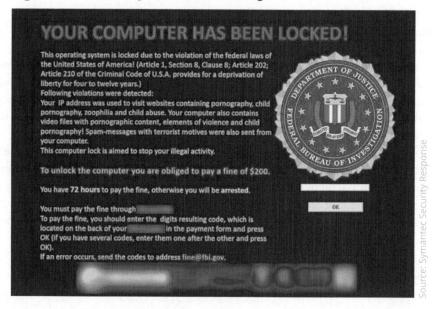

Figure 5-2   Blocking ransomware variation

Note 3

Ransomware attackers have determined the optimal price point for a ransom: the amount must be small enough that most victims will begrudgingly pay to have their systems unblocked, but large enough that when thousands of victims pay up, the attackers can garner a handsome sum. For individuals, the ransom is usually around $500. However, for enterprises, the price can be tens or even hundreds of millions of dollars. And some enterprising ransomware attackers have even set up help desks that victims can call to receive assistance in paying the ransom!

Locking Ransomware

Ransomware has continued to evolve from its earliest iterations. For example, as ransomware became more widespread, attackers dropped the pretense that the ransomware is from a reputable third party. Instead, they simply blocked the user's computer and demanded a fee for its release.

In recent years, a more malicious form of ransomware has arisen. Instead of just blocking the user from accessing the computer, this malware encrypts some or all the files on the device so that they cannot be opened (encrypting only some files helps the malware to evade initial detection). A benefit of this approach is that unlike blocking ransomware that prevented the device from being used and made it difficult to pay the ransom, the device remains functional so that the ransom can be more easily paid. This is called **locking ransomware**.

In a locking ransomware attack, after the files have been encrypted, a message appears telling the victim what has occurred and that a fee must be paid to receive a key to unlock them. Usually, the message contains a warning about the increased urgency for payment by claiming that the cost for the key increases every few hours. On some occasions, the threat actors claim that an ever-increasing number of the encrypted user files will be deleted and lost forever until the ransom is paid. And if the ransom is not paid by a specific deadline, then the key to unlock the files can never be purchased. Figure 5-3 shows a locking ransomware message.

Figure 5-3   Locking ransomware message

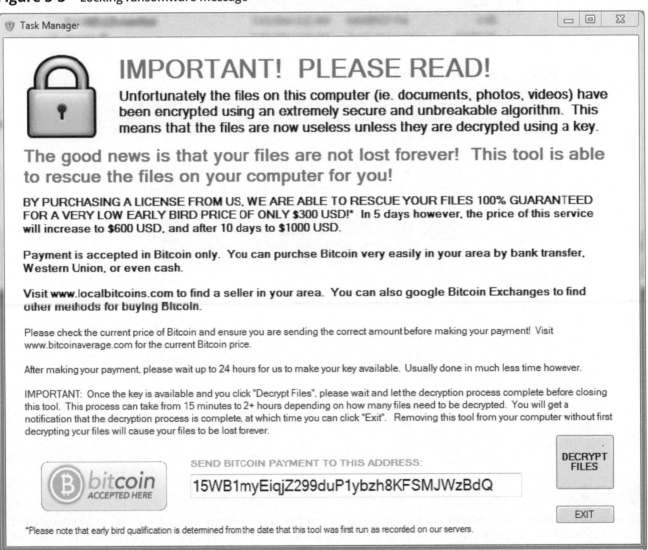

Note 4

With early locking ransomware attacks, threat actors only delivered the decryption key fewer than half of the times that a ransom was paid. However, this resulted in many victims not paying the ransom since word circulated that the risk was high of not getting the key. Threat actors have since learned that there is more to gain in the long run of making the key available after a ransom is paid. However, due to the nature of ransomware, the target's computer still may not function properly after the files have been decrypted. About 54 percent of organizations who paid the ransom reported system issues or corrupted data after using the decryption key.[1]

Soon attackers expanded the scope of the files that were infected: in addition to encrypting files on the device's local drive, new variants of locking ransomware encrypt all files on *any* network or storage device that is connected to that device. This includes secondary drives, USB drives, network-attached storage devices, network servers, and even cloud-based data repositories.

Attackers have now turned their ransomware attacks into blended attacks, which puts even more pressure on the victims to pay. Attackers first steal all the data they can get their hands on before locking up the files on the victim's device. If a victim refuses to pay for a decryption key, the threat actors threaten to publicly release the stolen information. This puts the victims in a bind: if they are able to restore their files themselves without purchasing the key, a public release of the files would still result in bad publicity, outrage from affected users, and hefty regulatory fines. And even paying the ransom does not prevent the threat actors from selling the stolen data later.

Recently threat actors have added yet another twist to ransomware attacks. Instead of merely threatening to publicly release stolen data if the victims do not pay the ransom, some attackers are adding extortion. In one event, a ransomware gang breached a network, stole the data, infected it with locking ransomware, and then contacted the victim threatening to sell the data to the highest bidder unless the victim paid a ransom of $50 million.

Today, ransomware is considered to be the most serious malware threat for several reasons:

- **Low barrier to entry.** Launching a ransomware attack is relatively inexpensive and does not require a high degree of skill. Threat actors can rent ransomware software for as little as $800 per month for their attacks.
- **Pervasive attacks.** Ransomware attacks occur with a very high frequency. Two out of every three organizations in 2021 experienced a successful attack, and ransomware is involved in one out of every four instances of a data breach.[2]
- **High impact.** The results of a ransomware attack are significant. About 37 percent of companies were forced to lay off employees due to a ransomware attack, 35 percent reported the resignation of senior-level managers following an attack, and 33 percent were forced to temporary suspend their business operations.[3]

Note 5

Originally the FBI did not support paying a ransom in any circumstances. It said, "The FBI does not advocate paying a ransom, in part because it does not guarantee an organization will regain access to its data. . . . Paying ransoms emboldens criminals to target other organizations and provides an alluring and lucrative enterprise to other criminals." However, later the FBI seemingly softened its stance by adding, "However, the FBI understands that when businesses are faced with an inability to function, executives will evaluate all options to protect their shareholders, employees, and customers."[4]

Eavesdrop

Another category of malware is that which eavesdrops or secretly listens to its targets. The two common types of eavesdropping malware are keyloggers and spyware.

Keylogger

A **keylogger** silently captures and stores each keystroke that a user types on the computer's keyboard. The threat actor can then search the captured text for any useful information such as passwords, credit card numbers, or personal information. A keylogger can be a software program or a small hardware device.

Software keyloggers are programs installed on the computer that silently capture sensitive information. However, software keyloggers, which conceal themselves so that the user cannot detect them, go far beyond just capturing a user's keystrokes. These programs can also make screen captures of everything that is on the user's screen and silently turn on the computer's web camera to record images of the user. A software keylogger is illustrated in Figure 5-4.

Figure 5-4   Software keylogger

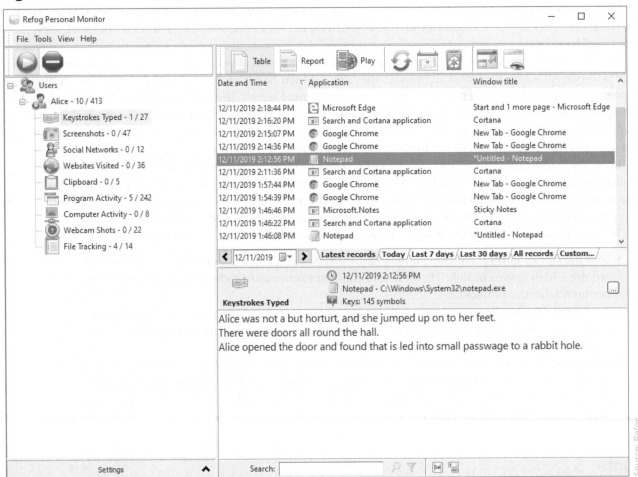

Source: Refog

Note 6

An advantage of software keyloggers is that they do not require physical access to the user's computer. This malware can be installed remotely and then routinely send captured information back to the attacker through the victim's own Internet connection.

For computers that are in a public location such as a library or computer lab but are "locked down" so that no software can be installed, a hardware keylogger can be used instead. These keyloggers are hardware devices inserted between the computer keyboard connection and USB port, as shown in Figure 5-5. Because the device resembles an ordinary keyboard connector and because the computer keyboard USB port is often on the back of the computer, a hardware keylogger can easily go undetected. In addition, the device is beyond the reach of the computer's anti-malware

Figure 5-5   Hardware keylogger

Hardware
keylogger

scanning software and thus raises no alarms. A disadvantage of a hardware keylogger is that the threat actor must install and then later return to physically remove the device to access the information it has stored, each time being careful not to be detected.

Spyware

Spyware is tracking software that is deployed without the consent or control of the user. Spyware typically secretly monitors users but, unlike a keylogger, makes no attempts to gather sensitive user keyboard input. It collects information without the user's approval by using the computer's resources, including programs already installed on the computer, to collect and distribute personal or sensitive information. Table 5-1 lists different technologies used by spyware.

Table 5-1   Technologies used by spyware

Technology	Description	Impact
Automatic download software	Used to download and install software without the user's interaction	Could install unauthorized applications
Passive tracking technologies	Used to gather information about user activities without installing any software	Could collect private information such as websites a user has visited
System-modifying software	Modifies or changes user configurations, such as the web browser home page or search page, default media player, or lower-level system functions	Changes configurations to settings that the user did not approve
Tracking software	Used to monitor user behavior or gather information about the user, sometimes including personally identifiable or other sensitive information	Could collect personal information that can be shared widely or stolen, resulting in fraud or identity theft

Caution

Not all spyware is necessarily malicious. For example, spyware monitoring tools can help parents keep track of the online activities of their children.

Masquerade

Some malware attempts to deceive the user and hide its true intentions by "masquerading" or pretending to be something else. Software in this category includes Trojans and remote access Trojans (RATs).

Trojan

According to ancient legend, the Greeks won the Trojan War by hiding soldiers in a large hollow wooden horse that was presented as a gift to the city of Troy. Once the horse was wheeled into the fortified city, the soldiers crept out of the horse during the night and attacked the unsuspecting defenders.

A computer Trojan is an executable program that masquerades as performing a benign activity but also does something malicious. For example, a user might download what is advertised as a calendar program, yet when it is installed, in addition to installing the calendar, it also installs malware that scans the system for credit card numbers and passwords, connects through the network to a remote system, and then transmits that information to the attacker.

Remote Access Trojan (RAT)

A special type of Trojan is a **remote access Trojan (RAT)**. A RAT has the basic functionality of a Trojan but also gives the threat agent unauthorized remote access to the victim's computer by using specially configured communication protocols. This creates an opening into the victim's computer, allowing the threat actor unrestricted access. The attacker can not only monitor what the user is doing but also can change computer settings, browse and copy files, and even use the computer to access other computers connected on the network.

Launch

Another category of malware is that which infects a computer to launch attacks on other computers. This includes a virus, worm, bloatware, and bot.

Virus

There are two types of viruses. These are a file-based virus and a fileless virus.

File-Based Virus　A biological virus is composed of tiny bits of genetic material enclosed by a protective shell. By themselves, viruses are lifeless and inert as they wait for a favorable environment in which to reproduce. When a virus encounters a host cell, the virus attaches itself to the outer wall of the cell, enters inside, travels to the cell's genome, merges with its genes, and then tricks the host's genome into making copies of itself.

> **Note 7**
>
> When the host cell is infected by a virus, the virus takes over the operation of that cell, converting it into a virtual factory to make more copies of the virus. The host cell rapidly produces millions of identical copies of the original virus. Biologists often say that viruses exist only to make more viruses.

In a similar fashion, a computer virus infects a computer with malware. A **file-based virus** is remarkably similar to a biological virus: it is malicious computer code that becomes part of a file.

Early viruses were relatively straightforward in how they infected files. One basic type of infection is the appender infection. The virus first attaches (appends) itself to the end of the infected file and inserts at the beginning of the file a "jump" instruction that points to the end of the file, which is the beginning of the virus code. When the program is launched, the jump instruction redirects control to the virus. Figure 5-6 shows how an appender infection works.

However, these types of viruses could be detected by virus scanners. Later file-based viruses went to greater lengths to avoid detection. Some of these techniques include split infections (dividing the malicious code itself into several parts with each part placed at random positions throughout the program code) or mutations (the virus changes its internal code to one of a set number of predefined mutations whenever it is executed). Some viruses even scan for the presence of files that security researchers typically use: if those files are present, the virus assumes it is being examined for weaknesses and automatically self-destructs by deleting itself.

Figure 5-6   Appender infection

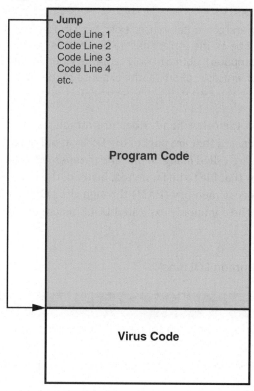

Each time the infected program is launched or the data file is opened—either by the user or the computer's OS—the virus first unloads its payload to perform a malicious action (delete files, prevent programs from launching, steal data to be sent to another computer, cause a computer to crash repeatedly, turn off the computer's security settings, etc.). Then the virus reproduces itself by inserting its code into another file, but only on the same computer: a virus can only replicate itself on the host computer where it is located and cannot automatically spread to another computer by itself. Instead, it must rely on the actions of users to spread it to other computers. Because viruses are attached to files, when a user transfers those infected files to other devices such as by sending an email attachment or inserting a USB flash drive into a computer, the virus then spreads. Thus, a virus must have two carriers: a file to which it attaches and a human to transport it to other devices.

A very large number of file types can contain a virus, and Table 5-2 lists some of the 50 different Microsoft Windows file types that can be infected with a virus.

Table 5-2   Windows file types that can be infected

File extension	Description
.docx or .xlsx	Microsoft Office user documents
.exe	Executable program file
.msi	Microsoft installer file
.msp	Windows installer patch file
.scr	Windows screen saver
.cpl	Windows Control Panel file
.msc	Microsoft Management Console file
.wsf	Windows script file
.ps1	Windows PowerShell script

> **Note 8**
>
> Several similarities between biological and computer viruses exist: both must enter their host passively (by relying on the action of an outside agent), both must be on the correct host (a horse virus cannot make a human sick, just as an Apple Mac virus cannot infect a Windows computer), both can only replicate when inside the host, both may remain dormant for a period of time, and both types of viruses replicate at the expense of the host.

Fileless Virus   A **fileless virus**, on the other hand, does not attach itself to a file. Instead, fileless viruses take advantage of native services and processes that are part of the OS to avoid detection and carry out its attacks. These native services used in a fileless virus are called *living-off-the-land binaries (LOLBins)*. Unlike a file-based virus, a fileless virus does not infect a file and wait for that file to be launched. Instead, the malicious code of a fileless virus is loaded directly in the computer's random access memory (RAM) through the LOLBins and then executed. For a computer running Microsoft Windows, some of the commonly exploited LOLBins are listed in Table 5-3.

Table 5-3   Microsoft Windows common LOLBins

Name	Description
PowerShell	A cross-platform and open source task automation and configuration management framework
Windows Management Instrumentation (WMI)	A Microsoft standard for accessing management information about devices
.NET Framework	A free, cross-platform, open source developer platform for building different types of applications
Macro	A series of instructions that can be grouped together as a single command to automate a complex set of tasks or a repeated series of tasks; can be written by using a macro scripting language, such as Visual Basic for Applications (VBA); and is stored within the user document (such as in an Excel .xlsx workbook or Word .docx file)

> **Note 9**
>
> Microsoft Windows LOLBins are often categorized into binaries (programs that end in .EXE), libraries (.DLL), and scripts (.VBS). By some estimates, 115 Windows LOLBins can be exploited by a fileless virus, while UNIX/Linux systems have 185 LOLBins.

There are several advantages of a fileless virus over a file-based virus: a fileless virus does not require that a specific type of file be stored on the computer's hard drive for the virus to infect, several LOLBins have extensive control and authority on a computer, fileless viruses can automatically launch, and they cannot be detected by anti-malware tools.

Worm

A second type of malware that has as its primary purpose to launch attacks in order to spread is a worm. A worm is a malicious program that uses a computer network to replicate and is sometimes called a "network virus." A worm is designed to enter a computer through the network and then take advantage of a vulnerability in an application or an OS on the host computer. Once the worm has exploited the vulnerability on one system, it immediately searches for another computer on the network that has the same vulnerability.

Note 10

One of the first wide-scale worm infections occurred in 1988. This worm exploited a misconfiguration in a program that allowed commands emailed to a remote system to be executed on that system. The worm also carried a payload containing a program that attempted to determine user passwords. Almost 6,000 computers, or 10 percent of the devices connected to the Internet at that time, were affected. The threat actor responsible was later convicted of federal crimes in connection with this incident.

Early worms were relatively benign and designed simply to spread quickly but not corrupt the systems they infected. These worms slowed down the network through which they were transmitted by replicating so quickly that they consumed all network resources. Today's worms can leave behind a payload on the systems they infect and cause harm, much like a virus. Actions that worms have performed include deleting files on the computer or allowing the computer to be remotely controlled by an attacker.

Note 11

Although viruses and worms are said to be automatically self-replicating, *where* they replicate is different. A virus self-replicates *on* the host computer but does not spread to other computers by itself. A worm self-replicates *between* computers (from one computer to another).

Bloatware

Bloatware is software that is installed on a device without the user requesting it. While bloatware by itself may not be harmful—some may in fact be useful—bloatware does have risks. First, the software could contain malware. Also, bloatware could become a platform for other malware to exploit if the bloatware contains a vulnerability.

One category of bloatware is software that comes preinstalled on a new device. Another category is software that a user does not intend to install but is installed as the result of overlooking the default installation options, as seen in Figure 5-7. This bloatware may inject advertising that obstructs content or interferes with web browsing, display pop-up or pop-under windows, change the default search engine or home page, add toolbars with no value for the user, or redirect browsers to another site.

Figure 5-7   Default installation options

Source: Oracle Corporation

Note 12

Most Android-based smartphones are designed to be "lean" by using a small amount of internal storage. One smartphone used only 256 megabytes (MB) of storage for both the Android OS and all apps. However, a new phone from a vendor uses a whopping 60 gigabytes (GB) of internal storage—even before any apps are downloaded and installed by the user! One reason for this huge footprint is bloatware. This phone vendor sells space in its devices to the highest bidder to preinstall bloatware, and it also sells space to the wireless carriers through whom the phone is purchased for their bloatware.

Bot

Another popular payload of malware is software that allows the infected computer to be placed under the remote control of an attacker for the purpose of launching attacks. This infected robot computer is known as a **bot** or *zombie*. When hundreds, thousands, or even millions of bot computers are gathered into a logical computer network, they create a *botnet* under the control of a *bot herder*.

Note 13

Due to the multitasking capabilities of modern computers, a computer can act as a bot while carrying out the tasks of its regular user. The user is completely unaware that their computer is being used for malicious activities.

Infected bot computers receive instructions through a command and control (C&C) structure from the bot herders regarding which computers to attack and how. There are a variety of ways for this communication to occur. A bot can receive its instructions by automatically signing into a bot-herding website where information has been placed that the bot knows how to interpret as commands, by signing in to a third-party website (this has an advantage of the bot herder not needing to have a direct affiliation with that website), or by commands sent via blogs, specially coded attack commands through posts on Twitter, or notes posted on social media sites.

Sidestep

The final category is that which attempts to help malware "sidestep" or evade detection. This includes logic bomb, rootkit, and backdoor.

Logic Bomb

A logic bomb is computer code that is typically added to a legitimate program but lies dormant and evades detection until a specific logical event triggers it. Once it is started, the program then deletes data or performs other malicious activities.

Note 14

Many logic bombs have been planted by disgruntled employees. For example, a Maryland government employee tried to destroy the contents of more than 4,000 servers by planting a logic bomb script that was scheduled to activate 90 days after he was terminated.

Logic bombs are difficult to detect before they are triggered. This is because logic bombs are often embedded in very large computer programs, some containing hundreds of thousands of lines of code. A trusted employee can easily insert a few lines of computer code into a long program without anyone detecting it. In addition, these programs are not routinely scanned for containing malicious actions.

Rootkits

A rootkit is malware that can hide its presence and the presence of other malware on the device. It does this by accessing lower layers of the OS or even using undocumented functions to make alterations. This enables the rootkit and any accompanying software to become undetectable by the OS or anti-malware scanning software.

Note 15

The risks of rootkits are significantly diminished today due to protections built into OSs.

Backdoor

A **backdoor** gives access to a computer, program, or service that circumvents any normal security protections. Backdoors that are installed on a computer allow the attacker to return later and bypass security settings.

Creating a legitimate backdoor is a common practice by developers, who may need to access a program or device on a regular basis, yet do not want to be hindered by continual requests for passwords or other security approvals. The intent is for the backdoor to be removed once the application is finalized. However, in some instances, backdoors have been left installed, and attackers have used them to bypass security.

Indicator of Attack (IoA)

There are different "tell-tale" signs regarding an attack. An indicator of attack (IoA) is a sign an attack is currently underway. This is different from an **indicator of compromise (IoC)**, which is evidence that an attack has already taken place. Not all attacks will generate these indicators. Table 5-4 lists several IoAs.

Table 5-4   Indicators of attack (IoAs)

Indicator	Description
Account lockout	A user account that is inaccessible through a normal login attempt can be an indication the account has been taken over by an attacker and is locking out a legitimate user.
Concurrent session usage	An indicator of attack in which both a legitimate user and an attacker are logged into the same account.
Blocked content	Data that is no longer accessible can be an IoA.
Impossible travel	Impossible travel is accessing a resource that is not possible due to geography; for example, a user who checks email from New York and then downloads a file from Los Angeles five minutes later is an example of impossible travel.
Resource consumption	System resources such as memory or processing capabilities that are suddenly depleted could indicate an attack.
Resource inaccessibility	A large-scale attack can block system resources from being accessed.
Out-of-cycle logging	Log records that do not correspond to actual events that have occurred can be an IoA.
Published/documented	Evidence from external sources of a current attack can be used to identify an attack.
Missing logs	Log files that have mysteriously been deleted is an indication of an ongoing attack taking place.

Two Rights & A Wrong

1. Blocking ransomware will encrypt one or more files with a key until a ransom is paid.
2. The two types of viruses are a file-based virus and a fileless virus.
3. A keylogger can be a software program or a small hardware device.

See the answers at the end of the module.

Application Vulnerabilities and Attacks

Certification

2.3 Explain various types of vulnerabilities.

2.4 Given a scenario, analyze indicators of malicious activity.

While attacks using malware typically add malicious software to an endpoint, another category of attacks specifically targets software applications that are already installed and running on the device. These attacks look for vulnerabilities in the application or manipulate the application in order to compromise it. Application attacks frequently result in privilege escalation. Privilege escalation allows the attacker to gain illicit access of elevated rights or privileges beyond what is entitled for a user. Privilege escalation can be either horizon (gaining access to rights of another account with similar privileges) or vertical (increasing the elevation of rights).

> **Note 16**
>
> In one year, 44 percent of all Microsoft vulnerabilities resulted in vertical privilege escalation.[5]

Application Vulnerabilities

There are several attacks that target vulnerabilities found in applications. Two of the most common vulnerabilities are buffer overflow and improper exception and error handling.

Buffer Overflow

Consider Tommaso, a teacher working in his office who manually grades a lengthy written examination by marking incorrect answers with a red pen. Because he is frequently interrupted in his grading by students, he places a ruler on the test question he is currently grading to indicate his "return point," or where he should resume the grading. Suppose that two devious students enter his office as he is grading final examinations. While one student distracts him, the second student silently slides the ruler down from question 4 to question 20. When Tommaso returns to grading, he will resume at the wrong "return point" and not look at the answers for questions 4 through 19.

This scenario is similar to how a threat actor may attempt to take advantage of a programming vulnerability. A storage buffer on a computer typically contains the memory location of the software program that was being executed when another function interrupted the process; that is, the storage buffer contains the "return address" where the computer's processor should resume once the new process has finished. An attacker can substitute their own "return address" in order to point to a different area in the computer's memory that contains their malware code.

A buffer overflow attack occurs when a process attempts to store data in RAM beyond the boundaries of a fixed-length storage buffer. This extra data overflows into the adjacent memory locations, or a "buffer overflow." Because the storage buffer typically contains the "return address" memory location of the software program being executed when another function interrupted the process, an attacker can overflow the buffer with a new address pointing to the attacker's malware code. These attacks are called injections or memory injections since they introduce something into RAM. A buffer overflow attack is shown in Figure 5-8. Buffer overflow vulnerabilities are often the result of programmers not adhering to secure program development practices.

> **Note 17**
>
> The "return address" is not the only element that can be altered in a buffer overflow attack, but it is one of the most common.

Figure 5-8   Buffer overflow attack

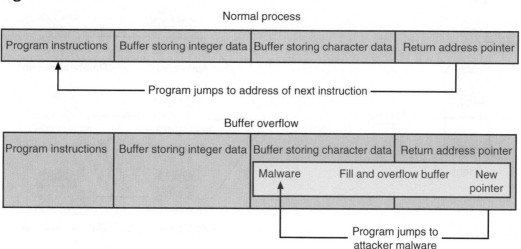

Normal process

| Program instructions | Buffer storing integer data | Buffer storing character data | Return address pointer |

Program jumps to address of next instruction

Buffer overflow

| Program instructions | Buffer storing integer data | Buffer storing character data | Return address pointer |

| | | Malware | Fill and overflow buffer | New pointer |

Program jumps to attacker malware

Improper Exception and Error Handling

A buffer overflow vulnerability is the result of poor coding on the part of software developers. Another vulnerability is likewise based on poor programing practices, specifically when an application does not properly check for exceptions that may occur when the program is running. Software that does not correctly "trap" an error condition could provide an attacker with underlying access to the system.

Suppose an attacker enters a string of characters that is much longer than expected. Because the software has not been designed for this input, the program could crash or suddenly halt its execution and then display an underlying OS prompt, giving an attacker access to the computer. This is known as improper exception and error handling.

Another improper handling situation is a NULL pointer/object dereference. (A *dereference* obtains from a pointer the address of a data item held in another location.) When an application dereferences a pointer that it expects to be valid but instead has a value of NULL, it typically causes a program to crash or exit. A NULL pointer/object dereference can occur through a number of flaws, including simple programming omissions.

A NULL pointer/object dereference can also be the result of a race condition. A race condition in software occurs when two concurrent threads of execution access a shared resource simultaneously, resulting in unintended consequences.

For example, in a program with two threads that have access to the same location in memory, Thread #1 stores the value A in that memory location. But since Thread #2 is also executing, it may overwrite the same memory location with the value Z. When Thread #1 retrieves the value stored, it is given Thread #2's Z instead of its own A. The software checks the state of a resource before using that resource, but the resource's state can change between the check and the use in a way that invalidates the results of the check. This is called a time of check (TOC) to time of use (TOU) race condition (sometimes combined together as "TOCTTOU," pronounced "TOCK-too"). This condition is often security-relevant: a threat actor who can influence the state of the resource between a check and use can negatively impact a number of shared resources such as files, memory, or variables in multithreaded programs. Such systems should be analyzed using a target of evaluation (TOE) approach. A TOE is a system, product, and its documentation that is the subject of a security evaluation.

Caution !

A typo of TOCTTOU is TOCCTOU and has been used in some influential documents, so the typo is repeated fairly frequently.

Application Attacks

A common type of attack is an application attack directed at programs running on Internet web servers, known as web-based attacks. A web server provides services that are implemented as "web applications" through software applications running on the server. A typical web application infrastructure is shown in Figure 5-9. The client's web

Figure 5-9   Web server application infrastructure

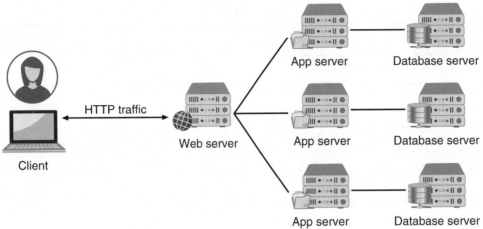

browser makes a request using the Hypertext Transport Protocol (HTTP) to a web server, which may be connected to one or more web application servers. These application servers run the specific "web apps," which in turn are directly connected to database servers on the internal network. Information from these database servers is retrieved and returned to the web server so that the information can be sent back to the user's web browser.

The multiple elements in a web application infrastructure provide multiple attack points: a single vulnerability could expose many other users who are accessing the web server. An attack could also compromise backend databases and app servers and the connected network infrastructure.

Web-based attacks frequently result in directory traversal. The "root" directory is a specific directory on a web server's file system, and users who access the server are usually restricted to the root directory and directories and files beneath the root directory, but they cannot access other directories. A directory traversal attack takes advantage of a vulnerability so that a user can move from the root directory to other restricted directories, viewing confidential files or entering commands to execute on the server.

Application web-based attacks include scripting attacks, injection attacks, request forgery attacks, and replay attacks.

Scripting

Most web applications create dynamic content based on input from the user. Figure 5-10 illustrates a fictitious web application that allows friends to share their favorite bookmarks with each other online. Users can enter their name, a description, and the URL of the bookmark and then receive a personalized "Thank You" screen. In Figure 5-11, the code that generates the "Thank You" screen is illustrated.

In a cross-site scripting (XSS) attack, a website that accepts user input without validating it (called "sanitizing") and uses that input in a response can be exploited. In the previous example, the input that the user enters for *Name* is not verified but instead is automatically added to a code segment that becomes part of an automated response. An attacker can take advantage of this in an XSS attack by tricking a valid website into feeding a malicious script to another user's web browser, which will then execute it.

> **Note 18**
>
> The term *cross-site scripting* refers to an attack using scripting that originates on one site (the web server) to impact another site (the user's computer).

Injection

In addition to cross-site attacks on web server applications, other attacks introduce new input by exploiting a vulnerability. One of the most common injection attacks, called SQL injection (SQLi), inserts statements to manipulate a database server. SQL stands for Structured Query Language, a language used to view and manipulate data that is stored in a relational database. SQLi targets SQL servers by introducing malicious commands.

Figure 5-10   Bookmark page that accepts user input

Figure 5-11   Input used in response

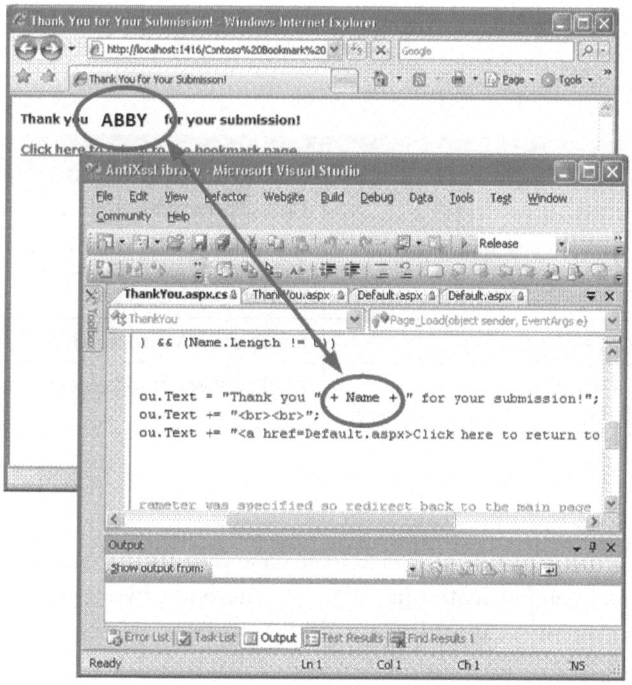

Consider a webpage that offers a solution for the user who has forgotten their password. An online form asks the user to enter their username, which is also their email address that is already on file. The submitted email address is compared to the stored email address and, if they match, a reset URL is emailed to that address.

If the email address entered by the user into the form is stored in the variable *$EMAIL*, then the underlying SQL statement to retrieve the stored email address from the database would be similar to:

SELECT fieldlist FROM table WHERE field = '$EMAIL'

The *WHERE* clause is meant to limit the database query to only display information when the condition is considered true (that is, when the email address in *$EMAIL* matches an address in the database).

An attacker using an SQL injection attack would begin by first entering a fictitious email address on this webpage that included a single quotation mark as part of the data, such as braden.thomas@fakemail.com'. If the message *E-mail Address Unknown* is displayed, it indicates that user input is being properly filtered and an SQL attack cannot be rendered on the site. However, if the error message *Server Failure* is displayed, it means that the user input is not being filtered and all user input is sent directly to the database. This is because the *Server Failure* message is due to a syntax error created by the additional single quotation mark in the fictitious email address.

Armed with the knowledge that input is sent unfiltered to the database, the attacker knows that anything they enter as a username in the form would be sent to and then processed by the SQL database. Now, instead of entering a username, the attacker would enter the following command, which would let them view all the email addresses in the database: whatever' or 'a'='a. This command is stored in the variable *$EMAIL*. The expanded SQL statement would read:

SELECT fieldlist FROM table WHERE field = 'whatever' or 'a'='a

These values are:

- **'whatever'.** This can be anything meaningless.
- **or.** The SQL *or* means that as long as either of the conditions are true, the entire statement is true and will be executed.
- **'a'='a'.** This is a statement that will always be true.

Because *'a'='a'* is always true, the *WHERE* clause is also true. It is not limited as it was when searching for a single email address before it would become true. The result can be that *all* user email addresses will then be displayed.

By entering crafted SQL statements as user input, information from the database can be extracted or the existing data can be manipulated. SQLi statements that can be entered and stored in *$EMAIL* and their pending results are shown in Table 5-5.

Table 5-5 SQLi statements

SQL injection statement	Result
whatever' AND email IS NULL; --	Determine the names of different fields in the database
whatever' AND 1=(SELECT COUNT(*) FROM tabname); —	Discover the name of the table
whatever' OR full name LIKE '%Mia%'	Find specific users
whatever'; DROP TABLE members; --	Erase the database table
whatever'; UPDATE members SET email = 'attacker-email@evil.net' WHERE email = 'Mia@good.com';	Mail password to attacker's email account

Request Forgery

Although some attacks have confusing names, that is not the case with the category of "request forgery." As its name suggests, it is a request that has been fabricated (a **forgery**). There are two types of request forgeries: a cross-site request forgery (CSRF) and a server-site request forgery (SSRF).

Cross-Site Request Forgery (CSRF) A **cross-site request forgery (CSRF)** takes advantage of an authentication "token" that a website sends to a user's web browser. If a user is currently authenticated on a website and is then tricked into loading another webpage, the new page inherits the identity and privileges of the victim, who may then perform an undesired function on the attacker's behalf. In other words, in a CSRF attack a *request* to a website is not from the authentic user but is a *forgery* that involves *crossing sites*.

Figure 5-12 illustrates a CSRF. Because a CSRF takes place on the client site, it is sometimes called a client-side request forgery.

Figure 5-12   Cross-site request forgery

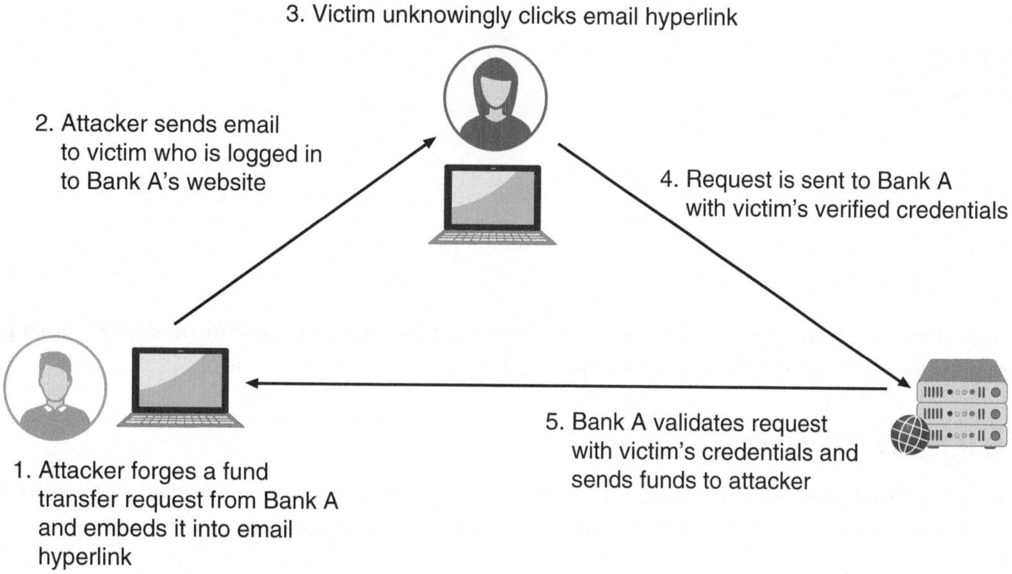

3. Victim unknowingly clicks email hyperlink

2. Attacker sends email to victim who is logged in to Bank A's website

4. Request is sent to Bank A with victim's verified credentials

1. Attacker forges a fund transfer request from Bank A and embeds it into email hyperlink

5. Bank A validates request with victim's credentials and sends funds to attacker

Server-Side Request Forgery (SSRF)   A **server-side request forgery (SSRF)** takes advantage of a trusting relationship between web servers (as opposed to a CSRF, which manipulates the trust from a user's browser to a server). SSRF attacks exploit how a web server processes external information received from another server. Some web applications are designed to read information from or write information to a specific URL. If an attacker can modify that target URL, they can potentially extract sensitive information from the application or inject untrusted input into it. Table 5-6 outlines the differences between a CSRF and a SSRF.

Table 5-6   CSRF and SSRF differences

Attack name	Attack target	Purpose of attack
CSRF	User	Force target to take action for attacker while pretending to be authorized user
SSRF	Web server	Gain access to sensitive data or inject harmful data

Replay

Whereas some attacks try to capture data sent between two users, a replay attack copies data and then uses it for an attack. Replay attacks are commonly used against digital identities—after intercepting and copying data, the threat actor retransmits selected and edited portions of the copied communications later to impersonate the legitimate user. Many digital identity replay attacks are between a user and an authentication server.

Two Rights & A Wrong

1. Privilege escalation can be either horizontal or vertical.

2. A buffer overflow attack occurs when a process attempts to store data in RAM beyond the boundaries of a fixed-length storage buffer.

3. An attacker who can access the root directory has conducted a directory traversal attack.

See the answers at the end of the module.

Securing Endpoint Devices

Certification

2.5 Explain the purpose of mitigation techniques used to secure the enterprise.

4.1 Given a scenario, apply common security techniques to computing resources.

4.4 Explain security alerting and monitoring concepts and tools.

There are various defenses that can be used to secure endpoint devices. These can be divided into protecting the endpoints from attacks and then hardening the endpoints for even greater protection.

Protecting Endpoints

Actively protecting computer endpoints can be done through different types of software installed on the endpoint. This software includes antivirus, web browser protections, and monitoring and response systems.

Antivirus

One of the first software protections was antivirus (AV) software. This software can examine a computer for file-based virus infections as well as monitor computer activity and scan new documents that might contain a virus. (Scanning is typically performed when files are opened, created, or closed.) If a virus is detected, options generally include cleaning the file of the virus, quarantining the infected file, or deleting the file. Log files created by AV products can also provide beneficial information regarding attacks.

Original AV products used signature-based monitoring, also called **static analysis**. The AV software scans files by attempting to match known virus patterns against potentially infected files (called string scanning). Other variations include wildcard scanning (a wildcard is allowed to skip bytes or ranges of bytes instead of looking for an exact match) and mismatch scanning (mismatches allow a set number of bytes in the string to be any value regardless of their position in the string).

> **Caution** !
>
> The weakness of signature-based monitoring is that the AV vendor must constantly be searching for new viruses, extracting virus signatures, and distributing those updated databases to all users. Any out-of-date signature database could result in an infection.

A newer approach to AV is heuristic monitoring (called **dynamic analysis**), which uses a variety of techniques to spot the characteristics of a virus instead of attempting to make matches. The difference between static analysis and dynamic analysis detection is similar to how airport security personnel in some nations screen for terrorists. A known terrorist attempting to go through security can be identified by comparing their face against photographs of known terrorists (static analysis). But what about a new terrorist for whom there is no photograph? Security personnel can look at the person's characteristics—holding a one-way ticket, not checking any luggage, showing extreme nervousness—as possible indicators that the individual may need to be questioned (dynamic analysis).

> **Note 19**
>
> One AV heuristic monitoring technique used is code emulation in which a virtual environment is created that simulates the CPU and memory of the computer. Any questionable program code is executed in the virtual environment (no actual virus code is executed by the real CPU) to determine if it is a virus.

Web Browsers

Web browsers have a degree of security that can protect endpoint computers. This security includes secure cookies and HTTP headers.

Secure Cookies   The Hypertext Transfer Protocol (HTTP) is the Internet-based protocol that is the foundation of all data exchanges on the web. It is a client-server protocol so that requests are initiated by the recipient or client, usually a web browser, to a web server.

One of the limitations of HTTP is that it is a stateless protocol. Unlike a stateful protocol, which "remembers" everything that occurs between the browser client and the server, a stateless protocol "forgets" what occurs when the session is interrupted or ends. There are three ways in which the stateless protocol HTTP can mimic a stateful protocol: use a URL extension so the state is sent as part of the URL as a response; use "hidden form fields" in which the state is sent to the client as part of the response and returned to the server as part of a form's hidden data; or use cookies. The server can store user-specific information in a file on the user's local computer and then retrieve it later in a file called a **cookie**.

> ### Note 20
> A cookie can contain a variety of information based on the user's preferences when visiting a website. For example, if a user inquires about a rental car at the car agency's website, that site might create a cookie that contains the user's travel itinerary. In addition, it may record the pages visited on a site to help the site customize the view for any future visits. Cookies can also store any personally identifiable information (name, email address, work address, telephone number, and so on) that was provided when visiting the site; however, a website cannot gain access to private information stored on the local computer.

There are several types of cookies. A first-party cookie is created from the website that a user is currently viewing; whenever the user returns to this site, that cookie is used by the site to view the user's preferences and better customize the browsing experience. Some websites attempt to place additional cookies on the local hard drive. These cookies often come from third parties that advertise on the site and want to record the user's preferences. These cookies are called third-party cookies. A session cookie is stored in RAM, instead of on the hard drive, and only lasts for the duration of visiting the website.

As a means of protection for cookies, a web browser can send a secure cookie. This cookie is only sent to the server with an encrypted request over the secure HTTPS protocol. This prevents an unauthorized person from intercepting a cookie that is being transmitted between the browser and the web server.

HTTP Response Headers   When a user visits a website through their web browser, the web server answers back with HTTP Response Headers. These headers tell the browser how to behave while communicating with the website. Several HTTP Response Headers can improve security; these are listed in Table 5-7.

Table 5-7   HTTP Response Headers

HTTP Response Header	Description	Protection
HTTP Strict Transport Security (HSTS)	Forces browser to communicate over more secure HTTPS instead of HTTP	Encrypts transmissions to prevent unauthorized user from intercepting
Content Security Policy (CSP)	Restricts the resources a user is allowed to load within the website	Protects against injection attacks
Cross Site Scripting Protection (X-XSS)	Prohibits a page from loading if it detects a cross-site scripting attack	Prevents XSS attacks
X-Frame-Options	Prevents attackers from "overlaying" their content on the webpage	Foils a threat actor's attempt to trick a user into providing personal information

Monitoring and Response Systems

It is important to monitor endpoints and then respond as needed. There are three types of monitoring and response systems for endpoint computers: host intrusion detection systems (HIDS), host intrusion prevention systems (HIPS), and endpoint detection and response (EDR).

Host Intrusion Detection Systems (HIDS)   A **host intrusion detection system (HIDS)** is a software-based application that runs on an endpoint computer and can detect that an attack has occurred. The primary function of a HIDS is automated detection, which saves someone from sorting through log files to find an indication of unusual behavior. HIDS can quickly detect evidence that an intrusion has occurred. Figure 5-13 shows a HIDS dashboard.

Figure 5-13   HIDS dashboard

Source: SolarWinds

A HIDS relies on agents installed directly on the endpoint, and these agents work closely with the OS to observe activity. HIDSs typically monitor endpoint computer functions such as system calls (a system call is an instruction that interrupts the program being executed and requests a service from the OS), file system access (ensures that all file openings are based on legitimate needs and are not the result of malicious activity), and host input/output (HIDS monitors all input and output communications to watch for malicious activity).

Host Intrusion Prevention Systems (HIPS)   As its name implies, an intrusion *prevention* system not only monitors to detect malicious activities but also attempts to stop it. A host intrusion prevention system (HIPS) monitors endpoint activity to immediately block a malicious attack by following specific rules. Activity that a HIPS watches for includes an event that attempts to control other programs, terminate programs, and install devices and drivers. When a HIPS blocks an action, it then alerts the user so an appropriate decision about what to do can be made.

Endpoint Detection and Response (EDR)   Endpoint detection and response (EDR) tools have a similar functionality to HIDS of monitoring endpoint events and of HIPS of taking immediate action. However, EDR tools are considered more robust than HIDS and HIPS. First, an EDR can aggregate data from multiple endpoint computers to a centralized database so that security professionals can further investigate and gain a better picture of events occurring across multiple endpoints instead of just on a single endpoint. This can help determine if an attack is more widespread across the enterprise and if more comprehensive and higher-level action needs to be taken. Second, EDR tools can perform more sophisticated analytics that identify patterns and detect anomalies. This can help detect unusual or unrecognized activities by performing baseline comparisons of normal behavior.

Hardening Endpoints

The next step after endpoints have been protected is to harden the endpoints for further protection. Hardening endpoints involves patch management and OS protections.

Patch Management

Early operating systems, such Microsoft Windows, Apple macOS, and Linux, were simply "program loaders" whose job was to launch applications. As more features and graphical user interfaces (GUIs) were added, operating systems became more complex.

> **Note 21**
>
> Today's Windows 11 is estimated to have over 50 million lines of code, Linux Debian has 68 million lines, and Apple macOS may have upward of 86 million lines of code. In contrast, Microsoft's first operating system, MS-DOS v1.0, had only 4,000 lines of code.

Due to the increased complexity of operating systems, unintentional vulnerabilities were introduced that could be exploited by attackers. In addition, new attack tools made what were once considered secure functions and services on operating systems now vulnerable. To address the vulnerabilities in operating systems that are uncovered after the software has been released to the general public as well as to provide ongoing additional features, operating system vendors deploy updates to users' computers through an automatic online update service. The user's computer interacts with the vendor's online update service to receive the latest updates.

One of the most important steps in securing an endpoint computer is patching, which is installing these software security updates. Threat actors often watch for the release of a patch and then immediately craft an attack around the vulnerability the patch addresses, knowing that many users and organizations are lax in applying patches.

Effective patch management involves two types of patch management tools to administer patches. The first type includes tools for patch distribution, while the second type involves patch reception.

Patch Distribution Modern operating systems, such as Red Hat Linux, Apple macOS, Ubuntu Linux, and Microsoft Windows, frequently distribute patches. These patches, however, can sometimes create new problems, such as preventing a custom application from running correctly. Organizations that have these types of applications usually test patches when they are released to ensure that they do not adversely affect any customized applications. In these instances, the organization delays the installation of a patch from the vendor's online update service until the patch is thoroughly tested. But how can an organization prevent its employees from installing the latest patch until it has passed testing and still ensure that all users download and install necessary patches?

The answer is to employ **automated patch management tools**. These tools are used to manage patches within the enterprise instead of relying on the vendor's online update service. Automated patch management tools typically consist of a component installed on one or more servers inside the corporate network. Because these servers can replicate information among themselves, usually only one of the servers must be connected to the vendor's online update service, as seen in Figure 5-14.

There are several advantages to automated patch management tools, including the following:

- Downloading patches from a local server instead of using the vendor's online update service can save bandwidth and time because each computer does not have to connect to an external server.
- Administrators can approve or decline updates for client systems, force updates to install by a specific date, and obtain reports on what updates each computer needs.
- Administrators can approve updates for "detection" only; this allows them to see which computers require the update without installing it.

Figure 5-14   Automated patch update service

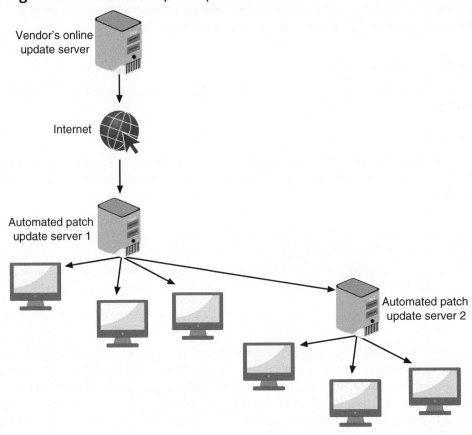

Patch Reception   Just as the patches must be distributed, they must also be received by the device. Prior versions of Microsoft Windows gave users several options regarding accepting or even rejecting patches. These options included *Download updates but let me choose whether to install them, Check for updates but let me choose whether to download and install them*, and *Never check for updates*. However, this approach frequently resulted in important security patches being ignored by users and putting their computers at risk.

The patch update options for Microsoft Windows 11 are far less lenient. Updates can also be delayed from one to five weeks. After that time, the updates will resume. Other options include setting a time range when the computer will restart after an update has been installed and optimizing delivery options that depend on the connection type. Apple macOS has similar features. Users can receive a notification that software updates are available, can choose when to install the updates, or choose to be reminded the next day.

Note 22

Threat actors will typically "reverse-engineer" patches to look for the vulnerability that is being fixed and then craft attacks based on that vulnerability, knowing that many users do not install patches as soon as they are available. Promptly installing patches is considered the most important step to protecting a device, so it is advised that they be configured so that patches are automatically downloaded and installed.

Operating Systems

There are several protections at the OS level that can provide enhanced protection. These include:

- **Disabling unnecessary ports and protocols.** One of the primary OS security configurations involves disabling ports/protocols or closing unused ports and disabling unnecessary protocols. This also includes turning off unneeded services, such as Microsoft Windows ASP.NET State Service, Portable Device Enumerator Service, and Apple macOS Spotlight Indexing.

- **Application allow list.** An increasingly popular approach to OS security is to employ application allow listing. This is approving in advance only specific applications to run on the OS so that any item not approved will not function. Application allow listing requires preapproval for an application to run. The inverse of an allow list is a deny list, or a listing of unapproved software so that any item not on the list can run. Although often overlooked, application allow listing is a powerful tool to combat attacks. The elite Tailored Access Operations (TAO) section of the National Security Agency (NSA) is responsible for compromising networks owned by hostile nations to spy on them. The head of the TAO spoke at a security conference about the best practices of security from the NSA's perspective (in his own words, "What can you do to defend yourself to make my life hard?") and said one of the most important steps was to employ application allow listing for the software that runs on servers.[6]

Note 23

Microsoft 11 Windows Defender offers built-in ransomware protection based on application allow listing called "controlled folder access" and allows only trusted apps to access protected folders. The apps can be executable files, scripts, or a dynamic-link library (DLL). There is a set of protected folders by default that typically contain user data (Documents, Pictures, Videos, Music, and Favorites) but users can also add additional folders to protect, and even add additional approved apps to access protected folders. In the event of a ransomware attack, a notification appears with a warning that an app attempted to make changes to a file in a protected folder. You explore using this feature in Hands-On Project 5-2.

- **Sandbox.** A sandbox is a "container" in which an application can be run so that it does not impact the underlying OS. Anything that occurs within the sandbox is not visible to other applications or the OS outside the sandbox. Also, the contents of the sandbox are not saved when it is closed. Sandboxes are often used when downloading or running suspicious programs to ensure that the endpoint will not become infected.

Two Rights & A Wrong

1. Cookies are a work-around of the stateless protocol HTTP.
2. A HIDS monitors endpoint activity to immediately block a malicious attack by following specific rules.
3. Dynamic analysis uses heuristic monitoring.

See the answers at the end of the module.

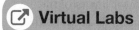 **Virtual Labs**   You're now ready to complete the simulations and live virtual machine labs for this module. The labs can be found in each module in MindTap.

Summary

- Malware (malicious software) is software designed to interfere with a computer's normal functions and can be used to commit an unwanted and harmful action. Although there has been no standard established for the classification of the different types of malware, the primary action that it performs can be used to group like instances together. These malware actions used for groupings, using common vernacular, are kidnap, eavesdrop, masquerade, launch, and sidestep.

- Some types of malware perform a "kidnapping" function by holding a user's device "hostage" until a ransom is paid. Ransomware is malicious software designed to extort money from victims in exchange for having their endpoint device restored to its normal working state. Blocking ransomware prevents the user from using their computer in a normal fashion by infecting the computer and then manipulating its OS in such a way as to block all normal access to the device. Locking ransomware encrypts some or all the files on the device so that they cannot be opened. New variants of locking ransomware encrypt all files on any network or attached device that is connected to that device. Blended ransomware attacks and extortion are new elements of ransomware attacks.

- Another category of malware is that which eavesdrops or secretly listens to its targets. A keylogger silently captures and stores each keystroke that a user types on the computer's keyboard so that the attacker can later search the captured text for any useful information. Keyloggers can be a software program or a small hardware device. Spyware typically secretly monitors users but unlike a keylogger makes no attempts to gather sensitive user keyboard input. It collects information without the user's approval by using the computer's resources, including programs already installed on the computer, to collect and distribute personal or sensitive information.

- Some malware attempts to deceive the user and hide its true intentions by "masquerading" or pretending to be something else. A computer Trojan is an executable program that masquerades as performing a benign activity but also does something malicious. A special type of Trojan is a remote access Trojan (RAT). A RAT has the basic functionality of a Trojan but also gives the threat agent unauthorized remote access to the victim's computer by using specially configured communication protocols.

- Another category of malware infects a computer to then launch attacks on other computers. A file-based virus is remarkably similar to a biological virus: it is malicious computer code that is attached to a file. Like its biological counterpart, a file-based virus reproduces itself on the same computer. A fileless virus does not attach itself to a file but takes advantage of native services and processes that are part of the OS to avoid detection and carry out its attacks. There are

several advantages of a fileless virus over a file-based virus: a fireless virus does not require that a specific type of file be stored on the computer's hard drive for the virus to infect, several LOLBins have extensive control and authority on a computer, fileless viruses can automatically launch, and they cannot be detected by anti-malware tools. A worm is a malicious program that uses a computer network to replicate. It is designed to enter a computer through the network and then take advantage of a vulnerability in an application or an OS on the host computer.

- Bloatware is software installed on a device without the user requesting it. While bloatware by itself may not be harmful, it does have risks. One category of bloatware is software that comes preinstalled on a new device. Another category is software that a user does not intend to install but is installed as the result of overlooking the default setup options. Another popular payload of malware is software that allows the infected computer to be placed under the remote control of an attacker for the purpose of launching attacks. This infected robot computer is known as a bot or zombie. When hundreds, thousands, or even millions of bot computers are gathered into a logical computer network, they create a botnet.

- Another category of malware is that which attempts to help malware evade detection. A logic bomb is computer code that is typically added to a legitimate program but lies dormant and evades detection until a specific logical event triggers it. Once it starts, the program deletes data or performs other malicious activities. A rootkit is malware that can hide its presence and the presence of other malware on the device. It does this by accessing lower layers of the OS or even using undocumented functions to make alterations. A backdoor gives access to a computer, program, or service that circumvents any normal security protections.

- An indicator of attack (IoA) is a sign an attack is currently underway. An indicator of compromise (IoC) is evidence that an attack has already taken place. Common IoAs include account lockout, concurrent session usage, blocked content, impossible travel, resource consumption, resource inaccessibility, out-of-cycle logging, published/documented, and missing logs.

- One category of attacks specifically targets software applications that are already installed and running on the device. These attacks look for vulnerabilities in the application or manipulate the application in order to compromise it. A buffer overflow attack occurs when a process attempts to store data in RAM beyond the boundaries of a fixed-length storage buffer. This extra data overflows into the adjacent memory locations. Another vulnerability is likewise based on poor programming practices, specifically when an application does not properly check for exceptions that may occur when the program is running. Software that does not correctly "trap" an error condition could provide an attacker with underlying access to the system. A race condition in software occurs when two concurrent threads of execution access a shared resource simultaneously, resulting in unintended consequences.

- A common type of attack is an application attack directed at programs running on Internet web servers, known as web-based attacks. Web-based attacks frequently result in directory traversal. In a cross-site scripting (XSS) attack, a website that accepts user input without validating it and uses that input in a response can be exploited. An attack called SQL injection (SQLi) inserts statements to manipulate a database server. Some attacks generate a request that has been fabricated or forged. A cross-site request forgery (CSRF) takes advantage of an authentication token that a website sends to a user's web browser. A server-side request forgery (SSRF) takes advantage of a trusting relationship between web servers. A replay attack copies data and then uses it for an attack.

- Various defenses can be used to secure endpoint devices. One of the first software protections was antivirus (AV) software. This software can examine a computer for file-based virus infections as well as monitor computer activity and scan new documents that might contain a virus. As a means of protection for cookies, a web browser can send a secure cookie, which is sent only to the server with an encrypted request. This prevents an unauthorized person from intercepting a cookie that is being transmitted between the browser and the web server. HTTP Response Headers tell the browser how to behave while communicating with the website, and different HTTP Response Headers can improve security.

- A host intrusion detection system (HIDS) is a software-based application that runs on an endpoint computer and can detect that an attack has occurred. A host intrusion prevention system (HIPS) monitors endpoint activity to immediately block a malicious attack by following specific rules. Activity that a HIPS watches for includes an event that attempts to control other programs, terminate programs, or install devices and drivers. Endpoint detection and response (EDR) tools have a similar functionality to HIDS of monitoring endpoint events and of HIPS of taking immediate action but are more robust than either HIDS or HIPS.

- One of the most important steps in securing an endpoint computer is patching, which is installing software security updates. Automated patch management tools are used to manage patches within the enterprise instead of relying on the vendor's online update service.

- Several protections at the OS level can provide enhanced protection. One of the primary OS security configurations involves disabling ports/protocols or closing unused ports and disabling unnecessary protocols. An application allow listing is approving in advance only specific applications to run on the OS so that any item not approved will not function. A sandbox is a container in which an application can be run so that it does not impact the underlying OS. Anything that occurs within the sandbox is not visible to other applications or the OS outside the sandbox.

Key Terms

account lockout	cross-site scripting	host intrusion prevention
antivirus (AV)	(XSS)	system (HIPS)
application allow listing	directory traversal	impossible travel
bloatware	disabling ports/protocols	indicator of attack (IoA)
blocked content	endpoint detection and	injection
buffer overflow attack	response (EDR)	keylogger
concurrent session usage	forgery	logic bomb

malware
memory injection
missing logs
out-of-cycle logging
patching
privilege escalation
published/documented
race condition
ransomware

replay
resource consumption
resource inaccessibility
rootkit
sandbox
secure cookie
spyware
SQL injection (SQLi)
target of evaluation (TOE)

time of check (TOC) to time of use
  (TOU)
Trojan
virus
web-based attacks
workstation
worm

Review Questions

1. What word is the currently accepted term that is used today to refer to network-connected hardware devices?

   a. Host
   b. Endpoint
   c. Device
   d. Client

2. Which of the following is NOT a feature of blocking ransomware?

   a. A message on the user's screen appears pretending to be from a reputable third party.
   b. It prevents a user from using their computer in a normal fashion.
   c. It can be defeated by a double power cycle.
   d. It is the earliest form of ransomware.

3. Cillian is explaining to an intern why ransomware is considered to be the most serious malware threat. Which of the follow reasons would Cillian NOT give?

   a. Once a device is infected with ransomware, it will never function normally.
   b. Launching a ransomware attack is relatively inexpensive and does not require a high degree of skill.
   c. Ransomware attacks occur with a very high frequency.
   d. Attacks from ransomware have a high impact on organizations.

4. Finn's team leader has just texted him that an employee, who violated company policy by bringing in a file on a USB flash drive, has just reported that their computer is infected with locking ransomware. Why would Finn consider this a serious situation?

   a. It sets a precedent by encouraging other employees to violate company policy.
   b. It can encrypt all files on any network that is connected to the employee's computer.

   c. The organization may be forced to pay up to $500 for the ransom.
   d. The employee would have to wait at least an hour before their computer could be restored.

5. What is the difference between a keylogger and spyware?

   a. A keylogger operates much faster than spyware.
   b. Spyware is illegal while a keylogger is not.
   c. Spyware typically secretly monitors users but unlike a keylogger makes no attempts to gather sensitive user keyboard input.
   d. Spyware can be installed using a hardware device while a keylogger cannot.

6. Which of the following is NOT a technology used by spyware?

   a. Tracking software
   b. System-modifying software
   c. Active tracking technologies
   d. Automatic download of software

7. Which of the following is NOT true about RATs?

   a. A RAT gives the threat agent unauthorized remote access to the victim's computer by using specially configured communication protocols.
   b. A RAT and a worm have the same basic function.
   c. A RAT allows the attacker to not only monitor what the user is doing but also can change computer settings, browse and copy files, and even use the computer to access other computers connected on the network.
   d. A RAT creates an opening into the victim's computer, allowing the threat actor unrestricted access.

8. Which of the following types of computer viruses is malicious computer code that becomes part of a file?

   a. File-based virus
   b. Jump virus
   c. Fileless virus
   d. RAM-Check virus

9. Which of the following is NOT a Microsoft Windows common LOLBin?

    a. DLR
    b. .NET Framework
    c. Macro
    d. PowerShell

10. Which of the following is sometimes called a "network virus" because it enters a computer to move through the network?

    a. Fileless virus
    b. Worm
    c. Trojan
    d. File-based virus

11. Which of these would NOT be considered the result of a logic bomb?

    a. Send an email to Rowan's inbox each Monday morning with the agenda of that week's department meeting.
    b. If the company's stock price drops below $50, then credit Oscar's retirement account with one additional year of retirement credit.
    c. Erase the hard drives of all the servers 90 days after Alfredo's name is removed from the list of current employees.
    d. Delete all human resource records regarding Augustine one month after he leaves the company.

12. Which of the following attacks is based on a website accepting user input without sanitizing it?

    a. RSS
    b. XSS
    c. iSQL
    d. SSXRS

13. Which of the following attacks is based on the principle that when a user is currently authenticated on a website and then loads another webpage, the new page inherits the identity and privileges of the first website?

    a. SSFR
    b. DLLS
    c. CSRF
    d. DRCR

14. Which of the following manipulates the trusting relationship between web servers?

    a. SSRF
    b. CSRF
    c. EXMAL
    d. SCSI

15. Which type of memory vulnerability attack manipulates the "return address" of the memory location of a software program?

    a. Pointer attack
    b. Stuffing attack
    c. Integer overwrite
    d. Buffer overflow attack

16. What race condition can result in a NULL pointer/object dereference?

    a. Conflict race condition
    b. Value-based race condition
    c. Thread race condition
    d. Time of check (TOC) to time of use (TOU)

17. Which of the following would NOT be considered an IoA?

    a. Resource manipulation
    b. Out-of-cycle logging
    c. Account lockout
    d. Blocked content

18. Nollaig is reviewing the steps that an attacker took when they compromised a web server and accessed confidential files. What type of attack was this?

    a. Directory traversal
    b. Account overflow
    c. Race condition
    d. TOE

19. Which of the following is NOT correct about a secure cookie?

    a. It is a means of protection of a web browser.
    b. A secure cookie is only sent to the server with an encrypted request.
    c. It uses the HTTPS protocol.
    d. It prevents an unauthorized person from intercepting a cookie that is being transmitted.

20. Which statement regarding a keylogger is NOT true?

    a. Software keyloggers can be designed to send captured information automatically back to the attacker through the Internet.
    b. Hardware keyloggers are installed between the keyboard connector and computer keyboard USB port.
    c. Software keyloggers are generally easy to detect.
    d. Keyloggers can be used to capture passwords, credit card numbers, or personal information.

Hands-On Projects

Project 5-1: Downloading and Running Microsoft Safety Scanner

Estimated Time: 20 minutes
Objective: Scan a computer for malware.
Description: Microsoft offers a free tool that can scan a computer for malware and then remove it. In this project, you download and run Microsoft Safety Scanner.

1. Open your web browser and enter the URL **docs.microsoft.com/en-us/microsoft-365/security/intelligence/safety-scanner-download**. (If you are not able to access the site through the web address, use a search engine to search for "Microsoft Safety Scanner Download.")
2. Read the information on this webpage about the scanner.
3. Click the link **Download Microsoft Safety Scanner (64-bit)**.
4. After the MSERT.exe file downloads, open the file by double-clicking it.

> **Caution** !
>
> Note where you saved this download. Microsoft Safety Scanner is a portable executable and will not appear in the Windows Start menu or as an icon on the desktop.

5. Answer **Yes** if asked **Do you want to allow this app to make changes to your device?**
6. When the End user license agreement appears, click in the box **Accept all terms of the preceding license agreement** and click **Next**.
7. When the **Welcome to the Microsoft Safety Scanner** window appears, click **Next**.
8. When the **Scan type** window appears, if necessary, click **Quick scan**. Click **Next**. Microsoft Safety Scanner performs a limited scan of the computer. This scan may take up to five minutes to complete depending on the computer's configuration.
9. Review the **Scan results** window that appears when the scan is completed. If any suspicious files or malware are detected, you may be asked to conduct a full scan.
10. How easy was this scanner to use? Is this something that you would recommend to a friend? Why or why not?

> **Note** 24
>
> Microsoft Safety Scanner can be downloaded and executed at any time. It only scans when manually launched by a user. A downloaded version is available for use up to 10 days after being downloaded; after this it expires. It is recommended that users always download the latest version of this tool before each scan.

11. Click **Finish**.
12. Close all windows.

Project 5-2: Configuring Microsoft Windows Security—Part 1

Estimated Time: 25 minutes
Objective: Explore Microsoft Windows security configurations.
Description: It is important that security settings be properly configured on a computer to protect it. In this project, you examine several security settings on a Microsoft Windows 11 computer using the Windows interface.

> **Caution** !
>
> This project shows how to configure Windows security for a personal computer. If this computer is part of a computer lab or office, these settings should not be changed without the proper permissions.

1. Click **Start** and then click **Settings**.
2. Click **Privacy & security**.
3. Click **Windows Security**.
4. Note the Protection areas and if any actions are necessary.
5. Click **Open Windows Security**.
6. Click **Virus & threat protection**. Note that a Quick scan of the computer can also be performed from this window.
7. Under **Virus & threat protection settings**, click **Manage settings**.
8. Be sure that all of the options are set to On.
9. Click the **Back** button to return to the **Virus & threat protection** screen.
10. Under **Virus & threat protection updates**, click **Protection updates**.
11. Click **Check for updates** to be sure that the latest updates have been downloaded and applied.
12. Minimize the **Virus & threat protection** window.
13. Click **Windows Update** to display the screen for managing patches.
14. If any updates need to be installed, click **Install now**.
15. Under **More options**, view the **Pause updates** pull-down menu to pause downloading updates. How many options are available to pause? Why might someone pause these updates? Set your time to pause to the minimum setting.
16. Click the **right arrow** next to **Update history**.
17. View the updates that have already been installed. How many are there? What are the dates for these updates? How frequently have they occurred?
18. Scroll down to **Definition Updates**. These are the virus signature updates for the native Microsoft Defender Antivirus software.
19. Click the **Virus & Threat Protection** icon to maximize it.
20. Under **Ransomware protection**, click **Manage ransomware protection.**
21. Microsoft Windows Defender offers built-in protection against ransomware. This is called *Controlled folder access*. Turn on **Controlled folder access** and, if necessary, click **Yes**.
22. Click **Protected folders** and, if necessary, click **Yes** to see the folders that are now protected.
23. How valuable is Controlled folder access? How easy is it to use for protection against ransomware?
24. Close all windows.

Project 5-3: Configuring Microsoft Windows Security—Part 2

Estimated Time: 25 minutes
Objective: Use ConfigureDefender.
Description: As seen from the prior project, Windows security settings are found across several different screens. This can make it easy to overlook important settings and time-consuming to fine-tune the settings, especially when configuring the Microsoft Defender virus and threat protection product. A third-party tool called ConfigureDefender provides an easier interface. In this project, you download and use the ConfigureDefender product.

Note 25

ConfigureDefender is not installed on the computer but runs as a stand-alone application.

1. Open your web browser and enter the URL **github.com/AndyFul/ConfigureDefender**. (If you are no longer able to access the program through the URL, use a search engine and search for "ConfigureDefender.")
2. Click **ConfigureDefender.exe**.
3. Click **Download**.
4. Open the file after the download has completed.
5. Answer **Yes** if asked **Do you want to allow this app to make changes to your device?**
6. The ConfigureDefender app now launches, as shown in Figure 5-15.

Figure 5-15   ConfigureDefender

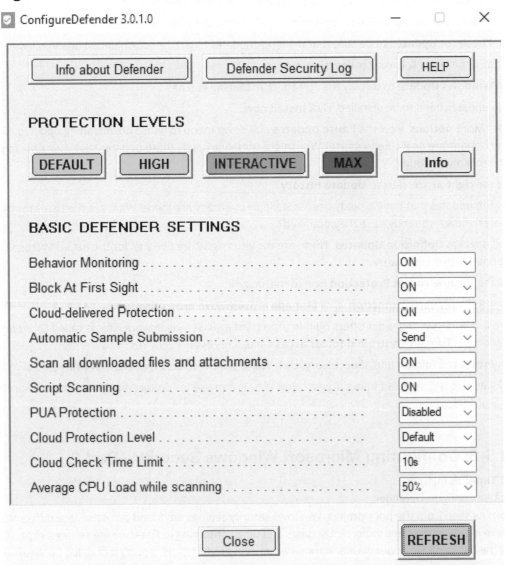

7. Scroll down through the settings. Were you aware that there were so many different options for Windows Defender?

8. Click the **Info** button to see the different protection levels. Close this window when finished reading.

9. Click the **HIGH** button and then close the pop-up box.

10. Scroll down through the settings. How much stronger are they than the Default settings?

11. Click the **MAX** button and then close the pop-up box.

12. Scroll down through the settings. How much stronger are they?

13. Finally, click either the **DEFAULT** or **HIGH** button to set your computer at the security level that you choose, or click **DEFAULT** to return to the basic security level.

14. How easy is ConfigureDefender to use? Would you recommend it to others?

15. Close all windows.

Project 5-4: Analyzing Files and URLs for File-Based Viruses Using VirusTotal—Part 1

Estimated Time: 30 minutes
Objective: Explore how to use VirusTotal.
Description: VirusTotal is a free online service that analyzes files and URLs to identify potential malware. VirusTotal combines 70 antivirus scanners and URL/domain blacklisting services along with other tools to identify malware. A wide range of files can be submitted to VirusTotal for examination, such as user data files and documents, executable programs, PDFs, and images. One of the uses of VirusTotal is to provide a "second opinion" on a file or URL that may have been flagged as suspicious by other scanning software. In this project, you use VirusTotal to scan a file and a URL.

1. First view several viruses from 20 years ago and observe their benign but annoying impact. Open your web browser and enter the URL **archive.org/details/malwaremuseum&tab=collection**. (If you are no longer able to access the site through the web address, use a search engine and search for "Malware Museum.")

2. All of the viruses have been rendered ineffective and will not harm a computer. Click several of the viruses and notice what they do.

3. When finished, close your web browser.

4. Use Microsoft Word to create a document that contains the above paragraph description about VirusTotal. Save the document as **VirusTotal.docx**.

5. Exit Word.

6. Open your web browser and enter the URL **www.virustotal.com**. (If you are no longer able to access the site through the web address, use a search engine and search for "Virus Total.")

7. If necessary, click the **FILE** tab.

8. Click **Choose file**.

9. Navigate to the location of **VirusTotal.docx** and click **Open**.

10. Click **Confirm upload**.

11. Wait until the upload and analysis is completed.

12. Scroll through the list of antivirus (AV) vendors that have been polled regarding this file. A green checkmark means no malware was detected.

13. Click the **DETAILS** tab and read through the analysis.

14. Use your browser's Back button to return to the VirusTotal home page.

15. Now you will analyze a website. Click **URL**.

16. Enter the URL of your school, place of employment, or another site with which you are familiar.

17. Wait until the analysis is completed.

18. Click the **DETAILS** tab and read through the analysis.

19. Click Scroll through the list of vendor analysis. Do any of these sites indicate **Unrated site** or **Malware site**?

20. How could VirusTotal be useful to users? How could it be useful to security researchers? Could it also be used by attackers to test their own malware before distributing it to ensure that it does not trigger an AV alert? What should be the protections against this?

21. Close all windows.

Project 5-5: Analyzing Virus Files Using VirusTotal—Part 2

Estimated Time: 20 minutes

Objective: Observe how VirusTotal identifies a virus.

Description: What happens when VirusTotal detects a file-based virus? In this project, you download a file that has a "signature" of a file-based virus into a sandbox and then upload it to VirusTotal.

Note 26

None of the actions in this project will harm the underlying computer.

1. Open your web browser.

2. Enter the URL **www.eicar.org/download-anti-malware-testfile**. (If you are no longer able to access the site through the web address, use a search engine and search for "Eicar Anti Malware.")

3. Scroll down to **Download area using the secure, SSL enabled protocol HTTPS**.

4. Click **eicar.com** to start the download.

5. Your anti-malware software on your personal computer should immediately flag this file as malicious and not allow you to download it. Because it cannot (and should not) be downloaded on your regular computer, you will instead want to use the Windows Sandbox you created in Module 1.

6. If you are using the Windows Sandbox, click **Start**, scroll down to Windows Sandbox, and then click **Windows Sandbox**.

7. First you will turn off the security protections in Windows Sandbox. Click **Start** and then **Windows Security**.

8. Click the three horizontal lines at the left of the screen to display the menu options.

9. Click **App & browser control**.

10. For each of the categories, click the **Off** button to turn off security. Remember this will only impact the security within the Windows Sandbox and will have no impact on the underlying computer.

11. Open Internet Explorer in the Windows Sandbox.

Note 27

Be sure to use the web browser in the Windows Sandbox and not the web browser in the underlying computer.

12. Enter the URL **www.eicar.org/download-anti-malware-testfile**.

13. Scroll down to **Download area using the secure, SSL enabled protocol HTTPS**.

14. Click **eicar.com** to start the download.

15. The anti-malware software within Windows Sandbox will now allow the file to be downloaded into the Sandbox.

16. Open another tab on the Internet Explorer web browser in Windows Sandbox and enter the URL **www.virustotal.com**. (If you are no longer able to access the site through the web address, use a search engine and search for "Virus Total.")

17. If necessary, click the **FILE** tab.

18. Click **Choose file**.

19. Navigate to the location of **Eicar.com** and click **Open**.

20. Click **Confirm upload**.

21. Wait until the upload and analysis is completed.

22. Scroll through the list of AV vendors that have been polled regarding this file. A green checkmark means no malware was detected.

23. Click the **DETAILS** tab and read through the analysis.

24. Close the Windows Sandbox. This will delete the Eicar.com file and reset the security settings to normal.

Project 5-6: Exploring Ransomware Sites

Estimated Time: 25 minutes
Objective: Research different ransomware sites.
Description: A variety of sites provide information about ransomware along with tools for counteracting some types of infection. In this project, you explore different ransomware sites.

1. Open your web browser and enter the URL **www.nomoreransom.org**. (If you are not able to access this site, open a search engine and search for "Nomoreransom.org.")

2. Click the **NO** button.

3. Read through the Prevention Advice. Do you think it is helpful?

4. Click **Crypto Sheriff**. How could this be useful to a user who has suffered a ransomware infection?

5. Click **Ransomware: Q&A**. Read through the information. Which statements would you agree with? Which statements would you disagree with?

6. Click **Decryption Tools**. This contains a list of different tools that may help restore a computer that has been infected by a specific type of ransomware.

7. Click one of the tools and then click **Download** to download it. Note that these tools change frequently based on the latest types of ransomware that are circulating.

8. Run the program to understand how these decryption tools function. Note that you will not be able to complete the process because there are no encrypted files on the computer. Close the program.

9. Now visit another site that provides ransomware information and tools. Open your web browser and enter the URL **id-ransomware.malwarehunterteam.com**.

10. What features does this site provide?

11. How could these sites be useful?

12. Close all windows.

Project 5-7: Using a Software Keylogger

Estimated Time: 30 minutes
Objective: Explore the features of a keylogger.
Description: A keylogger program captures everything that a user enters on a computer keyboard. In this project, you download and use a software keylogger.

Caution ❗

The purpose of this activity is to provide information regarding how these programs function in order that adequate defenses can be designed and implemented. These programs should never be used in a malicious fashion against another user.

1. Open your web browser and enter the URL **refog.com**. (If you are no longer able to access the program through the URL, use a search engine and search for "Refog Keylogger.")
2. Click **Features** to see the features of the product.
3. Click **Home**.
4. Click **Download**.
5. Click **Create an account** and enter the requested information.
6. Click **Download**.
7. When the file finishes downloading, run the installation program. Note that you may have to enter the password on the previous page to extract the files.
8. When prompted with **I'm going to use this software to monitor:** select **My own computer**.
9. Click **Hide program icon from Windows tray**. Click **Next**.
10. Click **I Agree**.
11. Click **Select All** and then **Next**.
12. Create a login and password for the online dashboard. Click **Activate**.
13. You will receive a message that the subscription has expired. Click **Yes** to install in offline mode.
14. Click **Install**.
15. Click **Restart Now**.
16. After the computer has restarted, use the keystroke combination **Ctrl+Alt+Shift+K** to launch Refog Keylogger.
17. Click **Tools** and then click **Settings**.
18. Note the default settings regarding what is captured.
19. Click **Back to log**.
20. Minimize Refog Keylogger.
21. Use your computer normally by opening a web browser to surf to a website. Open Microsoft Word and type several sentences. Open and close several programs on the computer.
22. Maximize Keylogger and note the information that was captured.
23. In the left pane, click through the different items that were captured.
24. Under Settings, click **Websites Visited**.
25. Under Websites Visited, click **Make website screenshots**.
26. Click **Apply**.
27. Open a web browser and surf to multiple websites.
28. Under Users, click **Websites visited**. Note the screen captures of the different sites.
29. What type of information would a software keylogger provide to a threat actor? How could it be used against the victim?
30. Click **File** and then **Exit** to close Keylogger.
31. You may uninstall Keylogger if you wish.
32. Close all windows.

Case Projects

Case Project 5-1: #TrendingCyber

Estimated Time: 15 minutes

Objective: Summarize your thoughts on the #TrendingCyber opener.

Description: Read again the opening #TrendingCyber in this module. Was this an attempt to circumvent a required disclosure of a breach? Or was it a valid means for Uber to find out about the vulnerability and patch it through its bug bounty program? Does the motivation of the threat actors define if their action is an attack or a disclosure of a vulnerability? Or does motivation matter here? If you were in Joseph's position, what would you have done? Why? Write a one-paragraph summary of your thoughts.

Case Project 5-2: Biological and File-Based Viruses

Estimated Time: 25 minutes

Objective: Identify similarities between biological and file-based viruses.

Description: The word *virus* comes from Latin, meaning a slimy liquid, poison, or poisonous secretion. In late Middle English, the term referred to the venom of a snake. The word later evolved from the discharge to the substances within the body that caused the infectious diseases producing the discharge. In 1799, Edward Jenner published his discovery that the "cow-pox virus" could actually be used as a vaccine against smallpox. As biological science continued to advance, the word *virus* became even more specific when referring to tiny infectious agents—even smaller than bacteria—that replicate in living cells. This new field of virology exploded in the 1930s when electronic microscopes allowed scientists to see viruses for the first time. Since then, scientists have continued to identify and name new biological viruses. Combating viruses by developing vaccines has many parallels to how malicious file-based viruses are identified and removed from a computer. Using the Internet, research these two types of viruses and find the similarities between combating biological and computer viruses. Write a one- to two-paragraph summary of your research.

Case Project 5-3: Living-Off-the-Land Binaries (LOLBins)

Estimated Time: 25 minutes

Objective: Research living-off-the-land binaries.

Description: Fileless viruses take advantage of native services and processes that are part of the OS to avoid detection and carry out their attacks. These native services used in a fileless virus are called living-off-the-land binaries (LOLBins). Use the Internet to research fileless viruses and LOLBins. When did fileless viruses first appear? How do they compare with file-based viruses? What are the defenses against fileless viruses? Write a one-page paper on your research.

Case Project 5-4: Infamous Logic Bombs

Estimated Time: 30 minutes

Objective: Research logic bombs.

Description: Research the Internet for examples of logic bombs. Select four logic bombs and write a report about them. Who was responsible? When did the bombs go off? What was the damage? What was the penalty for the person responsible? Did the organization make any changes after the attack? How can they be prevented?

Case Project 5-5: Indicators of Compromise (IoCs)

Estimated Time: 30 minutes.

Objective: Research indicators of compromise.

Description: There are different "tell-tale" signs regarding an attack. An indicator of attack (IoA) is a sign an attack is currently underway. This is different from an IoC, which is evidence that an attack has already taken place. Research IoCs and identify at least six. Create a table similar to Table 5-2 that lists the IoC and a brief description of it.

Case Project 5-6: External Software Component Attacks

Estimated Time: 40 minutes

Objective: Research attacks that target external software components.

Description: In addition to attacking software directly, threat actors also target external software components. One component is an application program interface (API), which is a link provided by an OS, web browser, or other platform that allows a developer access to resources at a high level. An example of an API is when a user visits a website and the message "This site wants to know your location" appears. The website is attempting to use the geolocation API available in the web browser. APIs relieve the developer from the need to write code for specific hardware and software. Because APIs provide direct access to data and an entry point to an application's functions, they are attractive targets for attackers looking for vulnerabilities in the API in an API attack. Another type of attack that targets external software components is a device driver attack. A device driver is software that controls and operates an external hardware device that is connected to a computer. Device drivers are specific to both the OS and the hardware device. Threat actors may attempt to alter a device driver for use in an attack (called device driver manipulation). An attacker may use shimming, or transparently adding a small coding library that intercepts calls made by the device and changes the parameters passed between the device and the device driver. This refactoring (changing the design of existing code) can be difficult to detect yet serves as a real threat. Use the Internet to research API and device driver attacks. How can threat actors manipulate these components? How common are these attacks? What are the defenses against them? Write a one-page paper on your research.

Case Project 5-7: Paying or Not Paying a Ransom

Estimated Time: 30 minutes

Objective: Research paying a ransom.

Description: There is much debate over whether or not a business should pay a ransom after encountering a ransomware attack. These reasons are given for not paying a ransom:

- If all victims stopped making ransomware payments, then the attacks would diminish.
- If attackers release stolen data, it can still damage the corporate brand.
- It funds more ransomware attacks.
- It will not stop the ransomware attacker from returning again later.
- Paying does not guarantee that the right encryption keys will be provided (although they usually are).
- Using cryptocurrency to pay the ransom can be difficult and sometimes risky.

  However, businesses counter with reasons a ransom should be paid:

- It avoids regulatory fines for losing important data.
- No highly confidential information is lost.
- Paying the ransom is usually the least costly option.
- The public does not have to be told about it.
- Everything can get back to normal quickly.
- It is often covered by cyber insurance.

What do you think? Research the pros and cons of paying a ransom. Should businesses be prohibited by law from paying a ransom? What would be the impact if the business was not able to restore its locked data? Should it be left as a business decision whether or not to pay? Take a position on one side of this issue and write a one-page document supporting your position.

Case Project 5-8: Stopping Ransomware

Estimated Time: 30 minutes

Objective: Research how to stop ransomware.

Description: A proposal to stop ransomware is to regulate and even shut down the cryptocurrency exchanges that accept and process the ransomware payments. Despite the fact that digital currencies are not anonymous, there is a growing cry for them to be regulated. The Ransomware Task Force, made up of more than 60 experts from government, industry, education, and the health and nonprofit sectors, released a report (securityandtechnology.org /ransomwaretaskforce/report/) that calls for sweeping recommendations to the public and private sectors on combatting ransomware. One of its recommendations is that the cryptocurrency sector that enables ransomware crime should be more closely regulated: "Governments should require cryptocurrency exchanges, crypto kiosks, and over-the-counter (OTC) trading 'desks' to comply with existing laws, including Know Your Customer (KYC), Anti-Money Laundering (AML), and Combatting Financing of Terrorism (CFT) laws." Would regulating cryptocurrency stop ransomware? Or would threat actors turn to another means of processing ransoms? If this is not the solution, how can ransomware be ended? Research how to stop ransomware and write a one-page paper on your findings.

Case Project 5-9: Bay Point Ridge Security

Estimated Time: 45 minutes
Objective: Research application attacks.
Description: Bay Point Ridge Security (BPRS) is a managed service provider (MSP) that manages networks, computers, cloud resources, and information security for small-to-medium enterprises (SMEs) in the region. BPRS provides internships to students who are in their final year of the security degree program at the local college and has recently hired you.

BPRS is preparing a presentation to the monthly meeting of IT professionals and has asked you to do research on application attacks.

1. Create a PowerPoint presentation on XSS, SQLi, CSRF and SSRF. Compare and contrast each attack. Your presentation should be at least 10 to 12 slides in length.

2. As a follow-up to your presentation, you have been asked to write a one-page report on race conditions. Use the Internet to research race conditions and how they can best be addressed.

Two Rights & A Wrong: Answers

Malware Attacks

1. Blocking ransomware will encrypt one or more files with a key until a ransom is paid.
2. The two types of viruses are a file-based virus and a fileless virus.
3. A keylogger can be a software program or a small hardware device.

Answer: The wrong statement is #1.
Explanation: Locking ransomware will encrypt one or more files with a key until a ransom is paid.

Application Vulnerabilities and Attacks

1. Privilege escalation can be either horizontal or vertical.
2. A buffer overflow attack occurs when a process attempts to store data in RAM beyond the boundaries of a fixed-length storage buffer.
3. An attacker who can access the root directory has conducted a directory traversal attack.

Answer: The wrong statement is #3.
Explanation: An attacker who can access other directories besides the root directory has conducted a directory traversal attack.

Securing Endpoint Devices

1. Cookies are a work-around of the stateless protocol HTTP.
2. A HIDS monitors endpoint activity to immediately block a malicious attack by following specific rules.
3. Dynamic analysis uses heuristic monitoring.

Answer: The wrong statement is #2.
Explanation: A HIPS monitors endpoint activity to immediately block a malicious attack by following specific rules.

References

1. "Ransomware: The true cost to business 2022," *Cyberreason*, accessed Feb. 21, 2023, https://www.cybereason.com/ransomware-the-true-cost-to-business-2022.

2. Kerner, Sean Michael, "Ransomware trends, statistics and facts in 2023," *TechTarget*, Jan. 30, 2023, accessed Feb. 5, 2023, https://www.techtarget.com/searchsecurity/feature /Ransomware-trends-statistics-and-facts.

3. "Ransomware: The true cost to business 2022," *Cyberreason*, accessed Feb. 21, 2023, https://www.cybereason.com/ransomware-the-true-cost-to-business-2022.

4. "High-impact ransomware attacks threaten U.S. businesses and organizations," Public Service Announcement, Federal Bureau of Investigation, Oct 2, 2019, accessed Feb. 21, 2023, https://www.ic3.gov /media/2019/191002.aspx.

5. Haber, Morey, "Privilege escalation attack and defense explained," *BeyondTrust*, Mar. 2, 2021, retrieved Feb. 4, 2023, https://www.beyondtrust.com/blog/entry/privilege-escalation-attack-defense-explained.

6. Horowitz, Michael, "Defending a network from the NSA," *Computerworld*, Feb. 1, 2016, accessed Feb. 21, 2023, http://www.computerworld.com/article/3028025/security/defending-a-network-from-the-nsa.html.

Module 6

Mobile and Embedded Device Security

Module Objectives

After completing this module, you should be able to do the following:

1 List and compare the different types of mobile devices and their risks

2 Explain the ways to secure a mobile device

3 Describe the vulnerabilities and security considerations of embedded and specialized devices

4 Explain how application security can provide protections

#TrendingCyber

"One size fits all" may apply to free T-shirts, but not to small device cryptography. Recently the winner of a contest for a new encryption standard for small devices was announced. This standard will soon start to be implemented across a wide range of devices.

Encryption and decryption are resource-intensive tasks. These tasks require significant processing and storage capacities—which is what small devices and sensors lack. Due to their diminutive size and limited power (they are usually powered by tiny, embedded batteries), tiny sensors and actuators such as implanted medical devices, stress detectors inside roads and bridges, and keyless entry fobs for vehicles cannot use the same cryptographic software that a standard computer uses. These devices require their own specialized cryptography to protect information gathered and transmitted by them. In other words, lightweight electronics require lightweight cryptographic algorithms.

In 2018, the National Institute of Standards and Technology (NIST) launched a competitive program to crown a new cryptography standard for tiny devices. NIST began by working with a wide range of industries and other organizations to understand the needs of these devices. Then a proposal was published that contained several criteria that had to be met by those making a submission. The specialized cryptography first and foremost had to provide strong encryption for lightweight electronics. But NIST wanted other factors, namely performance and flexibility in terms of speed, size, and energy consumption.

NIST invited the world's cryptography community to submit products to be evaluated. A total of 57 submissions were initially received. NIST next employed a multiround public review process in which cryptographers examined and attempted to find weaknesses in each of the candidates. Eventually, 10 finalists were identified, and they received even more scrutiny.

Finally, in early 2023, the winner was announced: Ascon. This cryptographic algorithm was developed in 2014 by a team of cryptographers from Graz University of Technology (Austria), Radboud University (The Netherlands), Infineon Technologies (Germany), and Lamarr Security Research (Austria). Ascon had the additional advantage of being selected in 2019 as the primary choice for lightweight authenticated encryption in a separate competition by a group of international cryptologic researchers known as CAESAR (Competition for Authenticated Encryption: Security, Applicability, and Robustness). Because Ascon had withstood several years of intense examination by cryptographers, it became a leading candidate and was eventually chosen.

Like many cryptographic solutions today, Ascon is a "family" of seven different technologies. As a family, these variants provide a range of functionality that can give designers different options for different tasks. Two of these tasks are among the most important in lightweight cryptography. The first is authenticated encryption with associated data (AEAD). AEAD protects the confidentiality of a message, but it also allows extra information to be included without being encrypted. This extra information may include the header of a message or a device's IP address. AEAD can be used in applications such as vehicle-to-vehicle communications or in identification tags that track packages in warehouses. The second task is hashing. Hashing, which creates a digital fingerprint of a message, can be used in lightweight cryptography to determine whether a software update is appropriate or has downloaded correctly.

Ascon is not intended to replace standard cryptography on devices that do not have the resource constraints of small devices. And Ascon is also not primarily designed to be used for post-quantum encryption. Although one of the Ascon variants was found to offer a measure of resistance to the attacks that might come from a powerful quantum computer, that was not a criterion being evaluated.

Because Ascon includes multiple variants, the final NIST standards may not include all of them. The NIST team is working with Ascon's designers and the cryptography community to finalize the details. The standard is expected to be formally released in late 2023 and will then soon start to be incorporated into a wide range of small devices.

Imagine one evening you are driving home listening to the satellite radio in your car. Suddenly a text message comes to your smartphone and is immediately transferred to your car's infotainment system. The message is displayed on a console and converted into audio that is played to you. A friend says that they are unexpectedly detained and asks if you could drive to their new house to let the dog out. The text contains a link to a map to the house, which your car's global positioning system (GPS) then displays and begins to give you turn-by-turn instructions. After a short distance, the GPS alerts you to an accident ahead that is causing a backup and reroutes you.

When you arrive at the house, your car parallel-parks itself on the street. You get out of your car, and it automatically locks as it senses you are walking away. As you walk toward the front porch, a doorbell with a security camera turns on and records your visit. Your smartwatch suddenly vibrates and a text message with a code appears; your friend has remotely configured the wireless door lock to let you into the house after you enter this code. When you walk into the house, the lights automatically turn on, music begins to play through the smart speakers, and the thermostat, which senses you have entered, adjusts the temperature. Before you let the dog out the back door, you first check to be sure that the dog's collar has its remote wireless tracker attached just in case the dog gets under the fence.

"Interesting science fiction" is likely how someone living just 10 short years ago would have reacted to this scenario. But today it's how we live. And it is all based on a dizzying array of sensors, miniature devices, and mobile technologies that seem to multiply overnight. Users have flocked to these devices and made them part of their everyday lives.

However, so too have attackers been drawn to these devices. Threat actors have targeted these devices for their valuable personal data that reveals patterns of users' lives, such as when they are away from home. Attackers also manipulate these devices, such as turning on an indoor security camera to spy on occupants without their knowledge. Compromising these devices is not difficult because the security on them is usually scant or even nonexistent.

In this module on device security, you explore mobile, embedded, and specialized device security. You begin by looking at securing mobile devices. Next, you explore embedded systems and Internet of Things devices. Finally, you examine how application software that runs on these and other devices can be securely designed and coded.

Securing Mobile Devices

Certification

2.3 Explain various types of vulnerabilities.

4.1 Given a scenario, apply common security techniques to computing resources.

There are different types of mobile devices, and they have security risks associated with them. Yet a variety of techniques and technologies can be applied for protecting them.

Introduction to Mobile Devices

There are a variety of mobile devices, which in turn may be connected through different technologies. There are also different ways by which mobile devices are deployed in the enterprise.

Types of Mobile Devices

There are several types of mobile devices. These include tablets, smartphones, wearables, and portable computers.

Tablets   **Tablets** are portable computing devices first introduced in 2010. Designed for user convenience, tablets are thinner, lighter, easier to carry, and more intuitive to use than other types of computers. Tablets are often classified by their screen size. The two most common categories of tablet screen sizes are 5–8.5 inches (12.7–21.5 cm) and 8.5–10 inches (21.5–25.4 cm). The weight of tablets is generally less than 1.5 pounds (0.68 kg), and they are less than 1/2 inch (1.2 cm) thick. Figure 6-1 shows a typical tablet device.

Figure 6-1   Tablet device

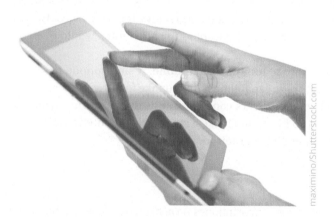

maximino/Shutterstock.com

Note 1

Tablets have a sensor called an accelerometer that senses vibrations and movements. It can determine the orientation of the device so that the screen image is always displayed upright.

Tablets generally lack a built-in keyboard or mouse. Instead, they rely on a touch screen that is manipulated with touch gestures for user input. Table 6-1 lists the touch gestures for an Apple tablet. Some tablets also support a separate pencil that can be used for drawing, note-taking, and document markup.

Table 6-1 Apple touch gestures

Gesture name	Action	Usage
Tap	Lightly striking the screen.	Make a selection.
Double tap	Two quick taps in succession.	Zoom in or out of content or an image.
Flick	Place finger on the screen and quickly "swipe" in the desired direction.	Scroll or pan quickly.
Drag	Place finger on the screen and move it in the desired direction.	Scroll or move the viewing area.
Pinch open	Place thumb and finger close together on the screen and move them apart.	Zoom in.
Pinch close	Place thumb and finger a short distance apart on the screen and move them toward each other.	Zoom out.
Touch and hold	Touch the screen until the action occurs.	Display an information bubble or magnify content.
Two-finger scroll	Move two fingers together in the same direction.	Scroll content in an element with overflow capability.

Although early tablets were primarily display devices with limited computing power, today tablets are powerful enough to be alternatives to standard laptop computers, with large storage capacities and powerful processors that can run a variety of third-party apps. The most popular operating systems (OSs) for tablets are Apple iPadOS, Google Android, and Microsoft Windows.

Smartphones   The earliest cellular telephones only had the ability to make phone calls. Soon additional features were added, so that these devices were called "feature phones." The features added included the integration of a camera, an MP3 music player, or the ability to send and receive text messages. However, many feature phones incorporated only a single feature, so that a user who wanted to take photos would need to purchase a specific model that had a camera.

The feature phone has given way to today's **smartphone**. A smartphone has a touchscreen display, one or more powerful cameras, and external storage capabilities. And, unlike feature phones, a smartphone has an OS, which gives it a much broader range of functionality. Users can install apps that perform a wide variety of functions for productivity, social networking, music, and so forth, much like a standard computer. Smartphones also can access the Internet, often through different means depending on their location.

> **Note 2**
>
> Due to their power and flexibility, today's smartphones have been described as "handheld personal computers that also happen to make phone calls."

Wearables   Another class of mobile technology consists of devices that can be worn by the user instead of carried. Known as **wearables**, these devices can provide even greater flexibility and mobility.

The most popular wearable technology is a smartwatch. Early smartwatches were just a means to receive smartphone notifications on the user's wrist. However, today wearables have significantly evolved to a much higher-level device. A modern smartwatch can still receive notifications of a phone call or text message, but they can also be used to manage media playback on a smartphone, to serve as a contactless payment system, and even to call emergency services if the watch detects the user has fallen. Figure 6-2 displays a smartwatch.

Another popular type of wearable is a fitness tracker. Originally designed to monitor and record physical activity, such as counting steps, they likewise have evolved into sophisticated health-monitoring devices. Modern fitness

Figure 6-2   Smartwatch

Alexey Boldin/Shutterstock.com

trackers can provide continual heart rate monitoring, GPS tracking, oxygen consumption, repetition counting (for weight training), and sleep monitoring.

Many fitness trackers and smartwatches use two different colors of LED lights on the underside of the device to take readings on the human body and then measure the light absorption with photodiodes. Green LED lights are used when the wearer is exercising (such as running or bicycle riding) by flashing a green light onto the wrist hundreds of times per second. Human blood absorbs green light so the heart rate can be determined by measuring the changes in green light absorption (a method called photoplethysmography or PPG). Red LED lights are used when the wearer is not exercising. Human blood reflects red light so about every 10 minutes the red LEDs flash to measure the resting heart rate. The reason for having two different-colored LEDs is due to accuracy and battery life. Green LEDs are more accurate, which is more important when assessing a rapid heart rate than a sedentary heart rate. But since green LEDs require more power, red LEDs are also used to save battery life.

Portable Computers   As a class, portable computers are devices that closely mirror the functionality of standard desktop computers. These portable computers have similar hardware (keyboard, hard drive, RAM, etc.) and run the same OS (Windows, Apple macOS, or Linux) and application software (Microsoft Office, web browsers, etc.) that are found on a general-purpose desktop computer. The primary difference is that portable computers are smaller, self-contained devices that can easily be transported from one location to another while operating on battery power.

A laptop computer is regarded as the earliest portable computer. A laptop is designed to replicate the abilities of a desktop computer with the same or only slightly less processing power yet is small enough to be used on a lap or small table. A notebook computer is a smaller version of a laptop computer and is considered a lightweight personal computer. Notebook computers typically weigh less than laptops and are small enough to fit easily inside a briefcase. A convertible or 2-in-1 computer can take on a variety of physical "poses" due to a flexible hinge: convertibles can be folded to form a laptop, tablet, stand, or tent. Figure 6-3 illustrates the different convertible computer poses.

> **Note 3**
>
> The first laptop computers were anything but portable. The Osborne 1, released in 1981, was called a "luggable computer" that weighed a whopping 24.5 pounds (11.1 kg). It also had no battery and only a 5-inch (13 cm) cathode-ray tube (CRT) screen.

Another type of computing device that resembles a laptop computer is a web-based computer. It contains a limited version of an OS and a web browser with an integrated media player. Web-based computers are Internet focused. Traditional software applications cannot be installed and there is limited user storage. Instead, the device accesses online web apps and saves user files on the web. The most common OSs for web-based computers are the Google Chrome OS and Microsoft Windows in S Mode.

Figure 6-3   Convertible poses

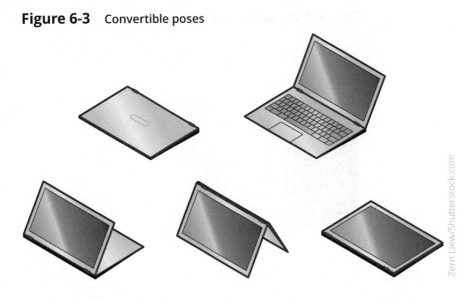

Zern Liew/Shutterstock.com

Mobile Device Connectivity Methods

Different connectivity methods are used to connect mobile devices to networks. These include:

- **Cellular.** Almost all mobile devices rely on a cellular network for connectivity. A cellular network is divided into smaller geographical areas of coverage (cells) that are hexagon shaped. At the center of each cell is a cell transmitter to which the mobile devices in that cell send and receive signals, and the transmitters in turn are connected to a mobile telecommunication switching office (MTSO). The MTSO controls all the transmitters in the cellular network and serves as the link between the cellular network and other networks. This is illustrated in Figure 6-4. The current cellular technology is 5G (fifth generation) that delivers higher speeds but has a smaller cell footprint.

Figure 6-4   Cellular network

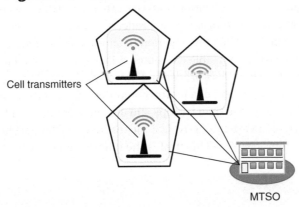

Cell transmitters

MTSO

- **Wi-Fi.** A wireless local area network (WLAN), commonly called **Wi-Fi**, is designed to replace or supplement a wired local area network (LAN). Devices such as tablets, laptop computers, and smartphones that are within range of a centrally located connection device can send and receive information at varying transmission speeds.
- **Bluetooth.** Bluetooth is the name given to a wireless technology that uses short-range radio frequency transmissions and provides rapid device pairings. Virtually all smartphones and portable computers, and an increasing number of standard desktop computers, have Bluetooth capabilities to connect to other devices.

- **USB connections.** Different types and sizes of Universal Serial Bus (USB) connectors on mobile devices can be used for data transfer between devices. The standard connection type on mobile devices is USB Type-C.

Note 4

The European Union (EU) has passed a regulation that by the end of 2024 all mobile phones, tablets, and cameras sold in the EU will have to be equipped with a USB Type-C charging port, and this will be extended to laptop computers in early 2026. The stated purpose is to reduce e-waste and to empower consumers to make more sustainable choices.

Enterprise Deployment Models

Due to the widespread use of mobile devices, it is not always feasible to require employees to carry company-owned smartphones along with their own personal cell phones. Many organizations have adopted an enterprise deployment model as it relates to mobile devices. These are listed in Table 6-2.

Table 6-2   Enterprise deployment models

Model name	Description	Employee actions	Business actions
Bring your own device (BYOD)	Allows users to use their own personal mobile devices for business purposes.	Employees have full responsibility for choosing and supporting the device.	This model is popular with smaller companies or those with a temporary staff.
Corporate owned, personally enabled (COPE)	Employees choose from a selection of company-approved devices.	Employees are supplied the device chosen and paid for by the company, but they can also use it for personal activities.	Company decides level of choice and freedom for employees.
Choose your own device (CYOD)	Employees choose from a limited selection of approved devices but pay the upfront cost of the device while the business owns the contract.	Employees are offered a suite of choices that the company has approved for security, reliability, and durability.	Company often provides a stipend to pay monthly fees to wireless carrier.
Corporate-owned	The device is purchased and owned by the enterprise.	Employees use the phone only for company-related business.	Enterprise is responsible for all aspects of the device.

There are several benefits of the BYOD, COPE, and CYOD models for the enterprise:

- **Management flexibility.** BYOD and CYOD ease the management burden by eliminating the need to select a wireless data carrier and manage plans for employees.
- **Less oversight.** Businesses do not need to monitor employee telecommunications usage for overages or extra charges.
- **Cost savings.** Because employees are responsible for their own mobile device purchases and wireless data plans (BYOD) or receive a small monthly stipend (CYOD), the company can save money.
- **Simplified IT infrastructure.** By using the existing cellular telephony network, companies do not have to support a remote data network for employees.
- **Reduced internal service.** BYOD, COPE, and CYOD reduce the strain on IT help desks because users will be primarily contacting their wireless data carrier for support.
- **Increased employee performance.** Employees are more likely to be productive while traveling or working away from the office if they are comfortable with their device.

In addition, users are eager to accept this flexibility. User benefits include:

- **Choice of device.** Users like the freedom of choosing the type of mobile device with BYOD, COPE, and CYOD instead of being forced to accept a corporate device that may not meet their individual needs (corporate-owned).
- **Choice of carrier.** Most users have identified a specific wireless data carrier they want to use and often resist being forced to use a carrier with whom they have experienced a poor past relationship.
- **Convenience.** Because almost all users already have their own device, the BYOD, COPE, and CYOD models provide the convenience of carrying only a single device.

Mobile Device Risks

Enterprises are increasingly relying on mobile devices, particularly as more employees are working from home or have a hybrid work setup between home and the office. Consider the following results from a recent survey[1]:

- Four out of every 10 employees work from home or on the road most of the time.
- Over 58 percent of organizations reported that they had more employees using mobile devices than one year prior.
- When asked how critical (on a 10-point scale) mobile devices were to the smooth operation of their organization, 91 percent answered seven or above (and 78 percent answered eight or higher).

However, the increasing reliance of businesses on mobile devices means that employees must have access to sensitive data (53 percent of organizations said that mobile devices have access to more sensitive data than one year ago). This has heightened the interest of threat actors toward mobile devices. Because employees now have access to much of the same data—customer lists, banking details, employees' personal data, billing information—through their mobile devices as they once had sitting in an office that had extensive security protections, it is not surprising that attacks are increasing on mobile devices. In the same survey, 45 percent of organizations admitted to suffering a compromise due to a mobile device, which is a compound annual growth rate of 14 percent over the last five years. About 73 percent described the impact of the attack as major, and over two out of every five organizations said that it had lasting repercussions.

There are several security risks associated with using mobile devices. These include mobile device vulnerabilities, connection vulnerabilities, and accessing untrusted content.

Mobile Device Vulnerabilities

There are several vulnerabilities inherent to mobile devices. Mobile device vulnerabilities include physical security, limited updates, location tracking, and unauthorized recording.

Physical Security   The greatest asset of a mobile device—its portability—is also one of its greatest vulnerabilities. Unlike desktop computers, mobile devices by their very nature are designed to be used in a wide variety of locations, both public (coffee shops, hotels, and conference centers) and private (employee homes and cars). Yet all these locations are outside of the enterprise's protected physical perimeter of walls, security guards, and locked doors. Mobile devices are routinely lost or stolen. On average, a laptop is stolen every 53 seconds, and 70 million smartphones are lost annually.[2]

Unless properly protected, any data on a stolen or lost device could be retrieved by a thief. Of greater concern is that the device itself can serve as an entry point into viewing corporate data or infiltrating the corporate data network.

Limited Updates   Security patches and updates for Apple iOS and Google Android, the two dominant mobile OSs, are distributed through **over-the-air (OTA) updates**. These updates include both modifying the device's firmware and updating the OS software.

Apple commits to providing OTA updates for its iPhones for at least four years after the OS is released. Apple iOS updates can be set to occur automatically or manually by the user, either through the device itself or by connecting it to a computer through which the update is downloaded.

However, OTA updates for Android OSs vary considerably. Mobile hardware devices developed and sold by Google receive Android OTA updates for three years after the device is first released. Other original equipment manufacturers (OEMs) are required to provide OTAs for at least two years. However, after two years, many OEMs are hesitant to distribute Google updates because it limits their ability to differentiate themselves from competitors if all versions of Android start to look the same through updates. Also, because OEMs want to sell as many devices as possible, they have no financial incentive to update mobile devices that users would then continue to use indefinitely.

Whereas users once regularly purchased new mobile devices about every two years, that is no longer the case. Due to the high cost of some mobile devices, more users are keeping their devices for longer periods of time. This can result in a mobile device being used that is no longer receiving OTA security updates and thus has become vulnerable.

Location Tracking   GPS is a satellite-based navigation system that provides information to a GPS receiver anywhere on (or near) Earth where there is an unobstructed line of sight to four or more GPS satellites. Mobile devices with GPS capabilities typically support geolocation, or the process of identifying the geographical location of the device.

> **Note 5**
>
> Geolocation is covered in Module 2.

Geolocation has several advantages. Location services are used extensively by social media, navigation systems, weather systems, and other mobile-aware applications. Geolocation can identify the location of a close friend or display the address of the nearest coffee shop. It can also be used to reduce bank card fraud. When a user makes a purchase at a specific store, the bank can immediately check the location of the user's authorized cell phone. If the cell phone and the bank card are in the same place, then that can be one item of several to validate the legitimacy of the purchase; however, if the cell phone is in Nashville and someone is trying to make a purchase in a store in Tampa, then the payment may be rejected.

> **Note 6**
>
> In 2021, a Mexican regulation took effect that requires financial institutions to collect and store customers' geolocation data when opening an account or conducting transactions on digital platforms. Customers must provide consent for the collection and storage of their geolocation data or else they will be denied access.

However, mobile devices using geolocation are at increased risk of targeted physical attacks. An attacker can determine where the user with the mobile device is currently located and use that information to follow the user to steal the mobile device or inflict harm upon the person. In addition, attackers can craft attacks by compiling over time a list of people with whom the user associates and the types of activities they perform.

A related risk is GPS tagging (also called geo-tagging), which is adding geographical identification data to media such as digital photos taken on a mobile device. A user who, for example, posts a photo on a social networking site may inadvertently be identifying a specific private location to anyone who can access the photo.

Unauthorized Recording   Video cameras ("webcams") and microphones on mobile devices have been a frequent target of attackers. By infecting a device with malware, a threat actor can secretly spy on an unsuspecting victim and record conversations or videos.

Connection Vulnerabilities

Vulnerabilities in mobile device connections can also be exploited by threat actors. These vulnerabilities are summarized in Table 6-3.

Accessing Untrusted Content

Accessing untrusted content is also a mobile device risk since it can introduce malware into the device. Untrusted content includes unapproved apps, messages, and Quick Response (QR) codes.

Table 6-3 Connection vulnerabilities

Name	Description	Vulnerability
Tethering	A mobile device with an active Internet connection can be used to share that connection with other mobile devices through Bluetooth or Wi-Fi.	An unsecured mobile device may infect other tethered mobile devices or the corporate network.
USB On-the-Go (OTG)	An OTG mobile device with a USB connection can function as either a host (to which other devices may be connected such as a USB flash drive) for external media access or as a peripheral (such as a mass storage device) to another host.	Connecting a malicious flash drive that is infected with malware to a mobile device could result in an infection, just as using a device as a peripheral while connected to an infected computer could allow malware to be sent to the device.
Malicious USB cable	A USB cable could be embedded with a Wi-Fi controller that can receive commands from a nearby device to send malicious commands to the connected mobile device.	The device will recognize the cable as a human interface device (similar to a mouse or keyboard), giving the attacker enough permissions to exploit the system.
Public Wi-Fi	Public Wi-Fi is generally free and can be found in restaurants, airports, and other locations where users can access the Internet.	Because public Wi-Fi locations are beyond the control of the organization, attackers could eavesdrop on data transmissions and view sensitive information.

Unapproved Apps   Normally users cannot download and install unapproved apps on their iOS or Android device. This is because users are required to access the Apple App Store or Google Play Store (or other Android store) to download an app; in fact, Apple devices can only download from the App Store. However, users can circumvent the installed built-in limitations on their smartphone (called **jailbreaking** on Apple iOS devices or **rooting** on Android devices). Jailbreaking and rooting give access to the underlying OS and file system of the mobile device with full permissions, essentially bypassing all security protections. Often this is done to download apps from an unofficial and unapproved third-party (**sideloading**). Because these apps have not been vetted (apps on official stores must be examined and approved before they are available), these "rogue" apps often contain malware that cannot be trapped by the smartphone's security protections.

However, in late 2022, the EU passed the Digital Markets Act (DMA), applicable in May 2023. It requires Apple and similar providers to offer alternatives to their own third-party app stores. Apple unsuccessfully argued that this will cause its iPhones to be at a high risk of infections since Apple will not be able to weed out apps that contain malware.

Messaging   Another means by which untrusted content can invade mobile devices is through short message service (SMS), which are text messages of a maximum of 160 characters; multimedia messaging service (MMS), which provides for pictures, video, or audio to be included in text messages; or **rich communication services (RCS)**, which can convert a texting app into a live chat platform and supports pictures, videos, locations, stickers, and emojis. Threat actors can send SMS texts that contain links to untrusted content or send a specially crafted MMS or RCS video that can introduce malware into the device.

> **Note 7**
>
> SMS and MMS are covered in Module 1.

Quick Response (QR) Codes   Mobile devices also have the ability to access untrusted content that other types of computing devices generally do not have. One example is **Quick Response (QR)** codes. These codes are a matrix or two-dimensional barcode consisting of black modules (square dots) arranged in a square grid on a white background. QR codes can store website URLs, plaintext, phone numbers, email addresses, or virtually any alphanumeric data up to 4,296 characters, which can be read by an imaging device such as a mobile device's camera. A QR code for www.cengage.com is illustrated in Figure 6-5.

Figure 6-5 QR code

Source: qrstuff.com

An attacker can create an advertisement listing a reputable website, such as a bank, but include a QR code that contains a malicious URL. Once the user snaps a picture of the QR code using their mobile device's camera, the code directs the web browser on their mobile device to the attacker's imposter website or to a site that immediately downloads malware.

Protecting Mobile Devices

Several steps can be taken to make mobile devices more resilient to attacks (called hardening mobile devices). These include properly configuring the device and using mobile management tools.

Device Configuration

Several configurations should be considered when setting up a mobile device for use. These include using strong authentication, containerization, and enabling loss or theft services.

Strong Authentication   Verifying the authenticity of the user of a mobile device involves different configurations. These include requiring a strong passcode and restricting unauthorized users with a screen lock.

Passcode. Almost all mobile devices have options for configuring different types of passcodes that must be entered before access will be granted. Although passwords are the most secure option, most users unfortunately opt not to configure their device with a password. This is primarily due to the time needed to enter the password and the difficulty of entering a complex password on the device's small on-screen virtual keyboard.

Another option is to use a **personal identification number (PIN)**. Unlike a password that can be comprised of letters, numbers, and characters, a PIN is made up of numbers only. Although the length of the PIN can usually range from 4 to 16 numbers on a smartphone, many users choose to set a short four-digit PIN, like those used with a bank's automated teller machine (ATM). However, short PIN codes provide only a limited amount of security. An analysis of 3.4 million users' four-digit (0000–9999) PINs that were compromised revealed that users create predictable PIN patterns. The PIN *1234* was used in more than one out of every 10 PINs. Table 6-4 lists the five most common PINs and their frequency of use. Of the 10,000 potential PIN combinations, 26.83 percent of all PINs could be guessed by attempting just the top 20 most frequent PINs.[3]

Table 6-4   Most common PINs

PIN	Frequency of use
1234	10.71%
1111	6.01%
0000	1.88%
1212	1.19%
7777	0.74%

Note 8

The research also revealed that the least common PIN was *8068*, which appeared in only 25 of the 3.4 million PINs.

A third option is to use a fingerprint or facial recognition to unlock the mobile device. For example, several smartphone devices have the fingerprint sensor on the back of the phone. This allows the user to access the fingerprint reader without the need to move their index finger from the back of the phone (where the index finger is normally located while holding the phone) to the front.

Note ⑨

Accessing a device through fingerprint, face, or voice is called biometrics and is covered in Module 7.

A final option is to draw or swipe a specific pattern connecting dots to unlock the device. This is illustrated in Figure 6-6. Swipe patterns can be detected by threat actors who watch a user draw the pattern or observe any lingering "smear" on the screen.

Figure 6-6   Swipe pattern

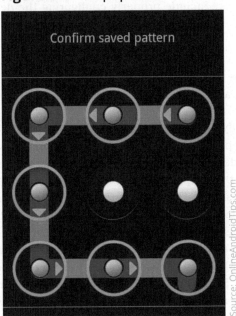

Source: OnlineAndroidTips.com

Screen lock. Once a user has been authenticated, typically the smartphone will remain available until a set time of inactivity, at which time the user must authenticate again. These screen locks have a variety of configuration settings. Most mobile devices can be set to have the screen automatically lock after anywhere from 5 seconds to 50 minutes of inactivity.

Some mobile devices can even be configured so that as long as the device is in a secure setting it stays unlocked. Google Android OS's feature called Smart Lock will keep a device unlocked as long as it is in the user's pocket or bag, connected to a trusted device, or located in a specific place.

Containerization   With the exception of corporate-owned devices, each of the other enterprise deployment models (BYOD, COPE, and CYOD) permit the user of a mobile device to use it for both business and personal needs. However, this may result in the "co-mingling" of critical business data with personal photos, downloads, and SMS texts, something that is not desirable to either the enterprise or the user.

An option on mobile devices that contain both personal and corporate data is segmentation, which is separating business apps and data from personal apps and data. This can be done by using "containerization" in which business and personal "containers" are created and managed. There are several advantages to segmenting by containerization on a mobile device used for both business and personal needs. It helps companies avoid data ownership privacy issues and legal concerns regarding a user's personal data stored on the device. In addition, it allows companies to delete only business data, when necessary, without touching personal data.

Enable Loss or Theft Services   One of the greatest risks of a mobile device is its loss or theft. Unprotected devices can be used to access corporate networks or view sensitive data stored on them. If a mobile device is lost or stolen, several security features can be used to locate the device or limit the damage. Many of these can be configured through a feature in the OS or an installed third-party app. These features are listed in Table 6-5.

Table 6-5   Security features for locating lost or stolen mobile devices

Security feature	Explanation
Alarm	The device can generate an alarm even if it is on mute.
Last known location	If the battery is charged to less than a specific percentage, the device's last known location can be indicated on an online map.
Locate	The current location of the device can be pinpointed on a map through the device's GPS.
Remote lockout	The mobile device can be remotely locked and a custom message sent that is displayed on the login screen.
Thief picture	A thief who enters an incorrect passcode three times will have their picture taken through the device's on-board camera and emailed to the owner.

If a lost or stolen device cannot be located, it may be necessary to perform a "remote wipe," which will erase sensitive data stored on the mobile device. This ensures that even if a thief accesses the device, no sensitive data will be compromised.

Caution !

If a theft does occur, do not resist or chase the thief. Instead, take note of the suspect's description, including any identifying characteristics and clothing, and then call the authorities. Also contact the organization or wireless carrier and change all passwords for accounts accessed on the device.

Mobile Management Tools

When using mobile devices in the enterprise, several support tools can facilitate the management of the devices. These include mobile device management, mobile application management, mobile content management, and unified endpoint management.

Mobile Device Management   Mobile device management (MDM) tools allow a device to be managed remotely by an organization. MDM typically involves a server component, which sends out management commands to the mobile devices, and a client component, which runs on the mobile device to receive and implement the management commands. An administrator can then perform OTA updates or configuration changes to one device, groups of devices, or all devices.

Some of the features that MDM tools provide include the ability to:

- Apply or modify default device settings
- Approve or quarantine new mobile devices
- Configure email, calendar, contacts, and Wi-Fi profile settings
- Detect and restrict jailbroken and rooted devices
- Display an acceptable use policy that requires consent before allowing access
- Distribute and manage public and corporate apps
- Enforce encryption settings, antivirus updates, and patch management
- Enforce **geofencing**, which is using the device's GPS to define geographical boundaries where an app can be used
- Securely share and update documents and corporate policies
- Selectively erase corporate data while leaving personal data intact
- Send SMS texts to selected users or groups of users (called **push notification services**)

Mobile Application Management (MAM)   Whereas MDM focuses on the device, **mobile application management (MAM)** covers application management, which comprises the tools and services responsible for distributing and controlling access to apps. These apps can be internally developed or commercially available apps.

> **Note 10**
>
> MDM provides a high degree of control over the device but a lower level of control on the apps, whereas MAM gives a higher level of control over apps but less control over the device.

Mobile Content Management (MCM)   Content management is used to support the creation and subsequent editing and modification of digital content by multiple employees. It can include tracking editing history, version control (recording changes and "rolling back" to a previous version, if necessary), indexing, and searching. A **mobile content management (MCM)** system is tuned to provide content management to hundreds or even thousands of mobile devices used by employees in an enterprise.

Unified Endpoint Management (UEM)   All of the capabilities in MDM, MAM, and MCM can be supported by **unified endpoint management (UEM)**. UEM is a group or class of software tools with a single management interface for mobile devices as well as computer devices. It provides capabilities for managing and securing mobile devices, applications, and content.

> **Two Rights & A Wrong**
>
> 1. MDM tools allow a device to be managed remotely by an organization.
> 2. COPE allows users to use their own personal mobile devices for business purposes.
> 3. Circumventing the installed built-in limitations on an Apple iPhone is called jailbreaking.
>
> See the answers at the end of the module.

Embedded Systems and Specialized Devices

> **Certification**
>
> 3.1 Compare and contrast security implications of different architecture models.
>
> 4.1 Given a scenario, apply common security techniques to computing resources.

Not all computing systems are desktop or mobile devices designed for direct human input. Computing capabilities can be integrated into a variety of different devices that receive automated machine input. An embedded system is computer hardware and software contained within a larger system that is designed for a specific function. There are different types of devices, and the protection of these devices needs to be considered.

Types of Devices

There are several categories of embedded and specialized devices. These include the hardware and software that can be used to create these devices, industrial systems, specialized systems, and Internet of Things devices.

Hardware and Software

Hardware and software components are easily available for an industrious user to create their own specialized device. One of the most common hardware components is the Raspberry Pi. This is a low-cost, credit-card-sized computer motherboard, as shown in Figure 6-7. This motherboard has different hardware ports that can connect to a range of peripherals. Figure 6-8 shows the Raspberry Pi components and ports. The Raspberry Pi can perform almost any task that a standard computer device can, such as browsing the Internet, playing high-definition video, creating spreadsheets, and playing games. It can also be used to control a specialized device.

Figure 6-7   Raspberry Pi

Source: Raspberry Pi Foundation

Figure 6-8   Raspberry Pi components and ports

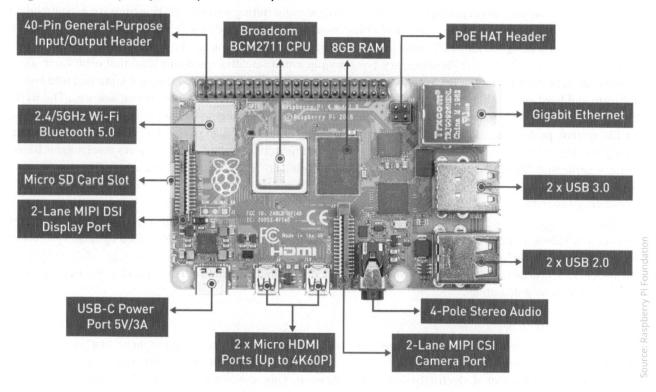

Source: Raspberry Pi Foundation

A device similar to the Raspberry Pi is the Arduino. Unlike the Raspberry Pi, which can function as a complete computer, the Arduino is designed as a controller for other devices: it has an 8-bit microcontroller instead of a 64-bit microprocessor on the Raspberry Pi, a limited amount of RAM, and no operating system but can only run programs that were compiled for the Arduino platform, most of which must be written in the C++ programming language. Although both the Raspberry Pi and Arduino can be used to interact with other specialized devices, such as control a robot, build a weather station, broadcast an FM radio signal, or build an automatic plant-watering device, the Arduino is generally considered a better solution for this type of interaction. It only has a single USB port, a power input, and a set of input/output pins for connections but consumes very little power.

Although the Raspberry Pi and Arduino are small motherboards, a **field-programmable gate array (FPGA)** is a hardware "chip" or integrated circuit (IC) that can be programed by the user ("field programmable") to carry out one or more logical operations. (ICs on standard computers as well as a Raspberry Pi and Arduino cannot be user programmed.) Specifically, a FPGA is an IC that consists of internal hardware blocks with user-programmable interconnects to customize operations for a specific application. A user can write software that loads onto the FPGA chip and executes functions, and that software can later be replaced or deleted.

Note 11

FPGAs are used in aerospace and defense, medical electronics, digital television, consumer electronics, industrial motor control, scientific instruments, cybersecurity systems, and wireless communications. Microsoft is now using FPGAs in its data centers to run its Bing search algorithms.

An even smaller component than the Raspberry Pi or Arduino is a **system on a chip (SoC)**. A SoC combines all the required electronic circuits of the various computer components on a single IC chip (the Raspberry Pi and Arduino are tiny motherboards that contain ICs, one of which is a SoC). SoCs often use a real-time operating system (RTOS) that is a specifically designed OS for a SoC in an embedded or specialized system. Standard computer systems, such as a laptop with a mouse and a keyboard or a tablet with a touch screen, typically receive irregular "bursts" of input data from a user or a network connection. Embedded systems, on the other hand, receive very large amounts of data very quickly, such as an aircraft preparing to land on a runway at night during a storm. RTOS is tuned to accommodate very high volumes of data that must be immediately processed for critical decision making (called high availability).

Because a RTOS is designed for a SoC, there are instances in which protecting and improving the functionality and security of a RTOS (hardening RTOS) is necessary. For example, small satellites (picosatellites) that orbit Earth use a RTOS for their on-board computers. Because these satellites cannot be accessed once they are launched into space, the software and hardware architectures are different from large spacecrafts and require special features. The RTOS on a picosatellite requires simplified structures and functions. Reliability-enhancing technologies are introduced to the kernel, file system, protocol stack, and application programming interface design of the RTOS. In addition, radiation hardening to mitigate the effects of these rays in outer space, fault detection, isolation and recovery mechanisms based on memory hardening, OS self-inspection, and hardware monitoring are all implemented as part of RTOS hardening.

Industrial Systems

Industrial control systems (ICSs) collect, monitor, and process real-time data so that machines can directly control devices such as valves, pumps, and motors without the need for human intervention. Often ICSs manage systems at remote locations. Multiple ICSs are managed by a larger supervisory control and data acquisition (SCADA) system. SCADA systems are crucial today for industrial organizations. They help to maintain efficiency and provide information on issues to help reduce downtime.

Specialized Systems

Several types of specialized systems are designed for specific applications. One example measures the amount of utilities consumed. Traditionally households have had utilities such as electricity and water measured by an analog meter that records the amount of electricity or water being used. This requires an employee from the utility to visit each home and read from the meter the amount that was consumed for the month so that a bill can be sent to the occupant. Digital smart meters are replacing these analog meters. Smart meters have several advantages over analog meters, and these are listed in Table 6-6.

Other specialized systems include medical systems, aircraft, and vehicles. The progression of specialized systems in automobiles is an example of how these systems have dramatically changed human-to-machine interaction. The first automobile embedded systems appeared in mass-production vehicles in the mid-1970s in response to regulations calling for higher fuel economy and emission standards and handled basic functions such as engine ignition timing

Table 6-6   Analog meters versus smart meters

Action	Analog meter	Smart meter
Meter readings	Employee must visit the dwelling each month to read the meter.	Meter readings are transmitted daily, hourly, or even by the minute to the utility company.
Servicing	Annual servicing is required in order to maintain accuracy.	Battery is replaced every 20 years.
Tamper protection	Data must be analyzed over long periods to identify anomalies.	Can alert utility in the event of tampering or theft.
Emergency communication	None available	Transmits "last gasp" notification of a problem to utility company.

and transmission shifting. By the 1980s, more sophisticated computerized engine-management systems enabled the use of reliable electronic fuel-injection systems and, later, active safety systems such as anti-lock braking and traction and stability control features were added, all controlled by embedded systems. Today embedded systems in cars use sonar, radar, and laser emitters to control brakes, steering, and the throttle to perform functions such as blind-spot and pedestrian collision warnings, automated braking, safe distance-keeping, and fully automated parking. Some of the embedded systems in cars are shown in Figure 6-9.

Figure 6-9   Embedded systems in cars

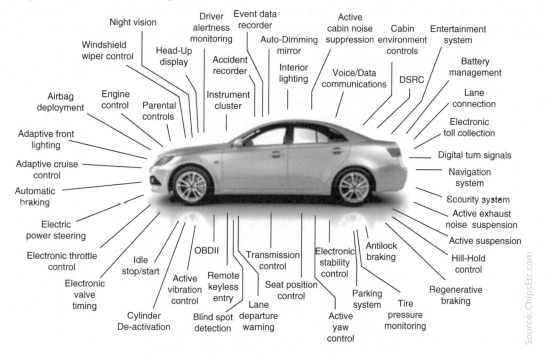

Source: ChipsEtc.com

Internet of Things

The Telecommunication Standardization Sector of the International Telecommunication Union (ITU-T) defines the **Internet of Things (IoT)** as "A global infrastructure for the information society, enabling advanced services by interconnecting (physical and virtual) things based on existing and evolving interoperable information and communication technologies."[4] More simply put, the IoT is connecting any device to the Internet for the purpose of sending and receiving data to be acted upon.

Although this definition could encompass laptop computers and tablets, more often IoT refers to devices that heretofore were not considered as computing devices connected to a data network. IoT devices are spurring home automation with items such as thermostats, coffee makers, tire sensors, slow cookers, keyless entry systems, washing machines, electric toothbrushes, headphones, and light bulbs, to name just a few. It is estimated that in 2022, the average number of connected devices per household was 22. The total number of IoT devices by 2025 is estimated to be 27 billion.[5]

Security Considerations

Despite the fact that ICS and SCADA systems, specialized systems, and IoT devices are widely used and will continue to grow exponentially, there are significant security concerns surrounding these systems and devices. Overall, these devices have a low resilience ("toughness") to resist attacks. Improving the security of these systems begins with knowing the security constraints. There are also specific hardening techniques and technologies for ICS and SCADA systems, some of which are being addressed by new legislation and regulations.

Security Constraints

Several constraints (limitations) make security a challenge for embedded systems and specialized devices. One typical constraint involves adding cryptography to these systems and devices. To perform their computations, cryptographic algorithms require both time and energy. Ideally, a cryptographic algorithm should have **low latency**, or a small amount of time that occurs between when a byte is input into a cryptographic algorithm and the time the output is obtained.

However, time and energy are both typically in short supply for small, low-power devices. Some algorithms require multiple (even 10 or higher) "cycles" on sections of the plaintext, each of which draws power and delays the output. One way to decrease latency is to make the cryptographic algorithm run faster—though this increases power consumption, which is either not available to low-power devices or would slow down the normal operations of the device.

This results in a resource versus security constraint, or a limitation in providing strong cryptography due to the tug-of-war between the available resources (time and energy) and the security provided by cryptography. The resource versus security constraint is illustrated in Figure 6-10. Table 6-7 lists additional security constraints.

> **Note 12**
>
> Resource versus security constraints are covered in Module 3.

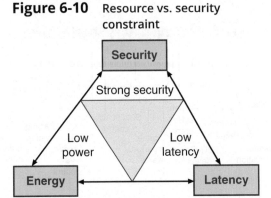

Figure 6-10   Resource vs. security constraint

Table 6-7   Security constraints for embedded systems and specialized devices

Constraint	Explanation
Power	To prolong battery life, devices and systems are optimized to draw very low levels of power and thus lack the ability to perform strong security measures.
Compute	Due to their size, small devices typically possess low processing capabilities, which restricts complex and comprehensive security measures.

Constraint	Explanation
Inability to patch	Few, if any, devices have been designed with the capacity for being updated to address exposed security vulnerabilities.
Patch availability	Many manufacturers do not produce patches for these devices.
Cost	Most developers are concerned primarily with making products as inexpensive as possible, which means leaving out all security protections.
Ease of recovery	A compromised sensor may have difficulty recovering to its normal state following an attack.
Responsiveness	Because many IoT devices require almost immediate responsiveness to inputs, adding security features to the device may impact its responsiveness.
Scalability	Attempting to increase the size and scope of a tiny IoT device often introduces new vulnerabilities.
Ease of deployment	A process for an accelerated rollout of devices at a faster pace than they can be secured can produce security issues.
Risk transference	Shifting risk and responsibility from one area of oversight to another can result in gaping security holes.
Availability	Ensuring timely and reliable access to IoT devices can be hampered if the device is overburdened with security constraints.

Hardening ICS and SCADA Systems

Several steps can be taken to harden SCADA and ICS systems. These include:

- Clearly define security roles, responsibilities, and authorities for managers, system administrators, and users.
- Identify security requirements.
- Conduct physical security surveys and assess all remote sites connected to the SCADA network to evaluate their security.
- Disconnect unnecessary connections to the SCADA network.
- Do not rely on proprietary protocols to protect the network.
- Document network architecture and identify systems that serve critical functions or contain sensitive information that require additional levels of protection.
- Establish clear policies and conduct training around the policies.
- Test to identify and evaluate possible attack scenarios.
- Evaluate and strengthen the security of all connections to the SCADA network.
- Remove or disable unnecessary services.
- Identify all connections to SCADA networks.
- Implement internal and external intrusion detection systems and incident monitoring.
- Implement the security features provided by device and system vendors.
- Perform technical audits of all SCADA devices and networks, and any other connected networks, to identify security concerns.

Legislation

Due to the importance of protecting IoT devices, federal and state laws have recently been passed to address their protection. At the federal level, the Internet of Things (IoT) Cybersecurity Improvement Act of 2020 requires agencies to increase cybersecurity for IoT devices owned or controlled by the federal government. In 2022, the EU passed the Cyber Resilience Act (CRA) that sets common security standards for connected devices and service.

At the state level, California and Oregon passed state laws addressing IoT security that went into effect in 2020. Both state laws require that connected devices be equipped with "reasonable security features" appropriate for the nature and function of the device and the information the device collects, contains, or transmits. Devices must be designed to protect both the device itself and any information contained within the device from unauthorized access, destruction, use, modification, or disclosure.

> **Caution** ❗
>
> When defining a "reasonable security feature," both California and Oregon laws say that this may consist of a prepro-grammed password that is unique to each device manufactured or that the device contains a security feature that requires a user to create a new means of authentication before accessing it for the first time. Beyond this example, however, neither law provides clear guidance as to what else could constitute a "reasonable security feature."

Regulations

In addition to federal and state laws, regulatory bodies have begun mandating protections on IoT devices. One example involves medical device manufacturers. Medical devices, such as insulin pumps, magnetic resonance imaging (MRI) devices, and heart rate monitors, have all been targets for attacks. One survey found that 88 percent of these types of medical IoT devices were involved in data breaches,[6] and 56 percent had experienced a cyberattack involving one of these Internet-connected devices over a 24-month period.[7]

However, the security on these critical medical devices—in which an attack may result in the death of the patient—is considered substandard. One medical device manufacturer experiences 114 million intrusion attempts each month, and only one out of every three medical facilities even keep an inventory of their devices. This led to a warning by the Federal Bureau of Investigation (FBI) in 2022 that unpatched and outdated devices pose a significant cybersecurity threat to U.S. healthcare.

In late 2022, the U.S. Food and Drug Administration (FDA) gained new powers from legislators to set minimum security standards for medical-device manufacturers. These standards include provisions that new devices must include a software bill of materials, which lists the components included in software, and that devices must also be able to accept patches and updates.

> **Note** 13
>
> Although the FDA's new legal powers take effect in early 2023, the agency has not yet indicated when it will begin exercis-ing and enforcing them.

> **Two Rights & A Wrong**
>
> 1. Multiple SCADAs are controlled by an ICS.
> 2. Power, compute, and availability are all security constraints for embedded systems and specialized devices.
> 3. RTOS is tuned to accommodate very high volumes of data that must be immediately processed for critical decision making.
>
> See the answers at the end of the module.

Application Security

> **Certification**
>
> 4.1 Given a scenario, apply common security techniques to computing resources.
>
> 4.3 Explain various activities associated with vulnerability management.

Protecting mobile devices through device configuration and mobile management tools, considering security restraints, and taking steps to harden ICS and SCADA systems as well as IoT devices are all important steps in information security. But an additional step is *critical* in securing *all* devices.

Endpoint devices all run applications (software programs). An unsecure application can open the door for attackers to exploit that application, the data that it uses, and even the underlying OS. Table 6-8 lists different attacks that can be launched using vulnerabilities in applications.

Table 6-8   Attacks based on application vulnerabilities

Attack	Description	Defense
Executable files attack	Trick the vulnerable application into modifying or creating executable files on the system	Prevent the application from creating or modifying executable files for its proper function
System tampering	Use the vulnerable application to modify special sensitive areas of the operating system (Microsoft Windows registry keys, system startup files, etc.) and take advantage of those modifications	Do not allow applications to modify special areas of the OS
Process spawning control	Trick the vulnerable application into spawning executable files on the system	Take away the process spawning ability from the application

The best steps taken to impose strict security on devices can all be negated by an application that contains vulnerabilities. Instead of reacting to an application with vulnerabilities, proactively preventing applications from having these vulnerabilities begins when the application is being developed and written. Following the basic steps for coding secure applications will significantly reduce the number of application vulnerabilities and thus reduce application attacks.

Note 14

Application vulnerabilities and applications attacks are covered in Module 5.

Application security involves knowing application development concepts, using secure coding techniques, and performing code testing.

Application Development Concepts

There are two levels of application development concepts. These include general concepts that apply to all application development and those that apply to a more rigorous security-based approach.

General Concepts

Developing an application requires several different stages. These stages include:

- **Development.** At the development stage, the requirements for the application are established and it is confirmed that the application meets the intended business needs before the actual coding begins.
- **Testing.** The testing stage thoroughly tests the application for any errors that could result in a security vulnerability.
- **Staging.** Staging tests to verify that the code functions as intended.
- **Production.** In the production stage, the application is released to be used in its actual setting.

An **application development lifecycle model** is a conceptual model that describes the different stages involved in creating an application. There are two major application development lifecycle models.

The **waterfall model** uses a sequential design process: as each stage is fully completed, the developers move on to the next stage. This means that once a stage is finished, developers cannot go back to a previous stage without starting over again. For example, in the waterfall model, quality assurance (QA; verification of quality) occurs only after the application has been tested and before it is finally placed in production. However, this makes any issues uncovered by QA difficult to address since it is at the end of the process. The waterfall model demands extensive planning in the very beginning and requires that it be followed carefully.

The **agile model** was designed to overcome the disadvantages of the waterfall model. Instead of following a rigid sequential design process, the agile model takes an incremental approach. Developers might start with a simplistic project design and begin to work on small modules. The work on these modules is done in short (weekly or monthly) "sprints," and at the end of each sprint, the project's priorities are again evaluated as tests are being run. This approach allows for software issues to be incrementally discovered so that feedback and changes can be incorporated into the design before the next sprint is started.

SecDevOps

One specific type of software methodology that follows the agile model and heavily incorporates secure coding practices and techniques to create secure software applications is called **SecDevOps**. SecDevOps (also known as DevSecOps and DevOpsSec) is the process of integrating secure development best practices and methodologies into application software development and deployment processes using the agile model. It is a set of best practices designed to help organizations implant secure coding deep in the heart of their applications.

SecDevOps is often promoted in terms of its elasticity (flexibility or resilience in code development) and its scalability (expandability from small projects to very large projects). However, the cornerstone of SecDevOps is automation. With standard application development, security teams often find themselves stuck with time-consuming manual tasks. SecDevOps, on the other hand, applies what is called automated courses of action to develop the code as quickly and securely as possible. This automation enables continuous monitoring (examining the processes in real time instead of at the end of a stage), continuous validation (ongoing approvals of the code), continuous integration (ensuring that security features are incorporated at each stage), continuous delivery (moving the code to each stage as it is completed), and continuous deployment (continual code implementation).

The SecDevOps methodology also includes concepts such as immutable systems (once a value or configuration is employed as part of an application, it is not modified; if changes are necessary, a new system must be created), infrastructure as code (managing a hardware and software infrastructure using the same principles as developing computer code), and baselining (creating a starting point for comparison purposes in order to apply targets and goals to measure success).

> ### Note 15
>
> Because SecDevOps is based on the agile method, it involves continuous modifications throughout the process. With these continual changes, it is important to use tools that support change management or creating a plan for documenting changes to the application. One tool for change management is version control software that allows changes to be automatically recorded and if necessary "rolled back" to a previous version of the software.

Secure Coding Techniques

There are several coding techniques that should be used to create secure applications and limit data exposure or disclosing sensitive data to attackers. These techniques include, for example, determining how encryption will be implemented and ensuring that memory management is handled correctly so as not to introduce memory vulnerabilities. Other techniques are summarized in Table 6-9.

Code Testing

Testing is one of the most important steps in SecDevOps. Instead of testing only after the application is completed, testing should be performed much earlier during the implementation and verification phases of a software development process. Testing involves static code analysis and dynamic code analysis.

Table 6-9   Secure coding techniques

Coding technique	Description	Security advantage
Input validation	Accounting for errors such as incorrect user input (entering a file name for a file that does not exist)	Can prevent cross-site scripting (XSS) and cross-site request forgery (CSRF) attacks
Normalization	Organizing data within a database to minimize redundancy	Reduces footprint of data exposed to attackers
Stored procedure	A subroutine available to applications that access a relational database	Eliminates the need to write a subroutine that could have vulnerabilities
Code signing	Digitally signing applications	Confirms the software author and guarantees the code has not been altered or corrupted
Obfuscation/camouflaged code	Writing an application in such a way that its inner functionality is difficult for an outsider to understand	Helps prevent an attacker from understanding a program's function
Dead code	A section of an application that executes but performs no meaningful function	Provides an unnecessary attack vector for attackers
Server-side execution and validation or client-side execution and validation	Input validation generally uses the server to perform validation but can also have the client perform validation by the user's web browser	Adds another validation to the process
Code reuse of third-party libraries and SDKs	Using existing software in a new application; a software development kit (SDK) is a set of tools used to write applications	Existing libraries that have already been vetted as secure eliminate the need to write new code

Note 16

Edsger W. Dijkstra, a famous software engineer, once said, "Program testing can be used to show the presence of bugs, but never to show their absence!"

Static Code Analysis

Analysis and testing of the software should occur from a security perspective before the source code is even compiled. These tests are called static code analysis. Figure 6-11 illustrates an automated static code analysis tool.

Note 17

Automated static code analysis may also be accompanied by manual peer reviews. In these reviews, software engineers and developers are paired together or in larger teams to laboriously examine each line of source code looking for vulnerabilities.

Dynamic Code Analysis

Security testing should also be performed after the source code is compiled (a process called dynamic code analysis or runtime verification) and when all components are integrated and running. This testing typically uses a tool or suite of prebuilt attacks or testing tools that specifically monitor the application's behavior for memory corruption, user privilege issues, and other critical security problems.

Figure 6-11 Automated static code analysis tool

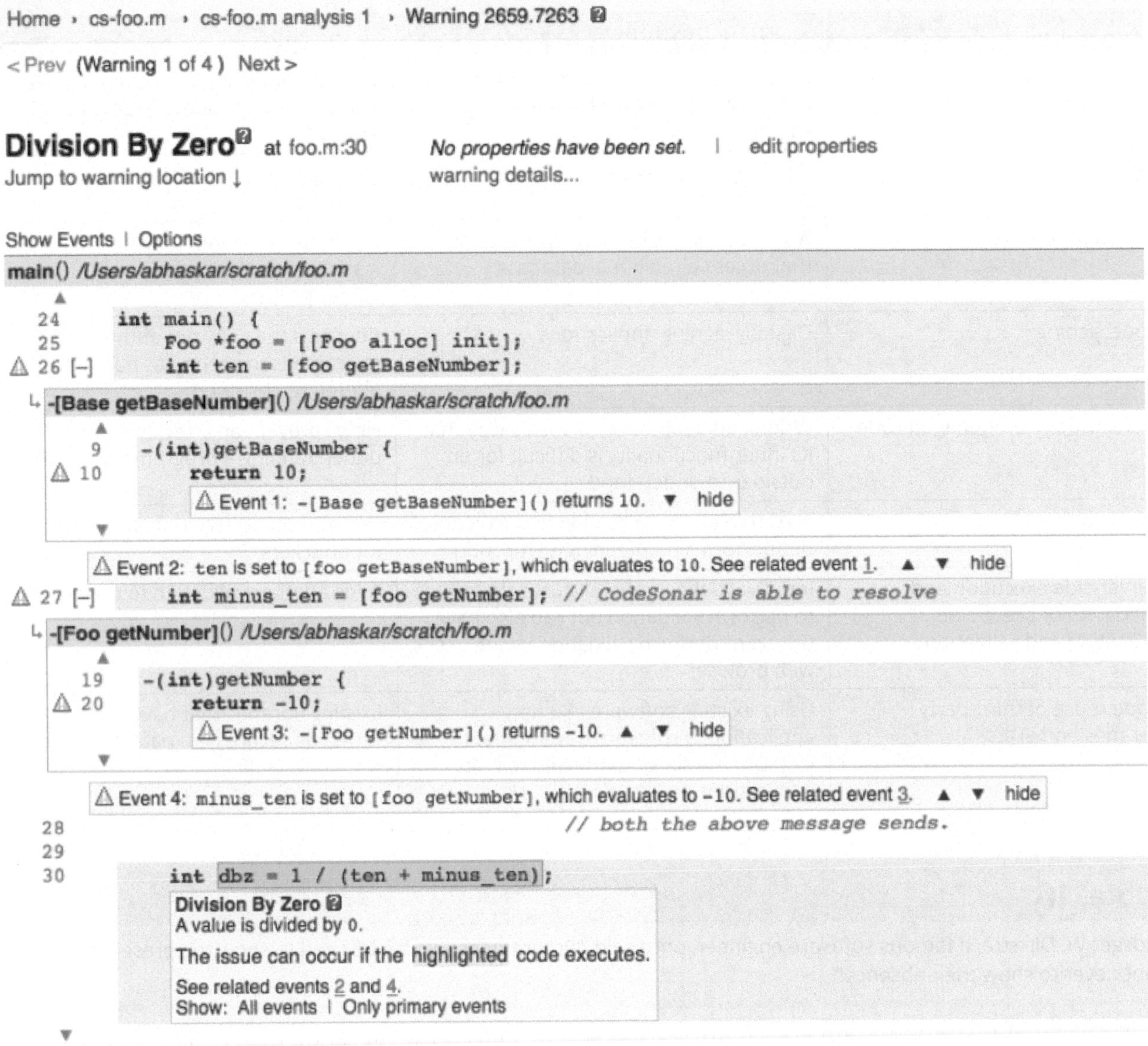

Home › cs-foo.m › cs-foo.m analysis 1 › Warning 2659.7263 ▣

< Prev (Warning 1 of 4) Next >

Division By Zero▣ at foo.m:30   *No properties have been set.* | edit properties
Jump to warning location ↓   warning details...

Show Events | Options
main() */Users/abhaskar/scratch/foo.m*

```
24      int main() {
25          Foo *foo = [[Foo alloc] init];
⚠ 26 [–]     int ten = [foo getBaseNumber];
```
  ┕ **-[Base getBaseNumber]**() */Users/abhaskar/scratch/foo.m*

```
9       -(int)getBaseNumber {
⚠ 10        return 10;
```
          ⚠ Event 1: -[Base getBaseNumber]() returns 10. ▼ hide

      ⚠ Event 2: ten is set to [foo getBaseNumber], which evaluates to 10. See related event 1. ▲ ▼ hide
```
⚠ 27 [–]     int minus_ten = [foo getNumber]; // CodeSonar is able to resolve
```
  ┕ **-[Foo getNumber]**() */Users/abhaskar/scratch/foo.m*

```
19      -(int)getNumber {
⚠ 20        return -10;
```
          ⚠ Event 3: -[Foo getNumber]() returns -10. ▲ ▼ hide

      ⚠ Event 4: minus_ten is set to [foo getNumber], which evaluates to -10. See related event 3. ▲ ▼ hide
```
                                        // both the above message sends.
28
29
30          int dbz = 1 / (ten + minus_ten);
```
            Division By Zero ▣
            A value is divided by 0.

            The issue can occur if the highlighted code executes.

            See related events 2 and 4.
            Show: All events | Only primary events

Some of the most common dynamic code analysis tools use a process called **fuzzing**. Fuzzing provides random input to a program in an attempt to trigger exceptions, such as memory corruption, program crashes, or security breaches. An advantage of fuzzing is that it produces a record of what input triggered the exception so it can be reproduced to track down the problem within the code. Fuzzing test software consists of an execution engine and an input generator, which usually allows the tester to configure the types of inputs. Figure 6-12 illustrates a fuzzer input generator.

Caution ❗

A single pass of a fuzzer is unlikely to find all exceptions in software due to the randomness in the fuzzing process. The mutation of the inputs relies on randomness to determine where to mutate input and what to mutate. Fuzzers require multiple trials and statistical tests.

Figure 6-12 Fuzzer input generator

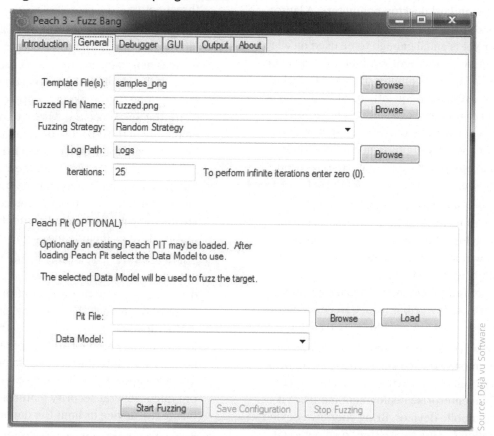

Source: Déjà vu Software

Two Rights & A Wrong

1. The waterfall model uses a sequential design process.
2. Dynamic code analysis should occur before the source code is compiled.
3. SecDevOps has elasticity and scalability.

See the answers at the end of the module.

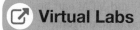 **Virtual Labs**   You're now ready to complete the simulations and live virtual machine labs for this module. The labs can be found in each module in MindTap.

Summary

- There are several types of mobile devices. Tablet computers are portable computing devices smaller than portable computers, larger than smartphones, and focused on ease of use. Tablets generally lack a built-in keyboard and rely on a touch screen. A smartphone includes an operating system that allows it to run apps and access the Internet, and it offers a broad range of functionality. Another class of mobile technology is wearable technology, devices that can be worn by the user instead of being carried.

- Portable computers are devices with functionality similar to standard desktop computers. A laptop is designed to replicate the abilities of a desktop computer yet is small enough to be used on a lap or small table. A notebook computer is a smaller version of a laptop computer designed to include only the most basic frequently used features of a standard computer in a smaller size that is easy to carry. A convertible or 2-in-1 computer can be used in a variety of physical configurations. Web-based computers are designed to be used primarily while connected to the Internet.

- Different connectivity methods are used to connect mobile devices to networks. A cellular network divides the coverage area into cells. Wi-Fi is a wireless local area network standard. Bluetooth is wireless technology that uses short-range radio frequency transmissions and provides rapid device pairings. USB connectors on mobile devices are used for data transfer.

- It is not always feasible to require an employee to carry a company-owned smartphone along with a personal cell phone. Many organizations have adopted an enterprise deployment model as it relates to mobile devices. Bring your own device (BYOD) allows users to use their own personal mobile devices for business purposes. Corporate owned, personally enabled (COPE) gives employees a choice from a selection of company-approved devices. Choose your own device (CYOD) gives employees a limited selection of approved devices, though the employee pays the upfront cost of the device while the business owns the contract. Corporate-owned devices are purchased and owned by the enterprise.

- Several risks are associated with using mobile devices. Mobile devices are used in a wide variety of locations outside of the organization's normal physical perimeter. Devices can easily be lost or stolen, and any unprotected data on the device can be retrieved by a thief. A stolen device can also be used as an entry point into the corporate network. As mobile devices age, they may no longer receive security updates. Geolocation, or the process of identifying the geographical location of a device, can be helpful but also is a security risk because it can identify the location of a person carrying a mobile device. Video cameras and microphones on mobile devices have been used by attackers to secretly "spy" on an unsuspecting victim. Vulnerabilities in mobile device connections can also be exploited by threat actors.

- Mobile devices have the ability to access untrusted content that other types of computing devices generally cannot. Users can circumvent the installed built-in limitations on their smartphone (jailbreaking on Apple iOS devices or rooting on Android devices) to download from an unofficial third-party app store (sideloading) or even write their own custom firmware to run on their device. Because these apps have not been approved, they may contain security vulnerabilities or even malicious code. Other means by which untrusted content can invade mobile devices include messaging and QR codes.

- There are several security considerations when initially setting up a mobile device. Mobile devices have options for configuring different types of passcodes that must be entered as authentication credentials and setting screen lock options. Personal and corporate data can be separated into different containers and each managed appropriately. If a mobile device is lost or stolen, several security features can be used to locate the device or limit the damage.

- Several support tools can facilitate the management of mobile devices in the enterprise. Mobile device management (MDM) tools allow a device to be managed remotely by an organization. Mobile application management (MAM) covers application management, which comprises the tools and services responsible for distributing and controlling access to apps. A mobile content management (MCM) system provides content management to mobile devices used by employees in an enterprise. All of the capabilities in MDM, MAM, and MCM can be supported by unified endpoint management (UEM).

- There are several categories of embedded and specialized devices. Hardware and software components are easily available for an industrious user to create their own specialized device. A system on a chip (SoC) combines all the required electronic circuits of the various computer components on a single IC chip. SoCs often use a real-time operating system (RTOS) that is specifically designed for an SoC in an embedded or specialized system.

- Industrial control systems (ICSs) collect, monitor, and process real-time data so that machines can directly control devices such as valves, pumps, and motors without the need for human intervention. Often ICSs manage systems at remote locations. Multiple ICSs are managed by a larger supervisory control and data acquisition (SCADA) system. Several types of specialized systems are designed for specific applications. The Internet of Things (IoT) is connecting any device to the Internet for the purpose of sending and receiving data to be acted upon.

- Security in embedded systems and specialized devices is often lacking. Several constraints make security a challenge for these systems. To address security in these devices, governments have begun to enact legislation to require stronger security on embedded systems and specialized devices. In addition, regulatory bodies are now setting minimum standards for these devices.

- Virtually any steps taken to impose strict security on devices can be negated by an application that contains vulnerabilities. Instead of reacting to an application with vulnerabilities, proactively preventing applications from having these vulnerabilities begins when the application is being developed and written. Developing an application requires several stages. An application development lifecycle model is a conceptual model that describes the different stages involved in creating an application.

- One specific type of software methodology that incorporates secure coding practices and techniques to create secure software applications is called SecDevOps. Several coding techniques should be used to create secure applications and limit data exposure or disclosing sensitive data to attackers. Testing is one of the most important steps in SecDevOps. Analysis and testing of the software should occur from a security perspective before the source code is even compiled. These tests are called static code analysis. Security testing should also be performed after the source code is compiled (a process called dynamic code analysis).

Key Terms

availability	embedded system	power
bring your own device (BYOD)	hardening mobile devices	real-time operating system (RTOS)
cellular	hardening RTOS	resilience
choose your own device (CYOD)	high availability	responsiveness
compute	inability to patch	risk transference
corporate owned, personally enabled (COPE)	industrial control systems (ICSs)	scalability
cost	input validation	sideloading
dynamic code analysis	Internet of Things (IoT)	static code analysis
ease of deployment	jailbreaking	supervisory control and data acquisition (SCADA)
ease of recovery	mobile device management (MDM)	
	patch availability	

Review Questions

1. Ahmet is explaining to his team members the security constraints that have made it a challenge to protect a new embedded system. Which of the following would Ahmet NOT include as a constraint?

   a. Authentication
   b. Cost
   c. Power
   d. Ease of use

2. Yusuf has been asked to experiment with different hardware to create a controller for a new device on the factory floor. He needs a credit-card-sized motherboard that has a microcontroller instead of a microprocessor. Which would be the best solution?

   a. SoC
   b. Raspberry Pi
   c. Arduino
   d. FPGA

3. Musa needs a tool with a single management interface that provides capabilities for managing and securing mobile devices, applications, and content. Which tool would be the best solution?

   a. UEM
   b. MDM
   c. MCCM
   d. MMAM

4. In a job interview, Deniz asks about the company policy regarding smartphones. She is told that employees may choose from a limited list of approved devices but that she must pay for the device herself; however, the company will provide her with a monthly stipend. Which type of enterprise deployment model does this company support?

   a. BYOD
   b. DYOD
   c. CYOD
   d. Corporate-owned

5. Eren has been asked to provide information regarding adding a new class of Android smartphones to a list of approved devices. One of the considerations is how frequently the smartphones receive firmware OTA updates. Which of the following reasons would Eren NOT list in their report as a factor in the frequency of Android firmware OTA updates?

   a. OEMs are hesitant to distribute Google updates because it limits their ability to differentiate themselves from competitors if all versions of Android start to look the same through updates.
   b. Because many of the OEMs have modified Android, they are reluctant to distribute updates that could potentially conflict with their changes.
   c. Wireless carriers are reluctant to provide firmware OTA updates because of the bandwidth it consumes on their wireless networks.
   d. Because OEMs want to sell as many devices as possible, they have no financial incentive to update mobile devices that users would then continue to use indefinitely.

6. What is the process of identifying the geographical location of a mobile device?

   a. Geotracking
   b. Geolocation
   c. GeoID
   d. Geomonitoring

7. Which of the following is NOT an advantage of COPE for an enterprise?

   a. Simplified IT infrastructure
   b. Cost savings
   c. Flexibility in management
   d. More oversight

8. Ceyhun received a request by a technician for a new portable computer. The technician noted that they wanted USB OTG support and asked Ceyhun's advice regarding it. Which of the following would Ceyhun NOT tell them is an advantage?

   a. A device connected via USB OTG can function as a peripheral for external media access.
   b. A device connected via USB OTG can function as a host.
   c. USB OTG is only available for connecting Android devices to a portable computer.
   d. Connecting a mobile device to an infected computer using USB OTG could allow malware to be sent to that device.

9. Ozan has received a phone call from his supervisor that a new employee has attempted to download and install an unapproved app that allows her to circumvent the built-in limitations on her Android smartphone. What is this called?

   a. Rooting
   b. Sideloading
   c. Jailbreaking
   d. Ducking

10. What is another name for runtime verification?

   a. Static code analysis
   b. Dynamic code analysis
   c. Fuzzering
   d. Weighted code analysis

11. What is dead code?

   a. A block of code that does not run.
   b. Code that has been tagged to be removed from an application.
   c. A branch in a code that calls in a subroutine but always returns a null value.
   d. A section of an application that executes but performs no meaningful function.

12. Cahill is writing an application using SecDevOps and wants to prevent XSS and CSRF attacks. What coding technique would he use?

   a. Obfuscation
   b. Code signing
   c. Input validation
   d. Normalization

13. What does containerization do?

    a. It splits operating system functions only on specific brands of mobile devices.

    b. It places all keys in a special vault.

    c. It slows down a mobile device to half speed.

    d. It separates personal data from corporate data.

14. What allows a device to be managed remotely?

    a. MDM

    b. MAM

    c. MRM

    d. MWM

15. Which of these is NOT a security feature for locating a lost or stolen mobile device?

    a. Remote lockout

    b. Last known good configuration

    c. Alarm

    d. Thief picture

16. What enforces the location in which an app can function by tracking the location of the mobile device?

    a. Location resource management

    b. Geofencing

    c. GPS tagging

    d. Graphical management tracking (GMT)

17. Which of these is considered the strongest type of passcode to use on a mobile device?

    a. Password

    b. PIN

    c. Fingerprint swipe

    d. Draw connecting-dots pattern

18. Which of the following is NOT a means by which untrusted content can be sent to a mobile device?

    a. SMS

    b. MMS

    c. RCS

    d. XRX

19. Which tool manages the distribution and control of apps?

    a. MAM

    b. MDM

    c. MCM

    d. MFM

20. Which type of OS is typically found on an embedded system?

    a. SoC

    b. RTOS

    c. OTG

    d. COPE

Hands-On Projects

Caution !

If you are concerned about installing any of the software in these projects on your regular computer, you can instead use the Windows Sandbox created in the Chapter 1 Hands-On Projects. Software installed within the virtual machine will not impact the host computer.

Project 6-1: Creating and Using Quick Response Codes

Estimated Time: 25 minutes

Objective: Demonstrate the risks of using Quick Response codes.

Description: Quick Response (QR) codes can be read by an imaging device such as a mobile device's camera or online. However, they pose a security risk. In this project, you create and use QR codes.

1. Use your web browser to go to **www.qrstuff.com**. (If you are no longer able to access the site through this URL, use a search engine and search for "Qrstuff.")

2. First, create a QR code. Under **DATA TYPE**, select **Website URL** is selected.

3. Under **CODE CONTENT**, enter the URL **http://www.cengage.com**. Watch how the **QR CODE PREVIEW** changes as you type.

4. Click **Next step** until the **TRACKING & ANALYTICS** page opens.

5. Under **Encoding Options**, select **Static - Embed URL into code as is**.

6. Click the **Download** button to download an image of the QR code.

7. Navigate to the location of the download and open the image. Is there anything you can tell by looking at this code? How could a threat actor use this to their advantage? Where could malicious QR codes be used? Is there any protection for the user when using QR codes?

8. Now use an online reader to interpret the QR code. Use your web browser to go to **blog.qr4.nl/Online-QR-Code-Decoder.aspx**. (The location of content on the Internet may change without warning. If you are no longer able to access the program through this URL, use a search engine and search for "Free Online QR Code Reader.")

9. Click **Choose File**.

10. Navigate to the location of the QR code that you downloaded on your computer and click **Open**.

11. Click **Upload**.

12. In the text box, what is displayed? How could an attacker use a QR code to direct a victim to a malicious website?

13. Use your web browser to go to **www.qrcode-monkey.com**. (If you are no longer able to access the program through this URL, use a search engine and search for "QRcodemonkey.")

14. Click **LOCATION**.

15. On the map, drag the pointer to an address with which you are familiar. Note how the **Latitude** and **Longitude** change.

16. Click **Create QR Code**.

17. Click **Download PNG** and then click **Save** to download this QR code to your computer.

18. Navigate to the location of the download and open the image. How does it look different from the previous QR code? Is there anything you can tell by looking at this code?

19. Use your web browser to return to **blog.qr4.nl/Online-QR-Code-Decoder.aspx**.

20. Click **Choose File**.

21. Navigate to the location of the map QR code that you downloaded on your computer and click **Open**.

22. Click **Upload**.

23. In the text box, a URL will be displayed. Paste this URL into a web browser.

24. What does the browser display? How could an attacker use this for a malicious attack?

25. Return to **www.qrstuff.com**.

26. Click each option under **DATA TYPE** to view the different items that can be created by a QR code. Select three and indicate how an attacker could use them.

27. Close all windows.

Project 6-2: Using Online Security Bulletins

Estimated Time: 25 minutes
Objective: Explore online security bulletins.
Description: Operating systems have made security bulletins available in a searchable online database. All security professionals need to be familiar with using this database. In this project, you explore these online databases.

1. Open your web browser and enter the URL **portal.msrc.microsoft.com/en-us/**. (The location of content on the Internet may change without warning. If you are no longer able to access the program through the above URL, use a search engine and search for "Microsoft Security Response Center.")

2. Click **Vulnerabilities** to display a list of recent vulnerabilities.

3. Click a **CVE Number** to read the information. Is this information helpful to understanding a vulnerability?

4. Click the popout window icon next to the CVE number. How helpful is this information?

5. Return to the MSRC page.

6. Click **Security Update Guide**.

7. Adjust the dates so that they are more encompassing.

8. Now click **Release Notes** next to a vulnerability. Is this information helpful?

9. How useful is this information? Is it presented in a format that is helpful?

10. Now compare the Microsoft database with Apple's. Enter the URL **support.apple.com/en-us/ HT201222**. (The location of content on the Internet may change without warning. If you are no longer able to access the program through the above URL, use a search engine and search for "Apple Security Updates.")

11. Scroll down through the list of Apple security updates. How does this list compare with the updates from Microsoft?

12. Select a recent event under **Name and information link**.

13. Read the information about the update. How does this information compare with Microsoft's information? Why is there such a difference? Which provides better information for security professionals?

14. Close all windows.

Project 6-3: Installing NoxPlayer Android Emulator

Estimated Time: 20 minutes
Objective: Install an Android emulator.
Description: In this project, you install an Android emulator on a personal computer.

1. Use your web browser to go to **www.bignox.com**. (The location of content on the Internet may change without warning. If you are no longer able to access the program through this URL, use a search engine and search for "NoxPlayer.")

2. Download the latest version of NoxPlayer.

3. When the download is complete, launch the installation file and accept the defaults to install the software.

4. Launch NoxPlayer.

5. Click the **System settings** icon.

6. Under **Performance settings**, click the down arrow to view the different options.

7. Under **Resolution setting**, change from the default **Tablet** to **Mobile phone**. What are the screen resolutions now?

8. Click **Device**.

9. Click the down arrow under **Mobile phone model** and select a different mobile phone to emulate.

10. How could this application be used for software testing? Are the features easy to use? What suggestions do you have for improvement?

11. Close all windows.

Case Projects

Case Project 6-1: #TrendingCyber

Estimated Time: 15 minutes
Objective: Summarize your thoughts on the #TrendingCyber opener.
Description: Read again the opening #TrendingCyber in this module. Why would NIST use a contest to determine a lightweight standard? Why would they not create their own algorithms instead? What are the advantages and disadvantages of each approach? Write a one-paragraph summary of your thoughts.

Case Project 6-2: Unified Endpoint Management Tools

Estimated Time: 25 minutes
Objective: Research unified endpoint management tools.
Description: Use the Internet to identify and compare three different unified endpoint management tools. Create a table that lists their various features. Which of the tools would you recommend for a small business with 10 employees who use smartphones but has a single person managing IT services? Why?

Case Project 6-3: Enterprise Deployment Model Comparison

Estimated Time: 30 minutes
Objective: Research different enterprise deployment models.
Description: Research the different enterprise deployment models listed in Table 6-2. Create a detailed table listing their typical features, how they are used, and their advantages and disadvantages to both the enterprise as well as to the employee. Which of them is the most secure option? Which is the least secure option? Which of them is most advantageous for the enterprise? Which would you prefer to use? Which would you recommend for your school or place of employment? Why? Create a one-paragraph summary along with your table.

Case Project 6-4: Fuzzers

Estimated Time: 25 minutes
Objective: Research fuzzers.
Description: Use the Internet to locate three different fuzzers. Create a table that compares the different features of each of these input generators. What are the strengths of each? What are the weaknesses? Which would you recommend? Why?

Case Project 6-5: Real-Time Operating System

Estimated Time: 15 minutes
Objective: Research real-time operating systems.
Description: Research information on a real-time operating system (RTOS) and identify three different systems. Create a table listing their features, security, strengths, weaknesses, and overall value. How difficult are they to program and use? What are some interesting uses for each?

Case Project 6-6: Rooting and Jailbreaking

Estimated Time: 25 minutes
Objective: Research the dangers of rooting and jailbreaking.
Description: Research Android rooting and Apple jailbreaking. What privileges can be obtained by rooting and jailbreaking? What are the advantages? What are the disadvantages? Can a device that has been broken return to its default state? If so, how? Finally, create a list of at least five reasons why rooting and jailbreaking are considered harmful in a corporate environment.

Case Project 6-7: Internet of Things Regulations

Estimated Time: 25 minutes

Objective: Research Internet of Things regulations.

Description: Use the Internet to research Internet of Things (IoT) regulations, like those to be implemented by the FDA. How comprehensive are these regulations? Will they dramatically improve the security of these devices? Which additional regulations would you like to see implemented? Why? Write a one-page paper on the information that you find.

Case Project 6-8: Mini PCs

Estimated Time: 20 minutes

Objective: Research Mini PCs.

Description: A new class of computers has recently become very popular. Known as Mini PCs, these devices can be used in place of standard desktop computers but are portable and can easily be carried in a backpack or purse. Although small in size (4.9 × 4.5 × 1.6 inches or 126 × 113 × 42 mm) they have powerful processors and large amounts of memory and storage and can support multiple monitors and support Bluetooth and Wi-Fi along with gigabit network ports. Some experts are predicting that these are the next class of computers between desktops and laptops. Research Mini PCs. Identify four different models and create a table of their features including costs. Do you think these will one day replace desktop computers? Why or why not?

Case Project 6-9: Bay Point Ridge Security

Estimated Time: 45 minutes

Objective: Protect mobile devices.

Description: Bay Point Ridge Security (BPRS) is a managed service provider (MSP) that manages networks, computers, cloud resources, and information security for small-to-medium enterprises (SMEs) in the region. BPRS provides internships to students who are in their final year of the security degree program at the local college and has recently hired you.

A local museum provides patrons with mobile devices that contain prerecorded information that can be listened to while viewing the museum's artifacts. Recently an incident occurred in which a patron circumvented the security on the device and, because it was not examined after it was turned in, the next patron who tried to use it was exposed to inappropriate content. The executive board of the museum wants something to be done to prevent this from recurring and also wants to ensure that all employee mobile devices are also secure. They have asked BPRS to make a presentation about mobile device security, and you have been given this assignment.

1. Create a PowerPoint presentation for the staff about the security risks of mobile technology and steps to be taken to secure mobile devices. Be sure to cover these from the perspective of the organization, the IT department, and the user. Your presentation should contain at least 10–12 slides.

2. After the presentation, the IT director at the museum has asked BPRS for recommendations on using MDM, MAM, MCM, and/or UEM. Write a one-page memo listing the features of these tools and how they could be used to help the museum.

Two Rights & A Wrong: Answers

Securing Mobile Devices

1. MDM tools allow a device to be managed remotely by an organization.
2. COPE allows users to use their own personal mobile devices for business purposes.
3. Circumventing the installed built-in limitations on an Apple iPhone is called jailbreaking.

Answer: The wrong statement is #2.

Explanation: BYOD allows users to use their own personal mobile devices for business purposes.

Embedded Systems and Specialized Devices

1. Multiple SCADAs are controlled by an ICS.
2. Power, compute, and availability are all security constraints for embedded systems and specialized devices.
3. RTOS is tuned to accommodate very high volumes of data that must be immediately processed for critical decision making.

Answer: The wrong statement is #1.

Explanation: Multiple ICSs are managed by a larger supervisory control and data acquisition (SCADA) system.

Application Security

1. The waterfall model uses a sequential design process.
2. Dynamic code analysis should occur before the source code is compiled.
3. SecDevOps has elasticity and scalability.

Answer: The wrong statement is #2.

Explanation: Static code analysis should occur prior to compilation.

References

1. "Mobile Security Index 2022," Verizon Wireless, accessed Feb. 11, 2023, https://www.verizon.com/business/resources/reports/mobile-security-index/.
2. Horn, Elaine, "Mobile device security: Startling statistics on data loss and data breaches," *ChannelProNetwork*, accessed Feb. 11, 2023, https://www.channelpronetwork.com/article/mobile-device-security-startling-statistics-data-loss-and-data-breaches#:~:text=70%20million%20smartphones%20are%20lost,and%2024%20percent%20from%20conferences.
3. "Pin analysis," DataGenetics, accessed Mar. 10, 2014, http://datagenetics.com/blog/september32012/index.html.
4. "Overview of the Internet of Things, Series y: Global information infrastructure, internet protocol aspects and next-generation networks - Next generation networks – Frameworks and functional architecture models," Jun. 2012, Retrieved May 18, 2017, www.itu.int/rec/T-REC-Y.2060-201206-I.
5. "How many IoT devices are there in 2023? [all you need to know]," TechJury, Feb. 7, 2023, accessed Feb. 11, 2023, https://techjury.net/blog/how-many-iot-devices-are-there/#gref.
6. Burkey, Annie, "Medical devices are a weak link in hospital cyber defenses, putting patients in the crossfire: study," Fierce Healthcare, Aug. 18, 2022, accessed Feb. 15, 2023, https://www.fiercehealthcare.com/health-tech/cyberattack-revolving-doors-medical-devices-put-patients-crossfire.
7. Rundle, James, "Medical-device makers face push to protect their wares from hacks," *WSJ Pro*, Feb. 13, 2023, accessed Feb. 13, 2023, https://www.wsj.com/articles/medical-device-makers-face-push-to-protect-their-wares-from-hacks-32e84445.

Module 7

Identity and Access Management (IAM)

Module Objectives

After completing this module, you should be able to do the following:

1 Describe different types of authentication credentials

2 List authentication best practices

3 Define access controls and explain how they can be used

#TrendingCyber

Passwords are essential for keeping out unauthorized users. But what happens when someone passes away and family members who need access to important accounts are unable to because they are password-protected, and nobody knows the password?

According to estate-planning attorneys, this problem of heirs not being to access accounts because of passwords became more common during the COVID-19 pandemic: many individuals fell ill and died suddenly without providing passwords to their protected information. These attorneys have said that when someone does not arrange in advance who can access protected accounts and how they can be accessed, it results in "a big mess and a lot of stress" for those left behind.

While at one time a recommendation was for users to write down their passwords and give that to a family member, that recommendation is no longer considered a good option. First, many accounts require users to periodically change passwords. Updating a list every time a password is changed and then sending it to family members is time-consuming and apt to be forgotten. Second, writing down passwords in general is not recommended due to the risk of a misplaced list or the list being viewed by someone who would be tempted to use it. For example, an unscrupulous person hired to clean a house or paint a room may be able to rifle through desk drawers looking for valuables or important information. Also, a nosy relative could use the passwords to snoop on the user without their knowledge. And because a safe deposit box at a bank may not be readily accessible to heirs upon a death (the laws vary by state), storing a list of passwords in a bank is also not recommended.

Several of the major tech platforms are now providing solutions in these circumstances. A living user can designate one or more "digital-legacy contacts" who can download data, such as text messages and photos, or access profiles upon the user's death. An advantage of this approach is that the actual password to the platform itself is not shared with anyone. However, it may restrict what can be accessible upon death.

Google's Inactive Account Manager provides the broadest range of options. A living user can decide what happens to their data after they have stopped using their account for a certain period (users decide the length of that period). Google will send an email when the account reaches the inactive time limit to up to 10 people. Also, what specific data the designees can access—such as YouTube videos, photos, emails, and other documents—can also be designated. However, the designees cannot send emails from the Google account in the user's name. If the Inactive Account Manager is not set up in advance, it is necessary to upload a death certificate and work with Google to close the account and receive any of its content.

Meta provides a more limited option for its platforms. Facebook users can select a digital-legacy contact to look after a "memorialized" account or choose to have that profile deleted after someone informs Meta of a death. In both cases, the fastest way to notify Facebook is with an uploaded death certificate. However, a digital-legacy contact cannot be set on Instagram in advance.

Apple allows a digital-legacy contact to access most of the data in the deceased's iCloud account. Once this is set up using an iPhone, the designees are given an access key. Upon death, a designee can log in and upload a death certificate to view the deceased's call history, health data, notes, and iCloud backups, but they will not have access to passwords stored in an iCloud Keychain. If no digital-legacy contact is made in advance, Apple requires a court order to give an heir access to the deceased's Apple ID and data.

Some online password managers also allow for digital-legacy contacts. 1Password has "shared vaults" that are shareable folders that designated friends or family members with granted access can view. The service also lets users print out an Emergency Kit document with space for login information and a Quick Response code that sends heirs to 1Password's website where they can sign into the account. LastPass permits users to designate a list of trusted people and invite them to create an account. In the event of the user's death, a trusted contact can request emergency access to the password vault. And a wait time can be set, during which access can be denied to the emergency contacts if the user is still alive and capable of accessing the account. And because smartphones are commonly used to verify a login attempt, users should also share with their designees how to access their phone.

The very foundation of security is keeping the bad guys out while letting the good guys in. Virtually every device that you use—laptop, smartphone, even a web server—has some means for you to prove you have approval to use that device. And once approved, you are not granted complete access to everything on the device. On a web server, you are not given access to another user's account, and even on your own computer you are restricted from accessing protected parts of the operating system (OS).

In information security, **identity and access management (IAM)** is the technologies that provide control over user validation and the resources that may be accessed. IAM ensures that the right users access the right digital resources at the right time and for the right reasons.

This final module about device security looks at how devices can be accessed by authorized users and restrict what users can do on the devices. First, you look at the different types of authentication credentials that can be used to verify a user's identity. Then you look at best practices for authentication. Finally, you explore limiting privileges through access controls.

Types of Authentication Credentials

Certification

2.5 Explain the purpose of mitigation techniques used to secure the enterprise.

4.6 Given a scenario, implement and maintain identity and access management.

In information security, IAM requires a user accessing a device to first provide some type of unique digital identity. This identity serves to differentiate the user from all other users. But it also requires the user to provide proof that they *are* this unique user, called **identity proofing**. Just as anyone knocking on a front door could claim to be a local utility repair person (identity), asking them to display an ID card would prove they are who they claim to be (identity proofing). Identity proofing is also called **authentication**, which is the process of ensuring that the person or system desiring access to resources is authentic or "genuine" and not an imposter.

Consider this scenario: Riker, Peyton, and Paolo work on a local military base and each afternoon they go to the gym on the base to exercise. As they reach the entrance to the building, each must press their finger to the fingerprint reader to enter the building (a "no tailgating" policy is strictly enforced). As they walk to the receptionist's desk, Riker holds up his ID card to the reader so the door to the locker room opens for him. As Peyton searches for his card, the receptionist, Li, waves him through to the locker room because she knows him. Riker laughs and says to Li, "It's only because of Peyton's flaming red hair that you recognize him, and it runs in his family!" Paolo, however, is new to the base and must sign in. After Li compares his signature to his membership application on file, she then allows him to enter. In the locker room, each of them opens their locker using a combination lock with a series of numbers that they have memorized.

In this scenario, the three men have been demonstrated to be authentic and not an imposter by the seven separate elements listed in Table 7-1. Because only the real or "authentic" person possesses one or more of these elements, these can be considered as types of authentication credentials.

Table 7-1   Elements that prove authenticity

Element	Description	Scenario example
Somewhere you are	Restricted location	Restricted military base
Something you are	Unique biological characteristic that cannot be changed	Fingerprint reader to enter building
Something you have	Possession of an item that nobody else has	Riker's ID card
Someone you know	Validated by another person	Li knows Peyton
Something you exhibit	Genetically determined characteristic	Peyton's flaming red hair
Something you can do	Perform an activity that cannot be exactly copied	Paolo's signature
Something you know	Knowledge that nobody else possesses	Combination to unlock locker

Note ①

Three of these elements (something you know, something you have, and something you are) are called *factors*, while the remaining four (somewhere you are, something you can do, something you exhibit, and someone you know) are called *attributes*. The element *something you exhibit* is often linked to more specialized attributes than hair color in the scenario and may even include neurological traits that can be identified by specialized medical equipment.

Any of these elements can be used as an authentication credential. However, the most common credentials found in IAM are something you know, something you have, something you are, and something you can do.

Caution ❗

The word *identity* in IAM covers both identity proofing and authentication.

Something You Know: Passwords

The most common IAM authentication credential is providing information that only the user knows. A password is a secret combination of letters, numbers, and/or characters. Passwords are universally used for authentication and work in a standard format across devices and sites. However, passwords provide weak protection and are constantly under attack.

Note 2

The person credited with inventing the computer password, Fernando "Corby" Corbato, who passed away in late 2019, was a researcher for the Massachusetts Institute of Technology and worked on the Compatible Time-Sharing System (CTSS), which allowed multiple users to share computer time. He devised a way to isolate users from each other with password-protected user accounts. In his later years, Corbato lamented that passwords had become problematic. He said that the Internet made logins with passwords "kind of a nightmare."

How Passwords Work

Consider a user who is creating a new account for an online bank. The user would first create (or in some instances be assigned) a username for the account before creating a password that satisfies the bank's necessary minimum password requirements. The username and password are then transmitted to the bank's server.

The server will convert the password to a scrambled set of characters to be stored. Technically, this scrambling is performed by a one-way hash algorithm that creates a message digest of the password. The reason why the original unscrambled password is not stored by the server is for security: an attacker who could steal this list of unscrambled passwords would then have immediate unfettered access to all accounts. Finally, the username and digest (scrambled password) would be stored along with other usernames and digests. Creating a password is illustrated in Figure 7-1.

Figure 7-1   Creating a password

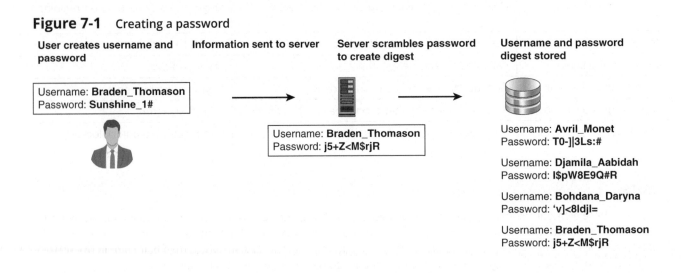

Note 3

Hashes are covered in Module 3.

The next time that the user logs into their bank account, they would enter both the username and password. This information is sent to the bank's server, which again creates a message digest on the password just entered by using the same one-way hash used originally when the account was created. The bank's server then looks for a match by comparing this just-created digest with the original stored digest. If the two scrambled digests match, then the user is authenticated and access is granted. Retrieving a password is illustrated in Figure 7-2.

Figure 7-2 Retrieving a password

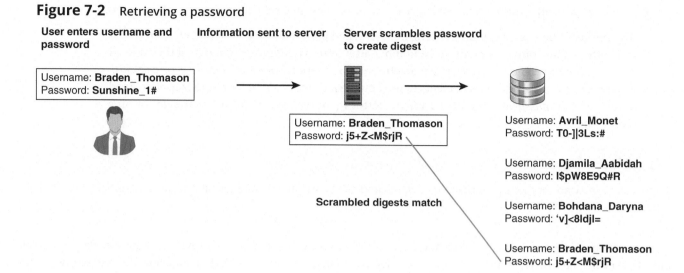

Password Weaknesses

The *security* of passwords is based on human memory: unless tricked by social engineering to reveal a password, a user's memory is considered a secure repository for passwords. This is because human memory cannot be compromised through a vulnerability the same way in which a technology device can be compromised.

However, the *weakness* of passwords is also based on human memory: human beings can memorize only a limited number of items. And the longer and more complex the item, the more difficult it is to remember. Passwords place heavy loads on human memory in multiple ways:

- The most effective passwords are long and complex. However, these are difficult for users to memorize and then accurately recall when needed.
- Users must remember multiple passwords for many different accounts. Most users have accounts for different computers and mobile devices at work, school, and home; multiple email accounts; online banking; Internet site accounts; and so on. According to one study, in the United States, the average number of online accounts registered to a single email address was 130. The average number of accounts per Internet user is estimated to be 207.[1]
- For the highest level of security, each account password should be unique, which further strains human memory.
- Many information security policies mandate that passwords expire after a set period of time, such as every 45 to 60 days, when a new one must be created. Some security policies even prevent a previously used password from being recycled and used again, forcing users to repeatedly memorize new passwords.

Because of the burdens that passwords place on human memory, users take shortcuts to help them memorize and recall their passwords, thus creating passwords that are vulnerable to attacks (weak passwords). Weak passwords often use a common word as a password (*princess*), a short word (*tabletop*), a predictable sequence of characters (*123456*), or personal information (*Hannah*) in a password. Another common shortcut that dramatically weakens passwords is to reuse the same password (or a slight derivation of it) for multiple accounts: although this makes it easier for the user, it also makes it easier for an attacker who compromises one account to then access all other accounts that use the same password.

Even when users attempt to create stronger passwords, they generally follow predictable patterns:

- **Appending.** When users combine letters, numbers, and punctuation (character sets), they do it in a pattern. Most often they only add a number after letters (*caitlin1* or *cheer99*). If they add all three character sets, it is in the sequence letters+punctuation+number (*braden.8* or *chris#6*).
- **Replacing.** Users also use replacements in predictable patterns. Generally, a zero is used instead of the letter *o* (*passw0rd*), the digit *1* for the letter *I* (*soc1al_med1a*), or a dollar sign for an *s* (*be$tfriend*).

> **Caution** !
>
> Attackers are aware of these patterns in passwords and can search for them, making it faster and easier to crack the password.

Security professionals decry the widespread use of weak passwords since they provide an easy attack vector. Four out of every five enterprise data breaches are caused by weak passwords, and half of all users use one password for all their accounts. And when forced to create a new password, two out of every three users create a password that is like the one they are replacing. The 10 most common passwords in 2023 are listed in Table 7-2, and three of the top four common passwords in this list have remained the same for over six years.[2]

Table 7-2   Ten most common passwords

Rank	Password
1	123456
2	123456789
3	qwerty
4	password
5	12345
6	qwerty123
7	1q2w3e
8	12345678
9	111111
10	1234567890

A noted security expert summarized the password problem well by stating:

> The problem is that the average user can't and won't even try to remember complex enough passwords to prevent attacks. As bad as passwords are, users will go out of the way to make it worse. If you ask them to choose a password, they'll choose a lousy one. If you force them to choose a good one, they'll write it [down] and change it back to the password they changed it from the last month. And they'll choose the same password for multiple applications.[3]

> **Note** 4
>
> A recent study looked at users who had been told that the password to their account had been stolen in a data breach. Only one-third of the users then changed their passwords. And the users were in no rush to change their passwords: only 3 percent changed their password within 30 days after the breach, while 12 percent waited between 60 and 90 days. Incredibly, only 14 percent of users changed their password to a *stronger* password; all others created passwords that were actually weaker or the same strength as the stolen password by reusing character sequences from their previous password or creating a new password that was similar to other passwords they use.

Password Attacks

There are different types of password attacks. Some attacks typically have very limited success at compromising an account, but they do not require much effort on the part of the threat actor. In some cases, the attacker may determine the user's password by more of a "lucky guess" than a focused and systematic attack. Other attacks are high outcome attacks in which there is a high degree of success, but these require much more time and effort.

Low-Outcome Attacks   There are two types of low-outcome attacks. These are online brute force attacks and password spraying.

Online Brute Force Attack   In an online automated brute force attack, every possible combination of letters, numbers, and characters is combined to attempt to determine the user's password. The same account is continuously attacked ("pounded") by entering different passwords. However, an online brute force attack is rarely used because it is a low-outcome attack and is impractical. Even at two or three tries per second, it could take thousands of years to guess the right password. In addition, most accounts can be set to disable all logins after a limited number of incorrect attempts (such as five), thus putting an end to the threat.

Password Spraying Attack   Instead of trying every possible combination to attempt to find the correct password, another type of password attack instead uses a type of "targeted guessing." A password spraying attack takes one or a small number of commonly used passwords (*password1* or *123456*) and then uses this same password when trying to log in to several different user accounts. Because this targeted guess is spread across many different accounts, instead of attempting multiple password variations on a single account, it is much less likely to raise any alarms or lock out the user account from too many failed password attempts. Although password spraying may result in occasional successes, it is still considered a low-outcome attack.

High-Outcome Attacks   There are other types of attacks that can produce a high number of compromised passwords. These attacks are focused on compromising and then attacking one of the key elements of password technology: the password digest files. Attackers set their sights on obtaining the file of password digests from a website or a device. Once that file is in the hands of the threat actors, it can be loaded onto their own computers and then exploited through sophisticated software called password crackers, which is designed to uncover the passwords.

However, password crackers do not "unravel" a digest to determine the underlying password; rather, they *compare* digests created from their known passwords to the digests in the stolen password file of unknown user passwords. When the digests match, the password has been "cracked." For example, using a password cracker, an attacker might take the word *Sunday* and create the digest *2602ab347f0ba5c63a0c936eba832ec5*. The cracking software then compares this digest against the digests from the stolen file. If a match of digests occurs, then the attacker knows the password is *Sunday*. Password crackers differ as to how known digests (called "candidates") are created.

Note 5

"Cracking" passwords is just matching digests.

How do threat actors obtain these valuable password digest files? At one time, attackers were forced to attempt to break through the security of a device like a web server to steal the file. However, if they were not successful, they would not be able to generate an attack.

A watershed moment in password attacks occurred in late 2009. An attacker using an SQL injection attack broke into a server belonging to a developer of several popular social media applications. This server contained more than 32 million user passwords, all in cleartext. These passwords were later posted on the Internet. Attackers quickly seized upon this opportunity. This "treasure-trove" collection of passwords gave attackers, for the first time, a large corpus of real-world passwords that could be utilized.

> ### Note 6
>
> These password collections also provided attackers advanced insight into the strategic thinking of how users create passwords. For example, on those occasions when users mix uppercase and lowercase letters in passwords, users tend to capitalize at the beginning of the password, much like writing a sentence. Likewise, punctuation and numbers are more likely to appear at the end of the password, again mimicking standard sentence writing. And a high percentage of passwords were comprised of a name and date, such as *Braden2008*. Such insights are valuable in attacks, significantly reducing the amount of time needed to break a password when compared to a raw brute force attack.

Since this initial theft, attackers who have stolen password digest files have routinely posted them on the Internet for other threat actors to download and use. Many of these websites also crack the submitted password digest files so that attackers have a readymade collection to download. One website boasts over 1.45 *trillion* cracked digests. Using stolen password digests as candidate passwords is the foundation of password cracking today, and almost all password cracking software tools accept these stolen lists as input.

High-outcome attacks based on password digest files include offline brute force attacks, dictionary attacks, credential stuffing, and rule attacks.

Offline Brute Force Attack   An offline brute force attack begins with a stolen password digests file. After loading this file onto their computer, the attacker then uses password cracking software to create candidate digests of every possible combination of letters, numbers, and characters. These are then matched against those in a stolen digest file looking for a match. This is the slowest yet most thorough method.

> ### Note 7
>
> When cracking passwords using a brute force attack, attackers often use computers with multiple graphics processing units (GPUs). Whereas the central processing unit (CPU) of a computer can do a wide variety of tasks, a GPU, which is separate from the CPU, is used to render screen displays on computers. GPUs are very good at performing video processing, which involves the repetitive work of performing the same function over and over on large groups of pixels on the screen. This makes GPUs superior to CPUs at repetitive tasks like breaking passwords.

Dictionary Attack   A variation of an offline brute force attack is a **dictionary attack**. Instead of using a wide range of candidate digests, a dictionary attack uses common dictionary words and phrases as candidates and then compares them against those in a stolen digest file. Dictionary attacks are successful because users often create passwords from simple dictionary words.

Credential Stuffing   Knowing from where the password digest was stolen gave threat actors the ability to log into accounts on that site. That is, if the password digest file came from example.com, then attackers could crack passwords to use on accounts on example.com. But because most users repeat their passwords on multiple accounts, attackers do not have to limit their attacks to only the site from which the password digest was stolen: they could inject the username and password on *any* site, hoping that the user had repeated the same username and password on it, too. This type of attack is known as **credential stuffing**, or the injection of stolen username and password credentials across multiple websites.

Rule Attack   A **rule attack** conducts a statistical analysis on the stolen passwords. The results of this analysis are then used to create a **mask** of the format of the candidate password. A mask of *?u ?l ?l ?l ?l ?d ?d ?d ?d* (u = uppercase, l = lowercase, and d = digit) would tell the password cracking program, "Use an uppercase letter for the first position, a lowercase letter for the next four positions, and digits for the remaining four positions." Using a mask will significantly reduce the time needed to crack a password. There are three basic steps in a rule attack:

1. A small sample of the stolen password plaintext file is obtained.
2. Statistical analysis is performed on the sample to determine the length and character sets of the passwords, as seen in Figure 7-3.

Figure 7-3   Rule attack statistical analysis

```
[*] Length Statistics...
[+]                              8: 62% (612522)
[+]                              6: 18% (183307)
[+]                              7: 14% (146152)
[+]                              5: 02% (26438)
[+]                              4: 01% (15088)
[+]                              3: 00% (2497)
[+]                              2: 00% (308)
[+]                              1: 00% (113)

[*] Charset statistics...
[+]              loweralphanum: 47% (470580)
[+]                 loweralpha: 46% (459208)
[+]                    numeric: 05% (56637)
```

3. A series of masks are generated that will be most successful in cracking the highest percentage of passwords. This is illustrated in Figure 7-4.

Figure 7-4   Rule attack generated masks

```
[*] Advanced Mask statistics...
[+]           ?l?l?l?l?l?l?l?l: 04% (688053)
[+]             ?l?l?l?l?l?l?l: 04% (601257)
[+]           ?l?l?l?l?l?l?l?l: 04% (585093)
[+]         ?l?l?l?l?l?l?l?l?l: 03% (516862)
[+]             ?d?d?d?d?d?d?d: 03% (487437)
[+]       ?d?d?d?d?d?d?d?d?d?d: 03% (478224)
[+]           ?d?d?d?d?d?d?d?d: 02% (428306)
[+]           ?l?l?l?l?l?l?d?d: 02% (420326)
[+]         ?l?l?l?l?l?l?l?l?l: 02% (416961)
[+]               ?d?d?d?d?d?d: 02% (390546)
[+]         ?d?d?d?d?d?d?d?d?d: 02% (307540)
[+]           ?l?l?l?l?l?d?d: 02% (292318)
[+]         ?l?l?l?l?l?l?l?d?d: 01% (273640)
```

Note 8

A rule attack is not intended to crack every password, but instead gives the highest probability of the largest number of passwords that can be broken.

Most threat actors do not use a single password attack tool but use several of these in combination. Table 7-3 lists a common sequence of attack tools on passwords.

Table 7-3   Common sequence of password attack tools

Order	Password attack	Explanation
1	Custom wordlist	Download a stolen password digest
2	Custom wordlist using rule attack	Generate password statistics using a rule attack to create specialized masks
3	Dictionary attack	Perform a dictionary attack on passwords
4	Dictionary attack using rules	Conduct a refined dictionary attack using results from a rule attack
5	Updated custom wordlist using rules	Input any cracked passwords from previous steps to create more refined rules
6	Hybrid attack	Perform a focused dictionary attack with a mask attack
7	Mask attack	Conduct a mask attack on harder passwords that have not already been cracked
8	Brute force attack	Last-resort effort on any remaining passwords

> **Note 9**
>
> Note that Table 7-3 assumes that a sample of the passwords in plaintext can be examined; if this is not available, then most attacks will skip to Step 3, which results in enough cracked passwords so that rules can be developed for the next step.

Something You Have: Tokens and Security Keys

Another type of authentication credential is based on the approved user having a specific item in their possession (something you have). The most common items that are used for this type of authentication are tokens, security keys, and smart cards.

Tokens

A *token* is some type of object. There are two types of authentication tokens: hardware tokens and software tokens. These are also called hard/soft authentication tokens.

Hardware Tokens   One type of hardware token is a windowed token, which is typically a small device (usually one that can be affixed to a keychain, called a key fob) with a window display. A windowed token is shown in Figure 7-5. A windowed token does not display a static value that never changes; instead, the value dynamically changes. This value is a **one-time password (OTP)** that can be used only once or for a limited period of time.

Figure 7-5   Windowed token

There are two types of OTPs. A time-based one-time password (TOTP) changes after a set period of time, such as every 30 to 60 seconds (this code is valid for only the brief period that it is displayed on the token). When the user logs in, they enter their username along with the code currently being displayed on the token. Instead of changing after a set number of seconds, an HMAC-based one-time password (HOTP) is "event-driven" and changes when a specific event occurs, such as when a user enters a personal identification number (PIN) on the token's keypad, which triggers the token to create a random code. For example, after entering the PIN *1729*, the code *833854* is displayed.

While windowed tokens have some advantages, such as creating dynamic OTPs, they do require the most steps to complete the authentication process. Once an OTP is received, it must then be manually entered on the endpoint device. And because the OTP is valid for only a short time, the user must enter it quickly.

Software Tokens   Instead of using a separate physical hardware device like a windowed token, today software-based tokens are becoming increasingly popular. Because smartphones are ubiquitous and carried by users virtually everywhere, they can be used for authentication without the need for an additional physical device. Two categories of software tokens are those that generate OTPs and those that supplement passwords.

Software OTP   A software OTP is generated through an app on a user's smartphone. This serves to replace a hardware token while providing an OTP for authentication.

Password Supplements   Instead of generating a dynamic OTP on a smartphone, more often today a password supplement is generated. This supplement is used along with a standard static password and is created once a valid username and password has been entered. Because this involves combining more than one type of authentication credential—both what a user knows (the password) and what the user has (the smartphone)—this is called multifactor authentication (MFA).

One type of password supplement is an authentication app installed on the user's smartphone that simply requests the user's approval. Whenever a user attempts to log in to an account by entering a username and password, a message is displayed on the phone (called a push notification) through the authentication app that asks them to approve or deny the request. Using an authentication app is seen in Figure 7-6.

Figure 7-6   Authentication app

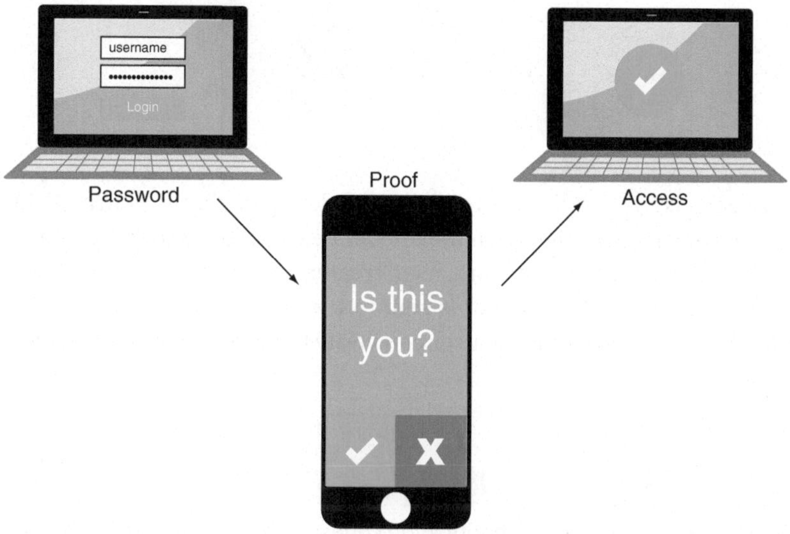

A more common option instead of a separate authentication app is for the user to receive an authentication code in an SMS text sent to their smartphone. After entering a username and password, a text message with an authentication code is sent and the user must enter that code on the website to complete the authentication process.

Despite its convenience and ability to reach a wide range of users, using a SMS text sent to a smartphone for authentication is not considered a secure option. An SMS text can be "phished" (a user is tricked into providing the code to an attacker through a phishing attack) and SMS texts can be intercepted. A new type of attack on SMS text authentication codes is "MFA fatigue." In this attack, a threat actor runs a script that attempts to log in repeatedly with stolen credentials, generating a seemingly endless stream of MFA push notifications sent to the user's smartphone. In many cases, the target will simply accept the MFA push notification in order to stop being bothered. If this does not occur, then the attacker will contact the target through email, through another text message, or by phone, pretending to be IT support and alerting the user to a supposed MFA malfunction. The target is asked to approve the notification to turn it off.

Note 10

In early 2023, Twitter announced that it would provide SMS authentication codes only to paid subscribers. Nonpaying Twitter users can still have MFA, but it will only be available through a software authentication app installed on the user's smartphone. Twitter claims that the change is because SMS authentication has been abused by attackers. However, a question has been raised that if this is vulnerable, why would it still be available to paid subscribers? Others have noted that this policy shift will save Twitter money because the company currently pays to send SMS texts for MFA.

Security Keys

A more secure option that is gaining acceptance is using a dedicated token key, known as a security key. As seen in Figure 7-7, a security key is a dongle that is inserted into the USB port (Windows and Apple) or Lightning port (Apple) or held near the device (such as a smartphone using near-field communication [NFC]). The key contains all the necessary cryptographic information to authenticate the user.

Figure 7-7   Security keys

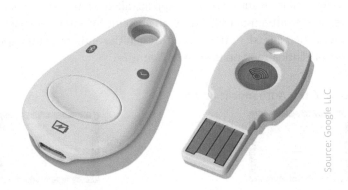

Source: Google LLC

One feature of security keys is attestation. Attestation is a key pair that is "burned" into the security key during manufacturing time and is specific to a device model. It can be used to cryptographically prove that a user has a specific model of device when it is registered. When a user creates a new credential key pair (that links to a specific service like Facebook or PayPal), the public key that is sent to the service is signed with the attestation private key. The service that is creating the new account for the user can verify that the attestation signature on the newly created public key came from the device.

> **Note 11**
>
> Because security keys do not transmit OTPs or authentication codes, many security professionals recommend that users consider security keys for authentication.

Smart Cards

A smart card is a credit-card-sized plastic card that can hold information to be used as part of the authentication process. Smart cards used for authentication generally require that the card be inserted into a card reader that is connected to the computer, although some cards are contactless cards that only require it to be in very close proximity to the reader. A smart card standard covering all U.S. government employees is called the Personal Identity Verification (PIV) standard.

Something You Are: Biometrics

In addition to authentication based on what a person knows or has, another category rests on the features and characteristics of an individual, known as biometrics. This type of authentication, something you are, involves physiological biometrics and cognitive biometrics.

Physiological Biometrics

Physiological means "relating to the way in which a body part functions." For authentication, physiological biometrics uses the way in which a body part uniquely functions in an individual. There are several unique characteristics of a person's body that can be used to authenticate a user. These can be divided into those that require specialized biometric scanners and those that use standard technology input devices for recognition. However, there are several issues regarding using biometrics.

Specialized Biometric Scanners   Some types of biometric authentication require specialized and dedicated biometric scanners that are used to inspect the person's features. A retinal scanner uses the human retina as a biometric identifier. The retina is a layer at the back (posterior) portion of the eyeball that contains cells sensitive to light, which trigger nerve impulses that pass these through the optic nerve to the brain, where a visual image is formed. Due to the complex structure of the capillaries that supply the retina with blood, each person's retina is unique.

Note 12

The network of blood vessels in the retina is so complex that even identical twins do not share a similar pattern. Even though retinal patterns may be altered in cases of diabetes, glaucoma, or retinal degenerative disorders, the retina generally remains unchanged through a person's lifetime.

A retinal scanner maps the unique patterns of a retina by directing a beam of low-energy infrared light (IR) into a person's eye as they look in the scanner's eyepiece (the beam cannot be detected by the user). Because retinal blood vessels are more absorbent of IR than the rest of the eye, the amount of reflection varies during the scan. This pattern of variations is recorded and used for comparison when the user attempts to authenticate.

Using a fingerprint as a biometric identifier has become the most common type of biometric authentication. Every user's fingerprint consists of several ridges and valleys, with ridges being the upper skin layer segments of the finger and valleys the lower segments. In one method of fingerprint scanning, the scanner locates the point where these ridges end and split, converts them into a unique series of numbers, and then stores the information as a template. A second method creates a template from selected locations on the finger.

There are two basic types of fingerprint scanners. A static fingerprint scanner requires the user to place the entire thumb or finger on a small oval window on the scanner. The scanner takes an optical "picture" of the fingerprint and compares it with the fingerprint image on file, as shown in Figure 7-8. The other type of scanner is known as a dynamic fingerprint scanner, which has a small slit or opening across which the finger is swiped.

Figure 7-8   Static fingerprint scanner

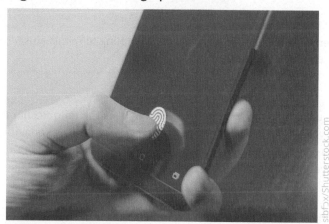

sibfax/Shutterstock.com

Note 13

Dynamic fingerprint scanners work on the same principle as stud finders that carpenters use to locate wood studs behind drywall. This is known as capacitive technology.

Another human characteristic that can be used for authentication is a person's vein (one of the "tubes" that form part of the blood circulation system in the human body that carries oxygen-depleted blood back toward the heart). Typically vein images in a user's palm or finger for authentication can be identified through a vein-scanning tablet.

A person's gait, or manner of walking, can also uniquely authenticate an individual. Research has shown that gait recognition can achieve over 99 percent accuracy. Typically, small sensors less than an inch in height can be placed on a floor at intervals of about 65 feet (20 meters) to measure gait.

Note 14

The payment provider Mastercard is working on developing a system that would uniquely identify mass transit passengers so that they do not need to swipe a transit card.

Standard Input Devices   Unlike some biometric identifiers that require specialized scanners, other types of biometrics can use standard computer input devices for recognition, such as a microphone or camera.

Because all users' voices are different, voice recognition, using a standard computer microphone, can be used to authenticate users based on the unique characteristics of a person's voice. Several characteristics make each person's voice unique, from the size of the head to age. These differences can be quantified to create a user voice template.

Caution !

Voice recognition is not to be confused with speech recognition, which accepts spoken words for input as if they had been typed on the keyboard.

One of the concerns regarding voice recognition is that an attacker could record the user's voice and then create a recording to use for authentication. However, this would be extremely difficult to do. Humans speak in phrases and sentences instead of isolated words. The phonetic cadence, or speaking two words together in a way that one word "bleeds" into the next word, becomes part of each user's speech pattern. It would be extremely difficult to capture several hours of someone's voice, parse it into separate words, and then combine the words in real time to defeat voice recognition security.

Note 15

To protect against even the remote possibility of an attacker attempting to mimic a user's voice, identification phrases can be selected that would rarely (if ever) come up in normal speech.

An iris scanner, which can use a standard computer webcam, uses the unique characteristic of the iris, which is a thin, circular structure in the eye. A human iris is seen in Figure 7-9. The iris is responsible for controlling the diameter and size of the pupils to regulate the amount of light reaching the retina. Iris recognition identifies the unique random patterns in an iris for authentication.

Figure 7-9   Iris

creativemarc/Shutterstock.com

Note 16

A person's eye color is actually the color of the iris, which is most often brown, blue, or green. In some cases, it can be hazel, gray, violet, or even pink.

A biometric authentication that is becoming increasingly popular—but also controversial—is facial recognition. Every person's face has several distinguishable "landmarks" that make up their facial features. These landmarks are called nodal points. Each human face has approximately 80 nodal points, such as the width of the nose, the depth of the eye sockets, the shape of the cheekbones, and the length of the jaw line. Using a standard computer webcam, facial recognition software can measure the nodal points and create a numerical code (faceprint) that represents the face.

Biometric Disadvantages   Using biometrics has several disadvantages. The cost for specialized biometric scanners can be high, particularly when they must be installed at each location where authentication is required. A second disadvantage is that biometric authentication is not foolproof: genuine users may be rejected (**false negative**) while imposters are accepted (**false positive**). Third, biometric systems can be "tricked." Security researchers have demonstrated that fingerprints can be collected from water glasses and used to trick fingerprint readers on smartphones. In addition, if digital biometric data, such as a fingerprint scan that has been converted into a value, is stolen then it cannot be reset like a password, leaving the victim unable to use biometrics ever again for authentication.

Note 17

To combat against the theft of digital biometric data, one identity provider now binds biometric login information to a user's specific device. If the data is stolen, it cannot be used on any other device.

A final concern with biometrics is the efficacy rate (efficacy is the benefit achieved). While biometrics can aid in authentication, some experts question the sacrifice of user privacy: as individuals provide their biometric characteristics, how can this data be kept secure? Who can have access to it? How can it be used? The trade-offs continue to be weighed across society.

Cognitive Biometrics

Whereas most biometrics considers a person's physical characteristics, the field of cognitive biometrics is related to the perception, thought process, and understanding of the user. Cognitive biometrics is considered to be much easier for the user to remember because it is based on the user's life experiences. This also makes it more difficult for an attacker to imitate. Cognitive biometrics is also called knowledge-based authentication.

One type of cognitive biometrics introduced by Microsoft is called Windows Picture Password for Windows touch-enabled devices. Users select a picture to use for which there should be at least 10 "points of interest" on the photograph that could serve as "landmarks" or places to touch, connect with a line, or draw a circle around. Specific gestures—tap, line, or circle—are then used to highlight any parts of the picture while these gestures are recorded. When logging in, a user reproduces those same gestures on the photograph, as illustrated in Figure 7-10. For an attacker to replicate these actions, they would need to know the parts of the image that were highlighted, and the order of the gestures, as well as the direction, and the starting and ending points, of the circles and lines. However, security researchers have found that one of the most common methods used in Picture Password was using a photo of a person and triple-tapping on the face, with the most common face tap being the eyes, followed by the nose and jaw.

Figure 7-10   Picture password authentication

Pressmaster/Shutterstock.com

Note 18

Other examples of cognitive biometrics include requiring someone to identify specific faces or recall "memorable events," such as taking a vacation, celebrating a personal achievement, or attending a special family dinner. The user is asked specific questions about that memorable event, such as what type of food was served, how old the person was when the event occurred, where the event was located, who was in attendance, and the reason for the event. The user authenticates by answering the same series of questions when logging in.

Something You Do: Behavioral Biometrics

Another type of authentication is based on actions that the user is uniquely qualified to perform, or something you do. This is sometimes called **behavioral biometrics**.

One type of behavioral biometrics is keystroke dynamics, which recognizes a user's unique typing rhythm. Keystroke dynamics uses two unique typing variables. The first is known as dwell time, which is the time it takes for a key to be pressed and then released. The second characteristic is flight time, or the time between keystrokes (both "down" when the key is pressed and "up" when the key is released are measured). After collecting multiple typing samples, a user template can be formed so that when the user enters their username and password when logging in, the typing rhythm is compared to the template. If both what was entered (the password) and how it was entered (the typing rhythm) are correct, then the user is authenticated; otherwise, they are rejected. This is shown in Figure 7-11.

Figure 7-11   Authentication by keystroke dynamics

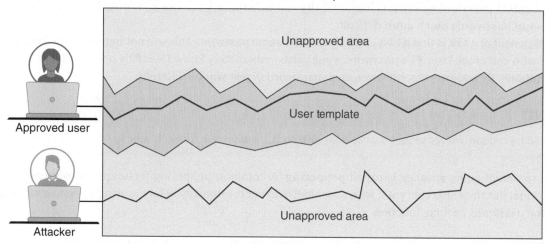

Keystroke dynamics hold a great deal of potential. Because this method requires no specialized hardware and because the user does not have to take any additional steps beyond entering a username and password, some security experts predict that keystroke dynamics will become more widespread in the near future.

Two Rights & A Wrong

1. "Somewhere you are" can be used as an authentication credential.
2. A password spraying attack has a very high potential for success.
3. Using SMS texts for MFA is not a secure option.

See the answers at the end of the module.

Authentication Best Practices

Certification

1.4 Explain the importance of using appropriate cryptographic solutions.

2.5 Explain the purpose of mitigation techniques used to secure the enterprise.

4.6 Given a scenario, implement and maintain identity and access management.

There are several authentication best practices. These can be divided into securing passwords and using secure authentication technologies.

Securing Passwords

Because passwords are so widely used—and widely attacked—much attention is focused on securing passwords. This includes protecting password digest files and managing passwords.

Protecting Password Digests

Besides securing servers so that the password digest files cannot be stolen, there are also additional steps that can be taken to protect the contents of the digests. These include salting and peppering along with key stretching.

Salting and Peppering   One means for an enterprise to protect stored digests is salting, which consists of a random string ("salt") that is used in hash algorithms. Passwords can be protected by adding this random string to the user's plaintext password before it is hashed. Salts make dictionary attacks and brute force attacks for cracking a large number of passwords much more difficult.

Another benefit of a salt is that if two users choose the same password, this will not help the attacker. Without salts, an attacker who can crack User #1's password would also immediately know User #2's password without performing any computations. By adding salts, however, each password digest will be different.

> **Caution** !
>
> Salts should be random (never sequential like *0001, 0002*, etc.) and unique for each user.

Another strengthening strategy is called **peppering**. A common peppering technique is to create the message digest as normal but then also encrypt it with a symmetrical encryption key before storing it. Peppering strategies do not affect the password hashing function.

Key Stretching   Using general-purpose hash algorithms like MD5 and SHA is not considered secure for creating digests because these hashing algorithms are designed to create a digest as quickly as possible. The fast speed of general-purpose hash algorithms works in an attacker's favor. When an attacker is creating candidate digests, a general-purpose hashing algorithm can rapidly create a very large number of passwords for matching purposes.

A more secure approach for creating password digests is to use a specialized password hash algorithm that is intentionally designed to be slower. This would then limit the ability of an attacker to crack passwords because it requires significantly more time to create each candidate digest, thus slowing down the entire cracking process. This is called key stretching. Whereas the increased time is a minor inconvenience when one user logs in and waits for the password digest to be generated, it can significantly reduce attackers' speed of generating candidates.

There are three common key stretching password hash algorithms. The algorithms bcrypt and PBKDF2 can be configured to require more time to create a digest. A network administrator can specify the number of iterations (rounds), which sets how "expensive" (in terms of computer time and/or resources) the password hash function will be. A newer key stretching algorithm, Argon2, can be configured based on several different parameters: adding a salt (which must be between 8 and 16 characters), the number of iterations (default of 3), and the memory usage (default parameter of 12).

> **Note** 19
>
> Using a general password algorithm, an attacker could generate about 95^8 candidate passwords in 5.5 hours. However, using bcrypt, in that same time only 71,000 candidate passwords could be generated.

Managing Passwords

While it is essential that password digest files be secured, it is likewise important that individual user passwords be kept safe. Solutions for managing passwords include enterprise password vaulting, user password managers, hardware password keys, and using password best practices.

Enterprise Password Vaulting   Enterprise-level password vaulting stores user password credentials in a highly protected database (vault) that is stored on the organization's network. However, password vaulting goes far beyond storing password credentials; it offers enhanced capabilities such as:

- Provide administrators complete authority over user passwords.
- Rotate and randomize passwords after access by a privileged user to enhance security.
- Grant access to critical assets with different levels of permissions assigned to users.
- Require users to document a valid reason for accessing a particular resource.
- Revoke access after a user session to safeguard privileged accounts from unauthorized access and misuse.
- Transfer orphaned accounts to other users in the network and provide access without revealing passwords.

User Password Managers   Unlike enterprise password vaulting that provides enhanced features needed by a large organization, a user password manager is a software application or online website that stores user passwords along with login information. Users can create and store multiple strong passwords in a single user "vault" file that is protected by one strong master password. They can retrieve individual passwords as needed from the vault. The value of using a password management application is that long, complex, and unique strong passwords can be easily created and used for all accounts.

However, password managers are more than a password-protected list of passwords: they typically include drag-and-drop capabilities, enhanced encryption, in-memory protection that prevents the OS cache from being exposed to reveal retrieved passwords, and timed clipboard clearing. Some password managers can even require that a secret key file be present when entering the master password to open the vault so that even if the vault file was stolen, it still could not be opened.

Hardware Password Keys   A weakness of vaults is that they are software based and could be susceptible to malware. More secure hardware-based solutions are also available in which to store passwords. They are called hardware **password keys**. Just as a security key can be used by itself for MFA, a password key can also be used as a separate storage facility for passwords. Figure 7-12 illustrates a password key. Password keys often serve as a hardware-based password manager, MFA security key, and file encryption device.

Figure 7-12   Password key

Source: OnlyKey

Password Best Practices   There are several best practices that should be followed for the creation and use of passwords. For example, all default passwords (standard preconfigured passwords) should be changed before a new device is placed into service. Password reuse (using the same password on multiple accounts) should be prohibited, since a threat actor who compromises one account would then have access to all other accounts. Password expiration (the point in time when a password is no longer valid) should not be utilized as a password best practice. Password age, the period of time that a password must be used before a user can change it, should be set to at least 1 to prevent a user from resetting an expired password with a new password then immediately reset it again to the old password. Provisioning (initially setting up user accounts) should include policies that address password best practices such as minimum password length, password age, and reuse while de-provisioning (removing user accounts) should also have policies such as accounts should be immediately suspended when an employee leaves the organization and the account be deleted 30 days later.

Note 20

In recognition of the difficulties surrounding expired passwords, a growing trend has been to drop this requirement. In 2019, Microsoft changed its long-held policy and recommended that password expiration be dropped and, in 2017, guidelines released by the National Institute of Standards and Technology (NIST) also recommended that password expiration should no longer be used. However, the Payment Card Industry (PCI) still requires that merchants and other providers change their passwords every 90 days. Some security professionals are calling for a modified password expiration so that the length of the password dictates its expiration. For example, a user who creates a 30-character password would not have to change that password for 2 years, while a password that is 15–25 characters in length would expire annually, and one of fewer than 15 characters would have to be reset every 90 days. One company that tried this approach found that calls to their help desk for password resets declined by 70 percent.

The most critical factor in a strong password is not complexity (the variation of its composition) but length (how many characters make up the password). A longer password is always more secure than a shorter password. This is because the longer a password is, the more attempts an attacker must make to break it. The formula for determining the number of possible passwords requires knowing only two items: the character set being used and the password length. Since the character set of most passwords is equal to the number of keys on a keyboard that can be used, the formula is *Number of keyboard keys ^ Password length = Total number of possible passwords*. Table 7-4 illustrates the number of possible passwords for different password lengths using a standard 95-key keyboard, along with the average attempts needed to break a password. Obviously, a longer password takes significantly more time to attempt to break than a short password.

Table 7-4   Number of possible passwords

Keyboard keys	Password length	Number of possible passwords	Average attempts to break password
95	2	9025	4513
95	3	857,375	428,688
95	4	81,450,625	40,725,313
95	5	7,737,809,375	3,868,904,688
95	6	735,091,890,625	367,545,945,313

Note 21

Users should not become confused by extravagant claims about the difficulty in breaking relatively short passwords. For example, one claim is that it would take 100 trillion years to break a password that is 18 characters in length and composed of numbers and uppercase and lowercase letters. However, this assumes that the password is a computer-generated random string to be broken by a brute force attack. But these are not the types of passwords that users memorize nor the types of attacks that threat actors use. A website notes that if a password contains words or names—which is common—or is used on multiple accounts, then the time to break an 18-character password is "Instantaneous!"!

Secure Authentication Technologies

There are several technologies that can enhance secure authentication. These include single sign-on and password-less systems.

Single Sign-On

Single sign-on holds great promise to relieve users of the burden of managing multiple passwords. It is important to understand single sign-on and the technologies that accompany it.

What Is Single Sign-On (SSO)?   One of the problems facing users today is the fact that if they have multiple accounts across multiple platforms that all should use a unique username and password. The difficulty in managing all of these different authentication credentials frequently causes users to compromise and select the least burdensome password and then use it for all accounts. A solution to this problem is to have one username and password to gain access to all accounts so that the user has only one username and password to remember.

This is the idea behind identity management, which is using a single authentication credential that is shared across multiple networks and has interoperability (the ability of systems to exchange information). When those networks are owned by different organizations, it is called federation (sometimes called federated identity management [FIM]). One application of federation is single sign-on (SSO), or using one authentication credential to access multiple accounts or applications. SSO holds the promise of reducing the number of usernames and passwords that users must memorize (potentially, to just one).

SSO Technologies There are several current technologies for SSO. These include Security Assertion Markup Language (SAML), Lightweight Directory Access Protocol (LDAP), and other federation systems.

Security Assertion Markup Language (SAML) Security Assertion Markup Language (SAML) is an XML standard that allows secure web domains to exchange user authentication and authorization data. This allows a user's login credentials to be stored with a single identity provider instead of being stored on each web service provider's server. SAML is used extensively for online e-commerce business-to-business (B2B) and business-to-consumer (B2C) transactions. The steps of a SAML transaction, which are illustrated in Figure 7-13, are:

1. The user attempts to reach a website of a service provider that requires a username and password.
2. The service provider generates a SAML authentication request that is then encoded and embedded into a URL.
3. The service provider sends a redirect URL to the user's browser that includes the encoded SAML authentication request, which is then sent to the identity provider.
4. The identity provider decodes the SAML request and extracts the embedded URL. The identity provider then attempts to authenticate the user either by asking for login credentials or by checking for valid session cookies.
5. The identity provider generates a SAML response that contains the authenticated user's username, which is then digitally signed using asymmetric cryptography.
6. The identity partner encodes the SAML response and returns that information to the user's browser.
7. Within the SAML response, there is a mechanism so that the user's browser can forward that information back to the service provider, either by displaying a form that requires the user to click a *Submit* button or by automatically sending to the service provider.
8. The service provider verifies the SAML response by using the identity provider's public key. If the response is successfully verified, the user is logged in.

Figure 7-13 SAML transaction

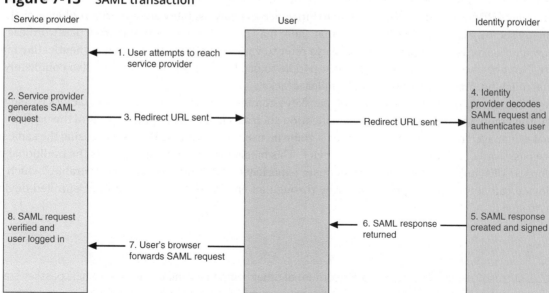

Lightweight Directory Access Protocol (LDAP)   A directory service is a database stored on the network itself that contains information about users and network devices. It contains information such as the user's name, telephone extension, email address, login name, and other facts. The directory service also keeps track of all the resources on the network and a user's privileges to those resources and grants or denies access based on the directory service information. Directory services make it much easier to grant privileges or permissions to network users.

The Lightweight Directory Access Protocol (LDAP) makes it possible for almost any application running on virtually any computer platform to obtain directory information. Because LDAP is an open protocol, applications need not worry about the type of server hosting the directory. LDAP is also the protocol or communication process that enables users to access a network resource through a directory service. Developers use LDAP to allow SSO if a single login were to grant the user access to all databases, apps, and devices on that server.

Other Federation Technologies   There are other federation technologies as well. These are listed in Table 7-5.

Table 7-5   Federation systems technologies

Name	Description	Explanation
OAuth (Open Authorization)	Open-source federation framework	OAuth 2.0 is a framework to support the development of authorization protocols.
OpenID	Open standard decentralized authentication protocol	Authentication protocol that can be used in OAuth 2.0 as a standard means to obtain a user identity.
Shibboleth	Open-source software package for designing SSO	Uses federation standards to provide SSO and exchanging attributes.

Note 22

OAuth relies on token credentials. A user sends their authentication credentials to a server (such as a web application server) and also authorizes the server to issue token credentials to a third-party server. These token credentials are used in place of transferring the user's username and password. The tokens are not generic but are for specific resources on a site for a limited period.

Passwordless Systems

Is it possible to have a strong and user-friendly authentication system that does not use passwords (passwordless)? For many years, technology platforms have said that the death of the password is right around the corner. However, these statements have turned out to be false. The promoted password alternatives, such as SSO, OAuth, and trusted platform modules (TPMs), were sometimes found to introduce as many usability and security problems as they solved. However, many security experts are now saying that there may be an alternative that is truly passwordless.

One new alternative is called **passkeys**. Passkeys refer to various methods for storing authenticating information in hardware. Not only are passkeys easier for most people to use than passwords, they are also completely resistant to credential phishing, credential stuffing, and similar attacks.

Passkeys do not rely on passwords. Instead, passkeys combine multiple authentication factors (usually a smartphone or laptop computer and a biometric authentication such as a facial scan or fingerprint of the user) into a single package that is managed by the device's OS. When signing in, users authenticate themselves using the same biometric or on-device password or PIN for unlocking their device. This mechanism completely replaces the traditional username and password or MFA and provides a much easier user experience. Passkeys are also "discoverable," which means an enrolled device can automatically push a passkey through an encrypted tunnel to another enrolled device that is attempting to sign in.

Note 23

In late 2022, Microsoft, Apple, Google, and a consortium of other companies unified around a single passkey standard.

> ## Two Rights & A Wrong
>
> **1.** Salting is encrypting a password digest before storing it.
>
> **2.** Password expiration is not a password best practice.
>
> **3.** Password length is more important than complexity.
>
> See the answers at the end of the module.

Access Controls

> ### Certification
>
> 2.5 Explain the purpose of mitigation techniques used to secure the enterprise.
>
> 4.6 Given a scenario, implement and maintain identity and access management.

It would be unthinkable for an employee, once they were allowed to enter a building by a security guard, to then be allowed free access to any office in that building. Rather, offices have door locks that restrict access to only those who have been preapproved with an appropriate key card.

In a similar fashion, a user who has been authenticated and can access a system does not have free reign to access any file or resource on that system. Instead, they must be preapproved to access resources and that access must be limited to what is only necessary for them to complete their work (least privilege).

> ### Note 24
>
> Most home users have full privileges on their personal computers so they can install programs, access files, or delete folders at will and give no thought to access control. In the enterprise, however, where multiple individuals could potentially have access to sensitive information, access control is essential.

As its name implies, access control is granting or denying approval to use specific resources once authenticated; it is controlling access. Some access can be based on time, such as just-in-time permissions (immediate elevation to higher-level permissions to perform a specific function before dropping back to normal levels), time-of-day restrictions (access levels that are bound to a specific window of time), and temporal accounts (one-time access). In any case, forethought must be given to why permissions are given, to whom, and what the impact may be (permission assignments and implications).

There are standard access control schemes and access control lists that are used to help enforce access control.

Access Control Schemes

Consider a system administrator who needs to act as an access control data custodian/steward. One afternoon, they must give a new employee access to specific servers and files. With hundreds of thousands of files scattered across a multitude of different servers, and with the new employee being given different access privileges to each file (for example, they can view one file but not edit it, but for a different file they can edit but not delete), controlling access could prove to be a daunting task.

However, this job is made easier by the fact that the hardware and software have a predefined framework that the administrator can use for controlling access. This framework, called an **access control scheme**, is embedded in the software and hardware. The administrator can use the appropriate scheme to configure the necessary level of control. Using these schemes is part of privileged access management, which is the technologies and strategies for controlling elevated (privileged) access and permissions.

Note 25

Access control schemes are variously referred to as access control models, methods, modes, techniques, or types. They are used by data custodians/stewards for access control but are neither created nor installed by them. Instead, these schemes are already part of the software and hardware.

There are five major access control schemes: Discretionary Access Control, Mandatory Access Control, Role-Based Access Control, Rule-Based Access Control, and Attribute-Based Access Control. There are also time-based access control schemes.

Discretionary Access Control (DAC)

The Discretionary Access Control (DAC) scheme is the least restrictive. With the DAC scheme, every object has an owner, who has total control over that object. Most importantly, the owner has discretion (the choice) as to who can access their objects and can grant permissions to other subjects over these objects. DAC is used on major OSs. Figure 7-14 illustrates the DAC that a Microsoft Windows owner has over an object. These controls can be configured so that another user can have full or limited access over a file, printer, or other object.

Figure 7-14   Windows Discretionary Access Control (DAC)

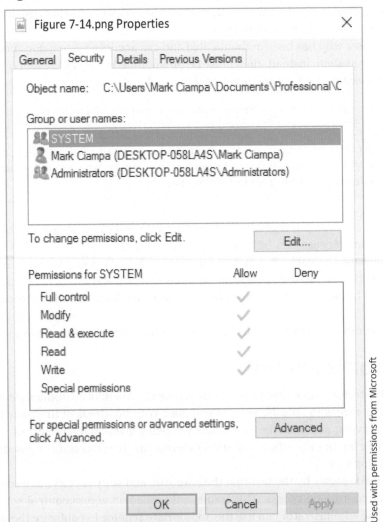

Used with permissions from Microsoft

DAC has two significant weaknesses. First, although it gives a degree of freedom to the subject, DAC poses risks in that it relies on decisions by the user to set the proper level of security. As a result, incorrect permissions might be granted to a subject or permissions might be given to an unauthorized subject. A second weakness is that a subject's permissions will be "inherited" by any programs that the subject executes. Threat actors often take advantage of this inheritance because users frequently have a high level of privileges. Malware that is downloaded onto a user's computer that uses the DAC scheme would then run at the same high level as the user's privileges.

Mandatory Access Control (MAC)

The opposite of DAC is the most restrictive access control scheme, Mandatory Access Control (MAC). MAC assigns users' access controls strictly according to the custodian's desires. This is considered the most restrictive access control scheme because the user has no freedom to set any controls or distribute access to other subjects.

There are two key elements to MAC:

- **Labels.** In a system using MAC, every entity is an object (laptops, files, projects, and so on) and is assigned a classification label. These labels represent the relative importance of the object, such as confidential, secret, and top secret. Subjects (users, processes, and so on) are assigned a privilege label (sometimes called a **clearance**).
- **Levels.** A hierarchy based on the labels is also used, both for objects and subjects. Top secret has a higher level than secret, which has a higher level than confidential.

MAC grants permissions by matching object labels with subject labels based on their respective levels. To determine if a file can be opened by a user, the object and subject labels are compared. The subject must have an equal or greater level than the object in order to be granted access. For example, if the object label is top secret, yet the subject has only a lower secret clearance, access is denied. Subjects cannot change the labels of objects or other subjects to modify the security settings.

Note 26

In the original MAC scheme, all objects and subjects were assigned a numeric access level and the access level of the subject had to be higher than that of the object for access to be granted. For example, if EMPLOYEES.XLSX was assigned Level 500 while SALARIES.XLSX was assigned Level 700, then a user with an assigned level of 600 could access EMPLOYEES.XLSX (Level 500) but not SALARIES.XLSX (Level 700). This scheme was later modified to use labels instead of numbers.

Microsoft Windows uses a MAC implementation called **Mandatory Integrity Control (MIC)** that ensures data integrity by controlling access to securable objects. A **security identifier (SID)** is a unique number issued to the user, group, or session. Each time a user logs in, the system retrieves the SID for that user from the database and then uses that SID to identify the user in all subsequent interactions with Windows security. Windows links the SID to an **integrity level**. Objects such as files, processes, services, and devices are assigned integrity levels—*low*, *medium*, *high*, and *system*—that determine their levels of protection or access. To write to or delete an object, the integrity level of the subject must be equal to or greater than the object's level. This ensures that processes running with a low integrity level cannot write to an object with a medium integrity level. MIC works in addition to Windows DAC: Windows first checks any requests against MIC and, if they pass, it then checks DAC.

Role-Based Access Control

The third access control scheme is Role-Based Access Control (RBAC) sometimes called **Non-Discretionary Access Control**. RBAC is considered a more "real-world" access control than the other schemes because the access under RBAC is based on a user's job function within an organization. Instead of setting permissions for each user or group, the RBAC scheme assigns permissions to particular roles in the organization and then assigns users to those roles. Objects are set to be a certain type, to which subjects with that particular role have access. For example, instead of creating a user account for Ahmed and assigning specific privileges to that account, the role *Business_Manager* can be created based on the privileges an individual in that job function should have. Then Ahmed and all other business managers in the organization can be assigned to that role. The users and objects inherit all the permissions for the role.

Rule-Based Access Control

The Rule-Based Access Control scheme, also called the Rule-Based Role-Based Access Control (RB-RBAC) scheme or "automated provisioning," can dynamically assign roles to subjects based on a set of rules. Each resource object contains a set of access properties based on the rules. When a user attempts to access that resource, the system checks the rules contained in that object to determine if the access is permissible.

Rule-Based Access Control is often used for managing user access to one or more systems, where business changes may trigger the application of the rules that specify access changes. For example, a subject on Network A wants to access objects on Network B, which is located on the other side of a router. This router contains the set of access control rules and can assign a certain role to the user, based on their network address or protocol, which will then determine whether they will be granted access. Similar to MAC, Rule-Based Access Control cannot be changed by users. All access permissions are controlled based on rules established by the custodian or system administrator.

Attribute-Based Access Control

While the Rule-Based Access Control scheme uses predefined rules, Attribute-Based Access Control (ABAC) uses more flexible policies that can combine attributes. These policies can take advantage of many different types of attributes, such as object, subject, and environment attributes. ABAC rules can be formatted using an *If-Then-Else* structure, so that a policy can be created such as *If this subject has the role of manager, then grant access else deny access.*

> **Note 27**
>
> ABAC systems can also enforce both DAC and MAC schemes.

Table 7-6 summarizes the features of the five access control schemes.

Table 7-6 Access control schemes

Name	Explanation	Description
Mandatory Access Control (MAC)	End-user cannot set controls	Most restrictive scheme
Discretionary Access Control (DAC)	Subject has total control over objects	Least restrictive scheme
Role-Based Access Control (RBAC)	Assigns permissions to particular roles in the organization and then users are assigned to roles	Considered a more "real-world" approach
Rule-Based Access Control	Dynamically assigns roles to subjects based on a set of rules defined by a custodian	Used for managing user access to one or more systems
Attribute-Based Access Control (ABAC)	Uses policies that can combine attributes	Most flexible scheme

Access Control Lists (ACLs)

An access control list (ACL) is a set of permissions (authorizations) that is attached to an object. This list specifies who are allowed to access an object and what operations they can perform on it. When a user requests to perform an operation on an object, the system checks the ACL for an approved entry in order to decide if the operation is allowed.

Although ACLs can be associated with any type of object, these lists are most often viewed in relation to files maintained by the OS. All OSs use a filesystem, which is a method for storing and organizing computer files to facilitate access. ACLs provide **filesystem permissions** for protecting files managed by the OS. ACLs have also been ported to SQL and relational database systems so that ACLs can provide database security as well.

Note 28

ACLs are the oldest and most basic form of access control. These became popular in the 1970s with the growth of multiuser systems, particularly UNIX systems, when it became necessary to limit access to files and data on shared systems. Later, as multiuser operating systems for personal use became popular, the concept of ACLs was added to them. Today all major OSs make use of ACLs at some level.

Although widely used, ACLs have limitations. First, using ACLs is not efficient. The ACL for each file, process, or resource must be checked every time the resource is accessed. They control not only user access to system resources but also application and system access. This means that in a typical computing session, ACLs are checked whenever a user accesses files, when applications are opened (along with the files and applications those applications open and modify), when the operating system performs certain functions, and so on. A second limitation to ACLs is that they can be difficult to manage in an enterprise setting where many users need to have different levels of access to many different resources. Selectively adding, deleting, and changing ACLs on individual files, or even groups of files, can be time-consuming and open to errors, particularly if changes must be made frequently.

Two Rights & A Wrong

1. Access control is granting or denying approval to use specific resources once a user has been authenticated.

2. Access control schemes are embedded in software and hardware.

3. DAC is the most restrictive access control scheme.

See the answers at the end of the module.

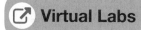 **Virtual Labs**   You're now ready to complete the simulations and live virtual machine labs for this module. The labs can be found in each module in MindTap.

Summary

- Identity and access management (IAM) is the technologies that provide control over user validation and the resources that may be accessed. IAM requires a user accessing a device to first provide some type of unique digital identity and then prove their genuineness (identity proofing), also known as authentication. There are three authentication credentials (something you know, something you have, and something you are) called factors while the remaining four (somewhere you are, something you can do, something you exhibit, and someone you know) are called attributes.

- The most common "something you know" type of authentication is a password. A password is a secret combination of letters, numbers, and/or characters that only the user should have knowledge of and is the most common type of authentication in use today. Passwords provide a weak degree of protection because they rely on human memory, and human beings have a finite limit to the number of items that they can memorize. Because of the burdens that passwords place on human memory, users create weak passwords to help them recall their passwords.

- There are different types of password attacks. Some attacks typically have very limited success at compromising an account, but they do not require much effort on the part of the threat actor. In an online automated brute force attack, every possible combination of letters, numbers, and characters is combined to attempt to determine the user's password. These attacks are rarely used because there is a low probability of success. A password spraying attack takes one or a small number of commonly used passwords and then uses this same password when trying to log in to several different user accounts. These attacks likewise have a low success rate.

- Other types of attacks can produce a high number of compromised passwords. These attacks are focused on password digest files. Password crackers compare digests created from known passwords to the digests in the stolen password file of unknown user passwords: when a match occurs, then the password is uncovered ("cracked"). An offline brute force attack uses password cracking software to create candidate digests of every possible combination of letters, numbers, and characters to compare against the digests in a password digest file. Instead of using a wide range of candidate digests, a dictionary attack uses common dictionary words and phrases as candidates and then compares them against those in a stolen digest file. Credential stuffing is the injection of stolen username and password credentials across multiple websites. A rule attack conducts a statistical analysis on the stolen passwords. Most threat actors do not use a single password attack tool but use several in combination.

- Another type of authentication credential is based on the approved user having a specific item in their possession (something you have). There are two types of authentication tokens: hardware tokens and software tokens. One type of hardware token is a windowed token, which is typically a small device with a window display that shows a one-time password (OTP). Instead of using a separate physical hardware device like a windowed token, today software-based tokens used with smartphones are becoming increasingly popular. Instead of generating a dynamic OTP on a smartphone, a password supplement is often generated. This supplement can be distributed through an authentication app or as an SMS text. Despite its convenience and ability to reach a wide range of users, using a SMS text sent to a smartphone for authentication is not considered a secure option.

- A more secure option that is gaining acceptance is using a dedicated token key, more commonly called a security key. A security key is a dongle that is inserted into the computer's port or held near the endpoint (such as a smartphone using near-field communication [NFC]). It contains all the necessary cryptographic information to authenticate the user. A smart card is a credit-card sized plastic card that can hold information to be used as part of the authentication process.

- The features and characteristics of the individual (something you are) can serve as authentication. Physiological biometrics uses a person's unique physical characteristics for authentication. This includes fingerprints, retinas, voice, iris, facial recognition, veins, and gait. There are disadvantages to biometrics. Cognitive biometrics is related to the perception, thought process, and understanding of the user. Cognitive biometrics is considered to be much easier for the user because it is based on the user's life experiences, which also makes it very difficult for an attacker to imitate. Behavioral biometrics, or something you do, authenticates by normal actions that the user performs. Behavioral biometric technologies include keystroke dynamics.

- There are several best practices for securing authentication credentials. One means for an enterprise to protect stored digests is salting, which consists of a random string that is used in hash algorithms. Peppering involves encrypting the password digest. Using general-purpose hash algorithms is not considered secure for creating digests. A better approach for creating password digests is to use a specialized password hash algorithm that is intentionally designed to be slower. This would then limit the ability of an attacker to crack passwords because it requires significantly more time to create each candidate digest, thus slowing down the entire cracking process. This is called key stretching.

- While it is essential that password digest files be secured, it is likewise important that individual user passwords be kept safe. Enterprise-level password vaulting stores user password credentials in a highly protected database (vault) that is stored on the organization's network. A user password manager is a software application or online web site that stores users' passwords along with login information. A hardware-based password key can also be used as a separate storage facility for passwords. Password best practices include changing all default passwords, prohibiting password reuse, not implementing password expiration, and extending password age. The most critical factor in a strong password is not complexity but length: a longer password is always more secure than a shorter password.

- Identity management is using a single authentication credential that is shared across multiple networks. When those networks are owned by different organizations, it is called federation. One application of federation is single sign-on (SSO) or using one authentication credential to access multiple accounts or applications. There are several current technologies for SSO. Security Assertion Markup Language (SAML) is an XML standard that allows secure web domains to exchange user authentication and authorization data. The Lightweight Directory Access Protocol (LDAP) is the protocol or communication process that enables users to access a network resource through a directory. OAuth (Open Authorization) is an open-source federation framework. After being promised for many years, authentication without using passwords, known as passwordless systems, are gaining headway.

- Access control is granting or denying approval to use specific resources; it is controlling access. Authentication, authorization, and accounting (AAA) provide a framework for controlling access to computer resources. Individuals are given different roles in relationship to access control objects or resources. These include data privacy officer, data custodian/steward, data owner, data controller, and data processor. Hardware and software have a predefined framework that the custodian can use for controlling access. This framework, called an access control scheme, can be used by a custodian/steward to configure the necessary level of control. Using these schemes is part of privileged access management, which is the technologies and strategies for controlling elevated (privileged) access. There are five major access control schemes: Discretionary Access Control, Mandatory Access Control, Role-Based Access Control, Rule-Based Access Control, and Attribute-Based Access Control.

- An access control list (ACL) is a set of permissions that is attached to an object. This list specifies which subjects are allowed to access the object and what operations they can perform on it. Although ACLs can be associated with any type of object, these lists are most often viewed in relation to files maintained by the OS. Although widely used, ACLs have limitations. First, using them is not efficient. A second limitation to ACLs is that they can be difficult to manage in an enterprise setting where many users need to have different levels of access to many different resources.

Key Terms

access control
access control list (ACL)
age
attestation
Attribute-Based Access Control
   (ABAC)
biometrics
brute force attack
complexity
default passwords
de-provisioning
Discretionary Access Control (DAC)
expiration
federation
hard/soft authentication tokens
identity and access management
   (IAM)
identity proofing

interoperability
just-in-time permissions
key stretching
least privilege
length
Lightweight Directory Access
   Protocol (LDAP)
Mandatory Access Control (MAC)
multifactor authentication (MFA)
OAuth (Open Authorization)
password
password manager
password spraying
password vaulting
passwordless
permission assignments and
   implications
permissions

provisioning
reuse
Role-Based Access Control
   (RBAC)
Rule-Based Access Control
salting
Security Assertion Markup
   Language (SAML)
security key
single sign-on (SSO)
something you are
something you have
something you know
somewhere you are
temporal accounts
time-of-day restrictions

Review Questions

1. How is SAML used?

   a. It serves as a backup to a directory server.
   b. It allows secure web domains to exchange user authentication and authorization data.
   c. It is an authenticator in IEEE 802.1x.
   d. It is no longer used because it has been replaced by LDAP.

2. Amahle is researching elements that can prove authenticity. Which of the following is based on unique biological characteristics?

   a. Something you exhibit
   b. Something you have
   c. Something you are
   d. Something about you

3. Which of the following elements is NOT true about passwords?

   a. The weakness of passwords is based on human memory.
   b. The most effective passwords are short but complex.
   c. For the highest level of security, each account should have a unique password.
   d. The security of passwords is based on human memory.

4. Imka has been asked to recommend a federation system technology that is an open-source federation framework and can support the development of authorization protocols. Which of these technologies would she recommend?

   a. OAuth
   b. Open ID
   c. Shibboleth
   d. NTLM

5. How is key stretching effective in resisting password attacks?

   a. It takes more time to generate candidate password digests.
   b. It requires the use of GPUs.
   c. It does not require the use of salts.
   d. The license fees are very expensive to purchase for use.

6. Which of these is NOT a key stretching algorithm?

   a. Argon2
   b. bcrypt
   c. PBKDF2
   d. MD5

7. Kholwa is explaining to her colleague how a password cracker works. Which of the following is a true statement about password crackers?

   a. Most states prohibit password crackers unless they are used to retrieve a lost password.
   b. Due to their advanced capabilities, they require only a small amount of computing power.
   c. A password cracker attempts to uncover the type of hash algorithm that created the digest because once it is known, the password is broken.
   d. Password crackers differ as to how candidates are created.

8. After a recent security breach, Lerato is investigating how the breach occurred. After examining log files, she discovered that the threat actor had used the same password on several different user accounts. What kind of attack was this?

   a. Password spraying attack
   b. Online brute force attack
   c. Offline brute force attack
   d. Dictionary attack

9. Why are dictionary attacks successful?

   a. Password crackers using a dictionary attack require less RAM than other types of password crackers.
   b. They link known words together in a "string" for faster processing.
   c. Users often create passwords from dictionary words.
   d. They use pregenerated rules to speed up the processing.

10. Which of the following is NOT true about a rule attack?

   a. A rule attack conducts a statistical analysis on the stolen passwords.
   b. Rule attacks are considered low-outcome attacks.
   c. The results of a rule attack are used to create a mask of the format of the candidate password.
   d. Using a mask will significantly reduce the time needed to crack a password.

11. Which of the following would a threat actor use last in attacks on a password digest?

   a. Brute force attack
   b. Custom wordlist
   c. Dictionary attack
   d. Dictionary attack using rules

12. Which of the following is NOT true about OTPs?

    a. They are displayed on security keys.
    b. An OTP can typically be used only once or for a limited period of time.
    c. They are dynamic and not static.
    d. There are two types of OTPs: TOTPs and HOTPs.

13. Which of the following is the least secure method for sending an authentication code?

    a. Authentication app
    b. Windowed token
    c. SMS text
    d. MFA push

14. Noxolo is researching human characteristics for biometric identification. Which of the following would she not find used for biometric identification?

    a. Retina
    b. Iris
    c. Weight
    d. Fingerprint

15. What type of biometrics is related to the perception, thought processes, and understanding of the user?

    a. Cognitive biometrics
    b. Standard biometrics
    c. Intelligence biometrics
    d. Behavioral biometrics

16. Which of the following is an authentication credential used to access multiple accounts or applications?

    a. SSO
    b. Credentialization
    c. Identification authentication
    d. Federal login

17. Which of the following is NOT true about password expiration?

    a. Both NIST and Microsoft no longer support it.
    b. It is not recommended for security.
    c. It should be set to at least one day.
    d. It is the point in time when a password is no longer valid.

18. Which of the following is NOT true about LDAP?

    a. It makes it possible for almost any application running on virtually any computer platform to obtain directory information.
    b. It is an open protocol.
    c. It is the protocol or communication process that enables users to access a network resource through a directory service.
    d. It cannot be used with SSO.

19. Mpho has been asked to look into security keys that have a feature of a key pair that is "burned" into the security key during manufacturing time and is specific to a device model. What feature is this?

    a. Authorization
    b. Authentication
    c. Attestation
    d. Accountability

20. Which access control scheme uses flexible policies that can combine attributes?

    a. ABAC
    b. RB-RBAC
    c. MAC
    d. DAC

Hands-On Projects

Caution

If you are concerned about installing any of the software in these projects on your regular computer, you can instead use the Windows Sandbox or install the software in the Windows virtual machine created in the Module 1 Hands-On Projects. Software installed within the virtual machine will not impact the host computer.

Project 7-1: Using an Online Password Cracker

Estimated Time: 25 minutes
Objective: Demonstrate that passwords can be cracked.
Description: In this project, you create a digest on a password and then crack it to demonstrate the speed of cracking weak passwords.

1. The first step is to use a general-purpose hash algorithm to create a password hash. Use your web browser to go to **www.fileformat.info/tool/hash.htm**. (The location of content on the Internet may change without warning; if you are no longer able to access the site through this URL, use a search engine and search for "Fileformat.info.")

2. Under **String hash**, enter the simple password **apple123** in the **Text:** line.

3. Click **Hash**.

4. Scroll down the page and copy the MD5 hash of this password to your Clipboard by selecting the text, right-clicking it, and choosing **Copy**.

5. Open a new tab on your web browser.

6. Go to **crackstation.net**.

7. Paste the MD5 hash of *apple123* into the text box below **Enter up to 20 non-salted hashes, one per line:**.

8. In the reCAPTCHA box, click the **I am not a robot** check box.

9. Click **Crack Hashes**.

10. How long did it take to crack this hash?

11. Click the browser tab to return to FileFormat.Info.

12. Under **String hash**, enter the longer password **applesauce1234** in the **Text:** line.

13. Click **Hash**.

14. Scroll down the page and copy the MD5 hash of this password to your Clipboard.

15. Click the browser tab to return to the CrackStation site.

16. Paste the MD5 hash of *applesauce1234* into the text box below **Enter up to 20 non-salted hashes, one per line:**.

17. In the reCAPTCHA box, click the **I am not a robot** check box.

18. Click **Crack Hashes**.

19. How long did it take this online rainbow table to crack this stronger password hash?

20. Click the browser tab to return to FileFormat.Info and experiment by entering new passwords, computing their hash, and testing them in the CrackStation site. If you are bold, enter a string hash that is similar to a real password that you use.

21. What does this tell you about the speed of password cracking tools? What does it tell you about how easy it is for attackers to crack weak passwords?

22. Close all windows.

Project 7-2: Using a Web-Based Password Manager

Estimated Time: 25 minutes
Objective: Use a web-based password manager.
Description: The drawback to using strong passwords is that they can be very difficult to remember, particularly when a unique password is used for each account that a user has. As another option, password manager programs allow users to create, store, and retrieve account information. One example of a web-based password storage program is Bitwarden, which is a free and open-source product. In this project, you create an account and use Bitwarden.

1. Use your web browser to go to **bitwarden.com**. (If you are no longer able to access the site through this URL, use a search engine and search for "Bitwarden.")

2. Click **View Plans & Pricing** and then click the **Personal** tab.

3. Under **Free**, click **Create Free Account**.

4. Enter the requested information and then click **Create account**.

5. Close Bitwarden.

6. Now go to your Bitwarden login page at **vault.bitwarden.com/#/**.

Caution !

The page from which you access your Bitwarden account is not the same as the page used for creating the account.

7. Enter your email address as your username and your master password.

8. Click **Log in**.

9. To add an account, click **New item**.

10. Under **What type of item is this?** select **Login**.

11. Enter the requested information as it applies to this account. Under **Name**, enter the name of this account. Under **Password**, note that there is a random password generator available. For **Authenticator key (TOTP)**, leave this blank. Under **Match detection**, select **Default match detection**.

12. The **Notes** section can be used for other information such as your random answers to the security questions for this site.

13. Click **Save**.

14. Now use Bitwarden to access this account. Click the three vertical dots next to the name of this account. From the drop-down menu, click **Launch**. You are now taken to this site.

15. Return to Bitwarden.

16. Click the three vertical dots next to the name of this account and click **Copy username**.

17. Return to your account and paste this username into the field.

18. Return to Bitwarden and click the three vertical dots and click **Copy password**.

19. Return to your account and paste the password into the field.

20. Log out of this account.

21. Now return to Bitwarden and enter a second account that you frequently use and then practice going to that account with the information stored in Bitwarden.

22. Log out of this account.

23. How easy is Bitwarden to use? Can you see how it can provide stronger security than memorizing weak passwords?

24. Log out of Bitwarden.

25. Close all windows.

Project 7-3: Using a Password Manager Application

Estimated Time: 25 minutes
Objective: Use a password manager.
Description: The drawback to using a web-based password manager is that its entire security depends on the strength of the website. For this reason, some security professionals prefer to use an application that is downloaded and stored on their computer instead. One example of a password manager application is KeePass Password Safe, which is an open-source product. In this project, you download and install KeePass.

1. Use your web browser to go to **keepass.info**, accept cookies, and then click **Downloads**.

2. Under **Getting KeePass**, locate the most recent version of Installer for Windows and click it to download the application. Save this file in a location such as your desktop, a folder designated by your instructor, or your portable USB flash drive. When the file finishes downloading, install the program. Accept the installation defaults.

3. Launch KeePass to display the opening screen.

4. Click **File** and **New** to start a password database. Enter a strong master password for the database to protect all the passwords in it. When prompted, enter the password again to confirm it.

5. Create a group by clicking **Group** and **Add Group** and then enter **Web Sites** and click **OK**.

6. Select the **Web Sites** group, click **Entry**, and then click **Add Entry**.

7. Enter a title for a website you use that requires a password under **Title**.

8. For **User name**, enter the username that you use to log in to this account.

9. Delete the entries **Password** and **Repeat** entries and enter the password that you use for this account and confirm it.

10. Enter the URL for this account in the **URL** box.

11. Click **OK**.

12. Click **File** and **Save**. Enter your last name as the file name and then click **Save**.

13. Exit KeePass.

14. Launch the KeePass application.

15. Enter your master password to open your password file.

16. If necessary, click the group to locate the account you just entered; it will be displayed in the right pane.

17. Click the Title of the site you just created.

18. Click the **Open URL(s)** icon in the toolbar to go to this site.

19. Click in the username field of this site that asks for your username.

20. Return to KeePass.

21. Click the **Perform Auto-Type** icon in the toolbar.

Note 29

The Perform Autotype feature will automatically enter your username and password into these fields in your online account. However, depending on how the website has been designed, they may not automatically populate these fields. As an alternative, you can drag and drop the username and password from KeePass into the account fields.

22. Because you can drag and drop your account information from KeePass, you do not have to memorize any account passwords and can instead create strong passwords for each account. Is this an application that would help users create and use strong passwords? What are the strengths of this program? What are the weaknesses? Would you use KeePass?

23. Close all windows.

Case Projects

Case Project 7-1: #TrendingCyber

Estimated Time: 15 minutes
Objective: Summarize your thoughts on the #TrendingCyber opener.
Description: Read again the opening #TrendingCyber in this module. Should all tech platforms have a universal "dig-ital-legacy contacts" policy? What should that policy look like? What about a person who was incapacitated and unable to access their information, but it was critical that the information be accessible? How could someone prove that they needed access? How could this be abused by threat actors? Write a one-paragraph summary of your thoughts.

Case Project 7-2: Passkey

Estimated Time: 30 minutes
Objective: Summarize the technology behind a passwordless system.
Description: One of the new passwordless technologies that is quickly gaining favor is Passkey from the FIDO Alliance (fidoalliance.org). Research the technology behind Passkey and how a user would implement it. What are your impres-sions? Does the technology appear to be sound? Is it user friendly? What happens if a user loses their smartphone? How could they then use Passkey? Write a one-page paper on your research.

Case Project 7-3: SIM Swap and Port Out Attacks

Estimated Time: 30 minutes
Objective: Research attacks on smartphones that can compromise MFA.
Description: Despite its convenience and ability to reach a wide range of users, using a SMS text sent to a smartphone for authentication is not considered a secure option. One attack is for a user to be tricked into providing the code received on a smartphone to an attacker through a phishing attack. Another concern are attacks through which SMS texts can be intercepted. The two common types of attacks that can intercept SMS texts are called port out attacks and SIM swap attacks. Research these two attacks. What are the user defenses against these attacks? Should the telecommunication carriers themselves be more restrictive about allowing someone to make these changes to a smartphone? Write a one-page paper on your research.

Case Project 7-4: Biometric Disadvantages: Crossover Error Rate

Estimated Time: 30 minutes
Objective: Research the disadvantages of biometric authentication.
Description: A disadvantage of biometric authentication is that it is not foolproof: genuine users may be rejected while imposters are accepted. The false acceptance rate (FAR) or false positive is the frequency at which imposters are accepted as genuine, while the false rejection rate (FRR) or false negative is the frequency that legitimate users are rejected. Biometric systems are tuned so that the FAR and FRR are equal over the size of the population (called the crossover error rate [CER]). Ideally the CER should be as low as possible to produce the lowest number of accepted imposter and rejected legitimate users. Research FAR, FRR, and CER. How do researchers arrive at these numbers? How can biometric systems be tuned to an acceptable CER? Write a one-page paper on your research.

Case Project 7-5: Biometric Disadvantages: Trickery

Estimated Time: 30 minutes
Objective: Research the disadvantages of biometric authentication.
Description: A disadvantage of biometric authentication is that these systems can be "tricked" into almost anyone. For example, security researchers have demonstrated that fingerprints can be collected from water glasses and

used to trick fingerprint readers on smartphones. Tricking an iris recognition system requires taking a picture of the authentic user's eye with a digital camera in "night" mode or with the infrared filter removed. The iris picture is then printed on a color laser printer. What are some other ways in which biometric authentication can be tricked? Use the Internet to find three examples of how these systems have been fooled. After researching these weaknesses, would you recommend using biometric authentication to a friend? Why or why not? Write a one-page paper on your research.

Case Project 7-6: Password Vaulting

Estimated Time: 30 minutes
Objective: Research password vaulting technologies.
Description: Enterprise-level password vaulting stores user password credentials in a highly protected database that is stored on the organization's network. However, password vaulting goes far beyond securely storing password credentials. Use the Internet to research password vaulting. Identify three products and compare their features and outline these features in a table. Which product would you recommend? Why?

Case Project 7-7: Testing Password Strength

Estimated Time: 30 minutes
Objective: Research password strength.
Description: How strong are your passwords? Various online tools can provide information on password strength, but not all feedback is the same. First, assign the numbers 1 through 3 to three passwords that are very similar (but not identical) to passwords you are currently using, and write down the number (not the password) on a piece of paper. Then, enter those passwords into these three online password testing services:

- How Secure Is My Password (www.security.org/how-secure-is-my-password/)
- Password Checker Online (password-checker.online-domain-tools.com)
- The Password Meter (www.passwordmeter.com)

Record next to each number the strength of that password as indicated by these three online tools. Then use each online password tester to modify the password by adding more random numbers or letters to increase its strength. How secure are your passwords? Would any of these tools encourage someone to create a stronger password? Which provided the best information? Create a one-paragraph summary of your findings.

Case Project 7-8: Password Requirements

Estimated Time: 20 minutes
Objective: Research password requirements.
Description: Visit the websites Password Requirements Shaming (password-shaming.tumblr.com) and Dumb Password Rules (dumbpasswordrules.com), which contain lists of password requirements for different websites that are considered weak. Read through several of the submissions. Select three that you consider the most egregious. Why are they the worst? Next, indicate what you would suggest to make the requirement stronger, but one that most users could meet. Write a one-paragraph summary.

Case Project 7-9: Password Managers

Estimated Time: 30 minutes
Objective: Research different password managers.
Description: Use the Internet to research four different password managers. Create a table comparing their features. Which is the easiest to use? Which has the most features? Which would you recommend to a friend?

Case Project 7-10: Create Your Own Cognitive Biometric Memorable Event

Estimated Time: 15 minutes

Objective: Create a cognitive biometric event.

Description: What type of cognitive biometric "memorable event" do you think would be effective? Design your own example that is different from those given in the module. There should be five steps, and each step should have at least seven options. The final step should be a fill-in-the-blank user response. Would this substitute for a password? Why or why not?

Case Project 7-11: Security Assertion Markup Language (SAML)

Estimated Time: 25 minutes

Objective: Research Security Assertion Markup Language (SAML).

Description: Use the Internet to research SAML. What are its features? How is it being used? What are its advantages and disadvantages? Write a one-page paper on your research.

Case Project 7-12: Log in with Other Sites

Estimated Time: 15 minutes

Objective: Research the risks of logging in with other site credentials.

Description: When logging in to an online account, sometimes the option is provided for the user to log in using a different set of authentication credentials, such as "Log in With Facebook" in which the user's Facebook username and password is used instead. Research the rewards and risks of logging in using authentication credentials from other sites. Is this like SSO? What are the advantages? What are the disadvantages? Is this safe? Would you recommend it? Write a one-page paper on your research.

Case Project 7-13: Biometric Laws

Estimated Time: 25 minutes

Objective: Research biometric state laws.

Description: Several states now have biometric laws, and others are considering similar legislation. Research these laws that are currently in place from three states. Compare the laws. Are they sufficient? What are their weaknesses? Finally, create your own law that you believe would protect the biometric data of users. Write a one-page paper on your research.

Case Project 7-14: Bay Point Ridge Security

Estimated Time: 45 minutes

Objective: Research password security.

Description: Bay Point Ridge Security (BPRS) is a managed service provider (MSP) that manages networks, computers, cloud resources, and information security for small-to-medium enterprises (SMEs) in the region. BPRS provides internships to students who are in their final year of the security degree program at the local college and has recently hired you.

You have been asked to make a presentation for a local community group about password security. The attendees do not have a technical background.

1. Create a PowerPoint presentation for the group about the risks of weak passwords and how to create strong passwords. Include information about security keys and how smartphones can be used for MFA. Your presentation should contain at least 10–12 slides.

2. After the presentation, the community group has asked for your recommendation on security keys. Use the Internet to identify two of each type that you would recommend and create a memo to the group that includes why you see these as being strong choices.

Two Rights & A Wrong: Answers

Types of Authentication Credentials

1. "Somewhere you are" can be used as an authentication credential.

2. A password spraying attack has a very high potential for success.

3. Using SMS texts for MFA is not a secure option.

Answer: The wrong statement is #2.

Explanation: Password spraying attacks have a low potential for success.

Authentication Best Practices

1. Salting is encrypting a password digest before storing it.

2. Password expiration is not a password best practice.

3. Password length is more important than complexity.

Answer: The wrong statement is #1.

Explanation: Peppering is encrypting a password digest before storing it.

Access Controls

1. Access control is granting or denying approval to use specific resources once a user has been authenticated.

2. Access control schemes are embedded in software and hardware.

3. DAC is the most restrictive access control scheme.

Answer: The wrong statement is #3

Explanation: DAC is the least restrictive access control scheme.

References

1. Le Bras, Tom, "Online overload – it's worse than you think," *Dashlane Blog*, accessed May 22, 2017, https://blog.dashlane.com/infographic-online-overload-its-worse-than-you-thought/.

2. Chang, Jenny, "55 important password statistics you should know: 2023 breaches & reuse data," *FinancesOnline*, Jan. 8, 2023, accessed Feb. 18, 2023, https://financesonline.com/password-statistics/.

3. Schneier, Bruce, *Secrets and lies: Digital security in a networked world* (New York: Wiley Computer Publishing), 2004.

Part 4
Infrastructure and Architectures

The modules in Part 4 deal with attacks and defenses of enterprise-level infrastructures and architectures. In Module 8, you learn about the threats against network infrastructures and how to perform security monitoring. Module 9 demonstrates how to protect a network through network security appliances and technologies. In Module 10, you learn how to manage wireless network security. Finally, in Module 11, cloud and virtualization security are discussed.

Module 8
Infrastructure Threats and Security Monitoring

Module 9
Infrastructure Security

Module 10
Wireless Network Attacks and Defenses

Module 11
Cloud and Virtualization Security

Infrastructure Threats and Security Monitoring

Module Objectives

After completing this module, you should be able to do the following:

1 Describe the different types of attacks on networks

2 Explain how to perform security monitoring and alerting

3 List and describe different email defenses

#TrendingCyber

What is the most critical computer network in the world? The answer may be a network that is out of this world. The computer network found on modern spacecraft would likely be one of the most critical computer networks because there is virtually no room for error: if something happens so that the network does not properly function, it would likely mean a catastrophe for the spacecraft and the astronauts on board. This is the reason a vulnerability recently found on the network used in modern spacecrafts has been the cause for alarm.

For many years, spacecraft had multiple computer networks installed. One network was used to transmit safety-critical and mission-critical instructions, such as transmitting steering and engine control messages to the various flight systems. On these computer networks, messages were sent and received at intervals as short as 40–50 milliseconds (ms). This fast speed was essential because a single delayed or dropped message could result in serious problems. The other spacecraft networks carried less critical traffic such as videoconferencing data. Segregating functions among different networks helps to ensure that critical messages were delivered in a timely fashion. However, having multiple computer networks added additional weight, took up valuable storage space, consumed power, and increased costs on the space-craft. But each of these four elements—weight, space, power, and cost—need to be kept to a minimum in outer space.

Modern spacecraft have moved away from multiple segregated computer networks. Instead, they use a single time-triggered Ethernet (TTE) network. Ethernet has been a standard for local area networks (LANs) since the 1980s, and TTE is built on it. TTE, first tested on a spacecraft in 2014, is called a mixed-criticality network. This single network is capable of routing traffic that has different levels of importance.

TTE provides two key benefits not available in regular Ethernet. First, it supports a "time-triggered paradigm" where all devices are tightly synchronized. They send messages at a predetermined schedule to reduce the time it takes data to move from one point to another (latency) down to hundreds of microseconds (µs). The second feature is fault tolerance. TTE replicates the entire network into multiple planes and forwards messages across all planes simultaneously for redundancy (most spacecraft have three planes).

However, in late 2022, security researchers published a study that demonstrated they were able to break TTE's isolation guarantees. They called their attack "PCspooF" because it injects program control frames (PCFs) into the TTE network. PCspooF is an attack that allows a noncritical device connected to a single plane to disrupt synchronization and communication between *all* TTE devices on *all* planes. These attacks caused TTE devices to lose synchronization for up to a second and drop 10 or more critical messages from reaching their destinations. While that may not sound like a large number of messages, on a spacecraft, losing just a small handful of messages can result in a catastrophic event.

The researchers used PCspooF on an actual avionics test bed as it guided a NASA-simulated crewed Orion capsule attempting to dock with a robotic spacecraft (this was part of NASA's Asteroid Redirect Mission, in which astronauts will attempt to change the orbit of an asteroid). The researchers conducted the test twice, once with no PCFs injected and again with the PCspooF attack. With no PCF injections, the simulated mission was completed successfully. Orion approached the robotic spacecraft at a relative velocity of 2–3 meters (6.5–10 feet) per second until it was approximately 300 meters (984 feet) away, aligned itself with the robotic spacecraft, and then proceeded straight at up to half a meter (1.6 feet) per second until the docking was complete.

However, when the PCspooF attack was launched, it caused messages to be dropped that introduced delays. This resulted in Orion deviating from its intended flight path. And rather than aligning with the robotic spacecraft, Orion swung underneath it at a distance of approximately 115 meters (377 feet). It also missed the limited time frame for docking. Finally, it floated away at a rate of 1–2 meters (3.2–6.5 feet) every second. These results demonstrated that PCspooF could not only disrupt the operation of critical systems and thwart the mission as a whole, but it also can threaten the safety of the crew, as uncontrolled maneuvers can easily cause collisions between space vehicles.

But TTE is not exclusively used on spacecraft. For many years it has been the preferred network used in helicopters, industrial control systems (ICSs), and energy-generation systems such as wind turbines. The vulnerabilities that PCspooF exploits can equally impact these devices and systems as well.

The security researchers provided several suggestions for preventing PCspooF. For its part, NASA said that it has taken "proactive measures to ensure potential risks on spacecraft from PCspooF are appropriately mitigated."

Whereas technology devices, like smartphones, tablets, and laptop computers, usually receive all the praise for ushering the world into a new and exciting era, in reality the invisible network that is connecting all these devices together should be receiving equal adoration. Imagine a smartphone that cannot connect to a network to receive messages or link to websites but, instead, can use only what is stored on that smartphone. Most users would quickly dump an unconnected smartphone in the nearest trash bin. Connectivity through networks has helped make today's devices revolutionary.

However, networks have also been responsible for the explosive growth of cyberattacks. They have opened the door for threat actors to reach across the world to launch attacks invisibly and instantaneously on any device connected to the Internet. And just as users surf the web without openly identifying themselves, attackers can likewise use anonymity to cloak their identity and prevent victims and law enforcement from identifying them.

This module begins a study of enterprise network attacks and defenses. First the module explores some of the common attacks that are launched against networks today. Then it looks at tools for monitoring and network security and raising alerts when that security is compromised. Finally, it explores email monitoring and security.

Attacks on Networks

Certification

2.4 Given a scenario, analyze indicators of malicious activity.

3.2 Given a scenario, apply security principles to secure enterprise infrastructure.

Threat actors place a high priority on targeting networks in their attacks. This is because exploiting a single network vulnerability could expose hundreds or thousands of devices. Several types of attacks target a network or a process that relies on a network. These can be grouped into on-path attacks, domain name system (DNS) attacks, distributed denial of service (DDoS) attacks, malicious coding and scripting attacks, Layer 2 attacks, and credential relay attacks.

On-Path Attacks

An on-path attack occurs when a threat actor positions themself in the middle between two communicating users or devices; that is, they are "on the path" of the information exchange that is taking place. In an on-path attack, the data stream from the originator will first reach the attacker before they forward data to the recipient.

There are two key advantages to an on-path attack. First, it can occur without the two targets knowing that an attacker is present. Second, it gives the attacker flexibility: they can either eavesdrop on the communication to gather valuable information or they can modify the message before sending it on to the recipient.

Three of the most common interception attacks are man-in-the-middle, session replay, and man-in-the-browser attacks.

Man-in-the-Middle (MITM)

Suppose that Angie, a high school student, is in danger of receiving a poor grade in math. Her teacher, Mr. Ferguson, mails a letter to Angie's parents requesting a conference regarding her performance. However, Angie waits for the mail and retrieves the letter from the mailbox before her parents come home. She forges her parent's signature on the original letter declining a conference and mails it back to her teacher. Angie then replaces the real letter with a counterfeit pretending to be from Mr. Ferguson that compliments Angie on her math work. The parents read the fake letter and tell Angie they are proud of her, while Mr. Ferguson is puzzled that Angie's parents are not concerned about her grades.

Angie has conducted a type of **man-in-the-middle (MITM)** attack. In a MITM, threat actor Eve will position herself into a communication between Alice and Bob, neither of whom can detect her presence. Eve can either passively eavesdrop on the conversation to collect information or actively impersonate Alice or Bob by sending false information to the other party, as seen in Figure 8-1.

Figure 8-1   MITM impersonation attack

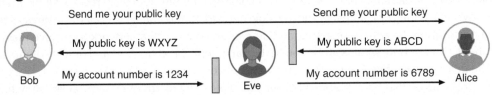

A threat actor faces two challenges in a typical MITM:

- **Intercepting traffic.** The first challenge is intercepting the traffic. In a typical HTTP transaction, there is a transmission control protocol (TCP) connection between the endpoint and the server. Using different techniques, the attacker can divide the original TCP connection into two new connections, one between the client and the attacker and the other between the attacker and the server. A threat actor could pretend to be an approved web application by altering packet headers in an Internet Protocol (IP) address. When targets attempt to access a URL connected to the application, they are instead sent to the attacker's website.
- **Decrypting transmissions.** The second challenge is to decrypt encrypted transmissions. An attacker could send a fake digital certificate to the target's computer associated with a compromised application to trick the computer into verifying the authenticity of the application. The attacker is then able to access any data entered by the victim.

Note 1

Detecting an active MITM attack can be difficult. Many security personnel instead focus on the result of an MITM attack, which is typically stealing data by impersonating an approved employee. Monitoring access to sensitive resources and failed login attempts followed by successful logins could be a sign of a successful MITM attack.

Session Replay

A replay attack is a variation of a MITM attack. Whereas a MITM attack alters and then sends the transmission immediately, a replay attack makes a copy of the legitimate transmission before sending it to the recipient. This copy is then used later when the threat actor "replays" the transmission.

A specific type of replay attack is a **session replay** attack, which involves intercepting and then using a session ID to impersonate a user. A session ID is a unique number that a web server assigns a specific user for the duration of that user's visit (session). Each time a website is visited, a new session ID is assigned and usually remains active as long as the browser is open. In some instances, after several minutes of inactivity, the server may generate a new session ID.

Most servers create complex session IDs by using the date, time of the visit, and other variables such as the device IP address, email, username, user ID, role, privilege level, access rights, language preferences, account ID, current state, last login, session timeouts, and other internal session details. Session IDs are usually at least 128 bits in length and hashed using a secure hash function like SHA-256. A sample session ID is *fa2e76d49a0475910504cb3ab7a1f626d174d2d*. Session IDs can be contained as part of a URL extension, by using "hidden form fields" in which the state is sent to the client as part of the response and returned to the server as part of a form's hidden data or as cookies.

Several techniques can be used for stealing an active session ID in a replay attack. These include network attacks (such as a MITM impersonation attack) and endpoint attacks (cross-site scripting, Trojans, and malicious JavaScript coding).

Man-in-the-Browser (MITB)

Like a MITM attack, a **man-in-the-browser (MITB)** attack intercepts communication between parties to steal or manipulate the data. Whereas a MITM attack occurs between two endpoints—such as between two users' laptops or a user's computer and a web server—a MITB attack occurs between a browser and the underlying computer. Specifically, a MITB attack seeks to intercept and then manipulate the communication between the web browser and the security mechanisms of the computer.

A MITB attack usually begins with a Trojan infecting the computer and installing an "extension" into the browser configuration so that when the browser is launched, the extension is activated. When a user enters the URL of a site, the extension checks to determine if this is a site that is targeted for attack. After the user logs in to the site, the extension waits for a specific webpage to be displayed in which a user enters information, such as the account number and password for an online financial institution (a favorite target of MITB attacks). When the user clicks "Submit," the extension captures all the data from the fields on the form and may even modify some of the entered data. The browser then proceeds to send the data to the server, which performs the transaction and generates a receipt that is sent back to the browser. The malicious extension again captures the receipt data and modifies it (with the data the user originally entered) so that it appears a legitimate transaction has occurred.

There are several advantages to a MITB attack for threat actors:

- Most MITB attacks are distributed through Trojan browser extensions, which provide a valid function to the user but also install the MITB malware, making it difficult to recognize that malicious code has been installed.
- Because MITB malware is selective as to which websites are targeted, an infected MITB browser might remain dormant for months until triggered by the user visiting a targeted site.
- MITB software resides exclusively within the web browser, making it difficult for standard anti-malware software to detect it.

Domain Name System (DNS) Attacks

The predecessor to today's Internet was the network ARPAnet. This network was completed in 1969 and linked together single computers located at each of four different sites (the University of California at Los Angeles, the Stanford Research Institute, the University of California at Santa Barbara, and the University of Utah) with a 50 Kbps connection. Referencing these computers was originally accomplished by assigning an identification number to each computer (IP addresses were not introduced until later). However, as additional computers were added to the network, it became more difficult for humans to accurately recall the identification number of each computer.

Note 2

On Labor Day in 1969, the first test of the ARPAnet was conducted. A switch was turned on and, to almost everyone's surprise, the network worked. Researchers in Los Angeles then attempted to type the word *login* on the computer in Stanford. A user pressed the letter *L* and it appeared on the screen in Stanford. Next, the letter *O* was pressed, and it too appeared. When the third letter *G* was typed, however, the network crashed.

What was needed was a naming system that would allow computers on a network to be assigned both numeric addresses and more friendly human-readable names composed of letters, numbers, and special symbols (called a symbolic name). In the early 1970s, each computer site began to assign simple names to network devices and also manage its own "host table" that mapped names to computer numbers. However, because each site attempted to maintain its own local host table, there were inconsistencies between the sites. A standard master table was then created that could be downloaded to each site.

When TCP/IP was developed, the table concept was expanded to a hierarchical name system for matching computer names and numbers. This is known as the **Domain Name System (DNS)**, which is the basis for domain name resolution of names to IP addresses used today.

Because of the important role it plays, DNS is a favorite target of threat actors. Domain Name System (DNS) attacks substitute a DNS address so that the computer is silently redirected to a different device. There are two common goals of a successful DNS attack:

- **URL redirection.** The goal of DNS attacks is usually a **URL redirection**: instead of the user reaching their intended site, they are redirected to another site. This site could be a fictitious site that looks identical to a bank or e-commerce site, so that a user would then enter their username, password, and credit card number—which would then be captured and used by the threat actor.
- **Domain reputation.** Online algorithms are continually evaluating the reputation of webpages, domains, and email service. A competitor could hire an attacker to use a DNS attack to cause a competitor's domain to earn a low domain reputation score, thus impacting sales. This is known as a **domain reputation attack**.

Attacks using DNS include DNS poisoning and DNS hijacking.

DNS Poisoning

As a holdover from the early days of TCP/IP when local host tables were used, today TCP/IP still first checks a local file. This file simply contains an IP address along with a corresponding host name, as seen in Figure 8-2. When a user enters a symbolic name, TCP/IP first checks the file to determine if there is an entry. If there is an entry, the corresponding IP address is returned; if no entry exists, the external DNS system is queried.

Figure 8-2   Local host file

127.0.0.1	localhost	
161.6.18.20	www.wku.edu	# Western Kentucky University
74.125.47.99	www.google.com	# My favorite search engine
216.77.188.41	www.att.net	# Internet service provider

Note 3

Host files are found in the */etc/* directory in UNIX, Linux, and macOS and are located in the *Windows\System32\drivers\etc* directory in Windows.

Attackers can target a local host file to create new entries that will redirect users to a fraudulent site. **DNS poisoning** modifies a local host file on a device to point to a different domain. However, instead of making several individual entries into the host file, threat actors will add a single entry that directs the computer to a DNS server that is under the control of the attackers. This DNS server contains all the attacker's malicious mappings. Thus, the threat actor can redirect *any* user request to a website that the attacker chooses. And since most users are unaware of the existence of a host file on their device, these infections can often go undetected for extended periods of time.

Note 4

Some governments use DNS poisoning to restrict their citizens from reading what they consider as unfavorable Internet content.

DNS Hijacking

Whereas DNS poisoning attempts to modify the local hosts file, **DNS hijacking** is intended to infect an external DNS server with IP addresses that point to malicious sites. This has the advantage of *all* users accessing this server to be redirected.

Instead of attempting to break into a DNS server to change its contents, attackers use a more basic approach. Because DNS servers exchange information among themselves (known as zone transfers), attackers will attempt to exploit a protocol flaw and convince the authentic DNS server to accept fraudulent DNS entries sent from the attacker's DNS server. If the DNS server does not correctly validate DNS responses to ensure that they have come from an authoritative source, it will store the fraudulent entries locally and will serve them to users and spread them to other DNS servers.

The process of a DNS poisoning attack from an attacker who has a domain name of www.evil.net with their own DNS server *ns.evil.net* is shown in Figure 8-3:

1. The attacker sends a request to a valid DNS server asking it to resolve the name *www.evil.net*.
2. Because the valid DNS server does not know the address, it asks the responsible name server, which is the attacker's *ns.evil.net*, for the address.
3. The name server *ns.evil.net* sends the address of not only *www.evil.net* but also all of its records (a zone transfer) to the valid DNS server, which then accepts them.
4. Any requests to the valid DNS server will now respond with the fraudulent addresses entered by the attacker.

Figure 8-3   DNS server poisoning

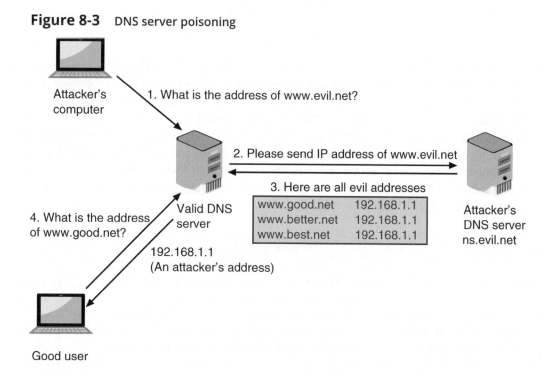

Distributed Denial of Service (DDoS) Attack

Suppose Gabe is having a conversation with Cora in a coffee shop when a "flash mob" of friends suddenly appears. (A flash mob is a large public gathering at which people perform an unusual or random act and then quickly disperse.) The friends all start talking to Gabe at the same time. He would be unable to continue his conversation with Cora because he is overwhelmed by the number of voices with which he would have to contend.

In a similar fashion, a technology-based **denial of service (DoS)** attack bombards a system with an extremely high number of "bogus" (fake) requests so that the system is overwhelmed and cannot respond to legitimate requests. DoS attacks today are distributed denial of service (DDoS) attacks: instead of only one source making a bogus request, a DDoS involves hundreds, thousands, or even millions of sources producing a torrent of fake requests. Targets of DDoS attacks include web servers, networks, cloud-based resources, and even infrastructure targets like electrical power grids.

There are two means by which attackers can generate massive amounts of data to overwhelm a system. The first is to use large numbers of compromised devices, each sending bogus requests. The devices that can be used in a DDoS attack are infected and controlled by threat actors so that users are completely unaware that their endpoints are part of a DDoS attack. These devices include typical computers and servers but also Internet of Things (IoT) devices like baby camera monitors and garage door openers. It is estimated that a botnet of only 1 million compromised IoT devices could easily send 4 terabits per second (Tbps) in a DDoS attack, which is the equivalent of streaming 800,000 high-definition movies simultaneously.

The second method is to use amplified attacks to increase the deluge of data. The most common amplified attacks are reflection attacks. Threat actors "point their data cannons" at a misconfigured Internet device or service in such a way that causes the device or service to reflect and generate an even *larger* payload at the ultimate target. One reflection amplification target is the Network Time Protocol (NTP), which is used for clock synchronization between computer systems so that all participating computers are within a few milliseconds of Coordinated Universal Time (UTC). By manipulating NTP, it can generate a 206-fold increase in throughput, meaning a modest 1 gigabyte of data initially sent is amplified through the reflection attack to over 206 gigabytes when it reaches the final victim. Another intermediary is memcachd, which is a database caching system for speeding up websites and networks. A memcached amplifier can deliver attacks *51,000* times their original size.

Malicious Coding and Scripting Attacks

Several successful network attacks come from malicious software code and scripts (called malicious code attacks). These attacks typically use PowerShell, Visual Basic for Applications, the coding language Python, and Linux/UNIX Bash.

PowerShell

PowerShell is a task automation and configuration management framework from Microsoft. Initially PowerShell was a Microsoft Windows component known as Windows PowerShell and was built on the Windows .NET framework (a developer platform that can be used to write apps in specific programming languages). In 2016, it was updated and released both as an open-source and a cross platform product running on Windows, macOS, and Linux platforms.

Administrative tasks in PowerShell are performed by **cmdlets** ("command-lets"), which are specialized .NET classes that implement a specific operation. PowerShell **providers** give access to data located in different data repositories, such as the file system or Windows registry. Users and developers can create and add their own cmdlets to Power-Shell. PowerShell also provides a hosting application program interface (API) so the PowerShell runtime can even be embedded inside other applications. On the Microsoft Windows platform, PowerShell has full access to a range of OS components and APIs. It can run locally on an endpoint or across a network accessing other endpoint devices.

The power and reach of PowerShell make it a prime target for threat actors. PowerShell allows attackers to inject code from the PowerShell environment into other processes without first storing any malicious code to the hard drive. This allows the commands to execute while bypassing security protections and leaves behind virtually no evidence. PowerShell can also be configured so that its commands are not detected by any anti-malware running on the computer. Because most applications flag PowerShell as a "trusted" application, its actions are rarely scrutinized.

> **Caution** !
>
> It is important to understand that these are not vulnerabilities but rather are features of PowerShell as a result of its tight integration with the .NET framework. It allows users an extremely powerful and easy means to access sensitive elements of an OS and is frequently used by developers and system administrators.

Visual Basic for Applications (VBA)

Visual Basic for Applications (VBA) is an "event-driven" Microsoft programming language. VBA allows both developers and users to automate processes that normally would take multiple steps or levels of steps. It can be used to control many tasks of the host application, including manipulating user interface features like toolbars, menus, forms, and dialog boxes.

VBA is built into most Microsoft Office applications (Word, Excel, and PowerPoint, for example) for both Windows and Apple macOS platforms. It is also included in select non-Microsoft products, such as AutoCAD, CorelDraw, and Libre-Office. VBA can even control one application from another application using Object Linking and Embedding (OLE) automation. For example, VBA can automatically create a Microsoft Word report from data in a Microsoft Excel spreadsheet.

VBA is most often used to create macros. A macro is a series of instructions that can be grouped together as a single command. Macros are used to automate a complex task or a repeated series of tasks. Macros are generally written by using VBA and are stored within the user document (such as in an Excel .xlsx worksheet or Word .docx file) and can be launched automatically when the document is opened.

Although macros date back to the late 1990s, they continue to be a key attack vector. Microsoft has reported that 98 percent of all Office-targeted threats are a result of macro-based malware, and it has warned users that Office macros, particularly in Excel, are still used to compromise Windows systems.[1]

> **Caution** !
>
> Unless there is a business requirement for macros, support for their use should be disabled across the Microsoft Office suite. If macros are required, only those that have been digitally signed by a trusted publisher should be allowed to execute. To prevent users or an adversary from bypassing macro security controls, all support for trusted documents and trusted locations should be disabled. Organizations can disable Trust Center settings and apply macro security controls using Group Policy settings.

Python

Python is a popular programming language that can run on several different OS platforms. Python's syntax allows programmers to write code that takes fewer lines than in other programming languages like Java and C++. Python also supports object-oriented programming. It has a large standard library in which developers can use routines created by other developers.

> **Note 8**
>
> Python was created in the late 1980s by a Dutch programmer as a side project during his Christmas vacation.

There are several best practices to follow when using Python so that the code does not contain vulnerabilities. These include using the latest version of Python, staying current on vulnerabilities within Python, being careful when formatting strings in Python, and downloading only vetted Python libraries. (A library is a collection of functions and methods that can perform actions so that the programmer does not have to write the code for it.)

Bash

Bash is the command language interpreter (called the "shell") for the Linux/UNIX OS. "Bash scripting" is using Bash to create a script (a script is essentially the same as a program, but it is **interpreted** and executed without the need for it to be first **compiled** into machine language). Exploits have taken advantage of vulnerabilities in Bash. For example, one vulnerability allowed attackers to remotely attach a malicious executable file to a variable (a value that changes) that is executed when Bash is invoked.

Layer 2 Attacks

In 1978, the International Organization for Standardization (ISO) released a set of specifications that was intended to describe how dissimilar computers could be connected together on a network. The ISO demonstrated that what happens on a network device when sending or receiving traffic can be best understood by portraying this transfer as a series of related steps. The ISO called its work the **Open Systems Interconnection (OSI)** reference model. After a revision in 1983, this OSI reference model is still used today.

The key to the OSI reference model is **layers**. The model breaks networking steps down into a series of seven layers. Within each layer, different networking tasks are performed, and each layer cooperates with the layer immediately above and below it. Each layer in the sending device corresponds to the same layer in the receiving device. The OSI model is shown in Figure 8-4.

Figure 8-4   OSI model

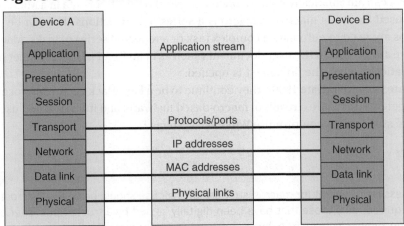

However, the OSI model was designed so that each layer is compartmentalized: different layers work without the knowledge and approval of the other layers. This means that if one layer is compromised, the other layers are unaware of any problem, which results in the entire communication being compromised.

Layer 2 of the OSI model is particularly weak in this regard and is a frequent target of threat actors. Layer 2, the Data Link Layer, is responsible for dividing the data into packets along with error detection and correction and performing physical addressing, data framing, and error detection and handling. A compromise at Layer 2 can impact the entire communication, as shown in Figure 8-5.

Figure 8-5 Layer 2 compromise

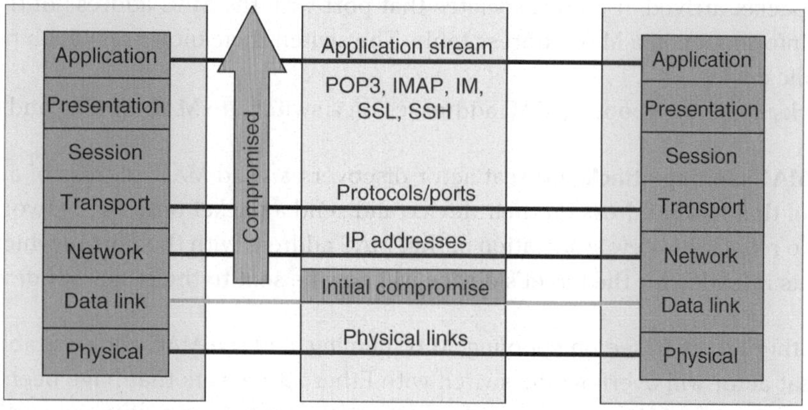

Note 9

There is not universal agreement on the usage of the terms *frame*, *packet*, *datagram*, and *segment*. The OSI uses the terms *protocol data unit (PDU)* and *service data unit (SDU)*. Usually an Ethernet frame is used for Data Link Layer (Layer 2) functions, an IP packet or datagram is at the Network Layer (Layer 3), and a segment is at the Transport Layer (Layer 4). However, this is not used consistently. Although some network certification exams do require specific terminology to be used in reference to these data units, the Security+ certification does not. To minimize confusion, the term *packet* may be used in the text in a generic sense of a unit of data.

Two of the common Layer 2 attacks are address resolution protocol poisoning and media access control attacks.

Address Resolution Protocol (ARP) Poisoning

The TCP/IP protocol suite requires that logical IP addresses be assigned to each device on a network, and these addresses can be changed as necessary. However, an Ethernet LAN uses the physical media access control (MAC) address that is permanently "burned" into a network interface card (NIC) to communicate. How can a physical MAC address be mapped to a logical and temporary IP address?

The answer for a device using TCP/IP on an Ethernet network to find the MAC address of another endpoint based on the IP address is the Address Resolution Protocol (ARP). If the IP address for an endpoint is known but the MAC address is not, the sending endpoint sends an ARP packet to all devices on the network that in effect says, "If this is your IP address, send me back your MAC address." The endpoint with that IP address sends back a packet with the MAC address so the packet can be correctly addressed. The IP address and the corresponding MAC address are stored in an ARP cache for future reference. In addition, all other endpoints that hear the ARP reply also cache that data.

Threat actors take advantage of a MAC address stored in a software ARP cache to change the data so that an IP address points to a different device. This attack is known as **ARP poisoning** and uses "spoofing," which is deceiving by impersonating another's identity.

Note 10

ARP poisoning is successful because there are no authentication procedures to verify ARP requests and replies.

Media Access Control Attacks

Besides ARP poisoning, there are other attacks that manipulate MAC addresses through spoofing. The target for these attacks is a network switch.

A network **switch** is a device that connects network devices and, unlike some other network devices, has a degree of "intelligence." Operating at the Layer 2 Data Link Layer, a switch can learn which device is connected to each of its ports. This learning is done by examining the MAC address of packets that it receives and observing at which of the switch's port that packet arrived. It then associates that port with the MAC address of the device connected to that port, storing that information in a MAC address table. The switch then knows on which port to forward packets intended for that specific device.

Two common attacks involving spoofing MAC addresses on a switch are MAC cloning and MAC flooding.

MAC Cloning   In a **MAC cloning attack**, a threat actor discovers a valid MAC address of a device connected to a switch. They then spoof that MAC address on their device and send a packet onto the network. The switch changes its MAC address table to reflect this new association of that MAC address with the port to which the attacker's device is connected. All packets intended for the target's device will now be sent to the attacker's device.

MAC Flooding   Another attack based on spoofing, MAC cloning, and the MAC address table of a switch is a **MAC flooding attack**. A threat actor will overflow the switch with Ethernet packets that have been spoofed so that every packet contains a different source MAC address, each appearing to come from a different endpoint. This can quickly consume all the memory, called the content addressable memory (CAM), for the MAC address table.

Once the MAC address table is full and cannot store an additional MAC address, the switch enters a failure mode, which is a predefined set of actions based on a failure of a network component. Table 8-1 lists the four types of failure modes. If a switch is in fail-open mode, it broadcasts frames to all ports. A threat actor could install software or a hardware device that captures and decodes packets on one client connected to the switch to view all traffic.

Table 8-1   Failure modes

Mode	Description	Explanation
Fail closed	Device shuts down when failure detected	Used when security concerns override the need for access
Fail open	Device remains open and operations continue as normal	Access is considered more important than security
Fail safe	Device is configured to protect all other components	Usually achieved through adding a separate device known as a bypass switch
Failover	Device can recover its functionality	Achieved through redundancy of devices

Note 11

A MAC flooding attack that consumes all the CAM on one switch will ultimately fill the CAM tables of adjacent switches.

Credential Relay Attack

As its name implies, a credential relay attack attempts to steal authentication credentials and then use them to access a system. Specifically, attackers intercept digests of user passwords as they are being transmitted and then relay the clients' credentials to impersonate the user. Most credential relay attacks involve a threat actor setting up their own device (a "machine-in-the-middle") and trick a user on their device (Device A) to attempt to authenticate to the attacker's bogus device. The attacker then captures the digest and uses it to access a valid device (Device B). A credential relay attack is shown in Figure 8-6.

Figure 8-6   Credential relay attack

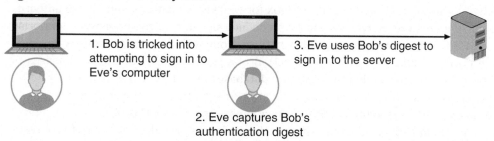

1. Bob is tricked into attempting to sign in to Eve's computer

2. Eve captures Bob's authentication digest

3. Eve uses Bob's digest to sign in to the server

Two Rights & A Wrong

1. An advantage of an on-path attack is that it can occur without the two targets knowing an attacker is present.

2. A session ID is a unique number that a web browser assigns a specific user for the duration of the user's visit to the site.

3. A MITB attack seeks to intercept and then manipulate the communication between the web browser and the security mechanisms of the computer.

See the answers at the end of the module.

Security Monitoring and Alerting

Certification

2.5 Explain the purpose of mitigation techniques used to secure the enterprise.

4.1 Given a scenario, apply common security techniques to computing resources.

4.4 Explain security alerting and monitoring concepts and tools.

4.5 Given a scenario, modify enterprise capabilities to enhance security.

Continual monitoring of the infrastructure for evidence of attacks is critical. This involves monitoring systems (devices), monitoring applications (programs), and monitoring infrastructures (networks). Once an attack is detected, an alert must be raised to ensure that proper defenses are in place. Security monitoring and alerting includes using monitoring methodologies and performing monitoring activities. There are several different tools for monitoring and alerting.

Monitoring Methodologies

Monitoring involves examining network traffic, activity, transactions, or behavior to detect security-related anomalies. There are four monitoring methodologies:

- **Anomaly monitoring. Anomaly monitoring** is designed for detecting statistical anomalies. First, a secure baseline of normal activities is compiled over time (a *baseline* is a reference set of data against which operational data is compared). Whenever there is a significant deviation from this baseline, an alarm is raised. An advantage of this approach is that it can detect the anomalies quickly without trying to first understand the underlying cause, but because normal behavior can change easily it is critical for baselines, after they have been created (establish baselines), to be distributed (deploy baselines) and updated (maintain baselines) on a timely basis.

- **Signature-based monitoring.** A second method, **signature-based monitoring**, examines network traffic, activity, transactions, or behavior to look for well-known patterns, much like antivirus scanning, to compare these activities against a predefined signature. Signature-based monitoring requires access to an updated database of signatures along with a means to actively compare and match current behavior against a collection of signatures. One of the weaknesses of signature-based monitoring is that the signature databases must be constantly updated.
- **Behavioral monitoring.** Rather than using statistics or signatures as the standard by which comparisons are made, **behavior-based monitoring** uses the "normal" processes and actions as the standard. Behavior-based monitoring continuously analyzes the behavior of processes and programs on a system and alerts the user if it detects any abnormal actions, at which point the user can decide whether to allow or block the activity. This is known as user behavior analytics or gathering data for monitoring user behavior. One of the advantages of behavior-based monitoring is that it is not necessary to update signature files or compile a baseline of statistical behavior before monitoring can take place. In addition, behavior-based monitoring can more quickly stop new attacks.
- **Heuristic monitoring.** Heuristic monitoring is founded on experience-based techniques and attempts to answer the question, *Will this do something harmful if it is allowed to execute?* Heuristic (from the Greek word for *find* or *discover*) monitoring uses an algorithm to determine if a threat exists. Table 8-2 illustrates how heuristic monitoring could trap an application that attempts to scan ports that the other methods might not catch.

Table 8-2   Methodology comparisons to trap port scanning application

Monitoring methodology	Trap application scanning ports?	Comments
Anomaly-based monitoring	Depends	Only if this application has tried to scan previously and a baseline has been established
Signature-based monitoring	Depends	Only if a signature of scanning by this application has been previously created
Behavior-based monitoring	Depends	Only if this action by the application is different from other applications
Heuristic monitoring	Yes	Alert is triggered if any application tries to scan multiple ports

Monitoring Activities

Several activities make up security monitoring and alerting. These are listed in Table 8-3.

Table 8-3   Monitoring activities

Activity	Description
Scanning	A frequent and ongoing process, often automated, that continuously searches for evidence of an attack
Reporting	Generating documentation on the results of monitoring activities
Quarantine	Isolating systems that have been compromised
Alerting	Detecting and notifying operators about meaningful events that may denote an attack
Alert tuning	"Tweaking" the alerting function to weed out false positives
Archiving	Retaining historical documents and records of monitoring

Tools for Monitoring and Alerting

Several tools can be used for monitoring and alerting. These include packet capture and replay tools, flow analysis tools, data loss prevention (DLP), Simple Network Management Protocol (SNMP) traps, log aggregation, security content automation protocols (SCAP), security information and event management (SIEM) tools, and security orchestration, automation, and response (SOAR) tools.

Note 12

Other applications that are not specific to monitoring and alerting can also provide valuation information. For example, antivirus software that discovers malware can likewise provide these functions.

Packet Capture and Replay Tools

Collecting and analyzing data packets that cross a network can provide a wealth of valuable information. This packet analysis typically examines the entire contents of the packet, which consists of both the header information and the payload. However, because all the information needed is rarely contained in a single packet, packet analysis involves the examination of multiple packets—often hundreds and even thousands of them—to "piece together" the information.

Note 13

Some of the common uses of packet analysis include troubleshooting network connectivity (determine packet loss, review TCP retransmission, and create graphs of high-latency packet responses), examining Application Layer sessions (captured packets can be used to view a full HTTP session for both requests and responses and even read email traffic) and solving Dynamic Host Configuration Protocol (DHCP) issues (examine DHCP client broadcasts, view DHCP offers with addresses and options, observe client requests for an address, and see the server's acknowledgment of the request).

Packet analysis can also be used extensively for security. Packet analysis can detect unusual behavior (such as a high number of DNS responses) that could indicate the presence of malware, search for unusual domains or IP address endpoints, and discover regular connections (beacons) to a threat actor's command and control (C&C) server.

Wireshark is a popular graphical user interface (GUI)–based packet capture and analysis tool. **Tcpdump** is a command-line packet analyzer. It displays TCP/IP packets and other packets being transmitted or received over a network and operates on UNIX and Linux operating systems, and various forks of it are available for Windows computers. However, the output from tcpdump can be voluminous and difficult to parse. **Tcpreplay** is a tool for editing packets and then "replaying" the packets back onto the network to observe their behavior.

Flow Analysis Tools

Although packet analysis is important, the time it takes to extract and examine raw data packets makes this process too slow to identify an attack. Is there a better way to know if a network attack has commenced?

Consider a homeowner who has received an extremely large bill. Upon investigation, they determine there was a hole in the water line, and they were being charged for water that they did not use but instead had leaked into the ground. To prevent this from occurring again, the homeowner uses a service from the local utility company. This service allows them to monitor water intake and generate an alert if that intake is above a normal level, as shown in Figure 8-7.

This same concept can apply to network traffic: if there is an unusual spike in network traffic leaving the network, it could indicate that a threat actor has compromised the network and is exfiltrating large amounts of confidential data. **Flow analysis** (also called network traffic analysis) is the process of monitoring the network's different devices and sounding an alert if it exceeds a predefined baseline.

Flow analysis has been performed for many years in order to troubleshoot network issues and identify performance bottlenecks by identifying which applications are "hogging" resources and bandwidth. The analysis usually looks at

Figure 8-7 Monitoring water intake

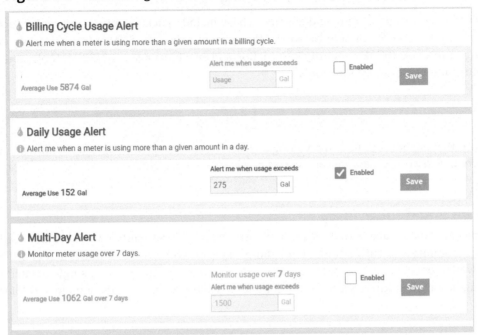

overall network utilization and speed by generating statistics based on the flow of data through the network. However, flow analysis for information security is different from traditional network traffic flow for several reasons:

- **Eliminates monitoring agents.** Threat actors often attempt to disable separate software monitoring agents that are installed on each network device in order to hide evidence of a data exfiltration. And some systems, such as database servers, application servers, DNS and DHCP servers, IoT devices, and embedded systems, cannot accept monitoring agents. However, by using network traffic analysis, the network data can be collected passively without the need of monitoring agents (called agentless) so that threat actors cannot interfere with the data collection.
- **Uses deep packet inspection.** Unlike traditional network traffic analysis that only looks at the flow of data through the network, network traffic analysis for security extracts metadata (data about data) from the network packets and then converts it into a readable format using what is called deep packet inspection. This can even facilitate decryption of application traffic and its contents so as to identify suspicious activities.
- **Provides richer information.** In addition to standard network analysis (such as identifying bottlenecks), deep packet inspection can identify what devices are active on the network, what applications and protocols they are using, and what data they are accessing. Also, alerts can be set to advise security administrators of any unusual activity or network anomalies.

Note 14

Flow analysis is often used in identifying a ransomware attack. Flow analysis can detect not only when data is being exfiltrated, but it can also determine multiple file names are being changed simultaneously, which is a typical indicator of a ransomware attack, and an alert can be generated in real time.

The output from a flow analysis network traffic analyst tool is shown in Figure 8-8.

Flow analysis data can be accumulated from different sources. NetFlow is a session sampling protocol feature on Cisco routers that collects IP network traffic as it enters or exits an interface and uses TCP/IP Internet Control Message

Figure 8-8   Network traffic analysis output

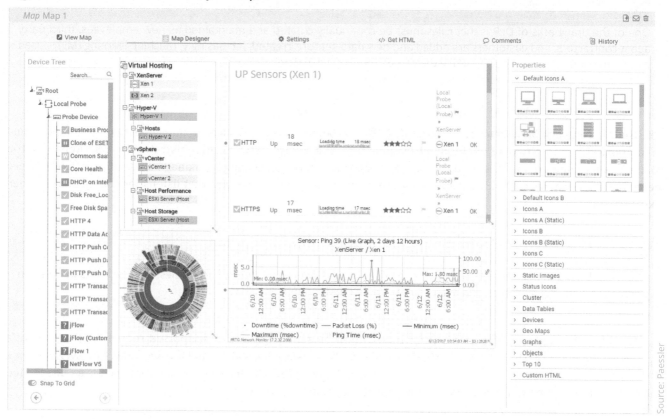

Protocol (ICMP) Echo request packets. sFlow is a packet sampling protocol that gives a statistical sampling instead of the actual flow of packets. IPfix (IP Flow Information Export) is similar to NetFlow but adds additional capabilities, such as integrating Simple Network Management Protocol (SNMP) information directly into the IPfix information so that all the information is available instead of the need to query the SNMP server separately.

Data Loss Prevention (DLP)

Another tool that can be used for monitoring and alerting focuses on watching confidential data. **Data loss prevention (DLP)** is a system of security tools used to recognize and identify data that is critical to the organization and ensure it is protected. This protection involves monitoring who is using the data, how it is being accessed, and sounding an alert and blocking the export of restricted data. DLP is considered as rights management, or the authority of the owner of the data to impose restrictions on its use.

Most DLP systems use content inspection. Content inspection is a security analysis of the transaction within its approved context. Content inspection looks at not only the security level of the data but also who is requesting it, where the data is stored, when it was requested, and where it is going. DLP systems can also use index matching. Documents that have been identified as needing protection, such as the program source code for a new software application, are analyzed by the DLP system and complex computations are conducted based on the analysis. Thereafter, if even a small part of that document is leaked, the DLP system can recognize the snippet as being from a protected document.

DLP begins with an administrator creating DLP rules based on the data (what is to be examined) and the policy (what to check for). DLPs can be configured to look for specific data (such as Social Security and credit card numbers), lines of computer software source code, words in a sequence (to prevent a report from leaving the network), maximum file sizes, and file types. These rules are then loaded into a DLP server.

If a policy violation is detected by the DLP agent, it is reported back to the DLP server. Different actions can then be taken. These could include blocking the data, redirecting it to an individual who can examine the request, quarantining the data until later, or alerting a supervisor of the request.

> ## Note 15
>
> One of the drawbacks of DLP is that rules must be continually created and maintained as new employees, third-party agent contractors, and customers are added and new data sets are created. Increasingly, machine learning (ML) is used by DLP to continually create and modify the criteria for protecting data.

Simple Network Management Protocol (SNMP) Traps

The **Simple Network Management Protocol (SNMP)** is a popular protocol used to manage network equipment and is supported by most network equipment manufacturers. It allows network administrators to remotely monitor, manage, and configure devices on the network. SNMP functions by exchanging management information between networked devices. Each SNMP-managed device must have an agent or a service that listens for commands and then executes them.

> ## Note 16
>
> SNMP can be found not only on core network devices such as switches, routers, and wireless access points but also on printers, copiers, fax machines, and even uninterruptible power supplies (UPSs).

Usually, a manager queries an agent for information by sending an SNMP-supported request in the form of a protocol data unit (PDU) to retrieve or to find variables and corresponding values that are available. However, a Simple Network Management Protocol (SNMP) trap is a special type of PDU. In this instance, an agent sends an unsolicited message or notification to the manager about critical events in the managed device.

Log Aggregation

A **log** is a record of the events occurring within an organization's systems and networks. Logs are composed of log entries, with each entry containing detailed information related to a specific event that has occurred. Many logs within an organization record events related to information security.

Almost every network device can—and does—produce a log. Whereas at one time each device had its own unique log format, today the **System Logging Protocol (Syslog)** is a means by which network devices can use a standard message format to communicate with a logging server. Devices can use a Syslog agent to send out notification messages under a wide range of specific conditions.

> ## Note 17
>
> Syslog works on all flavors of Unix and Linux, as well as macOS. Although Windows-based servers do not support Syslog natively, many third-party tools are available to allow Windows devices to communicate with a Syslog server.

Having a log format dramatically facilitates consolidating multiple logs together for analysis. This consolidation is known as log aggregation. Log aggregation enables security personnel to gather events from disparate sources into a single entity so that it can be searched and analyzed.

Security Content Automation Protocols (SCAP)

Security Content Automation Protocols (SCAP) is made up of several open security standards. These standards are considered security benchmarks, or a standard or point of reference against which they may be compared or assessed.

SCAP can help automate vulnerability management and determine whether the enterprise is compliant with required policies. SCAP is a collection of community-accepted security standards, hosted in open-source, online repositories. SCAP-compliant applications use these standards to check systems for vulnerabilities and misconfigurations. They can help report back with an overall score to evaluate the system's security posture and interoperate with other SCAP-validated scanners to provide results in a standardized format.

Security Information and Event Management (SIEM)

A Security Information and Event Management (SIEM) product (usually pronounced "seem" instead of "sim") consolidates real-time security monitoring and management of security information with analysis and reporting of security events. A SIEM product can be a separate device, software that runs on a computer, or even a service provided by a third party. A SIEM dashboard is shown in Figure 8-9.

Figure 8-9   SIEM dashboard

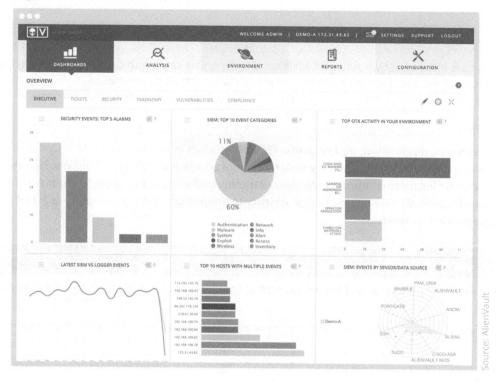

Source: AlienVault

The starting point of a SIEM is the data input. Data feeds into a SIEM are the standard packet captures of network activity and log collections. Because of the numerous network devices producing logs, SIEMs also perform log aggregation. A SIEM typically has the following features:

- **Aggregation.** SIEM aggregation combines data from multiple data sources, such as network security devices, servers, and software applications, to build a comprehensive picture of attacks.
- **Correlation.** The SIEM correlation feature searches the data acquired through SIEM aggregation to look for common characteristics, such as multiple attacks coming from a specific source.
- **Automated alerting and triggers.** SIEM automated alerting and triggers can inform security personnel of critical issues that need immediate attention. A sample trigger may be "Alert when a firewall, router, or switch indicates 40 or more drop/reject packet events occur from the same IP source address occurring within 60 seconds."
- **Time synchronization.** Because alerts occur over a wide spectrum of time, SIEM time synchronization can show the order of the events.
- **Event duplication.** When the same event occurs that is detected by multiple devices, each will generate an alert. The SIEM event duplication feature can help filter the multiple alerts into a single alarm.
- **Logs.** SIEM logs or records of events can be retained for future analysis and to show that the enterprise has been in compliance with regulations.

However, a SIEM goes beyond collecting and aggregating data. A SIEM can perform user behavior analysis. When a user's account suddenly acts in an unusual fashion, such as a lateral movement between assets, this could be an indication that a threat actor has compromised that account. A SIEM can then generate an alert for further investigation.

SIEMs can also perform sentiment analysis. Sentiment analysis is the process of computationally identifying and categorizing opinions, usually expressed in response to textual data, to determine the writer's attitude toward a particular topic. In other words, sentiment analysis is the interpretation and classification of emotions (positive, negative, and neutral) within text data using text analysis techniques. Sentiment analysis has been used when tracking postings threat actors make in discussion forums with other attackers to better determine the behavior and mindset of threat actors. This type of information can be valuable in determining their goals and actions and has even been used as a predictive power to alert against future attacks.

> **Note 18**
>
> Sentiment analysis is often used by businesses while conducting online chats with customers or examining Twitter and social media posts to identify customer sentiment toward products, brands, or services.

Security Orchestration, Automation, and Response (SOAR)

A **security orchestration, automation, and response (SOAR)** product is similar to a SIEM in that it is designed to help security teams manage and respond to the very high number of security warnings and alarms. However, SOARs take it a step further by combining more comprehensive data gathering and analytics in order to automate incident response. While a SIEM tends to generate more alerts than a security team may be able to respond to, a SOAR allows a security team to automate incident responses.

> **Two Rights & A Wrong**
>
> 1. Anomaly monitoring looks for well-known patterns to compare these activities against a predefined signature.
> 2. Flow analysis monitors the network's different devices and sounds an alert if it exceeds a predefined baseline.
> 3. A SIEM product consolidates real-time security monitoring and management of security information with analysis and reporting of security events.
>
> See the answers at the end of the module.

Email Monitoring and Security

> **Certification**
>
> 4.5 Given a scenario, modify enterprise capabilities to enhance security.

A sometimes-overlooked system that requires monitoring is the enterprise email system. Due to its widespread use and importance, email monitoring and security are of prime importance. This requires knowing the basics of how email works, the threats associated with email, and email defenses.

How Email Works

The basic components involved in sending and receiving email are the Mail User Agent (MUA) and Mail Transfer Agent (MTA). A MUA is what is used to read and send mail from an endpoint; this could be an app (like Thunderbird) or a webmail interface (like Gmail or Outlook). MTAs are programs that accept email messages from senders and route them toward their recipients.

Originally, email was sent to a mail server using the Simple Mail Transfer Protocol (SMTP). When it arrived at its destination, it was downloaded from the server using the Post Office Protocol (POP3). It was necessary for MUAs to use both SMTP and POP3 so that it could send user messages to the user's mail server (using SMTP) and could download messages intended for the user from the user's mail server (using POP3).

When Internet Access Message Protocol (IMAP) was introduced, it essentially replaced POP3. IMAP allows users to leave email on the mail server so that an email could be read from multiple endpoints (an email could be read on a smartphone when it was first received and then later referenced on a laptop). IMAP also allowed messages to be organized into folders that could again be accessed consistently from any endpoint. More recently, webmail has become more popular and widespread. Users can use a website as their MUA (such as Gmail) and no longer must configure endpoints with SMTP or IMAP server settings.

Note 19

Using email for political purposes helped first introduce email to the general public. Former President Jimmy Carter used a basic email system, which charged $4 per message, to coordinate strategies and send speeches during his 1976 presidential campaign.

As email is transferred from MTA to MTA, information is added to the **email header**. The email header contains information about the sender, recipient, email's route through MTAs, and various authentication details. Each MTA along the path adds its own information to the top of the email header. This means that when reading an email header, the final destination MTA information will be at the top of the header, and reading down through each subsequent header will ultimately end at the sender MTA header information. Figure 8-10 shows a partial email header.

Figure 8-10   Email header

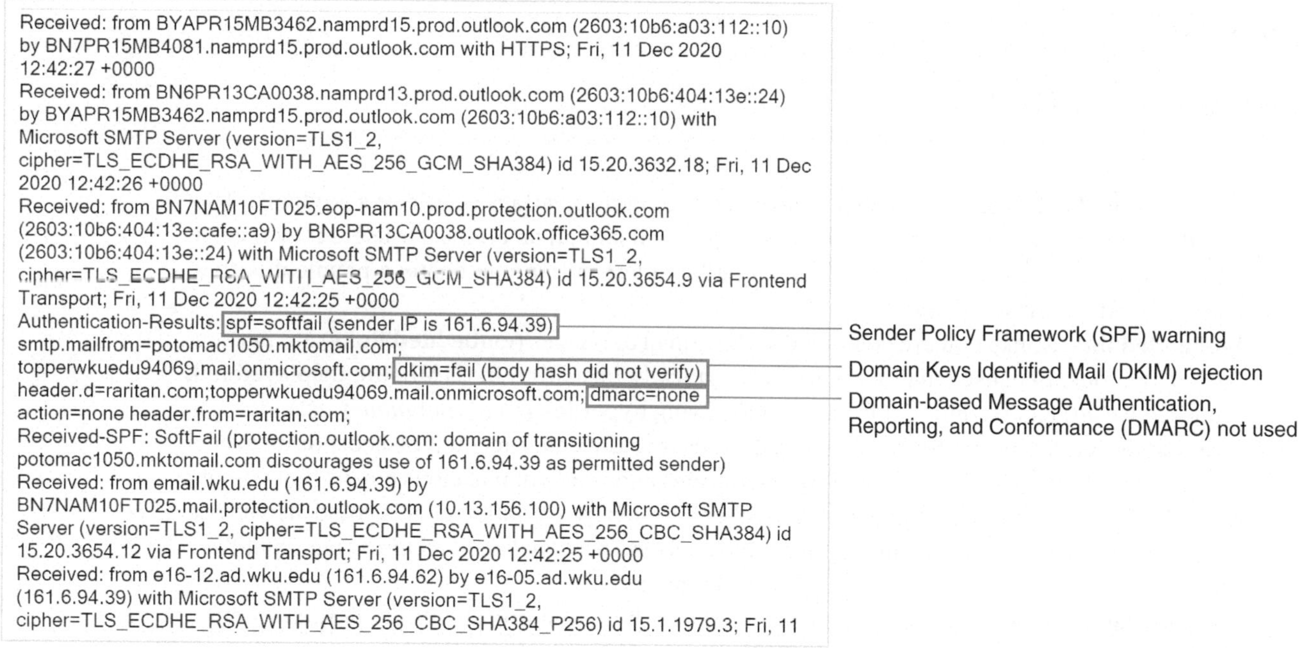

```
Received: from BYAPR15MB3462.namprd15.prod.outlook.com (2603:10b6:a03:112::10)
by BN7PR15MB4081.namprd15.prod.outlook.com with HTTPS; Fri, 11 Dec 2020
12:42:27 +0000
Received: from BN6PR13CA0038.namprd13.prod.outlook.com (2603:10b6:404:13e::24)
by BYAPR15MB3462.namprd15.prod.outlook.com (2603:10b6:a03:112::10) with
Microsoft SMTP Server (version=TLS1_2,
cipher=TLS_ECDHE_RSA_WITH_AES_256_GCM_SHA384) id 15.20.3632.18; Fri, 11 Dec
2020 12:42:26 +0000
Received: from BN7NAM10FT025.eop-nam10.prod.protection.outlook.com
(2603:10b6:404:13e:cafe::a9) by BN6PR13CA0038.outlook.office365.com
(2603:10b6:404:13e::24) with Microsoft SMTP Server (version=TLS1_2,
cipher=TLS_ECDHE_RSA_WITH_AES_256_GCM_SHA384) id 15.20.3654.9 via Frontend
Transport; Fri, 11 Dec 2020 12:42:25 +0000
Authentication-Results: spf=softfail (sender IP is 161.6.94.39)
smtp.mailfrom=potomac1050.mktomail.com;
topperwkuedu94069.mail.onmicrosoft.com; dkim=fail (body hash did not verify)
header.d=raritan.com;topperwkuedu94069.mail.onmicrosoft.com; dmarc=none
action=none header.from=raritan.com;
Received-SPF: SoftFail (protection.outlook.com: domain of transitioning
potomac1050.mktomail.com discourages use of 161.6.94.39 as permitted sender)
Received: from email.wku.edu (161.6.94.39) by
BN7NAM10FT025.mail.protection.outlook.com (10.13.156.100) with Microsoft SMTP
Server (version=TLS1_2, cipher=TLS_ECDHE_RSA_WITH_AES_256_CBC_SHA384) id
15.20.3654.12 via Frontend Transport; Fri, 11 Dec 2020 12:42:25 +0000
Received: from e16-12.ad.wku.edu (161.6.94.62) by e16-05.ad.wku.edu
(161.6.94.39) with Microsoft SMTP Server (version=TLS1_2,
cipher=TLS_ECDHE_RSA_WITH_AES_256_CBC_SHA384_P256) id 15.1.1979.3; Fri, 11
```

— Sender Policy Framework (SPF) warning

— Domain Keys Identified Mail (DKIM) rejection

— Domain-based Message Authentication, Reporting, and Conformance (DMARC) not used

Email headers also contain an analysis of the email by the MTA. Table 8-4 shows the different analysis categories and abbreviations used by Microsoft Office 365.

Table 8-4   Microsoft Office 365 email analysis

Abbreviation	Category
BULK	Bulk
DIMP	Domain impersonation
GIMP	Mailbox intelligence-based impersonation
HPHISH	High-confidence phishing
HSPM	High-confidence spam
MALW	Malware
PHSH	Phishing
SPM	Spam
SPOOF	Spoofing
UIMP	User impersonation
AMP	Anti-malware
SAP	Safe attachments
OSPM	Outbound spam

Email Threats

The threat most often associated with email is phishing. However, a variety of other threats are related to email. These include the following:

> **Note 20**
>
> Phishing is covered in Module 2.

- **Malicious payload.** Often the email message itself contains an attack (**malicious payload**). This could include an attachment that, upon opening it, will launch an attack. Or users may receive a fictious overdue invoice that demands immediate payment and, in haste, a payment is then made (called an invoice scam).
- **Embedded links.** Links that are contained within email messages (**embedded links**) are particularly dangerous. Because email messages are typically formatted in HTML, the displayed link (*your-bank.com*) can be different from the underlying hyperlink (*steal-your-money.net*).
- **Impersonation.** A threat actor who could gain access to the email account of a corporate executive could pretend to be that person (**impersonation**) and send out malicious emails that contain embedded links to sites belonging to the attacker. These impersonation emails could also have a malicious attachment with an email subject line such as *This attachment requires your immediate attention!* to trick the user into opening the attachment.
- **Forwarding.** There are several dangers associated with **forwarding** emails to another account. While some users want to "auto-forward" (automatically forward) all corporate emails to their personal user accounts for different reasons (enhanced spam filter, ease of access, etc.), there are risks with forwarding email messages. For example, sensitive email messages could be distributed outside the corporate email environment, making it easier for unauthorized individuals to read the messages. Also, if an email message forwarded from a corporate account was flagged as "Spam" by a user's personal email account, this could damage the "reputation score" of the corporate email that is used by email providers and spam filters. Also, if legal action is initiated and all email evidence must be surrendered, critical emails that may have been erased from a personal email account may not have a backup available as with a corporate email system.

> **Note 21**
>
> An analysis report by the U.S. Cybersecurity & Infrastructure Security Agency (CISA) titled "Strengthening Security Configurations to Defend Against Attackers Targeting Cloud Services" specifically mentions that threat actors are collecting sensitive information by taking advantage of email-forwarding rules that users had set up to forward work emails to their personal accounts. In one case, the CISA determined that the threat actors modified an existing email rule on a user's account originally set by the user to forward emails sent from a certain sender to a personal account. The threat actors modified the rule to redirect all emails to an account controlled by the threat actors.

Email Defenses

Different defenses can be used to address email threats. Spam and phishing filters can help address phishing attacks while strong endpoint anti-malware can be used to minimize malicious payloads. However, other email threats can only be addressed through improving user behavior, such as not clicking embedded links and not forwarding email to personal accounts. And some email threats—like impersonation based on a compromised account—have virtually no defenses.

There are also technology defenses used to address weaknesses inherent in the email system. For example, the original SMTP protocol had no provisions for security. All MTAs were expected to accept all messages from all senders and send the message along to another MTA. Although modern email is typically automatically encrypted from MTA to MTA as data in-transit using the protocol TLS (over port 993) or STARTTLS (port 143), this only protects email as it is being relayed from one MTA to another MTA along the delivery path; it does not address protection at the MTAs. If an email travels from the sender through three MTAs before reaching its recipient, any MTA along the way can alter the content of the message or change the header information.

There are different email defenses that can be used to protect email. These include Sender Policy Framework (SPF), Domain Keys Identified Mail (DKIM), and Domain-based Message Authentication, Reporting, and Conformance (DMARC). In addition, many organizations use a secure email gateway (SEG).

Sender Policy Framework (SPF)

It is important to protect against forged emails that pretend to come from one domain but actually come from another domain. Threat actors who can forge a domain can send fake messages that appear to come from an organization (spoofing), and a recipient who trusts the domain would likewise trust the email. Spoofed messages can be used for malicious purposes to communicate false information, distribute malware, and trick users into giving out sensitive information. In addition, it is important that valid email messages are not erroneously marked as spam, thus preventing their delivery to the recipient MTA.

Sender Policy Framework (SPF) is an email authentication method that identifies the MTA email servers that have been authorized to send email for a domain. SPF helps protect a domain from spoofing and also helps prevent messages from a valid domain from being marked as unwanted spam. If a domain does not use SPF, then receiving MTA email servers cannot verify that messages appearing to be from a domain actually are from that domain. This could result in the receiving MTA servers forwarding valid emails into the recipients' spam folders or even rejecting valid messages.

The administrative owner of a domain can set a TXT record in its DNS that states what servers are allowed to send mail on behalf of that domain. For example, in Figure 8-11, the Cengage.com SPF record indicates that email from cengage.com should only come from the servers specified, namely *Microsoft Outlook* and *PPHosted.com*. Those coming from a different domain are met with a "SoftFail" warning that says to trust this message less than normal but do not completely invalidate it based on this alone.

> **Note 22**
>
> The email header in Figure 8-10 indicates a SoftFail warning (*spf=softfail*).

However, SPF headers in an email are not infallible. Once generated, there is no means of protecting the information. This makes SPF useful to the MTA servers themselves while transmitting the email, but the protection does not extend beyond that. However, SPF is still an excellent tool for quickly identifying and intercepting spam.

Figure 8-11 Cengage SPF record

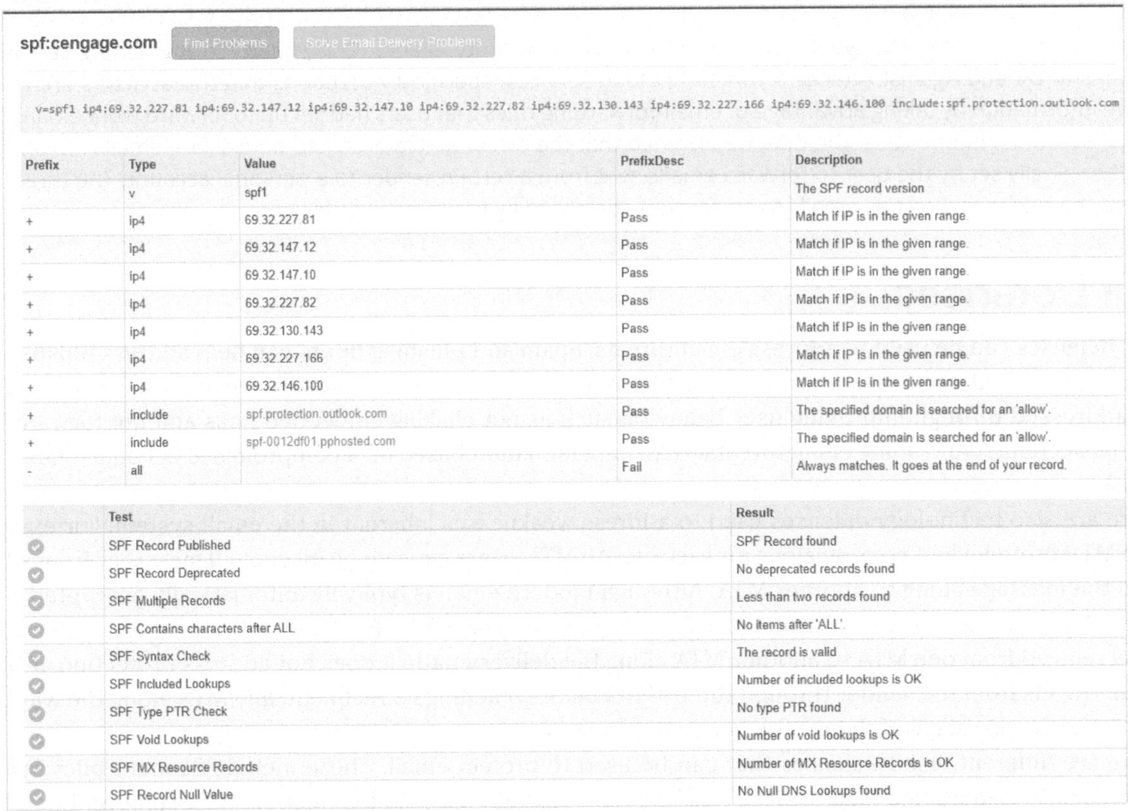

spf:cengage.com Find Problems Solve Email Delivery Problems

v=spf1 ip4:69.32.227.81 ip4:69.32.147.12 ip4:69.32.147.10 ip4:69.32.227.82 ip4:69.32.130.143 ip4:69.32.227.166 ip4:69.32.146.100 include:spf.protection.outlook.com

Prefix	Type	Value	PrefixDesc	Description
	v	spf1		The SPF record version
+	ip4	69.32.227.81	Pass	Match if IP is in the given range.
+	ip4	69.32.147.12	Pass	Match if IP is in the given range.
+	ip4	69.32.147.10	Pass	Match if IP is in the given range.
+	ip4	69.32.227.82	Pass	Match if IP is in the given range.
+	ip4	69.32.130.143	Pass	Match if IP is in the given range.
+	ip4	69.32.227.166	Pass	Match if IP is in the given range.
+	ip4	69.32.146.100	Pass	Match if IP is in the given range.
+	include	spf.protection.outlook.com	Pass	The specified domain is searched for an 'allow'.
+	include	spf-0012df01.pphosted.com	Pass	The specified domain is searched for an 'allow'.
-	all		Fail	Always matches. It goes at the end of your record.

	Test	Result
✓	SPF Record Published	SPF Record found
✓	SPF Record Deprecated	No deprecated records found
✓	SPF Multiple Records	Less than two records found
✓	SPF Contains characters after ALL	No items after 'ALL'.
✓	SPF Syntax Check	The record is valid
✓	SPF Included Lookups	Number of included lookups is OK
✓	SPF Type PTR Check	No type PTR found
✓	SPF Void Lookups	Number of void lookups is OK
✓	SPF MX Resource Records	Number of MX Resource Records is OK
✓	SPF Record Null Value	No Null DNS Lookups found

Source: MXToolbox

Domain Keys Identified Mail (DKIM)

Domain Keys Identified Mail (DKIM) is an authentication technique that validates the content of the email message itself. This validation is accomplished through a digital signature. The administrative owner of the sending domain can generate an asymmetric public/private key pair and store the public key in a TXT record on the domain's DNS. Mail servers on the outer boundary of the domain's infrastructure then use the private DKIM key to generate a digital signature (which is an encrypted digest created with a hash algorithm) of the entire message body, including all headers accumulated by the different MTAs. Recipients can decrypt the DKIM signature using the public DKIM key retrieved from the DNS to ensure that the digests match.

Note 23

The email header in Figure 8-10 indicates a DKIM rejection: *dkim=fail (body hash did not verify)*.

Domain-Based Message Authentication, Reporting, and Conformance (DMARC)

Domain-based Message Authentication, Reporting, and Conformance (DMARC) extends SPF and DKIM. It allows the administrative owner of a domain to publish a policy in their DNS records to specify which mechanism (DKIM, SPF, or both) is used when sending email from that domain. It also indicates how to check the *From:* field that is presented to end-users and a reporting mechanism for actions performed under those policies.

Note 24

The email header in Figure 8-10 indicates DMARC is not being used (*dmarc=none*).

Secure Email Gateway (SEG)

Many organizations filter all incoming email through a secure email gateway (SEG). An SEG acts as a "proxy" for the organization's email server. Any email sent to the organization will be redirected to the SEG, which can then filter and inspect the email for malicious content. Malicious email is deleted while approved email is forwarded to the corporate email server for delivery to the intended recipient. Configuring an SEG involves setting up its DNS MX record to point to the SEG.

Despite their widespread use, there are limitations to a SEG:

- **Single-layer security.** Some SEGs actually disable the built-in security protections offered by email providers like Google or Microsoft. This negates a defense-in-depth posture.
- **Exposing protections.** Because it is necessary to change an organization's DNS MX record to point to SEG, this may enable attackers to tailor attacks to circumvent the defense.
- **Multiple root domains.** While an organization may have its DNS MX record pointing to its SEG, other email products like Gmail and Office 365 also have a root domain whose DNS is managed by Google or Microsoft. Attackers that send emails to this root domain can bypass an SEG.

Two Rights & A Wrong

1. A MUA is what is used to read and send mail from an endpoint while MTAs are programs that accept email messages from senders and route them toward their recipients.

2. Each MTA along the path adds its own information to the top of the email header.

3. SPF is an authentication technique that validates the content of the email message itself.

See the answers at the end of the module.

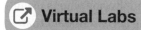 **Virtual Labs**   You're now ready to complete the simulations and live virtual machine labs for this module. The labs can be found in each module in MindTap.

Summary

- An on-path attack occurs when a threat actor is positioned in the middle of two communicating users or devices. There are different types of these attacks. A man-in-the-middle (MITM) attack intercepts legitimate communication and forges a fictitious response to the sender or eavesdrops on the conversation. A session replay attack intercepts and uses a session ID to impersonate a user. A man-in-the-browser (MITB) attack occurs between a browser and the underlying computer. A MITB attack seeks to intercept and then manipulate the communication between the web browser and the security mechanisms of the computer.

- Domain Name System (DNS) attacks substitute a DNS address so that the computer is silently redirected to a different device. DNS poisoning modifies a local lookup table on a device to point to a different domain, which is usually a malicious DNS server controlled by a threat actor that redirects traffic to a website designed to steal user information or infect the device with malware. DNS hijacking is intended to infect an external DNS server with IP addresses that point to malicious sites.

- A distributed denial of service (DDoS) attack involves a device being overwhelmed by a torrent of fake requests so that it cannot respond to legitimate requests for service. There are two means by which attackers can generate massive amounts of data to overwhelm a system. The first is to use large numbers of compromised devices, each sending bogus requests. The second method is to use amplified attacks to increase the deluge of data. The most common amplified attacks are reflection attacks in which attackers direct their initial data stream at a misconfigured Internet device or service in such a way that it causes the device or service to reflect and generate an even larger payload at the ultimate target.

- Several successful network attacks come from malicious software code and scripts. PowerShell is a task automation and configuration management framework from Microsoft. The power and reach of PowerShell make it a prime target for threat actors who use it to inject malware. Visual Basic for Applications (VBA) is an "event-driven" Microsoft programming language that is used to automate processes that normally would take multiple steps or levels of steps. VBA is most often used to create macros. A macro is a series of instructions that can be grouped together as a single command. Macros are still used to distribute malware. Python is a popular programming language that can run on different OS platforms. There are several "best practices" to follow when using Python so that the code does not contain vulnerabilities. Bash is the command language interpreter (called the "shell") for the Linux/UNIX OS. Bash scripting is using Bash to create a script. (A script is essentially the same as a program, but it is interpreted and executed without the need for it to be first compiled into machine language.)

- Layer 2 of the OSI model is particularly weak and is a frequent target of threat actors. ARP poisoning changes the ARP cache so the corresponding IP address is pointing to a different computer. In a MAC cloning attack, a threat actor discovers a valid MAC address of a device connected to a switch and then spoofs that MAC address on their device and sends a packet onto the network. The switch changes its MAC address table to reflect this new association of that MAC address with the port to which the attacker's device is connected. In a MAC flooding attack, a threat actor overflows the switch with Ethernet packets to consume all the memory for the MAC address table and enters a fail-open mode, broadcasting frames to all ports. A threat actor could then install software or a hardware device that captures and decodes packets on one client connected to the switch to view all traffic. A credential relay attack attempts to steal

authentication credentials and then use them to access a system.

- Continual monitoring of the infrastructure for evidence of attacks is critical. There are four monitoring methodologies: anomaly-based monitoring, signature-based monitoring, behavior-based monitoring, and heuristic monitoring. Several activities make up security monitoring and alerting. These include scanning, reporting, quarantine, alerting, alert tuning, and archiving.

- Several tools can be used for monitoring and alerting. Packet analysis tools can detect unusual behavior that could indicate the presence of malware, search for unusual domains or IP address endpoints, and discover regular connections to a threat actor's C&C server. Flow analysis (also called network traffic analysis) is the process of monitoring the network's devices and sounding an alert if it exceeds a predefined baseline. NetFlow is a session sampling protocol feature on Cisco routers that collects IP network traffic as it enters or exits an interface and uses ICMP Echo request packets.

- Data loss prevention (DLP) is a system of security tools used to recognize and identify data critical to the organization and ensure that it is protected. This protection involves monitoring who is using the data and how it is being accessed. Data that is considered critical to the organization or is confidential can be tagged as such. A user who attempts to access the data to disclose it to an unauthorized user will be prevented from doing so. A Simple Network Management Protocol (SNMP) trap agent sends an unsolicited message or notification to the manager about critical events in the managed device. Log aggregation enables security personnel to gather events from disparate sources into a single entity so that it can be searched and analyzed.

- Security content automation protocols (SCAP) is made up of several open security standards. These standards are considered security benchmarks, which are standards against which they may be compared or assessed. SCAP can help automate vulnerability management and determine whether the enterprise is compliant with required policies. A security information and event management (SIEM) product consolidates real-time security monitoring and management of security information with analysis and reporting of security events. A security orchestration, automation, and response (SOAR) product allows a security team to automate incident responses.

- A sometimes-overlooked system that requires monitoring is the email system. The basic components involved in sending and receiving email are the Mail User Agent (MUA) and Mail Transfer Agent (MTA). A MUA is what is used to read and send mail from an endpoint and could be an app or a webmail interface. MTAs are programs that accept email messages from senders and route them toward their recipients. As email is transferred from MTA to MTA, information is added to the email header. The email header contains information about the sender, recipient, email's route through MTAs, and various authentication details.

- There are a variety of threats related to email, yet different email defenses can also be used to protect email. These include Sender Policy Framework (SPF), Domain Keys Identified Mail (DKIM), and Domain-based Message Authentication, Reporting, and Conformance (DMARC). Many organizations filter all incoming email through a secure email gateway (SEG). An SEG acts as a "proxy" for the organization's email server. Any email sent to the organization will then be redirected to the SEG, which can filter and inspect the email for malicious content.

Key Terms

agentless
agents
alert tuning
alerting
amplified attacks
archiving
benchmark
credential relay attack
data loss prevention (DLP)
deploy baselines
distributed denial of service (DDoS)
Domain-based Message
   Authentication, Reporting, and
   Conformance (DMARC)

Domain Keys Identified Mail (DKIM)
Domain Name System (DNS) attacks
establish baselines
fail closed
fail open
failure mode
log aggregation
maintain baselines
malicious code attacks
monitoring applications
monitoring infrastructures
monitoring systems
NetFlow
on-path attack

quarantine
reflection attacks
reporting
scanning
secure baseline
secure email gateway (SEG)
Security Content Automation
   Protocols (SCAP)
Security Information and Event
   Management (SIEM)
Sender Policy Framework (SPF)
Simple Network Management
   Protocol (SNMP) trap
user behavior analytics

Review Questions

1. Which attack intercepts communications between a web browser and the underlying OS?

   a. MITM
   b. MRTR
   c. MTTR
   d. MITB

2. Himari needs to protect against potential attacks on DNS. What are the locations she would need to protect?

   a. Web server buffer and host DNS server
   b. Reply referrer and domain buffer
   c. Web browser and browser add-on
   d. Local host file and external DNS server

3. What is the result of an ARP poisoning attack?

   a. The ARP cache is compromised.
   b. Users cannot reach a DNS server.
   c. MAC addresses are altered.
   d. An internal DNS must be used instead of an external DNS.

4. Yua has discovered that the network switch is broadcasting all packets to all devices. She suspects it is the result of an attack that has overflowed the switch MAC address table. Which type of attack would she report?

   a. MAC spoofing attack
   b. MAC cloning attack
   c. MAC flooding attack
   d. MAC overflow attack

5. Sakura is explaining to a colleague the different types of DNS attacks. Which DNS attack would only impact a single user?

    a. DNS hijack attack
    b. DNS poisoning attack
    c. DNS overflow attack
    d. DNS resource attack

6. Which type of monitoring methodology looks for statistical deviations from a baseline?

    a. Behavioral monitoring
    b. Signature-based monitoring
    c. Anomaly monitoring
    d. Heuristic monitoring

7. Ichika suspects that there may be infected devices on the network that are sending regular beacons to a threat actor's C&C server. Which type of analysis would she use to determine if this is true?

    a. Traffic analysis
    b. Port analysis
    c. Packet analysis
    d. Probe analysis

8. Akari has been asked to install a packet analysis tool on a Linux web server. Because this server does not do anything unnecessary so it reduces the footprint that a threat actor could exploit, all applications on the server are command-line applications and there is no graphical user interface (GUI). Which tool would Akari install?

    a. Ethereal
    b. Tcpdump
    c. Network General
    d. Sniffer

9. Which of the following is NOT a reason that threat actors use PowerShell for attacks?

    a. It cannot be detected by anti-malware running on the computer.
    b. It leaves behind no evidence on a hard drive.
    c. It can be invoked prior to system boot.
    d. Most applications flag it as a trusted application.

10. Which attack uses the fewest number of computers to launch the attack?

    a. DoS
    b. DDoS
    c. DoSS
    d. DooS

11. Which of the following is used to write macros?

    a. PowerShell
    b. Python
    c. Bash
    d. VBA

12. Which of the following is NOT correct about an email header?

    a. As email is transferred from MTA to MTA, information is added to the email header.
    b. Email headers are encrypted to prevent someone from altering the contents.
    c. The email header contains information about the sender, recipient, email's route through MTAs, and various authentication details.
    d. Each MTA along the path adds its own information to the top of the email header.

13. Which of the following is NOT correct about forwarding emails?

    a. Corporations routinely allow employees to forward emails.
    b. Employees may "auto-forward" corporate emails to utilize enhanced spam filtering.
    c. Forwarded emails may not be available for email evidence.
    d. Unauthorized users could access forwarded emails.

14. Which of the following email defenses uses a digital signature?

    a. SPC
    b. DKIM
    c. DMARC
    d. It depends on whether or not the email payload has been encrypted.

15. Aoi uses the Python programming language and does not want her code to contain vulnerabilities. Which of the following best practices would she NOT use?

    a. Only use compiled and not interpreted Python code.
    b. Use the latest version of Python.
    c. Use caution when formatting strings.
    d. Download only vetted libraries.

16. What is Bash?

    a. The command-language interpreter for Linux/UNIX OSs
    b. The open-source scripting language that contains many vulnerabilities
    c. A substitute for SSH
    d. The underlying platform on which macOS is built

17. Which of the following is a tool for editing packets and then putting the packets back onto the network to observe their behavior?

    a. Tcpreplay
    b. Tcpdump
    c. Wireshark
    d. Packetdump

18. Which of the following is NOT a limitation of an SEG?

    a. Slow processing speed
    b. Single-layer security
    c. Multiple root domains
    d. Revealing protections

19. Amari has been asked to compare an organization's security against a set of open security standards. Which of the following would he choose?

    a. SCAP
    b. NFLOW
    c. SOAR
    d. SPF

20. What does an SNMP trap do that is different from the normal SNMP function?

    a. SNMP traps do not use PDU.
    b. SNMP traps can only respond to administrator queries once per hour.
    c. SNMP traps can send unsolicited messages.
    d. SNMP traps require authentication while normal SNMP does not.

Hands-On Projects

Caution !

If you are concerned about installing any of the software in these projects on your regular computer, you can instead use the Windows Sandbox used in the Module 1 Hands-On Projects. Software installed within the sandbox will not impact the host computer.

Project 8-1: DNS Poisoning

Estimated Time: 20 minutes
Objective: Demonstrate a DNS poisoning attack.
Description: Substituting a fraudulent IP address can be done by either attacking the Domain Name System (DNS) server or the local host table. Attackers can target a local hosts file to create new entries that redirect users to their fraudulent site. In this project, you add a fraudulent entry to the local hosts file.

1. Go to the Western Kentucky University website at **www.wku.edu**.

2. Go to the website of your school or business where you work.

3. Now find the IP address of the website of that school or business. Go to **ipaddress.com/ip_lookup/** and enter the domain name to receive the correct IP address.

Caution !

If your search reveals multiple IP addresses for that website, you will need to choose another website that only has a single IP address.

4. Verify the IP address of both sites. To reach the Western Kentucky University website by IP address, use your web browser to go to **https://161.6.94.74**.

Caution !

If your browser displays warning messages when searching by IP address, click through those messages and approve using the IP address.

5. Now go to the website of your school or business by entering **https://***IP_address*.

6. Click **Start** and then type **Notepad**.

7. In the search results, click **Run as administrator**. If you receive the message **Do you want to allow this app to make changes to the device?**, click **Yes**.

8. Click **File** and then **Open**. Click the **File Type** arrow to change from **Text Documents (*.txt)** to **All files (*.*)**.

9. Navigate to the file **C:\Windows\System32\drivers\etc\hosts** and open it.

10. At the end of the file following all hashtags (#) in the first column, enter the IP address of **161.6.94.74**. This is the IP address of Western Kentucky University.

11. Press **Tab** and enter **www.***name_of_your_school_or_business*. In this hosts table, the domain name of your school or business is now resolved to the IP address of Western Kentucky University.

12. Click **File** and then **Save**.

13. Open your web browser and then enter the URL of your school or business. What website appears?

14. Return to the hosts file and remove this entry.

15. Click **File** and then **Save**.

16. Close all windows.

Project 8-2: ARP Poisoning

Estimated Time: 20 minutes

Objective: Demonstrate an ARP poisoning attack.

Description: Attackers frequently modify the Address Resolution Protocol (ARP) table to redirect communications away from a valid device to an attacker's computer. In this project, you view the ARP table on your computer and make modifications to it. You will need to have another "target's" computer running on your network (and know the IP address), as well as a default gateway that serves as the switch to the network.

1. Open a Command Prompt window by right-clicking Start and selecting **Terminal (Admin)**.

2. To view your current ARP table, type **arp -a** and then press **Enter**. The Internet Address is the IP address of another device on the network while the Physical Address is the MAC address of that device.

3. To determine network addresses, type **ipconfig** and then press **Enter**.

4. Record the IP address of the default gateway.

5. Delete the ARP table entry of the default gateway by typing **arp -d** followed by the IP address of the gateway, such as **arp -d 192.168.1.1**, and then press **Enter**.

6. Create an automatic entry in the ARP table of the target's computer by typing **ping** followed by that computer's IP address, such as **ping 192.168.1.100**, and then press **Enter**.

7. Verify that this new entry is now listed in the ARP table by typing **arp -a** and then press **Enter**. Record the physical address of that computer.

8. Add that entry to the ARP table by entering **arp -s** followed by the IP address and then the MAC address.

9. Delete all entries from the ARP table by typing **arp -d**.

10. Close all windows.

Project 8-3: MAC Spoofing

Estimated Time: 20 minutes

Objective: Demonstrate a MAC spoofing attack.

Description: In a MAC cloning attack, a threat actor discovers a valid MAC address of a device connected to a switch. They then spoof that MAC address on their device and send a packet onto the network. In this activity, you spoof a MAC address.

1. Go to the Technitium website at **technitium.com/tmac/**. (If you are no longer able to access the program through this URL, use a search engine to search for "Technitium MAC address changer.")

2. Click **Download Now**.

3. Click **Direct Download**.

4. Save the file to your computer and then install the application.

5. Launch the application.

6. If necessary, click **Yes** to respond to the pop-up dialog box.

7. Scroll through the list of network connections on your computer.

8. Select the network connection that is your Internet connection.

9. Read the information on the **Information** tab.

10. Click **Random MAC Address** to display another MAC address that can be assigned to this device.

11. Click the down arrow in the box below the new random MAC address. Note the long list of different NIC vendors from which a MAC address can be chosen.

12. Click **(2C-30-33) Netgear**.

13. Look at the new MAC address under **Change MAC Address** and note the first three pairs of numbers. What does this correspond to?

14. Click **Why?** next to **Use '02' as first octet of MAC address**.

15. Read the explanation about why 02 should be used as the first octet.

16. If you want to change your MAC address, click **Change Now!** or close the application if you do not want to change the address.

17. How easy was it to spoof a MAC address? How can a threat actor use this in a MAC cloning attack?

18. Close all windows.

Project 8-4: Sentiment Analysis

Estimated Time: 25 minutes
Objective: Research sentiment analysis.
Description: Sentiment analysis is the process of computationally identifying and categorizing opinions, usually expressed in response to textual data, to determine the writer's attitude toward a particular topic. It has been used when tracking postings threat actors make to determine the behavior and mindset of threat actors and has even been used as a predictive power to alert against future attacks. In this project, you experiment with sentiment analysis to learn of its capabilities.

1. Open your web browser and enter the URL **https://monkeylearn.com**. (If you are no longer able to access the site through this web address, use a search engine to search for "MonkeyLearn.")

2. Click **RESOURCES** and then **Guides**. This webpage helps show how sentiment analysis fits into the context of artificial intelligence.

3. Click **Sentiment Analysis** and read through what it is, how it is useful, and how it can be performed.

4. Now create an account. Go to **https://app.monkeylearn.com/accounts/register/** and follow the instructions to create a MonkeyLearn account and then sign in.

5. Click **Explore**.

6. Click **Sentiment Analysis**.

7. Enter the text **I like sunshine.** and click **Classify Text**. What tag does it provide and what is the confidence level?

8. Enter several random phrases and perform an analysis on each.

9. Return to the Explore screen.

10. Select **Hotel Aspect**.

11. Search the Internet for a review of a hotel—one that you consider would be positive and another that would be negative—and paste the first review into the text box. Click **Classify Text**. Would you agree with the analysis? Do the same with the second review.

12. Return to the Explore screen.

13. Select **Sentiment Analysis**.

14. Use a search engine to search the Internet for *cybersecurity quotations.* Cut and paste several of these into the text box and analyze them.

15. Now enter statements from threat actors. Go to Google Images (**https://images.google.com**).

16. Enter the search word **ransomware** and press **Enter**.

17. Locate ransomware screens that contain messages from threat actors and enter these into the Sentiment Analysis text box for analysis. What is the sentiment analysis for these quotations from threat actors?

18. How could sentiment analysis be useful in identifying a threat actor's mindset? Do you think it could be used for predicting attacks?

19. Close all windows.

Case Projects

Case Project 8-1: #TrendingCyber

Estimated Time: 15 minutes
Objective: Summarize your thoughts on the #TrendingCyber opener.
Description: Read again the opening #TrendingCyber in this module. Should TTE have been tested more thoroughly before it was chosen for use on a spacecraft? Despite the limitations of weight, space, power, and cost that drove engineers to choose TTE over multiple segregated networks, is this a valid trade-off? Should there be a separate network to handle mission-critical functions? Why? Write a one-paragraph summary of your thoughts.

Case Project 8-2: DDoS Mitigation

Estimated Time: 25 minutes
Objective: Research DDoS mitigation.
Description: For websites, the only real protection against DDoS attacks is DDoS mitigation services. These services will detect abnormal network traffic that may signal an imminent DDoS attack and then reroute the traffic away from the target, either to be filtered or just discarded. This rerouting is most often done in one of two ways. The first method uses DNS redirection. This is accomplished by changing DNS records (specifically the CNAME and A record) to point to the IP address of the mitigation provider, where malicious requests are dropped while legitimate requests are forwarded back to the actual website. In some ways DNS redirection is similar to DNS poisoning. The second method is Border Gateway Protocol (BGP) routing that can divert all Network Layer packets, meaning that it is effective across all protocols to stop various types of Network and Application Layer attacks. However, DDoS mitigation services can be expensive. How do most organizations attempt to mitigate a sudden DDoS attack that is directed at their web servers? Use the Internet to research DDoS mitigation techniques, technologies, and third-party entities that provide mitigation services. Write a one-page paper on your research.

Case Project 8-3: PowerShell

Estimated Time: 25 minutes

Objective: Research PowerShell capabilities.

Description: PowerShell is an extremely powerful application. One recent attack illustrates how PowerShell can be used by threat actors. This attack started with a phishing email with the subject line "URGENT!" that contained an Excel attachment with a malicious embedded script. Once the user opened the attachment and approved the script to run its active content, it then decrypted and executed a PowerShell script. The script ran with the PowerShell parameters ExecutionPolicyByPass (allow the PowerShell script to run despite any system restrictions), WindowStyleHidden (run the script quietly without any notification to the user), and NoProfile (do not load the system's custom PowerShell environment). Is PowerShell too powerful? Should its capabilities be limited so as to prevent threat actors from utilizing this tool? Research PowerShell and how it has been used in attacks. Identify at least one recent attack that has used PowerShell. Write a one-page summary of your research.

Case Project 8-4: Tcpdump

Estimated Time: 20 minutes

Objective: Research Tcpdump.

Description: Tcpdump is a command-line packet analyzer. It displays TCP/IP packets and other packets being transmitted or received over a network and operates on UNIX and Linux operating systems, and various forks of it are available for Windows computers. Tcpdump's power and functionality can be seen by the large number of switches that are available for tcpdump. A complete list of tcpdump switches is available at www.tcpdump.org/manpages/tcpdump.1.html. Research Tcpdump and its capabilities. How does it compare with Wireshark? What are its advantages and disadvantages? Write a one-page summary of your research.

Case Project 8-5: Microsoft Macro Protections

Estimated Time: 25 minutes

Objective: Research Microsoft protections from malicious macros.

Description: Due to the impact of macro malware, Microsoft has implemented several protections:

- **Protected View.** Protected View is a read-only mode for an Office file in which most editing functions are disabled and macros will not launch. Files that are opened from an Internet location, received as an email attachment, opened from a potentially unsafe location, opened from another user's OneDrive storage, or have "active content" (macros or data connections) will display a Protected View warning message.
- **Trusted Documents.** A trusted document is a file that contains active content but will open without a warning. Users can designate files in the Office Trust Center as trusted. However, files opened from an unsafe location cannot be designated as a trusted document. Also, the ability to designate a trusted document can be turned off by the system administrator.
- **Trusted Location.** Files that are retrieved from a trusted location can be designated as safe and will not open in Protected View. It is recommended that if a user trusts a file that contains active content, it should be moved to a trusted location instead of changing the default Trust Center settings to allow macros.

Research these protections against macros. Write a one-page paper that lists each protection, their strengths and weaknesses, and how they are implemented.

Case Project 8-6: NetFlow

Estimated Time: 20 minutes

Objective: Research NetFlow.

Description: NetFlow is a session sampling protocol feature on Cisco routers that collects IP network traffic as it enters or exits an interface and uses TCP/IP ICMP Echo request packets. Research NetFlow. What are its strengths and weaknesses? How does it compare to other flow-analysis data-capture programs? Write a one-page paper on your research.

Case Project 8-7: Secure Email Gateways

Estimated Time: 25 minutes

Objective: Research secure email gateways.

Description: A SEG acts as a "proxy" for the organization's email server. Any email sent to the organization will be redirected to the SEG, which can then filter and inspect the email for malicious content. Use the Internet to identify three SEG products. Create a table that compares their strengths, weaknesses, features, and cost. Which would you recommend? Why? Write a one-page paper on your findings.

Case Project 8-8: DNS Services

Estimated Time: 25 minutes

Objective: Research DNS services.

Description: Many organizations offer a free domain name resolution service that resolves DNS requests through a worldwide network of redundant DNS servers. The claim is that this is faster and more reliable than using the DNS servers provided by Internet service providers (ISPs), and that these DNS servers improve security by maintaining a real-time blacklist of harmful websites and will warn users whenever they attempt to access a site containing potentially threatening content. They also say that using this service can reduce exposure to types of DNS poisoning attacks. Research free DNS services. Identify at least three providers and create a table comparing their features. Are the claims of providing improved security valid? How do they compare with your ISP's DNS service? Write a one-page paper on your research.

Case Project 8-9: DNS-over-HTTPS (DoH)

Estimated Time: 30 minutes

Objective: Research DNS-over-HTTPS (DoH).

Description: To protect DNS, some providers are using DNS-over-HTTPS, also called DoH. As its name implies, DoH uses HTTPS instead of HTTP to send DNS queries via an encrypted HTTPS connection (Port 443) rather than sending them in cleartext (Port 53). The encrypted DoH query is sent to a special DoH resolving server that aggregates all users' DoH queries and then translates them into regular unencrypted DNS queries for processing by DNS servers. However, DoH has become very controversial. Why? What are the advantages of DoH? What are its disadvantages? How does it compare with DNS-over-TLS (DoT)? Write a one-page paper on your research.

Case Project 8-10: Bay Point Ridge Security

Estimated Time: 40 minutes

Objective: Research email security.

Description: Bay Point Ridge Security (BPRS) is a managed service provider (MSP) that manages networks, computers, cloud resources, and information security for small-to-medium enterprises (SMEs) in the region. BPRS provides internships to students who are in their final year of the security degree program at the local college and has recently hired you.

A new client is concerned about their corporate email. Not only are too many malicious emails by-passing their defenses but, due to the sensitive nature of the contents of their emails, they believe that stronger security is needed.

1. Create a PowerPoint presentation on the various email technology defenses of SPF, DKIM, and DMARC. Include a summary of how each works, what are the strengths and the weaknesses, and how each is implemented. Your presentation should be at least 10 to 12 slides in length.

2. As a follow-up to your presentation, you have been asked to write a one-page report on SEGs along with a recommendation. Use the Internet to research SEGs and how they can best be used.

Two Rights & A Wrong: Answers

Attacks on Networks

1. An advantage of an on-path attack is that it can occur without the two targets knowing an attacker is present.

2. A session ID is a unique number that a web browser assigns a specific user for the duration of the user's visit to the site.

3. A MITB attack seeks to intercept and then manipulate the communication between the web browser and the security mechanisms of the computer.

Answer: The wrong statement is #2.

Explanation: A session ID is a unique number that a web server assigns a specific user for the duration of the user's visit to the site.

Security Monitoring and Alerting

1. Anomaly monitoring looks for well-known patterns to compare these activities against a predefined signature.

2. Flow analysis monitors the network's different devices and sounds an alert if it exceeds a predefined baseline.

3. A SIEM product consolidates real-time security monitoring and management of security information with analysis and reporting of security events.

Answer: The wrong statement is #1.

Explanation: Anomaly monitoring is designed for detecting statistical anomalies.

Email Monitoring and Security

1. A MUA is what is used to read and send mail from an endpoint while MTAs are programs that accept email messages from senders and route them toward their recipients.

2. Each MTA along the path adds its own information to the top of the email header.

3. SPF is an authentication technique that validates the content of the email message itself.

Answer: The wrong statement is #3.

Explanation: DKIM is an authentication technique that validates the content of the email message itself.

Reference

1. Thompson, Mia, "How to stay safe from Office macro-based malware with email security," *Solarwinds MSP*, Feb. 10, 2020, accessed Jun. 17, 2020, www.n-able.com/blog /how-stay-safe-office-macro-based-malware-email-security.

Infrastructure Security

Module Objectives

After completing this module, you should be able to do the following:

1 List the different types of security appliances and how they can be used

2 Describe security software protections

3 Explain how a secure design can aid in mitigating attacks

4 Describe different access technologies and how they can be used

#TrendingCyber

Ransomware attackers have increasingly become more aggressive in their extortion techniques. This has resulted in more calls for systems that hold confidential information to be physically separated from the Internet (called an "air gap") so that threat actors cannot reach highly confidential data. But will this technique work for preventing ransomware attacks?

Typically, ransomware attacks have two phases: the threat actors first steal the data and then lock it up with encryption. By stealing the data first, the threat actors then have leverage to pressure victims to pay the ransom—they can threaten to publish the stolen data if the victims do not pay. In order to avoid bad publicity and fines that can come from the release of the stolen data, many organizations that were at first reluctant to pay the ransom often choose to do so.

The FBI Internet Crime Complaint Center (IC3) publishes an annual Internet Crime Report. Regarding ransomware, the FBI says that "it has been challenging for the FBI to ascertain the true number of ransomware victims" because many attacks go unreported to law enforcement. However, of those reported in 2022, the FBI said that the total losses resulting from ransomware had decreased by about $15 million from the previous year. Part of this decrease is because more ransomware targets are refusing to pay large ransom demands.

But this increase by those targets who refuse to pay is not decreasing the number of incidents of ransomware attacks, according to the FBI. Instead, it is forcing the threat actors to become even more aggressive in their tactics. Attackers are now taking what some consider hostile actions in order to secure a ransom, knowing that a growing percentage of targets will refuse to pay.

This more aggressive behavior on the part of ransomware attackers can be seen clearly by two recent ransomware incidents. In the first ransomware attack, threat actors targeted the patient photo system related to radiation oncology treatment from a physician practice that was part of the Lehigh Valley Health Network (LVHN). After LVHN refused the attacker's demands to pay a ransom, the attackers then threatened to publish data stolen from the system. The threat actors told LVHN, "Our blog is followed by a lot of world media. The case will be widely publicized and will cause significant damage to your business" and "Your time is running out. We are ready to unleash our full power on you!"

The attackers then released three screenshots of cancer patients receiving radiation treatment and seven documents that included patient personal information. The medical photos were graphic and intimate, depicting patients' naked breasts in various angles and positions. While hospitals and health care facilities have long been a favorite target of ransomware attacks, security professionals say this demonstrates the attackers' desperation and willingness to go to ruthless extremes to pressure a target to pay.

The second example of escalation came when another ransomware gang in 2023 exfiltrated and then encrypted data from the Minneapolis Public Schools (MPS), which enrolls more than 36,000 students annually. The stolen data was from not only students but also staff and even parents, dating back to 1995. The attackers offered three options: anyone could pay $1 million to buy the stolen MPS data, the school district itself could pay the ransom and have the stolen data deleted, or someone could pay $50,000 to extend the ransom deadline by one day. The MPS refused to pay.

The attackers then published samples of the stolen data from the MPS. One sample included leaked screenshots of scans of handwritten notes that described allegations of a sexual assault, which included the names of a male student and two female students involved in the incident. But they did not stop there. Next, the threat actors posted a 50-minute video in which they appeared to scroll through and review the data they stole from the school.

The heinous nature of the release of this sensitive information has caused an outcry. While ransomware groups have performed unscrupulous tactics before, the targets were not cancer patients or schoolchildren. One professional noted, "We really haven't seen things like this before." Another said, "It follows closely patterns in kidnapping cases, where when victims' families refused to pay, the kidnappers might send an ear or other body part of the victim."

The escalation of these attacks has resurrected again the cry for computers and networks that contain sensitive information to be disconnected from the Internet. These air-gapped networks would make it impossible for threat actors to reach the data. This, some say, would ultimately deprive attackers of data and put an end to ransomware attacks once and for all.

But the history of air-gapped networks shows that this technique is unlikely to work.

While air-gapping computers or entire networks may prevent one type of infrastructure attack of threat actors entering a network to steal information, it still leaves open the door for other types of attacks. Social engineering is often used to infiltrate an air-gapped network. One trick that has been used was to leave an infected USB flash drive on the floor of a parking structure or on a bench outside the building that houses the air-gapped network. Unsuspecting employees picked up these flash drives and inserted them into a computer that was part of the air-gapped network in an attempt to discover the owner of the flash drive. But this resulted in the air-gapped network being infected. Another trick was to "pre-penetrate" the computers before they become separated through an air gap. This was done by hiding malware or back doors into software libraries that are used in producing applications—even antivirus software—that will eventually run on an air-gapped network. And attackers have even resorted to bribing or coercing an insider to download data from the network.

Security professionals have also noted the virtual impossibility of having an air-gapped network in today's remote or hybrid work environment. How would employees access data from an air-gapped network if they are working from home or live in another state? What about critical data that must interact with data that is not critical? How could that connection take place? And would organizations be able to even differentiate between critical data that requires an air-gapped network while deeming all other data as dispensable?

While cries for "Just air-gap it!" may sound like the solution to these heinous ransomware attacks, it's unlikely to solve the problem.

At one time, "information security" and "network security" were virtually synonymous. That was because the network was viewed as the "moat" around which endpoint devices could be kept safely inside while attackers were on the outside. A secure and impenetrable network was viewed as the key to keeping attackers at bay.

This approach, however, proved to be untenable. There were simply too many avenues into devices residing within the network that malware could enter. For example, users could insert an infected USB flash drive directly into their computer, thus bypassing the secure network "moat."

This is not to say that network security is not important. On the contrary, having a secure network is still considered essential. Even today, not all applications are designed and written with security in mind, so it falls on the network to provide protection. And because an attacker who can successfully penetrate a computer network could then access hundreds or even thousands of endpoints, servers, and storage devices, a secure network defense remains a critical element in any enterprise's overall security plan.

This module explores network infrastructure security. It investigates how to build a secure infrastructure through network security appliances and security software, network design, and access technologies.

Security Appliances

Certification

1.2 Summarize fundamental security concepts.

2.5 Explain the purpose of mitigation techniques used to secure the enterprise.

3.2 Given a scenario, apply security principles to secure enterprise infrastructure.

4.1 Given a scenario, apply common security techniques to computing resources.

There are multiple mitigation principles that can be used in securing information, some of which are listed in Table 9-1. These mitigation principles can be applied to protecting many different areas of information security but can particularly be applied to protecting a network infrastructure.

Table 9-1   Mitigation principles

Principle	Description
Gap analysis	A comparison of the organization's current state of information security with recommended controls
Segmentation	Dividing a network into multiple subnets or segments with each acting as its own small network to improve monitoring and enhance security
Isolation	Keeping multiple instances of an **attack surface** separate so that each instance can only see and affect itself
Least privilege	Granting access that is limited to what is only necessary for a device or user to complete their work
Configuration enforcement	Applying security measures to reduce unnecessary vulnerabilities
Decommissioning	Removing or dismantling a technology or service from a live production environment
Removal of unnecessary software	Deleting software that is not essential to an operation in order to eliminate an attack vector
Selection of effective controls	Choosing productive safeguards or countermeasures to limit the exposure of an asset to a danger
Device placement	Physically locating important devices in secure locations

Protecting an infrastructure begins by using security appliances (devices) to protect the network. There are two basic categories of appliances. Common networking devices typically have basic security features that can be utilized. However, devices that are designed primarily for security can give a higher level of protection.

Note **1**

An advantage of using both common networking devices and infrastructure hardware designed specifically for security together is that this can result in a layered security approach. A network with layered security makes it more difficult for an attacker because they must have the tools, knowledge, and skills to break through multiple and diverse layers. And a layered approach can also be useful in resisting a broader array of attacks.

Common Network Devices

Common network infrastructure devices are the basic or standard devices that are found in virtually any network. Although these are not considered security appliances, nevertheless they typically contain security features that can be used to provide a degree of network protection. However, insecure or improperly configured common network devices can be exploited so that their protections are circumvented. Thus, it is important that these devices be properly configured and secured to provide protection for resisting attacks (called hardening targets).

Common network devices are often classified based on their function in the seven-layer Open Systems Interconnection (OSI) reference model. And different protocol data units (PDUs) are represented at the various layers of the OSI model. These PDUs include bit (Physical), frame (Data Link), packet (Network), segment for Transmission Control Protocol and datagram for User Datagram Protocol (Transport), and data (Session, Presentation, and Application).

Note 2

The OSI reference model is covered in Module 8.

A once-common network device that is rarely used today is a hub. The common network devices found in modern networks include switches, routers, servers, and load balancers.

Legacy Hubs

Early local area networks (LANs) used a hub, which is a standard network device for connecting multiple network devices so that they function as a single network segment. Because hubs worked at the Physical Layer (Layer 1) of the OSI model, they did not read any of the data bits passing through them and thus were ignorant of the source and destination of the PDUs. A hub would only receive incoming data, regenerate the electrical signal, and then send all the PDUs received out to all other devices connected to the hub. Each device would then decide if the data was intended for it (and then retained it) or if it was for another device (and then ignored it). In essence, a hub was a multiport repeater: whatever it received, it then passed on. Because a hub repeated all PDUs to all the attached network devices, it significantly—and unnecessarily—increased network traffic.

But instead of containing security features, hubs were considered a security risk. A threat actor could install software or a hardware device that captured and decoded PDUs on a client connected to the hub and view all network traffic sent to all devices. This would enable the threat actor to read or capture sensitive communications. Because of their impact on network traffic and their inherent security risk, hubs are considered legacy devices and are rarely used today in enterprise networks.

Note 3

Hubs are still used in time-critical applications. Because hubs do not buffer frames before forwarding them, they are faster than switches. The typical frame delay of a hub is 100 to 350 billionth of a second (a nanosecond or ns) while the delay for a switch is about 10,000 ns.

Switches

Like a hub, a network switch is a device that connects network devices. However, unlike a hub, a switch has a degree of intelligence. Operating at the Data Link Layer (Layer 2), a switch can learn which device is connected to each of its ports by examining the media access control (MAC) address of frames that it receives and observing at which of the switch's port it arrived. It then associates that port with the MAC address of the device connected to that port, storing that information in a MAC address table. The switch then knows on which port to forward frames intended for that specific device.

This intelligence means that a switch not only improves network performance by limiting the number of packets distributed but also provides better security. A threat actor who installs software to capture frames on a computer attached to a switch will see only packets that are directed to that device and not those intended for any other network device as with a hub.

It is important for switches to be properly hardened to provide a high degree of security. Proper hardening of a switch includes implementing port security and configuring other switch defenses.

Port Security   A common attack against switches is a MAC flooding attack. These attacks overflow the switch with Ethernet frames that have been "spoofed" so that each frame contains a different source MAC address, each appearing to come from a different computer. This can quickly consume all the memory, so the switch is unable to store any additional MAC addresses, enters a fail-open mode, and functions like a hub, broadcasting PDUs to all ports. A threat actor could then capture PDUs on one client connected to the switch in order to view all traffic.

> **Note 4**
>
> MAC flooding attacks are covered in Module 8.

To counteract MAC flooding attacks, most switches have implemented a technology known as port security. Switches that support port security can be configured to limit the number of MAC addresses that can be learned on ports. Restricting the number of incoming MAC addresses for a port prevents overwhelming the MAC address table. If additional MAC addresses are sent to a switch, the port security feature can be configured to ignore the new MAC addresses while allowing normal traffic from the single preapproved MAC address (restrict mode), record new MAC addresses up to a specific limit (sticky mode), or block the port entirely (shutdown mode). MAC address tables can also be converted from a dynamic "learning" mode to a static "permanent" mode when necessary.

Another protection of port security prevents users from connecting their own unapproved devices to the network. A user who has only a single network connection in their office might be tempted to purchase a switch and plug it into that connection so that they can then attach multiple network devices to that switch. However, port security can usually prevent these unauthorized switches and the unauthorized devices connected to them from connecting to the corporate network.

Configuration Defenses   It is important that the necessary defenses be configured on a switch to harden it. Attacks and configuration defenses for switches are summarized in Table 9-2.

Table 9-2   Switch configuration defenses

Type of attack	Description	Security defense
MAC flooding	An attacker can overflow the switch's address table with fake MAC addresses, forcing it to act like a hub, sending packets to all devices.	Use a switch that can close ports with too many MAC addresses.
MAC address spoofing	If two devices have the same MAC address, a switch may send frames to each device. An attacker can change the MAC address on their device to match the target device's MAC address.	Configure the switch so that only one port can be assigned per MAC address.
ARP poisoning	The attacker sends a forged ARP packet to the source device, substituting the attacker's computer MAC address.	Use an ARP detection appliance.
Port mirroring	An attacker connects their device to the switch's port.	Secure the switch in a locked room.

Routers

Operating at the Network Layer (Layer 3), a router is a network device that can forward frames across different computer networks. When a router receives an incoming frame, it reads the destination address and then, using information in its routing table, sends it to the next network toward its destination.

Routers can also perform a security function by using an access control list (ACL). An ACL is like a set of permissions or rules that functions as a network filter to permit or restrict data flowing into and out of the router network interfaces. When an ACL is configured on an interface, the router analyzes the data passing through the interface, compares it to the criteria described in the ACL, and either permits the data to continue or prohibits it.

Note 5

Whereas a separate security device can provide more in-depth protection, these separate devices may slow the flow of data as the data must be routed through this device. A router using an ACL, on the other hand, can operate at the higher speed of the router and not delay network traffic.

On external routers that face the Internet, router ACLs can restrict known vulnerable protocols from entering the network. They can also be used to limit traffic entering the network from unapproved networks. Routers can even protect against devices that imitate another computer's IP address ("IP spoofing"). This defense is called **antispoofing**.

Note 6

Because IP spoofing attacks often utilize known unused and untrusted addresses, an external router ACL can block these addresses by designating a range of restricted IP addresses. However, antispoofing ACLs on external routers require frequent monitoring because the address ranges that are denied can frequently change.

Router ACLs can also be used on internal routers that process interior network traffic. These router ACLs are usually less restrictive but more specific than those on external router ACLs since the devices on the internal network are generally considered to be friendly. Internal router ACLs are often configured with explicit *permit* and *deny* statements for specific addresses and protocol services. Internal router ACLs can also limit devices on the network from performing IP spoofing by applying outbound ACLs that limit the traffic to known valid local IP addresses.

Servers

Whereas some attacks are directed at the network itself, other attacks are directed specifically at network servers. As its name implies, a server distributes resources and services to devices connected to the network. A single server can serve multiple devices, and a single device can access multiple servers. Common servers include database servers, print servers, email servers, file servers, application servers, web servers, and even game servers.

A compromised server may provide threat actors with access to its privileged contents. It could also give an opening for attacks to any of the devices that access the server. The basic steps for hardening a server include:

- **Apply patches to vulnerabilities.** Apply software patches immediately because unpatched server software is particularly vulnerable to threat actors.
- **Monitor the server.** Continually monitoring servers provides insight into the activity on the server and particularly who is using it.
- **Control access permissions.** Instituting the principle of least privilege is an effective way to verify that important programs, configurations, and other operations on the server are only accessible to those who need it.
- **Remove unnecessary software.** Server software is an attack vector, so it is important to remove software and applications that are not needed or are no longer in use.
- **Secure the server location.** Servers must be placed in a secure location that is locked and restricted only to approved staff.

Load Balancers

Load balancing is a technology that can help to evenly distribute work across a network. Requests that are received can be allocated across multiple devices such as servers. To the user, this distribution is transparent and appears as if a single server is providing the resources. Load-balancing technology reduces the probability of overloading a single server and ensures that each networked server benefits from having optimized bandwidth.

Load balancing can be performed either through software running on a computer or as a dedicated hardware device known as a load balancer. Load balancers are often grouped into two categories: Layer 4 load balancers and Layer 7 load balancers. Layer 4 load balancers act upon data found in the Network and Transport Layer protocols such as Internet Protocol (IP), Transmission Control Protocol (TCP), File Transfer Protocol (FTP), and User Datagram Protocol (UDP). Layer 7 load balancers distribute requests based on data found in Application Layer protocols such as HTTP.

The use of a load balancer also has security advantages. Because load balancers are generally located between routers and servers, they can detect and stop attacks directed at a server or application. A load balancer can be used to detect and prevent protocol attacks that could cripple a single server. Some load balancers can hide HTTP error pages or remove server identification headers from HTTP responses, denying attackers additional information about the internal network.

Infrastructure Security Hardware

Although hardened and properly configured common networking devices can provide a degree of security, specialized infrastructure hardware devices designed for information security can give a much higher level of protection. These devices include firewalls, proxy servers, deception and disruption instruments, and intrusion detection and prevention systems.

Note 7

The strongest infrastructure security hardware available cannot negate reckless actions made by users. Consider a successful attack on NASA's Jet Propulsion Laboratory (JPL) that resulted in 500 MB of data stolen that related to a Mars mission. A 49-page report by the NASA Office of Inspector General (OIG) revealed that although the NASA JPL network had multiple infrastructure security appliances installed, the point of entry into the network by the attackers was a $35 Raspberry Pi, small enough to fit in your hand, that a JPL employee connected to the network without authorization.

Firewalls

It is likely that no security appliance is more misunderstood than a firewall. Due to the nature of its name ("It's an impenetrable barrier!") and aided by inaccurate portrayals in movies, a firewall is often perceived by the general public as the ultimate security device that will block anything and everything that is malicious. Unfortunately, this is a wildly inaccurate perception. Firewalls are an important element in network security, but they fall far short of being the ultimate defense. It is important to understand the function of firewalls, as well as know the different categories and types of firewalls.

Firewall Functions   In building construction, a firewall is usually a brick, concrete, or masonry wall positioned vertically through all stories of commercial buildings, apartments, and other similar structures. Required by both national and local building codes, its purpose is to contain a fire and prevent it from spreading.

A computer firewall serves a similar purpose; it is designed to limit the spread of malware. A firewall functions by using bidirectional inspection of examining both outgoing and incoming network packets. It allows approved packets to pass through the firewall to its destination, but it can take different actions when it detects a suspicious packet. The actions are based on specific criteria to accept or deny packets (rules) and these firewalls are called **rule-based firewalls**. Firewall rules can contain parameters such as:

- **Source address.** The source address is the location of the origination of the packet (where the packet is *from*). Addresses can generally be indicated by a specific IP address or range of addresses, IP mask, MAC address, or host name.
- **Destination address.** This is the address the connection is attempting to reach (where the packet is going *to*). These addresses can be indicated in the same way as the source address.
- **Source port.** The source port is the TCP/IP port number being used to send packets of data through. Options for setting the source port often include a specific port number or a range of numbers.

- **Destination port.** This setting gives the port on the remote computer or device that the packets will use. Options include the same as for the source port. Restricting packets based on the source or destination port is called firewall port filtering.
- **Protocol.** The protocol defines the network protocol (such as *TCP, UDP, TCP or UDP, ICMP,* or *IP*) that is being used when sending or receiving packets of data, and restricting based on the protocol is known as firewall protocol filtering.
- **Direction.** This is the direction of traffic for the data packet (*Incoming, Outgoing,* or *Both*).
- **Priority.** The priority determines the order in which the rule is applied.
- **Time.** Rules can be set to only be active during a scheduled time.
- **Context.** A rule can be created that is unique for specific circumstances (contexts). For example, different rules may be in effect depending on whether a laptop is on-site or is remote.
- **Action.** The action setting indicates what the firewall should do when the conditions of the rule are met. Typical firewall rule actions are listed in Table 9-3.

Table 9-3 Typical firewall rule actions

Action	Description	Example	Comments
Allow	Explicitly allows traffic that matches the rule to pass	Permit incoming Address Resolution Protocol (ARP) traffic	Implicitly denies all other traffic unless explicitly allowed
Bypass	Allows traffic to bypass the firewall	Bypass based on IP, port, traffic direction, and protocol	Designed for media-intensive protocols or traffic from a trusted source
Deny	Explicitly blocks all traffic that matches the rule	Deny traffic from IP address	Generally drops the packet with no return message to the sender
Force Allow	Forcibly allows traffic that would normally be denied by other rules	Useful for determining if essential network services are able to communicate	Traffic will still be subject to inspection by other security appliances
Log Only	Traffic is logged but no other action is taken	Bypass rules do not generate log files but Log Only will	Occurs if the packet is not stopped by a Deny rule or an Allow rule that excludes It

Older firewalls often had each rule as a separate instruction that was processed in sequence so that firewall rules were essentially *IF-THEN-ELSE* constructions: *IF* these rule conditions are met, *THEN* the action occurs *ELSE* go on to the next rule. This made it important that not only the rules but also the sequencing of the rules be considered. For example, if Rule #13 allowed a TCP connection to a specific address but later Rule #27 was added to deny all TCP traffic, then TCP packets meeting Rule #13 would be allowed because it occurred first. More modern firewalls allow a priority order to be created to eliminate the confusion that often surrounded multiple conflicting rules.

A more flexible type of firewall than a rule-based firewall is a **policy-based firewall**. This type of firewall allows for more generic statements to be used instead of specific rules. For example, the policy statement *Allow management traffic from trusted networks* could translate into specific rules that allow traffic from *192.2.0.0/24* to *TCP Port 22* and *192.2.100.0/24* to *TCP Port 3389*.

In addition to filtering based on packets, firewalls can also apply **content/URL filtering**. The firewall can be used to monitor websites accessed through HTTP to create custom filtering profiles. The filtering can be performed by assessing webpages by their content category and then creating lists of approved or restricted URLs. This type of filtering is often available with consumer-oriented firewalls and advertised as a parental control feature that is easily configurable, as seen in Figure 9-1.

Figure 9-1 Content/URL filter

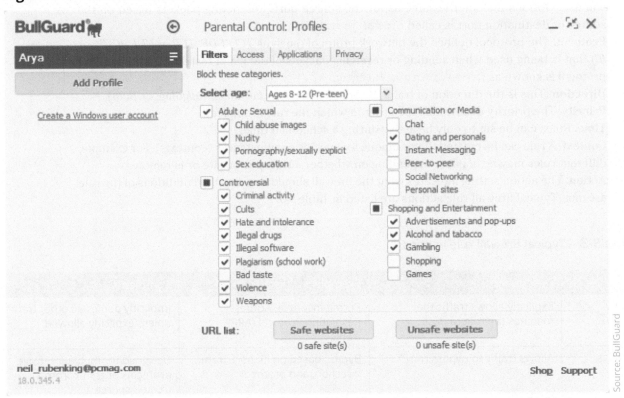

Source: BullGuard

Firewall Categories There are different categories of firewalls. These can be compared as opposites and include:

- **Hardware versus software.** A **software firewall** runs as a program or service on a device, such as a computer or router. **Hardware firewalls** are specialized separate devices that inspect traffic. Because they are specialized devices, hardware firewalls tend to have more features but are more expensive and can require more effort to configure and manage. However, a disadvantage of a software firewall is that a malware infection on the device on which it is running, such as a computer, could also compromise the software firewall. Whereas a hardware firewall also has underlying software, typically that footprint is smaller (to provide less of a target for attackers) or specialized.
- **Host versus appliance versus virtual.** A host-based firewall is a software firewall that runs on and protects a single endpoint device (a host). All modern OSs include a host-based firewall. These firewalls tend to be application-centric: users can create an opening in the firewall for a specific application. This is more secure than permanently opening a port in the firewall that will always remain open as opposed to a port that is only opened when the application requires it and is then closed. An **appliance firewall** is typically a separate hardware device designed to protect an entire network, as seen in Figure 9-2. A **virtual firewall** is one that runs in the cloud. Virtual firewalls are designed for public cloud environments in which deploying an appliance firewall would be difficult or even impossible.
- **Open source versus proprietary.** Some firewalls are freely available (**open-source firewall**) while other firewalls are owned by an entity that has an exclusive right to it (**proprietary firewall**). Open-source firewalls have been gaining wider acceptance as they have incorporated more features and are built on a secure foundation. For example, pfSense is built on the same underlying OS as many commercial products and is seen in Figure 9-3.
- **Stateful versus stateless. Stateless packet filtering** looks at a packet and permits or denies it based solely on the firewall rules. Stateless packet filtering operates at OSI Layer 3. **Stateful packet filtering** uses both the firewall rules and the state of the connection. A stateful

Figure 9-2   Appliance firewall

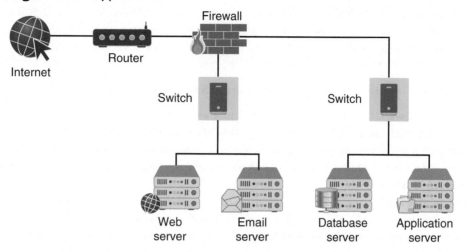

Figure 9-3   pfSense open-source firewall

Floating	LocalNetworks	WAN	LAN	DMZ	WAN2	L2TP VPN	IPsec	OpenVPN

Rules (Drag to Change Order)

	States	Protocol	Source	Port	Destination	Port	Gateway	Queue	Schedule	Description	Actions
Remote Administration											🗑
☐ ✓	6/803 KiB	IPv4 TCP	RemoteAdmin	*	This Firewall	admin ports	*	none		Allow firewall admin	⚓✏📋⊘🗑
VPN Rules											🗑
☐ ✓	0/0 B	IPv4 UDP	203.0.113.5	*	WAN address	1195	*	none		OpenVPN from Remote Site 2	⚓✏📋⊘🗑
☐ ✓	0/0 B	IPv4 UDP	203.0.113.5	*	WAN address	1194 (OpenVPN)	*	none		OpenVPN from Remote Site B	⚓✏📋⊘🗑
☐ ✓	0/0 B	IPv4 UDP	*	*	WAN address	1194 (OpenVPN)	*	none		Allow traffic to OpenVPN server	⚓✏📋⊘🗑
Public Services											🗑
☐ ✓	0/0 B	IPv4 TCP	*	*	10.3.0.15	80 (HTTP)	*	none		NAT HTTP to web server	⚓✏📋⊘🗑
☐ ✓	0/0 B	IPv4 TCP	bob	*	10.3.0.5	22 (SSH)	*	none		NAT Bob - SSH	⚓✏📋⊘🗑
☐ ✓	0/0 B	IPv4 TCP	sue	*	10.3.0.15	22 (SSH)	*	none		NAT Sue - SSH	⚓✏📋⊘🗑
Misc											🗑
☐ ✓	0/0 B	IPv4 TCP/UDP	WAN net	*	*	1812 - 1813	*	none		RADIUS from other test firewalls	⚓✏📋⊘🗑

Source: pfSense

packet-filtering firewall keeps a record of the state of a connection between an internal endpoint and an external device. It can be used to answer the question, "Did the internal device request this packet?" While a stateless packet filter firewall might allow a packet to pass through because it met all the necessary criteria (rules), a stateful packet filter would not let the packet pass if that internal endpoint did not first request it, such as information from an external web server. A stateful packet-filtering firewall is called a **Layer 4 firewall** because it can allow or deny traffic based on the state of the session.

- **Dedicated firewall versus network access control list (ACL).** Whereas dedicated firewalls are designed to exclusively permit or deny packets, this functionality of filtering packets can also be incorporated into other devices as well through a **network access control list**. Common network devices like switches and routers can have network ACLs that serve to check packets for entry approval into the network.

> **Note 8**
>
> ACLs are not specific devices but instead are a functionality that can be implemented across devices and software. For example, filesystem ACLs manage access to directories or files, and these are covered in Module 7.

Specialized Firewalls There are several specialized firewall appliances:

- **Web application firewall.** One specialized firewall is a web application firewall (WAF) that looks at the applications using HTTP. A web application firewall, which can be a separate hardware appliance or a software plug-in, can block specific websites or attacks that attempt to exploit known vulnerabilities in specific client software and can even block cross-site scripting and SQL injection attacks.
- **Next-generation firewall.** A next-generation firewall (NGFW) has additional functionality beyond a traditional firewall. NGFW can filter packets based on applications. NGFWs have visibility of applications by using **deep packet inspection** and thus can examine the payloads of packets and determine if they are carrying malware. In addition to basic firewall protections, filtering by applications, and deep packet inspection, NGFWs can also perform URL filtering and intrusion prevention services.
- **Unified threat management.** Unified threat management (UTM) is a device that combines several security functions. These include packet filtering, antispam, antiphishing, antispyware, encryption, intrusion protection, and web filtering.

> **Note 9**
>
> Often a device that performs services beyond that of a NGFW is called a UTM.

- **Layer 7 firewall**. Stateless firewalls operate at OSI Layer 3 and examine factors such as the source IP address, while stateful firewalls function at Layer 4 and look at the state of the connection. A Layer 7 firewall allows for more advanced traffic filtering. Layer 7 firewalls can investigate the contents of the packets to determine whether they contain malware.
- **Network address translation gateway**. Network address translation (NAT) is a technique that allows private IP addresses to be used on the public Internet. It does this by replacing a private IP address with a public IP address: as a packet leaves a network, NAT removes the private IP address from the sender's packet and replaces it with an alias IP public address and then maintains a record of the substitution; when a packet is returned, the process is reversed. A **network address translation gateway** is a cloud-based technology that performs NAT for cloud services. It can also provide a degree of security: it can mask the IP addresses of internal devices.

Proxy Servers

In the human world, a *proxy* is a person who is authorized to act as the substitute or agent on behalf of another person. For example, an individual who has been granted the power of attorney for a sick relative can make decisions and take actions on behalf of that person as a proxy.

There are also proxies that are used in computer networking. These devices act as substitutes on behalf of the primary device and are called proxy servers. A **forward proxy server** is a computer that intercepts user requests from the internal secure network and then processes the requests on behalf of the user. When an internal endpoint requests a service such as a file or a webpage from an external web server, it normally would connect directly with that remote server. In a network using a forward proxy server, the endpoint first connects to the proxy server, which checks its memory to see if a previous request already has been fulfilled and whether a copy of that file or page is residing on the proxy server in its temporary storage area (**cache**). If it is not, the proxy server connects to the external web server using its own IP address (instead of the internal endpoint's address) and requests the service. When the proxy server receives the requested item from the web server, the item is then forwarded to the requester.

A forward proxy server has several advantages, including increased speed (because it can cache material, a request can be served from the cache instead of retrieving the webpage through the Internet), reduced costs (it can reduce the amount of bandwidth usage because of the cache), and improved management (it can block specific webpages and/or entire websites). One of the primary advantages is stronger security. Acting as the intermediary, a proxy server can protect clients from malicious sites by denying the request. In addition, a proxy server can hide the IP address of client systems inside the secure network. Only the proxy server's IP address is used on the open Internet.

A **reverse proxy server** routes requests coming from an external network to the correct internal server. To the outside user, the IP address of the reverse proxy is the final IP address for requesting services; however, only the reverse proxy can access the internal servers. Forward proxy and reverse proxy servers are illustrated in Figure 9-4.

Figure 9-4   Forward and reverse proxy servers

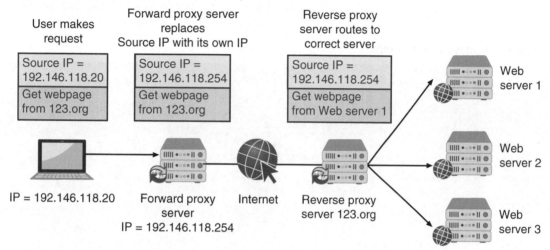

Deception and Disruption Instruments

Deception is the act of causing someone to accept as true that which is false. Deception can be used as a security defense: by directing the focus of threat actors away from a valuable asset to something that has little or no value, they can be tricked into thinking what they are attacking is truly valuable or that their attack is successful, when it is not. Creating network deception can involve creating and using lures while disruption can be accomplished with a sinkhole.

> **Note** ⑩
>
> Niccolo Machiavelli, an Italian Renaissance diplomat and philosopher who is often called the father of modern political science, once said, "Never attempt to win by force what can be won by deception."

Lures   In order to catch fish, typically a lure is used as bait to attract the fish. A fishing lure is an artificial bait; it is a replica that mimics the food fish eat. Using flashy colors, bright reflections, movements, vibrations, and even loud noises, it attracts the fish's attention and entices it into striking the lure. However, the result is the fish being caught on one of the lure's hooks. A fishing lure is seen in Figure 9-5.

Figure 9-5   Fishing lure

shadowcaster studio/
Shutterstock.com

In a similar fashion, a technology lure can serve as bait to attract threat actors. A honeypot lure is a computer located in an area with low security that serves as bait to threat actors. The honeypot is intentionally configured with security vulnerabilities so that it is open to attacks. Instead of capturing the attackers like a fish, security personnel generally have two other goals when using a honeypot:

- **Deflect.** A honeypot can deflect or redirect threat actors' attention away from legitimate servers by encouraging them to spend their time and energy on the decoy server, distracting their attention from the data on the actual server.
- **Discover.** A honeypot can trick threat actors into revealing their attack techniques. Once these techniques are discovered, it can then be determined if the real production systems could thwart such an attack.

Figure 9-6 shows the results from a honeypot dashboard; it lists attacker probes by time and country.

Figure 9-6   Honeypot dashboard

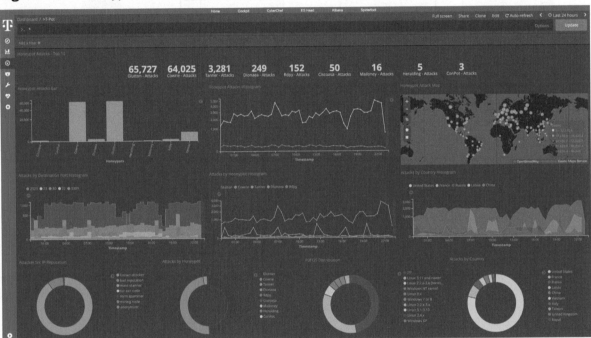

Note 11

The number of attempts against a honeypot is staggering. In one study, 10 honeypots around the world were created that simulated the Secure Shell (SSH) service. One of the honeypots started receiving login attempts just *52 seconds* after it went online. Once all 10 of the honeypots were discovered, a login attempt was made about every *15 seconds on each one*. At the end of one month, over 5 million attacks had been attempted on these honeypots.[1]

There are different types of honeypots. A low-interaction honeypot may only contain a login prompt. This type of honeypot only records login attempts and provides information on the threat actor's IP address of origin. A high-interaction honeypot is designed for capturing much more information from the threat actor. High-interaction honeypots typically have data files that appear to be authentic but are imitations of real data files (honeyfiles) along with fake telemetry. (Telemetry is the collection of data such as how certain software features are used, application crashes, and general usage statistics and behavior.) A honeyfile can reveal how threat actors exploit this data so that defenses can be created.

Similar to a honeypot, a honeynet is a network set up with intentional vulnerabilities. Its purpose is also to invite attacks so that the attacker's methods can be studied; that information can then be used to increase network security. A honeynet typically contains one or more honeypots.

Lures do not have to be limited to honeypots or honeynets; fake data can also be added to live production systems. For example, a fake record in a database that is stolen may help to pinpoint a specific weakness in security that allowed the attacker entry or if the thief was an insider. A lure that can provide more specific information on threat actors is called a honeytoken.

Caution !

Setting up a honeypot to attract threat actors can be dangerous. It is critical that there be no connection between the honeypot and the production network. A safer approach is to use a cloud service provider for setting up a honeypot.

Sinkholes   Another deception technique is to use **sinkholes**. A sinkhole is essentially a "bottomless pit" designed to steer unwanted traffic away from its intended destination to another device, deceiving the threat actor into thinking the attack is successful when the sinkhole is actually providing information about the attack. One type of sinkhole is a domain name service (DNS) sinkhole. A DNS sinkhole changes a normal DNS request to a preconfigured IP address that points to a firewall with a rule of *Deny* set for all packets so that every packet is dropped with no return information provided to the sender.

Note 12

DNS sinkholes are commonly used to counteract distributed denial-of-service (DDoS) attacks. Many enterprises contract with a DDoS mitigation service that helps identify DDoS traffic so that it is sent to a sinkhole while allowing legitimate traffic to reach its destination. Sinkholes are also used by law enforcement to stop a widespread ongoing attack by redirecting traffic away from the attacker's command and control (C&C) server to a sinkhole. As an added step, the sinkhole can save these packets for further examination in an attempt to identify the threat actors.

Intrusion Detection and Prevention Systems

An intrusion detection system (IDS) can detect an attack as it occurs and sound an alarm for security personnel to investigate to determine if further action is needed (known as a passive device attribute). An IDS analyzes a copy of the monitored traffic by comparing it against known attack patterns (signatures).

An intrusion prevention system (IPS) attempts to automatically block the attack as it occurs (active device attribute). It also looks for trends, or new attacks for which there is no existing signature. To identify attacks, an IPS may analyze **user behavior analytics**, which uses the "normal" processes and actions as the standard. This technique continuously analyzes the behavior of processes and programs on a system to determine if there is a nefarious action.

The interconnection points between the IDS/IPS and other devices (connectivity) can be different. An inline system is connected directly to the network to monitor the flow of data as it occurs and is typically used in an IPS. A **passive** system is connected to a port on a switch, which receives a copy of network traffic and is found in an IDS. Table 9-4 lists the differences between inline and passive systems.

Table 9-4   Inline versus passive IDS

Function	Inline	Passive
Connection	Directly to network	Connected to port on switch
Traffic flow	Routed through the device	Receives copy of traffic
Blocking	Can block attacks	Cannot block attacks
Detection error	May disrupt service	May cause false alarm

While IDS and IPS can be applied to endpoints (hosts), they are more commonly found on networks. These network-based systems are:

- **Network intrusion detection systems.** A network intrusion detection system (NIDS), similar to a software-based host intrusion detection system (HIDS), watches for attacks on the network. As network traffic moves through the network, NIDS sensors—usually installed on network devices such as firewalls and routers—gather information and report back to a central device.
- **Network intrusion prevention system.** A network intrusion prevention system (NIPS) not only monitors to detect malicious activities but also attempts to stop them, much like a HIDS.

One of the major differences between a NIDS and a NIPS is its location. A NIDS has NIDS sensors that monitor the traffic entering and leaving a firewall and reports back to the central device for analysis. A NIPS, on the other hand, would be located inline on the firewall itself. This allows the NIPS to act more quickly to block an attack.

Two Rights & A Wrong

1. Segmentation is dividing a network into multiple subnets with each acting as its own small network to improve monitoring and enhance security.

2. A rule-based firewall is more flexible than a policy-based firewall.

3. A forward proxy is a computer or an application program that intercepts user requests from the internal secure network and then processes that request on behalf of the user.

See the answers at the end of the module.

Software Security Protections

Certification

3.2 Given a scenario, apply security principles to secure enterprise infrastructure.

4.5 Given a scenario, modify enterprise capabilities to enhance security.

While hardware devices are most commonly used to protect an infrastructure network, there are also software security protections. These include web filtering, DNS filtering, file integrity monitoring, and extended detection and response (XDR).

Web Filtering

As its name implies, web filtering monitors the websites users are browsing so that the organization can either allow or block web traffic to protect against potential threats and enforce corporate policies. When a user requests a web resource, the web filter technology scans the requested website. If the website is considered safe, the web filter will allow access to the site; however, if the scan reveals a malicious or suspicious site, the web filtering technology will block access.

There are different types of web filtering software. These differences are based on the location of the filtering engine:

- **Browser scanning.** Web filters can be added to a web browser in the form of browser extensions or add-ons. Although filters are easy to implement, they are considered a "lightweight" solution not robust enough for use in an enterprise environment.
- **Agent-based scanning.** Web filtering software that resides on the endpoint device is called agent-based web filtering.
- **Centralized proxy scanning.** Instead of software residing on each endpoint that must be installed and managed, a more consolidated approach is preferable. This involves performing web filtering on a proxy appliance through which all requests are funneled. Known as centralized proxy scanning,

these proxy appliances can be standard forward proxy servers or specialized web proxy servers, whose only function is to examine web requests.

- **Cloud scanning.** A growing trend is to utilize a cloud-based solution through which all requests are channeled. By using cloud scanning, the engine can also filter traffic from remote users who are not located on the premises.

Note 13

Not all web scanning is software-based. There are separate network hardware appliances that perform web filtering, and other infrastructure security hardware such as firewalls and routers can also perform some levels of web filtering.

There are different methods that web filtering uses to identify malicious websites to create block rules, or criteria for which a website is inaccessible to users. One method is content categorization. Websites are classified into broad categories, such as *Education*, *Kid's Sites*, and *Sports*. These categories also include inappropriate or malicious sites, such as *Adult/Sexually Explicit*, *Criminal Activity*, and *Illegal Drugs*. There are over 1,000 content categories and web filtering software can block sites based on their category.

Another method is Universal Resource Locator (URL) scanning. This web filtering software uses a separate service. These services specialize in scanning the web for malicious websites and then create a database of URLs to be blocked. This service can be "in house," which is supported by the software vendor, or relies on a separate service (or both).

Note 14

Most malicious URL scanning services rely on Google Safe Browsing, which is constantly being updated with lists of unsafe web resources and is a free service.

The reputation score is another method used for web filtering. Each website can be assigned a web reputation score (WBRS) that reflects its relative safety. A website that is well trafficked, well known, and associated with several trusted IP addresses connecting back to it will earn a high WBRS. However, a relatively new URL may present a hazard and earn a lower score, while an unknown URL associated with a suspicious or malicious IP will be given an even lower WBRS.

Note 15

Some of the factors used in creating a WBRS include the URL category, age of a URL, its history, domain reputation, presence of downloadable files or code, previous association with malicious Internet objects, popularity, website owner, and presence on any block/allow lists.

DNS Filtering

Similar to web filtering, DNS filtering blocks harmful or inappropriate content. However, while web filtering blocks webpages, DNS filtering blocks entire domains. This means that DNS filtering is able to block all the webpages of an entire domain, even though they have different URLs. If the webpages *example.com/phishing*, *example.com/virus*, and *example.com/Trojan* were all detected as being malicious, with web filtering, three separate block rules would need to be invoked to block all three sites. But with DNS filtering, the entire domain *example.com* could be closed off with only one block rule.

Note 16

The Domain Name System matches domain names (*cengage.com*) with its corresponding IP address (69.32.208.75) through a process called "resolving" the domain.

Because all DNS queries go to a DNS resolver, these resolvers can also act as filters by refusing to resolve queries for certain domains. Typically, these malicious domains are found in a list of unapproved sites that a DNS can access. Suppose an employee receives a phishing email and is tricked into clicking a link that leads to *example.com/phishing*. The DNS query first goes to the organization's DNS resolving service that uses DNS filtering. Because that malicious site is on that organization's blocklist, the DNS resolver will fail to resolve the name, effectively blocking the request.

File Integrity Monitoring (FIM)

File integrity monitoring (FIM) is a technology designed to "keep an eye on" files to detect any changes within the files that may indicate a cyberattack. After establishing a baseline for "clean" files, a file integrity monitor examines files to see if they have changed, when the change occurred, how they changed, who changed them, and what can be done to restore those files if the changes are unauthorized.

Note 17

File integrity monitors are used for both detecting malware as well as maintaining compliance with industry-specific regulations. The Payment Card Industry Data Security Standard (PCI DSS) has no less than four requirements related to file integrity monitors. PCI DSS Requirement 10.5.5 states that organizations in compliance will "Use file integrity monitoring or change detection software on logs to ensure that existing log data cannot be changed without generating alerts (although new data being added should not cause an alert)."

The problem with file integrity monitors is the high volume of "noise," or too much unhelpful information. Files may change frequently for many different benign reasons with limited insight into whether a change poses a security risk. While file integrity monitors can be beneficial, they need to provide sufficient insight so that proper actions can be taken.

Extended Detection and Response (XDR)

Endpoint detection and response (EDR) tools monitor endpoint events by aggregating data from multiple endpoint computers to a centralized database. This gives a better picture of events occurring across multiple endpoints instead of just on a single endpoint. It can help determine if an attack is more widespread across the enterprise and if more comprehensive and higher-level action needs to be taken.

Note 18

EDR is covered in Module 5.

Whereas EDR aggregates data from multiple endpoints, extended detection and response (XDR) goes a step further by collecting and correlating data across various network appliances, including servers, email systems, cloud repositories, as well as endpoints. This data is then analyzed and correlated. By combining data from multiple sources, XDR gives a higher level of visibility and context to incidences, thus reducing false positives while revealing advanced threats. An XDR system typically involves software agents installed on devices that are connected to a cloud-based analysis engine.

Two Rights & A Wrong

1. Web filtering can be accomplished through browser scanning, agent-based scanning, centralized proxy scanning, or cloud scanning.
2. DNS filtering blocks entire domains.
3. EDR is more robust and provides greater protection than XDR.

See the answers at the end of the module.

Secure Infrastructure Design

Certification

1.2 Summarize fundamental security concepts.

3.1 Compare and contrast security implications of different architecture models.

3.2 Given a scenario, apply security principles to secure enterprise infrastructure.

Equally important to security appliances and software security protections is the proper design of the network; in many ways the design of the network may be even *more* important to keeping an infrastructure safe. While appliances and software can block isolated malicious attempts to enter the network, a secure design creates a foundation of a secure network. That is, security appliances and software are *reactive* while a secure design is considered *proactive*. Secure infrastructure design involves knowing what it is and the technologies used in designing a secure network: virtual LANs (VLANs), demilitarized zones (DMZs), and zero trust.

What Is Secure Infrastructure Design?

It would be unthinkable to have an office building in which anyone could freely enter any room or office. Instead, office buildings have different areas with different levels of access. While a lobby is generally an open area for almost anyone to initially enter the building, security guards and technology devices restrict access to other areas, such as only allowing approved personnel to their own offices. And within those areas, there are even more restrictions: a regular employee can enter their office but is restricted from entering the security operations center (SOC) that monitors and manages information security functions.

In a similar way, a network infrastructure should be designed like an office building, with some areas available for general access while other parts of the network having successively tighter restrictions. For example, a public-facing web server needs to be in an area in which anyone can access it, while a server with sensitive corporate accounting data must be in a highly restricted area of the network. And the most restricted level of all can be a network that has physical isolation from all other networks or the Internet. This is called an air-gapped network because it is physically separated from other networks. Creating these security zones of different levels of access creates a higher level of security through network design.

> **Note 19**
>
> "Air-gapped" was not a term that originated with network infrastructure. It has been used for many years in the field of electricity, referring to the space between two objects magnetically related (like the rotor and the stator in a dynamo) or between two objects electrically related (such as the gap between an electrode and the tip of a spark plug).

This infrastructure separation can be achieved in two different ways. The first is by **physical segmentation**. As the name implies, physical segmentation involves breaking down a larger computer network into a collection of smaller networks ("subnets"). A physical network appliance acts as the gateway into the subnet, controlling which traffic comes in and goes out. Physical segmentation is relatively straightforward to administer because the topology is fixed in the architecture. Logical segmentation creates subnets via "virtual networks" or through network addressing schemes. Logical segmentation is more flexible than physical segmentation because it requires no wiring or physical movement of network appliances to create the subnet, and automated provisioning can simplify the configuration of the smaller networks.

Virtual LANs (VLANs)

Physical segmentation of a network to create a subnet is often accomplished by using switches to divide the network into a hierarchy. Core switches reside at the top of the hierarchy and carry traffic between switches, while workgroup switches are connected directly to the devices on the network. It is often beneficial to group similar users together, such as all the members of an accounting department. However, grouping by user sometimes can be difficult because all users might not be in the same location and served by the same switch.

> **Note 20**
>
> Core switches must work faster than workgroup switches because core switches must handle the traffic of several workgroup switches.

Instead of physical segmentation, logical segmentation is an alternative that can segment a network by separating devices into logical groups. This is known as creating a **virtual LAN (VLAN)**. A VLAN allows scattered users to be logically grouped together even though they are physically attached to different switches. This can reduce network traffic and provide a degree of security. VLANs can be isolated so that sensitive data is transported only to members of the VLAN.

> **Note 21**
>
> Although network subnetting and VLANs are often considered to be similar, there are differences between them. Subnets are subdivisions of IP address classes (Class A, B, or C) and allow a single Class A, B, or C network to be used instead of multiple networks. VLANs are devices that are connected logically rather than physically, either through the port they are connected to or by their MAC address.

VLAN communication can take place in two ways. If multiple devices in the same VLAN are connected to the same switch, the switch itself can handle the transfer of packets to the members of the VLAN group. However, if VLAN members on one switch need to communicate with members connected to another switch, a special "tagging" protocol must be used, either a proprietary protocol or the vendor-neutral IEEE 802.1Q. These special protocols add a field to the packet that "tags" it as belonging to the VLAN.

> **Note 22**
>
> Another security advantage of VLANs is that they can be used to prevent direct communication between servers, which can bypass firewall or IDS inspection. Servers that are placed in separate VLANs will require that any traffic headed toward the default gateway for inter-VLAN routing be inspected.

Demilitarized Zone (DMZ)

Imagine a bank that located its automated teller machine (ATM) in the middle of their vault. This would be an open invitation for disaster by inviting every outside user to enter the secure vault to access the ATM. Instead, the ATM and the vault should be separated so that the ATM is in a public area that anyone can access, while the vault is restricted to trusted individuals. In a similar fashion, locating public-facing servers such as web and email servers inside the secure network is also unwise. An attacker must only break out of the security of the server to access the secure network.

To allow untrusted outside users access to resources such as web servers, most networks employ a **demilitarized zone (DMZ)**. The DMZ functions as a separate network that rests outside the secure network perimeter: untrusted outside users can access the DMZ but cannot enter the secure network.

Consider Figure 9-2 (shown earlier), which illustrates a DMZ containing a web server and an email server that are accessed by outside users. In this configuration, a single firewall with three network interfaces is used: the link to the Internet is on the first network interface, the DMZ is formed from the second network interface, and the secure internal LAN is based on the third network interface. However, this makes the firewall device a single point of failure for the network, and it also must take care of all the traffic to both the DMZ and internal network. A more secure approach is to have two firewalls, as seen in Figure 9-7. In this configuration, an attacker would have to breach two separate firewalls to reach the secure internal LAN. This type of configuration is called a screened subnet because it is using a device to limit the protected internal network from the open external network.

Figure 9-7   DMZ with two firewalls

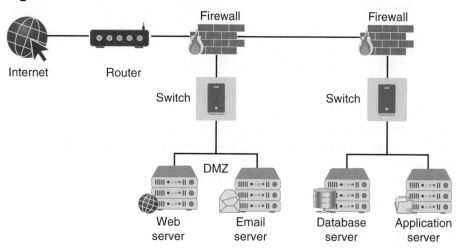

Caution (!)

Some consumer routers advertise support to configure a DMZ. However, this is not a DMZ. Rather, it allows only one local device to be exposed to the Internet for Internet gaming or videoconferencing by forwarding all the ports at the same time to that one device.

However, how should a DMZ be configured so that trusted administrators can still access the hardware and software in a DMZ? If a pathway is enabled for administrators to enter the zone, that same pathway, if compromised, can provide access to threat actors back to the secure network.

A common approach is to use a jump server, as shown in Figure 9-8. A jump server is a minimally configured administrator server (either physical or virtual) within the DMZ. Running only essential protocols and ports, it connects two dissimilar security zones while providing tightly restricted access between them. An administrator accesses the jump server, which is connected to the administrative interface of the devices within the DMZ.

Figure 9-8   Jump server

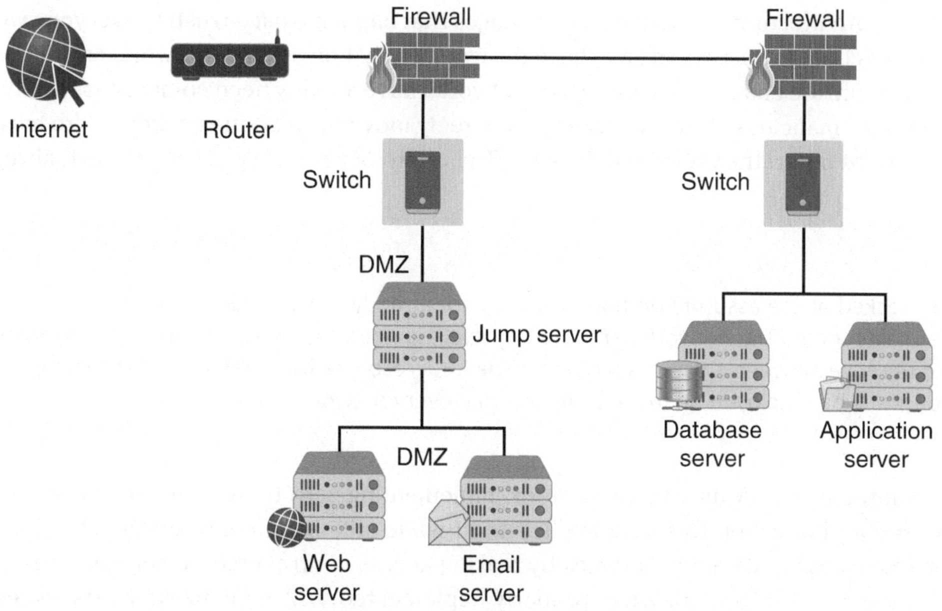

> **Caution** ⚠
>
> To further limit the vulnerabilities of a jump server, administrators should ensure that all jump server software is regularly updated, limit the programs that can run on it, implement multifactor authentication for logins, do not allow outbound access or severely restrict access from the jump server, and use ACLs to restrict access to specific authorized users.

In recent years, an additional security configuration has been used to limit risks when administering a DMZ. Instead of an administrator connecting to a jump server from just any computer, only a dedicated secure admin workstation (SAW) can be used to connect to the jump server. Using a SAW prevents an administrator's infected computer from compromising the jump server.

In addition to the DMZ, there are other security zones (separate subnets for enhanced security) that can also be used for security. These are listed in Table 9-5.

Table 9-5 Other security zones

Name	Description	Security benefits
Intranet	A private network that belongs to an organization that can only be accessed by approved internal users	Closed to the outside public, thus data is less vulnerable to external threat actors
Extranet	A private network that can also be accessed by authorized external customers, vendors, and partners	Can provide enhanced security for outside users compared to a publicly accessible website
Guest network	A separate open network that anyone can access without prior authorization	Permits access to general network resources like web surfing without using the secure network

Zero Trust

Most networks are based on a traditional security model that operates on the assumption that everything inside an organization's network can be trusted. It assumes that a user's identity has not been compromised, that all users within the network are trusted users, and that all users will act responsibly.

This assumption is false. The true assumption is that the network is already infected. Attackers are not trying to enter from the outside but are currently on the inside.

Zero trust is a strategic initiative about networks that is designed to prevent successful attacks by threat actors who are already within a network. As its name implies, zero trust attempts to eliminate the concept of trust from an organization's network architecture. Zero trust acknowledges that implicit trust—trusting everyone within a network— is a vulnerability. This is because networks have been designed so that once in the network, any users can freely move laterally to access or exfiltrate data. Yet because most networks have already been compromised and threat actors are "lurking in the shadows," malicious attackers likewise can freely move through the network. Zero trust is not designed to make a system trusted but, rather, to eliminate trust. The motto of zero trust is "Never trust, always verify."

> **Note** 23
>
> Many users are shocked at the assumption that attackers are already lurking inside a secure network. However, that has become the reality today. The network perimeter, by itself, is not a factor in determining internal trustworthiness, and there is no difference between an access request made for a resource from either inside the network or outside the network. Controls must be employed on the assumption that every network is untrusted.

A zero-trust architecture (ZTA) is a framework for implementing zero trust in an enterprise. Zero trust focuses on authentication and authorization to shrink implicit trust while still maintaining availability. The goal of ZTA is to prevent unauthorized access to data and services by making access control enforcement as precise and granular as possible (policy-driven access control). When properly implemented, ZTA minimizes threats against assets (threat scope reduction).

A user (called a subject) or another device (a system) requests access to a resource. The user is considered to be in an untrusted zone while the resource is in a secured zone that cannot be accessed without approval. Users are verified through adaptive identity, which takes into consideration more than just a username and password; it can also include the role of the user in the organization, their location, the resources being requested, and any prior behavior on the network that deviates from a baseline.

The policy engine is a component of the **policy decision point (PDP)** that provides input into the **policy enforcement point (PEP)** to make the decision whether to grant access for a request. The policy engine relies on policy automation that uses automated processes for referring to policies for approval. The control plane is used for communication while the data plane is used for the transfer of the resource if approved. A conceptual ZTA is illustrated in Figure 9-9.

Figure 9-9   Conceptual ZTA

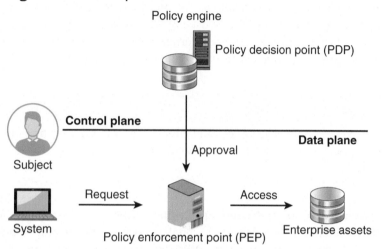

Note 24

In early 2022, an executive order from the president of the United States mandated that all government agencies must achieve specific zero-trust security goals by the end of fiscal year 2024.

Two Rights & A Wrong

1. Infrastructure separation can be achieved through physical segmentation or logical segmentation.
2. A VLAN allows scattered users to be logically grouped together even though they are physically attached to different switches.
3. ZTA uses a PEP to provide input into a PDP.

See the answers at the end of the module.

Access Technologies

Certification

3.2 Given a scenario, apply security principles to secure enterprise infrastructure.

4.5 Given a scenario, modify enterprise capabilities to enhance security.

Accessing a network infrastructure from a location other than the campus on which the organization is located is called remote access. At one time the means through which the remote access occurred (transport method) was a telephone dial-up connection through a modem; this has replaced (except in extreme instances) a direct connection through the Internet. Remote access always requires that the connection be secure (secure communication). This involves selecting the best networking protocol to use (protocol selection) and opening the right ports on devices so that the communication can occur (port selection).

However, not all access technologies are remote. Some access technologies involve local access but perform in a means that enhances security. Two of the common access technologies are virtual private network (VPN) and network access control (NAC).

Virtual Private Network (VPN)

A virtual private network (VPN) is a security technology that enables authorized users to use an unsecured public network, such as the Internet, as if it were a secure private network. It does this by encrypting all data that is transmitted between the remote endpoint and the network, not just specific documents or files. There are two common types of VPNs. A remote access VPN is a user-to-LAN connection used by remote users. The second type is a site-to-site VPN, in which multiple sites can connect to other sites over the Internet. Some VPNs allow the user to always stay connected instead of connecting and disconnecting from it. These are called always-on VPNs.

> **Note 25**
>
> Software-based VPNs are often used on mobile devices and offer the most flexibility in how network traffic is managed. However, hardware-based VPNs, typically used for site-to-site connections, are more secure, have better performance, and can offer more flexibility.

When using a VPN, there are two options depending on which traffic is to be protected. When all traffic is sent to the VPN concentrator and protected, this is called a full tunnel. However, not all traffic—such as web surfing or reading personal email—may need to be protected through a VPN. In this case, a split tunnel, or routing only some traffic over the secure VPN while other traffic directly accesses the Internet, may be used instead. This can help to preserve bandwidth and reduce the load on the VPN concentrator.

There are a variety of protocols that can be used for VPNs. The most common are IPsec and SSL or the weaker TLS. The Layer 2 Tunneling Protocol (L2TP) is a VPN protocol that does not offer any encryption or protection, so it is usually paired with IPsec (L2TP/IPsec). The current version of HTML, HTML5, can be used as a "clientless" VPN on an endpoint so that no additional software must be installed. Other popular VPN protocols include OpenVPN, SoftEther, WireGuard, SSTP, and IKEv2/IPsec.

> **Note 26**
>
> As protests in totalitarian states have increased, these governments have turned to controlling their citizens' access to the Internet as a means of controlling the information that protesters can receive and send to the outside world. Typically, this has involved blocking popular app stores so that encrypted social media apps cannot be downloaded and also turning off mobile access in areas where protests erupt. Protesters have turned to using VPNs to mask their IP addresses so that governments have a much more difficult time monitoring their activity or detecting a user's location. One nation-state has said they may make the sale of VPNs a criminal activity, and one official even called for the execution of those caught selling VPN services.

Network Access Control (NAC)

The waiting room at a doctor's office is an ideal location for the spread of germs: waiting patients are in a confined space, are ill, and typically have weakened immune systems. A sick patient in the waiting room could easily infect all other waiting patients. It is not uncommon today for a physician to post a nurse at the door of the waiting room to screen patients. Anyone who came to the waiting room with certain symptoms would be denied access (and rescheduled to a special after-hours appointment), given a prescription by the nurse for general medication, or directed to a separate quarantine room away from other patients.

This is the logic behind network access control (NAC). NAC examines the current state of an endpoint before it can connect to the network. Any device that does not meet a specified set of criteria, such as having the most current antivirus signature or the software firewall properly enabled, is denied access to the network, or given restricted access to computing resources, or connected to a "quarantine" network where the security deficiencies are corrected, after which the endpoint is connected to the normal network. The goal of NAC is to prevent computers with suboptimal security from potentially infecting other computers through the network.

Note 27

NAC also can be used to ensure that systems not owned by the organization, such as those owned by customers, visitors, and contractors, can be granted access without compromising security.

Some NAC systems use software agents installed on endpoints to gather information (called a host agent health check). An agent may be a permanent NAC agent and reside on end devices until uninstalled, or it may be a dissolvable NAC agent that disappears after reporting information to the NAC. Instead of installing agents on each device, the NAC technology can be embedded within a Microsoft Windows Active Directory domain controller. When a device joins the domain and a user logs in, NAC uses Active Directory to scan the device to verify that it complies with the necessary criteria. This is an agentless NAC because no additional software is required.

An example of the NAC process is illustrated in Figure 9-10:

1. The client performs a self-assessment using a System Health Agent (SHA) to determine its current security posture.

2. The assessment, known as a Statement of Health (SoH), is sent to a server called the Health Registration Authority (HRA). This server enforces the security policies of the network. It also integrates with other external authorities such as antivirus and patch management servers to retrieve current configuration information.

Figure 9-10   Network access control (NAC) process

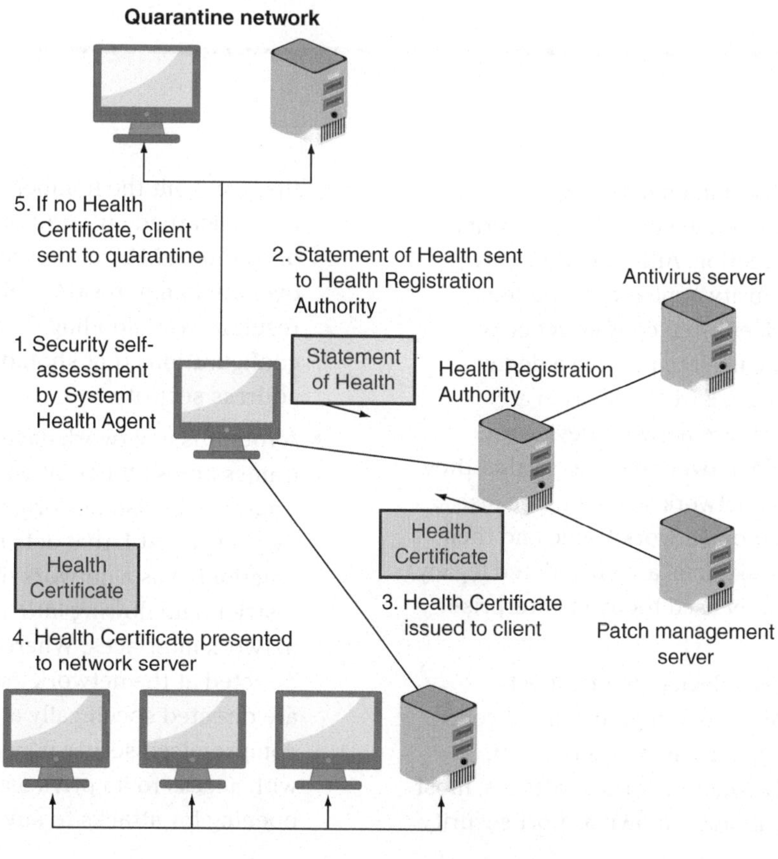

3. If the client is approved by the HRA, it is issued a Health Certificate.

4. The Health Certificate is then presented to the network servers to verify that the client's security condition has been approved.

5. If the client is not approved, it is connected to a quarantine network where the deficiencies are corrected and then the computer is allowed to connect to the network.

Note 28

There are two methods NAC uses for directing an infected endpoint away from the normal production network. Interestingly, each of these methods is also used by threat actors in their attacks. The first method is ARP poisoning and the second is DNS poisoning, each of which is covered in Module 8.

Two Rights & A Wrong

1. A VPN only encrypts documents and files.

2. L2TP is usually paired with IPsec.

3. NAC examines the current state of an endpoint before it can connect to the network.

See the answers at the end of the module.

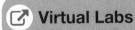 **Virtual Labs**   You're now ready to complete the simulations and live virtual machine labs for this module. The labs can be found in each module in MindTap.

Summary

- Networks use both common network infrastructure devices and specialized security appliances for protection. Although these are not considered security appliances, common infrastructure devices often contain security features that can be used to provide a degree of network protection. Early LANs used a hub, which is a standard network device for connecting multiple network devices so that they function as a single network segment. Because of their high impact on network traffic and their inherent security risk, hubs are considered legacy devices and are rarely used today in enterprise networks.

- A network switch is a device that connects network devices and has a degree of intelligence. A common attack against switches is a MAC flooding attack. To counteract these attacks, most switches have technology known as port security

- that can limit the number of MAC addresses that can be learned on ports. Restricting the number of incoming MAC addresses for a port prevents overwhelming the MAC address table that can result in MAC flooding. There are other switch configurations that should be implemented to address security.

- A router is a network device that can forward frames across different computer networks. Routers can also perform a security function by using an ACL that acts like a set of rules functioning as a network filter to permit or restrict data flowing into and out of the router network interfaces. Whereas some attacks are directed at the network itself, other attacks are directed specifically at network servers. A compromised server may provide threat actors with access to its privileged contents or give an opening for attacks to any of the devices that access the server. There are several basic steps for hardening a server. The use of a load balancer also has security advantages. Because load balancers are generally located between routers and servers, they can detect and stop attacks directed at a server or application.

- Security can be achieved through common devices by using the security features found in standard networking devices. Using both standard networking devices as well as security appliances can result in a layered security approach, which can significantly improve security.

- Although hardened and properly configured common networking devices can provide a degree of security, specialized infrastructure hardware devices designed for information security can give a much higher level of protection. A firewall is designed to limit the spread of malware. A firewall functions by bidirectional inspection by examining both outgoing and incoming network packets and allows approved packets to pass through but it can take different actions when it detects a suspicious packet. The actions are based on specific criteria or rules. Older firewalls often had each rule as a separate instruction that was processed in sequence, while modern firewalls allow a priority order. In addition to filtering based on packets, firewalls can also apply content/URL filtering.

- There are different categories of firewalls. Software firewalls run as a program or service on a device, while hardware firewalls are specialized separate devices that inspect traffic. A host-based firewall is a software firewall that runs on and protects a single endpoint device while an appliance firewall is typically a separate hardware device designed to protect an entire network. Some firewalls are freely available (open-source firewall) whereas other firewalls are owned by an entity that has an exclusive right to it (proprietary firewall).

- Stateless packet filtering on a firewall looks at a packet and permits or denies it based solely on the firewall rules. Stateful packet filtering uses both the firewall rules and the state of the connection. Whereas dedicated firewalls are designed to exclusively permit or deny packets, this functionality of filtering packets can also be incorporated into other devices as well through a network access control list.

- There are several specialized firewall appliances. A web application firewall (WAF) looks at applications using HTTP. A network address translation gateway is a cloud-based technology that performs NAT for cloud services. A next-generation firewall (NGFW) has additional functionality beyond a traditional firewall. Unified threat management (UTM) is a device that combines several security functions. These include packet filtering, antispam, antiphishing, antispyware, encryption, intrusion protection, and web filtering. A Layer 7 firewall allows for more advanced traffic filtering because it can investigate the contents of packets.

- A forward proxy is a computer or an application program that intercepts user requests from the internal secure network and then processes that request on behalf of the user. A reverse proxy routes requests coming from an external network to the correct internal server. Acting as the intermediary, a proxy server can provide a degree of protection.

- A honeypot is a computer located in an area with limited security that serves as bait to threat actors. The honeypot is intentionally configured with security vulnerabilities so that it is open to attacks. A high-interaction honeypot is usually configured with a default login and loaded with software, data files that appear to be authentic but are actually imitations of real data files called honeyfiles, and fake telemetry data. A honeynet is a network set up with intentional vulnerabilities. Fake data can also be added to live production systems, which is known as a honeytoken. A sinkhole is essentially a "bottomless pit" designed to steer unwanted traffic away from its intended destination to another device. One type of sinkhole is a DNS sinkhole.

- An intrusion detection system (IDS) can detect an attack as it occurs, while an intrusion prevention system (IPS) attempts to block the attack. An inline system is connected directly to the network and monitors the flow of data as it occurs. A passive system is connected to a port on a switch, which receives a copy of network traffic. A network intrusion detection system (NIDS), similar to a software-based host intrusion detection system (HIDS), watches for attacks on the network. A network intrusion prevention system (NIPS) not only monitors to detect malicious activities but also attempts to stop them.

- While hardware devices are most commonly used to protect an infrastructure network, there are also software security protections. Web filtering software monitors the websites users are browsing so that the organization can either allow or block web traffic to protect against potential threats and enforce corporate policies. There are different methods that web filtering uses to identify malicious websites to create block rules, or criteria for which a website is inaccessible to users. These include content categorization, URL scanning, and reputation scores. DNS filtering blocks harmful or inappropriate content. However, while web filtering blocks webpages, DNS filtering blocks entire domains. File integrity monitoring (FIM) is a technology designed to watch files to detect any changes within the files that may indicate a cyberattack. XDR collects and correlates data across various network appliances, including servers, email systems, cloud repositories, and endpoints.

- Equally important to security appliances and software security protections is the proper design of the network. The most restricted level of a network that has physical isolation from all other networks or the Internet is called an air-gapped network.

- A VLAN allows scattered users to be logically grouped together even though they are physically attached to different switches. This can reduce network traffic and provide a degree of security. A DMZ functions as a separate network that rests outside the secure network perimeter; untrusted outside users can access the DMZ but

cannot enter the secure network. In addition to a DMZ, there are other security zones or separate subnets for enhanced security that can also be used for security. Zero trust is a strategic initiative about networks that is designed to prevent successful attacks by threat actors who are already within a network. Zero trust attempts to eliminate the concept of trust from an organization's network architecture by acknowledging that implicit trust or trusting everyone within a network is a vulnerability.

- Accessing a network infrastructure from a location other than the campus on which the organization is located is called remote access. A VPN is a security technology that enables authorized users to use an unsecured public network, such as the Internet, as if it were a secure private network. It does this by encrypting all data that is transmitted between the remote endpoint and the network, not just specific documents or files. There are a variety of protocols that can be used for VPNs.

- Network access control (NAC) examines the current state of an endpoint before it can connect to the network. Any device that does not meet a specified set of criteria, such as having the most current antivirus signature or the software firewall properly enabled, is denied access to the network, or given restricted access to computing resources, or connected to a "quarantine" network where the security deficiencies are corrected. Some NAC systems use software installed on endpoints (agents), while other systems are agentless and do not require additional software to be installed.

Key Terms

active device attribute
adaptive identity
agent-based web filtering
air-gapped network
block rules
centralized proxy scanning
configuration enforcement
connectivity
content categorization
control plane
data plane

decommissioning
device placement
DNS filtering
extended detection and response (XDR)
file integrity monitoring (FIM)
firewall
firewall port filtering
firewall protocol filtering
gap analysis
hardening targets

honeyfiles
honeynet
honeypot
honeytoken
host-based firewall
inline
intrusion detection system (IDS)
intrusion prevention system (IPS)
isolation
jump server
Layer 4 firewall

Layer 7 firewall
load balancer
logical segmentation
network access control (NAC)
next generation firewall (NGFW)
NIDS sensors
passive device attribute
physical isolation
policy automation
policy engine
policy-driven access control
port security
port selection
protocol selection

proxy servers
remote access
removal of unnecessary software
reputation score
router
rules
screened subnet
secure communication
secured zone
security zones
segmentation
selection of effective controls
server
signatures

subject
switch
system
threat scope reduction
transport method
trends
unified threat management (UTM)
Universal Resource Locator (URL)
    scanning
virtual private network (VPN)
web application firewall (WAF)
web filtering
zero trust

Review Questions

1. Which of the following is NOT true about VPNs?

   a. It encrypts all data that is transmitted between the remote endpoint and the network.
   b. A remote access VPN is a user-to-LAN connection.
   c. A full tunnel routes only some traffic over the secure VPN.
   d. There are a variety of protocols that can be used for VPNs.

2. Which firewall rule action implicitly denies all other traffic unless explicitly allowed?

   a. Force Allow
   b. Force Deny
   c. Bypass
   d. Allow

3. Which of the following is NOT true about zero trust?

   a. Zero trust assumes that networks have already been infiltrated by threat actors.
   b. Zero trust is designed to make a system trusted.
   c. The motto of zero trust is "Never trust, always verify."
   d. Zero trust acknowledges that implicit trust is a vulnerability.

4. Maya is researching information on firewalls. She needs a firewall that allows for more generic statements instead of creating specific rules. What type of firewall should Maya consider purchasing that supports her need?

   a. Content/URL filtering firewall
   b. Policy-based firewall
   c. Hardware firewall
   d. Proprietary firewall

5. Astri is reviewing a log file of a new firewall. She notes that the log indicates packets are being dropped for incoming packets for which the internal endpoint did not initially create the request. What kind of firewall is this?

   a. Stateful packet filtering
   b. Connection-aware firewall
   c. Proxy firewall
   d. Packet-filtering firewall

6. What is a virtual firewall?

   a. A firewall that runs in the cloud
   b. A firewall that runs in an OS contained as part of an appliance
   c. A firewall that runs in a sandbox
   d. A firewall appliance that runs on a LAN

7. Which of these appliances provides the broadest protection by combining several security functions?

   a. NAT
   b. UTM
   c. WAF
   d. NGFW

8. Which firewall allows for the most advanced traffic filtering?

   a. Layer 4 firewall
   b. Layer 5 firewall
   c. Layer 6 firewall
   d. Layer 7 firewall

9. Ada is researching DDoS mitigations for her company. Which of the following should Ada consider?

    a. DDoS Prevention System (DPS)
    b. DNS sinkhole
    c. MAC pit
    d. IP denier

10. Which of the following devices routes requests coming from an external network to the correct internal server?

    a. Forward proxy server
    b. Reverse proxy server
    c. Lateral proxy server
    d. Neutral proxy server

11. Iben is preparing a presentation about DMZs. Which of the following would NOT be a true statement regarding a DMZ?

    a. It can be configured to have one or two firewalls.
    b. It contains servers that are used only by trusted internal users.
    c. It typically includes an email or web server.
    d. It provides an extra degree of security.

12. Tuva is documenting the different types of web filtering software her organization is using for scanning. Which of the following is NOT a type of web filtering scanning she would document?

    a. Cloud scanning
    b. Decentralized proxy scanning
    c. Agent-based scanning
    d. Browser scanning

13. Which of the following is NOT an example of infrastructure security hardware that can be used for protecting a network?

    a. IPS
    b. Proxy server
    c. NGFW
    d. Switch

14. Which of the following is NOT software-based security protection for an infrastructure network?

    a. DNS filtering
    b. Web filtering
    c. FIM
    d. RDR

15. Which device intercepts internal user requests and then processes those requests on behalf of the users?

    a. Intrusion prevention device
    b. Forward proxy server
    c. Reverse proxy server
    d. Host detection server

16. Oda needs to configure the VPN to preserve bandwidth. Which configuration would she choose?

    a. Narrow tunnel
    b. Wide tunnel
    c. Split tunnel
    d. Full tunnel

17. Which of the following is NOT a common network device that can be configured to provide a degree of security protection?

    a. Router
    b. Switch
    c. Endpoint
    d. Server

18. Which of the following is found on live production systems?

    a. Honeyhome
    b. Honeypot
    c. Honeynet
    d. Honeytoken

19. Which of the following is NOT used to create a web filtering block rule?

    a. Reputation score
    b. URL scanning
    c. DNS polling
    d. Content categorization

20. What is the advantage of XDR over EDR?

    a. XDR collects and correlates data across various network appliances.
    b. XDR is faster than EDR.
    c. The agent footprint of XDR is significantly smaller than an agent for EDR.
    d. XDR does not require user input.

Hands-On Projects

Caution !

If you are concerned about installing any of the software in these projects on your regular computer, you can instead use the Windows Sandbox created in the Module 1 Hands-On Projects. Software installed within the sandbox will not impact the computer.

Project 9-1: Using GlassWire Firewall

Estimated Time: 35 minutes
Objective: Explore the features of a firewall.
Description: GlassWire is a firewall and Security and Information Event Management (SIEM) product. In this activity, you will download and install GlassWire.

1. Use your web browser to go to **www.glasswire.com**. (If you are no longer able to access the site through the URL, use a search engine to search for "GlassWire.")
2. Click **Features** and scroll through the page to read about the different features and configuration options in this product.
3. Click **Download** and then click **DOWNLOAD GLASSWIRE** to download the file.
4. Navigate to the location of the downloaded file **GlassWireSetup.exe** and launch this program to install GlassWire by accepting the default settings.
5. Click **Finish** to run GlassWire.
6. Note that the information scrolls horizontally to the left regarding events that are occurring. Open a web browser and surf the Internet for several minutes.
7. Return to GlassWire.
8. Slide the scroller to the bottom of the screen to consolidate the views.
9. Click **Apps**. What information is given in the left pane? How can this be useful?
10. Click **Traffic** to view an analysis of the different traffic types.
11. Open a web browser and then arrange the GlassWire window and the browser window side by side on your computer screen.
12. Use your web browser to surf the web and watch the GlassWire screen as well. What can you learn from this?
13. Close the browser window and maximize GlassWire.
14. Click the **Firewall** button. What apps or services have recently gone through your firewall?
15. Click the **Usage** button to see a summary of the local Apps utilized, the Hosts accessed, and the Traffic Type.
16. Click **Alerts**. Scroll through any alerts that have been issued. What can you tell about them?
17. How valuable is this information from GlassWire?
18. Close all windows.

Project 9-2: Configuring Microsoft Windows Defender Firewall—Apps

Estimated Time: 25 minutes
Objective: Configure a host-based firewall.
Description: In this project, you explore configuration settings on Windows Firewall for allowing an app to penetrate the firewall.

1. Right-click **Start** and then click **Settings**.

2. Click **Privacy & security**.

3. Click **Windows Security**.

4. Click **Firewall & network protection**.

Note 29

Windows Firewall uses three different profiles: domain (when the computer is connected to a Windows domain), private (when connected to a private network, such as a work or home network), and public (used when connected to a public network, such as public Wi-Fi). A computer may use multiple profiles so that a business laptop computer may use the domain profile at work, the private profile when connected to the home network, and the public profile when connected to a public Wi-Fi network. Windows asks whether a network is public or private when you first connect to it.

5. Click **Allow an app through firewall**. Depending on your network configuration, click the type of network that says **(active)**.

6. The Microsoft Windows Defender host-based firewall is application-centric: users can create an opening in the firewall for each specific application. This is more secure than permanently opening a port in the firewall that will always remain open as opposed to a port that is only opened when the application requires it and is then closed. However, there is an issue with these types of firewalls in that installed apps routinely give themselves permissions through the firewall without making that clear to the user. Scroll down through the apps that have access through the firewall. Does this lengthy list surprise you? What are the security risks?

7. Click **File and Printer Sharing**.

8. Click **Details . . . .**

9. Read the description. Click **OK**.

10. Click **What are the risks of allowing an app to communicate?** What type of information is provided? How helpful is this information? How could it be improved?

11. Close the browser window.

12. Now add an app that can penetrate the firewall. Click **Change settings**.

13. Click **Allow another app . . . .**

14. See the apps that have been installed on this computer by clicking **Browse . . . .**

15. Scroll down and select an app and click **Open**.

16. Click **Network Types**. For this app, which network type would you select? Why?

17. Click **Cancel**.

18. Click **Cancel** on the **Add an app** window.

19. Click **Cancel** on the **Allow apps to communicate through Windows Defender Firewall**.

20. Close all windows.

Project 9-3: Configuring Microsoft Windows Defender Firewall—Ports

Estimated Time: 20 minutes
Objective: Configure port settings on a firewall.
Description: In this project, you explore configuration settings on Windows Firewall for opening a port on the firewall.

1. Right-click **Start** and then click **Settings**.

2. Click **Privacy & security**.

3. Click **Windows Security**.

4. Click **Firewall & network protection**.

5. Click **Advanced settings**.

6. In the **Windows Defender Firewall with Advanced Security on Local Computer** window, click **Inbound Rules** in the left pane. Expand the screen so you can see all of the columns.

7. Why do some apps have **Any** for **Remote Address** while other apps are more restrictive for these parameters?

8. Click **Outbound Rules** and view the same parameters.

9. Create a specific rule to open a firewall port. Click **Outbound Rules** in the left pane.

10. In the right pane, notice the different ways in which a firewall filter can be created. What is the advantage of **Filter by Profile**?

11. Click **New Rule**.

12. Note that there are four types of rules that can be created. Click **Custom** and then **Next**.

13. A custom rule can apply to all programs, a specific program, or a Windows service. Click **Customize** next to **Services**.

14. Click **Apply to this service** and scroll through the list of available services.

15. Click **Cancel**.

16. Be sure that **All programs** is selected and click **Next**.

17. Specific ports and protocols can be selected for this rule. Under **Protocol type**, select **TCP**. Note the **Protocol number** is automatically selected.

18. In **Local port**, select **Specific Ports**.

19. Enter **80**.

20. In **Remote port**, select **All ports**, if necessary.

21. Click **Next**.

22. Under **Which local IP addresses does this rule apply to?** Click **These IP addresses:**

23. Click **Add**.

24. Click **This IP address range**.

25. In the **From** box, enter **192.168.0.0**.

26. In the **To** box, enter **192.168.0.255** and click **OK**.

27. Click **Next**.

28. Read the three options for actions. Be sure that **Block the connection** is selected. Click **Next**.

29. Read the three options for when this rule applies. Click **Next**.

30. A name can be given to this rule. However, click the **Back** button and review each of the settings that were created for this rule. What type of rule have you just created? What will it block? Why?

31. Click **Cancel** and close all windows.

Project 9-4: Using a VPN

Estimated Time: 30 minutes
Objective: Configure and use a VPN.
Description: In this project, you will download and install a VPN.

1. Use your web browser to go to **protonvpn.com**.

2. Click **Get Proton VPN now**.

3. Under **Proton Free** click **Get Proton Free**.

4. Click **Continue with free**.

5. Enter the requested information to create a Proton Account and follow the steps to download and install the application.

6. If necessary, click the icon to launch ProtonVPN.

7. Enter your username and password. Turn off **Start and connect on boot**. Click **Login**.

8. Click **Take a Tour** to learn about its features.

9. Note that the free version only supports servers in three countries. Click the down arrow next to **United States** to see the list of servers.

10. Click **Quick Connect** to connect to a server. This will route your traffic through a Proton server to mask your data.

11. Notice that the **Connected** message displays on the map the server through which the data is routed.

12. In the **Countries** tab, click the rightmost icon to display the **Kill Switch** options. If necessary, turn **Kill Switch On**. This will disable the VPN if the connection is dropped.

13. Click the **Profiles** tab.

14. Note that you can connect either the **Fastest** or **Random** connection to a Proton server.

15. Click **Create Profile**.

16. Notice the options for creating an automatic profile that will be used whenever you launch ProtonVPN.

17. How easy is this VPN to use? What features are most prominent for security and privacy?

18. Close all windows.

Case Projects

Case Project 9-1: #TrendingCyber

Estimated Time: 15 minutes
Objective: Summarize your thoughts on the #TrendingCyber opener.
Description: Read again the opening #TrendingCyber in this module. If an air gap is not the solution to solving ransomware attacks, what could be the answer? Should paying a ransom be outlawed? Should all data be required to be encrypted? What would work? Write a one-paragraph summary of your thoughts.

Case Project 9-2: Hardening Security Appliances

Estimated Time: 25 minutes
Objective: Research how to harden security appliances.
Description: It is essential that security appliances be hardened. Not only does a misconfigured device allow threat actors an opening into the network, but it also provides a false sense of security that makes it difficult to realize a problem exists. One basic configuration management tool is to use standard naming conventions. Using the same conventions for assigning names to appliances (standard naming conventions) can eliminate confusion regarding the various appliances. These conventions will vary by organization, but an example is "Device names are limited to 15 characters by technical necessity. To ensure interoperability with other systems, only letters and numbers shall be used. Each device name shall have the following minimum structure: the first three characters are the appropriate unit identifier (mandatory); the next six numbers are the device's inventory control tag number (mandatory); the remaining six characters may be used at the discretion of the department, or not used at all (optional)." Another tool is to use a defined IP schema. An IP schema is a standard guide for assigning IP addresses to devices. This makes it easier to set up and troubleshoot devices and helps to eliminate overlapping or duplicate subnets and IP address

device assignments, avoid unnecessary complexity, and not waste IP address space. Finally, creating a visual mapping (diagram) of security appliances can likewise be valuable when new appliances are added or when troubleshooting is required. Write a short paragraph that summarizes your research on hardening security appliances. What are the risks of not following these best practices for hardening? Which of these three would you consider to be the most valuable? How could these be enforced in an organization? Write a one-page summary about these tools.

Case Project 9-3: Cloud-Based Honeypots

Estimated Time: 20 minutes
Objective: Research honeypot deception.
Description: Research cloud-based honeypots. What are their advantages? What are their disadvantages? When should they not be used? How could one be set up? Create a one-page paper of your research.

Case Project 9-4: Hardening a Jump Server

Estimated Time: 20 minutes
Objective: Determine how to configure a jump server.
Description: How should a jump server be configured? Create a list of configurations that you would use to set up a jump server that had the fewest risks.

Case Project 9-5: Researching Network Access Control

Estimated Time: 25 minutes
Objective: Research NAC from different vendors.
Description: Use the Internet to research the network access control (NAC) products from Microsoft and Cisco. How are they different? How are they similar? What are some of the options for each product? Which would you choose, and why? Write a one-page paper on your research.

Case Project 9-6: UTM Comparison

Estimated Time: 20 minutes
Objective: Identify UTM commercial products.
Description: Create a table of four UTM devices available today. Include the vendor name, pricing, a list of features, the type of protections it provides, etc. Based on your research, assign a value of 1–5 (lowest to highest) that you would give that UTM. Include a short explanation of why you gave it that ranking.

Case Project 9-7: Zero Trust

Estimated Time: 30 minutes
Objective: Explore zero trust.
Description: Use the Internet to research zero trust. What is it? What are its advantages? What are its disadvantages? What technologies does it require? Is it a long-term security solution? Is it widely accepted? What do you think about it? Write a one-page paper on your research.

Case Project 9-8: Network Firewall Comparison

Estimated Time: 15 minutes
Objective: Compare different types of firewalls.
Description: Use the Internet to identify three network firewalls and create a chart that compares their features. Note if they are rule-based or policy-based, perform stateless or stateful packet filtering, what additional features they include (IDS, content filtering, etc.), their costs, etc. Which would you recommend? Why?

Case Project 9-9: Load-Balancing Scheduling Protocols

Estimated Time: 25 minutes

Objective: Explore scheduling protocols.

Description: There are different scheduling protocols that are used in load balancers. In a round-robin scheduling protocol, the rotation applies to all devices equally. A scheduling protocol that distributes the load based on which devices can handle the load more efficiently is known as affinity scheduling. Affinity scheduling may be based on which load balancers have the least number of connections at a given point in time. Other scheduling protocols can use HTTP headers, cookies, or data within the application message itself to make a decision on distribution. Research these scheduling protocols. Which would you consider to be the most efficient? Which would provide the highest degree of security? Write a one-page paper on your research.

Case Project 9-10: Load-Balancing Configurations

Estimated Time: 25 minutes

Objective: Analyze load-balancing configurations.

Description: When multiple load balancers are used together to achieve high efficiency, they can be placed in different configurations. In an active–passive configuration, the primary load balancer distributes the network traffic to the most suitable server while the secondary load balancer operates in a "listening mode." This second load balancer constantly monitors the performance of the primary load balancer and will step in and take over the load-balancing duties should the primary load balancer start to experience difficulties or fail. The active–passive configuration allows for uninterrupted service and can also handle planned or unplanned service outages. In an active–active configuration, all load balancers are always active. Network traffic is combined and the load balancers then work together as a team. Load balancers in an active–active configuration can also remember previous requests from users and retain this information. In the event the user returns requesting the same information, the user is directed to the load balancer that previously served the request and the information can be immediately provided. Research these different configurations. Write a one-page summary of your research.

Case Project 9-11: Bridge Protocol Data Units

Estimated Time: 25 minutes

Objective: Research bridge protocol data units.

Description: A broadcast storm occurs in a misconfigured network when frames are broadcast, received, and rebroadcast by each switch. Broadcast storms can cripple a network in a matter of seconds to the point that no legitimate traffic can occur. Because the headers that a Layer 2 switch examines do not have a time to live (TTL) value, a packet could loop through the network indefinitely. Broadcast storm prevention can be accomplished by loop prevention, which uses the IEEE 802.1d standard spanning-tree protocol (STP). The STP uses an algorithm that creates a hierarchical "tree" layout that "spans" the entire network. It determines all the redundant paths that a switch has to communicate, recognizes the best path, and then blocks out all other paths. STP does this by sending out bridge protocol data units (BPDUs) that give information about the switch port (MAC address, priority, etc.). This enables switches in the STP to share information with other switches. BPDUs are also periodically sent to inform other switches of port changes. However, a threat actor can try to take advantage of the STP by sending out their own malicious BPDUs to the switch to change its configuration. Because BPDUs should only be exchanged between switches, a defense is to enable BPDU guard, which is a feature on the switch that creates an alert when a BPDU is received from an endpoint and not a switch. In such an instance, the port on the switch will be disabled and no traffic is sent or received by that port. Research BPDUs and BPDU guards. Explain how this can protect a network. Write a one-page paper on your research.

Case Project 9-12: Quality of Service (QoS)

Estimated Time: 25 minutes

Objective: Research Quality of Service.

Description: Quality of Service (QoS) is a set of network technologies used to guarantee its ability to dependably serve network resources and high-priority applications to endpoints. QoS technologies provide "differentiated" handling and capacity allocation to specific network traffic. A network administrator can assign the order in which packets are handled and the amount of bandwidth given to an application or traffic flow (called traffic shaping). The first step in QoS is that traffic must be classified or differentiated using various QoS tools. Classifying traffic according to the corporate policy allows organizations to ensure the consistency and adequacy of network resources for the most important applications. While traffic can be prioritized by port or IP address, this has obvious limitations. (It is unlikely that a specific IP address should always have high network capacity no matter what activity is being performed.) Instead, traffic should be viewed by the application or user, which can then result in a more meaningful classification of the data. Almost all firewalls today recognize QoS settings (this is done through configuring the "Type of Service" 8-bit field within an IP packet that is reserved for QoS markings). Research QoS. Can it be used to provide a higher degree of security? How? Write a one-page paper on your research.

Case Project 9-13: Bay Point Ridge Security

Estimated Time: 45 minutes
Objective: Research firewalls.
Description: Bay Point Ridge Security (BPRS) is a managed service provider (MSP) that manages networks, computers, cloud resources, and information security for small-to-medium enterprises (SMEs) in the region. BPRS provides internships to students who are in their final year of the security degree program at the local college and has recently hired you.

You have been asked to evaluate the security of a new client and you find that their firewalls are out of date and inadequate. Because of recent employee turnover, the security team has asked you to make a presentation directly to the senior management requesting funding for new appliances. The attendees of this meeting do not have a technical background.

1. Create a PowerPoint presentation about firewalls. Include their functions and different categories. Your presentation should contain at least 10–12 slides.

2. After the presentation, the senior management has asked for your recommendation regarding which specialized firewall (NGFW, WAF, or UTM) should be purchased. Create a memo to the group that gives your recommendation.

Two Rights & A Wrong: Answers

Security Appliances

1. Segmentation is dividing a network into multiple subnets with each acting as its own small network to improve monitoring and enhance security.

2. A rule-based firewall is more flexible than a policy-based firewall.

3. A forward proxy is a computer or an application program that intercepts user requests from the internal secure network and then processes that request on behalf of the user.

Answer: The wrong statement is #2.
Explanation: A policy-based firewall is more flexible than a rule-based firewall.

Software Security Protections

1. Web filtering can be accomplished through browser scanning, agent-based scanning, centralized proxy scanning, or cloud scanning.

2. DNS filtering blocks entire domains.

3. EDR is more robust and provides greater protection than XDR.

Answer: The wrong statement is #3.

Explanation: Extended detection and response (XDR) is more robust than endpoint detection and response (EDR) because it collects and correlates data across various network appliances as well as endpoints.

Secure Infrastructure Design

1. Infrastructure separation can be achieved through physical segmentation or logical segmentation.
2. A VLAN allows scattered users to be logically grouped together even though they are physically attached to different switches.
3. ZTA uses a PEP to provide input into a PDP.

Answer: The wrong statement is #3.

Explanation: Zero-trust architecture (ZTA) uses a policy decision point (PDP) to provide input into the policy enforcement point (PEP).

Access Technologies

1. A VPN only encrypts documents and files.
2. L2TP is usually paired with IPsec.
3. NAC examines the current state of an endpoint before it can connect to the network.

Answer: The wrong answer is #1.

Explanation: A VPN encrypts all data that is transmitted between the remote endpoint and the network, not just specific documents or files.

Reference

1. Boddy, Matt, "Exposed: Cyberattacks on cloud honeypots," *Sophos*, Apr. 9, 2019, accessed April 3, 2023, www.sophos.com/en-us/press-office/press-releases/2019/04/cybercriminals-attack-cloud-server-honeypot-within-52-seconds.aspx.

Module 10

Wireless Network Attacks and Defenses

Module Objectives

After completing this module, you should be able to do the following:

1 Describe the different types of wireless network attacks

2 List the vulnerabilities of WLAN security

3 Explain the solutions for securing a wireless network

#TrendingCyber

No technology has changed more in the last 25 years than the technology behind wireless local area networks (WLANs) or Wi-Fi. When introduced back in 1997, this technology supported data transmissions at a paltry 2 million bits per second (Mbps). Since then, Wi-Fi has gone through seven (and soon to be eight) different versions, with the next version designed to transmit at a whopping 46,210 Mbps. The growth in Wi-Fi technology in such a relatively short period of time has truly been astonishing.

One effect of this rapid growth is the very wide range of Wi-Fi hardware in use today based on different versions. While some users and organizations have rushed to the latest-and-greatest new devices that supported a brand-new version, others have simply stuck with what works. And sometimes this replacement has been forced: new versions have caused some hardware vendors to "orphan" devices that were based on previous versions so that their older devices are no longer manufactured or even supported. The end result of this uneven replacement is that there is a wide range of Wi-Fi devices in use today. And this is not just limited to Wi-Fi. Computers, networks, mobile devices, smartphones, and virtually every category of technology face the same issue of different generations of devices all in use at the same time.

This broad range of different technology equipment in use simultaneously has caused an unintended security problem. Older equipment, while still in use by at least a portion of users, is not always readily available for testing, making it virtually impossible to look for vulnerabilities or test new security patches.

Over a decade ago, this problem hit Intel Corporation extremely hard. Some of their older devices could not be located for security testing. These devices were so scarce that Intel's security researchers had to look on eBay to purchase outdated equipment offered for sale by users.

Intel determined that they must address this problem. They created a warehouse and laboratory in Costa Rica, where the company already had a research and development (R&D) lab, to store all its technology devices—both old and new—and make the devices available for remote testing. Called the Long-Term Retention Lab, it was fully functional by 2019. The lab gives Intel, which has over 100,000 employees worldwide, a centralized and secure location where security tests can be run from anywhere in the world. Intel engineers can request a device in a specific configuration for testing (the lab receives over 1,000 such requests each month). The equipment is then assembled by a technician and made accessible through cloud services. The lab runs 24 hours a day, seven days a week, typically with about 25 engineers working any given shift.

Access to the Long-Term Retention Lab building is strictly controlled. The lab's exact location is a secret. Nobody outside of Intel can have access, and any new employees must first be approved by senior managers. Surveillance cameras watch the equipment at all times.

The warehouse currently stores around 3,000 hardware and software items, dating back over 10 years. All new Intel technology is now built with the facility in mind. New equipment is sent to the lab before it is released to the general public (about 50 new devices arrive each week). Technical documentation is also created to allow engineers to support it for up to 10 years. Intel plans to expand the warehouse, nearly doubling the space to 27,000 square feet, so it can house up to 6,000 pieces of computer equipment.

But Intel found that just locating and shipping equipment to the lab was often not enough. Without documentation or a contact person knowledgeable about the equipment, it was difficult for technicians to properly configure it. Intel reached out to engineers who had long since moved on to other projects or had even left the company. These employees and former employees provided detailed information regarding the devices that they helped design years earlier. With their assistance, Intel was able to create detailed technical documentation on the older equipment.

The lab has become an integral part of Intel's security program. It has been especially useful when Intel is trying to replicate security vulnerabilities reported to it by outside researchers through its bug-bounty program. The lab also provides isolated systems for security research. Testing security vulnerabilities often causes systems to crash, which can result in data loss, so using live production systems is out of the question. The isolated lab is an ideal solution. The lab even brings commercial value to Intel. The company's research has shown that customers are more likely to buy technology from manufacturers that proactively test their products.

As one Intel security engineer said, "Hopefully, I will never find myself searching eBay for Intel hardware again."

Ubiquitous means "being everywhere." And perhaps that is the best word to describe wireless data networks: they are *everywhere*. When was the last time you were at a coffee shop that did not have Wi-Fi? Or a library? Or a hotel? Or an airplane? Or a sports stadium? The list goes on and on. Not only do we expect these wireless networks to be everywhere, but we demand it: a coffee shop that does not have Wi-Fi will have more than its share of empty seats.

And wireless technologies do not just provide convenient services for users; they have become essential drivers in today's economy. One measurement of the impact of a single wireless technology, Wi-Fi, is profound. A study was commissioned to assess the worldwide economic value of Wi-Fi by measuring its direct net contribution to the global gross domestic product (GDP) and to worldwide employment. The study estimated Wi-Fi's global economic value to be $1.96 trillion in 2018, increasing to $3.47 trillion by 2023; it will reach $4.34 trillion by 2025. And if worldwide availability of newer Wi-Fi versions is factored in, the value would increase to *$4.9 trillion* by 2025.[1]

But just as users are drawn to wireless data networks, so are attackers. Wi-Fi and other wireless data networks are tempting and often too-easy targets for attackers to compromise, despite the fact that modern devices have a wide range of security protections available. However, often these protections are overlooked or are misconfigured, or users are not aware of their importance.

After exploring wired infrastructure security in Module 9, this module explores wireless network security. You first investigate the attacks on wireless devices that are common today. Next, you explore vulnerabilities in wireless security. Finally, you examine several secure wireless protections.

Wireless Attacks

There are different wireless technologies behind connecting devices to wireless networks. While some networks are managed by the providers, most wireless technologies that are the basis for wireless networks found in a home or office are instead owned and managed by the users. Unfortunately, these wireless networks are all too often left unprotected or with only minimal security and are vulnerable to wireless network attacks.

The most common wireless technologies include cellular, Bluetooth, near field communication, radio frequency identification, and wireless local area networks.

Cellular Networks

The most widespread wireless networks are **cellular** networks. These networks are operated by telecommunication service providers and include name-brand consumer wireless cellular carriers. The three largest service providers operate nationwide wireless networks that cover almost the entire population of the United States, while smaller regional and local carriers (of which there are over 100) provide coverage across selected areas. They supplement nationwide coverage through roaming agreements with the large providers.

Note 1

Cellular networks are covered in Module 6.

The introduction of the faster 5G cellular service in 2018 has allowed service providers to offer fixed wireless service for Internet connectivity. This service is "fixed" in that the device that receives the wireless signal is stationary, although the user with a mobile device can freely roam yet remain connected to this fixed device. These fixed wireless services compete against wired cable connections and fiber optic solutions. One advantage of fixed wireless service is that it can provide Internet access to remote or rural areas that lack a wired infrastructure.

Telecommunication service providers own, maintain, and manage their own network equipment and facilities. Thus, end users are not responsible for configuring or securing these cellular networks.

Bluetooth Attacks

Bluetooth is the name given to a wireless technology that uses short-range radio frequency (RF) transmissions and provides rapid device pairings. Named after 10th-century Danish King Harald "Bluetooth" Gormsson, who was responsible for unifying Scandinavia, it was originally designed in 1994 by the cellular telephone company Ericsson to replace personal computer cables. However, Bluetooth has moved well beyond its original design.

Note 2

The name "Bluetooth" was only intended as a temporary codeword for the technology as it was being developed. When it came time to select a more serious name, it was proposed that RadioWire become the official name. However, a full trademark search on RadioWire could not be completed in time for the product launch, so Bluetooth was used instead as the official name.

Bluetooth is a personal area network (PAN) technology designed for data communication over short distances and enables users to connect wirelessly to a wide range of computing and telecommunications devices. It provides for virtually instantaneous connections with little user intervention between a Bluetooth-enabled device and receiver. Several of these Bluetooth-enabled products are listed in Table 10-1.

Table 10-1 Bluetooth products

Category	Bluetooth pairing	Usage
Automobile	Hands-free car system with cell phone	Drivers can speak commands to browse the cell phone's contact list, make and receive hands-free phone calls, or use its navigation system.
Home entertainment	Stereo headphones with portable music player	Users can create a playlist on a portable music player and listen through a set of wireless headphones or speakers.
Photographs	Digital camera with printer	Digital photos can be sent directly to a photo printer or from pictures taken on one cell phone to another phone.
Computer accessories	Computer with keyboard and mouse	Small travel mouse can be linked to a laptop or a full-size mouse and keyboard that can be connected to a desktop computer.
Sports and fitness	Heart-rate monitor with wristwatch	Those who exercise can track heart rates and blood oxygen levels.
Medical and health	Blood pressure monitors with smartphones	Patient information can be sent to a smartphone, which can then send an emergency phone message, if necessary.

Note 3

Bluetooth is also finding its way into some unlikely devices. A Victorinox Swiss Army pocketknife model has Bluetooth technology that can be used to remotely control a computer when projecting a PowerPoint presentation. Other unusual devices include Bluetooth-enabled toothbrushes, keychain breathalyzers, stethoscopes, and even trash cans that send reminders to take out the garbage.

The current version is Bluetooth 5.4, introduced in early 2023 (all Bluetooth devices are backward compatible with previous versions). There are two implementations of Bluetooth. **Bluetooth Basic Rate/Enhanced Data Rate (BR/EDR)**, sometimes called "Bluetooth Classic," is designed for devices needing short-range continuous connectivity (such as streaming music to a Bluetooth headset), while **Bluetooth Low Energy (LE)** is for devices that require short bursts of data over longer distances (such as inventory control devices at a retail store). The number of bits per second (bps) that Bluetooth LE can transmit is between 125 Kbps and 2 Mbps, while Bluetooth BR/EDR supports data rates from 1 Mbps to 3 Mbps.

Bluetooth devices are categorized by their "class," of which there are three classes. Each class can transmit over different distances. The advertised distance ranges for Class 1 devices are up to 328 feet (100 meters), Class 2 devices have a maximum range of 98 feet (30 meters), and Class 3 devices can send and receive up to 33 feet (10 meters).

Caution !

There are a number of factors that can impact the range of transmission. For Bluetooth, this includes the Physical Layer of the protocol, the receiver sensitivity, the device's transmit power, antenna gain, and path loss. Advertised ranges are generalizations of the range of transmission.

The primary type of Bluetooth network is a piconet. When two Bluetooth devices come within range of each other, after an initial pairing confirmation, they automatically connect whenever they meet. One device is the "broadcaster," and it controls all the wireless traffic. The other device is an "observer" that takes commands from the broadcaster. Observer devices that are connected to the piconet and are sending transmissions are active followers; devices that are connected but are not actively participating are parked followers. Devices can also switch roles so that an observer temporarily becomes a broadcaster but then switches back to an observer role or vice versa. An example of two piconets with multiple observers is illustrated in Figure 10-1.

Figure 10-1   Bluetooth piconets

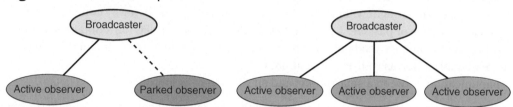

The network topology (the arrangement of the nodes of a communication network) of Bluetooth is usually point-to-point (one device connected to one device or, in the case of Bluetooth, one observer connected to one broadcaster) or point-to-multipoint (one device connected to multiple devices), as seen in Figure 10-1. The point-to-multipoint Bluetooth topology allows, for example, a single Bluetooth-enabled smartphone to control multiple Bluetooth devices (speaker, fitness tracker, etc.).

Bluetooth LE also supports a many-to-many topology, known as a mesh. Mesh topologies are often used to extend the range of a Bluetooth network. Instead of being limited to the range of a class, an observer can communicate with another broadcaster closer to the broadcaster, who can then send it on to yet another observer still closer to the broadcaster, until the packet reaches the broadcaster.

Note 4

The Bluetooth specification also allows for a device to be a member in two or more overlaying piconets that cover the same area. This group of piconets in which connections exist between different piconets is called a *scatternet*. However, scatternets are rarely used.

One of the primary features of Bluetooth is its ability for observers to connect to a broadcaster dynamically and automatically "on the fly" as needed whenever Bluetooth devices enter and leave the coverage area. However, this also opens the door for attacks on Bluetooth. Two common Bluetooth attacks are bluejacking and bluesnarfing.

Bluejacking

Bluejacking is an attack that sends unsolicited messages to Bluetooth-enabled devices. Usually bluejacking involves sending text messages, though images and sounds can also be transmitted. Bluejacking is usually considered more annoying than harmful because no data is stolen; however, many Bluetooth users resent receiving unsolicited messages.

Note 5

Bluejacking has been used for advertising purposes by vendors.

Bluesnarfing

Bluesnarfing is an attack that accesses unauthorized information from a wireless device through a Bluetooth connection. In a bluesnarfing attack, the attacker copies emails, calendars, contact lists, cell phone pictures, or videos by connecting to the Bluetooth device without the owner's knowledge or permission.

> **Note 6**
>
> Bluejacking and bluesnarfing can be mitigated by turning off Bluetooth when not needed, making the device nondiscoverable, or rejecting pairing requests from an unknown device.

Near Field Communication (NFC) Attacks

Near field communication (NFC) is a set of standards used to establish communication between devices in very close proximity. Once the devices are brought within 4 centimeters of each other, the two-way communication is established. Devices using NFC can be active or passive. A passive NFC device, such as an NFC tag, contains information that other devices can read but the tag neither reads other tags nor receives any information; it simply transmits data. Active NFC devices can read information as well as transmit data.

The NFC communication between a smartphone and an NFC tag is as follows:

1. The smartphone (interrogator) sends out a signal to the tag, which becomes powered by the energy in the interrogator's wireless signal.

> **Note 7**
>
> The ability of an NFC tag to be powered by the interrogator's signal allows tags to be very small in size because it is unnecessary for a tag to have its own battery or attached to another power source.

2. The interrogator and tag each create a high-frequency magnetic field from an internal antenna. Once the fields are created, a connection can be formed between the devices (known as magnetic induction). This is illustrated in Figure 10-2 (in this figure, the antennas are pictured outside of the interrogator and tag for clarity).

Figure 10-2 NFC magnetic induction

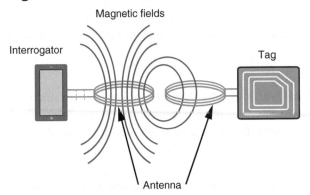

3. The interrogator sends a message to the tag to find out what type of communication the tag uses. When the tag responds, the interrogator sends its first commands based on that type.
4. When the tag receives the instruction, it checks to determine if the instruction is valid. If it is not, the tag ignores the communication. If it is a valid request, the tag responds with the requested information. For sensitive transactions, such as credit card payments, a secure communication channel is established, and all transmitted information is encrypted.

Examples of NFC use include the following:

- **Entertainment.** NFC devices can be used as a ticket to a stadium or concert, for purchasing food and beverages, and for downloading upcoming events by tapping a smart poster.
- **Office.** An NFC-enabled device can be used to enter an office, clock in and out on a factory floor, or purchase snacks from a vending machine.

- **Retail stores.** Coupons or customer reward cards can be provided by tapping the point-of-sale (PoS) terminal.
- **Transportation.** On a bus or train, NFC can be used to quickly pass through turnstiles and receive updated schedules by tapping the device on a kiosk.

Note 8

There are five types of NFC tags, Type 1 through Type 5, used in different settings. For example, Type 2 tags are often used for event tickets and transit passes while Type 5 is used to tag library books.

Consumer NFC devices are most often used as an alternative to paying cash or using a credit card in a retail store. Using NFC as a payment method is called a "contactless payment system." Users store payment card numbers in a "virtual wallet" on a watch or smartphone to pay for purchases at an NFC-enabled PoS checkout device. Figure 10-3 shows one such contactless payment system.

Figure 10-3   Contactless payment system

New Africa/Shutterstock.com

The use of NFC has risks because of the nature of this technology. The risks and defenses of using NFC are listed in Table 10-2.

Table 10-2   NFC risks and defenses

Vulnerability	Explanation	Defense
Eavesdropping	Unencrypted NFC communication between the device and terminal can be intercepted and viewed.	Because an attacker must be extremely close to pick up the signal, users should remain aware of their surroundings while making a payment.
Data theft	Attackers can "bump" a portable reader to a user's smartphone in a crowd to make an NFC connection and steal payment information stored on the phone.	This can be prevented by turning off NFC while in a large crowd.
Man-in-the-middle attack	An attacker can intercept the NFC communications between devices and forge a fictitious response.	Devices can be configured in pairing so one device can only send while the other can only receive.
Device theft	The theft of a smartphone could allow an attacker to use that phone for purchases.	Smartphones should be protected with passwords or strong PINs.

> ## Note 9
>
> There are other short-range wireless technologies besides NFC. Matter is a smarthome standard for connecting wireless devices such as security cameras and smart locks. Thread is another wireless protocol that is similar to Matter but is a mesh-based network technology, and Z-Wave technology is also mesh based. ZigBee, introduced in 2004, is a low-power, short-range, and low-data rate specification for occasional data or signal transmission from a sensor or Internet of Things (IoT) device.

Radio Frequency Identification (RFID) Attacks

Another wireless technology similar to NFC is radio frequency identification (RFID). RFID is commonly used to transmit information between employee identification badges, inventory tags, book labels, and other paper-based tags that can be detected by a proximity reader. For example, an RFID tag can easily be affixed to the inside of an ID badge and can be read by an RFID reader as the user walks through a turnstile with the badge in a pocket.

> ## Note 10
>
> RFID systems operate in one of three different bands: low frequency (LF), high frequency (HF), and ultra-high frequency (UHF).

Most RFID tags are passive and do not have their own power supply; instead, the electrical current induced in the antenna by the incoming signal from the transceiver provides enough power for the tag to send a response. Because it does not require a power supply, passive RFID tags can be very small, only 0.4 mm × 0.4 mm and thinner than a sheet of paper, as illustrated in Figure 10-4. The amount of data transmitted typically is limited to just an ID number. Passive tags have ranges from about 1/3 inch to 19 feet (10 millimeters to 6 meters). Active RFID tags must have their own power source.

Figure 10-4   RFID tag

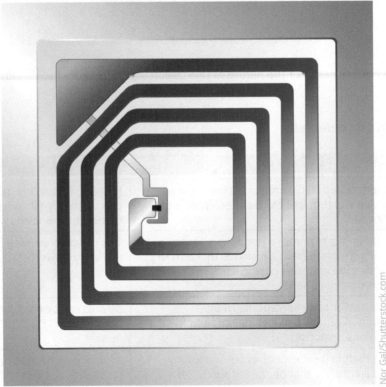

Nor Gal/Shutterstock.com

RFID tags are susceptible to different attacks. Table 10-3 lists several attacks that could occur in a retail store that uses RFID inventory tags.

Table 10-3   RFID attacks in retail stores

RFID attack type	Description of attack	Implications of RFID attack
Unauthorized tag access	A rogue RFID reader can determine the inventory on a store shelf to track the sales of specific items.	Sales information could be used by a rival product manufacturer to negotiate additional shelf space or better product placement.
Fake tags	Authentic RFID tags are replaced with fake tags that contain fictitious data about products that are not in inventory.	Fake tags undermine the integrity of the store's inventory system by showing data for items that do not exist.
Eavesdropping	Unauthorized users could listen in on communications between RFID tags and readers.	Confidential data, such as a politician's purchase of antidepressants, could be sold to a rival candidate in a "smear" campaign.
RFID cloning	RFID cloning (capturing data and then using it in a nefarious manner) can transfer the price from a $10 t-shirt to a $1,000 coat.	Thieves using a smartphone can capture and transfer RFID data from one tag to another, resulting in the theft of expensive items.

Besides paper-based tags, RFID technology can also be embedded into a chip. This is commonly found in contactless credit cards that allow cardholders to "wave" their cards in front of a contactless payment PoS terminal to complete a purchase. The information is sent from the chip to the terminal via RFID.

RFID technology is often found in devices that contain user identities or similar information. These identity devices include:

- **Enhanced Driver's License (EDL).** Drivers from Michigan, Minnesota, New York, Vermont, and Washington State may elect to have an EDL. An EDL card can be used as an alternative to a passport at some U.S. border crossings. EDLs use an RFID signal to send a unique code to a secure system. Using that code, the system then retrieves the owner's biographic and biometric data; however, no data other than the unique code is stored and transmitted from the EDL using RFID.
- **Passports.** RFID technology is embedded in the front cover of U.S. passports and contains data such as the holder's full name, address, and photo. The passport book front cover must be open for the RFID to transmit information; a closed passport book does not transmit information.
- **Hotel key card.** Hotel key cards use RFID LF. The information transmitted is typically the room number and the starting and ending dates of the stay and may include the number of people in the room.

As RFID technology is increasingly added to devices that contain user identities, the fear of eavesdropping RFID transmissions is often raised. However, this is not considered a high risk. The short range of RFID LF transmissions of only 4 inches (10 centimeters) makes it difficult for an attacker to steal RFID information simply by walking next to a target. And because a passport must be open in order to transmit, it would not be possible for an attacker to move close to a traveler who has a passport in a pocket to steal the information via RFID.

Note 11

Some wallets are advertised as providing "RFID Blocking Technology." These wallets typically state that "This product CAN block RFID signals from an id card, driver's license, credit/debit cards, and passports (working frequency 13.56 MHz). This product CANNOT block signals from some hotel room cards, some building access cards, and id badges (working frequency 125 KHz)."

Wireless Local Area Network Attacks

A wireless local area network (WLAN), commonly called Wi-Fi, is designed to replace or supplement a wired local area network (LAN). Devices such as tablets, laptop computers, and smartphones that are within range of a centrally located connection device can send and receive information at varying transmission speeds. It is important to know the different versions of Wi-Fi, identify the hardware necessary for a wireless network, and describe the different types of WLAN attacks directed at both the enterprise and consumers.

WLAN Versions

For computer networking and wireless communications, the most widely known and influential organization is the Institute of Electrical and Electronics Engineers (IEEE), which dates to 1884. In the early 1980s, the IEEE began work on developing computer network architecture standards. This work was called Project 802 and quickly expanded into several different categories of network technology.

Note 12

One of the most well-known IEEE standards is 802.3, which sets specifications for Ethernet local area network technology.

In 1990, the IEEE started work to develop a standard for WLANs operating at 1 and 2 Mbps. Several proposals were recommended before a draft was developed. This draft, which went through seven different revisions, took seven years to complete. In 1997, the IEEE approved the final draft, known as IEEE 802.11.

Although bandwidth of 2 Mbps was acceptable in 1990 for wireless networks, by 1997 it was no longer sufficient for network applications. The IEEE body revisited the 802.11 standard shortly after it was released to determine what changes could be made to increase the speed. In 1999, a new IEEE 802.11b amendment was created, which added two higher speeds (5.5 Mbps and 11 Mbps) to the original 802.11 standard. At the same time, the IEEE also issued another standard with even higher speeds, IEEE 802.11a, with a top speed of 54 Mbps.

This set the stage for successive—and very successful—new versions of Wi-Fi over the next 25 years. There were three driving forces behind creating these new versions. First, new wireless technologies are being continually developed that are incorporated into the new versions. Second, government organizations that control the usage of the electromagnetic spectrum through which the RF waves travel continue to open new parts of the frequency spectrum for unlicensed technologies like Wi-Fi transmissions. (Wi-Fi operates in the gigahertz or GHz frequency.) These new areas of the spectrum are less crowded with competing signals and provide higher speeds. Third, there is an ongoing need for increased security to prevent threat actors from eavesdropping or manipulating wireless signals. The result has been that new versions have significant improvements over previous versions in terms of increased speed, coverage area, resistance to interference, and stronger security.

However, the IEEE has used a confusing "alphabet soup" of terms to describe these new versions, such as IEEE 802.11n, 802.11ax, 802.11g, and 802.11ac. These terms do not indicate which version is newer (802.11n is not a newer version than 802.11ax) and proved to be confusing. To reduce this confusion, the Wi-Fi Alliance, a global nonprofit association designed to promote Wi-Fi, in 2018 adopted "consumer-friendly" version numbers. Table 10-4 compares the different WLAN versions.

Note 13

The next version of Wi-Fi is Wi-Fi 7 (IEEE 802.11be). It will also be called EHT (extremely high throughput) and can transmit at data rates exceeding 46 Gbps, a fourfold increase over Wi-Fi 6E. It may be ratified in 2024.

WLAN Hardware

For all its functionality, the number of hardware elements needed to operate a WLAN is surprisingly small. Endpoints must have a wireless client network interface card (**wireless adapter**) that performs the same functions as a wired adapter, with one major exception: there is no external cable connection (RJ-45). In its place is an embedded antenna to send and receive wireless signals.

Table 10-4   WLAN versions

IEEE name	Wi-Fi Alliance version	Ratification date	Frequency utilized (GHz)	Maximum data rate
802.11	None	1997	2.4	2 Mbps
802.11b	Wi-Fi 1	1999	2.4	11 Mbps
802.11a	Wi-Fi 2	1999	5	54 Mbps
802.11g	Wi-Fi 3	2003	2.4	54 Mbps
802.11n	Wi-Fi 4	2009	2.4 and 5	600 Mbps
802.11ac	Wi-Fi 5	2014	5	7.2 Gbps
802.11ax	Wi-Fi 6	2019	2.4 and 5	9.6 Gbps
802.11ax	Wi-Fi 6E	2020	2.4, 5, and 6	9.6 Gbps

The second hardware device needed is a wireless **access point (AP)**, which is a centrally located WLAN connection device that can send and receive information. It primarily consists of an antenna and a radio transmitter/receiver, special bridging software to interface wireless devices to other devices, and a wired network interface that allows it to connect by cable to a standard wired network. A WLAN using an AP is operating in what is called infrastructure mode.

An AP has two basic functions. First, it acts as the "base station" for the wireless network. All wireless devices with a wireless adapter transmit to the AP, which in turn redirects the signal, if necessary, to other wireless devices. The second function of an AP is to act as a bridge between the wireless and wired networks. The AP is connected to the wired network by a cable, allowing all the wireless devices access through the AP to the wired network (and vice versa). A typical WLAN setup is shown in Figure 10-5.

Figure 10-5   Typical WLAN setup

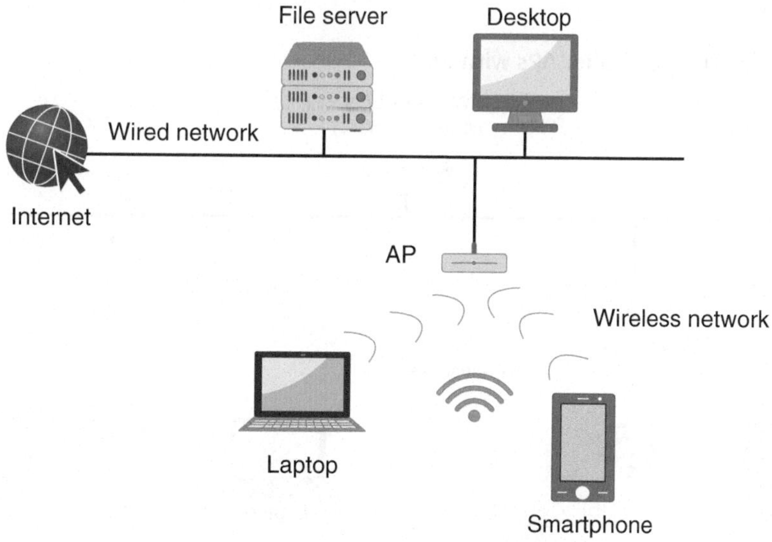

Note 14

A Wi-Fi network can also function without an AP so that the devices only communicate between themselves and cannot connect to another network. The IEEE calls this an Independent Basic Service Set (IBSS) or, more commonly, ad hoc mode. The Wi-Fi Alliance has created a similar technical specification called Wi-Fi Direct. However, this mode is rarely used.

For a small office or home, instead of using an enterprise-grade AP, another device is commonly used. This device combines multiple features into a single hardware device. These features often include those of an AP, firewall, router, and dynamic host configuration protocol (DHCP) server, along with other features. Strictly speaking, these devices are "residential WLAN gateways" as they serve as the entry point from the Internet into the wireless network. However, most vendors instead choose to label their products as simply **wireless routers**.

There are different types of enterprise APs. These include fat versus thin APs, controller versus stand-alone, and captive portal APs.

Fat versus Thin APs   Standard APs are autonomous, or independent, because they are separate from other network devices and even other autonomous APs. Autonomous APs have the intelligence required to manage wireless authentication, encryption, and other functions for the wireless client devices that they serve. Because everything is self-contained in these single devices, they are sometimes called "fat APs."

Although fat APs are functional for a small office setting in which there may be a handful of APs, what happens in a large enterprise or college campus where there can be hundreds or even thousands of APs? In this case, fat APs are not a viable option. Because each AP is autonomous, a single wireless network configuration change would require that each AP be reconfigured individually, which could take time and a large workforce to complete.

When multiple APs are widely deployed, a "thin AP" can be a better solution. These lightweight APs do not contain all the management and configuration functions found in fat APs. Much of the configuration is centralized in the wireless switch so that the network administrator can work directly with the switch from the wired network. This can also improve security because managing from a central location instead of visiting and configuring each fat AP reduces the risk of a security setting being overlooked.

Stand-alone versus Controller APs   Although thin APs can be managed from a switch, a further improvement can be made by managing from a device that is dedicated for configuring APs. Instead of installing stand-alone APs like fat or thin APs, **controller APs** can be managed through a dedicated wireless LAN controller (WLC). The WLC is the single device that can be configured and then these settings are automatically distributed to all controller APs (a remote office WLAN controller is used to manage multiple WLCs at remote sites from a central location). Controller APs with a WLC are shown in Figure 10-6.

Figure 10-6   Controller APs with WLC

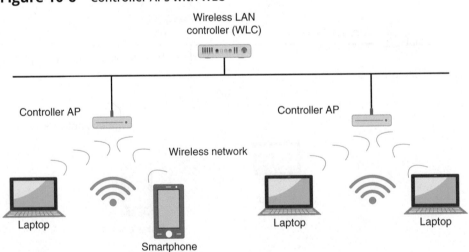

Note 15

Controller APs handle only the real-time medium access control (MAC) layer functionality within themselves; all other (non-real-time) MAC functionality is processed by the WLC. This type of division is referred to as a split MAC architecture.

Besides centralized management, controller APs provide other advantages over stand-alone APs. As wireless client devices move through a WLAN, a lengthy handoff procedure occurs during which one stand-alone AP transfers authentication information to another. Slow handoffs can be unacceptable on WLAN systems using time-dependent communication, such as voice or video. With controller APs, however, this handoff procedure is eliminated because all authentications are performed in the WLC. Another advantage of WLCs are the tools that many provide for monitoring the environment and providing information regarding the best locations for APs, wireless configuration settings, and power settings.

> **Caution** !
>
> There are disadvantages to controller APs. WLCs still do not provide true convergence (integration) of the wired and wireless networks but only ease some of the management burdens of WLANs. In addition, these devices are proprietary, which means all the thin APs and WLCs on a network must be from the same vendor to function cohesively.

Captive Portal APs   In a public area that is served by a WLAN, opening a web browser will rarely give immediate Internet access because the owner of the WLAN usually wants to advertise itself as providing this service, or wants the user to read and accept an acceptable use policy (AUP) before using the WLAN. Sometimes a "general" authentication, such as a password given to all current hotel guests, must be entered before being given access to the network. This type of information, approval, or authentication can be supported through a **captive portal AP**. A captive portal AP uses a standard web browser to provide information and gives the wireless user the opportunity to agree to a policy or present valid login credentials, providing a higher degree of security.

> **Caution** !
>
> When accessing a public WLAN, users should consider using a virtual private network (VPN) to encrypt all transmissions.

WLAN Enterprise Attacks

In a traditional wired network, a well-defined boundary or "hard edge" protects data and resources. There are two types of hard edges. The first is a network hard edge. A wired network typically has one point (or a limited number of points) through which data must pass from an external network to the secure internal network. This single data entry point makes it easier to defend the network because any attack must pass through this one point. Security appliances can be used to block attacks from entering the network. The combination of a single entry point plus security appliances that can defend it make up a network's hard edge, which protects important data and resources. This is illustrated in Figure 10-7.

The second hard edge is made up of the walls of the building that houses the enterprise. Because these walls keep out unauthorized personnel, attackers cannot access the network. In other words, the walls serve to physically separate computing resources from attackers.

The introduction of WLANs in enterprises, however, has changed these hard edges to "blurred edges." Instead of a network hard edge with a single data entry point, a WLAN can contain multiple entry points. As shown in Figure 10-8, the RF signals from APs create several data entry points into the network through which attackers can inject attacks or steal data. This makes it difficult to create a hard network edge. In addition, because RF signals extend beyond the boundaries of the building, the walls cannot be considered as a physical hard edge to keep away attackers. A threat actor sitting in a car well outside of the building's security perimeter can still easily pick up a wireless RF signal to eavesdrop on data transmissions or inject malware behind the firewall. An AP whose security settings have not been set or have been improperly configured can allow attackers access to the network.

Several different wireless attacks can be directed at the enterprise. These include rogue access points, evil twins, intercepting wireless data, and wireless denial attacks.

Rogue Access Point   Lejla is the manager of a recently opened retail storefront and wants to add wireless access in the employee break room. However, her employer's IT staff turns down her request for a wireless network.

Figure 10-7   Network hard edge

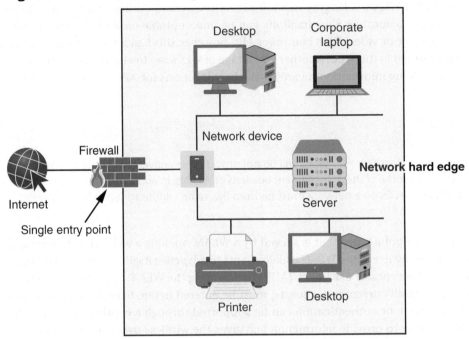

Figure 10-8   Network blurred edge

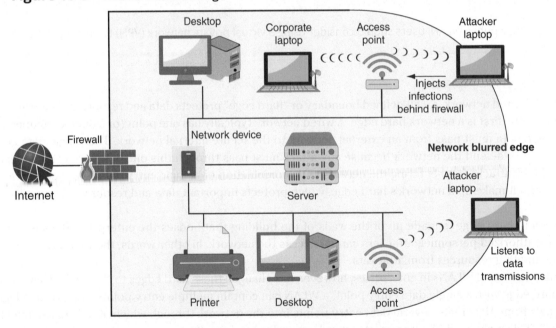

Lejla decides to take the matter into her own hands. She purchases an inexpensive wireless router, secretly brings it into the store, and connects it to the wired network, thus providing wireless access to her employees. Unfortunately, Lejla also has provided open access to an attacker sitting in their car in the parking lot, who picks up the wireless signal. This attacker can then circumvent the security protections of the company's network.

Lejla has installed a **rogue AP** (*rogue* means someone or something that is deceitful). A rogue AP is an unauthorized AP that allows an attacker to bypass many of the network security configurations and opens the network and its users to attacks. For example, although firewalls are typically used to restrict specific attacks from entering a network, an attacker who can access the network through a rogue AP is behind the firewall.

Note 16

Rogue APs do not even have to be separate network devices. The Microsoft Windows wireless Hosted Network function makes it possible to virtualize the physical wireless adapter into multiple virtual wireless adapters (virtual Wi-Fi) that can be accessed by a software-based wireless AP (SoftAP). This means that any computer can easily be turned into a rogue AP. However, smartphones using the mobile hotspot feature are not rogue devices since using this feature only transmits through the cellular network to the Internet and not through a Wi-Fi network like a corporate WLAN.

Evil Twin   Whereas a rogue AP is set up by an internal user, an evil twin is an AP that is set up by an attacker. This AP is designed to mimic an authorized AP, so a user's mobile device like a laptop or tablet will unknowingly connect to this evil twin instead. Attackers can then capture the transmissions from users to the evil twin AP.

Figure 10-9 illustrates rogue AP and evil twin attacks on an enterprise network, which further create a "blurred edge" to a corporate network.

Intercepting Wireless Data   One of the most common wireless attacks is intercepting and reading data that is being transmitted. An attacker can pick up the RF signal from an open or misconfigured AP and read any confidential wireless transmissions. To make matters worse, if the attacker manages to connect to the enterprise wired network through a rogue AP, they could also read broadcast and multicast wired network traffic that leaks from the wired network to the wireless network. Using a WLAN to read this data could yield significant information to an attacker regarding the wired enterprise network.

Wireless Denial Attacks   Attackers can attempt to deny a device access to the AP by performing a type of wireless denial attack. The three most common types of these attacks are jamming, a disassociation attack, and a duration field values attack.

Jamming   Because wireless devices operate using RF signals, there is the potential for signal interference. Although the wireless device itself may be the source of interference for other devices, attackers can leverage signals from other devices to disrupt valid wireless transmissions.

Note 17

Several types of devices transmit a radio signal that can cause incidental interference with a WLAN. These devices include microwave ovens, elevator motors, photocopying machines, and certain types of outdoor lighting systems, to name a few. These may cause errors or completely prevent transmission between a wireless device and an AP.

Attackers can use intentional RF interference to flood the RF spectrum with enough interference to prevent a device from effectively communicating with the AP. This attack prevents the transmission of data to or from network devices. In one type of wireless denial attack, an attacker can intentionally flood the RF spectrum with extraneous RF signal "noise" that creates interference and prevents communications from occurring, called jamming.

Note 18

Jamming attacks generally are rare because sophisticated and expensive equipment is necessary to flood the RF spectrum with enough interference to impact the network. In addition, because a very powerful transmitter must be used at a relatively close range to execute the attack, it is possible to identify the location of the transmitter and therefore identify the source of the attack.

Disassociation Attack   Another wireless denial attack takes advantage of an IEEE 802.11 design weakness. This weakness is the implicit trust of management frames that are transmitted across the wireless network, which include information such as the sender's source address. Because IEEE 802.11 requires no verification of the source device's identity (and so all management frames are sent in an unencrypted format), an attacker can easily craft a fictitious frame that pretends to come from a trusted client when it is in fact from a malicious attacker.

Figure 10-9   Rogue access point and evil twin attacks

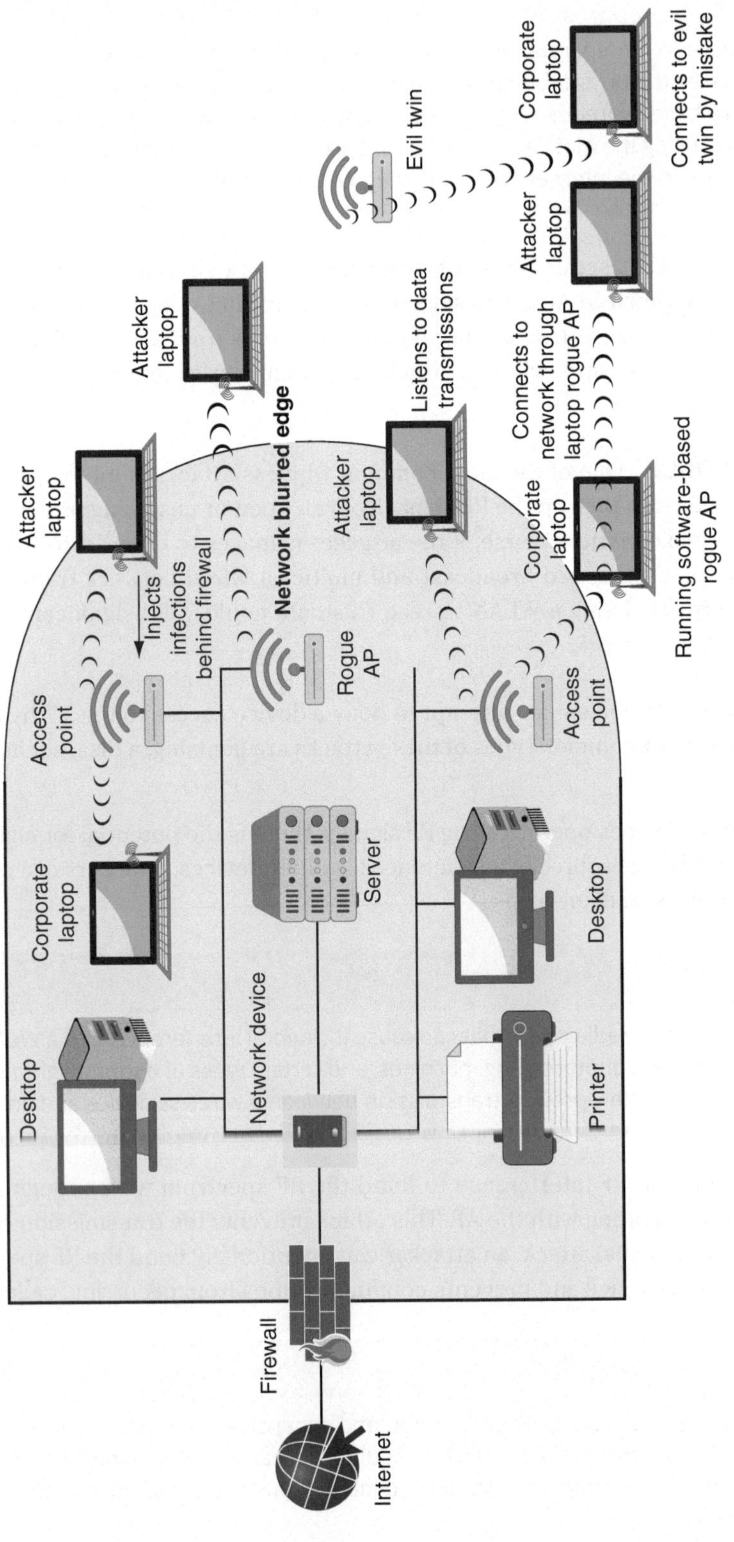

An attacker can "spoof" different types of frames to prevent a client from being able to remain connected to the WLAN. A client must be both authenticated and associated with an AP before being accepted into the wireless network and deauthenticated and disassociated when the client leaves the network. An attacker can create false deauthentication or disassociation management frames that appear to come from another client device, causing the client to disconnect from the AP (called a disassociation attack). Although the client device can send another authentication request to an AP, an attacker can continue to send spoofed frames to sever any reconnections.

Note 19

The amendment IEEE 802.11w was designed to protect against disassociation attacks. However, it only protects specific management frames instead of all management frames, requires updates to both the AP and the wireless clients, and might interfere with other security devices. For these reasons, it has not been widely implemented.

Duration Field Values Attack   A duration field values attack is another wireless attack designed to prevent access to a client. The 802.11 standard provides an option using the Request to Send/Clear to Send (RTS/CTS) protocol. An RTS frame is transmitted by a mobile device to an AP that contains a duration field indicating the length of time needed for both the transmission and the returning acknowledgment frame. The AP, as well as all stations that receive the RTS frame, are alerted that the medium will be reserved for a specific period. Each receiving station stores that information in its net allocation vector (NAV) field, and no station can transmit if the NAV contains a value other than zero. An attacker can send a frame with the duration field set to an arbitrarily high value (the maximum is 32,767), thus preventing other devices from transmitting for lengthy periods of time.

WLAN Consumer Attacks

Users face several risks from attacks on their home wireless networks. On an unsecured or improperly configured wireless router, attackers could:

- **Steal data.** On a computer in the home WLAN, an attacker could access any folder with file sharing enabled. This essentially provides an attacker full access to steal sensitive data from the computer.
- **Read wireless transmissions.** User names, passwords, credit card numbers, and other information sent over the WLAN could be captured by an attacker.
- **Inject malware.** Because attackers could access the network behind a firewall, they could inject viruses and other malware onto a computer.
- **Download harmful content.** In several instances, attackers have accessed a home computer through an unprotected WLAN and downloaded child pornography to the computer and then turned that computer into a file server to distribute the content. When authorities traced the files back to that computer, the unsuspecting owner had been arrested and their equipment confiscated.

Two Rights & A Wrong

1. Bluejacking is an attack that sends unsolicited messages to Bluetooth-enabled devices.
2. An RFID cloning attack involves replacing authentic RFID tags with fake tags.
3. A rogue AP is an unauthorized AP that allows an attacker to bypass many of the network security configurations.

See the answers at the end of the module.

Vulnerabilities of WLAN Security

Certification

2.2 Explain common threat vectors and attack surfaces.

From the outset of WLANs, it was recognized that wireless transmissions could be vulnerable to attackers. The IEEE implemented several wireless security protections within their standards while leaving other protections to be applied at the WLAN vendor's discretion. Several of these protections, though well intended, were vulnerable and led to attacks. These vulnerabilities can be divided into those based on Wired Equivalent Privacy (WEP), Wi-Fi Protected Setup (WPS), MAC address filtering, and Wi-Fi Protected Access (WPA).

Wired Equivalent Privacy (WEP)

Wired Equivalent Privacy (WEP) is an IEEE 802.11 security protocol designed to ensure that only authorized parties can view transmitted wireless information. WEP accomplishes this confidentiality by encrypting the transmissions. WEP relies on a shared secret key that is known only by the wireless client and the AP. The same secret key must be entered on the AP and on all devices before any transmissions can occur because it is used to encrypt any packets to be transmitted as well as decrypt packets that are received. IEEE 802.11 WEP shared secret keys must be a minimum of 64 bits in length. Most vendors add an option to use a longer 128-bit shared secret key for higher security.

The shared secret key is combined with an initialization vector (IV), which is a 24-bit value that changes each time a packet is encrypted. The IV and the key are combined and used as a seed for generating a random number necessary in the encryption process. The IV and encrypted ciphertext are both transmitted to the receiving device. Upon arrival, the receiving device first separates the IV from the encrypted text and then combines the IV with its own shared secret key to decrypt the data.

WEP has several security vulnerabilities. First, to encrypt packets, WEP can use only a 64-bit or 128-bit number, which is made up of a 24-bit IV and either a 40-bit or 104-bit default key. Even if a longer 128-bit number is used, the length of the IV remains at 24 bits. The relatively short length of the IV limits its strength since shorter keys are easier to break than longer keys.

Second, WEP implementation violates the cardinal rule of cryptography: anything that creates a detectable pattern must be avoided at all costs. This is because patterns provide an attacker with valuable information to break the encryption. The implementation of WEP creates a detectable pattern for attackers. Because IVs are 24-bit numbers, there are only 16,777,216 possible values. An AP transmitting at only 11 Mbps can send and receive 700 packets each second. If a different IV were used for each packet, then the IVs would start repeating in fewer than seven hours (a "busy" AP can produce duplicates in fewer than five hours). An attacker who captures packets for this length of time can see the duplication and use it to crack the code.

> ## Note 20
>
> Microsoft Windows 11 and updated versions of Windows 10 no longer support WEP and will not allow connections to occur between devices running these versions of Windows an AP. However, previous versions of Windows as well as current versions of Apple macOS still support WEP.

Wi-Fi Protected Setup (WPS)

Wi-Fi Protected Setup (WPS) is an optional means of configuring security on WLANs. It is designed to help users who have little or no knowledge of security to implement security quickly and easily on their WLANs.

There are two common WPS methods. The PIN method utilizes a Personal Identification Number (PIN) printed on a sticker of the wireless router or displayed through a software setup wizard. The user types the PIN into the wireless device (like a wireless tablet, laptop computer, or smartphone) and the security configuration automatically occurs. This is the mandatory model, and all devices certified for WPS must support it. The second method is the push-button method. The user pushes a button (usually an actual button on the wireless router and a virtual one displayed through a software setup wizard on the wireless device) and the security configuration takes place. Support for this model is mandatory for wireless routers and optional for connecting devices.

However, there are significant design and implementation flaws in WPS using the PIN method:

- There is no lockout limit for entering PINs, so an attacker can make an unlimited number of PIN attempts.
- The last PIN character is only a checksum.
- The wireless router reports the validity of the first and second halves of the PIN separately, so essentially an attacker must break only two short PIN values (a four-character PIN and a three-character PIN).

Due to the PIN being broken down into two shorter values, only 11,000 different PINs must be attempted before determining the correct value. If the attacker's computer can generate 1.3 PIN attempts per second (or 46 attempts per minute), the attacker can crack the PIN in less than four hours and become connected to the WLAN. This effectively defeats security restrictions that allow only authorized users to connect to the wireless network.

> **Caution** !
>
> Some wireless vendors are implementing additional security measures for WPS, such as limiting the number and frequency of PIN guesses. However, unless it can be verified that WPS supports these higher levels of security, it is recommended that WPS be disabled through the wireless router's configuration settings.

MAC Address Filtering

One means of protecting a WLAN is to control which devices are permitted to join the network. Wireless access control is intended to limit a user's admission to the AP: only those who are authorized can connect to the AP and thus become part of the wireless LAN.

The most common type of wireless access control is **Media Access Control (MAC) address filtering**. The MAC address is a hardware address that uniquely identifies each device on a network. The MAC address is a unique 48-bit number that is "burned" into the network interface card adapter when it is manufactured. The IEEE 802.11 standard permits controlling which devices can connect to the WLAN but does not specify how the control is to be implemented.

Since a wireless device can be identified by its MAC address, however, virtually all wireless AP vendors implement MAC address filtering as the means of access control. A wireless client device's MAC address is entered into software running on the AP, which is then used to permit or deny a device from connecting to the network. As shown in Figure 10-10, restrictions can be implemented by either listing a specific device to be allowed access into the network or listing a device to be blocked.

Figure 10-10   MAC address filtering

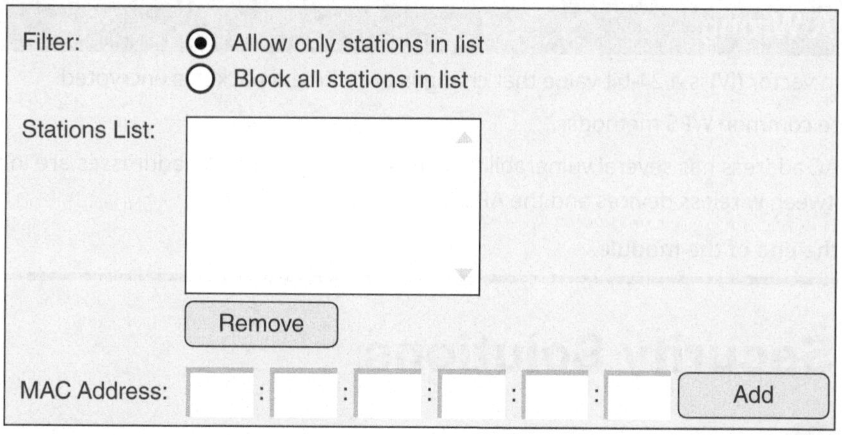

> **Note** 21
>
> MAC address filtering is usually implemented by permitting instead of preventing because it is not possible to know the MAC addresses of all the devices that are to be excluded.

Filtering by MAC address has several vulnerabilities. First, MAC addresses are initially exchanged between wireless devices and the AP in an unencrypted format. An attacker monitoring the airwaves could easily see the MAC address of an approved device and then substitute it on their own device. Another weakness of MAC address filtering is that managing several MAC addresses can pose significant challenges. The sheer number of users often makes it difficult to manage all the MAC addresses. As new users are added to the network and old users leave, keeping track of MAC address filtering demands almost constant attention. For this reason, MAC address filtering is not always practical in a large and dynamic wireless network.

Caution ❗

It is not uncommon to read of controlling access to the WLAN by hiding the *Service Set Identifier (SSID)* of the wireless network, which is the user-supplied network name of a wireless network and generally can be any alphanumeric string up to 32 characters. Although normally the SSID is broadcast so that any device can see it, the broadcast can be restricted so that only those users that know the "secret" SSID in advance would be allowed to access the network. However, the SSID can be easily discovered even when it is not contained in one type of transmitted frames (beacon frames) because it is transmitted in other management frames sent by the AP. Hiding SSID is not recommended as a security protection.

Wi-Fi Protected Access (WPA)

The Wi-Fi Alliance introduced **Wi-Fi Protected Access (WPA)** to fit into the existing WEP engine without requiring extensive hardware upgrades or replacements. There were two modes of WPA. WPA-Personal was designed for individuals or small office/home office (SOHO) settings, which typically have 10 or fewer employees. A more robust WPA-Enterprise was intended for larger enterprises, schools, and government agencies. WPA addresses both encryption and authentication.

A wireless network in which no authentication is required, such as at a local coffee shop, is using an open method. However, most WLANs need to restrict who can access the network through authentication. Authentication for WPA-Personal is accomplished by using a preshared key (PSK). In cryptography, a PSK is a value that has been previously shared using a secure communication channel between two parties. In a WLAN, a PSK is slightly different. It is a secret value that is manually entered on both the AP and each wireless device, making it essentially identical to the "shared secret" used in WEP. Because this secret key is not widely known, it can be assumed that only approved devices have the key value. Devices that have the secret key are then automatically authenticated by the AP. Although an improvement over previous WEP security technologies, WPA nevertheless has weaknesses and is not considered a secure option.

Two Rights & A Wrong

1. An initialization vector (IV) is a 24-bit value that changes each time a packet is encrypted.
2. There are three common WPS methods.
3. Filtering by MAC address has several vulnerabilities, most notably that MAC addresses are initially exchanged between wireless devices and the AP in an unencrypted format.

See the answers at the end of the module.

Wireless Security Solutions

Certification

4.1 Given a scenario, apply common security techniques to computing resources.

Despite the fact that there were vulnerabilities in some early wireless security protections, it is generally recognized that modern wireless security solutions are much more secure. Wi-Fi Protected Access 2 (WPA2) and Wi-Fi Protected Access 3 (WPA3) form the foundation of today's wireless security solutions. In addition, there are other wireless security protections.

Wi-Fi Protected Access 2 (WPA2)

Due to the shortcomings of WPA, a more robust wireless security standard was introduced by the IEEE, known as IEEE 802.11i. Shortly thereafter, the Wi-Fi Alliance introduced **Wi-Fi Protected Access 2 (WPA2)**, which is based on the final IEEE 802.11i standard and is almost identical to it. As with WPA, there are two modes of WPA2: WPA2-Personal for individuals or small offices and WPA2-Enterprise for larger enterprises, schools, and government agencies. WPA2 addresses the two major security areas of WLANs, namely, encryption and authentication.

AES-CCMP Encryption

The cryptographic wireless protocol (the standard used for wireless encryption) for WPA2 is the Counter Mode with Cipher Block Chaining Message Authentication Code Protocol (CCMP) and specifies the use of CCM (a general-purpose cipher mode algorithm providing data privacy) with AES. The Cipher Block Chaining Message Authentication Code (CBC-MAC) component of CCMP provides data integrity and authentication.

> ### Note 22
> CCM itself does not require that a specific block cipher be used, but the most secure cipher AES is mandated by the WPA2 standard. For this reason, CCMP for WLANs is sometimes designated as *AES-CCMP*.

IEEE 802.1x Authentication

Authentication for the WPA2-Enterprise model uses the IEEE 802.1x standard. This standard, originally developed for wired networks, provides a greater degree of security by implementing port-based authentication. IEEE 802.1x blocks all traffic on a port-by-port basis until the client is authenticated using credentials stored on an authentication server. This prevents an unauthenticated device from receiving any network traffic until its identity can be verified. It also strictly limits access to the device that provides the authentication to prevent attackers from reaching it. Figure 10-11 illustrates the steps in an 802.1x authentication procedure.

Figure 10-11   IEEE 802.1x process

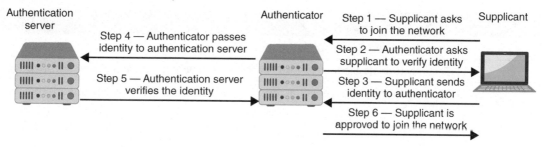

1. The device (called a **supplicant**) requests permission from the **authenticator** to join the network.
2. The authenticator asks the supplicant to verify its identity.
3. The supplicant sends identity information to the authenticator.
4. The authenticator passes the identity credentials on to an **authentication server**, whose only job is to verify the authentication of devices. The identity information is sent in an encrypted form.
5. The authentication server verifies or rejects the supplicant's identity and returns the information to the authenticator.
6. If approved, the supplicant can now join the network and transmit data.

> ### Note 23
> Although IEEE 802.1x is commonly used on wireless networks, it can be used for wired networks as well. For example, in a public conference room, an RJ-45 network connection may be accessible to both trusted employees and untrusted public users. IEEE 802.1x permits trusted employees to access both the secure internal corporate network and the Internet, while restricting public users to Internet access only from the same network connection.

It is important that the communication between the supplicant, authenticator, and authentication server in an IEEE 802.1x configuration be secure. The authentication wireless protocols (standards for confirming the identity of the user or system) for wireless networks is known as the Extensible Authentication Protocol (EAP). Despite "protocol" in its name, EAP is actually a framework for transporting authentication protocols instead of the authentication protocol itself. EAP essentially defines the format of the messages and uses four types of packets: *request*, *response*, *success*, and *failure*. Request packets are issued by the authenticator and ask for a response packet from the supplicant. Any number of request–response exchanges may be used to complete the authentication. If the authentication is successful, a success packet is sent to the supplicant; if not, a failure packet is sent.

Note 24

An EAP packet contains a field that indicates the function of the packet (such as response or request) and an identifier field used to match requests and responses. Response and request packets also have a field that indicates the type of data being transported (such as an authentication protocol) along with the data itself.

A common EAP protocol is Protected EAP (PEAP). PEAP is designed to simplify the deployment of 802.1x by using Microsoft Windows logins and passwords. PEAP is considered a more flexible EAP scheme because it creates an encrypted channel between the client and the authentication server, and the channel then protects the subsequent user authentication exchange. To create this channel, the PEAP client first authenticates the PEAP authentication server using enhanced authentication.

There are several EAP protocols supported in WPA2-Enterprise; the most common are listed in Table 10-5.

Table 10-5 Common EAP protocols supported by WPA2-Enterprise

EAP name	Description
EAP-TLS	Uses digital certificates for authentication
EAP-TTLS	Securely tunnels client password authentication within Transport Layer Security (TLS) records
EAP-FAST	Securely tunnels any credential form for authentication (such as a password or a token) using TLS

Note 25

There are over 40 EAP methods.

Wi-Fi Protected Access 3 (WPA3)

The next generation of Wi-Fi Protected Access (WPA) is known as **WPA3**. The goal of WPA3 is to deliver a suite of features to simplify security configuration for users while enhancing network security protections.

Caution !

WPA3, as well as WPA2, is officially neither a standard nor a protocol. WPA3 is a hardware certification program that specifies what existing standards a product must support in order to be labeled as "Wi-Fi CERTIFIED WPA3." This means that the device will be interoperable with other similar devices that have also obtained the WPA3 certified label.

Like WPA2, WPA3 has different modes: WPA3-Enterprise and WPA3-Personal. WPA3 also supports an optional mode with higher levels of security, known as WPA3-Enterprise 192-bit mode. There are several security improvements that are part of WPA3:

- WPA3 includes **Simultaneous Authentication of Equals (SAE)**. SAE is designed to increase security at the time of the handshake when keys are being exchanged. The result is that WPA3 can give stronger security even if short or weak passwords are used.
- Protected Management Frames (PMFs) mitigate against disassociation attacks.
- WPA3 has improved interaction capabilities with IoT devices. The older WPA2 was primarily designed to work with traditional mobile devices that had screens (like smartphones and laptops) in which the user could enter a password and configure the wireless settings. However, most IoT devices have no screens. WPA3 contains new ways to configure security for these types of devices.
- When using an open or public Wi-Fi network in airports and coffee shops, WPA3 will apply individualized data encryption so that every connection between a client and an AP/wireless router will be encrypted with a unique key. Known as **Opportunistic Wireless Encryption (OWE)**, this can mitigate against man-in-the-middle (MITM) attacks and is an optional WPA3 enhancement.
- **Wi-Fi Easy Connect** supersedes WPS by scanning a QR code or NFC tag to connect devices. This is likewise optional for WPA3.

Additional Wireless Security Protections

Other security steps can be taken to protect a wireless network. These include installation, configuration, and rogue AP system detection.

Installation

Most users, when installing a wireless LAN in a home or apartment, generally do not give much thought to determining the optimum location for the wireless router so that its RF signal coverage is uniform throughout the house but extends outside it as little as possible. Instead, these devices are typically placed wherever it is convenient, such as next to the Internet connection, near a desktop computer, or even tucked away on a bookcase that happens to have enough space to accommodate it. If the wireless signal does not reach into the far corners of the house or outside onto an outdoors deck, then those areas are simply recognized as being "dead space" and are just avoided when using the network.

However, when installing a WLAN for an organization, areas of dead space cannot be so easily tolerated. Whereas at home a user may simply move to another room for better reception, that may not always be possible in a building with multiple offices, locked doors, and private cubicles. This means important considerations must be taken into account when installing a new WLAN for an organization: all areas of a building should have adequate wireless coverage, all employees must have a reasonable amount of bandwidth, and, for security reasons, a minimum amount of wireless signal should "bleed" outside the walls of the building.

Ensuring that a WLAN can provide its intended functionality and meet its required design goals can best be achieved through a site survey. A site survey is an in-depth examination and analysis of a WLAN site. A site survey mainly addresses placing the AP in the optimum location.

There are several tools that can be used in a site survey for installation:

- **Heat maps.** A Wi-Fi heat map is a visual representation of the wireless signal coverage and strength. Wi-Fi heat maps are generally overlaid on top of a building or facility floorplan to help give a clear indication of where problem areas are located in relation to the collected site survey data. Figure 10-12 illustrates a heat map.
- **Wi-Fi analyzers.** A **Wi-Fi analyzer** tool helps to visualize the essential details of the wireless network. An analyzer can provide information such as signal strength, network health, channel bandwidth, channel coverage, data rate, and interference (noise).

Figure 10-12   Wi-Fi heat map

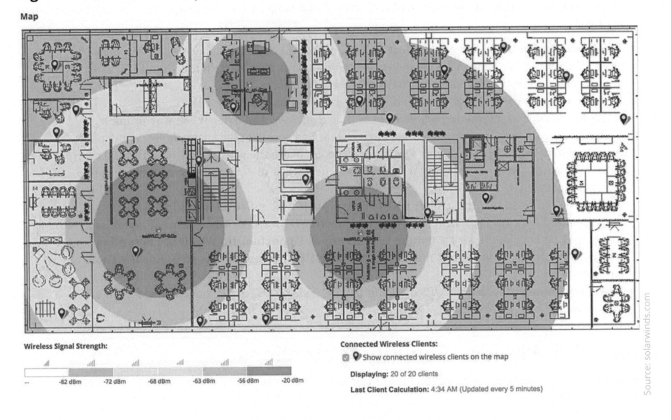

Wireless Signal Strength:

-82 dBm   -72 dBm   -68 dBm   -63 dBm   -56 dBm   -20 dBm

Connected Wireless Clients:

☑ 📍 Show connected wireless clients on the map

Displaying: 20 of 20 clients

Last Client Calculation: 4:34 AM (Updated every 5 minutes)

- **Channel overlays.** It is not uncommon for multiple APs attempting to utilize the same frequency (channel) that then causes interference. Software that illustrates these **channel overlays** can help visualize conflicting overlaps. Channel overlay software is seen in Figure 10-13.

Figure 10-13   Channel overlay software

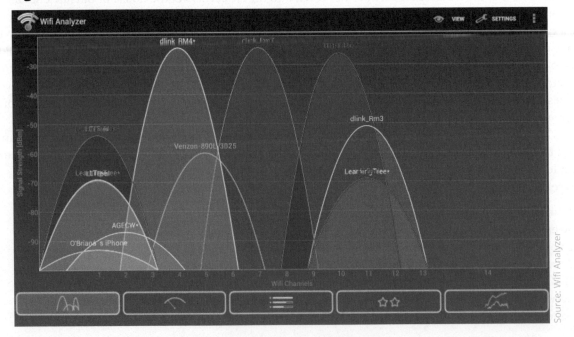

Note 26

Although the placement of a wireless router in a home or apartment may not have as many options as an office, there are some principles to keep in mind that can improve Wi-Fi service. If possible, place the wireless router in a central location so the wireless signal does not have to penetrate more than two rooms and two interior walls. Also, the higher the wireless router can be placed above the heads of people, the better; one human body can impact the signal about the same as one interior wall.

Configuration

Selecting the proper configuration options for the AP can also enhance security. Some of these settings are designed to limit the spread of the wireless RF signal so that a minimum amount of signal extends past the physical boundaries of the enterprise to be accessible to outsiders. AP configuration and device options include setting the signal strength and choosing the correct RF spectrum options. One device option is to select the best type of antenna and to correctly locate it.

Signal Strength Settings   A security feature on some APs is the ability to adjust the level of power at which the WLAN transmits. On devices with that feature, the power can be adjusted so that less of the signal leaves the premises and reaches outsiders. For IEEE WLANs, the maximum transmit power is 200 milliwatts (mW). APs that can adjust the power level usually permit the level to be adjusted in predefined increments, such as 1, 5, 20, 30, 40, 100, or 200 mW.

Spectrum Selection   Some APs provide the ability to adjust frequency spectrum settings. These include:

- **Frequency band.** An increasing number of APs support dual bands of spectrum. If one band is not being used, it should be disabled. If both bands are to be used, it is recommended that both be set to the same configuration settings.
- **Channel selection.** Some APs have an *Auto* mode in which the AP selects the optimum channel within the frequency band. On those devices in which this mode is not supported, it is important to choose a channel that is different from that of other nearby APs or sources of interference.
- **Channel width.** Channel width controls how much of the spectrum is available to transfer data. However, larger channels are more subject to interference and are more likely to interfere with other devices.

Antenna Placement and Type   APs use antennas that radiate out a signal in all directions. Because these devices are generally positioned to provide the broadest area of coverage, APs should be located near the middle of the coverage area. Generally, the AP can be secured to the ceiling or high on a wall. It is recommended that APs be mounted as high as possible for two reasons: (1) there may be fewer obstructions for the RF signal and (2) to prevent thieves from stealing the device.

For security purposes, the AP and its antenna should be positioned so that, when possible, a minimal amount of signal reaches beyond the security perimeter of the building or campus. Another option is to use a type of antenna that will focus its signal in a more concentrated direction toward authorized users instead of broadcasting it over a wide area.

Rogue AP System Detection

As the cost of consumer wireless routers has fallen, the problem of rogue APs has risen. Identifying these devices in an enterprise is known as rogue AP system detection. Several methods can be used to detect a rogue AP by continuously monitoring the RF airspace. This requires a special sensor called a wireless probe, a device that can monitor the airwaves for traffic. There are four types of wireless probes:

- **Wireless device probe.** A standard wireless device, such as a portable laptop computer, can be configured to act as a wireless probe. At regular intervals during the normal course of operation, the device can scan and record wireless signals within its range and report this information to a centralized database. This scanning is performed when the device is idle and not receiving any transmissions. When several mobile devices are used as wireless device probes, it can provide a high degree of accuracy in identifying rogue access points.

- **Desktop probe.** Instead of using a mobile wireless device as a probe, a desktop probe utilizes a standard desktop PC. A universal serial bus (USB) wireless adapter is plugged into the desktop computer to monitor the RF in the area for transmissions.
- **Access point probe.** Some AP vendors have included in their APs the functionality of detecting neighboring APs, friendly as well as rogue. However, this approach is not widely used. The range for a single AP to recognize other APs is limited because they are typically located so that their signals overlap only in such a way as to provide roaming to wireless users.
- **Dedicated probe.** A dedicated probe is designed to exclusively monitor the RF for transmissions. Unlike access point probes that serve as both an AP and a probe, dedicated probes only monitor the airwaves. Dedicated probes look much like standard access points.

Once a suspicious wireless signal is detected by a wireless probe, the information is sent to a centralized database where WLAN management system software compares it to a list of approved APs. Any device not on the list is considered a rogue AP. The WLAN management system can instruct the switch to disable the port to which the rogue AP is connected, thus severing its connection to the wired network.

Two Rights & A Wrong

1. There are three modes of WPA2: WPA2-Professional, WPA2-Enterprise, and WPA2 192-bit mode.
2. The encryption protocol used for WPA2 is the Counter Mode with Cipher Block Chaining Message Authentication Code Protocol (CCMP) and specifies the use of CCM (a general-purpose cipher mode algorithm providing data privacy) with AES.
3. EAP-TLS uses digital certificates for authentication.

See the answers at the end of the module.

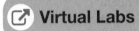 **Virtual Labs** You're now ready to complete the simulations and live virtual machine labs for this module. The labs can be found in each module in MindTap.

Summary

- There are different wireless technologies behind connecting devices to wireless networks. The most widespread wireless networks are cellular networks that are operated by telecommunication service providers and smaller regional and local carriers. Because the telecommunication service providers own, maintain, and manage their own network equipment and facilities, end-users are not responsible for configuring or securing these cellular networks. Bluetooth is a wireless technology that uses short-range RF transmissions. It enables users to connect wirelessly to a wide range of computing and telecommunications devices by providing

rapid "on-the-fly" connections between Bluetooth-enabled devices. The primary type of Bluetooth network topology is a piconet. Two of the common attacks on wireless Bluetooth technology are bluejacking, which is sending unsolicited messages, and bluesnarfing, or accessing unauthorized information from a wireless device through a Bluetooth connection.

- Near field communication (NFC) is a set of standards that can be used to establish communication between devices in close proximity. Once the devices are either tapped together or brought very close to each other, a two-way communication is established. NFC devices are increasingly used in contactless payment systems so that a consumer can pay for a purchase by simply tapping a store's payment terminal with their smartphone. There are risks with using NFC contactless payment systems because of the nature of this technology.

- A wireless technology similar to NFC is radio frequency identification (RFID). RFID is commonly used to transmit information between paper-based tags that can be detected by a proximity reader. Because RFID tags do not require a power supply, they can be very small and thinner than a sheet of paper. RFID tags are susceptible to some types of attacks.

- A wireless local area network (WLAN), commonly called Wi-Fi, is designed to replace or supplement a wired LAN. The IEEE has developed standards for WLANs and these have evolved through the years in terms of speed, coverage area, increased resistance to interference, and stronger security. An enterprise WLAN requires a wireless adapter and an AP for communications, whereas a home network uses a wireless router instead of an AP.

- There are different types of enterprise APs. A thin AP is a lightweight device that does not contain all the management and configuration functions found in fat APs. Much of the configuration is centralized in the wireless switch. Instead of installing stand-alone APs like fat or thin APs, controller APs can be managed through a dedicated wireless LAN controller (WLC). The WLC is the single device that can be configured and then these settings are automatically distributed to all controller APs. A captive portal AP uses a standard web browser to provide information and give the wireless user the opportunity to agree to a policy or present valid login credentials, providing a higher degree of security.

- In a traditional wired network, the security of the network itself along with the walls and doors of the secured building protect the data and resources. Because an RF signal can easily extend past the protective perimeter of a building and because an AP can provide unauthorized entry points into the network, WLANs are frequently the target of attackers. A rogue AP is an unauthorized AP that allows an attacker to bypass network security and opens the network and its users to attacks. An evil twin is an AP that is set up by an attacker to mimic an authorized AP and capture the transmissions from users. One of the most common wireless attacks is intercepting and reading data that is being transmitted. In addition, if the attacker manages to connect to the enterprise wired network through a rogue AP, they could also read broadcast and multicast wired network traffic. Attackers can attempt to deny a device access to the AP by performing a type of wireless denial attack. The three most common types of these attacks are jamming, a disassociation attack, and a duration field value attack. Consumer wireless networks that are not protected are subject to attackers stealing data, reading transmissions, or injecting malware behind the firewall.

- WLANs have always been recognized as attack vectors and the IEEE has implemented several wireless security protections. Despite their intended design, several of these protections were vulnerable to attacks. Wired Equivalent Privacy (WEP) was designed to ensure that only authorized parties can view transmitted wireless information by encrypting transmissions. WEP relies on a secret key that is shared between the wireless client device and the AP that is combined with an initialization vector (IV). However, WEP has several security vulnerabilities. Wi-Fi Protected Setup (WPS) is an optional means of configuring security on WLANs and is designed to help users who have little or no knowledge of security to implement security quickly and easily on their WLANs. However, there are significant design and implementation flaws in WPS.

- One method of controlling access to the WLAN so that only approved users can be accepted is to limit a device's access to the AP. Virtually all wireless AP vendors offer Media Access Control (MAC) address filtering. Filtering by MAC address, however, has several vulnerabilities. Wi-Fi Protected Access (WPA) was designed to fit into the existing WEP engine without requiring extensive hardware upgrades or replacements. Security vulnerabilities can be found in WPA.

- Wi-Fi Protected Access 2 (WPA2) is the second generation of WPA security. Encryption under WPA2 is accomplished by using AES-CCMP. The Cipher Block Chaining Message Authentication Code (CBC-MAC) component of CCMP provides data integrity and authentication. WPA2 authentication is accomplished by the IEEE

802.1x standard. Because it is important that the communication between the supplicant, authenticator, and authentication server in an IEEE 802.1x configuration be secure, a framework for transporting the authentication protocols is known as the Extensible Authentication Protocol (EAP). EAP is a framework for transporting authentication protocols by defining the format of the messages.

- The next generation of Wi-Fi Protected Access (WPA) is known as WPA3. The goal of WPA3 is to deliver a suite of features to simplify security configuration for users while enhancing network security protections. WPA3 also supports an optional mode with higher levels of security known as WPA3-Enterprise 192-bit mode. There are several security improvements that are part of WPA3.

- Other steps can be taken to protect a wireless network. Important considerations must be taken into account when installing a new WLAN for an organization: all areas of a building should have adequate wireless coverage, all employees must have a reasonable amount of bandwidth,

and, for security reasons, a minimum amount of wireless signal should "bleed" outside the walls of the building. Ensuring that a WLAN can provide its intended functionality and meet its required design goals can best be achieved through a site survey. A site survey is an in-depth examination and analysis of a WLAN site. A site survey mainly addresses placing the AP in the optimum location.

- Selecting the proper configuration options for the AP can also enhance security. Some of these settings are designed to limit the spread of the wireless RF signal so that a minimum amount of signal extends past the physical boundaries of the enterprise to be accessible to outsiders. AP configuration and device options include setting the signal strength and choosing the correct RF spectrum options. One device option is to select the best type of antenna and to correctly locate it.

- The problem of rogue Aps is of increasing concern to organizations. Several methods can be used to detect a rogue AP by continuously monitoring the RF airspace. This requires a special sensor called a wireless probe, a device that can monitor the airwaves for traffic.

Key Terms

bluejacking
bluesnarfing
Bluetooth
Cipher Block Chaining Message
    Authentication Code (CBC-MAC)
Counter Mode with Cipher
    Block Chaining Message
    Authentication Code Protocol
    (CCMP)

disassociation attack
duration field values attack
EAP-FAST
EAP-TLS
EAP-TTLS
evil twin
Extensible Authentication Protocol
    (EAP)
heat map

jamming
Protected EAP (PEAP)
radio frequency identification
    (RFID)
RFID cloning
rogue AP
site survey
wireless local area network (WLAN)

Review Questions

1. Simiso has been asked to research a new payment system for the retail stores that her company owns. Which technology is predominantly used for contactless payment systems that she will investigate?

   a. Bluetooth
   b. Near field communication (NFC)
   c. Wi-Fi
   d. Radio Frequency ID (RFID)

2. Muchaneta is investigating a security incident in which the smartphone of the CEO was compromised and confidential data was stolen. She suspects that it was an attack that used Bluetooth. Which attack would this be?

   a. Blueswiping
   b. Bluehiking
   c. Bluejacking
   d. Bluesnarfing

3. What is a difference between NFC and RFID?

   a. NFC is based on wireless technology while RFID is not.
   b. RFID is faster than NFC.
   c. NFC requires the sender to be very close to the receiver.
   d. NFC devices cannot pair as quickly as RFID devices.

4. Which of the following attacks transfers the data from one RFID tag to another?

   a. RFID swiping
   b. RFID cloning
   c. RFID duplicating
   d. RFID mirroring

5. Thubelihle has just been informed that an employee has tried to install their own wireless router in the employee lounge. Why is installing this rogue AP an issue?

   a. It uses the weaker IEEE 80211i protocol.
   b. It allows an attacker to bypass network security configurations.
   c. It conflicts with other network firewalls and can cause them to become disabled.
   d. It requires the use of vulnerable wireless probes on all mobile devices.

6. Zendaya is helping her neighbor install and configure a new wireless router. Her neighbor is reluctant to configure the settings on the device but just wants to accept the default settings. Which of these is NOT a reason Zendaya would give regarding the risks of an improperly configured wireless router?

   a. An attacker can steal data from any folder with file sharing enabled.
   b. Wireless devices could be susceptible to an INKSPOT attack.
   c. User names, passwords, credit card numbers, and other information sent over the WLAN could be captured by an attacker.
   d. Malware can be injected into a computer connected to the WLAN.

7. Which of these WPS methods is vulnerable?

   a. Push-button
   b. PIN
   c. NXC
   d. Click-to-send

8. Zuri is on vacation and visits a local coffee shop to enjoy a beverage and check her email through the free Wi-Fi. When she first connects, a screen appears asking her to agree to an acceptable use policy (AUP) before continuing. What type of AP portal has she encountered?

   a. Rogue portal
   b. Approval portal
   c. Limited portal
   d. Captive portal

9. Which of the following is NOT a wireless denial attack that attempts to prevent a user from accessing or using a WLAN?

   a. RTS/CTS replay attack
   b. Duration field values attack
   c. Disassociation attack
   d. Jamming

10. Nia is writing an email to an employee about a wireless attack that is designed to capture wireless transmissions from legitimate users. Which type of attack is she describing?

    a. NFC capture attack
    b. Evil twin attack
    c. WPA grab attack
    d. Sleeper attack

11. Which of these is a vulnerability of MAC address filtering in a WLAN?

    a. Not all operating systems support MACs.
    b. APs use IP addresses instead of MACs.
    c. The user must enter the MAC.
    d. MAC addresses are initially exchanged unencrypted.

12. Which of the following is NOT true about cellular networks?

    a. Using a cellular network requires extensive security configurations on the part of the user.
    b. Cellular networks are operated by telecommunication service providers.
    c. The telecommunication service providers of cellular networks own, maintain, and manage their own network equipment and facilities.
    d. The most widespread wireless networks are cellular networks.

13. Which of the following is NOT true about WLAN versions?

    a. New versions of WLANs have appeared regularly.
    b. Updated versions have resulted in increased speed, coverage area, and resistance to interference and stronger security.
    c. WLAN standards are set by the IEEE.
    d. WLAN-IEEE 8ax is the final version to be released.

14. Which of these is the encryption protocol for WPA2?

    a. IEEE 802.1x
    b. CCMP
    c. XAP
    d. CBC-MAC

15. Which mode provides the highest level of security?

    a. WEP mode
    b. WPA2-Enterprise mode
    c. WPA4-X mode
    d. WPA3-Enterprise 192-bit mode

16. Nala needs to purchase WLCs for the office. What type of AP must she also purchase that can be managed by a WLC?

    a. Stand-alone AP
    b. Controller AP
    c. Fat AP
    d. Any type of AP can be managed by a WLC.

17. Which WPA3 security feature is designed to increase security at the time of the handshake?

    a. WEP
    b. SAE
    c. OWE
    d. PXF

18. Hadiza is explaining the EAP to a new hire. What would be the best explanation of EAP?

    a. It is the transport protocol used in TCP/IP for authentication.
    b. It is a framework for transporting authentication protocols.
    c. It is a subset of WPA2.
    d. It is a technology used by IEEE 802.11 for encryption.

19. Makena has been asked to recommend an EAP for a system that uses both passwords and tokens with TLS. Which should she recommend?

    a. EAP-SSL
    b. EAP-TLS
    c. EAP-TTLS
    d. EAP-FAST

20. Which of these is a WPA3 technology that mitigates against association attacks?

    a. OWE
    b. SAE
    c. XR3
    d. PMF

Hands-On Projects

Caution !

If you are concerned about installing any of the software in these projects on your regular computer, you can instead use the Windows Sandbox created in the Module 1 Hands-On Projects. Software installed within the sandbox will not impact the computer.

Project 10-1: Using a Wireless Monitor Tool

Estimated Time: 30 minutes

Objective: Explore the features of a wireless monitor.

Description: Most Wi-Fi users are surprised to see just how far their wireless signal will reach and, if the network is unprotected, this makes it easy for an attacker hiding several hundred feet away to break into the network. There are several tools available that will show the different wireless signals from Wi-Fi networks that can be detected. In this project, you download and install the NirSoft WifiInfoView tool. You will need a computer with a wireless adapter, such as a laptop, to complete this project.

1. Use your web browser to go to **www.nirsoft.net/utils/wifi_information_view.html**. (If you are no longer able to access the site through the web address, use a search engine to search for "NirSoft WifiInfoView.")

2. Scroll down and click **Download WifiInfoView**. Choose 32-bit or 64-bit depending on your operating system.

3. Download the tool and, when finished, extract the files and then launch the program.

4. Wait until WifiInfoView displays all Wi-Fi networks that it detects.

5. Scan through all the information that is displayed. Does the amount of available information from Wi-Fi networks to which you are not connected surprise you?

6. Scroll back to the first column of information.

7. Under **SSID**, is there a service set identifier for each network? Why would an SSID not appear? Does disabling the broadcast of the SSID name give any enhanced level of security? Why not?

8. Note the value under the column **MAC Address**. How could a threat actor use this information?

9. Under **RSSI**, the signal strength is displayed (lower numbers indicate a stronger signal).

10. The **Frequency** column displays the frequency on which the network is transmitting, and the **Channel** column gives the corresponding channel. Click **Channel** to sort the channels. Is there any channel overlap? How could this be a problem?

11. Double-click the Wi-Fi network to which you are currently connected. A window of the available information that is being transmitted through the Wi-Fi is displayed. This is the information that anyone can see regarding your Wi-Fi network. Close this window.

12. Now select a network other than the one to which you are connected and double-click it to display information. After reading the information, close the window.

13. Scroll to the **Security** and **Cipher** columns. What security are the networks using?

14. Scroll to **WPS Support**. How many networks have WPS turned on? Is this secure?

15. What additional information do you find useful? What information would a threat actor find useful?

16. Close all windows.

Project 10-2: Viewing WLAN Security Information with Vistumbler

Estimated Time: 35 minutes

Objective: Observe the type of security information that is beaconed out from WLANs.

Description: Vistumbler can be used to display the security information that is beaconed out from WLANs. Note that Vistumbler does not allow you to "crack" any WLANs but instead only displays information. In this project, you use Vistumbler to view this information. This project works best when you are in an area in which you can pick up multiple WLAN signals.

1. Use your web browser to go to **www.vistumbler.net**. (The location of content on the Internet may change without warning. If you are no longer able to access the program through this URL, use a search engine and search for "Vistumbler.")

2. Click **EXE Installer** or **(Mirror)**.

3. Follow the prompts to download and install Vistumbler using the default settings.

4. If the program does not start after the installation is complete, launch Vistumbler.

Caution !

Some antivirus (AV) software may indicate that Vistumbler is a virus. It might be necessary to temporarily turn off your AV software for this project. Be sure to turn AV back on when the project is completed.

5. If necessary, expand the window to full screen.

6. Click **Scan Aps**. If no networks appear, click **Interface** and then select the appropriate wireless NIC interface.

7. Note the columns **Signal** and **High Signal**. How could they be used in a site survey?

8. Click **Graph 1**.

9. Click one of the Aps displayed at the bottom of the screen. Allow Vistumbler to accumulate data over several minutes. What information is displayed on this graph?

10. Click **Graph 2**.

11. Click another one of the Aps displayed at the bottom of the screen. Allow Vistumbler to accumulate data over several minutes. What information is displayed on this graph? How is this different from the previous graph?

12. Click **No Graph** to return to the previous screen.

13. Use the horizontal scroll bar to move to the right. Note the columns **Authentication**, **Encryption**, **Manufacturer**, and **Radio Type**. How would this information be useful to an attacker?

14. Use the horizontal scroll bar to move back to the far left.

15. In the left pane, expand the information under **Authentication**. What types are listed?

16. Expand the information under these types and note the information given for the wireless LAN signals.

17. In the left pane, expand the information under **Encryption**. What types are listed? Which types are most secure? Which types are least secure?

18. Expand the information under these types and note the information given for each WLAN.

19. Record the total number of different WLANs that you can detect, along with the number of encryption types. Which type is most common?

20. One of the features of Vistumbler is its ability to use audio and text-to-speech information so that the location and strength of WLANs can be detected without the need to constantly monitor the screen. Be sure that the speakers on the laptop computer are turned on.

21. Click **Options**.

22. Click **Speak Signals**. Vistumbler will "speak" the percentage of signal strength.

23. Now carry the laptop away from the AP and note the changes. How would this be helpful to an attacker?

24. Close Vistumbler.

25. Close all windows and do not save any data. If necessary, restart your AV software.

26. How does Vistumbler compare with WifiInfoView? Which is easier to use? Which tool gives more information?

Project 10-3: Configuring a Wireless Router

Estimated Time: 35 minutes

Objective: Explore the features of a wireless router.

Description: The ability to properly configure a wireless router is an important skill for end-users. In this project, you use an online emulator from TRENDnet to configure a wireless router.

1. Use your web browser to go to **https://www.trendnet.com/emulators/TEW-827DRU_v2.0R/basic_status.html**. (The location of content on the Internet may change without warning; if you are no longer able to access the program through this URL, use a search engine and search for "Trendnet Emulators.")

2. An emulated Setup screen is displayed, showing what a user would see when configuring an actual TRENDnet.

3. Be sure that the **BASIC** tab is selected in the left pane. Note the simulated **Network Status** information.

4. Click **Wireless** in the left pane and read the information displayed.

5. Under **Broadcast Network Name (SSID)**, note the two options. What would **Disable** do? Why is this not considered a strong security step (consider Step 7 of Hands-On Project 10-2)?

6. Under **Security**, note the default setting for **Security Mode**. Is this a good default option?

7. Under **Security**, use the pull-down menu to display the options for **Security Mode**. What does **WPA2-PSK** mean? What are the other options?

8. Under **WPA**, the **Pre-Shared Key** is the value that would be entered on this wireless router and on each of the wireless devices on the network. Click **Show Password** and then enter a strong key value.

9. In the left pane, click **Guest Network**. Read the information about a guest network. A guest network allows you to have an additional open network just for occasional guests that does not affect the main wireless network. How could this be an advantage?

10. Note the option under **Internet Access Only**. When would you select this option?

11. Note the option under **WLAN Partition**. Why is this not enabled by default?

12. Under **Security**, note that an option under **Security Mode** is **Disable**. Why would a guest network's security be turned off by default? (*Hint:* If it were turned on, what would the guests need before they could use the network?)

13. In the left pane, click **ADVANCED**.

14. Click **Security**.

15. Under **Access Control**, what is the **Enable Access Control** setting? Does it provide strong security if it were enabled?

16. Click **Setup**.

17. Click **Upload Firmware** and read through the information. When would you use this option?

18. How easy is this user interface to navigate? Does it provide enough information for a user to set up the security settings on this system?

19. Close all windows.

Project 10-4: Using Microsoft Windows Netsh Commands

Estimated time: 30 minutes
Objective: Use the Windows netsh feature.
Description: Microsoft Windows displays the network status of a device that is connected to a network, either a wired network or a Wi-Fi network. However, configuring different connection parameters is largely unavailable to users through the main interface. The Windows Network Shell (*netsh*) can be used to configure and display advanced network settings. Netsh is a command-line interface (CLI) that requires commands to be typed instead of selected from a menu. This gives netsh extended flexibility. In this project, you explore some of the *netsh* commands.

Note 27

For this project, you will need a computer running Microsoft Windows that has a wireless adapter and can access a Wi-Fi network.

1. In Microsoft Windows, right-click the **Start** button.

2. Select **Terminal (Admin)**. This will open the Windows command window in elevated privilege mode.

3. Type **netsh** and then press **Enter**. The command prompt will change to *netsh>*.

4. Type **wlan** (an abbreviation for *wireless local area network*) and then press **Enter**. The command prompt will change to *netsh wlan>*.

5. Type **show drivers** and then press **Enter** to display the wireless adapter information. It may be necessary to scroll back toward the top to see all the information.

6. Under **Radio types supported**, the different types of Wi-Fi networks to which this computer can connect are displayed. What is the maximum data rate of the highest level of radio type?

> **Note 28**
>
> The "radio types supported" are listed by their IEEE nomenclature. Refer to Table 10-4 for a listing of these and the corresponding Wi-Fi Alliance versions.

7. Under **Authentication and cipher supported in infrastructure mode**, which Wi-Fi Protected Access Personal is supported, WPA2 Personal or WPA3 Personal? Why is this version supported?

8. Next, view the WLAN interfaces for this computer. Type **show interfaces** and then press **Enter**. Record the SSID value and the name of the Profile.

9. Display all the available Wi-Fi networks to this computer. Type **show networks** and then press **Enter**.

10. Windows creates a profile for each network to which you connect. To display those profiles, type **show profiles** and then press **Enter**. If there is a profile of a network that you no longer use, type **delete profile name=**_profile-name_.

11. Now disconnect from your current WLAN by typing **disconnect** and then press **Enter**. Note the message you receive and observe the status in your system tray.

12. Reconnect to your network by typing **connect name=**_profile-name_ **ssid=**_ssid-name_ as previously recorded and then press **Enter**.

13. Netsh allows you to block specific networks. Select another network name that you currently are not connected to. Type **show networks**, press **Enter**, and then record the SSID of that network you want to block.

14. Type **add filter permission = block ssid=**_ssid-name_ **networktype = infrastructure** and then press **Enter**.

15. Type **show networks** and then press **Enter**. Does the network that you previously blocked appear in the list?

16. Now display the blocked network (but do not allow access to it). Type **set blockednetworks display=show** and then press **Enter**.

17. Type **show networks** and then press **Enter**. Does the network that you previously blocked appear in the list?

18. Click the wireless icon in your system tray. Does the network appear in this list?

19. Click the wireless icon in your system tray again. What appears next to the name of this blocked network?

20. Now re-enable access to the blocked network by typing **delete filter permission = block ssid=**_ssid-name_ **networktype = infrastructure** and then press **Enter**.

21. Netsh can also generate a detailed Wi-Fi network report. This report shows all the Wi-Fi events from the last three days and groups them by Wi-Fi connection sessions. It also shows the results of several network-related command-line scripts and a list of all the wireless adapters. Type **show wlanreport** and then press **Enter**.

22. Record the location to which the report was written.

23. Open a web browser and type the location of the report. For example, if the location is _C:\ProgramData\Microsoft\Windows\WlanReport\wlan-report-latest.html_, then enter into the web browser **file:/// C:\ProgramData\Microsoft\Windows\WlanReport\wlan-report-latest.html**.

24. Scan through the report for the information. Note that the first paragraph displayed allows you to hover over a session or click it. How could this information be helpful?

25. Type **Exit** and then press **Enter**.

26. Type **Exit** again and then press **Enter** to close the command window.

Case Projects

Case Project 10-1: #TrendingCyber

Estimated Time: 15 minutes

Objective: Summarize your thoughts on the #TrendingCyber opener.

Description: Read again the opening #TrendingCyber in this module. Should all manufacturers of hardware be required to have a facility like Intel's Long-Term Retention Lab? Or should there be a single universal lab that contains products across all vendors? Should a tax be added to the sale of all products to support such a lab? What would be the advantages and disadvantages? Write a one-paragraph summary of your thoughts.

Case Project 10-2: Comparisons of Contactless Payment Systems

Estimated Time: 20 minutes

Objective: Research the strengths and weaknesses of contactless payment systems.

Description: Three of the most popular contactless payment systems are Apple Pay, Google Pay, and Samsung Pay. Each of these has advantages and disadvantages. Using the Internet, research these three different systems. Create a table that lists each of the systems, features, strengths and weaknesses, ease of use, security, etc. Which of them would you recommend? In your opinion, what can be done to make these more popular? Write a one-paragraph summary to accompany your table.

Case Project 10-3: Bluetooth Range Estimator

Estimated Time: 20 minutes

Objective: Explore the different interferences that can occur using Bluetooth.

Description: The range at which a Bluetooth device can transmit depends on several different factors. It is good to understand the ranges in order to be aware of whether a Bluetooth-enabled device could be the victim of a bluejacking or bluesnarfing attack. Go to **www.bluetooth.com/learn-about-bluetooth/bluetooth-technology/range/** to explore the Bluetooth Range Estimator tool. First, watch the video and then read the details of each of the key factors. Then use the range estimator tool, changing the different parameters (receiver sensitivity, path loss, transmit power, transmitter antenna gain, and receiver antenna gain) to determine the estimated range. What does this tell you about Bluetooth ranges? How could this tool be used? Write a one-page paper on what you have learned

Case Project 10-4: EAP

Estimated Time: 20 minutes

Objective: Compare and contrast EAP solutions.

Description: Use the Internet to research information on the different EAP protocols (see Table 10-5). Write a brief description of each and indicate the relative strength of its security. Write a one-page paper on your research.

Case Project 10-5: WPA3 Features

Estimated Time: 25 minutes

Objective: Research WPA3.

Description: Use the Internet to research these WPA3 features: SAE, PMF, and OWE. What prior weaknesses in WPA security do each of these address? What are the primary advantages and disadvantages of each of these features? How do they enhance Wi-Fi security? Write a one-page paper on your research.

Case Project 10-6: Antennas

Estimated Time: 25 minutes

Objective: Gain a broader understanding of antennas.

Description: To many users, antennas are just one of life's great mysteries. They know from experience that any antenna is better than having no antenna, and that the higher the antenna is located, the better the reception will be. Yet the antenna is arguably one of the most important parts of a wireless network. Antennas play a vital role in both sending and receiving signals, and a properly positioned and functioning antenna can make all the difference between a WLAN operating at peak efficiency or a network that nobody can use. Use the Internet to research antennas for APs. What different types of antennas are used? What are their strengths? What are their weaknesses? Which types would be used to concentrate a signal to a more confined area? Write a one-page paper on what you find.

Case Project 10-7: Your Personal Wireless Security

Estimated Time: 25 minutes

Objective: Explore wireless security.

Description: Is the wireless network you own as secure as it should be? Examine your wireless network or that of a friend or neighbor and determine which security model it uses. Next, outline the steps it would take to move it to the next highest level. Estimate how much it would cost and how much time it would take to increase the level. Finally, estimate how long it would take you to replace all the data on your computer if an attacker corrupted it, and what you might lose. Would this be motivation to increase your current wireless security model? Write a one-page paper on your work.

Case Project 10-8: Wallet RFID Blocking Technology

Estimated Time: 20 minutes

Objective: Determine the security of RFID blocking technology.

Description: Some wallets are advertised as providing "RFID Blocking Technology." Research the blocking features in wallets that claim to have this protection. How does it work? What level of protection does it provide? Would you recommend it to your friends? Write a one-page paper on your research.

Case Project 10-9: WPA3-Enterprise 192-Bit Mode

Estimated Time: 20 minutes

Objective: Determine the security strength of WPA3-Enterprise 192-bit mode.

Description: Like WPA2, WPA3 has different modes, known as WPA3-Enterprise and WPA3-Personal. WPA3 also supports an optional mode with higher levels of security known as WPA3-Enterprise 192-bit mode. Research this mode. What are its additional features? How does it provide enhanced security for authentication, authentication encryption, key derivation, and management frame protection (MFP)? Who is using this stronger security mode? In what settings would you recommend it? Why? Write a one-page paper on your research.

Case Project 10-10: Wi-Fi 7

Estimated Time: 20 minutes

Objective: Research the new features of Wi-Fi 7.

Description: The next version of Wi-Fi will be IEEE 802.11be, also called Wi-Fi 7 and EHT (extremely high throughput). It will transmit at data rates exceeding 46 Gbps. It may be ratified in 2024. Research Wi-Fi 7. What are its proposed new features? What coverage area will it encompass? What are its requirements for hardware and software? What new security features will it have? Write a one-page paper on your research.

Case Project 10-11: Blocking WEP

Estimated Time: 20 minutes
Objective: Determine if WEP should be blocked by all operating systems.
Description: WEP has several security vulnerabilities and is considered dated. Microsoft Windows 11 and updated versions of Windows 10 no longer support WEP and will not allow connections to occur between devices and an AP. However, previous versions of Windows as well as current versions of Apple macOS still support WEP. Why does Apple choose not to block it? Due to its vulnerabilities, should all operating systems block WEP? What would be the advantages? What would be the disadvantages? Write a one-page paper about blocking WEP.

Case Project 10-12: Piggybacking on Home Wi-Fi

Estimated Time: 20 minutes
Objective: Assess the risks of piggybacking on home Wi-Fi.
Description: Comcast is a nationwide ISP offering its Xfinity product to consumers. The device from Comcast that consumers use to connect to the Internet also includes a Wi-Fi wireless gateway. However, this gateway broadcasts two Wi-Fi signals: one for the consumer and a second network signal that any Xfinity Internet customer can use without the customer's permission by simply signing on. This means that any Xfinity customer can use another customer's Wi-Fi service without first receiving approval. There is no means to disable this free service. How do you feel about Xfinity offering this service without the customer's express approval for others to access this second Wi-Fi signal? Would you want strangers accessing your Wi-Fi service without your knowledge or approval? What are the advantages? What are the risks?

Case Project 10-13: Bay Point Ridge Security

Estimated Time: 45 minutes
Objective: Research wireless security.
Description: Bay Point Ridge Security (BPRS) is a managed service provider (MSP) that manages networks, computers, cloud resources, and information security for small-to-medium enterprises (SMEs) in the region. BPRS provides internships to students who are in their final year of the security degree program at the local college and has recently hired you.

You have been asked to evaluate the wireless security of a new client and you find that it is not secure. You are now asked to make a presentation about wireless attacks and their options for security.

1. Create a PowerPoint presentation for the staff about the threats against WLANs and the weaknesses of Wi-Fi. Also include information about the more secure WPA2 and WPA3. Your presentation should contain at least 10–12 slides.

2. After the presentation, the client is trying to decide if they should install a captive portal for their customer WLAN. Create a memo to their management outlining the advantages and disadvantages, along with your recommendation.

Two Rights & A Wrong: Answers

Wireless Attacks

1. Bluejacking is an attack that sends unsolicited messages to Bluetooth-enabled devices.
2. An RFID cloning attack involves replacing authentic RFID tags with fake tags.
3. A rogue AP is an unauthorized AP that allows an attacker to bypass many of the network security configurations.

Answer: The wrong statement is #2.

Explanation: RFID cloning captures data transmitted via RFID and transfers it to another tag.

Vulnerabilities of WLAN Security

1. An initialization vector (IV) is a 24-bit value that changes each time a packet is encrypted.

2. There are three common WPS methods.

3. Filtering by MAC address has several vulnerabilities, most notably that MAC addresses are initially exchanged between wireless devices and the AP in an unencrypted format.

Answer: The wrong statement is #2.

Explanation: WPS has two methods: the PIN method and the push-button method.

Wireless Security Solutions

1. There are three modes of WPA2: WPA2-Professional, WPA2-Enterprise, and WPA2 192-bit mode.

2. The encryption protocol used for WPA2 is the Counter Mode with Cipher Block Chaining Message Authentication Code Protocol (CCMP) and specifies the use of CCM (a general-purpose cipher mode algorithm providing data privacy) with AES.

3. EAP-TLS uses digital certificates for authentication.

Answer: The wrong statement is #1.

Explanation: WPA3, not WPA2, has three modes.

Reference

1. The economic value of Wi-Fi: A global view (2021-2025)," *Wi-Fi Alliance*, Sep. 2021, accessed Mar. 28, 2023, https://www.wi-fi.org/download.php?file=/sites/default/files/private/The_Economic_Value_of_Wi-Fi-A_Global_View_2021-2025_202109.pdf.

Cloud and Virtualization Security

Module Objectives

After completing this module, you should be able to do the following:

1   List and describe the different types of clouds and their locations, architectures, and models

2   Describe cloud security controls

3   Explain virtualization security

#TrendingCyber

In 2003, Amazon was growing fast—very fast. In fact, its growth was so rapid that its information technology (IT) infrastructure could not keep up: by the time new servers and network appliances were ordered and installed, there was already a need for more equipment. Amazon recognized that staying ahead of its IT needs was critical but could not be accomplished just by buying more equipment. There had to be a better way for Amazon's infrastructure to efficiently scale up.

Amazon started exploring a radical idea: what if the software applications were decoupled from the local hardware infrastructure? That flexibility would allow for hardware to be used much more efficiently instead of "on-prem" servers sitting mostly idle just waiting for someone to launch the installed applications. Thus, the seeds of modern cloud computing were born.

But Amazon also realized that if there was value for them doing it, there could also be value to other businesses, too. (There is a persistent rumor that Amazon, after starting its internal cloud service, suddenly saw that they had excess capacity and then decided to sell it to others; Amazon says this is untrue, but they had planned from the outset to offer cloud services to others.) With the blessing of its CEO, Amazon launched its cloud computing infrastructure, known as Amazon Web Services (AWS), in 2006. Due to its popularity, Microsoft and Google soon followed with their own cloud services two years later.

Since then, cloud computing has taken the IT world by storm, with organizations scaling down or even abandoning their own data centers and using cloud services. Consider the ride-sharing app company Uber Technologies. Since its 2009 founding, Uber had resisted moving to the cloud and instead had primarily relied on its own server hardware. As its peers in the technology sector embraced cloud computing, Uber resisted the move and became an anomaly. But a tipping point came during the COVID-19 pandemic, when supply chain disruptions forced Uber to wait as long as one year to receive delivery of new hardware. This forced Uber to rethink the cloud.

In 2022, Uber decided to go all-in with cloud computing. It struck two seven-year cloud deals with two different cloud providers so they could move away from their own data centers (where 95 percent of its IT was housed) to a completely cloud-centric model. This will allow Uber to not only cut internal IT costs but also shift its engineers from managing data centers to more cutting-edge technology like artificial intelligence.

However, not everyone is enamored with cloud computing. Governments are now starting to raise alarms over the cloud.

In early 2023, the U.S. Treasury Department sounded warnings about potential risks caused by financial institutions relying on a small number of providers for cloud computing services. The Treasury said that these institutions, including banks, are increasing their use of cloud computing services but from only a small number of cloud providers. The department warned that a technical issue or a cyberattack on one of these cloud providers could impact all the banks that used that provider and immediately ripple down to consumers who could not access their money (although they also said that "there are open questions about the extent of that impact"). The Treasury is forming a task force to study the concentration in cloud computing services by financial institutions, with the possibility of eventually recommending new regulations to manage potential risks.

Around this same time, Ofcom, the United Kingdom's communications regulating body, said it was "particularly concerned" by the practices of AWS and Microsoft, which together control between 60 and 70 percent of the U.K. cloud market. If unchecked, according to Ofcom, the concentration of cloud computing supply in the hands of a few large U.S. companies could lead to British customers paying more for cloud services while smaller cloud providers could be squeezed out of the market. They have called for a probe into Microsoft and Amazon's dominance of the country's cloud computing market.

The European Union (EU) has taken it one step farther. In late 2023, a regulation called the Digital Operational Resilience Act (DORA) for the EU financial services sector was passed. It is designed to ensure that all participants in the financial system will have the necessary safeguards in place to mitigate cyberattacks and other risks. It also introduces an oversight framework for critical third-party providers like cloud service providers. While banks and other financial firms already have plans for IT security, more was needed so they stay resilient through a severe disruption, according to the EU. Regulators also expressed concern about the speed and scale at which banks, insurers, and investment firms are moving critical functions and market operations onto a handful of cloud platforms.

An "outsized influence" is something that has an unusually large, exaggerated, or extravagant impact. Since the first microcomputer appeared 50 years ago, there have been several devices and services that have had an outsized influence on technology. In addition to ever faster and more capable central processing units (CPUs), the list of devices and services include double data rate synchronous dynamic random access memory (DDR SDRAM), hard drives (HDDs) and solid-state drives (SSDs), local area networks (LANs), and even the lowly mouse.

Two services have had an outsized influence on enterprise-level IT over the last 20 years. The first is cloud computing, which is a completely different way of providing computing and network resources and paying for those resources. The second is virtualization, in which hardware is simulated by software.

In this final module on infrastructures, you explore cloud computing and virtualization. You will examine what both of these technologies are, how they function, and how they can be secured.

Introduction to Cloud Computing

Certification

3.1 Compare and contrast security implications of different architecture models.

Understanding cloud computing involves knowing what cloud computing is; the different types of clouds; cloud locations, architectures, and models; and how it is managed. It also involves knowing cloud-native microservices.

What Is Cloud Computing?

Forty years ago, as computing technology became widespread, enterprises employed an architectural model of computing in which servers and networking equipment were installed locally on an organization's campus. This required that the company purchase, install, and manage all the necessary hardware and software. As more resources were needed, more purchases were made and more personnel were hired to manage the technology.

This model resulted in several challenges for organizations. First, there were spiraling costs; as the organization grew, so did the need for purchasing ever more hardware and software and hiring more personnel. Also, due to constraints, most organizations could never reach the optimum level of IT that was needed. Supply chain issues prevented equipment from being delivered promptly and a lack of qualified personnel would "crimp" the IT department so that it could not provide the needed levels of technology and support that were demanded. And what happened when more hardware and personnel were needed for just a short period of time, such as around the holidays when consumers were making voluminous purchases—but once the holidays passed, the additional capacity was no longer needed until the next holiday season?

Because of these challenges, some enterprises turned to hosted services. In a hosted services environment, servers, storage, and the supporting networking infrastructure are shared by multiple enterprises over a remote network connection that had been contracted for a specific period. As more resources are needed (such as additional storage space or computing power), the enterprise contacts the hosted service and negotiates an additional fee as well as signs a new contract for those new services.

Today an entirely new approach for computing has gained widespread use. This approach is known as cloud computing. Although various definitions of cloud computing have been proposed, the definition from the National Institute of Standards and Technology (NIST) may be the most comprehensive: "Cloud computing is a model for enabling convenient, on-demand network access to a shared pool of configurable computing resources (e.g., networks, servers, storage, applications, and services) that can be rapidly provisioned and released with minimal management effort or service provider interaction."[1] In some ways, cloud computing is similar to hosted services but at a different scale. It supports multiple tenants online while providing rapid and even automatic scalability and elasticity. Entities that offer cloud computing are called **cloud service providers**.

Cloud computing is a much more flexible approach to computing resources. Cloud computing allows an almost endless array of servers, software, and network appliances to be quickly and easily configured as needed. And it is a pay-per-use computing model in which customers pay only for the online computing resources they need. As computing needs increase or decrease, cloud computing resources can be quickly scaled up or scaled back. Because cloud resources are available online, users from virtually anywhere around the world can access them by opening a web browser without the need for installing additional software. Cloud computing is illustrated in Figure 11-1, and Table 11-1 lists different advantages of cloud computing.

Figure 11-1   Cloud computing

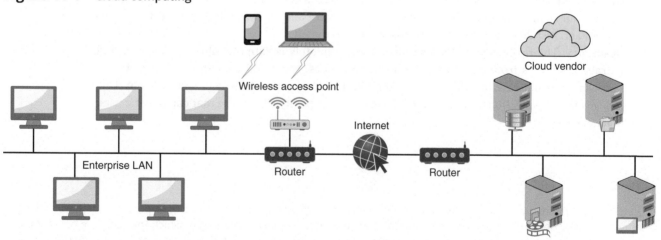

Table 11-1 Cloud computing advantages

Characteristic	Explanation
On-demand self-service	The consumer can make changes, such as increasing or decreasing computing resources, without requiring any human interaction from the service provider.
Universal client support	Virtually any networked device (desktop, laptop, smartphone, tablet, etc.) can access cloud computing resources.
Invisible resource pooling	The physical and virtual computing resources are pooled together to serve multiple, simultaneous consumers that are dynamically assigned or reassigned based on the consumers' needs; the customer has little or no control or knowledge of the physical location of the resources.
Immediate elasticity	Computing resources can be increased or decreased quickly to meet demands.
Metered services	Fees are based on the computing resources used.

Note 1

According to a recent survey, the top five reasons organizations gave for using the cloud were expanding existing and building new products and services, increasing efficiency and ability, creating new processes and workflow, mitigating business and regulatory risk, and expanding into new markets.[2]

One of the attractive features of cloud computing is cost savings. The savings available through cloud computing are due to these factors:

- **Elasticity and scalability.** Cloud computing gives organizations the ability to expand and reduce resources according to the specific service requirements. Users can create an ongoing infrastructure or provision any number of resources only for a specific task. For example, an e-commerce site may provision multiple servers to accommodate a large number of orders during the holiday season, and then drop those resources after the holidays when they are no longer needed.
- **Pay-per-use.** Organizations pay for cloud services when they are used, either for the short term (for computing power for one day or several months) or for a longer duration (for using cloud-based storage).
- **On demand.** Because cloud services are only activated when needed, they are not permanent parts of an IT infrastructure. This means that hardware and software do not need to be purchased and installed and IT staffing needs are also reduced.
- **Resiliency.** The resiliency of cloud services can completely isolate the failure of a server and storage resources from cloud users. If an issue occurs, the cloud provider will migrate the hardware and software to a different resource in the cloud without the user's knowledge. This relieves the organization from needing to have excess capacity sitting idle that can only be used in an emergency.

Note 2

Cloud computing involves shifting the bulk of the costs from *capital expenditures* (CapEx), or purchasing and installing servers, storage, networking, and related infrastructure, to *operating expenses* (OpEx), in which the costs are only for the usage of these resources. In some ways this is similar to the savings with using a ride-hailing service like Uber or Lyft to pay for transportation only when needed instead of purchasing, maintaining, and insuring a car.

Types of Clouds

There are different types of clouds. A **public cloud** is one in which the services and infrastructure are offered to all users with access provided remotely through the Internet. Unlike a public cloud that is open to anyone, a **community cloud** is a cloud that is open only to specific organizations that have common concerns. For example, because of the strict data requirements of the Health Insurance Portability and Accountability Act of 1996 (HIPAA), a community cloud open only to hospitals may be used. A **private cloud** is created and maintained on a private network. Although this type offers the highest level of security and control (because the company must purchase and maintain all the software and hardware), it also reduces cost savings. A **hybrid cloud** is a combination of public and private clouds.

Cloud Locations

The introduction of cloud computing has redefined the location of computing resources. Instead of using a centralized model in which equipment and personnel are located locally at the organization's campus, computing now takes place in several different locations (a decentralized model). These are listed in Table 11-2 and illustrated in Figure 11-2.

Table 11-2   Computing locations

Location	Description	Example
On-premises	Computing resources located on the campus of the organization ("on-prem")	Desktop computer, local area network, data center
Off-premises	A computing resource hosted and supported by a third party	Remote backup facility
Fog	A decentralized computing infrastructure in which data, compute capabilities, storage, and applications are located between the data source and the cloud	Automated guided vehicles on an industrial shop floor
Edge	Computing that is performed at or very near to the source of data instead of relying on the cloud or on-prem for processing	Internet of Things device
Cloud	A remote facility for computing	Artificial intelligence processing engine

Figure 11-2   Computing locations

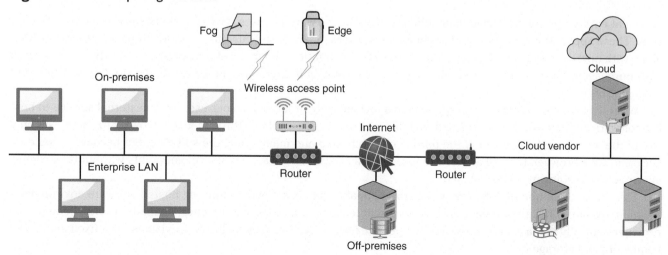

Cloud Architecture

Many elements make up cloud architecture. A sampling of these elements include:

- **Thin client.** A thin client is a computer that runs from resources stored on a central cloud server instead of a localized hard drive. Thin clients connect remotely to the cloud computing environment where applications and data are stored and where the processing takes place.
- **Transit gateway.** A transit gateway is an AWS technology that allows organizations to connect all existing virtual private clouds (VPCs), physical data centers, remote offices, and remote gateways into a single managed source. The transit gateway gives full control over all the resources, including network routing and security, VPCs, shared services, and other resources that may even span multiple AWS accounts. Transit gateways can consolidate edge connectivity and route it through a single cloud entry point.

Note 3

A transit gateway is considered a "hub-and-spoke" network topology that enables the user to monitor all activity.

- **Serverless infrastructure.** The term "serverless" is a misnomer. While there are servers (somewhere) performing a critical function, a serverless infrastructure is one in which the capacity planning, installation, setup, and management are all invisible to the user because the cloud provider handles them. Because the server resources of the cloud are inconspicuous to the end-user, this type of infrastructure is called serverless.

Note 4

Serverless essentially means that provisioning, deploying, and managing a physical server disappears from a list of concerns.

Cloud Models

There are several service models in cloud computing. These are Software as a Service, Platform as a Service, Infrastructure as a Service, and Anything as a Service.

Software as a Service (SaaS)

A typical enterprise must manage many different sets of software licenses for the various software applications it uses. These applications typically include human resources, finance, and customer relationship management (CRM), along with operating systems (OSs), productivity software, utilities, and many others. Significant costs are associated with purchasing these desktop or service licenses, installing and upgrading the software, distributing patches, and managing them.

What if as an alternative the enterprise paid a low monthly or annual fee per user for an external service to host the software on their own hardware? And what if it was then made available through a web browser to users? Not only would the enterprise be relieved of the burden of purchasing and maintaining the software, but because it could be accessed via a browser, then all authorized users could access it from any number of endpoints without the need for any specialized software to be installed.

This is the definition of **Software as a Service (SaaS)**. SaaS is a cloud computing hosted software environment. It eliminates any software purchase, installation, maintenance, upgrades, and patches; instead, the cloud computing provider centrally manages the software on a per-user basis. SaaS usually includes provisions for a fixed amount of bandwidth and storage.

Note 5

SaaS offers commercial and well-known software to users without any technical intervention from the IT staff. The software is offered as a complete *service* to users.

Platform as a Service (PaaS)

Platform as a Service (PaaS) provides a software platform on which the enterprise or users can build their own applications and then host them on the PaaS provider's infrastructure. The software platform can be used as a development framework to build and debug the app and then deploy it.

Note 6

PaaS can also provide "middleware" services like database and component services for use by the applications.

Unlike SaaS in which everything is transparent to the enterprise, PaaS provides a moderate degree of control for the enterprise over the cloud computing environment. However, the enterprise does not always need to monitor usage and manually add resources; rather, the cloud provider can guarantee elasticity and scalability.

Caution !

Not all applications developed for a traditional enterprise network may seamlessly migrate to PaaS. Often the most success is from new applications that are developed specifically on and for the cloud.

Infrastructure as a Service (IaaS)

Infrastructure as a Service (IaaS) provides unlimited "raw" computing, storage, and network resources that the enterprise can use to build their own virtual infrastructure in the cloud. The number of CPU processors and their speed, the amount of memory, the volume of storage, and the desired virtual networking resources like routers and switches can all be arranged to create the necessary virtual infrastructure. Enterprises can then load their own OSs (or "rent" them from the cloud provider) and software, web services, and database applications. Scaling and elasticity are not always automatically provided as with PaaS but, instead, are the enterprises' responsibility to monitor and request additional services.

How much of an enterprise's network architecture should be migrated to the cloud—and how much should remain on-prem? A traditional three-tier on-prem architecture is illustrated in Figure 11-3 (note that for simplicity no security appliances are illustrated). This multi-tiered design helps control connections, provide scaling, and increase security. An enterprise could migrate *Tier 1—Web servers* and *Tier 2—Application servers* to a cloud computing provider but keep *Tier 3—Database servers* on-prem for security. However, it could just as easily migrate all three tiers to the cloud computing provider. Such a decision will need to be based on several different factors.

Another question with IaaS involves using Layer 2 (switching) or Layer 3 (routing) when connecting to the virtual cloud network. Whereas Layer 2 is the simpler mode, in which the Ethernet MAC address and Virtual LAN (VLAN) information is used for forwarding, the disadvantage of Layer 2 networks is scalability. Using Layer 2 addressing and connectivity can result in a "flat" topology, which is unrealistic when there are a large number of endpoints. Instead, using routing and subnets to provide segmentation for the appropriate functions provides greater flexibility but at the cost of forwarding performance and network complexity.

Figure 11-3   Three-tier architecture

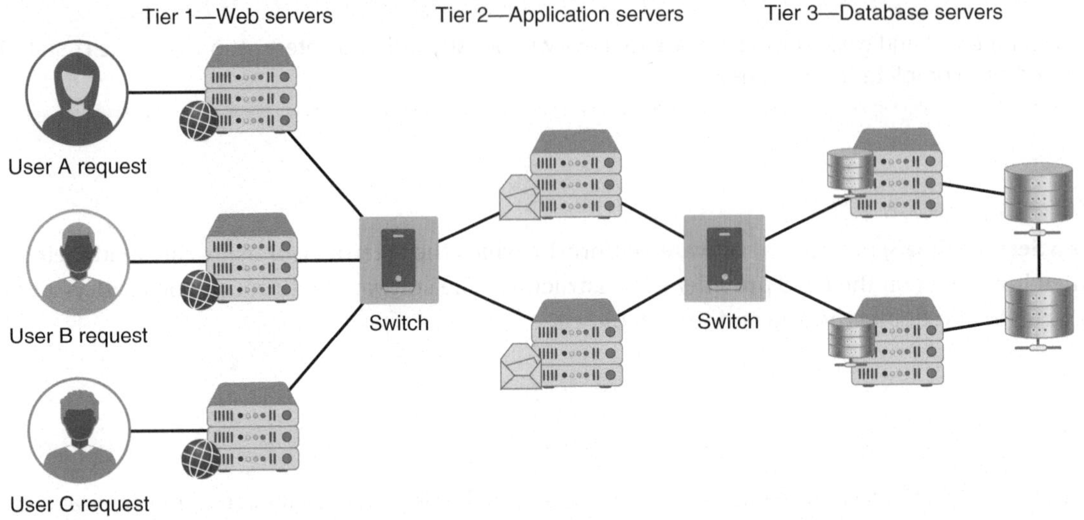

Tier 1—Web servers   Tier 2—Application servers   Tier 3—Database servers

User A request

User B request

Switch

Switch

User C request

Anything as a Service (XaaS)

Anything as a Service (XaaS) describes a broad category of subscription services related to cloud computing. XaaS is any IT function or digital component that can be transformed into a service for enterprise or user consumption. Today a vast number of products, tools, and technologies are being delivered as a service over the Internet. For example, **Security as a Service (SECaaS)** provides security services—such as intrusion detection and security information and event management (SIEM)—all delivered from the cloud to the enterprise. This relieves the enterprise from purchasing and managing security hardware and software.

> **Note 7**
>
> Examples of IT-based services include Communication as a Service (CaaS), Desktop as a Service (DaaS), and Healthcare as a Service (HaaS). One example of a non-IT service is a ride-sharing service like Uber and Lyft, called Transportation as a Service (TaaS).

Cloud Management

After implementing a cloud computing solution, it is necessary for an organization to provide ongoing management. Managing cloud resources can be more challenging than managing on-prem resources. Typically, a cloud computing infrastructure, consisting of a virtual network and related servers, encompasses many different cloud elements, and it is not uncommon for a large organization to contract with different cloud computing providers. Properly managing multiple services from multiple providers can be cumbersome.

Cloud management can be conducted by the local organization performing the work itself or by contracting with a third-party management service provider.

Local Management

One of the challenges when locally managing cloud computing is the question of how best to perform "services integration," or the combined management function of multiple services into a single entity. Services integration attempts to achieve a "boundary-less" approach, which involves integrating all users across the enterprise who are utilizing cloud computing. Services integration includes integrating SaaS and PaaS, on-prem applications, third-party gateways, and social media services. The goal is to be able to monitor a seamless flow of data and transactions across systems.

When managing cloud computing locally, it is important to have written resource policies in place. These policies must clearly outline who is the responsible party for cloud computing, what are their duties and responsibilities, how cloud computing can be used (and not used), and the processes for acquiring these resources.

Note 8

Because a cloud environment can be set up by virtually any employee using their own credit card, "shadow IT" cloud environments are a serious threat. One survey revealed that 93 percent of respondents said they continue to deal with shadow IT cloud computing, 82 percent have experienced security events as a result, and 71 percent said that employees are violating formal policies regarding cloud use by using cloud computing without authorization.[3]

Service Providers

Instead of relying on local effort to manage a cloud environment, many organizations turn to external third-party service providers. A managed service provider (MSP) delivers services, such as network, application, infrastructure, and security, through ongoing and regular support as well as active administration of those resources. In short, an MSP assumes the role of a traditional on-prem IT organization.

Note 9

MSPs are covered in Module 1.

An MSP can manage on the customers' premises, in the MSP's own data center ("hosting"), in a third-party data center, or in a cloud computing environment. "Pure-play" MSPs focus on a single vendor or technology, which is usually their own core offerings, while other MSPs include services from other types of providers.

A specialized type of MSP is a managed security service provider (MSSP). An MSSP can assist with or even fully assume the cybersecurity defenses by providing an organization with a negotiated amount of cybersecurity monitoring and management on the organization's own premises. These services typically include installing and monitoring antivirus and spam blocking, intrusion detection systems, firewalls, and virtual private networks (VPNs) An MSSP can also handle system changes, modifications, and upgrades.

Cloud-Native Microservices

Due to the nature of the cloud, the design of applications or services that are created specifically to exist in the cloud can be much more flexible. Traditional application design is often called "monolithic" because the entire program is developed as a single entity. While monolithic code writing and deploying was originally done for convenience because it all occurs at a single location in the office of the organization, these applications soon became larger and more complex as more features were added and requirements were expanded. This made management of these applications difficult for these reasons:

- As the applications became larger, deployment times became longer.
- The codebase became too large for any single developer or development team to fully understand.
- Due to the complexity, any modifications often resulted in other parts of the code being impacted so that the application became unstable, unsecure, or failed to function as designed.

The solution to monolithic application design is to divide it into smaller entities. These were not divided by *technical* processes but, rather, each entity is a specialized part of the code. This is known as microservices (also called a microservices architecture or cloud-native microservices because the application is both built and deployed using the cloud). A comparison of monolithic and microservices architectures is illustrated in Figure 11-4.

Figure 11-4 Monolithic versus microservices architecture

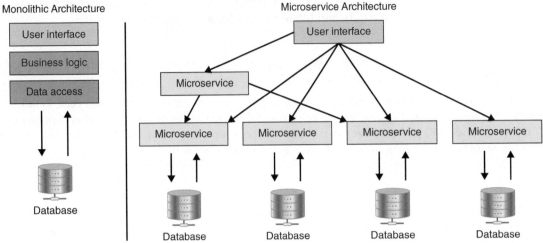

A microservices architecture has smaller and more specialized elements, each of which manages its own database, generates its own logs, and handles user authentication. These are performed by using **microservices APIs** and specialized APIs called RESTful APIs.

Note 10

Application programming interfaces (APIs) are covered in Module 5.

Using a microservices architecture has several advantages. The code can be updated more easily with new features and functionality added without rewriting the entire application. Also, teams of programmers can use different programming languages for different components. And components can be scaled up or back independently of one another, reducing the waste and cost associated with having to scale entire applications because a single feature is facing too much load.

Note 11

When the British Broadcasting Corporation (BBC) moved its monolithic on-demand video platform to a cloud computing environment using a microservices architecture, the final product was comprised of 30 separate microservices.

Two Rights & A Wrong

1. A community cloud is a cloud that is open only to specific organizations that have common concerns.
2. The edge computing location is performed at or very near the source of the data instead of relying on the cloud or on-prem for processing.
3. Infrastructure as a Service (IaaS) provides a software platform on which the enterprise or users can build their own applications and then host them.

See the answers at the end of the module.

Cloud Computing Security

2.3 Explain various types of vulnerabilities.

3.1 Compare and contrast security implications of different architecture models.

3.2 Given a scenario, apply security principles to secure enterprise infrastructure.

4.1 Given a scenario, apply common security techniques to computing resources.

Cloud computing provides several unique advantages for protection. However, it also has vulnerabilities, though these can be mitigated through cloud security controls.

Cloud-Based Security

Information security can be enhanced by using the cloud. These include using virtual security appliances, cloud access security brokers, and a secure access service edge.

Virtual Security Appliances

Just as physical security appliances are used in an on-prem network, virtual security devices in a cloud computing environment can also provide protection. These include cloud firewalls and secure web gateways.

Cloud Firewall   A cloud firewall is virtual software that functions in a similar manner to a physical security appliance by examining traffic into and out of the cloud. Sometimes called a public cloud firewall, next-gen firewall, or virtual firewall, these devices are deployed in the public cloud. They have several advantages over a physical appliance such as the ability to scale quickly as the need arises.

> **Caution !**
>
> When deploying a cloud firewall, the costs should be considered. Like cloud providers, third-party cloud firewall providers charge an hourly rate for the service. This is especially the case if the network has been "micro-segmented," with each segment requiring its own cloud firewall.

Secure Web Gateway (SWG)   A **secure web gateway (SWG)** combines several features into a single product. It examines both incoming and outgoing traffic and performs basic URL and monitoring web applications. A SWG also analyzes received traffic (even that encrypted by SSL), performs data loss prevention (DLP), and provides alerts to a monitoring device like a SIEM appliance. A SWG can be placed on endpoints, at the edge, or in the cloud.

Cloud Access Security Broker (CASB)

As with applications running in an on-prem environment, cloud-based applications must also be protected. However, there are several common misperceptions about applications running in the cloud. One misperception is that application security is entirely the cloud provider's responsibility. Another misconception is that the native "out of the box" security of the applications being licensed will provide adequate security. In addition, misconfigurations of the application setup and insecure APIs or interfaces can provide vulnerabilities for threat actors to exploit.

One security protection for cloud computing application security is to use a **cloud access security broker (CASB)**. A CASB is a set of software tools or services that resides between an enterprise's on-prem infrastructure and the cloud provider's infrastructure. Acting as the gatekeeper, a CASB ensures that the security policies of the enterprise extend to its data in the cloud. For example, if the enterprise has a policy for encrypting data, a CASB can enforce that control and ensure that data is encrypted when it is copied from the cloud to a local device. Another security protection is to use cloud-based DLP to extend the enterprise's policies to data stored in the cloud.

Secure Access Service Edge (SASE)

As the number of remote users increases along with SaaS applications, an organization's data is now moving in new ways. Instead of being confined to an on-prem data center, data moves from the local data center up to cloud services, which includes both public and hybrid clouds, and moves back down to branch offices before returning to the data center. With all this data movement, the need for a new approach for network security is clear.

A secure access service edge (SASE), pronounced "sassy," is the convergence of several security services into a single, cloud-delivered service model. SASE has been defined as security functions delivered as a service that are based on the identity of the user or system and its real-time usage context so that predefined enterprise security policies can be applied while continuously assessing security risks throughout the session. In other words, a SASE architecture identifies users and devices, applies policy-based security, and then delivers secure access to the appropriate application or data.

Various technologies combine to make up a SASE. These include SWG, CASB, zero-trust architecture (ZTA), and wide area networking (WAN) technologies. (WANs are a form of telecommunication networks that can connect devices from multiple remote locations and are established by telecommunication service providers that lease the network to businesses.) A subset of SASE that only includes the security components and not the WAN is called a **security services edge (SSE)**.

Note 12

By one estimate, in 2024 about 40 percent of enterprises will have explicit strategies to adopt SASE, an increase from less than 1 percent at the end of 2018.

Cloud Vulnerabilities

Although cloud firewalls, SWGs, CASBs, and SASEs can provide enhanced security using the cloud, there are also vulnerabilities associated with the cloud. Even though the organization is not tasked with securing the hardware in a public or hybrid cloud, leaving that duty to the cloud provider, nevertheless securing the use of the cloud has several unique challenges (called cloud-specific vulnerabilities). Several issues associated with cloud security are listed in Table 11-3.

Table 11-3 Cloud security issues

Security issue	Description
Unauthorized access to data	Improper cloud security configurations can result in data being left exposed.
Lack of visibility	Organizations have limited or no visibility into the security mechanisms of the cloud provider and thus cannot verify the effectiveness of security controls.
Insecure APIs	While APIs help cloud customers customize their PaaS by providing data recognition, access, and effective encryption, threat actors can exploit a vulnerable API.
Compliance regulations	Maintaining compliance requires that an organization know where their data is, who can access it, and how it is protected, but this can be difficult in an opaque cloud system where the transparency is lacking.
System vulnerabilities	A cloud infrastructure is prone to system vulnerabilities due to complex networks and multiple third-party platforms.

Two general vulnerabilities associated with using the cloud include responsibility matrix confusion and the lack of a cloud conceptual model.

Responsibility Matrix Confusion

One of the prominent challenges of cloud computing is recognizing who is responsible for which security element. A table that lists the various duties, called a responsibility matrix, shows that some security duties are always the responsibility of the organization, some are the specific duties of the cloud service provider, while others vary by type and may be shared between the two entities. Figure 11-5 illustrates a typical responsibility matrix. Because of these different responsibilities, this often creates areas of confusion resulting in security not being applied correctly.

Figure 11-5 Responsibility matrix

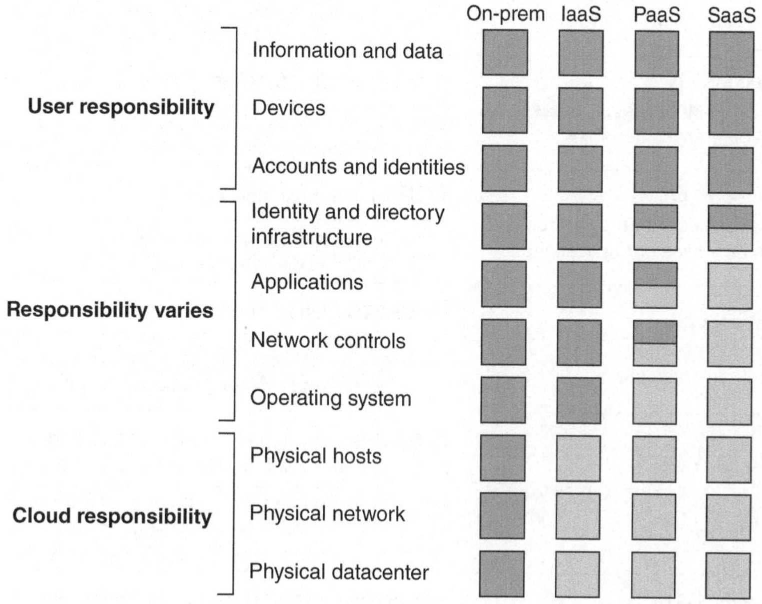

> **Note 13**
>
> A misunderstanding of the responsibility matrix leads to cloud misconfigurations. In a recent survey, 62 percent of security professionals said that the misconfiguration of a cloud platform is the biggest cloud security risk.[4]

Lack of Cloud Conceptual Model

Determining the correct security virtual device for the cloud can be challenging. A primary reason for this challenge is that physical networks neatly map to the Open Source Interconnection (OSI) seven-layer model that illustrates network functionality, as seen in Figure 11-6. When managing an on-prem infrastructure, it is relatively straightforward for a network administrator to understand what is being done at each layer, who is responsible for physical connectivity, who manages Layer 3 routing and control, and who has access to the upper layers. When a term like "Layer 3" is used to describe IP-based routing or when "Layer 7" is used to describe functions that are interacting at a software level, these are universally and uniformly applied. This enables security professionals to more easily identify the security appliances needed and understand how they interact with the other layers and appliances.

However, with cloud computing, the OSI model is no longer as useful—if at all. First, the cloud provider manages cabling, Internet connections, power, cooling, disks, redundancy, and physical security instead of the customer. Second, everything the cloud customer "sees" is abstract and virtual, and essentially exists only as code. Third, there is a higher level of interaction. An organization may create multiple cloud computing accounts with multiple cloud providers in order to separate environments from each other, each with different VPCs for different applications; multiple subnets for different functions; and a variety of storage, network, and compute configurations. The lack of a conceptual model like the OSI model makes selecting and managing security virtual devices more challenging.

Different cloud-based conceptual models are starting to be proposed. One model is shown in Table 11-4. However, no single model has been widely adapted, and it appears that no model will become the standard in the near future.

Figure 11-6 OSI seven-layer model

Layer	Application/Example
Application (7) Serves as the window for users and application processes to access the network services.	**End-user layer** Program that opens what was sent or creates what is to be sent
	Resource sharing • Remote file access • Remote printer access • Directory services • Network management
Presentation (6) Formats the data to be presented in the Application layer. It can be viewed as the "translator" for the network.	**Syntax layer** Encrypt and decrypt (if needed)
	Character code translation • Data conversion • Data compression • Data encryption • Character set translation
Session (5) Allows session establishment between processes running on different stations.	**Synch and send to ports** (logical ports)
	Session establishment, maintenance, and termination • Session support • Perform security, name recognition, logging, etc.
Transport (4) Ensures that messages are delivered error-free, in sequence, and with no losses or duplications.	**TCP** Host to host, flow control
	Message segmentation • Message acknowledgment • Message traffic control • Session multiplexing
Network (3) Controls the operations of the subnet, deciding which physical path the data takes	**Packets** ("letter," contains IP address)
	Routing • Subnet traffic control • Frame fragmentation • Logical–physical address mapping • Subnet usage accounting
Data Link (2) Provides error-free transfer of data frames from one node to another over the Physical layer.	**Frames** ("envelopes," contains MAC address) Network Interface Card (NIC) adapter—Switch—NIC adapter (end to end)
	Establishes and terminates the logical link between nodes • Frame traffic control • Frame sequencing • Frame acknowledgment • Frame delimiting • Frame error checking • Media access control
Physical (1) Concerned with the transmission and reception of the unstructured raw bit stream over the physical medium.	**Physical structure** Cables, hubs, etc.
	Data encoding • Physical medium attachment • Transmission technique • Baseband or broadband • Physical medium transmission bits and volts

Table 11-4 Proposed cloud-based conceptual model

Layer and name	Description	Party responsible
5—Application Experience	End-user facing interface	Customer
4—Native Service	Create, store, process	Customer
3—Software-Defined Datacenter	Create infrastructure	SaaS—Cloud computing provider PaaS and IaaS—Customer
2—Virtualization Software	Software that virtualizes the hardware	Cloud computing provider
1—Physical Infrastructure	Buildings, power, cables, hardware, utilities	Cloud computing provider

Cloud Security Controls

Despite these vulnerabilities, cloud security controls can mitigate the vulnerabilities (hardening cloud infrastructure). A security control exists to reduce or mitigate the risk to assets. A control can be a policy, procedure, technique, method, solution, plan, action, or device designed to help accomplish that goal. Some controls are inherent to the cloud computing platforms and offered by the cloud computing providers to their customers (**cloud native controls**) while other security controls are available from external sources (third-party vendors).

Securing cloud computing involves using controls such as conducting audits, utilizing regions and zones, implementing secrets management, and enforcing mitigations on the three function areas of cloud computing: storage, network, and compute. There are also special considerations for hybrid clouds.

Conduct Audits

A **cloud security audit** is an independent examination of cloud service controls. Once completed, the auditor renders an objective assessment of the security. A cloud auditor can evaluate the services provided by a cloud provider in terms of security controls, privacy impact, availability, and performance. An auditor can also review the integration of all the different elements that are used in the overall infrastructure, such as VPCs, physical data centers, remote offices, and remote gateways.

Audits are typically performed to verify the conformance to established standards so that the organization can be authenticated as being in compliance. Auditing is particularly important for federal agencies because of a requirement that agencies should include a contractual clause enabling third parties to assess security controls of cloud providers. The organization itself can also benefit from the independent audit by being made aware of any deficiencies that must be addressed.

Utilize Regions and Zones

Highly available systems are reliable because they can continue operating even when critical components fail. These systems are also resilient, meaning that they are able to simply handle failure without service disruption or data loss, and seamlessly recover from such a failure. In a cloud computing environment, reliability and resiliency are achieved through duplicating processes across one or more geographical areas. These are called **high availability across zones**.

Cloud provider Amazon Web Services (AWS) maintains multiple geographic *Regions*, including those in North America, South America, Europe, China, Asia Pacific, South Africa, and the Middle East. An *Availability Zone (AZ)* is one or more data centers within an AWS Region, each with redundant power, networking, and connectivity. By spreading their cloud infrastructure across several AZs, AWS clients can create systems that are more highly available, fault tolerant, and scalable than would be possible from using a single data center. And if an application is partitioned across multiple AZs, then organizations are better isolated and protected from issues like power outages, lightning strikes, tornadoes, and earthquakes.

> **Note 14**
>
> All AZs in an AWS Region are interconnected with high-bandwidth, low-latency networking over fully redundant, dedicated fiber connections. All AZs are physically separated from each other by a "meaningful distance" from any other AZ, although all are within 60 miles (100 km) of each other.

Implement Secrets Management

It is necessary for cloud-native microservices to communicate between themselves. However, cloud-based microservices must have the keys needed to access the other microservices, such as API keys, passwords, certificates, encryption keys, and tokens. How should these "secrets" be passed or accessed securely? Embedding the keys as part of the software code ("hard coding") is not a secure option.

The answer is to use **secrets management**. Secrets management enables strong security and improved management of a microservices-based architecture. It allows the entire cloud infrastructure to remain flexible and scalable without sacrificing security. A secrets manager provides a central repository and single source to manage, access, and audit secrets across a cloud infrastructure. Typical features of a secrets management system are listed in Table 11-5.

Table 11-5   Secrets management features

Feature	Description
Limited and automated replication	While secret data and secret names are "project-global" resources, the secret data is stored in regions, which the user can specify or the cloud provider can designate.
Secret-specific versioning	A secret can be pinned to a specific version of the code (like "v3.2").
Audit logging	Every interaction generates an audit entry in a log file that can be used to find abnormal access patterns that may indicate possible security breaches.
Default encryption	Data is encrypted in transit and at rest with AES-256-bit encryption keys.
Extensibility	One system is able to extend and integrate into other existing secrets management systems.

Cloud computing providers typically offer their own proprietary secrets management systems, and there are several third-party systems available.

Enforce Functional Area Mitigations

As mentioned, cloud computing has three functional areas: storage, network, and compute. Each of these has its own set of security mitigations and are listed in Table 11-6.

Table 11-6   Functional area controls

Functional area	Control	Description
Storage	Permissions	Enforce what actions can be taken on stored data (edit, delete, copy, etc.).
Storage	Encryption	Encrypt data at rest in the cloud.
Storage	Replication for high availability	Store multiple copies of critical data across regions and zones to protect against loss.
Network	Virtual networks	Create a virtual network that connects services and resources like virtual machines and database applications with each other via a secure, encrypted, and private network, as seen in Figure 11-7.
Network	Public and private subnets	Configure a VPC with a public subnet for public-facing web server applications and a different private subnet for back-end servers that are not publicly accessible.
Network	Segmentation	Create network segments to enforce rules for which services are permitted between accessible zones so that only designated endpoints belonging to other approved zones can reach them.
Network	API inspection and integration	Use automated API inspection and integration services for authentication, authorization, encryption, availability, and policy compliance of APIs.
Compute	Security groups	Use security groups to segment the different computing resources into logical groupings that form network perimeters.
Compute	Dynamic resource allocation	Deprovision computing resources when they are no longer needed.
Compute	Instance awareness	Implement instance awareness or the ability for security appliances to differentiate between different instances of cloud apps.
Compute	VPC endpoint	When creating a VPC endpoint, attach an endpoint policy that controls access to the service.

Hybrid Cloud Considerations

Hybrid clouds, which are a combination of public and private clouds, have several security advantages. By having both public and private storage options, organizations can secure their most sensitive and highly regulated data in the private cloud infrastructure under their control and store less-sensitive data on the public cloud. This can also avoid having a single point of failure in the event of a ransomware or another malware attack. In addition, with new regulations being enacted by foreign governments regarding where data must be hosted, hybrid clouds can readily comply with privacy and sovereignty regulations.

However, hybrid clouds also have special security challenges (called hybrid cloud considerations). This is due to their unique nature of spanning both public and private spaces. For example, whereas under a standard responsibility matrix there may be either user or cloud provider responsibility, with hybrid clouds there is often a shared security responsibility. It is important to fully understand who is responsible for which security elements.

Figure 11-7   Virtual network

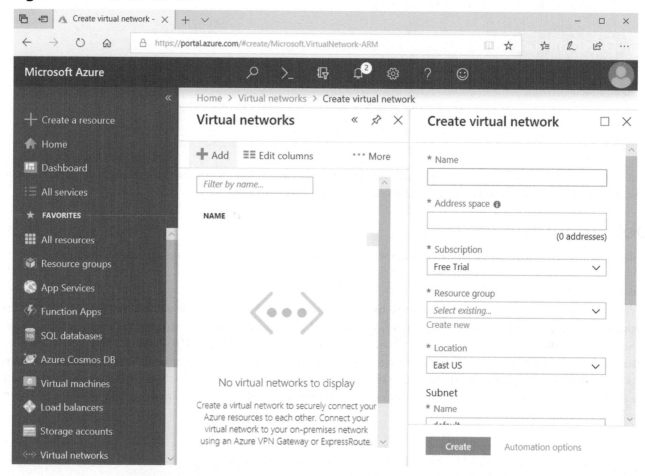

Although no two hybrid cloud environments look the same, there are general best security practices:

- Encrypt sensitive data and data traffic between the two clouds and inspect all encrypted traffic.
- Monitor and audit configurations and use automation, rather than manual management, to keep configurations aligned between the clouds.
- Run regular scans to identify weak points.
- Secure all endpoints.
- Enforce zero-trust security.

Note 15

Zero-trust security is covered in Module 9.

Two Rights & A Wrong

1. A SWG can be placed on endpoints, at the edge, or in the cloud.
2. An SSE includes SWG, CASB, ZTA, and WAN technologies.
3. Secrets management enables strong security and improved management of a microservices-based architecture.

See the answers at the end of the module.

Virtualization Security

Like cloud security, virtualization security also involves first an understanding of the topic along with specific examples. It includes specific steps to be taken to secure a virtualized environment.

Defining Virtualization

Understanding virtualization includes knowing what it is and how it can be used, along with its advantages.

What Is Virtualization?

Virtualization is a means of managing and presenting computer resources by function without regard to their physical layout or location. One type of virtualization in which an entire operating system environment is simulated is known as host virtualization. Instead of using a physical computer, a **virtual machine (VM)**, which is a simulated software-based emulation of a computer, is created instead. The "host system" (the OS installed on the computer's hardware) runs a VM monitor program that supports one or more "guest systems" (a foreign virtual OS) that run applications. For example, a computer that boots to Windows 11 (host) could support a VM of Linux (guest) as well as another Windows 11 (guest) system.

> **Note 16**
>
> Virtualization is not new. It was first developed by IBM in the 1960s for running multiple software "contexts" on its mainframe computers. It has gained popularity over the last 20 years as on-prem data centers used it for migrating away from physical servers to more economical VMs.

Virtualization is used to consolidate multiple physical servers into VMs that can run on a single physical computer. Because a typical server utilizes only about 10–15 percent of its capacity, multiple VMs can run on a single physical server. Virtualization is used extensively in cloud computing environments. It gives the flexibility necessary for rapid deployments. In fact, the adoption and popularity of cloud computing can be directly attributed to the widespread use of server virtualization.

The VM monitor program is called a **hypervisor**, which manages the VM operating systems. Hypervisors use a small layer of computer code in software or firmware to allocate resources in real time as needed, such as input/output functions and memory allocations. There are two types of hypervisors:

- **Type I.** Type I hypervisors run directly on the computer's hardware instead of the underlying operating system. Type I hypervisors are sometimes called "native" or "bare metal" hypervisors.
- **Type II.** Instead of running directly on the computer hardware, Type II hypervisors run on the host operating system, much like a regular application.

Type I and Type II hypervisors are illustrated in Figure 11-8.

One form of virtualization is containerization, which is a reduced instance of virtualization. With both Type I and Type II hypervisors, the entire guest operating system must be started and fully functioning before an application can be launched. A **container**, on the other hand, holds only the necessary OS components (such as binary files and libraries) that are needed for that specific application to run. And, in some instances, containers can even share

Figure 11-8   Type I and Type II hypervisors

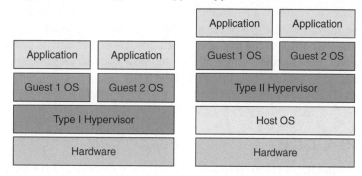

binary files and libraries. This not only reduces the necessary hard drive storage space and random access memory (RAM) needed but also allows for containers to start more quickly because the entire operating system does not have to be started. Containers can be easily moved from one computer to another. A container is illustrated in Figure 11-9.

Figure 11-9   Container

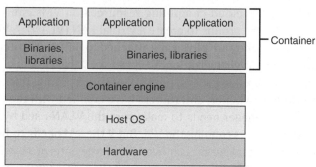

A common application of virtualization is **virtual desktop infrastructure (VDI)**. VDI is the process of running a user desktop inside a remote VM that resides on a server. This enables personalized desktops for each user to be available on any computer or device that can access the server so that their personalized desktop and files can be accessed as if they were sitting at their own computer. This allows mobile users to access their desktop from any location. It also provides flexibility: a user can access a Linux desktop using an Apple Mac computer in which the desktop is running on a Windows server. VDI also allows centralized management as opposed to the need for technical support personnel to access a system remotely or even visit a user's desk to troubleshoot, saving substantial time and money.

Advantages of Virtualization

Virtualization has several advantages. First, new virtual server machines can be quickly made available (host availability), and resources such as the amount of RAM or hard drive space can easily be expanded or contracted as needed (host elasticity). Also, virtualization can reduce costs. Instead of purchasing one physical server to run one network operating system and its applications, a single physical server can run multiple VMs and host multiple operating systems. This results in significant cost savings in that fewer physical computers must be purchased and maintained. In addition, the cost of electricity to run these servers as well as keep data center server rooms cool is also reduced.

Another advantage of server virtualization is that it can be beneficial in providing uninterrupted server access to users. Data centers must schedule planned "downtime" for servers to perform maintenance on the hardware or software. It is often difficult, however, to find a time when users will not be inconvenienced by the downtime. This can be addressed by virtualization that supports live migration; this technology enables a VM to be moved to a different physical computer with no impact to the users. The VM stores its current state onto a shared storage device immediately before the migration occurs. The VM is then reinstalled on another physical computer and accesses its storage with no noticeable interruption to users. Live migration can also be used for load balancing; if the demand for a service or application increases, network managers can quickly move this high-demand VM to another physical server with more RAM or CPU resources.

> **Caution** !
>
> Sometimes overlooked when migrating multiple physical servers to VMs is the need for increased bandwidth to the physical server that houses the VMs. Prior to the migration, each physical server had its own network connection; now, however, a single physical server must handle all the traffic for multiple VMs. Servers housing multiple VMs may need a 10 Gbps or even 100 Gbps Ethernet card to handle the increase in traffic.

Infrastructure as Code

Instances of virtualization are sometimes referred to as infrastructure as code. Three examples are software-defined networks, software-defined wide area networks, and software-defined visibility.

Software-Defined Network (SDN)

Virtualization has been an essential technology in changing the face of computing over the last decade. Racks of individual physical servers running a single application have been replaced by only a few hardware devices running multiple VMs, which are simulated software-based emulations of computers. VMs have made cloud computing possible; as computing needs increase or decrease, cloud computing resources on VMs can be quickly scaled up or back. Networks can also be configured into logical groups to create a virtual LAN (VLAN). A VLAN allows scattered users to be logically grouped together even though they are physically attached to different switches. The computing landscape today would simply not be possible without virtualization.

Yet VMs and virtual LANs run into a bottleneck: the physical network. Dating back over 40 years, networks comprised of physical hardware like bridges, switches, and routers have collided with the world of VMs and VLANs.

Consider this problem. A network manager needs to make sure the VLAN used by a VM is assigned to the same port on a switch as the physical server that is running the VM. But if the VM needs to be migrated, the manager must reconfigure the VLAN every time that a virtual server is moved. In a large enterprise, whenever a new VM is installed, it can take hours for managers to perform the necessary reconfiguration. In addition, these managers must configure each vendor's equipment separately, tweaking performance and security configurations for each session and application. This process is difficult to do with conventional network switches because the *control logic* for each switch is bundled together with the *switching logic.*

What is needed is for the flexibility of the virtual world to be applied to the network. This would allow the network manager to add, drop, and change network resources on the fly quickly and dynamically.

The solution is a software-defined network (SDN). A SDN virtualizes parts of the physical network so that it can be more quickly and easily reconfigured. This is accomplished by separating the *control plane* from the *data plane,* as illustrated in Figure 11-10. The control plane consists of one or more SDN servers and performs complex functions such as routing and security checks. It also defines the data flows through the data plane.

Figure 11-10 Software-defined network

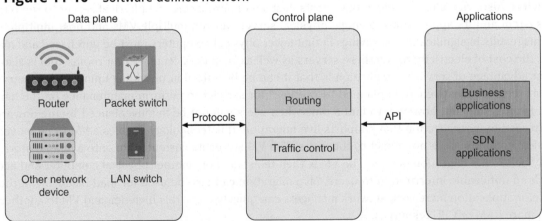

Note 17

In an SDN, the control plane is essentially an application running on a computer that can manage the physical plane.

If traffic needs to flow through the network, it first receives permission from the SDN controller, which verifies that the communication is permitted by the network policy of the enterprise. Once approved, the SDN controller computes a route for the flow to take and adds an entry for that flow in each of the switches along the path. Because all the complex networking functions are handled by the SDN controller, the switches simply manage "flow tables" whose entries are created by the controller. The communication between the SDN controller and the SDN switches uses a standardized protocol and API.

Note 18

The architecture of SDN is very flexible, using different types of switches from different vendors at different protocol layers. SDN controllers and switches can be implemented for Ethernet switches (Layer 2), Internet routers (Layer 3), transport (Layer 4) switching, or Application layer switching and routing.

With the decoupling of the control and data planes, SDN enables applications to deal with one "abstracted" network device without any care for the details of how the device operates. This is because the network applications see only a single API to the controller. This makes it possible to quickly create and deploy new applications to orchestrate network traffic flow to meet specific enterprise requirements for performance or security.

Note 19

From a security perspective, SDNs can provide stronger protection. SDN technology can simplify extending VLANs beyond just the perimeter of a building, which can help secure data. Also, an SDN can ensure that all network traffic is routed through a firewall. And because all network traffic flows through a single point, it can help capture data for NIDS and NIPS.

Software-Defined Wide Area Network (SD-WAN)

Whereas an SDN virtualizes a LAN, a software-defined wide area network (SD-WAN) is a virtualized service that connects and extends enterprise WAN networks over large geographical distances. SD-WAN is designed to solve challenges associated with a traditional WAN, such as integrating connectivity between the service provider and the organization. Because an SD-WAN is based on software rather than hardware, it can be configured to handle different kinds of traffic and conditions in real time. It can also adapt quickly to changing situations and offer better security and reliability than traditional WANs.

Software-Defined Visibility (SDV)

Software-defined visibility (SDV) is a framework that allows users to create programs in which critical security functions that previously required manual intervention can now be automated. As technology moves from a user interacting with a machine to a machine interacting with multiple machines, it is necessary to improve this interaction. SDV allows network administrators to automate multiple functions in a network infrastructure, including dynamic response to detected threat patterns, adjustments to traffic mode configurations for in-line security tools, and additional IT operations-management functions and capabilities.

Note 20

SDV relies on a set of APIs known as RESTful APIs, which use existing HTTP methods of GET, PUT, POST, and DELETE. RESTful APIs have become so foundational that they are sometimes called the "backbone of the Internet."

Security Concerns for Virtual Environments

Host virtualization also has several security-related advantages:

- The latest security updates can be downloaded and run in a VM to determine compatibility or the impact on other software or even hardware. This is used instead of installing the update on a production computer and then being forced to "roll back" to the previous configuration if it does not work properly.
- A "snapshot" of a state of a VM can be saved for later use. A user can make a snapshot before performing extensive modifications or alterations to the VM, and then the snapshot can be reloaded so that the VM is at the beginning state before the changes were made. Multiple snapshots can be made, all at different states, and loaded as needed.
- Testing the existing security configuration, known as security control testing, can be performed using a simulated network environment on a computer using multiple VMs. For example, one VM can virtually attack another VM on the same host system to determine vulnerabilities and security settings. This is possible because all the VMs can be connected through a virtual network.
- VMs can promote security segregation and isolation. Separating VMs from other machines can reduce the risk of infections transferring from one device to another.
- A VM can be used to test for potential malware. A suspicious program can be loaded into an isolated VM and executed (sandboxing). If the program is malware, it will impact only the VM, and it can easily be erased and a snapshot reinstalled. This is how antivirus software using heuristic detection can spot the characteristics of a virus.

Note 21

Threat actors have learned that when their malware is run in a sandbox, it most likely is being examined by a security professional. Many modern instances of malware will refuse to function or even self-destruct if it detects that it is being run in a sandbox.

However, there are security+ concerns for virtualized environments:

- Not all hypervisors have the necessary security controls to keep out determined attackers. If a single hypervisor is compromised, multiple virtual servers are at risk.
- Traditional security tools, such as antivirus, firewalls, and intrusion detection systems (IDSs), were designed for single physical servers and do not always adapt well to multiple VMs. Instead, "virtualized" versions can be used instead, such as a firewall virtual appliance that is optimized for VMs.
- VMs must be protected from both outside networks and other VMs on the same physical computer. In a network without VMs, external devices such as firewalls and IDS that reside between physical servers can help prevent one physical server from infecting another physical server, but no such physical devices exist between VMs.
- VMs may be able to "break out" from the contained environment and directly interact with the host operating system (called VM escape). It is important to have virtual machine escape protection so that a VM cannot directly interact with the host operating system and potentially infect it, which could then be transmitted to all other VMs running on the host operating system.
- Because multiple VMs share the same physical hardware, it may be possible that physical resources that are not properly "flushed" could result in a second VM accessing sensitive data left in that resource by the first VM. This is known as a resource reuse virtualization vulnerability.

Because VMs can easily and quickly be created and launched, this has led to virtual machine sprawl, or the widespread proliferation of VMs without proper oversight or management. It is often easy for a VM to be created and then forgotten. A guest OS that has remained dormant for a period may not contain the latest security updates, even though the underlying host operating system has been updated. When the guest is launched, it will be vulnerable until properly updated.

Combating VM sprawl is called virtual machine sprawl avoidance. Suggestions for limiting VM sprawl include performing regular audits to identify VMs that are no longer needed, using good naming conventions to be able to identify the purpose of a VM more easily, and periodically cleaning up VMs so that new processes can be easily added to an existing VM. Another option is to install a virtual machine manager, which can provide a dashboard of the status of the VMs. A virtual machine manager is seen in Figure 11-11.

Figure 11-11   Virtual machine manager

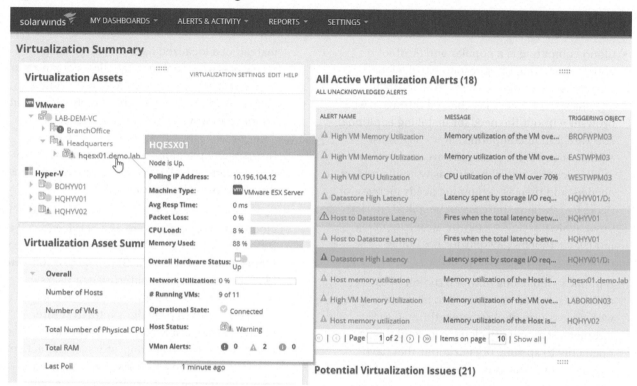

In addition to protecting VMs, container security is also important. Best practices for securing a container include always managing container-based processes using nonprivileged user accounts and using trusted images to create a container because a compromised image can more easily circumvent existing security measures.

Another practice is to use tools to harden the hosts. One tool is Security-Enhanced Linux (SELinux). This is a security architecture for Linux systems that allows administrators to have more control over who can access the system. SELinux defines access control lists (ACLs) for the applications, processes, and files on a system and then uses security policies (a set of rules) to enforce the access.

Note 22

SELinux was originally developed by the National Security Agency (NSA) as a series of patches to the Linux kernel. It was later integrated into the Linux kernel.

Two Rights & A Wrong

1. A host system runs a VM monitor program that supports one or more guest systems that run applications.
2. SDV allows network administrators to automate multiple functions in a network infrastructure.
3. Type II hypervisors run directly on the computer's hardware instead of the underlying operating system.

See the answers at the end of the module.

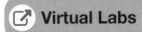 **Virtual Labs**   You're now ready to complete the simulations and live virtual machine labs for this module. The labs can be found in each module in MindTap.

Summary

- Cloud computing is a popular and flexible approach to computing resources. All cloud resources are available online from virtually anywhere, and access is achieved through a web browser without the need for installing additional software. Cloud computing allows an almost endless array of servers, software, and network appliances to be quickly and easily configured as needed, and then as computing needs increase or decrease, these resources can be quickly scaled up or scaled back. As a pay-per-use computing model, customers pay only for the online computing resources they need.

- A public cloud is one in which the services and infrastructure are offered to all users with access provided remotely through the Internet. A community cloud is a cloud that is open only to specific organizations that have common concerns. A private cloud is created and maintained on a private network. Although this type offers the highest level of security and control (because the company must purchase and maintain all the software and hardware), it also reduces cost savings. A hybrid cloud is a combination of public and private clouds.

- Cloud computing takes place in several different locations. On-premises is computing resources located on the campus of an organization while off-premises is a computing resource hosted and supported by a third party. Fog is a decentralized computing infrastructure in which data, compute capabilities, storage, and applications are located between the data source and the cloud. Edge is computing that is performed at or very near to the source of data instead of relying on the cloud or on-prem for processing.

- Many elements make up a cloud architecture. A thin client is a computer that runs from resources stored on a central cloud server instead of a localized hard drive. A transit gateway is a technology that allows organizations to connect all existing virtual private clouds (VPC), physical data centers, remote offices, and remote gateways into a single managed source. A serverless infrastructure is one in which the capacity planning, installation, setup, and management are all invisible to the user because the cloud provider handles them.

- Several different services models are available in cloud computing. Software as a Service (SaaS) is a cloud computing hosted software environment. Platform as a Service (PaaS) provides a software platform on which the enterprise or users can build their own applications and then host them on the PaaS provider's infrastructure. Infrastructure as a Service (IaaS) provides unlimited "raw" computing, storage, and network resources that the enterprise can use to build their own virtual infrastructure in the cloud. Anything as a Service (XaaS) describes a broad category of subscription services related to cloud computing. XaaS is any IT function or digital component that can be transformed into a service for enterprise or user consumption. Cloud management can be conducted by the local organization performing the work itself or by contracting with a third-party management service provider. Cloud-native microservices are applications built and deployed using the cloud.

- Information security can be enhanced by using the cloud. Just as physical security appliances are used in an on-prem network, virtual security devices in a cloud computing environment can also provide protection. A cloud firewall is virtual software that functions in a similar manner to a physical security appliance by examining traffic into and out of the cloud. A cloud access security broker (CASB) is a set of software tools or services that resides between an enterprise's on-prem infrastructure and the cloud provider's infrastructure. Acting as the gatekeeper, it ensures that the security policies of the enterprise extend to its data in the cloud. Secure access service edge (SASE) architecture identifies users and devices, applies policy-based security, and then delivers secure access to the appropriate application or data.

- Cloud computing has several potential security issues. One of the prominent challenges of cloud computing is recognizing who is responsible for which security element. A table that lists the various duties, called a responsibility matrix, shows different responsibilities, which often creates areas of confusion. The lack of a conceptual model like the OSI model also makes selecting and managing security virtual devices more challenging.

- Mitigating cloud vulnerabilities involves using security controls. Some controls are inherent to the cloud computing platforms and offered by the cloud computing providers to their customers (cloud-native controls) while other security controls are available from external sources (third-party solutions). One control is a cloud security audit conducted as an independent examination of cloud service controls. Once completed, the auditor renders an objective assessment of the security. Another control uses regions and zones. In a cloud computing environment, reliability and resiliency is achieved through duplicating processes across one or more geographical areas. This is called high availability across zones. Secrets management enables strong security and improved management of a microservices-based architecture. It allows the entire cloud infrastructure to remain flexible and scalable without sacrificing security. Cloud computing has three functional areas: storage, network, and compute. Each of these has its own set of security mitigations. Hybrid clouds, which are a combination of public and private clouds, have several security advantages but also pose challenges.

- Virtualization is a means of managing and presenting computer resources by function without regard to their physical layout or location. One type of virtualization in which an entire operating system environment is simulated is known as host virtualization. Instead of using a physical computer, a virtual machine (VM), which is a simulated software-based emulation of a computer, is created instead. Virtualization is used to consolidate multiple physical servers into VMs that can run on a single physical computer. Virtualization is used extensively in cloud computing environments. The VM monitor program is called a hypervisor, which manages the VM operating systems. A reduced instance of virtualization is a container. A container holds only the necessary OS components such as binary files and libraries that are needed for that specific application to run.

- Instances of virtualization are sometimes referred to as infrastructure as code. A software-defined network (SDN) virtualizes parts of the physical local area network so that it can be more quickly and easily reconfigured by separating the control plane from the data plane. A software-defined wide area network (SD-WAN) is a virtualized service that connects and extends enterprise WAN networks over large geographical distances. Software-defined visibility (SDV) is a framework that allows users to create programs in which critical security functions that previously required manual intervention can now be automated.

- There are security concerns for virtualized environments. One concern is that VMs may be able to "escape" from the contained environment and directly interact with the host operating system. It is important to have virtual machine escape protection so that a VM cannot directly interact with the host operating system and potentially infect it, which could then be transmitted to all other VMs running on the host operating system. Another concern is that VMs can easily and quickly be created and launched, leading to virtual machine sprawl, or the widespread proliferation of VMs without proper oversight or management, increasing security vulnerabilities. Combating VM sprawl is called virtual machine sprawl avoidance. In addition to protecting VMs, container security is also important.

Key Terms

centralized
cloud computing
cloud specific vulnerabilities
containerization
decentralized
hardening cloud infrastructure
hybrid cloud considerations

infrastructure as code
microservices
on-premises
resource reuse
responsibility matrix
secure access service edge (SASE)
Security-Enhanced Linux (SELinux)

serverless
software-defined network (SDN)
software-defined wide area
    network (SD-WAN)
third-party vendors
virtualization
VM escape

Review Questions

1. Which of the following is NOT a characteristic of cloud computing?

   a. Metered services
   b. Delayed elasticity
   c. On-demand self-service
   d. Universal client support

2. Alois is creating a report for his team about the cost savings associated with cloud computing. Which of the following would NOT be included in his report on the cost savings?

   a. Reduction in broadband costs
   b. Resiliency
   c. Scalability
   d. Pay-per-use

3. Lyam is completing a requisition form for the IT staff to create a type of cloud that would only be accessible to other HR managers like Lyam who are employed at manufacturing plants. The form asks for the type of cloud that is needed. Which type of cloud would best fit this need?

   a. Public cloud
   b. Group cloud
   c. Hybrid cloud
   d. Community cloud

4. Mael is working on a project to deploy automated guided vehicles on the industrial shop floor of the manufacturing plant in which he works. What location of computing would be best for this project?

   a. Remote
   b. Edge
   c. Off-premises
   d. Fog

5. Alderic is frustrated that his company is using so many different cloud services that span multiple cloud provider accounts and even different cloud providers. He wants to implement a technology to give full control and visibility over all the cloud resources, including network routing and security. What product does he need?

   a. Thin virtual visibility appliance (TVVA)
   b. SWG
   c. CASB
   d. Transit gateway

6. What does the term "serverless" mean in cloud computing?

   a. The cloud network configuration does not require any servers.
   b. Server resources of the cloud are inconspicuous to the end-user.
   c. Servers are run as VMs.
   d. All appliances are virtual and do not interact with physical servers.

7. Arsene has been given a project to manage the development of a new company app. He wants to use a cloud model to facilitate the development and deployment. Which cloud model should he likely choose?

   a. SaaS
   b. XaaS
   c. IaaS
   d. PaaS

8. Which cloud model requires the highest level of IT responsibilities?

   a. IaaS
   b. SaaS
   c. PaaS
   d. Hybrid cloud

9. The CEO is frustrated by the high costs associated with security at the organization and wants to look at a third party assuming part of their cybersecurity defenses. Emeric has been asked to look into acquiring requests for proposals (RFPs) from different third parties. What are these third-party organizations called?

   a. MXIAs
   b. MPSs
   c. MSSPs
   d. MSSOs

10. Which of the following is NOT true about microservices?

   a. It is a solution to monolithic application design by dividing it into smaller entities.
   b. It is also called cloud-native microservices.
   c. It is used when the application is developed locally and then imported into the cloud.
   d. The division of the application is not by technical processes.

11. Which of the following is NOT correct about high availability across zones?

   a. In a cloud computing environment, reliability and resiliency are achieved through duplicating processes across one or more geographical areas.
   b. An Availability Zone (AZ) is one or more data centers within a Region, each with redundant power, networking, and connectivity.
   c. They are more highly available, fault tolerant, and scalable than would be possible with a single data center.
   d. They require that specific security appliances be located on-prem so that the local data center can be considered as a qualified Zone.

12. Which of these is NOT created and managed by a microservices API?

   a. User experience (UX)
   b. Database
   c. Logs
   d. Authentication

13. Which of the following is true about secrets management?

   a. It does not provide a central repository.
   b. It can only be used on-prem for security but has a connection to the cloud.
   c. It requires AES-512.
   d. It cannot be audited for security purposes.

14. Based on a common responsibility matrix, which of the following is a cloud service provider NOT responsible for?

   a. Devices
   b. Physical hosts
   c. Physical datacenters
   d. Physical network

15. Which of the following includes ZTA?

   a. SWG
   b. CASB
   c. SASE
   d. RCSC

16. Which type of hypervisor runs directly on a computer's hardware?

   a. Type I
   b. Type II
   c. Type III
   d. Type IV

17. Which of the following is NOT correct about containers?

   a. Containers start more quickly.
   b. Containers reduce the necessary hard drive storage space to function.
   c. Containers require a full OS whenever APIs cannot be used.
   d. Containers include components like binary files and libraries.

18. Which of the following virtualizes parts of a physical local network?

   a. SDN
   b. SDV
   c. VDI
   d. SD-WAN

19. Which of the following will NOT protect containers?

   a. Use a hardened OS.
   b. Use reduced-visibility images to limit the risk of a compromise.
   c. Only use containers in a protected cloud environment.
   d. Eliminate APIs.

20. What do SDN, SD-WAN, and SDV all have in common?

   a. They were all developed in the 1970s.
   b. They are all infrastructure as code.
   c. They require a public cloud.
   d. Specific REST-R-APIs must be used with each of them.

Hands-On Projects

Caution

If you are concerned about installing any of the software in these projects on your regular computer, you can instead use the Windows Sandbox created in the Module 1 Hands-On Projects. Software installed within the virtual machine will not impact the host computer.

Project 11-1: Creating a Fedora Virtual Machine

Estimate Time: 30 minutes
Objective: Create a Fedora VM using VirtualBox.
Description: In this project, you will download and install VirtualBox to create a Fedora virtual machine.

1. Use your web browser to go to **www.virtualbox.org**. (The location of content on the Internet may change without warning. If you are no longer able to access the program through this URL, use a search engine to search for "Oracle virtualbox").
2. Click **Downloads**.
3. Click **Windows hosts** or the platform that you are using.
4. Download and install the software.
5. If necessary, launch VirtualBox.
6. Next, download an image to serve as the guest OS. Go to **fedoraproject.org**.
7. Click **Get Fedora**.
8. Click **Workstation**.
9. Click **Download now**.
10. Under **For Intel and AMD x86_64 systems**, click **iso** and then click the **Download** button.
11. Return to VirtualBox.
12. Create a new Fedora VM. Click **New**.
13. Under **Name:** enter **Fedora**.
14. Click the arrow next to **ISO Image**.
15. Navigate to the Fedora image and select it.
16. Click **Open**.
17. Click **Next**.
18. Under **Hardware**, the memory and processors can be adjusted, if necessary. Click **Next**.
19. Under **Virtual Hard disk**, click **Next**.
20. Click **Finish**.
21. In the left pane a **Fedora** VM now appears. Double-click on it to launch the VM.
22. Select **Start Fedora – Workstation** and press **Enter**.
23. The Fedora operating system will launch as a VM. You can navigate through the Fedora VM as the guest OS.
24. Close the Fedora VM. You are presented with three options regarding saving your work. Click **Power off the machine** to not save any work.
25. Close all windows.

Project 11-2: Creating a Windows Virtual Machine

Estimate Time: 30 minutes
Objective: Create a Windows 11 VM using VirtualBox.
Description: In this project, you will create a Windows virtual machine.

1. Download a Windows image to serve as the guest OS. Go to **www.microsoft.com/software-download/ windows11**.

2. Under **Download Windows 11 Disk Image (ISO) for x64 devices**, select **Windows 11 (multi-edition ISO for x64 devices)**.

3. Click **Download**.

4. Follow the instructions to download the Windows 11 disk image.

5. Launch VirtualBox.

6. Click **New**.

7. Under **Name**, enter the name **Win11VM**.

8. Under **ISO Image**, navigate to the Windows 11 disk image.

9. Click **Next**.

10. Under **Password**, note the password for this VM.

11. Click **Next**.

12. Under **Hardware**, the memory and processors can be adjusted, if necessary. Click **Next**.

13. Under **Virtual Hard disk**, click **Next**.

14. Click **Finish**.

15. In the left pane, **Win11VM** now appears. Double-click it to launch the VM.

16. You are now running a Windows 11 VM.

17. When finished, close this VM. You do not need to save any work.

18. Close all windows.

Case Projects

Case Project 11-1: #TrendingCyber

Estimated Time: 15 minutes
Objective: Summarize your thoughts on the #TrendingCyber opener.
Description: Read again the opening #TrendingCyber in this module. Should governments attempt to regulate cloud computing? Will this result in more cloud computing services? Or will it weaken existing cloud providers? Will additional cloud services provide a higher level of service than is now available? What are the risks of government regulations? Write a one-paragraph summary of your thoughts.

Case Project 11-2: Secrets Management Systems

Estimated Time: 25 minutes
Objective: Research secrets management.
Description: Cloud computing providers typically offer their own proprietary secrets management systems, and there are several third-party systems available. Identify two proprietary secrets management systems from cloud providers and two third-party systems. Research each and then create a document outlining how they are used, their strengths, and their weaknesses.

Case Project 11-3: Comparing Managed Security Service Providers (MSSPs)

Estimated Time: 20 minutes
Objective: Compare MSSPs.
Description: Identify three MSSPs and research the services that they provide. Create a document that outlines the services provided by each MSSP. Would you support contracting with an MSSP for part of an organization's security functions? Would you support using an MSSP for all security functions? Write a one-page paper arguing both the pros and cons of using MSSPs.

Case Project 11-4: Create a Cloud Conceptual Model

Estimated Time: 30 minutes
Objective: Design a cloud conceptual model.
Description: Use the Internet to research different cloud conceptual models and identify at least three. Then create your own model. Draw the different layers and label each along with how each layer would function.

Case Project 11-5: Cloud Provider Security Protections

Estimated Time: 25 minutes
Objective: Research cloud provider security protections.
Description: It is important that enterprises require specific cloud provider guarantees to enhance information security. For example, many enterprises require that the means be in place by which authorized users are given access while threat actors are denied. Also, some enterprises require that the customer's data must be isolated from that of other customers, and the highest level of application availability and security must be maintained. And other providers demand that all transmissions to and from the cloud must be adequately protected. What are other cloud provider security protections that you would require to keep your data on the cloud safe? Research different cloud provider security protections. Create a table of at least five different protections, how they would be implemented, and why you would require each protection.

Case Project 11-6: Secure Web Gateways (SWGs)

Estimated Time: 25 minutes
Objective: Research secure web gateways.
Description: A secure web gateway (SWG) combines several features into a single product. It examines both incoming and outgoing traffic and performs basic URL and monitoring web applications. Use the Internet to research SWG. What are its strengths? What are its weaknesses? How are they typically used? What protections do they provide? Write a one-page paper on your research.

Case Project 11-7: Cloud Access Security Brokers (CASBs)

Estimated Time: 25 minutes
Objective: Explore CASBs.
Description: One security protection for cloud computing application security is to use a cloud access security broker (CASB). A CASB is a set of software tools or services that resides between an enterprise's on-prem infrastructure and the cloud provider's infrastructure. Acting as the gatekeeper, a CASB ensures that the security policies of the enterprise extend to its data in the cloud. Research CASBs and write a one-page paper on how they function, their relative strengths and weaknesses, and the security that they can provide.

Case Project 11-8: Secure Access Service Edge (SASE)

Estimated Time: 25 minutes

Objective: Research SASE security protections.

Description: A secure access service edge (SASE) is the convergence of several security services into a single, cloud-delivered service model. Various technologies combine to make up a SASE. These include SWG, CASB, zero-trust architecture (ZTA), and wide area networking (WAN) technologies, among others. A SASE architecture identifies users and devices, applies policy-based security, and then delivers secure access to the appropriate application or data. Use the Internet to research SASE technology and write a one-page paper on how it is implemented and the protections that it provides.

Case Project 11-9: Bay Point Ridge Security

Estimated Time: 45 minutes

Objective: Research microservices.

Description: Bay Point Ridge Security (BPRS) is a managed service provider (MSP) that manages networks, computers, cloud resources, and information security for small-to-medium enterprises (SMEs) in the region. BPRS provides internships to students who are in their final year of the security degree program at the local college and has recently hired you.

BPRS is preparing a presentation for the monthly luncheon meeting of area IT professionals and has asked you to do research on cloud-native microservices.

1. Create a PowerPoint presentation on cloud-native microservices and how they are used in a cloud environment. Your presentation should be at least 10 to 12 slides in length.

2. As a follow-up to your presentation, you have been asked to write a one-page report on using microservices APIs and specialized RESTful APIs. Use the Internet to research microservices APIs and how they are used.

Two Rights & A Wrong: Answers

Introduction to Cloud Computing

1. A community cloud is a cloud that is open only to specific organizations that have common concerns.
2. The edge computing location is performed at or very near the source of the data instead of relying on the cloud or on-prem for processing.
3. Infrastructure as a Service (IaaS) provides a software platform on which the enterprise or users can build their own applications and then host them.

Answer: The wrong statement is #3.

Explanation: Platform as a Service (PaaS) provides a software platform on which the enterprise or users can build their own applications and then host them.

Cloud Computing Security

1. A SWG can be placed on endpoints, at the edge, or in the cloud.
2. An SSE includes SWG, CASB, ZTA, and WAN technologies.
3. Secrets management enables strong security and improved management of a microservices-based architecture.

Answer: The wrong statement is #2.

Explanation: A SASE includes SWG, CASB, ZTA, and WAN technologies while an SSE does not have WAN technologies.

Virtualization Security

1. A host system runs a VM monitor program that supports one or more guest systems that run applications.

2. SDV allows network administrators to automate multiple functions in a network infrastructure.

3. Type II hypervisors run directly on the computer's hardware instead of the underlying operating system.

Answer: The wrong statement is #3.

Explanation: Type I hypervisors run directly on the computer's hardware instead of the underlying operating system.

References

1. Mell, Peter, and Grance, Tim, "The NIST definition of cloud computing," NIST Computer Security Division Computer Security Resource Center, Oct. 7, 2009, accessed Apr. 11, 2023, http://csrc.nist.gov/groups/SNS/cloud-computing/.

2. "The state of cloud-native security report 2023," *Paloalto*, retrieved Apr. 5, 2023, https://start.paloaltonetworks.com/state-of-cloud-native-security-2023.html.

3. Donovan, Fred, "Shadow IT plagues organizations, undermining cloud security," *HIT Infrastructure*, Feb. 21, 2019, accessed Apr. 20, 2023, https://hitinfrastructure.com/news/shadow-it-plagues-organizations-undermining-cloud-security.

4. "2022 cloud security report," *Cybersecurity Insiders*, retrieved Apr. 5, 2023, https://cyberinsiders.wpenginepowered.com/wp-content/uploads/2022/05/2022-Cloud-Security-Report-Fortinet-Final-7b50d436.pdf.

Part 5
Operations and Management

A security operations center (SOC) is the unit of an organization responsible for protecting it against cyber threats by continuously monitoring its defenses and investigating any potential security incidents. The modules in this final part deal with the operations and management functions of a typical SOC. In Module 12, you learn about vulnerability scanning and assessments. Module 13 looks at preparing and investigating attacks. In Module 14, you learn about security operations. Finally, Module 15 discusses information security management.

Module 12
Vulnerability Management

Module 13
Incident Preparation and Investigation

Module 14
Oversight and Operations

Module 15
Information Security Management

Vulnerability Management

Module Objectives

After completing this module you will be able to do the following:

1 List the reasons for conducting a vulnerability scan

2 Describe the different scanning decisions and how to run a vulnerability scan

3 Explain how to use audits and assessments

#TrendingCyber

Cybersecurity threat intelligence is a booming segment within the cybersecurity industry. The commercial market for these products and services is valued at over $5 billion globally, and it is predicted to triple over the next five years.

Threat intelligence helps address a major challenge facing all organizations, namely identifying and understanding all relevant cybersecurity threats. Some threat intelligence data can be extracted from an organization's own security devices, such as a firewall log that captures the external IP addresses of a threat actor attempting a brute-force attack on passwords or a spam filter that can identify emails containing a phishing URL. These IP addresses and URLs, known as indicators of compromise (IoCs), can then be fed into the organization's security information and event management (SIEM) tool or an intrusion detection system (IDS) to protect against attacks. But this localized threat intelligence data can be only a small fraction of the total threat landscape, since this data is the result of only the attacks that the organization has witnessed. Instead of only relying on their own threat intelligence, most organizations turn to external sources that can provide a broader range of data to reveal patterns and trends.

There are several sources of external threat intelligence data. Open-source threat intelligence typically consists of public lists of IoCs. Another source is a collaboration between trusted organizations in the same industry in which the members share threat information with each other. But one of the most popular sources is threat intelligence data purchased from security providers. These providers not only send this data as electronic "feeds" for their customers' security appliances, but they also provide in-depth research. Some providers give specialized services for specific market sectors, such as government or financial services. A recent survey of security professionals in North America and the United Kingdom found that 44 percent of respondents say that paid threat intelligence is the primary source of data for their organization.

But how accurate is this data from threat intelligence providers? It has been hard to answer that question. Providers have not shared their information with outsiders or researchers so that it can be evaluated. In fact, they rarely even advertise what their services cost (estimates range up to $650,000 annually, depending on the size of the organization).

However, recently some security researchers were able to analyze and compare paid threat intelligence data.[1] And what they found was surprising.

When comparing threat intelligence feeds from different paid sources, the researchers discovered that very little if any overlap; that is, a threat identified from one paid source was not identified by another paid source. In fact, only 1.3 percent of the IoCs from Paid Source #1 were found in Paid Source #2. In one analysis, the researchers tracked 22 threat actors in two separate feeds and found only 2.5 to 4.0 percent of the indicators were in both threat intelligence feeds. The highest level of duplication was only 21 percent—and that was only the IP address of a specific threat actor. The researchers concluded that each paid threat intelligence source is observing different indicators of cybersecurity incidents so that information from one paid source is not found in the feed from another paid source.

And when the researchers looked at the timeliness of the information, they found that one threat intelligence paid source identified a threat one month sooner than another source, which could leave organizations subscribing to the second source unprotected for 30 days. Although it could be assumed that paid sources would provide the information more quickly than other types of sources, they were faster in only half of the cases that were analyzed. That means that half of the time the open-source and shared threat intelligence sources were faster in publishing their alerts.

Another surprising insight was how the subscriber organizations use the data. Many organizations highly value the more selective and curated threat intelligence data from a paid source—but not just because it is used for network detection of attacks. Rather, they value the data because it decreases the time that their internal analysts must spend pouring over the data (open-source and shared threat intelligence usually contain very large volumes of data that must be internally analyzed).

While threat intelligence data is critical for organizations, the researchers concluded that the value of this data from paid sources may not be as high as it should be.

A laurel is a shrub traditionally used to weave wreaths and crowns that were symbols of victory in the sporting events of ancient Greece. This gave rise to the expression "rest on one's laurels," which means to be so satisfied with what has already been achieved that no further effort is needed.

Pity the poor organization today that thinks for even a moment they can rest on their laurels about their information security defenses. The SoC at one major shipping port recently reported that they are the target of about 40 million attempted cyberattacks each month. With this continual barrage of attacks occurring around the clock that probe for the tiniest crack in defenses to exploit, all organizations must continually look for vulnerabilities in their own defenses.

This is a process known as **vulnerability management**. Also called "infrastructure risk visibility and assurance," it is an ongoing examination of the organization's security. Vulnerability management seeks to answer such questions as "Where are we exposed?", "What should we prioritize?", "Are we reducing our exposure over time?", and even "How do we compare with our peers?"

In this module, you examine the security vulnerability management process. First, you study running a vulnerability scan and how to address the results. Then, you explore different types of audits and assessments, particularly penetration testing.

Vulnerability Scanning

> ### Certification
>
> ---
> 4.3 Explain various activities associated with vulnerability management.
> ---

As its name implies, "vulnerability scanning" is an examination of the organization's security to uncover weaknesses. Vulnerability scanning is a higher-level ongoing evaluation of the protections that are in place and is an important tool that organizations regularly use to protect their assets. Vulnerability scanning involves understanding the basics of a vulnerability scan, the sources of data needed for a scan, knowing the decisions that must be made regarding scans, running a scan, analyzing scan reports, and addressing the reported vulnerabilities.

Vulnerability Scan Basics

There are foundational concepts regarding a vulnerability scan. These include defining a vulnerability scan, understanding application package monitoring, and knowing the challenges associated with a scan.

What Is a Vulnerability Scan?

A vulnerability scan is an ongoing automated process used to identify weaknesses and monitor information security progress. It is an assessment that is designed to be a cyclical and continual scanning and monitoring process. Its purpose is to find weaknesses and address them to reduce the attack surface. As such, it serves as a system/process audit on both the devices that are used and the processes to protect those devices.

Application Package Monitoring

One specialized type of vulnerability scan examines applications. Because applications, especially cloud native apps, are a gateway to servers and networks, they present an ideal attack vector for threat actors to exploit. This is particularly true since many applications use **open-source libraries**. A "library" is a collection of precompiled and reusable files, functions, scripts, routines, and similar resources that are used by computer programmers for software development. "Open source" initially referred to software for which the source code was "open" for anyone to examine, but over time it was applied to anything that could be freely used without restrictions.

Note 1

The phrase "open source" came out of a strategy session in 1998 by about a half dozen Linux software developers who wanted to take advantage of an announcement by Netscape that it was planning to give away the source code of its browser. The developers wanted to persuade the corporate world about the superiority of an open software development process but found that the phrase "free software" that had been used previously carried a stigma of being inferior. After a brainstorming session, the label "open source" was agreed upon.

Because these libraries are not owned and controlled by any single entity, attackers frequently infect open-source libraries with their malware. The malware then replicates whenever a programmer downloads and uses that library in their application.

Note 2

Over 80 percent of app vulnerabilities can be attributed to vulnerabilities in indirect dependencies such as open-source libraries.

It is essential for organizations to analyze cloud apps, particularly as more apps rely on open-source libraries. Analyzing these apps can be done using package monitoring tools, which continuously analyze apps for vulnerabilities. Some application package monitoring tools even have a dashboard that provides an at-a-glance view of the applications' current security features, as well as a more detailed audit view to show where security configurations should be modified.

Vulnerability Scan Challenges

Despite its importance, several challenges are associated with vulnerability scanning. Some of these can even be considered as risks and include the following:

- **Volume of scan data.** Vulnerability scans can produce large amounts of data that must be analyzed.
- **Identification of vulnerabilities.** A vulnerability scanner must be able to perform two tasks: (1) locate and identify devices, software, open ports, and other system information and (2) correlate that information with known vulnerabilities from one or more repositories of vulnerabilities. Not every identified system element may be an actual vulnerability and, if a system element is not part of the vulnerability repository, then a weakness may be overlooked.

- **Technical limitations.** Vulnerability scanning that is configured to be aggressive or intrusive can impact performance or even stability of the systems being scanned. Scanning could also cause bandwidth issues on networks. These technical limitations of a vulnerability scan could have an effect on the timeliness and usefulness of the scan.
- **Remediations.** Due to several factors, such as a high cost to remediate or a very low risk of exploitation, not all identified vulnerabilities may be addressed. The process for making these determinations can often be challenging and highly debated.

Sources of Threat Intelligence

Threat intelligence is data that is collected, processed, and analyzed to understand a threat actor's motives, targets, and attack behaviors. Threat intelligence enables organizations to make faster, more informed data-based security decisions. This changes behavior from being reactive to proactive.

Threat intelligence is especially vital to vulnerability scanning. Vulnerability scanning involves looking for the presence of a threat by comparing what is scanned against a set of known threats. This approach is signature-based because it compares a vulnerability scan against a set of known threat signatures. Signature-based monitoring requires access to an updated repository of signatures. Repositories about an existing threat should include the context, mechanisms, indicators, implications, and actionable advice.

But how are these known threats identified and compiled into a repository? There are three primary sources of threat intelligence: proprietary sources, information-sharing organizations, and open-source intelligence.

Proprietary

A "proprietor" is the owner of something, so proprietary relates to ownership. Some threat intelligence data is owned by an entity and is not available to outsiders. These entities can be the enterprise itself or an outside third party.

Enterprise Data   Because corporate enterprises and organizations are under continual attack, they can gather their own data on attacks directed at them. Using this data, they can then write their own rules for use in a vulnerability scanner. In addition to the enterprise gathering its own data from attacks and application package monitoring, it can also look to its bug bounty programs or search the dark web for data as additional indicators of attacks (IoAs).

Bug Bounty Programs   A common practice of large enterprises is to pay security researchers who uncover security bugs in their products and then privately report the bugs so that they can be patched before threat actors find them. This is called a bug bounty program or a responsible disclosure program. Organizations can use the data gathered from their bug bounty program as input into the vulnerability scanner to search for these weaknesses in the organization's defenses.

> ## Note 3
>
> Google, who started its bug bounty program in 2010, pays from $100 to $31,337 per reported bug. In 2022, Google paid over $29 million in bounties (compared to 2017 when it only paid $2.8 million). Zerodium, on the other hand, pays up to $2.5 million for information on a single vulnerability. Google even maintains a bug bounty "Leaderboard" hall of fame listing those who have revealed the most bugs.

Dark Web   The web has three levels, as illustrated in Figure 12-1: the **clear web**, which includes ordinary websites (social media, ecommerce, news, and similar sites) that most users access regularly and can be located by a search engine; the **deep web**, which are exclusive and protected websites (such as corporate email, material behind a digital paywall, and cloud hosting services) that are hidden from a search engine and cannot be accessed without valid credentials; and the dark web. The dark web is like the deep web in that it is beyond the reach of a normal search engine, but it is the domain of threat actors. Using special software such as Tor or I2P (Invisible Internet Project), it masks the user's identity to allow for malicious activity such as selling drugs and stolen personal information and buying and selling malicious software used for attacks. Some security professionals and enterprise organizations use the dark web on a limited basis to look for information about the latest types of attacks.

Figure 12-1 Dark web

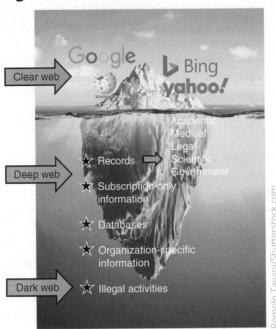

> **Caution** ❗
>
> Finding information on the dark web is difficult. First, it requires using Tor or IP2, which prevents a device's IP address being traced. Second, although there are some dark web search engines, they are unlike regular search engines such as Google. Dark web search engines are difficult to use and notoriously inaccurate. One reason is that merchants who buy and sell stolen data or illicit drugs are constantly on the run and their dark websites appear and then suddenly disappear with no warning. Finally, dark websites use a naming structure that results in URLs such as *p6f47s5p3dq3qkd.onion*. All of these are hurdles that keep out anyone who does not understand these inner workings.

Third-Party Data   Many enterprises lack the time and expertise to research the latest threats and then write the rules to detect those threats. As an alternative, proprietary vulnerability scanners (as opposed to free or open-source scanners) typically offer their own threat intelligence as a paid subscription service. These are known as proprietary third-party sources. The threat intelligence data from these sources are based on the information they collect from their own customers and the work of their threat research teams. These teams are tasked with mapping different types of attacks and the latest threats, suspicious behaviors, vulnerabilities, and exploits they uncover across the entire threat landscape. These are then regularly published and distributed to their customers as direct threat feeds that serve as input into the scanning software to be used in comparison with the enterprise's security defenses.

Information Sharing Organizations

Information sharing organizations gather, collate, analyze, and then distribute threat intelligence. The sources of their information are often from similar organizations that have gathered their own threat intelligence information.

> **Note** ④
>
> Information sharing is sometimes called "crowd-sourced threat intelligence."

Sharing threat intelligence information has two advantages. First, organizations can leverage the collective knowledge, experience, and capabilities of other organizations in their "sharing community" to gain a more complete understanding of the threats they face. Second, by correlating and analyzing cyber threat information from multiple sources, an organization can also enrich its own existing information and make it more actionable. For example, an organization can independently confirm their own observations with other sharing members and improve the overall quality of the threat information through the reduction of ambiguity and errors. Threat intelligence data is often collected and then disseminated through public information sharing centers.

> ## Note 5
>
> Different categories of organizations share threat intelligence. These include Information Sharing and Analysis Centers (ISACs), Information Sharing and Analysis Organizations (ISAOs), and industry groups.

A typical threat intelligence information sharing center is the U.S. Department of Homeland Security (DHS) Cyber Information Sharing and Collaboration Program (CISCP). The CISCP "enables actionable, relevant, and timely unclassified information exchange through trusted public-private partnerships across all critical infrastructure sectors." With the DHS serving as the coordinator, the CISCP enables its members (called "partners") to not only share threat and vulnerability information but also take advantage of the DHS's cyber resources. Some of the CISCP services include the following:

- **Analyst-to-analyst technical exchanges.** Partners can share and receive information on threat actor tactics, techniques, and procedures (TTPs) and emerging trends.
- **CISCP analytical products.** A portal can be accessed through which partners can receive analysis of products and threats.
- **Cross-industry orchestration.** Partners can share lessons learned and their expertise with peers across common sectors.
- **Digital malware analysis.** Suspected malware can be submitted to be analyzed and then used to generate malware analysis reports to mitigate threats and attack vectors.

> ## Note 6
>
> The CISCP program is free to join and use. Those interested must agree to a Cyber Information Sharing and Collaboration Agreement (CISCA), which enables DHS and its partners to exchange anonymized information. Once partners sign the agreement, DHS coordinates an on-boarding session to customize how DHS and the organization can exchange information.

There are generally two concerns around public information sharing centers. These are the privacy of shared information and the speed at which the information is shared.

Privacy   A concern about using public information sharing centers is that of privacy. An organization that is the victim of an attack must be careful not to share proprietary or sensitive information when providing IoCs and attack details. As a safeguard, most public information sharing centers have protections in place to prevent the disclosure of proprietary information. For example, Table 12-1 lists the privacy protections of the CISCP.

Table 12-1   CISCP privacy protections

Protection	Explanation	Example
Cybersecurity Information Sharing Act (CISA)	CISA is a federal law passed in 2015 that provides authority for cybersecurity information sharing between the private sector, state, and local governments and the federal government.	CISA requires a nonfederal entity to remove any information from a cyber threat indicator that it knows at the time of sharing to be personal information of a specific individual or information that identifies a specific individual that is not directly related to a cybersecurity threat.

(continues)

Table 12-1 CISCP privacy protections *(Continued)*

Protection	Explanation	Example
Freedom of Information Act (FOIA)	FOIA was passed in 1967 and provides the public the right to request access to records from any federal agency.	Although federal agencies are required to disclose any information requested under the FOIA, there are nine exemptions, one of which protects interests such as personal privacy.
Traffic-Light Protocol (TLP)	TLP is a set of designations used to ensure that sensitive information is shared only with the appropriate audience.	TLP uses four colors (red, amber, green, and white) to indicate the expected sharing limitations the recipients should apply.
Protected Critical Infrastructure Information (PCII)	The PCII Act of 2002 protects private-sector infrastructure information that is voluntarily shared with the government for the purposes of homeland security.	To qualify for PCII protections, information must be related to the security of the critical infrastructure, voluntarily submitted, and not submitted in place of compliance with a regulatory requirement.

> **Caution** !
>
> When participating in information sharing, organizations must be careful not to share sensitive customer and company data. To guard against this, organizations should share only top-level data and not individual customer records and take care to clean any provided information to ensure it does not contain private information, confidential company data, or industry secrets.

Speed Threat intelligence information must be distributed as quickly as possible to others. To rely on email alerts that require a human to read them and then react takes far too much time. As an alternative, **Automated Indicator Sharing (AIS)** can be used instead. AIS enables the exchange of cyber threat indicators between parties through computer-to-computer communication, not email communication. Threat indicators such as malicious IP addresses or the sender address of a phishing email can be quickly distributed to enable others to repel these attacks.

> **Note** 7
>
> Those participating in AIS generally are connected to a managed system controlled by the public information sharing center that allows bidirectional sharing of cyber threat indicators. Not only do participants receive indicators, but they can also share indicators they have observed in their own network defenses to the public center, which then distributes them to all participants.

Two tools facilitate AIS. **Structured Threat Information Expression (STIX)** is a language and format used to exchange cyber threat intelligence. All information about a threat can be represented with objects and descriptive relationships. STIX information can be visually represented for a security analyst to view or can be stored in a lightweight format to be used by a computer. **Trusted Automated Exchange of Intelligence Information (TAXII)** is an application protocol for exchanging cyber threat intelligence over Hypertext Transfer Protocol Secure (HTTPS). TAXII defines an application protocol interface (API) and a set of requirements for TAXII clients and servers. There are several standardized threat intelligence sharing formats, which are listed in Table 12-2.

Table 12-2   Standardized threat intelligence sharing formats

Format abbreviation	Format name	Description
CAPEC	Common Attack Pattern Enumeration and Classification	A comprehensive dictionary and classification taxonomy of known attacks.
CybOX	Cyber Observable eXpression	A language that provides a common structure for representing cyber observables across and among the operational areas of enterprise cybersecurity.
IODEF	Incident Object Description Exchange Format	A data representation that provides a framework for sharing information commonly exchanged by computer security incident response teams (CSIRTs).
IDMEF	Intrusion Detection Message Exchange Format	An experimental format is used to define data formats and exchange procedures for sharing information of interest to intrusion detection and response systems and to management systems.
MAEC	Malware Attribute Enumeration and Characterization	A standard for creating and providing a language for sharing structured information about malware based on attributes such as behaviors, artifacts, and attack patterns.
OpenC2	OASIS Open Command and Control	A format for documents, specifications, lexicons, or other artifacts to fulfill the needs of cybersecurity command and control in a standardized manner.
STIX	Structured Threat Information eXpression	A language and format used to exchange cyber threat intelligence so that all information about a threat can be represented with objects and descriptive relationships.
TAXII	Trusted Automated eXchange of Indicator Information	An application protocol for exchanging cyber threat intelligence over HTTPS.
VERIZ	Vocabulary for Event Recording and Incident Sharing	A set of metrics designed to provide a common language for describing security incidents in a structured and repeatable manner.

Open-Source Intelligence (OSINT)

Open-Source Intelligence (OSINT) is threat intelligence data that has been legally gathered from free and public sources. While in practice this usually means information found on the Internet, any public information falls into the category of OSINT.

Note 8

In 2023, the U.S. government announced that it was pursuing a plan to create new laws to address cybersecurity. The plan reiterates several priorities that have frequently been listed by various senior cybersecurity officials, such as urging more collaboration and sharing threat intelligence with the private sector.

Besides threat feeds, OSINT is often used to create cybersecurity **threat maps** that illustrate cyber threats overlaid on a diagrammatic representation of a geographical area. Figure 12-2 illustrates a threat map. Threat maps help in visualizing attacks and provide a limited amount of context of the source and the target countries, the attack types, and historical and near real-time data about threats.

Figure 12-2 Threat map

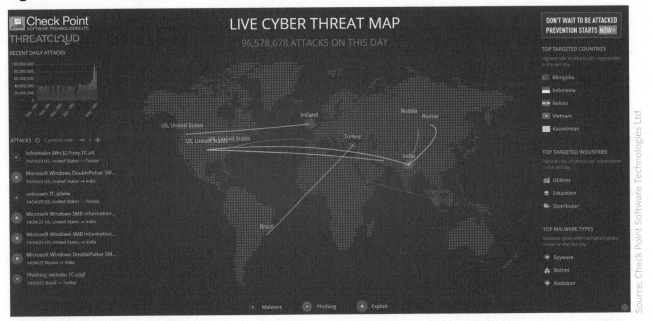

Caution !

Threat maps may look impressive, but in reality they provide limited valuable information. Many maps claim that they show data in real time, but most are simply a playback of previous attacks. Because threat maps show anonymized data, it is impossible to know the identity of the attackers or the victims. Also, threat actors usually mask their real locations so what is displayed on a threat map is incorrect. As a result, many cybersecurity professionals question the value of threat maps.

Scanning Decisions

Several questions must be answered prior to conducting a vulnerability scan if that scan is to be impactful. These prerequisite decisions include determining what should be scanned, how it should be scanned, and when the scan should occur.

What Should Be Scanned?

One of the first decisions before conducting a scan is to determine what should be scanned. This involves assigning a value to data to determine the important data and identify where that data is located.

Assigning Data Value   "Shouldn't we just scan everything?" would seem to be the response regarding what data needs to be scanned. However, not all data is the same: some data is critical and must be protected at all costs (such as research and development data) while other data is of lesser importance (like marketing data). A vulnerability scan can be made to primarily focus on the critical data elements with frequent scans while not neglecting other data elements with less-frequent scans. Thus, before performing a vulnerability scan, it is important to know the value of specific data.

Note 9

The measure of the importance of data can often be gauged by asking the basic question, "What would an unexpected loss or disclosure of this information mean to us?"

Determining the value of data can be aided by first categorizing data into distinct classifications and then protecting these classifications accordingly. Instead of grouping data into categories such as customer data, financial data, and human resources data—which may have varying levels of importance and thus need different levels of control—it is far more beneficial to use data classifications to group like data that needs similar protections. These classifications include confidential, private, sensitive, critical, public, and restricted.

> **Note 10**
>
> When considering to which classification a data element should be assigned, not only should the confidentiality of the data be considered but also the integrity and availability.

There are also various data types, which are not to be confused with a data category. Similar data types would be categorized into a single data classification. The different data types include regulated, intellectual property, trade secret, and enterprise information. Once data has been properly identified, then its value can be determined and the type and frequency of a vulnerability scan can be calculated.

> **Note 11**
>
> Data classifications and types of data are covered in Module 2.

Identifying Data Locations   In addition to knowing the relative value of the data, knowing the location of that data is important. This ensures that specific devices containing high-value data can be scanned more frequently. Table 12-3 lists the types of vulnerability scans that can be made over common assets that typically contain or transmit important data.

Table 12-3 Types of vulnerability scans over assets

Asset	Description
Network	Can identify possible network security attacks and vulnerable systems on wired networks
Endpoint	Can locate and identify vulnerabilities in servers, workstations, or other network endpoints and provide visibility into the configuration settings and patch history of the endpoints
Wireless network	Can identify rogue access points and validate that the wireless network is secure
Database	May identify the weak points in a database
Applications	Web applications and other software assets can be scanned in order to detect known software vulnerabilities and erroneous configurations

However, to create this list of assets to scan, an asset inventory or listing of all significant assets needs to be consulted. For those organizations that maintain an up-to-date asset inventory through regular asset management, the asset inventory can be reviewed to identify the systems that should be scanned. However, what if no asset inventory is available, or it is out of date so that it cannot be trusted as accurate?

Although it is possible to use a vulnerability scanning tool to run a full vulnerability scan of all devices on the entire network, this can take a significant amount of time to both find assets and assess their vulnerabilities. Fortunately, most vulnerability scanning tools allow for an inventory scan that only searches for devices attached to the network or for the location of specific software on the devices. Figure 12-3 shows a hardware asset management screen, and Figure 12-4 illustrates a software asset management screen.

Figure 12-3   Hardware asset management screen

Figure 12-4   Software asset management screen

How Should It Be Scanned?

Another scanning decision involves how the data and assets should be scanned. Two categories of options include active versus passive scanning and internal versus external scanning.

Active versus Passive Scanning   It is necessary for a vulnerability scan to collect data on the assets that are to be examined. For example, data such as the device name, IP address, operating system (OS) version, installed software, patches applied, and so on, are all needed to then determine if there is a vulnerability. Extracting this data is called **enumeration** and is intended to build a picture of the endpoint and network (**mapping**).

There are two different approaches to gathering this data. **Active scanning** sends test traffic transmissions into the network and monitors the responses of the endpoints. **Passive scanning**, on the other hand, does not send any transmissions but instead only listens for normal traffic to learn the needed information.

A primary advantage of conducting active scanning over passive scanning is that active scanning can accelerate the collection of the data; it is not necessary to wait for normal network traffic to or from each asset to generate a complete profile of information. In addition, not all parts of a network may always be available, which can limit the ability to passively monitor traffic.

Note 12

Some active scanners can also immediately take action if a serious vulnerability is uncovered (such as blocking an open port) or even launch a simulated attack to observe the response.

However, there are disadvantages to active scanning. These disadvantages include the following:

- Smaller networks can become overloaded with high volumes of test traffic.
- Sending test traffic increases the risk of the endpoints malfunctioning if incompatible queries are sent.
- Some devices such as Internet of Things (IoT) devices may not be able to perform their normal tasks while receiving and returning test traffic and could become overloaded.
- Many IoT devices are proprietary and may react differently to test traffic.

Internal versus External Scanning   Another option regarding how the assets should be scanned involves the "vantage point" of the scan. An **internal vulnerability scan** is performed from the vantage point inside the internal network; that is, it is launched and then conducted from inside the corporate network. An internal vulnerability scan typically has the primary benefit of identifying at-risk systems.

An **external vulnerability scan** is performed from the vantage point outside the network. It targets specific IP addresses that are within the network to identify vulnerabilities. An external scan can also detect open ports and protocols.

When Should It Be Scanned?

Another consideration is when and how frequently a vulnerability scan should be conducted. The optimum frequency for vulnerability scanning is continual: all systems are scanned all the time. However, different constraints call for scanning on a routine basis instead of around the clock. These constraints include the following:

- **Technical constraints.** Limitations based on technology (technical constraints) can dictate how frequently a scan may be performed. For an organization with a very large network with many devices, it simply may not be possible to scan the entire network within a desired time period. Other technical constraints include limitations on network bandwidth and vulnerability scan software license limitations. When dealing with technical constraints, spreading out the scans to run at specific times may be a necessary alternative.
- **Workflow interruptions.** Continual vulnerability scans may impact the response time of a system so that the daily workflow or normal business processes are hindered. Moving the scans to "off hours" such as nights or weekends can limit the interruptions.

- **Regulatory requirements.** Specific regulations can dictate how frequently a vulnerability scan must be performed. For example, some regulatory bodies state how often vulnerability scans must be conducted.
- **Risk appetite.** A final consideration is the organization's tolerance for exposure to a vulnerability (**risk appetite**). The risk appetite for different systems may be different: those systems with sensitive data for which there is a low-risk appetite may be scanned more frequently than those systems that contain only public data and have a high-risk appetite.

> **Caution** (!)
>
> When determining the risk appetite, longer intervals between scans results in a greater risk for a vulnerability to be exploited.

Running a Vulnerability Scan

Because a vulnerability scan is an automated continual process, several tools can be used for running the scan. Running the vulnerability scan itself involves configuring the software and then executing the scan.

Vulnerability Scanning Tools

There are several categories of vulnerability scanning tools. These categories include tools that focus on website and application scanning, port scanning, infrastructure vulnerability scanning, and cloud scanning. Some of the most popular vulnerability scanning tools include the following:

- **Open Vulnerability Assessment Scanner (OpenVAS).** OpenVAS is considered a full-featured vulnerability scanner that currently includes over 50,000 vulnerability tests and receives daily updates. Greenbone Networks has maintained OpenVAS since 2009 and serves as part of Greenbone's proprietary vulnerability management system. However, OpenVAS itself has been contributed as open source under the GNU General Public License (GNU GPL).
- **Invicti.** Invicti is a tool for scanning website applications for vulnerabilities and is a type of application package monitoring tool. It provides a detailed directory structure breakdown and remediation guidance for discovered vulnerabilities. Scans can be triggered on a scheduled or ad-hoc basis. Figure 12-5 displays the Invicti tool.

Figure 12-5 Invicti application vulnerability scanner

- **Nexpose.** Nexpose is a well-known vulnerability scanner from Rapid7. A Nexpose Community Edition is a scaled-down version of Rapid7's more comprehensive vulnerability scanner. The Community Edition will run on physical machines under either Windows or Linux and is also available as a virtual appliance to run within a virtual machine. However, the Community Edition has several limitations: only a maximum of 32 IP addresses can be scanned and it can only be used for 12 months.
- **Nessus.** Perhaps the best-known and most widely used vulnerability scanner is Nessus. It is a product of Tenable and contains a wide array of prebuilt templates. Nessus advertises that new plug-ins are available as soon as 24 hours after a new vulnerability is disclosed. Nessus has a free version that will only scan 16 IP addresses.

After selecting a vulnerability scanning tool, the software plug-ins need to be updated and the vulnerability and threat feeds need to be accessed.

Plug-In Updates   As attacks continue to evolve, vulnerability scan software must be "nimble" so that information regarding new attacks can be regularly added and updated. Many vulnerability scan products are modular in nature instead of comprising a single enormous software package. These module updates, known as a "plug-in," can be downloaded and installed as needed. However, plug-ins generally go beyond basic updates. Many plug-ins contain advanced vulnerability information, a set of remediation actions, and updated algorithms to test for the presence of the security issue.

> **Note 13**
>
> The number of plug-ins continues to grow exponentially. In one 24-month period, the number of Nessus vulnerability scanner plug-ins grew from 149,780 to 185,609.

Vulnerability and Threat Feeds   To provide a set of vulnerabilities to vulnerability scan software, there are various vulnerability feeds, which are sources of data related to potential or current threats that provide this data. Some feeds are proprietary from third parties. Other feeds are from information sharing organizations or OSINT. Some of the best-known vulnerability feeds are the NIST National Vulnerability Database (NVD), MITRE Common Vulnerabilities and Exposures (CVE), AlienVault, and FBI InfraGard Portal. Vulnerability scanning tools allow for these feeds to be input into the scanning software.

Configuring the Scan Software

Configuring vulnerability scan software involves setting specific parameters so that the scan meets the intended objective. These parameters include the scope, sensitivity levels, and data types.

Scope   The **scope** of a vulnerability scan is the target devices to be scanned. This generally include a range of hosts or subnets, as shown in Figure 12-6. The scope of a scan should be designed to meet the intended goals of the scan. If a specific vulnerability for Windows 11 computers is being targeted in the scan, for example, then it makes sense to only scan systems running that OS.

> **Note 14**
>
> Limiting the scope can also reduce the impact on the overall performance of the network.

The scope can be set by using environmental variables, which are variables whose values are set outside the program, typically through functionality built into the OS or a microservice. An environmental variable, for example, can point to a directory that is to be excluded from a scan.

Figure 12-6   Vulnerability scan scope

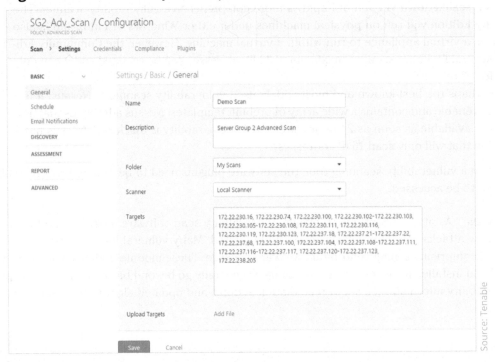

Sensitivity Level   While the scope represents the breadth of the scan, the **sensitivity level** is the depth of a scan. That is, what type of vulnerabilities are being searched for? While a general scan may search for all vulnerabilities, often a scan is looking for a specific type of vulnerability. The sensitivity configuration variable can be used to limit how deeply a system is examined.

Data Type   Another configuration setting specifies the data types to be scanned. Like the sensitivity level, this can be used to "drill down" when searching for a specific vulnerability in a known file type instead of searching all files on a system.

Executing the Scan

When executing the scan, different scanner options can impact running the scan. These are server-based versus agent-based scans and credentialed versus noncredentialed scans. However, before attempting a scan, the scanner permissions and access should be reviewed. It is also important to properly configure other network appliances when running a scan.

Scanner Permissions and Access   A well-protected network ideally should hinder or even block a scanner from performing a vulnerability scan, just as it would prevent a threat actor from conducting their own scan for recon-naissance. In such cases, the network security would prevent the vulnerability scanner from being able to accurately examine the devices on the network. It may be necessary for network security to have appropriate scanner permissions added so that it is able to access the devices on the network.

Yet just as the scanner needs permissions to access the network, from another standpoint, an additional set of scanner permissions are also needed. These are permissions for a user to access and use the scanner itself.

It is no surprise that a vulnerability scanner may uncover significant vulnerabilities, to the extent that if executed on a system not owned by the organization, it would allow the tester access to the system via uncovered vulnerabilities. This obviously raises serious legal and ethical issues. Testers using a vulnerability scanner should have permissions from internal supervisors to use the software, and this software should only be used to access approved systems.

Server-Based versus Agent-Based Scans   Suppose you want to invite a group of your friends out to share a pizza late one night at a new restaurant. You open your smartphone, bring up a web browser, and search for the time that the restaurant closes. Once you find that information, you post it on your social media account so that your friends will see it.

You have just used the two means of accessing Internet information. *Pull* is when you are seeking information, such as the answer to a question, so you *pull* that information into you. *Push* is when you are using the Internet in a more passive way and content comes to you. By posting the information about the restaurant's closing time in your social media account, it is then *pushed* to your friends.

Vulnerability scanners have traditionally used a pull approach: a scanner manager connects to a scanner engine that probes each system for information that is then gathered (pulled) back for analysis. This is known as **server-based** (pull) **scanner technology**, as shown in Figure 12-7.

Figure 12-7   Server-based scanner technology

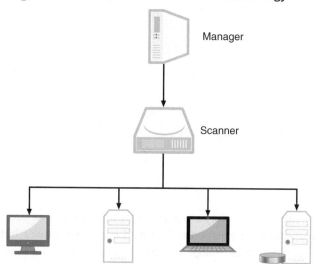

However, today a push option is becoming increasingly popular. Software agents that reside on a system send (push) their information back to the manager. This is known as **agent-based** (push) **scanner technology**. Agent-based scanner technology is shown in Figure 12-8. Agent-based scanners tend to have less impact on network performance. However, the software agents could become the target of threat actors so that they would not accurately report the true status of a compromised computer.

Figure 12-8   Agent-based scanner technology

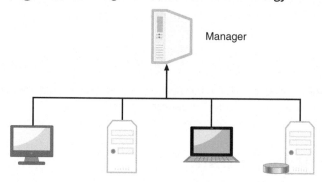

Credentialed versus Noncredentialed Scan   A threat actor who can compromise a network can cause a significant degree of harm. Yet a threat actor who can compromise a network and has in their possession valid authentication credentials (usernames and passwords, certificates, public keys, etc.) can potentially cause catastrophic harm. Which of these should a vulnerability scan imitate: a threat actor who does not have stolen credentials or one who does?

Fortunately, most vulnerability scanners allow for both types of scans. A **credentialed scan** is a scan for which valid authentication credentials are supplied to the vulnerability scanner to mimic the work of a threat actor who possesses these credentials, while a **noncredentialed scan** provides no such authentication information. Figure 12-9 shows the credentials that can be entered for a credentialed scan.

Figure 12-9   Credentialed scan

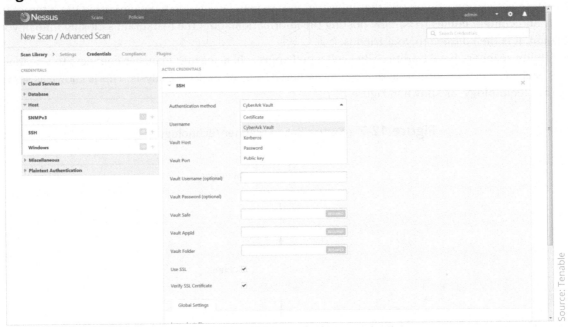

Source: Tenable

Noncredentialed scans run faster because they are performing fundamental actions such as looking for open ports and finding software that will respond to requests. Credentialed scans are slower but can provide a deeper insight into the system by being able to access a fuller range of software installed on the system and examine the software's configuration settings and current security posture.

Network Appliance Configurations   Vulnerability scanners should set off alarms on security appliances such as intrusion detection systems (IDSs), intrusion prevention systems (IPSs), and firewalls. One approach is to mitigate these alarms by instructing the IDS/IPS to ignore attacks originating at the vulnerability scanner and to also configure the vulnerability scanner to correspond to the IDS/IPS.

However, a preferred approach is to use this as an opportunity to validate the behavior of both the vulnerability scanner and IDS/IPS. By knowing that the vulnerability scanner should set off alarms on other security appliances, it is possible to predict the behavior of the IDS/IPS in response to the vulnerability scanner. Analyzing the behavior of both devices can serve as a check to ensure that they are operating properly.

Note 15

If you choose to have the IDS/IPS not ignore the vulnerability scanner, you should configure the IDS/IPS to record the predicted events but set them to a very low priority for generating alerts.

Analyzing Vulnerability Scans

Once the vulnerability scan is completed, the results need to first be validated and then reported.

Validation

When examining results of a vulnerability scan, it is important to validate its results for confirmation. Has the vulnerability scan identified genuine vulnerabilities and not missed any? If the scan were 100 percent accurate, then the organization would know that a future attack would accurately trigger an alarm (**true positive**) while the absence of an attack would not trigger an alarm (**true negative**). However, it is possible that the scan could generate an error. There are two types of these errors. A false positive is an alarm that is raised when there is no problem, while a false negative is the failure to raise an alarm when there is an issue.

Note 16

False positives and false negatives were terms that are used frequently in the debate over using a nose swab or a throat swab when testing for the COVID-19 virus. Throat swabs tend to yield more false positives (telling people they are infected when they are not) while nasal swabs often result in more false negatives (telling people they are not infected when indeed they are).

Vulnerability scans may produce false positives for several reasons; for example, scan options may not have been well defined or missed in a configuration review, or the scanner might not recognize a control that is already in place to address an existing vulnerability. The result of a false positive in a vulnerability scan is it creates a large amount of unnecessary work looking for a vulnerability for which none exists. Security professionals should attempt to identify false positives in a scan report, especially those that would require extensive effort to address.

The result of a false negative, however, is much more serious: the scan overlooked an existing vulnerability that a threat actor may find and exploit. One means of identifying false negatives is to correlate the vulnerability scan data with several internal data points. The most common are related log files. Because a log is simply a record of events that occur, system event logs document any unsuccessful events and the most significant successful events. The types of information recorded might include the date and time of the event; a description of the event; its status, error codes, and service name; and the user or system that was responsible for launching the event. Log reviews, or an analysis of log data, can be used to identify false negatives.

Note 17

Logs can be particularly helpful internal data points when correlating with vulnerability scan results. For example, if a scan indicates that a vulnerability in a software application was found on a specific device but a follow-up investigation revealed that the application was no longer vulnerable, log files could indicate whether that program's configuration had been changed between the time of the scan and the follow-up analysis.

Reporting

Distributing the results of the scan to the appropriate parties is known as reporting. Usually, different levels of available reports should be distributed to different audiences. Table 12-4 describes the report types and audiences.

Table 12-4   Vulnerability scan reporting

Audience	Level of report	Explanation
Management	A general report that outlines the impact to the organization	Management will be interested in how the latest scan compares with previous scans, how serious are the vulnerabilities, and how long it will take to address these latest vulnerabilities.
System and network engineers	A technical report that outlines what needs to be addressed	Engineers will want a listing of the devices with vulnerabilities and specific details regarding how to fix the problems.
Application developers	A report that lists the applications that contain vulnerabilities and what those vulnerabilities are	Developers will want to know which of their applications are vulnerable and as much as possible the location of that vulnerability in their code.
Security teams	A very specific report as it relates to the technical security details	Security teams want to know what systems were vulnerable, the details as to why they could be exploited, and what remediation steps are necessary.

Note 18

Today vulnerability scan software can provide extensive information through reporting to assist different audiences. For example, for a website that contains a SQL injection vulnerability, the vulnerability scan software can provide application developers the name of the application, the input to the web application that triggered the vulnerability and the corresponding output, and even the specific variable within the application that resulted in the compromise.

There are also different means of distributing reports. Reports can automatically be distributed via email to specific audiences. They can also be sent at different times, such as when a scan is completed or once each week. Another option is for individuals to be given direct access to the vulnerability scan software so that they can read the reports on demand as a type of manual report distribution.

Addressing Vulnerabilities

The final step in vulnerability scanning is to address any issues that were uncovered. This involves remediating vulnerabilities. To remediate vulnerabilities, the first step is to prioritize the vulnerabilities. Then action steps should be taken to address those vulnerabilities that have been prioritized as most important.

Prioritize Vulnerabilities

Consider a vulnerability scan that produces the results shown in Figure 12-10 in which there are 20 vulnerabilities listed. Although there are (thankfully) no critical vulnerabilities, nevertheless there are multiple high, medium, and low vulnerabilities. But where do you begin? Do you start with the high vulnerabilities and work your way down through all the low vulnerabilities? Or is there a better approach to take?

Figure 12-10   Results of vulnerability scan

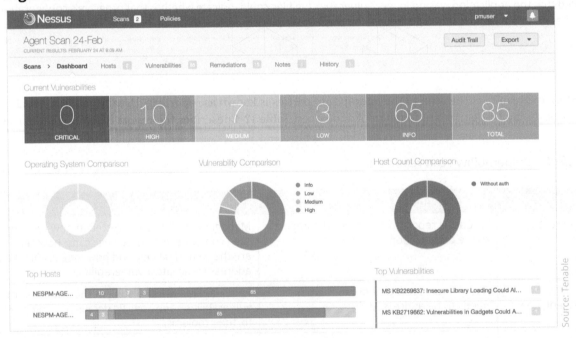

Source: Tenable

It is important to remember the principle that *it is rarely possible, and often not desirable, to address all vulnerabilities*. This is because not all vulnerabilities are as potentially damaging as other vulnerabilities. And despite the rating of medium given to a vulnerability by a scanner, to one organization this vulnerability may be critical while to another it is not worth the effort to fix. Also, because many vulnerabilities are complex to unravel and take an extended amount of time to address, there may not be enough time to solve all of them. So, beginning with the high vulnerabilities and working down through the low vulnerabilities may not always be the best plan of action.

Instead, it is necessary to prioritize (treat one item as more important than another) the vulnerabilities so that the most critical vulnerabilities are addressed early on, while others will wait until later or not even be addressed. There are criteria used for prioritizing vulnerabilities. These include the following:

- **Common Vulnerability Scoring System** (CVSS). The Common Vulnerability Scoring System (CVSS) contains numeric scores generated using a complex formula that considers such variables as the access vector, attack complexity, authentication, confidentiality of the data, and the system's integrity and availability. The vulnerabilities with the highest numeric CVSS scores are generally considered to require early attention.

- **Common Weakness Enumeration** (CWE). The Common Weakness Enumeration (CWE) is another categorical system for hardware and software weaknesses and vulnerabilities. The CWE rankings are based on a vulnerability classification system or categories of similar vulnerabilities. The CWE has over 600 different categories with rankings, including classes for buffer overflows, directory tree traversal errors, race conditions, cross-site scripting, hard-coded passwords, and insecure random numbers.

Prioritizing vulnerabilities is an inexact and sometimes difficult process. However, attention should first be directed toward those that are determined to be critical (can cause the greatest degree of harm) to the specific organization and that the difficulty and time for implementing the correction is reasonable.

Take Action Steps

Once the vulnerabilities are prioritized, a series of action steps can be taken to actively address these uncovered vulnerabilities. These action steps include the following:

- **Patch and harden.** Vulnerabilities should first be addressed by **patching** systems that are missing existing software updates. This is the easiest, quickest, and most economical approach and generally will address a high number of exposed vulnerabilities. After patching, the systems should be hardened as necessary with new hardware or software.

- **Address difficult vulnerabilities.** Some vulnerabilities that need to be addressed will not have a quick and easy solution; instead, the options are very difficult or impractical at the present time. In these cases, it may be necessary to determine an alternative action (**compensating control**), such as removing an endpoint from the network.

- **Identify exceptions and exemptions.** In some cases, it may be necessary to declare that certain vulnerabilities fall outside the bounds of what the organization will address (exceptions and exemptions). This may be due to a low exposure factor (exposure factor is a subjective estimate of the loss to an asset if the specific threat occurs) or low industry/organizational impact (a determination that an attack will have a small effect). In some cases, it may be appropriate to pay a third-party for insurance so that if an attack occurs based on the vulnerability, the organization will be compensated for it. Different organizations will approach these exceptions and exemptions differently based on their willingness to assume a level of risk in order to achieve a result (risk tolerance).

- **Analyze network segmentation.** The work of a threat actor to penetrate a system often follows a similar pattern. The threat actors first conduct reconnaissance against the systems, looking for vulnerabilities, and when a path to a vulnerability is exposed, they gain access to the system through it. Once initial access is gained, they escalate to more advanced resources by tunneling through the network looking for additional systems they can access from their elevated position. In order to thwart this movement by threat actors, it is important that network **segmentation** be utilized. Network segmentation is designed to architect a network so that parts can be cordoned off or segmented into isolated sections. This allows an organization to treat different segments of the network differently based on the classification of the data in that segment: low-risk segments may have fewer restrictions while high-risk segments are more heavily protected. Vulnerability scans can be used to identify vulnerabilities in network segmentation, and several regulatory requirements even mandate that segmentation controls be scanned.

> **Note 19**
>
> Network segmentation is covered in Module 9.

- **Verify mitigation.** It is important to corroborate that the vulnerabilities have indeed been properly addressed (validation of remediation). This is done by performing another vulnerability scan (rescanning) followed by an analysis of the results (audit) for validation of their accuracy (verification). In addition, once the changes have been approved and applied to the production system, these changes need to be formally communicated and recorded.

Two Rights & A Wrong

1. Threat intelligence is data that is collected, processed, and analyzed to understand a threat actor's motives, targets, and attack behaviors.
2. A false positive is the failure to raise an alarm when there is an issue.
3. It is rarely possible, and often not desirable, to address all the vulnerabilities found in a vulnerability scan.

See the answers at the end of the module.

Audits and Assessments

Certification

4.3 Explain various activities associated with vulnerability management.

5.5 Explain types and purposes of audits and assessments.

Just as a vulnerability scan is an evaluation by the organization of its ability to resist attacks, there are other types of evaluations on the organization's information security. These are known as audits and assessments. An **audit** is an examination of results to verify their accuracy. Someone performs this other than the person responsible for producing the results. An assessment is a judgment made about those results. An assessment goes further than an audit: it involves actions necessary to make what was assessed brought back into conformity with the required standards.

Audits and assessments can be internal and external. In addition, one specific type of audit is a penetration test.

Internal Audits

Most organizations perform audits by company employees known as internal audits. These are also known as self-assessments because they are "inward focused" on the organization itself. The goal of internal audits is to identify the actions needed to put what was assessed back into compliance or conformity to mandated standards.

One example of a group performing internal audits is an audit committee. An audit committee is one of the major operating committees of a company's board of directors. The audit committee oversees the organization's financial statements and reporting by providing proof (attestation) that the organization is in compliance with required standards. At least one person on the committee must qualify as a financial expert. All U.S. publicly traded companies must maintain a qualified audit committee to be listed on a stock exchange.

External Assessments

External assessments are performed by professionals from outside the organization. Because they are not employees whose welfare could be jeopardized by a poor review, these professionals perform an independent third-party audit. Their assessments or examinations of the organization are often to ensure that the company is compliant with regulatory requirements as set forth by outside bodies. There are numerous federal regulatory agencies as well as regulatory organizations that are industry specific.

Penetration Testing

One specialized form of audits and assessments is a penetration test. It is important to know what a penetration test is, the types of testers, the levels of reconnaissance, and how a penetration test compares with a vulnerability scan.

What Is a Penetration Test?

In information security, one specific type of audit and assessment is penetration testing ("pen test"). By its very nature, a penetration test attempts to uncover vulnerabilities and then exploit them, just as a threat actor would. Unlike a vulnerability scan that is considered a defensive assessment because it only looks at the protections of a system, a penetration test is an offensive assessment that probes the system for weaknesses.

Penetration testing involves a significant amount of time and resources. So, the question is sometimes asked, "Why spend the time and effort to perform a penetration test? Why can't we just do a vulnerability scan of our network defenses to find vulnerabilities?"

While a vulnerability scan of network defenses can help find vulnerabilities, the type of vulnerabilities revealed is different from a penetration test. A vulnerability scan may find only "surface" problems to be addressed. This is because many scans are entirely automated and provide only a limited verification of any discovered vulnerabilities. A penetration test, on the other hand, can go further to find and exploit "deep" vulnerabilities using manual techniques.

These deep vulnerabilities can only be exposed through *actual attacks that use the mindset of a threat actor*. Both elements are important. First, the attacks must be the same (or remarkably similar) as those used by a threat actor; anything less will not uncover the deep vulnerabilities that an attacker can find. Second, the attacks should follow the thinking of threat actors. Understanding their thinking helps to better perceive what assets they are seeking, how they may craft the attack, and even how determined they are to obtain assets. Without having an attacker's mindset, it is difficult to find these deep vulnerabilities.

> ## Note 20
>
> Some security professionals believe organizations that do not have a solid cybersecurity defense should not consider a pen test as the first step. Instead, a general scan should first be conducted to reveal and address surface vulnerabilities. Once this analysis is completed, a more thorough pen test can then be performed.

While most often a penetration test is an attempt to actively attack an information technology (IT) system as a threat actor would, penetration testing is not limited to IT. Many penetration tests are not technical but examine the physical environment (physical penetration testing), probing for weaknesses in physical security controls such as fencing and lighting to determine if the testers can enter restricted areas. Penetration tests that probe both technical and physical weaknesses are integrated penetration tests.

Types of Testers

A question that is often debated is who should conduct the penetration test. Should it be conducted by in-house employees or an external consultant? Or is there another option? What are the advantages and disadvantages to each approach?

Internal Security Personnel   Using internal employees to conduct a penetration test has advantages in some cases. First, there is little or no additional cost. Also, the test can be conducted much more quickly. Finally, an in-house penetration test can be used to enhance the training of employees and raise the awareness of security risks. When conducting an in-house pen test, an organization often divides security employees into opposing teams to conduct a "war game" scenario. Table 12-5 lists the composition and duties of the teams in a pen test war game.

Table 12-5   Penetration testing war game teams

Team name	Role	Duties	Explanation
Red Team	Attackers	Scans for vulnerabilities and then exploits them	Has prior and in-depth knowledge of existing security, which may provide an unfair advantage
Blue Team	Defenders	Monitors for Red Team attacks and shores up defenses as necessary	Scans log files, traffic analysis, and other data to look for signs of an attack
White Team	Referees	Enforces the rules of the penetration testing	Makes notes of the Blue Team's responses and the Red Team's attacks
Purple Team	Bridge	Provides real-time feedback between the Red and Blue Teams to enhance the testing	The Blue Team receives information that can be used to prioritize and improve their ability to detect attacks while the Red Team learns more about technologies and mechanisms used in the defense

Note 21

Sometimes organizations add an incentive called a capture the flag (CTF) exercise. A series of challenges with varying degrees of difficulty are outlined in advance. When one challenge is solved, a "flag" is given to the pen tester, and the points are totaled once the time has expired. The winning player or team is the one that earns the highest score. CTF events are often hosted at information security conferences or by schools.

However, using internal security employees to conduct a penetration test has several disadvantages:

- **Inside knowledge.** Employees often have in-depth knowledge of the network and its devices. A threat actor, on the other hand, would not have the same knowledge, so an attack from employees would not truly simulate that of a threat actor.
- **Lack of expertise.** Employees may not have the credentials needed to perform a comprehensive test. Their lack of expertise may result in few deep vulnerabilities being exposed.
- **Reluctance to reveal.** Employees may be reluctant to reveal a vulnerability discovered in a network or system that they or a fellow employee have been charged with protecting.

External Consultants   Contracting with an external third-party pen testing consultant to conduct a penetration test offers the following advantages:

- **Expertise.** External contractors that conduct penetration tests have the technical and business expertise to conduct a thorough test.
- **Credentials.** Pen test contractors usually employ people who hold several security certifications to validate their pen testing knowledge and experience.
- **Experience.** Because they have conducted numerous penetration tests, contractors know what to look for and how to take advantage of a vulnerability.
- **Focus.** Reputable penetration testing firms generally deliver expert security services and are highly focused on the task.

Penetration testing using external consultants is often classified based on the level of knowledge of the environment and access provided in advance of the pen test. These levels are described in Table 12-6.

Table 12-6 Penetration testing levels

Level name	Description	Main task	Advantages	Disadvantages
Unknown environment	Testers have no knowledge of the network and no special privileges	Attempt to penetrate the network	Emulate exactly what a threat actor would do and see	If testers cannot penetrate the network, then no test can occur
Partially known environment	Testers are given limited knowledge of the network and some elevated privileges	Focus on systems with the greatest risk and value to the organization	More efficiently assess security instead of spending time trying to compromise the network and then determining which systems to attack	This "head start" does not allow testers to truly emulate what a threat actor may do
Known environment	Testers are given full knowledge of the network and the source code of applications	Identify potential points of weakness	Focus directly on systems to test for penetration	This approach does not provide a full picture of the network's vulnerabilities

Caution !

A disadvantage of using an external consultant is the usage of the information that is uncovered. A contractor who conducts a pen test will not only learn about an organization's network and system vulnerabilities but may also receive extremely sensitive information about these systems and how to access them. Such knowledge could be sold to a competitor by an unscrupulous employee of the third-party contractor. As a protection, most penetration testing contracts will contain a nondisclosure agreement (NDA) that states all client information related to the test will be treated as highly confidential and at the end of the test, all data and storage media is either destroyed or given back to the client.

Levels of Reconnaissance

One of the first tasks of testers with unknown or partially unknown environments is to perform preliminary information gathering from outside the organization. This reconnaissance is called **footprinting**.

There are two methods by which this information is gathered. Active reconnaissance involves directly probing for vulnerabilities and useful information, much like a threat actor would do. For example, unprotected wireless data transmissions from wireless local area networks can often be used to gather information or even circumvent security protections. The disadvantage of active reconnaissance in a pen test is that the probes are likely to alert those security professionals within the enterprise who did not know about the pen test that something unusual is occurring. This may result in them "locking down" the network to become more restrictive and thus more difficult to probe.

Instead of active reconnaissance, passive reconnaissance takes an entirely different approach: the tester uses tools that do not raise any alarms. This may include searching online for publicly accessible information like OSINT that can reveal valuable insight about the system.

Note 22

Active reconnaissance relies on traffic being sent to the targeted system, while passive reconnaissance calls for the tester to quietly "make do" with whatever information they can accumulate from public sources.

Penetration Test versus Vulnerability Scan

There are differences between a penetration test and a vulnerability scan. A penetration test is a single event using a manual process. A vulnerability scan, on the other hand, is a frequent and ongoing process that is automated to continuously identify vulnerabilities and monitor cybersecurity progress. In other words, a vulnerability assessment is a cyclical and continual process of ongoing scanning and continuous monitoring to reduce the attack surface while a penetration test seeks to discover deep vulnerabilities. Table 12-7 contrasts a vulnerability scan with a penetration test.

Table 12-7   Vulnerability scan versus penetration test

	Vulnerability scan	Penetration test
Purpose	Reduce attack surface	Identify deep vulnerabilities
Procedure	Scan to find weaknesses and then mitigate	Act like a threat agent to find vulnerabilities to exploit
Frequency	Usually ongoing scanning and continuous monitoring	When required by regulatory body or on a predetermined schedule
Personnel	Internal security personnel	External third parties or internal security personnel
Process	Usually automated with handful of manual processes	Entirely manual process
Goal	Identify risks by scanning systems and networks	Gain unauthorized access and exploit vulnerabilities
Final report audience	Executive summary for less technical audience, technical details for security professionals	Several different audiences

Note 23

A growing trend by global organizations is to create cybersecurity digital dashboards to help top executives make sense of the cybersecurity and privacy risks the organization faces from around the world. These platforms analyze vulnerability scans and penetration tests that identify corporate cybersecurity vulnerabilities along with information from privacy-compliance firms. The dashboard also assigns priority scores based on how critical a new project is and the types of risks that have been identified. For example, if the company is creating a new website and the legal counsel states that the site must include a message asking visitors for permission to collect their personal data, the dashboard will flag it as a risk until that message is created.

Two Rights & A Wrong

1. An assessment is an examination of results to verify their accuracy.

2. A penetration test looks for deep vulnerabilities that can only be exposed through actual attacks that use the mindset of a threat actor.

3. In a partially known environment, testers are given limited knowledge of the network and only some elevated privileges.

See the answers at the end of the module.

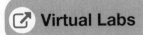 **Virtual Labs**   You're now ready to complete the simulations and live virtual machine labs for this module. The labs can be found in each module in MindTap.

Summary

- A vulnerability scan is an ongoing automated process used to identify weaknesses and monitor information security progress. It is an assessment designed to be a cyclical and continual scanning and monitoring process. The purpose of a scan is to find weaknesses and address them to reduce the attack surface. It serves as a system/process audit on both the devices that are used and the processes to protect those devices.

- Vulnerability management is also called infrastructure risk visibility and assurance. Its purpose is to be an ongoing examination of the organization's security instead of a specifically scheduled or even annual event. It is not designed to expose deep vulnerabilities as a pen test can, but it provides an ongoing evaluation of the protections in place. One specialized type of vulnerability scan examines applications. Analyzing these apps can be done using package monitoring tools. Despite its importance, several challenges are associated with vulnerability scanning.

- Threat intelligence is data that is collected, processed, and analyzed to understand a threat actor's motives, targets, and attack behaviors. There are three primary sources of threat intelligence. Some threat intelligence data is owned by an entity and is not available to outsiders. These entities can be the enterprise itself or an outside third party. Information sharing organizations gather, collate, analyze, and then distribute threat intelligence. The sources of their information are often from similar organizations that have gathered threat intelligence information based on their own organization. Open-Source Intelligence (OSINT) is threat intelligence data that has been legally gathered from free and public sources.

- Several decisions must be made prior to conducting a scan if the scan is to be impactful. One of the first decisions before conducting a scan is to determine what should be scanned. In addition to knowing the relative importance of the data, knowing the location of that data is also important so that specific systems with high-value data can be scanned more frequently. Another consideration is when and how frequently a vulnerability scan should be conducted. The optimum frequency for vulnerability scanning is continual: all systems are scanned all the time. However, different constraints call for scanning on a routine basis instead of around the clock.

- Because a vulnerability scan is an automated continual process, different tools can be used for running the scan. There are several categories of vulnerability scanning tools, such as tools that focus on website and application scanning, port scanning, infrastructure vulnerability scanning, and cloud scanning. Many vulnerability scan products are modular in nature instead of a single enormous software package. These module updates, known as "plug-ins," can be downloaded and installed as needed. To provide a set of vulnerabilities to vulnerability scan software, there are various vulnerability feeds, which are sources of data related to potential or current threats that provide this data. Configuring vulnerability scan software involves setting specific parameters so that the scan meets the intended objective. These parameters include the scope, sensitivity levels, and data types.

- When executing the scan, different scanner options can impact running the scan. A well-protected network ideally should hinder or even block a scanner from performing a vulnerability scan, just as it would prevent a threat actor from conducting their own scan for reconnaissance. It may be necessary for network security to have appropriate scanner permissions added so that it can access the devices on the network. A credentialed scan is a scan for which valid authentication credentials are supplied to the vulnerability scanner to mimic the work of a threat actor who possesses these credentials, while a noncredentialed scan provides no such authentication information. Vulnerability scanners should set off alarms on security appliances. One approach is to mitigate these alarms by instructing the IDS/IPS to ignore attacks originating at the vulnerability scanner. However, a preferred approach is to use this as an opportunity to validate the behavior of both the vulnerability scanner and IDS/IPS.

- Once the vulnerability scan is completed, the results need to be validated and then reported. Validating a scan involves looking for two types of errors: false positives and false negatives. Different levels of reports are usually available that should be distributed to different audiences. The final step in executing a vulnerability scan is to remediate any uncovered vulnerabilities. Not all vulnerabilities are as potentially damaging as other vulnerabilities. Despite the rating of medium given to a vulnerability by a scanner, to one organization this vulnerability may be critical while to another it is not worth the effort to fix. Because many vulnerabilities are complex to unravel and take an extended amount of time to address, there may not be enough time to solve all of them. Vulnerabilities need to be prioritized so that the most important vulnerabilities are addressed early on, while others can wait until later or not even addressed. There are several criteria used for prioritizing vulnerabilities.

- Once a priority order of addressing vulnerabilities is established, the next step is to work toward correcting the vulnerabilities. This includes patching, hardening, addressing difficult vulnerabilities, identifying exceptions and exemptions, analyzing network segmentation, and verifying the mitigation.

- Just as a vulnerability scan is an evaluation by the organization of its ability to resist attacks, there are other types of evaluations on the organization's information security. These are known as audits and assessments. An audit is an examination of results to verify their accuracy. Someone performs this other than the person responsible for producing the results. An assessment is a judgment made about those results. An assessment goes further than an audit: it involves actions necessary to make what was assessed brought back into conformity with the required standards. Most organizations perform audits by company employees known as internal audits. External assessments are performed by professionals from outside the organization.

- One specialized form of audits and assessments is a penetration test. A penetration test attempts to uncover vulnerabilities and then exploit them, just as a threat actor would. Unlike a vulnerability scan that is considered a defensive assessment in that it only looks at the protections of a system, a penetration test is an offensive assessment that probes the system for weaknesses. Using internal employees to conduct a penetration test has advantages in some cases but several disadvantages. Contracting with an external third-party pen testing consultant to conduct a penetration test is the preferred option. There are two methods by which this information is gathered. Active reconnaissance involves directly probing for vulnerabilities and useful information, much like a threat actor would do. When using passive reconnaissance, the tester uses tools that do not raise any alarms.

Key Terms

active reconnaissance
assessment
attestation
audit
audit committee
bug bounty program
Common Vulnerability Scoring
System (CVSS)
Common Weakness Enumeration
(CWE)
compliance
dark web
defensive
environmental variables
examinations
exceptions and exemptions
exposure factor

external assessments
false negative
false positive
independent third-party audit
industry/organizational impact
information sharing organizations
insurance
integrated penetration tests
internal audits
known environment
offensive
Open-Source Intelligence (OSINT)
package monitoring
partially known environment
passive reconnaissance
penetration testing
physical penetration testing

prioritize
proprietary
regulatory
reporting
rescanning
responsible disclosure
program
risk tolerance
self-assessments
system/process audit
third-party sources
threat feeds
unknown environment
validation of remediation
verification
vulnerability classification
vulnerability scan

Review Questions

1. Which of the following is NOT true regarding a vulnerability scan?

   a. It is an ongoing automated process used to identify weaknesses and monitor information security progress.

   b. Its purpose is to find weaknesses and address them in order to reduce the attack surface.

   c. It is an assessment that is designed to be a cyclical and continual scanning and monitoring process.

   d. It audits only the devices that are used but not the processes to protect devices.

2. Why are open-source libraries vulnerable?

   a. These libraries are not owned and controlled by any single entity.

   b. They use coding tools that are considered inferior to standardized tools.

   c. They are "stubs" that cannot be properly verified for malware.

   d. Their platforms are known to be owned and managed by threat actors.

3. Isai needs to continuously analyze apps for vulnerabilities and wants a dashboard that the security team can use to monitor the applications' current security features. What tool would Isai select?

   a. App evaluator

   b. Cloud native control (CNC)

   c. Program tester

   d. Package monitoring

4. Which of the following is NOT a challenge of running a vulnerability scan?

   a. Remediations

   b. Technical limitations

   c. Identification of vulnerabilities

   d. Low volume of scan data

5. Which of the following is NOT true about threat intelligence?

   a. Threat intelligence is data that is collected, processed, and analyzed to understand a threat actor's motives, targets, and attack behaviors.

   b. Threat intelligence enables organizations to make faster, more informed data-based security decisions.

   c. Threat intelligence is especially vital to penetration testing.

   d. Threat intelligence changes behavior from being reactive to proactive.

6. Kostyantyn has been asked to explore part of the web that is the domain of threat actors to look for information about the latest types of attacks. What area of the web will he explore?

   a. Dark web

   b. Deep web

   c. Black web

   d. Restricted web

7. Where do third-party sources get their threat intelligence data?

   a. From government contractors

   b. From the information they collect from their own customers

   c. From free and public sources

   d. From paid informants

8. Which of the following is NOT an advantage of an organization sharing threat intelligence information?

   a. Organizations can enrich their own existing information and make it more actionable.

   b. Organizations can independently confirm their own observations with other sharing members and improve the overall quality of the threat information through the reduction of ambiguity and errors.

   c. Organizations can leverage the collective knowledge, experience, and capabilities of other organizations in their sharing community to gain a more complete understanding of the threats they face.

   d. Organizations can identify third-party OSINT providers more quickly to purchase their threat feeds.

9. Artem has been asked to identify an application protocol for exchanging cyber threat intelligence over HTTPS. Which protocol would he choose?

   a. STIX

   b. CybOX

   c. TAXII

   d. IODEF

10. Which of the following is used to create cybersecurity threat maps?

   a. Information sharing organizations

   b. Proprietary enterprises

   c. OSINT

   d. Third-party data sharing organizations (3DSO)

11. Which of the following does NOT apply to a vulnerability scan?

    a. Identify vulnerabilities by scanning systems and networks.

    b. Scan to find weaknesses and then mitigate.

    c. Are usually automated with a handful of manual processes.

    d. Act like a threat actor to find vulnerabilities to exploit.

12. Which of the following is NOT a type of vulnerability scan over an asset?

    a. Operating system

    b. Wireless network

    c. Endpoint

    d. Network

13. Bohdan is explaining to an intern some of the disadvantages to active scanning. Which of the following would Bohdan NOT give as a disadvantage?

    a. IoT devices may react differently to test traffic.

    b. Sending test traffic increases the risk of the endpoints malfunctioning if incompatible queries are sent.

    c. Smaller networks can become overloaded with high volumes of test traffic.

    d. Active scanning can accelerate the collection of data.

14. Which type of vulnerability scan is performed from the vantage point outside the network?

    a. Remote vulnerability scan

    b. External vulnerability scan

    c. Network vulnerability scan

    d. Internal vulnerability scan

15. Arkady has been asked to explain to a manager why the SOC is not performing vulnerability scans continuously over all systems. Which of the following would NOT be a reason Arkady would give?

    a. Expense

    b. Workflow interruptions

    c. Risk appetite

    d. Technical constraints

16. Which of the following do plug-ins NOT contain?

    a. Advanced vulnerability information

    b. Listing of vulnerable local IP addresses

    c. Remediation actions

    d. Updated algorithms

17. Borysko needs to specify which devices need to be included in the next vulnerability scan. What parameter must he set?

    a. Sensitivity level

    b. Region

    c. Scope

    d. NET-SCAN

18. Danylo is examining the results of a vulnerability scan and is prioritizing the list of vulnerabilities. He wants to use a system that will assign a numeric score to each vulnerability. Which system will Danylo use?

    a. CRV

    b. VDSS

    c. RDV

    d. CVSS

19. Which of the following is considered the best-known and most widely used vulnerability scanner?

    a. Nessus

    b. VAX

    c. RCAP

    d. Invicti

20. What is the first step that should be taken after deciding which vulnerability scanning tool to use?

    a. Set the scope.

    b. Determine the sensitivity level.

    c. Update the plug-ins.

    d. Execute the scan.

Hands-On Projects

Project 12-1: Exploring Common Vulnerabilities and Exposures (CVE)

Estimated Time: 25 minutes

Objective: Research CVE.

Description: Vulnerability feeds are available to provide updated information to scanning software about the latest vulnerabilities. One of the most highly regarded is the Common Vulnerabilities and Exposures (CVE). These can also be manually examined for information on the latest vulnerabilities. In this project, you learn more about CVE and view CVE information.

1. Open your web browser and enter the URL **https://cve.org**. (If you are no longer able to access the site through this web address, use a search engine to search for "Mitre CVE.")

2. Click **Resources & Support** in the top menu.

3. Click **FAQs** and read through this overview, expanding the items where necessary.

4. Click **About** in the top menu.

5. Watch the video **CVE Program Overview**. In your own words, how would you describe it? How does it work? What advantages does it provide?

6. In the **About** box, expand **Process**.

7. Click **CVE Record Lifecycle**.

8. Read through the steps and expand items where necessary.

9. Searches can be performed through either entering specific CVE IDs or by keyword. Click the breakout icon next to **CVE List keyword search**.

10. Enter a generic vulnerability such as **passwords** and then click **Submit** to display the CVE entries. How many relate to this topic?

11. Select several of the CVE entries and read through the material.

12. Locate a CVE entry that contains the tag *Disputed*. Click this entry. Under *Description*, click ****DISPUTED**** to read about what constitutes a disputed CVE. Who would dispute a CVE? Why?

13. Return to the CVE page with the description of the CVE you selected. Click **Search CVE List**.

14. Enter a different vulnerability and select several entries to read through its details.

15. Close all windows.

Project 12-2: Exploring the National Vulnerability Database (NVD)

Estimated Time: 30 minutes
Objective: Use the NVD.
Description: The National Vulnerability Database (NVD) is managed by the U.S. government as a repository for vulnerability management data and contains software flaws, misconfigurations, product names, and their impacts. In this project, you explore the NVD.

1. Open your web browser and enter the URL **https://nvd.nist.gov**. (If you are no longer able to access the site through this web address, use a search engine to search for "NIST NVD.")

2. Click the plus sign next to **General**.

3. Click **FAQ**.

4. Click **General FAQs**.

5. Read through the material. In your own words, how does the MITRE CVE compare with the NIST NVD? When would you use the CVE? When would you use the NVD? How frequently is the NVD updated? Is this often enough?

6. Return to the home page by clicking the Back button as many times as necessary.

7. Click the plus sign next to **General**.

8. Click **NVD Dashboard** to view the latest information. Do the numbers surprise you? How does the number of vulnerabilities under the score distribution compare? Is that what you would have expected?

9. Scroll through the *Last 20 Scored Vulnerability IDs & Summaries*. Have you heard of any of these vulnerabilities? How will they be distributed to the public at large?

10. Return to the home page.

11. Click the plus sign next to **General**.

12. Click **Visualizations** to display graphical information.

13. Click **Vulnerabilities – CVE**.

14. Click **Description Summary Word** to display a bar graph of the most common words used as part of a vulnerability description. Hover over the three highest bars to view the three most frequent words used. Is this what you would have expected?

15. Return to the Vulnerability Visualizations page. Select each of the other graphs and study the information presented. How could a security professional use this information?

16. Return to the NVD Visualizations page. Click **Products – CPE**. Which vendor has the highest number of total products that appears in the NVD? View other vendors by hovering over the bars. What do you find interesting about this distribution?

17. Return to the home page by clicking the Back button as many times as necessary.

18. Click the plus sign next to **Other Sites**.

19. Click **Checklist (NCP) Repository**.

20. This displays a form through which you can search for benchmarks/secure configuration guides. Select different parameters to view different guides, and then select one to view in detail. Is this information helpful?

21. Return to the home page by clicking the Back button as many times as necessary.

22. Click the plus sign next to **Search**.

23. Click **Vulnerability Search**.

24. Enter **passwords**. How many vulnerabilities are found? Select several of these to read through the information.

25. Select a different vulnerability to search the NVD database. How useful is this information?

26. Close all windows.

Case Projects

Case Project 12-1: #TrendingCyber

Estimated Time: 15 minutes
Objective: Summarize your thoughts on the #TrendingCyber opener.
Description: Read again the opening #TrendingCyber in this module. Why are there variations between the paid threat intelligence feeds? What risks would this cause for the subscriber? Should these security providers be more transparent about their feeds? Should they allow security researchers to analyze the feeds? Or should there be a rating system for the different feeds? Write a one-paragraph summary of your thoughts.

Case Project 12-2: Vulnerability Feed

Estimated Time: 15 minutes
Objective: Analyze features in vulnerability feeds.
Description: Visit the website abuse.ch and research the different features that are available for a vulnerability feed. How up to date does the information appear to be? How many malware instances have been submitted? What strengths are there of this feed? What weaknesses exist? And how could a threat actor use this site? Write a one-page paper on your research.

Case Project 12-3: Nessus

Estimated Time: 20 minutes

Objective: Explore the features of Nessus.

Description: Perhaps the best-known and most widely used vulnerability scanner is Nessus, which contains a wide array of prebuilt templates. Nessus advertises that new plug-ins are available as soon as 24 hours after a new vulnerability is disclosed. Visit the Nessus website at **www.tenable.com/products/nessus** and read the information on Nessus. Write a one-page paper on your research about Nessus. You can also download the free Nessus Essentials software and run a vulnerability scan on a maximum of 16 IP addresses.

Case Project 12-4: Scanning Decisions

Estimated Time: 25 minutes

Objective: Determine how to make decisions about vulnerability scanning.

Description: Identify a network at your school or business or a personal network to evaluate and develop the scanning decisions if you were to perform a vulnerability scan on it. Include what should be scanned (data classification, asset criticality, and network segmentation), how it should be scanned (active vs. passive scanning and internal vs. external), and when it should be scanned. For each of these, have a justification as to why you made this decision and the weakness of the alternative. Create a one-page paper on your scanning decisions.

Case Project 12-5: Balancing Business Processes and Scanning

Estimated Time: 20 minutes

Objective: Create a rationale for balancing business processes and vulnerability scanning.

Description: Suppose you work for a company that is resisting implementing changes to vulnerabilities identified by a vulnerability scan. Your company states that the business process interruption would be significant and could potentially cause significant downtime to address a vulnerability that possibly would never even be exploited. Create a one-page memo to your manager about the importance of addressing vulnerabilities and your recommendations for balancing business processes and cybersecurity.

Case Project 12-6: False Positives and False Negatives

Estimated Time: 15 minutes

Objective: Research false positives and false negatives.

Description: Use the Internet to research false positives and false negatives. Which is worse? If a doctor gives information to a patient about the results of a diagnostic test, is a false positive or a false negative worse? What about facial recognition scanning for a criminal? Which is worse for a vulnerability scan, a false positive or a false negative? Write a one-page paper on your findings and analysis.

Case Project 12-7: Penetration Testing Products

Estimated Time: 25 minutes

Objective: Research penetration testing products.

Description: Use the Internet to research pen test products. Select three products and create a table that compares their features. Be sure to include such elements as how often they are updated, the systems they run on, and available tools. Based on your analysis, which would you recommend? Why?

Case Project 12-8: Threat Actor Tactics

Estimated Time: 20 minutes

Objective: Research threat actor tactics.

Description: Most users are unaware of how threat actors work and their various tactics. Read the article "Tales From the Trenches; a Lockbit Ransomware Story" at **https://www.mcafee.com/blogs/other-blogs/mcafee-labs/tales-from-the-trenches-a-lockbit-ransomware-story/**. This article contains detailed information about the tactics of threat actors for a particular strain of ransomware. Although some of the information is very technical in nature, it does give a good picture of the advanced skills and strategies used today. Write a one-paragraph summary of what you have learned about their tactics.

Case Project 12-9: Cyber Exposure Platforms

Estimated Time: 30 minutes
Objective: Research cyber exposure platforms.
Description: The concept of all an organization's servers residing in an on-premise data center that serves resources to desktop computers is a historical relic. Computer servers, networks, and endpoints have evolved more rapidly over the last decade than perhaps in any time in the history of information technology. Cloud computing, mobile smartphones, virtual machines, and Internet of Things (IoT) devices, just to name a few, have dramatically increased today's enterprise's IT capabilities—and correspondingly have dramatically increased its attack surface. This is shown in Figure 12-11.

Figure 12-11   Today's enterprise IT

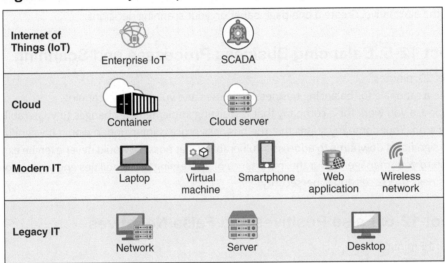

However, performing static vulnerability scans, in the eyes of many security professionals, may no longer provide the visibility into system and network vulnerabilities that they once did. Legacy scans that are ad hoc and siloed are usually labor intensive and expensive, resulting in limited deployments and incomplete visibility. These scans often lack comprehensive, continuous, and accurate visibility into where vulnerabilities reside and how businesses might be impacted. And without this visibility, it is difficult or even impossible to prioritize and manage risks.

Among the specific limitations of legacy vulnerability management are a focus on traditional assets. Legacy vulnerability scanning focuses on traditional IT assets such as network infrastructures, servers, and desktop computers. These tools are not always designed to discover and scan new assets such as cloud instances, containers, web applications, and IoT devices. Another limitation is reliance on active scanning technologies. Active vulnerability scanning tools, while essential, can only capture a snapshot at a single point in time. They often entirely miss devices that are not always connected to the corporate network or that do not have static IP addresses (such as smartphones or remote employees' laptop computers), short-lived assets such as containers, and resources like cloud repositories. Vulnerability scanning was simply not designed for today's dynamic assets and does not always give an accurate picture of their security.

As a result, advanced vulnerability scanning tools and processes have recently been introduced to reflect the changes in IT. A new category of security tools, sometimes called *cyber exposure platforms*, are specifically designed to continuously perform asset inventory and then assess not only traditional IT infrastructures and devices but also cloud, mobile, IoT, and other assets across the entire organization. In addition, these tools can help quickly evaluate vulnerabilities, prioritize issues, take appropriate corrective steps, and finally measure and report on the vulnerability from both a technical and business perspective.

Use the Internet to research cyber exposure platforms. How do they function? What are their advantages? What are their disadvantages? Is this the future of vulnerability scanning? Write a one-page paper on your research.

Case Project 12-10: Crowdsourced Penetration Testers

Estimated Time: 30 minutes
Objective: Research crowdsourced penetration testers.
Description: A bug bounty is a monetary reward given for uncovering a software vulnerability. Most software developers offer some type of bug bounty, ranging from several thousand dollars to millions of dollars. Bug bounty programs take advantage of crowdsourcing, which involves obtaining input into a project by enlisting the services of a large number of individuals through the Internet. Recently some third-party organizations have begun offering crowdsourced pen testing. Instead of contracting with a single external pen tester consulting organization, crowdsourced pen testing involves a large group of individuals who are not regular employees of an organization. These hand-picked crowdsourced members of the security community test the security of an organization. Some of the advantages of crowdsourced pen testers are faster testing that can result in quicker remediation of vulnerabilities, the ability to rotate teams so different individuals test the system, and the option of conducting multiple pen tests simultaneously. Research crowdsourced penetration testing. Identify several examples of these services. Would you recommend an external third party performing a pen test on your organization? What are the risks? Write a one-page paper on your research.

Case Project 12-11: Penetration Testing Scope

Estimated Time: 30 minutes
Objective: Research penetration testing scopes.
Description: For a pen test, the scope is what should be tested. Scope involves several elements that define the relevant test boundaries. Because laws vary among states, provinces, and countries, it is important to identify the physical location of the targets and, if necessary, adjust the scope of the test. For instance, countries in the European Union (EU) have more stringent laws surrounding the privacy of individuals, which can change how a social engineering engagement would be executed. In addition to these boundaries, other boundaries should be considered. For example, does the pen test include physical security, such as fencing, cameras, and guards? Are there limitations on who should be targeted by social engineering attacks (such as excluding specific C-suite executives)? Should there be limits on spear-phishing messages, such as those that contain offers for drugs or pornographic material?

The importance of determining the scope of pen testing can be illustrated by a recent event. Two security contractors from Coalfire, a penetration testing company that frequently does security assessments for federal agencies and for state and local governments, were arrested in Adel, Iowa, as they attempted to gain access to the Dallas County Courthouse. They claimed to be conducting a penetration test to determine how vulnerable county court records were and to measure law enforcement's response to a break-in. However, because the Iowa state court officials who ordered the test never told county officials about it, the penetration testers were arrested and went to jail. The state officials later apologized to Dallas County, citing confusion over just what Coalfire was going to test, although later both parties said there were "different interpretations" of the scope of the pen test. How could this incident have been avoided? What documentation is needed to perform a penetration test? Who should be aware of a test taking place? Write a one-page summary of penetration testing scopes.

Case Project 12-12: Bay Point Ridge Security

Estimated Time: 45 minutes
Objective: Research vulnerability scans and pen tests.
Description: Bay Point Ridge Security (BPRS) is a managed service provider (MSP) that manages networks, computers, cloud resources, and information security for small-to-medium enterprises (SMEs) in the region. BPRS provides internships to students who are in their final year of the security degree program at the local college and has recently hired you.

You have been asked to work with a new client who is reluctant to allow a vulnerability scan and a penetration test on their systems. They do not want any weaknesses to be exposed and instead are only interested in building what they consider stronger security.

1. Create a PowerPoint presentation about vulnerability scans and pen testing. Include the functions of each and how they could help the client create stronger defenses. Your presentation should contain at least 10–12 slides.

2. After the presentation, the senior management is confused why not all vulnerabilities should be immediately addressed. Create a memo that explains why it is not always possible to address all vulnerabilities and what your recommendation would be to decide which to address and why.

Two Rights & A Wrong: Answers

Vulnerability Scanning

1. Threat intelligence is data that is collected, processed, and analyzed to understand a threat actor's motives, targets, and attack behaviors.

2. A false positive is the failure to raise an alarm when there is an issue.

3. It is rarely possible, and often not desirable, to address all the vulnerabilities found in a vulnerability scan.

Answer: The wrong answer is #2.

Explanation: A false positive is an alarm that is raised when there is no problem, while a false negative is the failure to raise an alarm when there is an issue.

Audits and Assessments

1. An assessment is an examination of results to verify their accuracy.

2. A penetration test looks for deep vulnerabilities that can only be exposed through actual attacks that use the mindset of a threat actor.

3. In a partially known environment, testers are given limited knowledge of the network and only some elevated privileges.

Answer: The wrong answer is #1.

Explanation: An audit is an examination of results to verify its accuracy. Someone performs this other than the person responsible for producing the results. An assessment is a judgment made about those results.

Reference

1. Bouwman, Xander; Griffioen, Harm; Egbers, Jelle; Doerr, Christian; Klievink, Bram; van Eeten, Michel, "A different cup of TI?: The added value of commercial threat intelligence," *29th USENIX Security Symposium*, retrieved Aug. 8, 2020, https://www.cyber-threat-intelligence.com/publications/Usenix2020-PaidCTI.pdf.

Module 13

Incident Preparation and Investigation

Module Objectives

After completing this module, you should be able to do the following:

1   Explain how to prepare for a cyber incident
2   Describe how to achieve resilience through redundancy
3   Describe how to conduct an analysis of an incident

#TrendingCyber

Investigating a cyber incident involves examining data found on hardware devices for information about the attack and preserving evidence for law enforcement. But security investigators are not the only ones who are interested in looking at hardware data: threat actors would love to get their hands on this data to assist them in crafting their attacks. Thus, this type of data should be carefully protected. However, recently security researchers found valuable data from network hardware devices that have been decommissioned and sold on the secondary market. The number of decommissioned devices with data and the type of data that was retrieved are alarming.

There have been many studies and cautionary tales of secondhand computing equipment being sold on the secondary market that still contained the previous owner's data. This data can be very personal and sensitive, including not only contact information and intimate photos but also medical history and financial data. Studies have consistently shown that a majority of used hard drives, USB flash drives, secure digital (SD) and other memory cards, and mobile devices such as phones and tablets purchased secondhand have had incomplete data wiping or no wiping before being resold.

However, one category of hardware that has not been examined for sensitive data is used routers. Operating at the Network layer (Layer 3), a router is a network device that can forward frames across different computer networks. Replacing a router from an equipment rack with a new device is a regular occurrence in many large business networking environments. It would be assumed that these seasoned enterprise networking and security professionals would be aware of the aforementioned studies and would take active steps to erase all data on decommissioned routers.

But that is not the case.

Security researchers at the security software company ESET stumbled across this problem entirely by accident. They were working on a project to set up a lab for testing real-world attacks against multiple attack surfaces like email and industrial control systems (ICSs). The researchers decided to use hardware devices that would mimic typical current production environments. Since many businesses were not using state-of-the-art equipment but equipment that was one or two versions behind, the researchers chose to purchase older and widely deployed hardware from the secondary market. One category of equipment that they bought was core routers of various sizes and from different vendors, which were purchased for only $50 to $150.

Much to their surprise, the ESET researchers found that one of the first routers to arrive that originally belonged to a "reputable, major, Silicon Valley-based, household-name software vendor with a global footprint" contained sensitive corporate data. This discovery temporarily diverted the path of their research to instead investigate if this was a widespread problem. Their budget allowed them to purchase a total of 18 used routers, covering a range of models from three of the largest name-brand vendors (Cisco, Fortinet, and Juniper Networks).

Of these 18 core routers, one was dead on arrival and two devices were a mirrored pair from a cluster configuration of which only one could be used. Five of the routers had their contents properly wiped clean, and two of the routers were hardened so that it was almost impossible to retrieve any data. That left nine core routers to examine. The researchers decided not to make any "heroic efforts," such as using data recovery or specialized digital forensic software, to view the data. Nor did they open the cases to extract components. Instead, they used only standard router operating system commands and utilities supplied by the device manufacturers to examine the router's contents.

The data they found first allowed them to determine the previous owners of the routers. Two of the routers came from a multinational technology company and from a telecom, each with over 10,000 employees and annual revenue exceeding $1 billion.

As they dug deeper, the routers gave up more secrets. They revealed customer data (on 22 percent of the routers), exposed data allowing third-party connections to the network (33 percent), showed credentials for connecting to other networks as a trusted party (44 percent), listed itemized connection details for specific applications (89 percent), provided router-to-router authentication keys (89 percent), and exposed one or more IPsec or VPN credentials, or hashed root passwords (100 percent).

The data uncovered included lists of application types and network locations and, in some cases, information on remote cloud applications hosted in specific remote data centers, complete with information on which ports or access control mechanisms were used and from which networks. Additionally, there were firewall rules that were used to block or allow certain access from other networks and at the times of day they could be accessed.

What could a threat actor do with these types of corporate secrets? They could plan and execute an attack with inside information that is normally visible only to internal personnel who have security clearances. With this level of detail, impersonating network or internal hosts would be far simpler for an attacker, especially since the devices contained VPN credentials or other easily cracked authentication tokens. The data also revealed the organization's approach to security in general. By noting how detailed or vague their security defenses were on these devices, a reasonable guess could be made about the security levels in the rest of the environment.

This research demonstrated that organizations, both large and small, are not properly wiping their equipment. Instead of attempting to cajole organizations to do a better job of wiping their network equipment of sensitive data, the researchers instead offered recommendations for the hardware vendors. First, they suggested that these vendors should provide to the public—at no charge—full and complete instructions for securely wiping devices, even for devices that are no longer sold or supported. Second, the secure-wipe instructions should use similar language and terms not just across a vendor's product lines and models but also across the industry as a whole so that instructions are clear and unambiguous. Third, in future designs, the vendors should consider only using easily removable media, such as a CompactFlash (CF) card, SD card, USB flash drive, or solid-state drives (SSDs), to store sensitive configuration information. The media could then be removed prior to decommissioning.

Because the researchers could identify the organizations who previously owned the routers, they attempted to notify the former owners of these issues so that they could be addressed before other routers were decommissioned and sold. While some organizations were responsive, other previous owners were very difficult or even impossible to reach. After two months of effort, they still had no response from some of the owners. The researchers then tried to contact the organizations via LinkedIn. While this resulted in more success, it still left two organizations who never replied to any inquiries. In the words of the ESET researchers, "We got the distinct impression that neither really wanted to hear from us."[1]

Each day around the world natural disasters strike with little if any warning: hurricanes, droughts, floods, earthquakes, and windstorms, just to name a few, are common. In 2022, on average there were 1.15 "notable disaster events" *daily*, for a total of 421 events. The most devastating event was a hurricane that resulted in 157 deaths and a $95.5 billion economic loss of which only 54 percent ($52.5 billion) was covered by insurance. The worldwide global economic loss due to all natural disasters for 2022 was $313 billion, up from $232 billion just three years before.

And one-half of all dollar losses occurred in the United States.[2] Not all disasters are acts of nature: sabotage, terrorism, industrial mishaps, chemical spills, and transportation accidents are but a few of the events that round out a long list of disasters.

One more disaster to add to this list is a successful cyberattack. Like natural disasters and human-made disasters, a cyberattack can cripple an unprepared organization. Unfortunately, preparation for such an event is woefully lacking. Over half of small businesses have no plan in place to react to a cyberattack because they think they are too small to be targeted. However, such is not the case: businesses large and small are under attack today. And about 60 percent of small companies that suffer a cyberattack are out of business within six months of the attack.[3]

The ability of an organization to maintain its operations and services in the face of natural disasters, human-made disasters, and cyberattacks is crucial if it is to survive. But this does not happen by accident. It calls for advanced preparation. And it requires investigation after an incident to learn from mistakes and address vulnerabilities.

In this module, you learn about these two steps of preparation and investigation. You first learn about basic steps in preparing for an attack. Next, you explore how to perform an investigation following a cyber event.

Preparatory Plans

Certification

3.4 Explain the importance of resilience and recovery in security architecture.

4.8 Explain appropriate incident response activities.

5.1 Summarize elements of effective security governance.

5.2 Explain elements of the risk management process.

Preparing for a cyber event is absolutely essential. This preparation involves business continuity and incident response planning.

Business Continuity Planning

It is important to know what business continuity planning involves. A business impact analysis and a disaster recovery plan are closely associated with business continuity.

Business Continuity Plan (BCP)

Business continuity can be defined as the ability of an organization to maintain its operations and services in the face of a disruptive event or a major disaster. These disasters may be environmental disasters (like floods, hurricanes, and tornados), human-made disasters (like industrial mishaps, chemical spills, and terrorist attacks), or a cyberattack. Although most disasters that threaten an organization are external disasters (like environmental disasters), some are internal (like a fire in a data center).

Business continuity planning is the process an organization undertakes in advance to determine a plan of action to protect itself in the event of a disaster. The outcome of this planning is a business continuity plan (BCP), which is a strategic document that provides alternative modes of operation for business activities that, if interrupted, could result in a significant loss to the enterprise. Creating a BCP involves identifying exposure to threats, creating preventive and recovery procedures, and then testing them to determine if they are sufficient. In short, a BCP is designed to ensure that an organization can continue to function (continuity of operations) in the event of an environmental disaster or human-made disaster. In other words, it is *recovery planning*.

> **Note 1**
>
> BCP may also include succession planning, which is determining in advance who will be authorized to take over in the event of the incapacitation or death of key employees.

A BCP should include the following elements:

- **High availability.** A BCP should address high availability, which is the ability to withstand all outages—planned and unplanned outages and environmental and internal disasters—while providing continuous processing for critical applications. For example, a high-availability solution for critical e-commerce servers and databases could require a fully automated failover to a backup system so that sales can continue functioning without any disruption.
- **Scalability.** Organizations continue to grow and expand on a regular basis. A BCP that only looks at the organization as it stands today will find that the plan is out of date tomorrow. Instead, a BCP must have the capability to cover increased capacity; in other words, a BCP must have scalability.
- **Diversity.** Just as a BCP must have scalability as capacity increases, it must also include diversity as different technologies, third-party vendors, controls, and even cryptographic solutions are added.
- **On-prem and cloud.** As more and more resources are moved from on-premises to the cloud, a BCP should have the flexibility to address this movement without needing to rewrite the plan regularly.

Similar to creating a BCP is **continuity of operation planning (COOP)**. This is a federal initiative that is intended to encourage organizations (and departments within an organization) to address how critical operations will continue under a broad range of negative circumstances. A COOP plan addresses emergencies from an "all-hazards approach" instead of focusing more narrowly on a specific event. It is designed to establish requirements for ensuring that critical functions continue and even includes how personnel and resources can be relocated in case of emergencies.

Business Impact Analysis (BIA)

One important tool for creating a BCP is a business impact analysis (BIA). A BIA identifies business processes and functions and then quantifies the impact a loss of these functions may have on business operations. These impacts include the impact on property (tangible assets), finance (monetary funding), safety (physical protection), reputation (status), and even life (well-being). By identifying the critical processes and functions through a site risk assessment (a detailed evaluation of the processes performed at a site and how they can be impacted), a BIA can then be the foundation for a functional recovery plan that addresses the steps to be taken to restore those processes, if necessary.

> **Caution !**
>
> It is sometimes assumed by an organization with remote sites that all sites perform essentially the same functions as the main headquarters. However, that is not always the case. A third-party vendor was hired to perform a BIA but was told to only look at the headquarters. The vendor convinced the organization to examine all the sites. They found that the headquarters performed over 80 different functions, of which half were centrally managed and implemented. The other 40 functions could be performed at the satellite offices in various combinations, which would have been overlooked if the BIA were not conducted at each site.

A BIA is designed to identify those processes that are critically important to an enterprise. A BIA will help determine the **mission-essential function** or the activity that serves as the core purpose of the enterprise. For example, a mission-essential function for a hospital could be to *Deliver healthcare services to individuals and their families*, while a nonessential function is to *Generate and distribute a monthly online newsletter*. In addition, a BIA can also help in the identification of critical systems that in turn support the mission-essential function. In a hospital setting, a critical system could be *Maintain an emergency room facility for the community*. Whereas this is a critical system, it is not the core purpose of the hospital.

Identifying the **single point of failure**, which is a component or entity in a system that, if it no longer functions, will disable the entire system, is also a goal of a BIA. A patient information database in a hospital could be considered a single point of failure. Minimizing these single failure points results in a system that can function for an extended period with little downtime. This availability is often expressed as a percentage of uptime in a year. Table 13-1 lists the percentage availability and the corresponding downtimes.

Table 13-1   Percentage availability and downtimes

Percentage availability	Name	Weekly downtime	Monthly downtime	Yearly downtime
90%	One Nine	16.8 hours	72 hours	36.5 days
99%	Two Nines	1.68 hours	7.20 hours	3.65 days
99.9%	Three Nines	10.1 minutes	43.2 minutes	8.76 hours
99.99%	Four Nines	1.01 minutes	4.32 minutes	52.56 minutes
99.999%	Five Nines	6.05 seconds	25.9 seconds	5.26 minutes
99.9999%	Six Nines	0.605 second	2.59 seconds	31.5 seconds

Note 2

Because privacy of data is of high importance today, many BIAs also contain a privacy impact assessment, which is used to identify and mitigate privacy risks. This includes an examination of what personally identifiable information (PII) is being collected, the reasons it is collected, and the safeguards regarding how the data will be accessed, shared, and stored. A privacy threshold assessment can determine if a system contains PII, whether a privacy impact assessment is required, and if any other privacy requirements apply to the IT system.

Disaster Recovery Plan (DRP)

Whereas a BCP looks at the needs of the business as a whole in recovering from a catastrophe, a subset of it focuses on continuity in the context of information technology (IT). This is called a disaster recovery plan (DRP), which is involved with restoring IT functions and services. A DRP is a written document that details the process for restoring IT resources following an event that causes a significant disruption in service. Comprehensive in scope, a DRP is intended to be a detailed document that is updated regularly.

Most DRPs cover a standard set of topics. One common topic is the sequence in restoring systems. After a disaster has occurred, what should be the sequence in which different systems are reinstated (**restoration order**)? That is, which systems should have priority and be restored before other systems? There are several factors that may be considered. One factor is obvious dependencies; that is, the network must be restored before applications that rely on the network are restored. A second factor is the processes that are of fundamental importance to an enterprise; critical systems that support the mission-essential function and those systems that require high availability need to be restored before other systems. Another factor is the alternative business practices, or those "workaround" activities that can temporarily substitute for normal business activities; that is, how long a manual workaround process can meet the temporary needs without causing bigger problems such as unmanageable backlogs.

Incident Response Planning

Successful information security attacks are inevitable. It is important to prepare in advance for an incident. There are different steps to take in preparation: creating an incident response plan, performing testing exercises, and studying attack frameworks.

Creating an Incident Response Plan

System weaknesses that lead to successful attacks mean that a formal plan of action is essential. An **incident response plan** is a set of written instructions for reacting to an information security incident. Without such a plan, enterprises are at risk of being unable to quickly identify the attack, contain its spread, recover, and learn from the attack to improve defenses.

The action steps to be taken when an incident occurs, called the incident response process, also make up the elements of an incident response plan. These are listed in Table 13-2.

Table 13-2   Incident response process

Action step	Description
Preparation	Equipping IT staff, management, and users to handle potential incidents when they arise
Detection	Determining whether an event is actually a security incident
Analysis	Collecting data from tools and systems to identify indicators of compromise
Containment	Limiting the damage of the incident and isolating those systems that are impacted to prevent further damage
Eradication	Finding the cause of the incident and temporarily removing any systems that may be causing damage
Recovery	After ensuring no threat remains, permitting affected systems to return to normal operation
Lessons learned	Completing incident documentation, performing detailed analysis to increase security, and improving future response efforts

An incident response plan should also contain the following information:

- **Definitions.** The plan should provide clear descriptions of the types and categories of documented incident definitions, which outline in detail what is—and is not—an incident that requires a response.
- **Incident response teams.** An incident response team is responsible for responding to security incidents. In addition to technical specialists who can address specific threats, it should also include members who are public-relations employees and managers who can guide enterprise executives on appropriate communication. Each member should have clearly designated duties, roles, and responsibilities in the team.
- **Reporting requirements.** The reporting requirements indicate to whom information should be distributed and at what point the security event has escalated to the degree that specific actions should be implemented. It is particularly important today for an incident response plan to identify the relevant stakeholders within the organization who need to be initially informed of an incident and then kept up to date. Known as stakeholder management, it includes areas such as operations, legal, technical, finance, and even human resources.

Performing Testing Exercises

It is important to test an incident response plan by conducting simulated testing exercises to make necessary adjustments. The different types of exercises are summarized in Table 13-3.

Table 13-3   Incident response testing exercises

Exercise Name	Description	Example
Tabletop	A monthly 30-minute discussion of a scenario conducted in an informal and stress-free environment.	This scenario is presented: An employee casually remarks about how generous it is of a vendor to provide the box of USB drives on the conference room table, embossed with the company logo. After making some inquiries, you find the vendor did not provide USB drives to employees. What do you now do?
Walkthrough	A review by IT personnel of the steps of the plan by paying particular attention to the IT systems and services that may be targeted in an attack.	A technician with knowledge of the current system will walk through the proposed recovery procedures to determine if there are omissions, gaps, errors, or false assumptions.
Simulation	A hands-on simulation exercise using a realistic scenario to thoroughly test each step of the plan.	A simulation of a senior vice president who opens a malicious attachment and introduces malware into the network is presented.
Fail over	Testing the process of temporarily switching to backup procedures after an attack.	The connection to a server is terminated to determine if the backup server will take over.
Parallel processing	Conducting the same tests simultaneously in multiple environments.	A test of an attack against a firewall at the main campus is also conducted at a remote site to determine if the same procedures are applicable.

Note 3

During the first few months of the COVID-19 pandemic, many medical professionals around the world who were active in combating the disease participated online in a tabletop game called Pandemic. The players collaborated (not competed) to contain outbreaks around the world and search for cures. Each player chose a role like a scientist, researcher, or medic, each with unique abilities, and had to work together to develop cures before the diseases overwhelmed them. Many medical professionals reported that playing the game was therapeutic and a boost to morale.

Studying Attack Frameworks

An information security **framework** is a series of documented processes used to define policies and procedures for implementation and management of security controls in an enterprise environment. About 84 percent of U.S. organizations use a security framework, and 44 percent use multiple frameworks.[4] Frameworks can also be studied about how attacks occur, called exploitation frameworks. These serve as models of the thinking and actions of today's threat actors. Three common attack frameworks include:

- **MITRE ATT&CK.** MITRE ATT&CK is a knowledge base of attacker techniques that have been broken down and classified in detail. The attacks are offensively oriented actions that can be used against particular platforms. The focus of ATT&CK is not on the tools and malware that attackers use but on how they interact with systems during an operation. These techniques are arranged into a set of tactics to help explain and provide context for the technique. Figure 13-1 displays a sample of the ATT&CK framework.
- **The Diamond Model of Intrusion Analysis.** The Diamond Model of Intrusion Analysis is a framework for examining network intrusion events. This framework derives its name and shape from the four core interconnected elements that comprise any event: adversary, infrastructure, capability, and victim. Analyzing security incidents involves piecing together the Diamond using information collected about these four facets to understand the threat in its full context. Figure 13-2 illustrates the Diamond Model.

Figure 13-1   MITRE ATT&CK framework

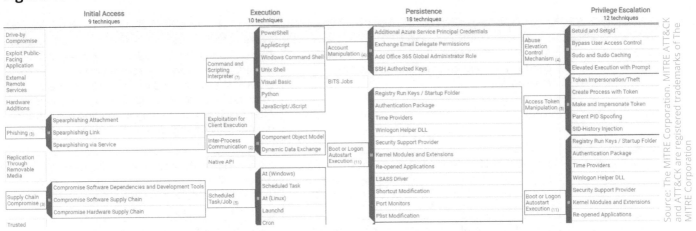

Figure 13-2   Diamond Model of Intrusion Analysis

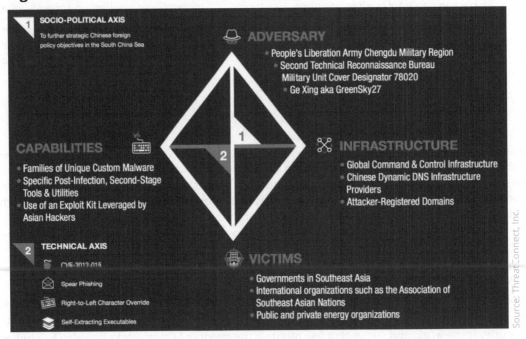

- **Cyber Kill Chain.** A *kill chain* is a military term used to describe the systematic process to target and engage an enemy. An attacker who attempts to break into a web server or computer network actually follows these same steps. Known as the Cyber Kill Chain, it outlines the steps of an attack. Figure 13-3 shows the Cyber Kill Chain. Its underlying purpose is to illustrate that attacks are an integrated and end-to-end process like a "chain." Disrupting any one of the steps will interrupt the entire attack process, but the ability to disrupt the early steps of the chain is the most effective and least costly.

Figure 13-3 Cyber Kill Chain

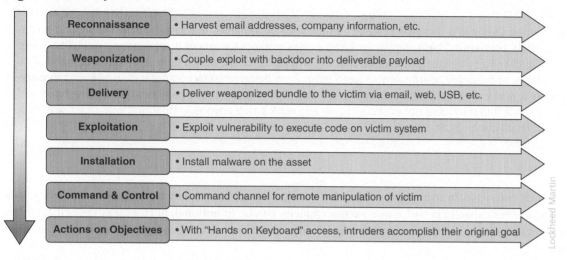

Reconnaissance	• Harvest email addresses, company information, etc.
Weaponization	• Couple exploit with backdoor into deliverable payload
Delivery	• Deliver weaponized bundle to the victim via email, web, USB, etc.
Exploitation	• Exploit vulnerability to execute code on victim system
Installation	• Install malware on the asset
Command & Control	• Command channel for remote manipulation of victim
Actions on Objectives	• With "Hands on Keyboard" access, intruders accomplish their original goal

Lockheed Martin

Note 4

The Cyber Kill Chain was first introduced by researchers at Lockheed Martin in 2011, which later trademarked the term, "Cyber Kill Chain."

Two Rights & A Wrong

1. A business continuity plan is the development of a strategic document that provides alternative modes of operation for business activities that, if interrupted, could result in a significant loss to the enterprise.

2. Parallel processing testing involves conducting the same test simultaneously in different environments.

3. The Cyber Kill Chain is a knowledge base of attacker techniques that have been broken down and classified in detail.

See the answers at the end of the module.

Resilience Through Redundancy

Certification

3.4 Explain the importance of resilience and recovery in security architecture.

5.2 Explain elements of the risk management process.

Capacity planning is the process of forecasting the need for future resources. This is achieved by analyzing the maximum capacity of the current environment and then using tools to measure it against future requirements to determine if more capacity should be added and when. Capacity planning involves not only calculating future human resources (people capacity planning) but also includes predicting the number of devices needed (technology capacity planning) and the size of the network (infrastructure capacity planning). Capacity planning is designed to prevent overprovisioning (having too many resources that are underutilized) and underprovisioning (having too few resources to meet necessary needs).

> **Note 5**
>
> Overprovisioning of employees was a common practice by technology companies that grew rapidly during and imme-
> diately after the COVID-19 pandemic. These companies hired excess workers for one of three reasons: to build a "deep
> bench" of employees who could immediately replace a departing employee, to hire workers ahead of future demand while
> applicants were available, or to simply hoard talent to keep them from being hired by competitors. However, this often
> resulted in new workers who were underutilized. Stories were common of internal company recruiters being hired and
> paid $190,000 annually but told they were not expected to do any work hiring anyone in their first year of employment
> because they were still just "learning the ropes."

While poor planning can result in over-provisioning that can lead to idle resources running below capacity, this does not mean that all excess capacity is bad. Some excess capacity can be intentional. In IT, excess capacity is often found by having duplicated equipment. One example is using multiple different devices to host or serve an application or a service, known as platform diversity.

Equipment **redundancy** (extra components not strictly necessary) can provide **resilience** (elasticity or flexibility) in the case of a cyberattack. The goal of this redundancy is to reduce a variable known as the mean time to recovery. Some systems are designed to have a mean value of zero, which means they have redundant components that can take over the instant the primary component fails.

Resilience through redundancy can also aid in incident preparation. Redundancy in information security usually involves duplicated servers, drives, networks, power, sites, clouds, and data.

> **Note 6**
>
> Because most endpoint devices, like desktop or laptop computers, are ubiquitous commodity items today, there is little
> need for redundancy for these devices. If necessary, the entire device can be quickly replaced in the event of a corrup-
> tion or failure.

Servers

Because servers play such a key role in a network infrastructure, the loss of one or more servers that support a criti-cal application can have a significant impact. There needs to be high availability in servers so that they are always accessible.

In the past, some organizations would stockpile spare parts to replace a part that was contaminated due to an attack or because of an equipment failure; sometimes entire redundant servers were used as standbys. However, the time it takes to install a new part or add a new server to the network and then load software and backup data was often more than an organization could tolerate.

A different approach that some organizations take is to design the network infrastructure so that multiple servers are incorporated into the network yet appear to users and applications as a single computing resource. One method to do this is by clustering or combining two or more devices to appear as a single unit. A server cluster is the com-bination of two or more servers that are interconnected to appear as one, as shown in Figure 13-4. These servers are connected through both a public cluster connection so that clients see them as a single unit as well as a private cluster connection so that the servers can exchange data when necessary.

Figure 13-4   Server cluster

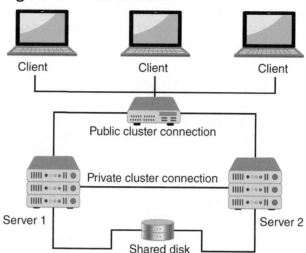

Note 7

Clustering is not the same as load balancing, which is covered in Module 9. Load balancing distributes a workload across multiple servers to improve performance. Server clustering, on the other hand, combines multiple servers to function as a single entity.

There are two types of server clusters. In an asymmetric server cluster, a standby server exists only to take over for another server in the event of its failure. The standby server performs no useful work other than to be ready if it is needed. In a symmetric server cluster, every server in the cluster performs useful work. If one server fails, the remaining servers continue to perform their normal work as well as that of the failed server.

Today, however, just as virtualization has reduced the number of physical servers that are needed in a data center, so too has virtualization impacted the number of server clusters that are needed for server redundancy. Because a virtualized image can be quickly moved to another physical server, the need for server clusters supporting large numbers of physical servers for disaster recovery has diminished. Tools are available so that as one virtual machine is shut down, a copy of that virtual machine is automatically launched.

Drives

There are two primary types of drives that are used to store data. There are also hardware redundancies for these drives known as RAID and SAN multipath.

Types of Drives

For over 40 years **hard disk drives (HDDs)**, which use spinning platters, actuator arms with read/write heads, and motors to store and retrieve data, were the mainstay of computer storage. However, today computers use **solid-state drives (SSDs)**, which essentially store data on chips instead of magnetic platters. Because SSDs lack moving parts, they are more resistant to failure and thus are more reliable than HDDs. Most servers utilize both HDDs and SSDs: the server boots from an SSD (due to its speed and reliability) but stores its data on an HDD (due to the lower cost of these drives).

Note 8

Data accumulated over 10 years on 230,921 HDDs and SSDs confirm that SSDs are more durable than HDDs. One study found that over their first four years of service, SSDs fail at a lower rate than HDDs overall. In the fifth year, HDD failure rates begin going up much more quickly, while SSDs continue to fail at roughly the same rate (about 1 percent) as they did in prior years. Another study of 17,155 failed drives revealed that HDDs typically fail in less than three years.

What steps can be taken when a drive fails? As with almost all electronic computing equipment, attempting to repair it is essentially out of the question. This means that a common metric (standard of measurement) for mechanical systems known as mean time to repair (MTTR), or the average time needed to restore to working order a failed component or device and return it to production status, is meaningless.

> ## Note 9
>
> The abbreviation MTTR is often used to represent four different measurements: the "R" can stand for repair, recovery, respond, or resolve. While these four metrics overlap, they each have their own meaning and nuance.

Because a drive cannot be repaired, some organizations maintain a stockpile of HDDs as spare parts to replace those that fail. Yet how many spare HDDs should an organization keep on hand? A metric that can be used to answer this question is mean time between failures (MTBF). MTBF refers to the average amount of time until a component fails, cannot be repaired, and must be replaced. Calculating the MTBF involves taking the total time measured divided by the total number of failures observed. For example, if 15,400 hard drive units were run for 1000 hours each and that resulted in 11 failures, the MTBF would be (15,400 × 1000) hours/11, or 1.4 million hours. This MTBF rating can be used to determine the number of spare hard drives that should be available for a quick replacement. If an organization had 1000 hard drives operating continuously with an MTBF rating of 1.4 million hours, it could be expected that one drive would fail every 58 days, or 19 failures over three years. This data can help an organization know how many spare hard drives are needed.

> ## Caution !
>
> The MTBF certainly does not indicate that a single hard drive is expected to last 1.4 million hours (159 years)! MTBF is a statistical measure and, as such, cannot predict anything for a single unit.

RAID

A system of hard drives based on redundancy can be achieved through using a technology known as **RAID (Redundant Array of Independent Drives** or **Redundant Array of Inexpensive Disks)**, which uses multiple hard drives for increased reliability and performance. RAID can be implemented through either software or hardware. Software-based RAID is implemented at the operating system (OS) level, while hardware-based RAID requires a specialized hardware controller either on the client computer or on the array that holds the RAID drives. RAID can support either multiple HDDs or SSDs.

> ## Caution !
>
> Although some motherboards have built-in RAID, this is simply BIOS-assisted software RAID and is usually proprietary and nonstandard. It is commonly known as "fake RAID."

There are several standard RAID configurations (called levels). Additional levels include "nested" levels that often combine two other RAID levels. For example, RAID Level 10 is a combination of RAID Level 0 and Level 1. With nested RAID, the elements can be either individual disks or entire RAIDs. The most common levels of RAID are Levels 0, 1, 5, 6, and 10. Descriptions of several of these common levels include:

- **RAID Level 0 (striped disk array without fault tolerance).** RAID Level 0 technology is based on "striping." Striping partitions divide the storage space of each hard drive into smaller sections (*stripes*), which can be as small as 512 bytes or as large as several megabytes. Data written to the stripes is alternated across the drives, as shown in Figure 13-5. Although RAID Level 0 uses multiple drives, it is not fault-tolerant; if one of the drives fails, all the data on that drive is lost.

Figure 13-5   RAID Level 0

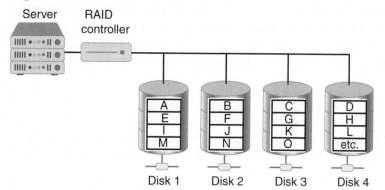

- **RAID Level 1 (mirroring).** RAID Level 1 uses *disk mirroring*. Disk mirroring involves connecting multiple drives in the server to the same disk controller card. When a request is made to write data to the drive, the controller sends that request to each drive; when a read action is required, the data is read twice, once from each drive. By "mirroring" the action on the primary drive, the other drives become exact duplicates. In case the primary drive fails, the other drives take over with no loss of data. This is shown in Figure 13-6. A variation of RAID Level 1 is to include disk duplexing. Instead of having a single disk controller card that is attached to all hard drives, disk duplexing has separate cards for each disk. A single controller card failure affects only one drive. This additional redundancy protects against controller card failures.

Figure 13-6   RAID Level 1

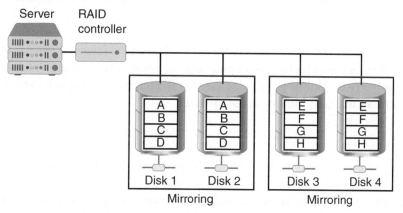

- **RAID 5 (independent disks with distributed parity).** RAID Level 5 distributes *parity* data (a type of error checking) across all drives instead of using a separate drive to hold the parity error checking information. Data is always stored on one drive while its parity information is stored on another drive, as shown in Figure 13-7. Distributing parity across other disks provides an additional degree of protection.

Figure 13-7   RAID Level 5

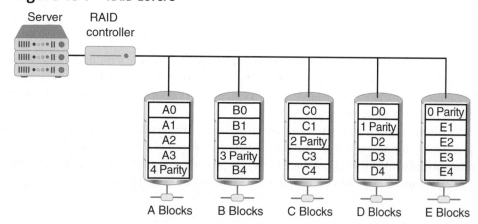

Different levels of RAID have different use cases. For example, RAID Level 0 is good for noncritical storage of data that must be read/written at high speed, such as on an image retouching or a video editing station. RAID Level 1 is best for mission-critical storage, such as for accounting systems. It is also suitable for small servers in which only two data drives will be used. RAID Level 5 is a good all-around system that combines efficient storage with excellent security and decent performance. It is best for file and application servers that have a limited number of data drives.

> **Caution** !
>
> Although all levels of RAID except Level 0 can offer protection from a single drive failure, RAID is not intended to replace data backups but rather to provide an immediate, live copy of data in the event of a drive failure.

SAN Multipath

In the enterprise, the standard data storage facilities and networking protocols cannot always cope with the need to store and transmit large volumes of data. Most organizations have turned to using a **storage area network (SAN)**, which is a dedicated network storage facility that provides access to data storage over a high-speed network. SANs consolidate different storage facilities that appear to the server as a single pool of locally attached devices.

> **Note 10**
>
> SANs can also support SAN-to-SAN replication: a SAN at Site A can update a duplicate SAN at Site B to serve as a backup copy. This type of replication does not impact the performance of normal servers and thus is very efficient.

"Multipath" is a technique for creating more than one physical path between devices and a SAN. If one path is interrupted (due to a cable break or a technician unplugging the wrong cable), multipath would simply redirect the broken connection to another path. Multipath can also assist with increasing the speed of a SAN by spreading connections across multiple paths so that a bottleneck is not created.

Networks

Due to the critical nature of connectivity today, redundant networks also may be necessary. A redundant network waits in the background during normal operations and uses a replication scheme to keep its copy of the live network information current. If a disaster occurs, the redundant network automatically launches so that it is transparent to users. A redundant network ensures that network services are always accessible.

> **Note 11**
>
> Some enterprises contract with more than one Internet service provider (ISP) for remote site network connectivity. In case the primary ISP is no longer available, the secondary ISP will be used. Enterprises can elect to use redundant fiber-optic lines to the different ISPs, each of which takes a diverse path through an area.

Virtually all network hardware components can be duplicated to provide a redundant network. The network interface card (NIC) adapter on a server that performs a critical function can have up to 32 physical adapters installed and then is configured into one or more software-based virtual network adapters. This is called NIC teaming and provides redundancy as well as faster performance.

Some manufacturers offer switches and routers that have a primary active port as well as a standby failover network port for physical redundancy. If a special packet is not detected in a specific time frame on the primary port, the failover port automatically takes over. Load balancers can provide a degree of network redundancy by blocking traffic to servers that are not functioning. Also, multiple redundant switches and routers can be integrated into the network infrastructure. Virtual software-defined network (SDN) controllers can increase network reliability and may lessen the need for redundant equipment. One technique that an SDN controller can use to increase network reliability is to set up multiple paths between the origin and the destination so that the network is not impacted by the outage of a single link.

Note 12

SDN is covered in Module 11.

Power

Maintaining electrical power is essential when planning for redundancy. Critical devices like servers can be fitted with a dual power supply so that if one power supply fails, the other can take over. A dual power supply is shown in Figure 13-8. A managed power distribution unit (PDU) is a device fitted with multiple electrical outputs and is designed to distribute electric power, especially to racks of computers and networking equipment located within a data center.

Figure 13-8   Dual power supply

Source: Athena Power

An **uninterruptible power supply (UPS)** is a device that maintains power to equipment in case of an interruption in the primary electrical power source. A UPS is more than just a big battery, however. UPS systems can also communicate with the network OS on a server to ensure that an orderly shutdown occurs. Specifically, if the power goes down, a UPS can send a message to the network administrator to indicate that the power has failed, notify all users that they must finish their work immediately and log off, prevent any new users from logging on, and disconnect users and shut down the server.

There are two primary types of UPSs.

- **Off-line UPS.** An **off-line UPS** is considered the least expensive and simplest solution. During normal operation, the equipment being protected is served by the standard primary power source. The off-line UPS battery charger is also connected to the primary power source to charge its battery. If power is interrupted, the UPS quickly (usually within a few milliseconds) begins supplying power to the equipment. When the primary power is restored, the UPS automatically switches back into standby mode.
- **On-line UPS.** An **on-line UPS** is always running off its battery while the main power runs the battery charger. An advantage of an on-line UPS is that it is not affected by dips or sags in voltage. An on-line UPS can clean the electrical power before it reaches the server to ensure that a correct and constant level of power is delivered to the server. The on-line UPS can also serve as a surge protector, which keeps intense spikes of electrical current, common during thunderstorms, from reaching systems.

Because a UPS can supply power only for a limited amount of time, many organizations turn to a backup generator to create power. Backup generators can be powered by diesel, natural gas, or propane gas to generate electricity. Unlike portable residential backup generators, commercial backup generators are permanently installed as part of the building's power infrastructure. They include automatic transfer switches that can instantly detect the loss of a building's primary power and switch to the backup generator.

Sites

Just as redundancies can be planned for servers, drives, networks, and power, it can also be planned for the entire site. A major disaster such as a flood or hurricane can inflict such extensive damage to a building that the organization must temporarily move to another location. Many organizations maintain redundant recovery sites in case this occurs. Three basic types of redundant sites are used:

- **Hot site.** A hot site is generally run by a commercial disaster recovery service that allows a business to continue computer and network operations to maintain business continuity. A hot site is essentially a duplicate of the production site and has all the equipment needed for an organization to continue running, including office space and furniture, telephone jacks, computer equipment, and a live telecommunications link. Data backups of information can be quickly moved to the hot site and, in some instances, the production site automatically synchronizes all its data with the hot site so that all data is immediately accessible. If the organization's on-prem data processing center becomes inoperable, typically all data processing operations can be moved to a hot site within an hour.

- **Cold site.** A cold site provides office space, but the customer must provide and install all the equipment needed to continue operations. In addition, there are no backups of data immediately available at this site. A cold site is less expensive but requires more time to get an enterprise in full operation after a disaster.

- **Warm site.** A warm site has all the equipment installed but does not have active Internet or telecommunications facilities and does not have current backups of data. This type of site is much less expensive than constantly maintaining those connections as required for a hot site; however, the amount of time needed to turn on the connections and install the backups can be as much as half a day or more.

> **Note 13**
>
> Businesses usually have an annual contract with a company that offers hot and cold site services with a monthly service charge. Some services also offer data backup services so that all company data is available regardless of whether a hot site or cold site is used.

However, it is important when creating alternate sites to consider geographic dispersal. Instead of all sites being clustered in a limited geographic area, they should be distributed across a larger area to mitigate the impact of environmental disasters (like hurricanes and tornados) and human-made disasters (like terrorist attacks and transport accidents).

Clouds

In the past, some organizations backed up their applications and data to the cloud and then, if a disaster were to occur, it would be restored to hardware in a hot, cold, or warm site. However, due to the ubiquity and universal access of cloud computing, it is rarely necessary to restore the data to a site. Instead, users directly access backed-up applications and data through the normal cloud computing infrastructure.

However, resilience is still important when using cloud computing. There are two considerations for cloud resilience. The first is the location of the data stored in the cloud. Geographic dispersal should also be taken into account when using cloud computing. This can be achieved through duplicating processes across one or more geographical areas, called high availability across zones.

> **Note 14**
>
> High availability across zones is covered in Module 11.

The second consideration is to spread cloud computing across multiple cloud providers. Known as using multicloud systems, this has the advantage of an organization being able to tolerate a critical issue that could occur with a single cloud provider. Companies that cannot tolerate downtime can distribute essential assets and data across multiple cloud providers to ensure that if one cloud ceases to function the business can continue to operate as normal.

Note 15

Increasingly, governments around the world are sounding alarms that businesses are consolidating their cloud activities to a small handful of cloud providers. These organizations are encouraged to consider multicloud systems, as discussed in Module 11.

Data

Resilience for data is simple: just make a copy of it. However, there are numerous questions about copying data. How often should it be done (frequency)? How can the data copy be restored if the original is tarnished (recovery)? Should the data copy be made unintelligible to outsiders (**encryption**)? And what about mission-critical environments in which no delays between a restoration from the copied data be tolerated?

The answer to these and other data copy questions often hinge on data copy calculations. And there are different types of data copy techniques.

Data Copy Calculations

Two calculations are used regarding when data copies should be performed. The first is known as the recovery point objective (RPO), which is defined as the maximum length of time that an organization can tolerate between copies. Simply put, RPO is the "age" of the data that an organization wants the ability to restore in the event of a disaster. For example, if an RPO is one hour, this means that an organization wants to be able to restore systems back to the state they were in no longer than one hour ago. Thus, it is necessary to make copies at least every hour because any data created or modified after that time will be lost.

Related to the RPO is the recovery time objective (RTO). The RTO is the length of time it will take to recover the data that has been copied. An RTO of 10 minutes means that data can be restored within that timeframe.

Types of Data Copies

Copying data has changed dramatically in recent years. Whereas at one time, data copies were made only as a scheduled event, today copies are made as a continuous process. Both are considered necessary for comprehensive protection.

Scheduled Event: Backup   A backup is a single scheduled event. The data is copied and then stored so that it can be used in the event of a disaster. The frequency of a backup, because it is a single scheduled event, is generally once per day (often at night when the impact on most users is limited).

A key consideration with backups is where the data copy should be stored. A copy stored onsite or where the data is actually being used has the advantage of being immediately available; however, the disadvantages of storing a backup onsite during an environmental or human-made disaster that impacts the site center will likewise impact the backup.

Another option is to store the copy offsite away from the production facility. However, there are security concerns (transporting data over long distances increases the risk of theft) or concern about a delay in accessing the media in the event the data backup must be quickly restored.

Note 16

One of the most secure offsite backup facilities is in a former salt mine facility in Kansas. It is 650 feet (198 meters) or about 45 stories beneath the surface. The facility is encased in solid stone and covers the equivalent of 35 football fields with over 1.7 million square feet (.52 million square meters) of storage space. The temperature and humidity levels remain constant year-round. The site protects against natural disasters (tornado, hurricane, flood, etc.) as well as human-made disasters (explosion, fire, civil unrest, etc.). It serves as the largest single storage facility for the movie and television film industry worldwide.

Continuous: Replication   An alternative to a single scheduled event is to continuously copy data, known as replication. There are two techniques for data replication. A snapshot takes a "picture" of the state of the data repeatedly. In the event of a failure, the data can be restored from a specific point in time based on the snapshot taken at that time. Journaling makes a copy of the data whenever a change to the data occurs.

Snapshots and journaling are often replicated across multiple sites so that a disaster at one site will not destroy the backup. Also, they have a very low RTO, often to the extent that users do not even realize that data was restored. Table 13-4 lists some of the differences between backups and replication.

> **Note 17**
>
> Many replication products even let users restore their own documents. A user who accidentally deletes a file can search the system by entering the name of the document and then view the results through an interface that looks like a web search engine. Clicking the desired file then restores it. For security purposes, users may search only for documents for which they have permissions.

Table 13-4   Backups versus replication

	Backup	Replication
Description	Makes a copy of data as an event at a specific point in time	Continuously copies data and is duplicated across multiple sites
Purpose	To provide long-term archival of business records	To quickly restore corrupted data
Use case	Used for all enterprise devices from endpoints to servers	Used for mission-critical applications that must always be available
Technology	Relies on specialized backup software	Uses snapshots or journaling
Recovery time	Long	Immediate
Cost	Relatively inexpensive	Requires sizeable investment in another infrastructure to continuously capture, store, and retrieve

> **Note 18**
>
> For home users, the best approach is a cloud-based journaling solution. Software monitors what files have changed and automatically updates the files with the most recent versions, and these are then stored online in the cloud. If users instead choose to make their own backups, they should follow the 3-2-1 backup plan by always maintaining three different copies of backups (that does not count the original data itself) by using at least two different types of media on which to store these backups (a separate hard drive, an external hard drive, a USB device, etc.) and storing one of the backups offsite.

> **Two Rights & A Wrong**
>
> 1. Redundancy in information security usually involves duplicated servers, drives, networks, power, sites, clouds, and data.
> 2. Clustering distributes a workload across multiple servers.
> 3. MTTR is meaningless when it comes to HDDs.
>
> See the answers at the end of the module.

Incident Investigation

After a cybersecurity incident occurs, it must be fully investigated. This is to not only pinpoint how it occurred so that future incidents can be prevented but also for regulatory compliance reporting. However, all too often this investigation only examines superficial causes and does not dig deeply enough to fully determine exactly *what* happened, *how* it happened, and most importantly *why* it happened. **Root-cause analysis (RCA)** is the process of discovering the origin (root) cause of the security event.

> **Note 19**
>
> Consider a government agency of 2,000 employees that an attacker was able to infiltrate through an accountant who used the same password for work as well as their social media. RCA would investigate not just the results of the attack or what the threat actors did but would dig for the origin of the attack all the way down to the accountant's computer and reuse of passwords.

Incident investigation involves analyzing data sources and performing a digital forensics investigation.

Data Sources

There are several sources of data that can provide helpful clues in uncovering how an incident occurred. These data sources include log files and data from other sources.

Log Files

A log is a record of events that occur. Security logs are particularly important for an incident investigation because they can reveal the type of attack that was directed at the network and how it successfully circumvented existing security defenses. Logs that typically provide the most beneficial security data for an investigation are listed in Table 13-5.

Table 13-5   Types of log files

Device	Explanation
Firewall logs	These logs can be used to determine whether new IP addresses are attempting to probe the network and if stronger firewall rules are necessary to block them. Outgoing connections, incoming connections, denied traffic, and permitted traffic should all be recorded.
Intrusion detection systems (IDS)/ intrusion prevention systems (IPS) logs	These record detailed security log information on suspicious behavior as well as any attacks that are detected. In addition, these logs also record any actions IPS used to stop the attacks.
Application logs	These log files can give information about attacks focused on different applications. If an application log identifies an app that has been the source of a compromise, software can be used to create a dump file, which is a snapshot of the process that was executing and any modules that were loaded for an app at a specific point in time. Dump file output is seen in Figure 13-9.
Endpoint logs	These can provide a wide range of reports and alerts with events classified by their severity level, such as system events, software installations, removable disk activity, Windows Registry changes, and login and session activity.

(continues)

Table 13-5 *(Continued)*

Device	Explanation
OS-specific security logs	OS logs typically record system events that are operational actions performed by OS components, such as shutting down the system or starting a service, and audit records that contain security event information such as successful and failed authentication attempts, file accesses, security policy changes, account creation and deletion, and use of privileges.
Network logs	These logs can come from different appliances, such as router and switch logs that provide general information about network traffic.
Metadata logs	Metadata is "data about data," or data that describes information about other data.

Figure 13-9 Dump file output

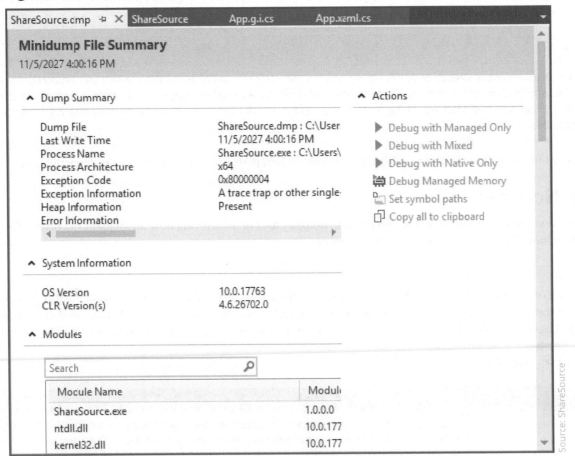

Source: ShareSource

There are several problems associated with log management, or transmitting, collecting, analyzing, and disposing of log data. This is due to the following:

- **Multiple devices generate logs.** Virtually every network device, both standard network devices and network security devices, can create logs. And each device may interpret an event in a different context, so that a router looks at a single event differently than a firewall does. This can create a confusing mix of log data.
- **Very large volume of data.** Because each device generates its own data, a very large amount of data can accumulate in a very short period of time. In addition, many devices record all events, even those that are not security related, which increases the amount of data that is generated. Filtering through this large volume of data can be overwhelming.
- **Different log formats.** Perhaps the biggest obstacle to log management is that different devices record log information in different formats and even with different data captured. Combining multiple logs, each with a different format, can be a major challenge.

Other Data Sources

Data accumulated from other sources can also provide useful information. One source is data from a **vulnerability scan**. In addition, security information and event management (SIEM) products that consolidate real-time security monitoring and management of security information with analysis and reporting of security events can be a valuable source. A SIEM dashboard can provide information collected from its sensors. This information includes alerts, trends, sensitivity, and correlation data.

Another source is from network Internet Protocol (IP) monitors. Various IP software monitors can provide insight into an incident by creating automated reports on activity without the need for a user to manually analyze the data. NetFlow is a session sampling protocol feature on Cisco routers that collects IP network traffic as it enters or exits an interface and uses TCP/IP Internet Control Message Protocol (ICMP) Echo request packets. sFlow is a packet capture sampling protocol that generates information based on capturing packets. It gives a statistical sampling instead of the actual flow of packets. IPFIX (IP Flow Information Export) is similar to NetFlow but adds additional capabilities, such as integrating Simple Network Management Protocol (SNMP) information directly into the IPFIX information so that all the information is available instead of requiring separate queries to the SNMP server.

Digital Forensics

Digital forensics is an important element in incident investigation. In fact, many users equate incident investigation with digital forensics, although they are not exactly the same: forensics is one important part of incident investigation. Understanding digital forensics involves knowing what it is and the steps for conducting a procedure.

What Is Digital Forensics?

In a general sense, **forensics** is the application of science to questions that are of interest to the legal profession. One example of forensics (and which most users associate with forensics) is analyzing evidence from a murder scene. A subset of forensics is digital forensics. Digital forensics involves the retrieval of difficult-to-obtain data, which is usually hidden, altered, or even deleted by the perpetrator. A digital forensics specialist searches for evidence pertaining to cybercrime or to damage that occurred during a cyber incident. In short, it is using technology to hunt for technology-based evidence.

Digital forensics is often confused with e-discovery, although they are not the same. When preparing for trial, both the prosecution and the defense engage in what is called "discovery." This is the formal process of exchanging information between the two parties about witnesses and evidence that will be presented at a trial, as seen in Figure 13-10. Discovery, since its inception in 1938, enables the parties to know before the trial begins what evidence may be presented.

Figure 13-10   Presentation of evidence

Gorodenkoff/Shutterstock.com

Note 20

Despite what is commonly seen in movies when a last-minute witness suddenly appears, discovery is designed to prevent this "trial by ambush," where one side does not learn of the other side's evidence until after trial begins and there is no time to obtain counterevidence.

Unlike previous years when discovery involved the exchange of a limited number of paper documents, today discovery involves an enormous volume of tens of thousands (or more) of documents that are in electronic format (emails, spreadsheets, PDFs, Word documents, etc.). Sifting through this massive repository of electronic documents can be a daunting task. E-discovery is the electronic counterpart of manually sifting through documents in discovery. Electronic documents are uploaded to an e-discovery platform in which software can quickly search for information based on key terms, much like using a web browser to search the Internet.

Forensics Procedures

When responding to an incident that requires an examination using digital forensics, five basic steps are followed, which are similar to those of standard forensics. The steps are to secure the crime scene, preserve the evidence, document the chain of custody, examine for evidence, and generate a report.

Secure the Scene   When an on-prem illegal or unauthorized incident occurs that involves technology, action must be taken immediately. A delay of even a few minutes can allow digital evidence to be overwritten in the normal function of the device, become contaminated by other users, or give the perpetrator time to destroy the evidence. A digital forensics incident response team is contacted and, upon arrival, their first job is to secure the scene. This involves documenting the physical surroundings, identifying and tagging all cables connected to the device, and taking custody of the device along with any peripherals.

Preserve the Evidence   The next task is preservation of evidence or ensuring that important proof is not corrupted or even destroyed. Preserving evidence can also help mitigate nonrepudiation, or a denial by the perpetrator that they were involved or did anything wrong.

Evidence from a suspected device should be placed in bags that have tags or identifying labels that record a description of the item, a numeric identifier, date, collection location, and other relevant information. These bags are then sealed to serve as protection against evidence being altered. One type of seal that is commonly used is a tamper-evident seal that cannot be removed and reapplied without leaving obvious visual evidence. If the seal or tape is lifted or removed, a clearly visible *OPENED* message appears on the packaging. For additional traceability and security, the tape is often labeled with a unique sequential number every 9 inches (22 centimeters). Tamper-evident tape is shown in Figure 13-11.

Figure 13-11   Tamper-evident tape

Source: American Casting MFG

Depending on the type and severity of the incident, it may be necessary to immediately involve the judicial system to help collect and preserve the digital evidence. This ensures that the integrity of the evidence is maintained and can be held up in a court of law (admissibility). Once data has been identified, it can be placed under a legal hold, meaning that it cannot be modified, deleted, erased, or otherwise destroyed.

Caution !

There is a tendency to issue legal holds that are too broad in scope. For example, to place a legal hold on all email correspondence may result in retaining thousands or millions of unneeded messages and associated attachments, while placing a legal hold on all portable devices, requiring them to be locked away, makes them useless to the organization. Instead, appropriate filters should be used to capture only data that is relevant.

Document Chain of Custody   As soon as the team begins its work, it must start and maintain a strict chain of custody. Documenting the evidence from the very beginning is called provenance. The chain of custody documents that the evidence was always under strict control and no unauthorized person was given the opportunity to corrupt the evidence. A chain of custody includes documenting all the serial numbers of the systems involved, who handled and had custody of the systems and for what length of time, how the computer was shipped, and any other steps in the process. In short, a chain of custody is a detailed document describing where the evidence was at all times from the beginning of the investigation.

Caution !

Gaps in a chain of custody can result in severe legal consequences. Courts have dismissed cases involving computer forensics because a secure chain of custody could not be verified.

A chain of custody form helps to document that evidence was under strict control at all times and no unauthorized person was given the opportunity to corrupt it, as shown in Figure 13-12.

Examine for Evidence   When examining a device for evidence, there are specialized tools that should be used to gather evidence (acquisition). It is important that these tools be used properly.

Digital Forensics Tools   There are different software digital forensics tools available for analysis. These tools are specialized for digital forensics to capture the system image, or a snapshot of the current state of these elements that contains all current settings and data. One common software tool is a mirror-image backup, also called a bit-stream backup. This is an evidence-grade backup because its accuracy meets evidence standards.

A mirror-image backup is not the same as a normal copy of the data. Standard file copies or backups include only files. Mirror-image backups replicate all sectors of a computer hard drive, including all files and any hidden data storage areas. It will also capture the swap file or pagefile that contains data that has been moved from RAM to the drive due to a lack of RAM space, and this should be examined for evidence.

Caution !

Using a standard copy procedure can miss significant data and can taint the evidence. For example, copying a file may change file date information on the source drive, which is information that is often critical in a computer forensics investigation.

Figure 13-12   Chain of custody form

Property Record Number:
_____

EVIDENCE CHAIN OF CUSTODY TRACKING FORM

Case Number: _____ Offense: _____

Submitting Official: (Name/ID#) _____

Date/Time Seized: _____Location of Seizure: _____

Description of Evidence

Item #	Quantity	Description of Item (Model, Serial #, Condition, Marks, Scratches)

Chain of Custody

Item #	Date/Time	Released by (Signature & ID#)	Received by (Signature & ID#)	Comments/Location

Final Disposal Authority

Item(s) #: _____ on this document pertaining to (suspect): _____
is/are no longer needed as evidence and is/are authorized for disposal by (check appropriate disposal method)

☐ Return to Owner   ☐ Auction/Destroy/Divert

Name & ID# of Authorizing Official: _____ Signature: _____ Date: _____

Witness to Destruction of Evidence

Item(s) #: _____ on this document were destroyed by Evidence Custodian _____ ID#:_____
in my presence on (date) _____.

Name & ID# of Witness to destruction: _____ Signature: _____ Date: _____

Release to Lawful Owner

Item(s) #: _____ on this document was/were released by Evidence Custodian
_____ ID#:_____ to

Name _____

Address: _____ City: _____ State: _____ Zip Code: _____

Telephone Number: (_____)_____

Under penalty of law, I certify that I am the lawful owner of the above item(s).

Signature: _____ Date: _____

Copy of Government-issued photo identification is attached. ☐ Yes ☐ No

This Evidence Chain-of-Custody form is to be retained as a permanent record.

Products are available that package multiple digital forensics tools into a single suite that has a common user interface and can more easily exchange information among the different tools. Two of the most common forensic suites are EnCase (shown in Figure 13-13) and FTK Imager. Other popular forensics software tools are memdump, a Linux utility that "dumps" system memory; WinHex, a hexadecimal editor that can be used for forensics; and Autopsy, a digital forensics platform.

Instead of gathering different forensics software tools, a digital forensic workstation, which is a computer that is specially configured to perform forensics activities, can be used instead. Digital forensic workstations are typically configured with the latest computer hardware, such as multiple-gigabit network ports and USB ports, along with "hot swap" bays to hold multiple drives for examination.

Figure 13-13   EnCase software

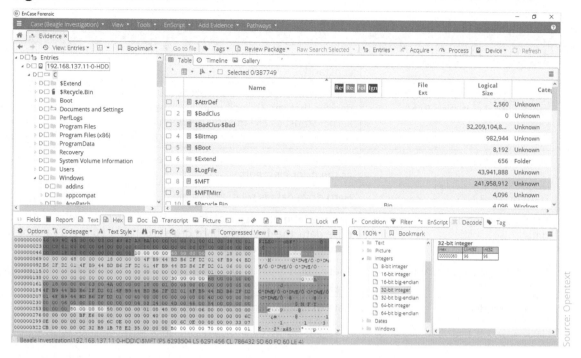

Source: Opentext

Note 21

Digital forensic workstations are expensive. Depending on the options installed, such a workstation might cost over $20,000.

There are also specialized hardware tools for digital forensics investigations. Mobile device forensics tools are designed to perform forensics on smartphones, tablets, and other similar devices. Because mobile devices are almost continually in a user's possession, they can accurately reveal the user's actions. Digital forensic information that can be extracted from a mobile device includes the following:

- **Call detail records.** This information can reveal the date and time a telephone call was started and ended, the terminating and originating cell phone towers that were used, whether the call was outgoing or incoming, the call's duration, who was called, and who made the call.
- **Global positioning system (GPS) data.** GPS data can accurately pinpoint the location of a user and what activities were performed in a specific location.
- **App data.** Many apps store and access data such as media files, contact lists, and a gallery of all the photos on the device.
- **Short Message Service (SMS) texts.** Text messaging is a popular means of communication. It leaves electronic records of dialogue that can be used as evidence.
- **Photos and videos.** Media recorded as photos and videos on a mobile device can often contain incriminating evidence.

Acquisition of Evidence   When examining technology devices that may contain evidence, called artifacts, it is critical to follow a specific order. This is because different data sources have different degrees of preservation. An **order of volatility** must be followed to preserve the most fragile data first. Table 13-6 lists the order of volatility.

Table 13-6 Order of volatility

Order	Examples	Description
1	Registers and CPU cache	Registers and the CPU cache are extremely volatile and change constantly.
2	Routing tables, ARP cache, process table, kernel statistics, RAM	The network routing and process tables have data located on network devices that can change quickly while the system is in operation, and kernel statistics are moving between cache and main memory, which make them highly volatile. RAM information can be lost if power is lost.
3	Temporary file systems	Temporary file systems are not subject to the degree of rapid changes as the prior elements.
4	Hard drive	Hard drive data is relatively stable.
5	Remote logging and monitoring data	Although remote logging and monitoring are more volatile than hard drive data, the data on a hard drive is considered more valuable and should be preserved first.
6	Physical configuration and network topology	These items are not considered volatile and do not have a significant impact on an investigation.
7	Archival media	Data that has been preserved in archival form is not volatile.

Note 22

The first two levels are considered the most volatile because they can change very quickly. A cache is a type of high-speed memory that stores recently used information so that it can be quickly accessed again at a later time. After retrieving this volatile data, the next focus is on the hard drive.

An additional source of hidden clues can be gleaned from metadata. Some electronic files may contain hundreds of pieces of such information. Examples of metadata include the file type, authorship, and edit history. Another example of metadata is the date and time that a file was created or accessed.

Generate a Report Upon completion of the examination, a detailed written description of the acquisition and analysis of the evidence is required (reporting). It lists the steps that were taken and any evidence that was uncovered in the forensic investigation. When using products that package multiple digital forensics tools into a single suite, a report can be automatically generated.

Two Rights & A Wrong

1. The first step in a digital forensics procedure is to preserve the evidence.
2. E-discovery is the electronic counterpart of manually sifting through documents in discovery.
3. The chain of custody documents that the evidence was always under strict control and no unauthorized person was given the opportunity to corrupt the evidence.

See the answers at the end of the module.

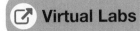 **Virtual Labs** You're now ready to complete the simulations and live virtual machine labs for this module. The labs can be found in each module in MindTap.

Summary

- The ability of an organization to maintain its operations and services in the face of natural disasters, human-made disasters, and cyberattacks is crucial if it is to survive. This calls for advanced preparation as well as investigation after an incident to learn from mistakes and address vulnerabilities. There are several types of preparatory plans that assist in advanced preparation. Business continuity is the ability of an organization to maintain its operations and services in the face of a disruptive event. A business continuity plan (BCP) is a document that provides alternative modes of operation for business activities. One important tool in BCP is a business impact analysis (BIA), which analyzes the most important mission-essential business functions and identifies critical systems and single points of failure. A disaster recovery plan (DRP) involves the steps for restoring IT functions and services to their former state. Most DRPs also cover a standard set of topics, and one common topic is the sequence in which different systems are reinstated.

- An incident response plan is a set of written instructions for reacting to an information security incident. Without such a plan, enterprises are at risk of being unable to quickly identify the attack, contain its spread, recover, and learn from the attack to improve defenses. The action steps to be taken when an incident occurs, called the incident response process, also make up the elements of an incident response plan. It is important to test an incident response plan by conducting simulated testing exercises to make necessary adjustments. The different types of exercises are tabletop, walkthrough, simulation, fail over, and parallel processing. An information security framework is a series of documented processes used to define policies and procedures for implementation and management of security controls in an enterprise environment. Frameworks can also be studied about how attacks occur, called exploitation frameworks, and can serve as models of the thinking and actions of threat actors.

- Equipment redundancy can provide resilience in the case of a cyberattack. Due to their ubiquity, endpoints rarely require hardware redundancy. Because servers play such a key role in a network infrastructure, the loss of a single server that supports a critical application can have a significant impact. A common approach is for the organization to design the network infrastructure so that multiple servers are incorporated into the network yet appear to users and applications as a single computing resource. One method of doing this is by using a server cluster, which is the combination of two or more servers that are interconnected to appear as one. A system of drives based on redundancy can be achieved through using a technology known as RAID, which uses multiple hard disk drives for increased reliability and performance. SAN multipath, a technique for creating more than one physical path between devices and a SAN, can also be used to provide redundancy.

- Most network hardware components can be duplicated to provide a redundant network. Maintaining electrical power is also essential when planning for redundancy. An uninterruptible power supply (UPS) is a device that maintains power to equipment in the event of an interruption in the primary electrical power source. Because a UPS can supply power for a limited amount of time, some organizations turn to a backup generator to create power. Redundancy can also be planned for the entire site. A major disaster such as a flood or hurricane can inflict such extensive damage to a building that the organization may have to temporarily move to another location. Many organizations maintain redundant sites in case this occurs. Three basic types of redundant sites are used: hot sites, cold sites, and warm sites. Resilience is important when using cloud computing. There are two considerations for cloud resilience: the location of the data stored in the cloud and using multiple cloud providers.

- Perhaps the most important redundancy is that of the data itself, which is accomplished through copying data. Two calculations are used regarding when data copies should be performed. The recovery point objective (RPO) is the maximum length of time that an organization can tolerate between data copies. The recovery time objective (RTO) is the length of time it will take to recover data that has been copied. A backup is a single scheduled event. The data is copied and then stored so that it can be used in the event of a disaster. A key consideration with backups is where the data copy should be stored, either onsite or offsite. An alternative to a single scheduled event is to continuously copy data (replication). There are two techniques for data replication: a snapshot takes a "picture" of the state of the data repeatedly, while journaling makes a copy of the data whenever a change to the data occurs.

- Following a cybersecurity incident, it should be fully investigated to not only pinpoint how it occurred so that future incidents can be prevented but also for regulatory compliance reporting. There are several sources of data that can provide helpful clues in uncovering how an incident occurred. A log is a record of events that occur, and security logs are particularly important for incident investigation because they can reveal the type of attack that was directed at the network and how it successfully circumvented existing security defenses. Logs that typically provide the most beneficial security data for an investigation are firewall logs, Intrusion detection systems (IDS)/intrusion prevention systems (IPS) logs, application logs, endpoint logs, OS-specific security logs, network logs, and metadata logs. Other data sources include vulnerability scans, dashboards, automated reports, and packet captures.

- Digital forensics involves the retrieval of difficult-to-obtain data, which is usually hidden, altered,

or even deleted by the perpetrator. A digital forensics specialist searches for evidence pertaining to cybercrime or to damage that occurred during a cyber incident. E-discovery is using technology to find important information in electronic documents. When responding to an incident that requires an examination using digital forensics, five basic steps are followed. The first step is to secure the scene, if necessary, by documenting the physical surroundings, identifying and tagging all cables connected to the device, and taking custody of the device along with any peripherals. The next task is preservation of evidence or ensuring that important proof is not corrupted or even destroyed.

- As soon as the digital forensics team begins its work, it must start and maintain a strict chain of custody. Documenting the evidence from the very beginning is called provenance. The chain of custody documents that the evidence was always under strict control and no unauthorized person was given the opportunity to corrupt the evidence. When examining a device for evidence, there are specialized tools that should be used to gather evidence. There are different software digital forensics tools available for analysis. These tools are specialized for digital forensics to capture the system image, or a snapshot of the current state of these elements that contains all current settings and data. There are also specialized hardware tools for digital forensics investigations. When examining technology devices that may contain evidence, called artifacts, it is critical to follow a specific order. This is because different data sources have different degrees of preservation. Upon completion of the examination, a detailed written description of the acquisition and analysis of the evidence is required.

Key Terms

acquisition	business impact analysis (BIA)	dashboard
analysis	capacity planning	detection
application logs	chain of custody	digital forensics
automated reports	clustering	disaster recovery plan (DRP)
backup	cold site	e-discovery
business continuity	containment	endpoint logs
business continuity plan (BCP)	continuity of operations	eradication

fail over
firewall logs
frequency
generator
geographic dispersal
high availability
hot site
incident response process
infrastructure capacity planning
intrusion detection systems (IDS)/
    intrusion prevention systems
    (IPS) logs
journaling
legal hold
lessons learned

log
mean time between failures
    (MTBF)
mean time to repair (MTTR)
metadata logs
multi-cloud systems
network logs
offsite
onsite
OS-specific security logs
packet capture
parallel processing
people capacity planning
platform diversity
preparation

preservation of evidence
recovery
recovery point objective (RPO)
recovery time objective (RTO)
replication
reporting
root cause analysis (RCA)
simulation
snapshot
tabletop
technology capacity planning
testing
uninterruptible power supply (UPS)
walkthrough
warm site

Review Questions

1. Mary Alice has been asked to help develop an outline of procedures to follow in the event of a major IT incident or an incident that directly impacts IT. What type of planning is this?

   a. Business impact analysis planning
   b. IT contingency planning
   c. Disaster recovery planning
   d. Risk IT planning

2. Which of the following is NOT an element that should be part of a BCP?

   a. High availability
   b. Simplicity
   c. Diversity
   d. Scalability

3. Which of the following is a federal initiative that is designed to encourage organizations to address how critical operations will continue under a broad range of negative circumstances?

   a. COOP
   b. BAIA
   c. MFTF
   d. PRPR

4. Bracha is completing a request for proposal (RFP) to be sent to different vendors. The RFP mandates that the annual downtime be the lowest possible. What name will Bracha include on her RFP?

   a. Zero Nines
   b. Nine Nines
   c. Six Nines
   d. Ninety-Nine Nines

5. Eden is creating an incident response plan. Which process involves completing incident documentation, performing detailed analysis to increase security, and improving future response efforts?

   a. Mission-essential functions
   b. Recovery objectives
   c. Lessons learned
   d. Tactical summary

6. Which of the following is NOT an item that should be included in an incident response plan?

   a. Definitions
   b. Incident response team composition
   c. Reporting requirements
   d. Alternative business practices

7. Hannah is planning incident response testing exercises for the next year. This exercise will be a monthly 30-minute discussion of a scenario conducted in an informal and stress-free environment. What is the name of this exercise?

   a. Simulation
   b. Tabletop
   c. Walkthrough
   d. Relaxed scenario event (RSE)

8. Chaya is helping an intern understand RAID. Which of the following is NOT something that Chaya will say about RAID?

   a. It can be implemented in hardware or software.
   b. Nested levels can combine other RAID levels.
   c. It is designed primarily to back up data.
   d. The most common levels of RAID are Levels 0, 1, 5, 6, and 10.

9. Which of the following frameworks is used for examining network intrusion events?

    a. Attack Network Vector (ANV)
    b. MITRE ATT&CK
    c. Cyber Kill Chain
    d. The Diamond Model of Intrusion Analysis

10. Which of the following is used to provide server redundancy?

    a. Load balancing
    b. Server resource sharing (SRS)
    c. Clustering
    d. Server conflagration

11. What device is always running off its battery while the main power runs the battery charger?

    a. Remote UPS
    b. Backup UPS
    c. Off-line UPS
    d. On-line UPS

12. Which type of site is essentially a duplicate of the production site and has all the equipment needed for an organization to continue running?

    a. Cold site
    b. Warm site
    c. Hot site
    d. Mixed site

13. Emma is reading the documentation for the new UPS that just arrived. Which of the following will the new UPS NOT perform?

    a. Prevent certain applications from launching that will consume too much power.
    b. Disconnect users and shut down the server.
    c. Prevent any new users from logging on.
    d. Notify all users that they must finish their work immediately and log off.

14. What is the definition of RPO?

    a. The maximum length of time that can be tolerated between backups.
    b. Length of time it will take to recover data that has been backed up.
    c. The frequency that data should be backed up.
    d. How a backup utility reads an archive bit.

15. Shai is designing the specifications for a new file server. Which of the following configurations will be the most effective?

    a. Boot from HDD, store data on SSD
    b. Boot from SSD, store data on HDD
    c. Boot from either HDD or SSD, store data on SSD
    d. Boot from either HDD or SSD, store data on HDD

16. Noa is writing an email to her team leader about her concerns that all of the organization's cloud resources are isolated on a single cloud provider. Noa believes that the company's cloud resources need to be spread across more than one cloud provider. What system is Noa advocating?

    a. Spread-cloud system
    b. Multicloud system
    c. Dispersed-cloud system
    d. Spectrum-cloud system

17. Which type of data copy makes a copy whenever a change to the data occurs?

    a. Disk copy
    b. Backup
    c. Snapshot
    d. Journaling

18. Which of the following is the process of discovering the origin (root) cause of a security event?

    a. TBS
    b. XRX
    c. BGP
    d. RCA

19. Which of the following logs contains data that describes information about other data?

    a. Application log
    b. Network log
    c. Metadata log
    d. Endpoint log

20. Which of the following is NOT true about digital forensics?

    a. Digital forensics is a subset of forensics, which is the application of science to questions that are of interest to the legal profession.
    b. Digital forensics involves the retrieval of difficult-to-obtain data, which is usually hidden, altered, or even deleted by the perpetrator.
    c. Digital forensics is often confused with e-discovery, although they are not the same.
    d. Digital forensics has evolved so that virtually anyone can perform it.

Hands-On Projects

Caution !

If you are concerned about installing any of the software in these projects on your regular computer, you can instead use the Windows Sandbox in the Module 1 Hands-On Projects. Software installed within the virtual machine will not impact the host computer.

Project 13-1: Using Windows File History to Perform Data Backups

Estimated Time: 30 minutes

Objective: Perform data backups on a Windows 11 computer.

Description: A software backup utility called File History is a Microsoft Windows 11 tool for backing up user files locally instead of in the cloud. Once configured, File History will automatically back up files to a storage device on a schedule. Note that File History is designed to back up user files and does not create a system image of the drive. In this project, you examine the configuration settings for File History.

1. Connect an external storage device such as a large-capacity USB flash drive or external hard drive to the computer as a repository for the backups. (You cannot back up files to the same drive that contains the user files.)

2. Enter **Control Panel** in the search bar.

3. Click **System and Security**.

4. Click **File History**.

5. If necessary click **Turn on**.

6. Click **Advanced settings**.

7. Click the down arrow under **Save copies of files**. Note the default setting is **Every hour (default)**. Scroll through the other options. Which would you consider the best option for you? Why?

8. Click the down arrow under **Keep saved versions**. Note the default setting is **Forever (default)**. Scroll through the other options. What is the advantage to having backups kept indefinitely? What is the disadvantage? Which would you consider the best option for you? Why?

9. Click the **Back** arrow and look at the list of items that File History automatically backs up under **Copy files from**. By default, File History is set to back up important folders in the user account's home folder, such as Desktop, Libraries (Documents, Downloads, Music, Pictures, Videos, and so on), and Favorites. Do these folders include all your important data?

10. Click **Exclude folders**.

11. Click **Add** and select a folder that does not contain your important data such as **Downloads**. Click **Select folder**.

12. Click the **Back** arrow to return to the File History window.

13. Click **Advanced settings** again.

14. Under **Event logs**, click **Open File History event logs to view recent events or errors**. This allows you to see the log of any errors that may have occurred during the backup. Why is this important? How often should this log be viewed?

15. How easy is File History to use? Would you recommend it as a basic file backup software utility? Why or why not?

16. Close all windows.

Project 13-2: Viewing and Changing the Backup Archive Bit

Estimated Time: 30 minutes

Objective: Manipulate the backup archive bit.

Description: One of the keys to backing up files is to know which files need to be backed up. Backup software can internally designate which files have already been backed up by setting an archive bit in the properties of the file. A file with the archive bit cleared (set to 0) indicates that the file has been backed up. However, when the contents of that file are changed, the archive bit is set (to 1), meaning that this modified file now needs to be backed up. In this project, you view and change the backup archive bit.

1. Start Microsoft Word and create a document that contains your name and today's date.
2. Save this document as **Bittest.docx** and then close Microsoft Word.
3. Enter **cmd** in the Windows search box and then press **Enter**. The Command Prompt window opens.
4. Navigate to the folder that contains **Bittest.docx**.
5. Type **attrib/?** and then press **Enter** to display the options for this command.
6. Type **attrib Bittest.docx** and then press **Enter**. The attributes for this file are displayed. The A indicates that the bit is set, and the file should be backed up.
7. You can clear the archive bit like the backup software does after it copies the file. Type **attrib –a Bittest.docx** and then press **Enter**.
8. Now look at the setting of the archive bit. Type **attrib Bittest.docx** and then press **Enter**. Has it been cleared?
9. Close the Command Prompt window.

Project 13-3: Viewing Windows Hidden Data

Estimated Time: 30 minutes

Objective: Search for hidden Windows data.

Description: Hidden data can be helpful to a computer forensics investigator. In this project, you will download and use a program to search for hidden data.

1. Use your web browser to go to **www.briggsoft.com**. (The location of content on the Internet may change without warning. If you are no longer able to access the program through the above URL, use a search engine and search for "Directory Snoop.")
2. Scroll down to the current version of **Directory Snoop** and click **Download** above **Free Trial**.
3. Follow the default installation procedures to install Directory Snoop.
4. Launch Directory Snoop.
5. Depending on the file system on your computer, click **FAT Module** or **NTFS Module**.
6. Under Select Drive, click **C:** or the drive letter of your hard drive. If the **RawDisk Driver** dialog box appears, click **Install Driver**, click **OK**, and then select the appropriate drive again.
7. Click to select a file and display its contents, preferably a user-created document (like a Microsoft Word file). Scroll down under **Text data** to view the contents that you can read.
8. Select other files to look for hidden data. Did you discover anything that might be useful to a computer forensics specialist?
9. Create a text document using Notepad. Click the **Start** button, enter **Notepad** in the Search box, and then click the app.
10. Enter the text **Now is the time for all good men to come to the aid of their country**.
11. Save the document on your desktop as **Country.txt**.
12. Exit Notepad.
13. Now delete this file. Right-click **Start**, click **File Explorer**, and then navigate to **Country.txt**.

14. Right-click **Country.txt** and then click **Delete**.

15. Now search for information contained in the file you just deleted. Return to **Directory Snoop**, click the top-level node for the **C:** drive, and then click the **Search** icon.

16. Click **Files**.

17. Enter **country** as the item that you are searching for.

18. Click **Search in slack area also**.

19. Click **OK**. Was the program able to find this data? Why or why not?

20. Close all windows.

Project 13-4: Viewing a Network Log

Estimated Time: 30 minutes
Objective: View the Google network log.
Description: A network log contains a wealth of data that can be used for not only troubleshooting but also digital forensics. In this project, you will view the Google Chrome web browser log.

1. Open a Chrome web browser.

2. Click the three vertical buttons at the top right.

3. Click the **Customize and control Google Chrome** button (three dots), and then click **More tools**.

4. Click **Developer tools**.

5. Click the **Network** tab at the top.

6. You will now record your network activity. Note that the red dot indicates recording is taking place.

7. Navigate to several different websites. Note the captured data in the pane.

8. If necessary, click the **All** button to see all the network activity.

9. In the pane under **Name**, click any event to open the detailed window.

10. Click **Headers**. Read through the data provided in the pane.

11. Scroll down to **User-Agent**. Note the information regarding web browsers that is found here.

12. Navigate to a website in which you must enter a username and password.

13. Enter a valid username but use **XXXXXXXX** as the password.

14. Click the red button to stop the network log capture.

15. Click the **Download** button to save this file as a .HAR (HTTP Archive) file.

16. Minimize the Chrome browser window.

17. Navigate to the .HAR file.

18. Right-click the file name.

19. Click **Open With**.

20. Select **Notepad** or a similar text editor.

21. You can now view the contents of the file.

22. Now search for **XXXXXXXX**, which is the fictitious password just entered.

23. This reveals that a network log can contain sensitive data. What protections should there be to prevent a malicious tech support person from requesting a user create an .HAR file and send it to them for analysis?

24. Close all windows.

Case Projects

Case Project 13-1: #TrendingCyber

Estimated Time: 15 minutes
Objective: Summarize your thoughts on the #TrendingCyber opener.
Description: Read again the opening #TrendingCyber in this module. Which of the three recommendations by the security researchers to the hardware vendors do you think would be most effective? Which would be the least effective? What other recommendation would you make for preventing data from being left on network equipment sold on the secondhand market? Write a one-paragraph summary of your thoughts.

Case Project 13-2: Personal Disaster Recovery Plan

Estimated Time: 20 minutes
Objective: Perform a personal disaster recovery plan.
Description: Create a one-page document of a personal disaster recovery plan (DRP) for your home computer. Be sure to include what needs to be protected and why. Does your DRP show that what you are doing to protect your assets is sufficient? Should any changes be made as to how you are currently protecting your assets?

Case Project 13-3: RAID Level 6 Costs

Estimated Time: 15 minutes
Objective: Research RAID Level 6.
Description: Use the Internet to research the costs of adding RAID Level 6 to a computer, which is generally recognized as the best general RAID level. Create a chart that lists the features, costs, and operating systems supported for this level. Would you purchase this for your computer? Why or why not?

Case Project 13-4: Personal Backup Procedures

Estimated Time: 20 minutes
Objective: Design a backup procedure.
Description: What are your personal data backup procedures? Write a one-paragraph description of how you back up your data, what data you back up, how often you perform a backup, where your backup is stored, etc. Use the information in this module to compare it with your current backup procedures. Write a second paragraph that identifies the strengths and weaknesses of your current procedures. Finally, write a third paragraph that outlines how you could change your current procedures to make your backups more secure.

Case Project 13-5: Comparing Terminology

Estimated Time: 20 minutes
Objective: Compare different terms used for business continuity plans.
Description: A business continuity plan (BCP) may sometimes be confusing due to conflicting terminology. Because BCPs are used across a wide range of industries and by different regulatory groups and agencies, many of these use their own unique terminology that is similar to BCP but slightly different. Several of the terms that are similar to or related to a BCP but have different meanings include Resumption Planning, Contingency Actions, Emergency Response, and Disaster Recovery. Research three of these and compare them in the context of a BCP. Write a one-page paper on your research.

Case Project 13-6: Cloud Digital Forensics

Estimated Time: 30 minutes

Objective: Research the challenges of cloud forensics.

Description: If a cyber incident is the result of a breach of cloud-based resources, it is not possible to secure the scene as in an on-prem incident. When dealing with a cloud incident, the following should be considered:

- A primary concern is to ensure that the digital evidence has not been tampered with by third parties so it can be admissible in a court of law. In Software as a Service (SaaS) and Platform as a Service (PaaS) models because customers do not have control of the hardware, they must depend on the cloud service providers to accumulate log data. A **right to audit clause** in a cloud contract gives the customer the legal right to review the logs, and these should also be negotiated in advance.
- When a cloud customer is notified by its cloud service provider that an incident occurred, the immediate response from the customer's in-house legal and IT teams will be to ask for details about the scope of the impact. However, unless they are contractually obligated, the cloud provider may take weeks or even months to provide its client with details as they perform an investigation. However, once the cloud customer has been notified, the "clock has started ticking" regarding data breach notification law deadlines. This can place the cloud customer in an awkward situation.
- The regulatory/jurisdiction laws that govern the site in which the cloud data resides may present difficulties. For example, a court order issued in a jurisdiction where the cloud data center is located will likely not be applicable to another jurisdiction in another country.

Research how an organization would conduct cloud digital forensics. What additional challenges can you find? Is it possible to even perform cloud digital forensics? Write a one-page paper on your research.

Case Project 13-7: Consumer Replication Services

Estimated Time: 30 minutes

Objective: Research consumer-based replication services.

Description: The most comprehensive data copy solution for most users is an online replication service, sometimes called a *continuous cloud backup*. Data copy occurs continually without any intervention by the user. Software monitors what files have changed and automatically updates the backed-up files with the most recent versions. These copies are stored online in the cloud. There are several cloud-based services available that provide features similar to these:

- **Automatic continuous backup.** Once the initial backup is completed, any new or modified files are also backed up. Usually the backup software will "sleep" while the computer is being used and perform backups only when there is no user activity. This helps to lessen any impact on the computer's performance or Internet speed.
- **Universal access.** Files backed up through online services can be made available to another computer.
- **Optional program file backup.** In addition to user data files, these services can also back up all program and operating system files.
- **Delayed deletion.** Files that are copied to the online server will remain accessible for up to 30 days before they are deleted. This allows a user to have a longer window of opportunity to restore a deleted file.
- **Online or hardware-based restore.** If a file or the entire computer must be restored, this can be done online. Some services also provide the option of shipping to the user the backup files on a separate hardware device.

Search for three different consumer replication services. Research these services and note their features. Create a table that lists each service and compares their features. Be sure to also include costs. Which would you recommend? Why?

Case Project 13-8: Solutions to Log Management

Estimated Time: 30 minutes
Objective: Research different solutions to log management.
Description: There are several problems associated with log management. However, there are different solutions to these problems. These are listed in Table 13-7.

Table 13-7   Log management tools

Solution	Description
syslog	syslog (system logging protocol) is a standard to send system log or event messages to a server.
nxlog	nxlog is a multi-platform log management tool and supports various platforms, log sources, and formats.
rsyslog	rsyslog (rocket-fast system for log processing) is an open-source utility for forwarding log messages in an IP network on UNIX devices.
syslog-ng	syslog-ng is an open-source utility for UNIX devices that includes content filtering.
journalctl	journalctl is a Linux utility for querying and displaying log files.

Research each of these five solutions and write a detailed report on how they can be used, their strengths and weaknesses, and how they address a specific log management issue.

Case Project 13-9: Log Sources

Estimated Time: 30 minutes
Objective: Research different sources of log data.
Description: In addition to the log sources listed in Table 13-5, there are other log files that contain valuable information. These are listed in Table 13-8.

Table 13-8   Network device log sources

Device	Explanation
Web servers	Web servers are usually the primary target of attackers. These logs can provide valuable information about the type of attack that can help in configuring good security on the server.
DHCP servers	DHCP server logs can identify new systems that mysteriously appear and then disappear as part of the network. They can also show what hardware device had which IP address at a specific time.
VPN concentrators	VPN logs can be monitored for attempted unauthorized access to the network.
Proxies	As intermediate hosts access websites, these devices keep a log of all URLs that are accessed through them. This information can be useful when determining if a zombie is "calling home."
Domain Name System (DNS)	A DNS log can create entries in a log for all queries that are received. Some DNS servers also can create logs for error and alert messages.
Email servers	Email servers can show the latest malware attacks that are being launched through the use of attachments.
Routers and switches	Router and switch logs provide general information about network traffic.

Use the Internet to reach each of these log sources. Create a table that lists how they would be used in investigating a cyber incident.

Case Project 13-10: SOAR Log Sources

Estimated Time: 40 minutes

Objective: Research SOAR runbooks and playbooks.

Description: There are several important steps that should be taken when responding to an incident in order to recoup from it (called response and recovery controls). One step is to take advantage of security orchestration, automation, and response (SOAR) elements.

> **Note 23**
>
> SOAR is covered in Module 8.

Two elements that are closely associated with using SOARs are a SOAR playbook and a runbook. A **playbook** is a linear-style checklist of required steps and actions needed to successfully respond to specific incident types and threats. These playbooks give a top-down step-by-step approach to an incident response by establishing formalized incident response processes and procedures. A playbook can help ensure that required steps are systematically followed, particularly when it is necessary to comply with regulatory frameworks. Although playbooks support both human tasks and automated actions, most organizations use playbooks to document processes and procedures that rely heavily on manual tasks, such as breach notification or malware reverse engineering.

A **runbook** is a series of automated conditional steps (like threat containment) that are part of an incident response procedure. Whereas a playbook focuses more on manual steps to be performed, a runbook is usually actions that are performed automatically. These automated responses can help to speed up the assessment and containment of incidences. While runbooks can also include human decision making as required, generally, however, most runbooks are automated action-based steps.

> **Caution !**
>
> Playbooks are not exclusively manual procedures, nor are runbooks exclusively automated procedures. However, playbooks are predominantly manual while runbooks are mostly automated.

Most SOAR platforms have different preconfigured "out-of-the-box" playbooks that are based on industry best practices and recognized standards. These playbooks identify and automate responses to frequent enterprise incidents, including phishing, compromised accounts, and malware. Organizations can craft their own customized playbooks, which are more simplified or advanced than preconfigured playbooks. This gives the organization freedom to react to an incident that is in accordance with regulations or compliance measures that more directly apply to them.

Used together, runbooks and playbooks provide organizations with streamlined methods for orchestrating incident response and to document different security processes. Multiple runbooks and playbooks can even be assigned to a single incident so that the correct type and level of automation and orchestration can be delivered.

Use the Internet to research SOAR runbooks and playbooks. Write a one-page paper on your research regarding how these products can be used.

Case Project 13-11: Bay Point Ridge Security

Estimated Time: 45 minutes

Objective: Research vulnerability scans and pen tests.

Description: Bay Point Ridge Security (BPRS) is a managed service provider (MSP) that manages networks, computers, cloud resources, and information security for small-to-medium enterprises (SMEs) in the region. BPRS provides internships to students who are in their final year of the security degree program at the local college and has recently hired you.

You have been asked to lead a workshop for small businesses on digital forensics.

1. Create a PowerPoint presentation about digital forensics, including what it is and the different forensics procedures. Your presentation should contain at least 10–12 slides.

2. After the presentation, the senior management is confused about the difference between forensics and e-discovery. Create a memo that explains the differences and how each would be used in different settings.

Two Rights & A Wrong: Answers

Preparatory Plans

1. A business continuity plan is the development of a strategic document that provides alternative modes of operation for business activities that, if interrupted, could result in a significant loss to the enterprise.
2. Parallel processing testing involves conducting the same test simultaneously in different environments.
3. The Cyber Kill Chain is a knowledge base of attacker techniques that have been broken down and classified in detail.

Answer: The wrong answer is #3.

Explanation: The Cyber Kill Chain outlines the steps of an attack.

Resilience Through Redundancy

1. Redundancy in information security usually involves duplicated servers, drives, networks, power, sites, clouds, and data.
2. Clustering distributes a workload across multiple servers.
3. MTTR is meaningless when it comes to HDDs.

Answer: The wrong answer is #2.

Explanation: Clustering combines two or more devices to appear as a single unit.

Incident Investigation

1. The first step in a digital forensics procedure is to preserve the evidence.
2. E-discovery is the electronic counterpart of manually sifting through documents in discovery.
3. The chain of custody documents that the evidence was always under strict control and no unauthorized person was given the opportunity to corrupt the evidence.

Answer: The wrong answer is #1.

Explanation: The first step in a digital forensics procedure is to secure the scene.

References

1. Camp, Cameron, "How I (could've) stolen your corporate secrets for $100," *ESET*. Apr. 2023, accessed Apr. 22, 2023, https://www.welivesecurity.com/wp-content/uploads/2023/04/used_routers_corporate_secrets. pdf.
2. "2023 Weather, climate and catastrophe insight," *AON*, accessed Apr. 22, 2023, https://www.aon.com/getmedia/f34ec133-3175-406c-9e0b-25cea768c5cf/20230125-weather-climate-catastrophe-insight.pdf.
3. Shepherd, Maddie, "30 Surprising small business cyber security statistics," *Fundera*, Jan. 23, 2023, accessed Apr 22, 2023, https://www.fundera.com/resources/small-business-cyber-security-statistics.
4. Watson, Melanie, "What are the top 4 cybersecurity frameworks?" *IT Governance*, Jan. 17, 2019, accessed Sep. 13, 2019, www.itgovernanceusa.com/blog/top-4-cybersecurity-frameworks.

Oversight and Operations

Module Objectives

After completing this module, you should be able to do the following:

1 Describe information security governance and compliance

2 Explain the security operations of automation, orchestration, and threat hunting

3 Describe how artificial intelligence is used in information security

#TrendingCyber

The marriage of technology and sports has a long history. For decades fans have come to enjoy baseball electronic scoreboards, football instant replays, and soccer jumbotrons to enhance their experiences. But in recent years, the infusion of technology into sports has gone to levels that were virtually unimaginable just a few short years ago and burrows even deeper every year. This has started to raise several questions about the privacy of sports data and how it should be used.

Technology has often been introduced into sports in a clandestine fashion to gain a competitive edge. In 1956, the Cleveland Browns of the National Football League (NFL) were approached by two inventors who had developed a small radio receiver. These inventors suggested that the Browns place the device in the quarterback's helmet to relay calls directly instead of sending in plays through substitute players. This system was first used secretly in an exhibition game. The opposing team soon noticed that the Browns were not substituting as often as they had before, and eventually spotted the transmitter behind a wooden light post on the sideline. Other teams quickly scrambled to devise their own transmitters, but none were as effective as the Browns' device (although it was not uncommon for a Browns' quarterback to occasionally hear a nearby taxi dispatcher on the receiver instead of their head coach). After three more games using the receiver, the NFL commissioner banned its use leaguewide. It was not until 1994 that the NFL approved a new version of a radio receiver for all teams to improve the pace of the game. Today coaches can talk to their quarterbacks and a designated defensive player via encrypted wireless communication to prevent opposing teams from listening in.

As fans have become more tech-savvy, the sports leagues have worked to satisfy their cravings for information by sharing data once reserved for the teams and leagues. Today, every NFL football stadium has up to 30 ultra wideband (UWB) receivers to gather real-time data during the game. Players on the field have two or three radio-frequency identification (RFID) tags installed in their shoulder pads, and RFID tags are also found on the officials, pylons, first-down markers and chains, and even in the football itself. An estimated 250 devices are used during a game for tracking and data accumulation, and three operators are required at every game to verify that all tracking systems are functioning properly. The tracking system captures player data such as their location on the field, speed, distance traveled, and acceleration, each measured 10 times per second. The raw data is sent to the cloud and processed to create player participation reports, calculate performance metrics, chart individual movements within inches (centimeters), and generate other advanced statistics. More than 200 new data points are collected on each play of every football game.

However, the data gathered during an NFL game pales in comparison to other sports. During the FIFA Soccer 2022 World Cup, each stadium employed 12 cameras using four-dimensional optical tracking. Unlike the NFL, which only tracked movement based on two or three RFID trackers in players' shoulder pads, soccer players had *29 points* on their bodies that were tracked during a match. This was to aid referees in calling an offside penalty. Yet this data also proved to be very valuable in revealing an athlete's performance on the field. Players at the World Cup could view their own data and performance analysis through an app created just for tournament athletes. Over 400 athletes downloaded the app, and they could choose to upload their game statistics to social media for the public to view.

However, this flood of sports data is having a profound impact on sports and their athletes.

First, the accumulation and analysis of this data has dramatically changed the game itself. At one time, technology was used primarily to report on *what* happened during a game. However, in the past 15 years, technology has changed *how* games are played. Consider the sport of baseball. Today home runs (and corresponding strikeouts) have reached record highs. This is because while using technology to gather and analyze reams of data, baseball teams found that sacrificing contact for power ultimately leads to more runs. Bunts and stolen bases have been cast aside as foolish risks. Starting pitchers work fewer innings and have been replaced by an endless parade of relievers pushing limits of how fast humans can throw a baseball. Technology has also changed football. Just over a decade ago, professional football teams took 62 percent of snaps from under center; today teams take 64 percent of their offensive snaps out of the shotgun. Every professional football passing record is owned by an athlete who is still playing today or just recently retired because passing consistently yields more yards than running. This has resulted in dramatic changes in how games are played.

Second, serious questions are being raised about the privacy of an athlete's data and how it should be used. What if a team uses data analytics on data collected from an athlete to predict the likelihood of a player getting injured? Should that be used for future contract negotiations? Would an athlete feel pressured to upload their performance data to social media if players on the opposing team uploaded their data and then charged the athlete with having "something to hide"? Should data be collected on athletes not only during a game but also during pregame warmups and postgame activities? What about collecting daily nutrition and sleep data? And should this data be shared with bettors who are seeking to know if an athlete will be subpar in an upcoming game due to lack of sleep?

This may only be the tip of the iceberg regarding how in the future an athlete's private data may be used. As one professional said, "This technology will be doing things that we cannot really imagine yet."

Consider the composition of the word *oversight*: "over" means above and "sight" is looking at but not touching. Oversight, which is a reviewing and monitoring of processes, policies, plans, programs, or projects, looks at these from above but does not necessarily become involved in their operations. The goal of oversight is to ensure that what is being done is achieving expected results; complies with applicable policies, laws, regulations, and ethical standards; and even represents good value for the money being spent.

Operations, on the other hand, is the opposite of oversight. In information security, it is the hour-by-hour work "in the trenches" of configuring appliances, applying controls, and reacting to cyber incidents.

Both oversight and operations are important: oversight watches and reviews while operations executes and implements. In this module, you study oversight and operations as they apply to information security.

Administration

Certification

5.1 Summarize elements of effective security governance.

5.4 Summarize elements of effective security compliance.

Oversight is often linked to "administration," which is the process of running a business or organization by performing executive-level duties. Two key duties of modern administration as it relates to information security are governance and compliance.

Governance

Governance in information security requires knowing what it is, its architectures, and the mechanisms for applying it.

What Is Governance?

Governance refers to the structures, systems, and practices an organization has in place to assign, oversee, and report. These three activities include the following:

- **Assign.** Governance is involved in assigning decision-making responsibilities, defining how decisions are to be made, and establishing the organization's strategic direction.
- **Oversee.** Overseeing the delivery of its services; the implementation of its policies, plans, programs, and projects; and the monitoring and mitigation of risks is a key element of governance.
- **Report.** Governance involves reporting on performance toward achieving intended results and then using that performance information to drive ongoing improvements and corrective actions (monitoring and revising).

There are several basic principles of good governance. These are summarized in Table 14-1.

Table 14-1   Principles of good governance

Principle	Explanation
Accountability	The obligation of an individual, a group, or an organization to answer for a responsibility that has been conferred.
Leadership	"Setting the tone," which plays a crucial role in encouraging an organization's personnel to embrace good governance practices.
Integrity	Acting in a way that is impartial and ethical, reflected in part through compliance with legislation, regulations, and policies, as well as through the instilling of high standards of professionalism at all levels of an organization.
Stewardship	The act of responsibly looking after resources on behalf of the organization and is demonstrated by maintaining or improving an organization's capacity to serve the public interest over time.
Transparency	Achieved when decisions and actions are open, meaning that stakeholders, including the public and employees, have access to full, accurate, and clear information on public matters.

Governance Architectures

Different architectures perform governance responsibilities. These include bodies and roles

Bodies   Governance bodies can be either internal to the organization or external. Those that are external can be categorized by their proximity to the organization: some cover just the immediate area (local/regional body), whereas others cover an entire nation (national body) or are worldwide in scope (global body). Some governance bodies are centralized, in which all authority is vested into a single group, whereas others are decentralized so that planning and decision making are distributed to smaller groups within it. Table 14-2 lists various typical governance bodies.

Table 14-2   Governance bodies

Name	Scope	Description
Board	Internal	Composed of internal directors who approve strategic organizational goals and policies.
Committee	Internal	The board governance committee is a subset of the board of directors that manages governance issues.
Government entity	External	National governments direct organizations through governance directives.
Regulatory	External	Regulatory agencies are responsible for distributing and enforcing government directives.
Legal	Internal	Internal corporate legal departments interpret internal and external governance policies.
Industry	External	Different industries create and audit governance policies for organizations that make up that industry.

Roles Because data is the lifeblood of information technology (IT), there are specific roles and responsibilities for those who have governance over systems and data. In this context, an **object** is a specific resource, such as a file or a hardware device; a **subject** is a user or a process functioning on behalf of the user that attempts to access an object; and an **operation** is the action that is taken by the subject over the object. For example, a user (subject) may attempt to delete (operation) a file (object). The different governance roles in relation to system and data resources are summarized in Table 14-3.

Table 14-3 System and data roles

Role	Description	Duties	Example
Data privacy officer (DPO)	Manager who oversees data privacy compliance and manages data risk	Ensures the enterprise complies with data privacy laws and its own privacy policies	Decides that users can have permission to access the file SALARY.XLSX
Custodian/ steward	Individual to whom day-to-day actions have been assigned by the owner	Periodically reviews security settings and maintains records of access by end-users	Sets and reviews security settings on SALARY.XLSX
Owner	Person responsible for the information	Determines the level of security needed for the data and delegates security duties as required	Determines that the file SALARY.XLSX can be read only by department managers
Controller	Principal party for collecting the data	Acquire user's consent, store the data, and manage consent or revoking access	Gathers data for SALARY.XLSX and identifies where it is stored
Processor	Proxy who acts on behalf of data controller	Person or agency that holds and processes personal data for a third party but does not make decisions about using the data and is not responsible for the data	Manages the SALARY.XLSX file on behalf of data controller

Figure 14-1 illustrates selected roles and terminology.

Figure 14-1 System and data roles and terminology

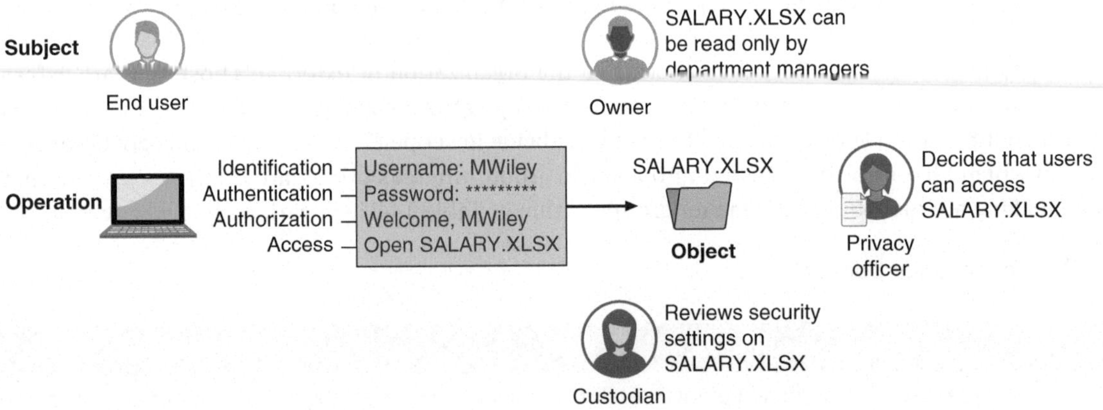

Governance Mechanisms

There are several mechanisms for applying governance in an organization. These include policies, procedures, standards, and guidelines.

Policies The uppermost level of a governance mechanism is perhaps the most elusive to define. This is because the word for this mechanism can have different meanings in different contexts. A policy is a formal statement that outlines specific requirements or rules that must be met based on a decision by a governing body. It outlines the principle that should be followed by its intended audience and addresses issues concerning the achievement of the overall purpose of the organization.

Note 1

A policy should link with the strategic objectives of the organization, such as improved service quality, reduced costs, or fewer workplace injuries.

However, if the question "What is a security policy?" were posed to both a manager and a security technician, the answers would likely be different. A manager might say that a security policy is a set of management statements that defines an organization's philosophy of how to safeguard its information. A security technician, on the other hand, might respond that a security policy is the technical configuration settings in a system. These two responses are not conflicting but are approached from two different standpoints. In fact, they are complementary: a written policy dictates what technology configuration settings should be used.

A further confusion can be attributed to the name of the Microsoft Windows process of assigning these privileges to a group of common users. Controls over user and computer accounts can be set through a feature known as Group Policy. Group Policy settings can be made on an individual computer (Local Group Policy) but will only apply to that computer, while settings applied to users in a domain will apply to all users (Domain Group Policy).

Several different policies (formal written statements) relate to information security. An acceptable-use policy (AUP) defines the actions users may perform while accessing systems and networking equipment. The users are not limited to employees but also include vendors, contractors, or visitors, each with different privileges. AUPs typically cover all computer use, including mobile devices. Other security policies include business continuity policies, disaster recovery policies, incident response policies, and a software development lifecycle (SDLC) policy that outlines how applications should be developed.

Note 2

The purpose of security policies is not to serve as a motivational tool to force users to practice safe security techniques. The results from research have indicated that the specific elements of a security policy do not have an impact on user behavior. Relying on a security policy as the exclusive defense mechanism will not provide adequate security for an organization.

Procedures   A procedure provides detailed mandatory steps that a user needs to follow to comply with a policy. Its goal is to inform employees how to carry out (implement) a policy. Procedures often contain written instructions in logically numbered steps and sometimes are in the form of a checklist. A common information security procedure is called an incident response playbook. A playbook lists specific actions to take for threats.

An example of a procedure is employee onboarding, or the tasks associated with hiring a new employee. These steps may include requiring new hires to sign an employee **nondisclosure agreement (NDA)** to make clear to employees that they may not disclose trade secrets and confidential information without permission. In addition, the setup and account configuration tasks for providing access to new employees should be outlined. These steps may include selecting and then installing the new computer, creating email mailboxes, adding user accounts to groups, and creating necessary folders.

Employee offboarding entails actions to be taken when an employee leaves an enterprise. When an employee leaves an organization, that employee's accounts should be immediately disabled (but not necessarily deleted). The necessary steps should include backing up all employee files from the local computer and file server, archiving email, forwarding email to a manager or coworker, hiding the name from the email address book, and so on.

Note 3

Orphaned accounts are user accounts that remain active after an employee has left an organization and are a serious security risk. For example, an employee who left under unfavorable circumstances might be tempted to "get even" with the organization by stealing or erasing sensitive information through their account. To assist with controlling dormant accounts, *account expiration* can be used. Account expiration is the process of setting a user's account to expire. Account expiration can be explicit, in that the account expires on a set date, or it can be based on a specific number of days of inactivity.

Standards In the context of governance, a standard specifies the uniform uses of specific technologies or settings for secure configurations. Standards can come from within the organization. However, often standards are issued by an external third party.

An example of a standard as it relates to information security is the **Payment Card Industry Data Security Standard (PCI DSS)**. The PCI DSS compliance standard was introduced to provide a minimum degree of security for handling customer card information. Requirement 11 of the latest standard (PCI DSS 3.2.1) states that organizations must "Regularly test security systems and processes" using both vulnerability scans and penetration tests. A partial list of the PCI DSS Requirement 11 standards is shown in Table 14-4.

Table 14-4 PCI DSS Requirement 11 standards

Standard	Description	Frequency
11.1	Implement processes to test for the presence of wireless access points (802.11) and detect and identify all authorized and unauthorized wireless access points.	Quarterly
11.2	Run internal and external network vulnerability scans to address vulnerabilities and perform rescans as needed until passing scans are achieved. External scans must be performed by an Approved Scanning Vendor (ASV), while scans conducted after network changes and internal scans may be performed by internal staff.	At least quarterly and after any significant change in the network
11.3	Develop and implement a methodology for penetration testing that includes external and internal testing. If segmentation is used to reduce PCI DSS scope, perform penetration tests to verify that the segmentation methods are operational and effective. Service providers using segmentation must confirm PCI DSS scope by performing penetration testing on segmentation controls.	At least annually and after any significant upgrade or modification; service providers must perform penetration testing at least every six months and after making changes to controls

Note 4

PCI DSS version 3.2.1, which has been in place since early 2018, will be replaced by version 4.0 that goes into effect on March 31, 2024. While some requirements will be effective immediately, many will not be required for another 12 months, giving businesses a year-long transition period to implement the more challenging requirements. Version 4.0 has 63 new requirements addressing such topics as phishing, social engineering, and evolving attacks against e-commerce payment applications.

Different standards are common in information security. These include password standards, access control standards, physical security standards, and encryption standards.

Guidelines A guideline provides general guidance and support for policies, standards, or procedures. A guideline gives the user guidance and additional information to help conform to more specific requirements. However, a guideline is voluntary while policies, standards, and procedures are considered mandatory.

Compliance

Related to governance is the topic of compliance. It is important to understand the definition of compliance and how organizations monitor it. One particular area of importance today with compliance is protecting user privacy.

Defining Compliance

Compliance is the process of ensuring that an organization adheres to laws and regulations related to information security and user data privacy. Many different types of organizations are required to comply with different security regulations and standards. These include the following:

- Companies that handle personal data of European citizens need to comply with the General Data Protection Regulation (GDPR).
- Financial institutions, retailers, and e-commerce companies need to comply with the PCI DSS standard that protects payment card data.
- Healthcare organizations must comply with Healthcare Insurance Portability and Accountability Act (HIPAA) regulations that protect patient health information.

Compliance is important from both a positive and negative perspective ("carrot and stick"). Positively, it provides "best practices" to follow to minimize the risk of a cyber incident. Negatively, it relies on penalties for noncompliance or not following compliance standards. These penalties include fines (monetary penalties), sanctions (other penalties such as withholding payments), reputational damage (negative perceptions of the organization), loss of license (withdrawal of a permit to function), or contractual impacts (suspending or even terminating contracts).

Compliance Monitoring

Compliance monitoring refers to the quality assurance tests that organizations perform to determine how well their business operations meet security regulations and standards. This need to monitor regulatory compliance performance is often itself a regulatory requirement. Compliance monitoring ensures that in information security an organization is practicing due care (taking reasonable steps to secure and protect its assets, reputation, and finances) and due diligence (identifying and mitigating risks brought on by third parties). Compliance monitoring involves having a process to verify conformity and generating appropriate analysis (reporting). This monitoring process can be either internal or external.

Internal Compliance Monitoring   Compliance monitoring can be performed by the organization itself (internal compliance monitoring). Typically, a dedicated compliance team will be responsible for tracking compliance and monitoring day-to-day activities by using relevant automation compliance tools. Instead of performing random manual "spot checks," automation compliance tools provide organizations with a continual evaluation of workflows. These tools work by first categorizing and then collecting and analyzing data at various points in its lifecycle; if the automation software recognizes a relative spike or drop in the data, an alert can be generated and sent to the appropriate stakeholders. These tools can also generate an internal compliance report that can be provided to an auditor that verifies compliance. A dashboard of an automation compliance tool is seen in Figure 14-2.

Figure 14-2   Automation compliance tool

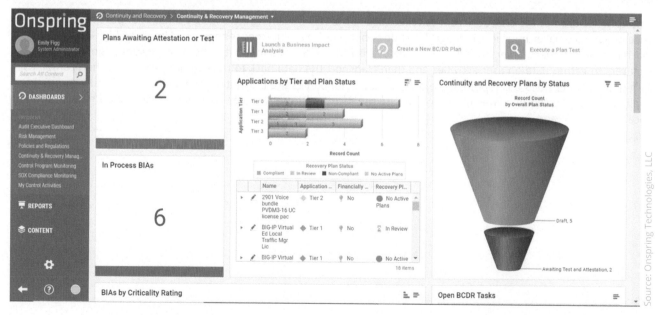

> **Note 5**
>
> Categorization of data is important because not all data needs the same protections. This is governed according to applicable regulations. For example, specific types of patient data need to be protected according to HIPAA regulations.

External Compliance Monitoring   Compliance monitoring can also be performed by a professional third party (external compliance monitoring and reporting). These entities can examine the protections set by the organization and then create an external compliance report. These reports serve as an official attestation (verification of its truth or authenticity) of compliance monitoring. Reports typically require a statement of the acknowledgment of the organization's responsibility for establishing and maintaining effective internal controls as they relate to compliance.

Securing Data Privacy Through Compliance

One of the most important protections that can be established through compliance is that of securing user data privacy. It is important to understand the types of user data that is collected and the current protections in place.

Types of Data Collection   There are two types of data collections of user private data that occur. The first is an *overt* and *legitimate* gathering of this data by an organization. For example, an organization may have a valid business need to ask a customer for their address and mobile phone number, and then keep this data on file. And the request for the data comes from asking the customer to provide it; it is not collected surreptitiously (secretly).

The second type of data collection is a *concealed* and *questionable* collection of user data. It is concealed because it is often collected in secret without the user's clear knowledge and express permission; it is questionable because there is not a clear business case for gathering it.

Many organizations today take advantage of the fact that every time a user interacts with technology, they leave behind a "data trail," which is a digital record of their activity. This includes obvious activities such as sending an email, browsing the Internet, and making a purchase—or *any* activity using technology. But today, data is predominantly collected by using tracking features (trackers) that are embedded in virtually every app on a smartphone; in fact, the average app has *six* trackers. Trackers allow third parties to collect data from the user's interaction with the app along with exactly where the user is located throughout the day. As more and more activities of a user's everyday life are performed electronically using more and more interconnected devices, the volume of data compiled on each user grows exponentially each day.

> **Note 6**
>
> Smartphones are not the only devices that collect user data. It is becoming increasingly difficult to purchase an appliance or even a smaller household "gadget" that does not require an Internet connection. Almost all high-end washing machines, dishwashers, dryers, refrigerators, and ovens require Wi-Fi connectivity. These connections allow the manufacturers to gather data on user activities and then transport the data back to the company—which it then combines with other data to build a comprehensive profile. Some companies are now intentionally disabling features until the appliance is connected to a Wi-Fi network—despite the fact that these features have been available on regular appliances *for over 75 years.*

There are significant issues raised with how both types of private data are collected and then used. These often overlap and are summarized in Table 14-5.

Table 14-5   Issues regarding how private data is collected and used

Issue	Explanation
The data is gathered and kept in secret.	Users have no formal rights to find out what private information is being gathered, who gathers it, or how it is being used.
The accuracy of the data cannot be verified.	Because users do not have the right to correct or control what personal information is gathered, its accuracy may be suspect. In some cases, inaccurate or incomplete data may lead to erroneous decisions made about individuals without any verification.
Identity theft can impact the accuracy of data.	Victims of identity theft will often have information added to their profile that was the result of actions by the identity thieves, and even this vulnerable group has no right to see or correct the information.
Unknown factors can impact overall ratings.	Ratings are often created from combining thousands of individual factors or data streams, including race, religion, age, gender, household income, zip code, presence of medical conditions, transactional purchase information from retailers, and hundreds more data points about individual consumers. How these different factors impact a person's overall rating is unknown.
Informed consent is usually missing or is misunderstood.	Statements in a privacy policy such as "We may share your information for marketing purposes with third parties" is not clearly informed consent to freely allow the use of personal data. Often users are not even asked for permission to gather their information.
Data is being used for increasingly important decisions.	Private data is being used on an ever-increasing basis to determine eligibility in significant life opportunities, such as jobs, consumer credit, insurance, and identity verification.
Targeted ads based on private data can lead to discrimination.	Targeted advertising can perpetuate and reinforce harmful stereotypes. For example, research has shown that online employment ads for science, technology, engineering, and mathematics are disproportionately shown to men and hidden from women.

Current Data Protections   Different legal protections are in place to protect the privacy of user data. To violate these protections may have significant ramifications (legal implications). Currently there are no universal protections (global data protections) to which all nations adhere. There are, however, protections that apply to a country or group of countries (national data protections).

In the European Union (EU), data protections cover what are called data subjects, which is any living individual whose personal data is collected and stored by an organization. The fundamental EU principle of data protection is the right to be forgotten, which means that data subjects have a legal right to have their private data erased. The regulation states, "The data subject shall have the right to obtain from the controller the erasure of personal data concerning him or her without undue delay and the controller shall have the obligation to erase personal data without undue delay."

Note 7

"Undue delay" is interpreted to be about 30 days.

The United States, however, has no "right to be forgotten" regulation. This is in part due to the fact that the ownership or legal possession and control of the data has not been firmly established. Different states have passed privacy laws so that they are local/regional data protections, but these vary widely. This means that U.S. data protections primarily are those established as industry regulations that an organization follows to be in compliance. These regulations typically outline the tasks of a controller versus a processor, how organizations should monitor collected data (data inventory), and the length of time data should be kept (retention).

> **Caution** (!)
>
> Some entities try to differentiate between data privacy, data security, and data protection. However, there are no clear and agreed-upon definitions for these terms, and they often are contradictory. Users should be cautioned about using these terms in a rigid fashion.

Two Rights & A Wrong

1. Governance refers to the structures, systems, and practices an organization has in place to assign, oversee, and report.
2. A custodian is a proxy who acts on behalf of a data controller.
3. A procedure provides detailed mandatory steps that a user needs to follow in order to comply with a policy.

See the answers at the end of the module.

Security Operations

Certification

4.7 Explain the importance of automation and orchestration related to secure operations.

4.8 Explain appropriate incident response activities.

In most organizations, information security defenders make up the **security operations center (SOC)**, pronounced "sock." While at one time this was a room (center) in which all the security personnel were housed, today with the growth of required defenses and the number of employees working remotely, a SOC is more of a *function* than a location. The members of a SOC team are responsible for multiple tasks, including proactive monitoring, incident response and recovery, remediation activities, compliance, and coordination.

There are different tools that a modern SOC uses today. These include automation, orchestration, threat hunting, and artificial intelligence.

Automation

There is a need for information security automation due to its many benefits. These can be illustrated through a variety of use cases.

Need for Security Automation

Organizations must collect global threat intelligence across all attack vectors outside of their network as well as their own data from within. Finding the linkages (correlations) from multiple external and internal data sources can result in more accurate results and reduces the likelihood of false positives. And this data correlation analysis must also be able to scale (increase) to meet ever-increasing threats. Although SOCs can collect voluminous amounts of this threat data, it is of limited value unless it can be quickly organized into actionable steps. With the high number of attacks and corresponding large volumes of data, it is virtually impossible to perform the necessary correlations manually.

Yet to the surprise of many users, information security has traditionally been more manual than automated for many years. Security personnel have been forced to work manually to search for evidence of attacks, uncover the techniques used by the malware, and then configure devices for protection. Although these security *devices* are obviously automated, the *work* done by security personnel has been highly manual.

However, in recent years, a shift has occurred in which more automation is becoming available to security personnel. Instead of relying on human power to battle attacks, automation is providing significant advancements. This helps to streamline and speed up security processes to provide the needed insights in a timely fashion.

Note 8

Security automation "levels the playing field" against threat actors who use automation for their attacks, reduces the volume of threats, and allows for faster prevention of zero-day attacks of previously unknown threats.

Benefits of Automation

Cybersecurity automation provides multiple advantages. The primary benefit is that automation can generate faster protection. Once a threat is identified, protections can be created and quickly distributed to networks, endpoints, and the cloud—something that is not possible with a manual process. Other benefits of automation are listed in Table 14-6.

Table 14-6   Benefits of security automation

Benefit	Explanation
Produce time efficiency	Automation can improve productivity by reducing the needed time to complete a task.
Enforce baselines	Security automation can ensure that required baselines are imposed.
Distribute standard infrastructure configurations	Unlike a technician who can easily miss a configuration setting when performing a task manually, automation can distribute infrastructure configurations to all devices.
Securely scale	Adding additional appliances to scale operations can be performed more securely through automation.
Improve staff retention	Due to the laborious nature of sifting through massive amounts of data, security automation can reduce the stress and "burnout" fatigue of workers and thus improve retention.
Reduce reaction time	Automation can dramatically decrease the time needed to react to an attack.
Generate workforce multiplier	Security automation gives staff the ability to be more productive.

Note 9

Services are available to help organizations identify security tasks for automation. This is done by tracking every task conducted during a security incident to identify what tasks need to be automated.

However, there are other considerations when using advanced security automation. Automation, particularly when interconnecting appliances, introduces complications (complexity), requires continual monitoring (ongoing support), and is more expensive (cost). A piece of equipment that develops a problem, if not immediately addressed, can cause additional future problems (technical debt). And if controls are not properly built in, automation can introduce an over-reliance so that an issue with the automation could cause the entire process to abruptly cease (single point of failure).

Use Cases for Security Automation

Several use cases demonstrate the advantages of security automation. These use cases include enhanced software development, improved provisioning, using security groups, and other use cases.

Enhanced Software Development   Security automation can be used to enhance software development to create more secure code. This includes using continuous integration, delivery, and deployment; using integrations and application programming interfaces; scripting; and guardrails.

Continuous Integration, Delivery, and Deployment   Software development has long been considered a highly manual process. As such, it has always been ripe for the introduction of security vulnerabilities due to human errors. However, implementing an automated process can not only produce code more quickly, but the code itself will be more secure. Table 14-7 lists the basic processes found in enhancing software development by automation.

Table 14-7 Automated software development processes

Process name	Description	Advantage	Explanation
Continuous integration (CI)	Developers merge their changes back to the main branch of code as often as possible, even several times each day.	Changes are validated by creating a build and running automated tests against it so that any problems can easily be identified as coming from a smaller segment of code.	Continuously integrating different changes from different developers prevents surprises on release day at the end of the project when all changes are merged.
Continuous delivery (CD or CDE)	Developers automatically deploy all code changes to a testing and/or production environment after the source code has been compiled (build stage).	An extension of continuous integration, it allows application deployment more quickly and easily while making troubleshooting easier as small batches of code are released.	Software can be released daily or weekly based on business requirements.
Continuous deployment (CD)	Every change that passes all stages of the production pipeline is immediately released to customers.	No human intervention is needed and only a failed test will prevent a new change to be deployed to production.	An excellent way to accelerate feedback loop with customers and take pressure off developers because there is not a single release day.

Figure 14-3 illustrates continuous integration, continuous deployment, and continuous development.

Figure 14-3   Continuous integration, continuous deployment, and continuous development

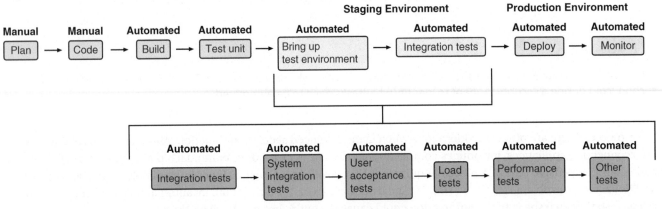

Application Programming Interface Integration   Uber, Airbnb, Instagram, and WhatsApp exemplify the modern business environment. These tech corporations are forerunners of the sharing economy and digital disruption with valuations exceeding $1 billion. They are seen as being more agile and able to adapt faster and adjust better to changing market conditions than large enterprises. In fact, they are often held up as models for today's business environment.

One driving factor that helped these companies succeed was how they created their customer and internal platforms. Instead of writing all software code from scratch, they relied heavily on **application programming interfaces (APIs)**. An API is a link provided by an operating system (OS), web browser, or other platform that allows a developer access to resources at a high level. An example of an API is when a user visits a website and the message *This site wants to know your location* appears. The website is attempting to use the geolocation API available in the web browser. APIs relieve the developer from the need to write code for specific hardware and software. Because APIs provide direct access to data and an entry point to an application's functions, they can be used to create code much more rapidly.

This use of APIs has led to what is called integrations and application programming interfaces (APIs), also called **integration platform as a service (iPaaS)**. This is a set of automated tools for connecting software applications that are deployed in different environments. API integration is used to integrate on-premises applications and data with cloud applications and data. It provides prebuilt connectors and business technologies that ease the development of integration flows and API management. It also offers custom development kits for linking legacy applications with mobile and social applications.

> **Note 10**
>
> As attractive as API integration is, it is also a target for attackers looking to exploit vulnerabilities in the API, called an API attack. API vulnerabilities are particularly attractive because they can have a broad impact and may take a long time to discover. In 2018, Facebook found a vulnerability in its API code that had made it possible for attackers to steal access tokens and take over the accounts of 30 million users. It took Facebook 14 months before they discovered the API vulnerability. API abuses are becoming a common type of web application attack resulting in a data breach.

Scripting   By its very nature, a script, which is a short "snippet" of code, is ideal for automation. In fact, it is often argued that scripting languages were specifically developed for automation tasks. This is because they often have features not found in formal programming languages. These features include simple mechanisms for invoking other programs, less strict language requirements such as no type system (a type system are rules that assign a property to variables and expressions), and no requirement to declare variables. In addition, the language runtime of a scripting language is usually included in the installation of the OS on the target systems. For example, Shell, Perl, and Python are widely available on most UNIX and Linux OSs, making both development and deployment of automation scripts a fast and easy process. Common scripting languages include JavaScript, PHP, Python, and Ruby.

Guardrails   Motorists are familiar with guardrails, which are designed to be a safety barrier to prevent a car from leaving the roadway and crashing into an object. Roadway guardrails are seen in Figure 14-4.

Figure 14-4   Roadway guardrails

Shahjehan/Shutterstock.com

> **Note 11**
>
> Roadway guardrails are more than just the metal barrier itself. Guardrails function as a system, which includes the guardrail itself, the posts, the soil that the posts are driven in, the connection of the guardrail to the posts, the end terminal, and the anchoring system at the end terminal. All these elements have a bearing on how the guardrail will function upon impact.

Security guardrails are "automations" that constantly watch cloud deployments, find deviations from desired baselines, and can even automatically remediate issues. Guardrails leverage cloud APIs and automation to build automated security without adding friction to slow down the development processes.

Improved Provisioning   **Provisioning** is the process of creating and setting up an IT infrastructure. It includes the steps required to manage user and system access to various resources. Provisioning is an early stage in the deployment of servers, applications, network components, storage, edge devices, and more.

> **Note 12**
>
> Provisioning is not the same as configuration management, although they both are steps in the deployment process. Once a system has been provisioned, the next step is to configure the system and maintain it over time.

Traditionally, provisioning has been a manual process that required both managerial approval and technical implementation, usually involving multiple individuals. This resulted in long delays of weeks or even months to be completed. This was particularly the case for onboarding new employees.

Automated provisioning has streamlined the provisioning process, whether it is provisioning for individuals (user automation provisioning) or systems (resource automation provisioning). Automated user provisioning automatically grants and manages users' access to the systems, applications, and resources of an organization by granting employees access based on their positions and permission levels (enabling services and access). The organization can use IT and telecommunication services through predefined procedures to achieve automated provisioning. For example, when a new hire is onboarded, an identity management platform automatically assigns their role and gives them access to the applications needed to execute their responsibilities. If the employee later changes positions, then automated provisioning can change their accounts and access to reflect that.

Utilize Security Groups   In cloud computing, automated security groups function like a virtual firewall that allows control over all inbound and outbound traffic to a particular cloud resource, such as a load balancer or database. Security groups are associated with network interfaces so that any changes are reflected immediately and automatically once the configuration is completed. For example, it can quickly deny ingress traffic from threat actors (disabling services and access).

> **Caution** !
>
> Security groups are not highly granular. For example, traffic cannot be restricted by a specific Internet Protocol (IP) address. Network access control lists are better suited for this task.

Other Automation Use Cases   There are additional use cases for security automation. These include the following:

- **Escalation.** Information security automation allows for the rapid detection of a threat incident so that its importance can immediately be elevated, thus reducing the time needed to mitigate the threat. This is known as automatic escalation.
- **Continuous integration and testing.** Using a manual process to add new network and security appliances and then test their configurations often results in a "one-and-done" approach. Rarely are the systems tested again until a problem develops. Automation, on the other hand, can help security personnel perform continuous integration and testing.
- **Ticket creation.** A **ticket** is a special document or record that represents an incident, alert, request, or event that requires action from the SOC. It often contains additional contextual details and may also include relevant contact information of the individual who created the ticket. This is because tickets are usually employee generated. A benefit of security automation is automatic ticket creation from a security event. This eliminates the need for a staff member to take time to analyze a situation to determine if it has escalated to the point of requiring a ticket; instead, an automated system can evaluate the level of threat and create a ticket.

Note 13

There are many advanced use cases for security automation. These include analyzing threat feeds, data enrichment, threat feed combination, and automated malware signature creation, to name a few.

Orchestration

An orchestra is a large instrumental ensemble (group) that plays a variety of types of music. Composed of four families of instruments (strings, brass, woodwinds, and percussion), a full symphony orchestra can have over 100 members, while a smaller chamber orchestra may still have up to 40 different members, depending on the music being played.

Note 14

A symphony orchestra is defined by its string family; without the strings, it would be classified as a band.

In recent years, the concept of a musical orchestra in which many varied instruments all work together, called orchestration, has made its way into information security. Security orchestration involves the automation and combination of many different individual tasks and processes. In contrast to security automation that only automates one task, workflow orchestration involves organizing many tasks into a functional process (workflow) that is automated. In other words, orchestration is automation used for entire processes instead of for a single task.

Caution !

Although on occasion security literature will use security automation and orchestration synonymously, this is incorrect. Security automation is setting a single security operations-related task to run on its own without the need for human intervention, whereas orchestration is automating multiple tasks that make up an entire process.

The various tasks that make up information security orchestration are large and complex scenarios, and these tasks often cross multiple platforms. This automated coordination involves hardware, software, middleware, and services. It uses multiple automated (and sometimes semi-automated) tasks to automatically execute a complex process or workflow.

Note 15

The purpose of orchestration is to streamline and optimize repeatable processes and ensure the correct execution of tasks. Whenever a process becomes repeatable and its tasks have the capability of being automated, orchestration can be used to optimize the process and eliminate redundancies, speed up completion time, and reduce errors.

Workflow orchestration has given rise to a new type of cybersecurity platform known as a security orchestration, automation, and response (SOAR) platform. SOAR is a combination of software programs and tools that allow organizations to synthesize and automate a range of security operations, threat intelligence, and incident response in a single platform. Consider a threat actor who is attempting to use a brute-force attack against a login prompt. Normally this would result in a human security administrator receiving an alert. The administrator would then have to open the firewall app and manually block the IP address of the attacker. However, when using a SOAR platform, the SOAR can automatically and immediately block the IP address of a computer that is attempting to brute-force a login. Figure 14-5 illustrates a SOAR dashboard in which it displays a "Dollars saved" amount, which is a common feature in SOAR dashboards.

Figure 14-5   SOAR dashboard

Source: Metron Labs

> **Note 16**
>
> SOARs are covered in Module 8.

Threat Hunting

Information security threat hunting has become an important process for protecting networks and endpoints. Threat hunting involves understanding what it is, the different levels, and the processes and tactics used.

What Is Threat Hunting?

Reactive is defined as responding to an event that has already occurred. It is an action based on something that happened in the past. *Proactive* is taking steps in anticipation of a future event that has not yet occurred. In a reactive mode, problems are solved as they arise, and this can even spark creativity while focusing on a solution. A proactive mode, on the other hand, attempts to address problems before they become an issue; however, being proactive may result in lost time if the event never occurs or has a much smaller impact than anticipated.

While both reactive and proactive actions are necessary, information security has for many years been considered solely reactive: following a successful infiltration by the threat actors, steps will be taken to fix the problem. This obviously is too late to prevent damage from occurring.

However, that posture is now changing: information security is becoming more proactive than reactive. This can most clearly be seen in threat hunting. Threat hunting is an emergent activity that combines a proactive, repetitive (iterative), and predominantly human (instead of automated) identification of a cyber invasion to an IT network or endpoints. This invasion has thus far evaded detection by existing security controls. Threat hunting assumes that the network is already infected, and attackers are not trying to enter from the outside but are currently inside.

Despite the fact that the roles of a threat hunter and other security roles may have similarities and may sometimes overlap, they actually are quite different. These differences in roles are listed in Table 14-8.

Table 14-8   Security roles

Title	Role	Goal	Task	Driving force	Timeframe
Incident responder	Reactive	Secure environment after alarm has been raised	Minimize impact of attack on the organization through formal process	Business continuity	Immediate
Penetration tester	Proactive	Secure environment through controlled offensive exercises	Mimic actions of threat actors to test and validate security posture	Uncover vulnerabilities	Soon
Threat hunter	Proactive	Identify suspicious activity before alarm has been raised	Seek evidence of malicious behavior	Prevent infection from spreading	Longer

Note 17

Threat hunting has been described as "incident response—but without the incident!"

Levels of Threat Hunting

Not all threat hunting occurs at the same threat-hunting level. An organization that practices threat hunting may not be doing it effectively or efficiently. Table 14-9 lists the levels of "maturity" of threat hunting along with the people, processes, and tools needed.

Table 14-9   Levels of threat hunting

Threat-hunting level	People	Processes	Tools
Initial (Level 1)	Existing SOC personnel	Ad-hoc hunts with little data collected	Standard SOC reactive tools with little automation
Managed (Level 2)	Threat hunting performed by volunteer	Uses basic threat feeds with indicators of compromise; hunts only occasionally	Searching for text strings and automatic matching of IoC
Defined (Level 3)	Dedicated threat hunter	Formal hunting process that occurs regularly with data collection from key areas	Uses statistical analysis techniques
Quantitatively Managed (Level 4)	SOC analysts rotated into threat hunting team	Hunts occur frequently with moderate data collection	Use of dashboards and visualization tools
Optimized (Level 5)	Threat-hunting teams integrated across a SOC with proper resources integration into process	Hunts occur continuously and data shared across security community	Takes advantage of machine learning

Note 18

Threat hunters should continue to strive for the highest level and, once there, maintain that level, which can be challenging.

Threat-Hunting Process and Tactics

Although threat hunting will vary from one organization to the next, there are fundamental steps in the process of threat hunting and tactics. These include the following:

- **Select the attack model.** It is important for an organization to decide how it envisions the process that the threat actors use in order to compromise their assets. This helps define the philosophy of how threat hunting will occur and identify who the threat actors are and how they function (called profiling threat actors and activities). It is also important for an organization to select an attack model and use that as a foundation for their threat hunting.

- **Identify the most concerning threats.** Not all potential threats are of the same importance. A variety of factors should be considered when identifying the threats that are of the highest level of concern. Depending on the threat model chosen, this step involves going through each of the phases in the model to identify the attacker activities that are most concerning.

- **Create a calendar.** The next step is to create a calendar of how frequently to hunt for specific threats. Those activities that are found near the end of the particular threat model that is chosen are those of the highest importance because these are the activities that the attacker is about to implement to achieve their desired result, and thus they need to be identified and stopped immediately. The various activities can be organized as having a low impact, medium impact, or high impact. High-impact activities should be hunted for more frequently than those with a lower impact.

- **Generate a hypothesis.** A **hypothesis** is a tentative assumption that is made and will then be tested to determine if it is valid. Threat hunting begins with a threat hunter asking basic questions, such as "How would a threat actor infiltrate our network?" For example, a hypothesis of looking for an instance of ransomware may be, "We hypothesize that if our network is infected with WannaCry ransomware we will see an increase in the rate of file renaming."

- **Investigate the hypothesis.** Once the hypothesis is developed, the threat hunter "follows up" on it by investigating through different tools and techniques.

- **Act on results.** After the hypothesis has been examined, it will be found to be either true or false. If the hypothesis is found to be false—for example, there is no increase in the rate of file renaming—it may be concluded that the ransomware has not infected the system. However, this is not an indication of failure; rather, it simply means that there is no indication of an infiltration based on the specifics of the hypothesis. However, it *only* indicates that there is no indication based on the specific hypothesis under investigation. There could be evidence elsewhere that must be uncovered. What happens if a hypothesis is proven correct? First, this information should be turned over to the SOC so that the infiltration can be "rooted out" and more secure defensive barriers erected. Second, when possible, successful hunts should be automated to maximize the efficient use of the threat-hunting team's time. This can also limit the need to continuously repeat the same hunts.

Artificial Intelligence

One of the most talked-about topics in recent memory is artificial intelligence (AI). However, to the surprise of many users, AI is nothing new in information security: it has played a prominent role in security defenses for well over half a decade. It is important to understand the definition of AI, how it is used in information security, and the risks associated with it.

Defining Artificial Intelligence (AI)

A *buzzword* is defined as a term that has quickly spread beyond its original field so that those outside the field use the word imprecisely and pretentiously. IT is renowned for these tech terms used in conversations by those who want to show off their knowledge but lack a clear understanding of the term's real meaning. For example, some users mistakenly talk about a computer "virus" when they mean malware in general or refer to the "cloud" as only remote storage. A current buzzword is "artificial intelligence." This term has quickly become fashionable in popular culture; however, few users can define exactly what it is.

When defining artificial intelligence, it is important to understand that it is not a term used in isolation; rather, it is directly related to other similar—and equally confusing—terminology. The best way to define AI is to see it in the context of these other terms:

- **Data analytics. Data analytics** is a fixed process that examines large data sets to draw conclusions about the information they contain. Researchers manually create algorithms designed to learn patterns and correlations from historical data. Data analytics relies on human interaction to query data, identify trends, and test assumptions. Insights gained can then be used to anticipate future events. For example, an online retailer collects historical data on customer behavior, product searches, purchase histories, and more. Applying techniques using advanced tools, they then sift through the data to identify patterns and trends (sometimes called "data mining") to identify the most popular products or search terms. This information can help prepare for a surge in future orders by increasing the inventory of that product.

- **Artificial intelligence.** A subset of data analytics is **artificial intelligence (AI)**. While AI involves data analytics, it is autonomous: it works on its own without immediate or continual human assistance. In other words, data analytics creates algorithms designed to learn patterns and correlations from data, which AI can then use itself to create predictive models. AI systems are iterative and dynamic: they get "smarter" as they analyze more data, and they become increasingly capable and autonomous. In short, AI refers to technologies that can understand and act by themselves based on acquired and derived information; they are "artificially" intelligent. An online retailer might use AI to automate the process of "data mining" instead of manually creating the algorithms each time.

- **Machine learning. Machine learning (ML)** is a subset of AI. It uses statistical techniques to give computer systems the ability to "learn" or progressively improve their performance using data rather than being explicitly programmed by a human. An ML system can then create a refined algorithm for the next iteration. ML works best when aimed at a specific task rather than a wide-ranging mission.

The relationships among data analytics, AI, and ML are illustrated in Figure 14-6.

Figure 14-6   Data analytics, AI, and ML relationship

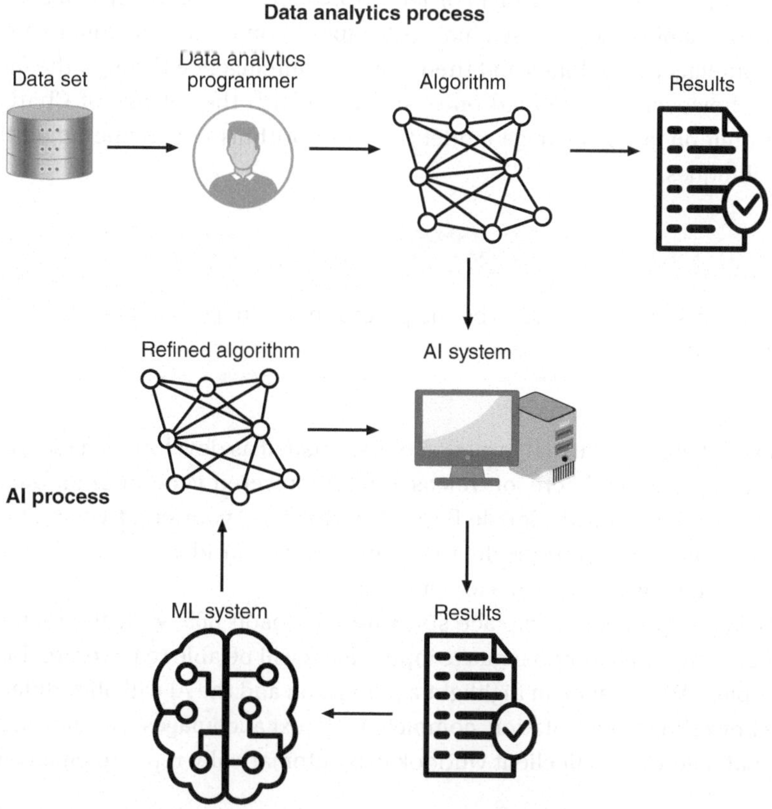

Note 19

These definitions and relationships continue to evolve. Some experts say that data analytics also uses ML in both AI and data analytics, but how it is used and the goals are slightly different. Other experts define data science as the study of data to extract meaningful insights for businesses and say it is the overarching term but define data analytics as a branch and not a subset.

There are three types of AI systems:

- **Assisted intelligence.** This type of AI system is widely available and improves what people and organizations are already doing.
- **Augmented intelligence.** These AI systems are emerging today. They enable people and organizations to do things they could not have done otherwise.
- **Autonomous intelligence.** This type of AI system is being developed for the future and features machines that act entirely on their own. An example of this type of system will be self-driving vehicles.

Note 20

There are other, related systems besides AI. Expert systems are programs designed to solve problems within specialized domains while neural networks use a biologically inspired programming paradigm that enables a computer to learn from observational data.

History of AI

The birth of AI can be traced all the way back to the beginning of digital computers. Shortly after their development in the 1940s, scientists, mathematicians, and philosophers began talking about machines that could "think" and act on their own.

Renowned British mathematician Alan Turing explored the mathematical possibility of AI, suggesting that because humans use available information as well as reason in order to solve problems and make decisions, why can't machines do the same? This became the framework of his seminal 1950 paper, "Computing Machinery and Intelligence," in which he discussed how to build intelligent machines and then test their intelligence through the famous "Turing Test."

To the general public, however, AI exploded onto the scene with the release of ChatGPT in November 2022. ChatGPT is an AI chatbot built on large language model (LLM) algorithms and is fine-tuned through supervised and reinforcement learning techniques.

Note 21

Natural Language Processing is sometimes said to be the process of teaching computers to understand linguistics and in doing so many LLMs are used.

Since the introduction of ChatGPT, a virtual "arms race" has ensued as developers have tried to outdo one another by incorporating AI into their products. Microsoft released an AI-powered version of its Bing search engine in early 2023, and Google immediately followed with Google Bard, described as "your creative and helpful collaborator, here to supercharge your imagination, boost your productivity, and bring your ideas to life." Microsoft then announced a new multibillion-dollar investment in ChatGPT maker Open AI.

Microsoft is now infusing its popular workplace software, Microsoft 365, with the technology behind ChatGPT, called Microsoft 365 Copilot. Through natural-language input, users will be able to generate documents, presentations, and original text. For example, a Word user can highlight a paragraph and the AI will offer different options for a rewritten version of it. An entire PowerPoint presentation, complete with text and images, can automatically be created based on the text from a document, and the email client Outlook can automatically reply to emails in depth using the same "voice" of the email recipient. AI features are also being added to the Windows OS as well to assist users in changing Windows settings, rearranging windows, and opening apps.

AI Uses in Information Security

Organizations face many challenges relating to information security, such as:

- Hundreds, thousands, or hundreds of thousands of endpoint devices per organization
- Large numbers of daily vulnerabilities including unknown zero-day vulnerabilities
- Massive amounts of security-related data that is generated hourly
- A serious shortage of trained security personnel

AI is ideally suited to address many of these challenges. AI technologies currently exist to properly train a self-learning AI system to gather data continuously and independently from millions—or even billions—of data points that can be immediately analyzed to identify patterns of an attack. AI can assist organizations *before* an attack (provide visibility and identify threats and anomalies early in the attack cycle, automatically investigate all anomalies, and identify high-risk attack behaviors), *during* an attack (force-multiply the security team with automated root-cause analysis to help them understand the full scope of the threat, automate incident workflow and remediation continuously, and collect ongoing evidence for forensics), and *after* an attack (continuously tune detection mechanisms based on lessons learned and adapt models to respond with increasing accuracy to future threats).

Table 14-10 lists several of the specific security tasks that AI can perform.

Table 14-10   AI security tasks

Task	Explanation
Analyze controls	AI systems can provide insight into current controls and their strengths and particular weaknesses and identify gaps in controls.
Reduce threat exposure	Because threat actors regularly change their tactics, AI-based security systems can provide up-to-date information of global and industry-specific threats to help the organization make critical prioritization decisions based on what could be used and what is likely to be used in an attack.
Conduct asset inventory	AI systems can help organizations gain a more accurate inventory of all devices, users, and applications with access to information systems and also provide assistance in categorization and the measurement of business criticality.
Perform breach risk prediction	Accounting for IT asset inventory, threat exposure, and controls effectiveness, AI-based systems can predict how and where an organization is most likely to be breached so that organizations can plan for resource and tool allocation toward areas of weakness while configuring and enhancing existing controls.
Manage incident response	When a security incident occurs, AI systems can provide an improved context of the attack to help prioritize and quickly respond to security alerts.
Provide descriptive explanations	Because securing "buy-in" from stakeholders across the organization for information security, AI systems can help provide understanding of the impact of various security systems and reporting to end-users, security operations, chief information security officer, auditors, chief information officer, chief executive officer, and board of directors.

Note 22

AI information security tools based on ChatGPT started appearing soon after the chatbot's release. BurpGPT is an AI vulnerability scanner that "leverages the power of AI to detect security vulnerabilities that traditional scanners might miss." It offers customizable prompts that enable tailored web traffic analysis to meet the specific needs of each user. PentestGPT is a ChatGPT-based penetration testing tool.

Security AI Risks

Although the use of AI in cybersecurity is important and growing, there are risks associated with using AI in security. These include the following:

- AI needs huge volumes of high-quality data to function accurately; however, many organizations do not have enough, or good enough, data.
- AI tends to generate too many false positives.
- It can be hard to "tune" an AI system for the specific needs of individual customers, especially smaller organizations without extensive data.
- There is a lack of transparency in how the AI system makes decisions, so this can be a challenge for the SOC that needs to understand these decisions in order to make their own subsequent choices.
- The algorithmic models can degrade over time if they are not properly maintained by data analytics experts.

However, risks of security AI are not limited to SOC operations. Threat actors themselves can attack AI systems and take advantage of AI. This is called adversarial artificial intelligence and includes the following:

- **Compromise the algorithms.** Just as all hardware and software is subject to being infiltrated by threat actors, AI-powered security applications and their devices likewise have vulnerabilities. These could be attacked and compromised and then the algorithms altered by threat actors to ignore attacks, much like a rootkit can instruct an OS to ignore malicious actions.
- **Taint ML training data.** Attackers can attempt to alter the training data that is used by ML in order to produce false negatives to cloak themselves.
- **Use AI maliciously.** Threat actors themselves can turn to using AI for attacks in order to circumvent defenses. Attackers can use AI to break through defenses and develop mutating malware that changes its structure to avoid detection.

Note 23

In early 2023, two security researchers acknowledged that ChatGPT helped them win the Zero Day Initiative's "hack-a-thon" that was designed to disrupt, break into, and take over Internet of Things (IoT) devices and industrial control systems (ICSs). After detecting several potential weak points, the researchers used ChatGPT to help write code to chain the vulnerabilities together, saving hours of manual development. The researchers won the contest prize of $123,000.

Two Rights & A Wrong

1. Complexity, ongoing support, cost, technical debt, and single point of failure are all risks of using automation in information security.

2. Security guardrails are automations that constantly watch cloud deployments, find deviations from desired baselines, and can even automatically remediate issues.

3. Threat hunting is an emergent activity that combines a reactive, repetitive (iterative), and predominantly human (instead of automated) identification of a cyber invasion to an IT network or endpoints.

See the answers at the end of the module.

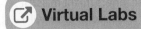 **Virtual Labs**   You're now ready to complete the simulations and live virtual machine labs for this module. The labs can be found in each module in MindTap.

Summary

- Governance refers to the structures, systems, and practices an organization has in place to assign, oversee, and report. Different architectures perform governance responsibilities. Governance bodies can be either internal to the organization or external. There are specific roles and responsibilities for those who have governance over systems and data and several mechanisms for applying governance in an organization. A policy is a formal statement that outlines specific requirements or rules that must be met based on a decision by a governing body. It outlines the principle that should be followed by its intended audience and should address issues concerning the achievement of the overall purpose of the organization. A procedure provides detailed mandatory steps that a user needs to follow in order to comply with a policy. A standard specifies the uniform uses of specific technologies or settings for secure configurations while a guideline provides general guidance and support for policies, standards, or procedures.

- Compliance is the process of ensuring that an organization adheres to laws and regulations related to information security and user data privacy. Compliance monitoring refers to the quality assurance tests that organizations perform to determine how well their business operations meet security regulations and standards. Compliance monitoring can be performed by the organization itself (internal compliance monitoring). Typically, a dedicated compliance team will be responsible for tracking compliance and monitoring day-to-day activities by using relevant automation compliance tools. Compliance monitoring can also be performed by a professional third party (external compliance monitoring and reporting). These entities can examine the protections set by the organization and then create an external compliance report.

- Data from users can be collected openly and to satisfy a legitimate business need or gathered secretly and for questionable usage. Significant issues are raised with how private data is collected and then used. Due to these issues, different legal protections are in place to protect the privacy of user data. Currently there are no universal or global data protections to which all nations adhere. There are, however, protections that apply to a country or group of countries called national data protections.

- Security defenders operate in an organization's SOC, which is responsible for detecting, analyzing, and responding to cybersecurity incidents. Although security devices are obviously automated, the work done by security personnel has in the past been highly manual. In recent years, a shift has occurred in which more automation is becoming available to security personnel. Cybersecurity automation provides multiple advantages. The primary benefit is that automation can generate faster protection. Once a threat is identified, protections can be created and quickly distributed to networks, endpoints, and the cloud, something that is not possible with a manual process.

- Several use cases demonstrate the advantages of security automation. Security automation can be used to enhance software development to create more secure code. This includes using continuous integration, delivery, and deployment and using integrations and application programming interfaces, scripting, and guardrails. Provisioning is the process of creating and setting up an IT infrastructure. Automated provisioning has streamlined the provisioning process, whether it is provisioning for individuals or systems. In cloud computing, automated security groups function like a virtual firewall that allows control over all inbound and outbound traffic to a particular cloud resource, such as a load balancer or database.

- Security orchestration involves the automation and combination of many different individual tasks and processes. In contrast to security automation that only automates one task, workflow orchestration involves organizing many tasks into a functional process (workflow) that is automated, typically using automated processes along with manual technology processes. Threat hunting is an emergent activity that combines a proactive, repetitive, and predominantly human identification of a cyber invasion to an IT network or endpoints. This invasion has thus far evaded detection by existing security controls. Threat hunting assumes that the network is already infected, and attackers are not trying to enter from the outside but are currently inside. Although threat hunting will vary from one organization to the next, there are fundamental steps in the process of threat hunting and tactics. These include selecting the attack model, identifying the most concerning threats, creating a calendar, generating a hypothesis, investigating the hypothesis, and then acting on the results.

- While AI involves data analytics, it is autonomous and works on its own without immediate or continual human assistance.

AI systems are iterative and dynamic: they get "smarter" as they analyze more data, and they become increasingly capable and autonomous. AI is ideally suited to address many of the challenges of information security. AI technologies currently exist to properly train a self-learning AI system to gather data continuously and independently from billions of data points that can be immediately analyzed to identify patterns of an attack. AI can assist organizations before an attack, during an attack, and after an attack. Although the use of AI in cybersecurity is important and growing, there are risks associated with using AI in security.

Key Terms

acceptable-use policy (AUP)
acknowledgment
attestation
automated provisioning
automation compliance tools
board
centralized
committee
complexity
compliance
compliance monitoring
continuous integration and testing
contractual impacts
controller
cost
custodian/steward
data inventory
data subjects
decentralized
disabling services and access
distribute standard infrastructure
    configurations
due care
due diligence
enabling services and access
enforce baselines
escalation

external compliance monitoring
    and reporting
fines
generate workforce multiplier
global body
global data protections
governance
government entity
guardrails
guideline
improve staff retention
industry
integrations and application
    programming interfaces (API)
internal compliance monitoring
internal compliance report
legal
legal implications
local/regional body
local/regional data protections
loss of license
monitoring and revising
national body
national data protections
noncompliance
offboarding
onboarding

ongoing support
orchestration
owner
ownership
playbook
policy
procedure
processor
produce time efficiency
reduce reaction time
regulatory
reputational damage
resource automation provisioning
retention
right to be forgotten
sanctions
securely scale
security groups
single point of failure
software development lifecycle
    (SDLC) policy
standard
technical debt
threat hunting
ticket creation
user automation provisioning

Review Questions

1. Which of the following is correct about security automation?

   a. Security operations have been more manual than automated for many years.

   b. Security automation requires both AI and ML.

   c. Security automation has been used since the very beginning of cybersecurity.

   d. Threat hunting relies heavily on cybersecurity automation.

2. Alois is explaining to his parents his new position in a SOC. Which of the following would Alois NOT say about a SOC?

   a. It houses the IT security team.

   b. It is responsible for detecting and analyzing cybersecurity incidents.

   c. It uses strictly automatic processes.

   d. A SOC responds to cybersecurity incidents.

3. Matheo is explaining to a new intern about the security automation used in the SOC. Which of the following would he NOT say regarding security automation?

   a. Using manual cybersecurity processes by a SOC will tip the balance in favor of attackers.

   b. Modern cyberattacks are highly automated so defenses need to be automated.

   c. Cybersecurity automation is now required by most certification bodies.

   d. Time spent on manual processes allows threat actors time to spread their malware.

4. What is data correlation?

   a. Finding linkages from multiple data sources.

   b. A requirement for using ML.

   c. A dated technology no longer used due to the introduction of security information and event management.

   d. Using a minimum of three external and three internal data sources to understand a zero-day attack.

5. Which of the following is NOT correct about governance?

   a. Governance refers to the structures, systems, and practices an organization has in place to assign, oversee, and report.

   b. Governance is involved in assigning decision-making responsibilities, defining how decisions are to be made, and establishing the organization's strategic direction.

   c. Governance is not concerned with overseeing the delivery of services; the implementation of its policies, plans, programs, and projects; and the monitoring and mitigation of risks.

   d. Governance involves reporting on performance toward achieving intended results and then using that performance information to drive ongoing improvements and corrective actions.

6. Which of the following is composed of internal directors who approve strategic organizational goals and policies?

   a. Panel

   b. Committee

   c. Board

   d. Council

7. Who is the principal party for collecting data?

   a. Custodian/steward

   b. Owner

   c. Controller

   d. Processor

8. Which policy defines the actions users may perform while accessing systems and networking equipment?

   a. ACXT

   b. RSRS

   c. BAC

   d. AUP

9. Which policy outlines how applications should be developed?

   a. SORA

   b. SCAP

   c. SDLC

   d. SARC

10. Which of the following is voluntary and not mandatory?

    a. Guideline

    b. Policy

    c. Standard

    d. Procedure

11. Lyam is researching scripting. Which of the following is NOT correct about scripting?

    a. JavaScript, PHP, Python, and Ruby are common scripting languages.
    b. The language runtime of a scripting language is usually included in the installation of the OS.
    c. Scripting has features not found in formal programming languages.
    d. Scripting should not be used for automation.

12. Which of the following is NOT correct about guardrails?

    a. Guardrails can automatically remediate issues.
    b. Guardrails add friction to slow down the development process.
    c. Guardrails constantly watch cloud deployments.
    d. Guardrails leverage cloud APIs and automation.

13. What is another name for integrations and application programming interfaces?

    a. APIaaS
    b. PaaS
    c. SaaS
    d. iPaaS

14. Which of the following involves the automation and combination of many different tasks and processes?

    a. Multitask combination (MTC)
    b. Cybersecurity automation
    c. Orchestration
    d. Autoflow

15. Which of the following platforms can take immediate action when it detects a malicious action?

    a. SIEM
    b. SOAR
    c. RSOC
    d. SAII

16. Which threat-hunting level hunts continuously and shares data across the security community?

    a. Managed
    b. Defined
    c. Quantitatively Managed
    d. Optimized

17. Which of the following is NOT a risk associated with using AI in cybersecurity?

    a. Attackers can attempt to alter the training data that is used by ML in order to produce false negatives to cloak themselves.
    b. The time needed for AI to provide indicators of attacks (IoA) but not indicators of compromise (IoC) is considered too slow to be useful today.
    c. Threat actors may turn to using AI for attacks in order to circumvent defenses.
    d. AI-powered security applications and their devices likewise have vulnerabilities that could be attacked and compromised so that threat actors could alter the algorithms to ignore attacks.

18. Which of the following is NOT a characteristic of threat hunting?

    a. Recursive
    b. Predominantly human
    c. Iterative
    d. Proactive

19. AI is a subset of which domain?

    a. ML
    b. Data analytics
    c. SOC
    d. Threat hunting

20. Which of the following is NOT an information security task that AI can perform?

    a. Perform breach risk prediction
    b. Conduct asset inventory
    c. Reduce threat exposure
    d. Configure controls

Hands-On Projects

Caution !

If you are concerned about installing any of the software in these projects on your regular computer, you can instead use the Windows Sandbox created in the Module 1 Hands-On Projects. Software installed within the virtual machine will not impact the host computer.

Project 14-1: Web Browser Privacy Settings

Estimated Time: 30 minutes
Objective: Set browser privacy settings.
Description: In this project, you view web browser privacy settings using a Google Chrome web browser.

1. Open a Chrome web browser and go to **www.cengage.com**.
2. Note that although you did not enter *https://*, nevertheless Google created a secure connection. Why would it do that? What are the advantages?
3. Click the padlock icon in the browser address bar to open the window about this connection.
4. Click **Cookies and site data**. How many cookies are used with this site? Does this number surprise you?
5. Click **Manage cookies and site data**.
6. Scroll down the list of cookies that were set from visiting this page. Are any of the names familiar to you?
7. Click the three vertical buttons next to one of the listed sites. What are the options?
8. Click **Done**.
9. Click the padlock icon in the browser address bar to open the window about this connection.
10. Note that the information provided says **Connection is secure**.
11. Click **Connection is secure** and read what this means. How should you use this when visiting a website that asks for information such as a credit card number?
12. Click **Certificate is valid** to view the digital certificate information for this site.
13. Read the **Certificate Information** about this digital certificate.
14. Click the **Details** tab and look at each of the fields and their values.
15. Click **Subject's Public Key** to display the public key associated with this website. How is the public key used?
16. Click **Issuer**. What third-party entity issued this digital certificate? What is the status of this certificate?
17. Click the **Close** button.
18. Click the three dots on the right side of the web browser and then click **Settings**.
19. Click **Privacy and security** in the left pane.
20. Click **Get started** under the **Take the Privacy Guide**.
21. Read through all of the screens. Is this information helpful? Click **Done** when finished.
22. Click **Check now** under **Safety check**. Note the different safety settings that are available.
23. Click **Cookies and other site data**. Note that different cookie settings can be selected here. Which settings would you choose? Why?
24. Click **See all cookies and site data**. Scroll through the list of cookies that are on this computer. Does the number surprise you?
25. What did you learn from examining these web browser settings? What changes would you make for improved privacy?
26. Close all windows.

Project 14-2: Using a Nonpersistent Web Browser

Estimated Time: 30 minutes

Objective: Use a browser that protects user privacy.

Description: Nonpersistence tools are those that are used to ensure that unwanted data is not carried forward but instead a clean image is used. This helps protect user privacy. One common tool is a web browser that retains no information such as cookies, history, passwords, or any other data and requires no installation but runs from a USB flash drive. In this project, you download and install a nonpersistent web browser.

1. Use your web browser to go to **www.browzar.com** (if you are no longer able to access the program through this URL, use a search engine and search for "Browzar").
2. Click **Key Features** and read about the features of Browzar.
3. Click **Help & FAQs** and read the questions and answers.
4. Click **Download now – it's FREE!**
5. Choose one of the available themes and click **Download**.
6. Click **Accept**.
7. Click **Download**.
8. Click the downloaded file to run Browzar. Note that no installation is required and it can be run from a USB flash drive.
9. From Browzar, go to **www.google.com**.
10. Enter **Cengage** in the search bar to search for information about Cengage.
11. Now click the red **X** in the upper-right corner to close the browser. What information appears in the pop-up window? What happened when you closed the browser?
12. Launch Browzar again.
13. Click **Tools**.
14. Click **Secure delete**.
15. Click **More**. What additional protections does Secure Delete give?
16. Close all windows.

Project 14-3: Using Windows Local Security Policy

Estimated Time: 30 minutes

Objective: Configure the Windows security policy.

Description: The Local Group Policy Editor is a Microsoft Management Console (MMC) snap-in that gives a single user interface through which all the Computer Configuration and User Configuration settings of Local Group Policy objects can be managed. The Local Security Policy settings are among the security settings contained in the Local Group Policy Editor. An administrator can use these to set policies that are applied to the computer. In this project, you view and change local security policy settings.

> **Caution** (!)
>
> You will need to be an administrator to open the Local Group Policy Editor.

1. Click **Start**.
2. Type **secpol.msc** into the Search box and then click **secpol**.

Note 24

If your computer is already joined to a domain, then searching for secpol.msc might not launch the application. If this is the case, click **Start** and type **mmc.msc**. On the File menu, click **Add/Remove** snap-in and then click **Add**. In **Add Standalone Snap-in**, double-click **Group Policy Object Editor**. If an error message occurs when launching the application, your version of Windows does not natively support secpol.msc and it may be necessary to download secpol.msc from the Internet.

3. First create a policy regarding passwords. Expand **Account Policies** in the left pane and then expand **Password Policy**.

4. Double-click **Enforce password history** in the right pane. This setting defines how many previously used passwords Windows will record. This prevents users from "recycling" old passwords.

5. Change **passwords remembered** to **4** and then click **OK**.

6. Double-click **Maximum password age** in the right pane. The default value is 42, meaning that users must change their password after 42 days.

7. Change **days** to **30** and then click **OK**.

8. Double-click **Minimum password length** in the right pane. The default value is a length of 8 characters.

9. Change **characters** to **10** and then click **OK**.

10. Double-click **Password must meet complexity requirements** in the right pane. This setting forces a password to include at least two opposite case letters, a number, and a special character (such as a punctuation mark).

11. Click **Enabled** and then click **OK**.

12. Double-click **Store passwords using reversible encryption** in the right pane. Because passwords should be stored in an encrypted format, this setting should not be enabled.

13. If necessary, click **Disabled** and then click **OK**.

14. In the left pane, click **Account lockout policy**.

15. Double-click **Account lockout threshold** in the right pane. This is the number of times that a user can enter an incorrect password before Windows will lock the account from being accessed. (This prevents an attacker from attempting to guess the password with unlimited attempts.)

16. Change **invalid login attempts** to **5** and then click **OK**.

17. Note that the Local Security Policy suggests changes to the **Account lockout duration** and the **Reset account lockout counter after** values to 30 minutes. Click **OK**.

18. Expand **Local Policies** in the left pane and then click **Audit Policy**.

19. Double-click **Audit account logon events**.

20. Check both **Success** and **Failure** and then click **OK**.

21. Right-click **Security Settings** in the left pane.

22. Click **Reload** to have these policies applied.

23. Close all windows.

Case Project 14-1: #TrendingCyber

Estimated Time: 15 minutes
Objective: Summarize your thoughts on the #TrendingCyber opener.
Description: Read again the opening #TrendingCyber in this module. What type of protections should exist for an athlete's data? Should the athlete own the data or the team for which they play? What are the arguments for each side? Should teams be prohibited from using predictive analytics to determine if an athlete could suffer an injury? Should athletes be prohibited from using predictive analytics to determine their future value to a team? Write a one-paragraph summary of your thoughts.

Case Project 14-2: Threat-Hunting Hypothesis

Estimated Time: 25 minutes
Objective: Identify threat-hunting hypotheses.
Description: Use the Internet to locate four different threat-hunting hypotheses. Next, determine the tools and techniques that you would use in order to determine if these hypotheses are valid. Finally, address the actions that you would take if each of the hypotheses were determined to be valid. Create a table of your findings.

Case Project 14-3: Challenges of Threat Hunting

Estimated Time: 25 minutes
Objective: Research the challenges surrounding threat hunting.
Description: Despite the allure of seeking out hidden attackers, threat hunting has several significant challenges associated with it. Threat hunters must be able to differentiate and identify two key elements. Historical evidence of an infection (artifacts) is an IoC. When detected by threat hunting, it suggests malicious activity is occurring. The descriptions of adversary behavior that IoCs indicate are called Tactics, Techniques, and Procedures (TTPs). IoCs are known knowns, while TTPs are known unknowns. Most automated network and endpoint security controls utilize signature and rule-based alerting for IoCs such as malware hashes. However, targeting TTPs is significantly more difficult and labor-intensive. For defenders, calculating hash values is a trivial indicator (and can be easily automated), while determining TTPs is very difficult and labor-intensive.

Research the difficulties and challenges of threat hunting. Write a one-page paper on your research.

Case Project 14-4: Threat-Hunting Prerequisites

Estimated Time: 25 minutes
Objective: Research the tools that a threat hunter needs.
Description: There are various techniques used in threat hunting. These include:

- **Searching.** Searching is the most basic method of querying a set of collected data such as a log file. The search criteria should be specific enough so that the results returned are not unmanageable but general enough so that no adversary activities are missed. When possible, wildcard (*) characters should be used.
- **Clustering.** Clustering is a form of statistical analysis that separates groups (clusters) of similar data points from a larger set based on specific characteristics.
- **Grouping.** Grouping identifies when multiple unique data points appear together based on specific criteria, for example, multiple events occurring in a specific time window. Unlike clustering, grouping requires an explicit set of data points as input.

- **Stack counting.** Stack counting (stacking) is the application of frequency analysis (how often something occurs) to large sets of data to identify outliers.
- **Supervised machine learning.** Machine learning uses algorithms and statistical models to progressively improve performance of a specific task. This could be identifying anomalous data that could indicate adversary activities. In supervised machine learning, a set of training data is fed into the algorithm with each data point (normal and anomalous) labeled with the desired output. Unsupervised machine learning is provided with "unlabeled" data, so the algorithm uses techniques like clustering and grouping to categorize the outputs instead.

There are a variety of tools that will be used within these processes. These include threat intelligence feeds, sources through which manual lookups can be performed, threat intelligence platforms, and tracking of developing standards. These various types of sources should be combined for integrated intelligence. In addition, these tools allow for an investigation of how the malware functions (executable process analysis).

What should be the prerequisites for a threat hunter? What level of statistics should they be familiar with? What are the other qualifications of a threat hunter? Use the Internet to research the qualifications for threat hunters. Review online job search sites that advertise for a threat hunter. Compare these with the types of courses offered at your school or another school. Create a "path" of courses that someone interested in threat hunting should take. Write a one-page paper on your research.

Case Project 14-5: Clean Desk Space Policy

Estimated Time: 25 minutes
Objective: Write a clean desk space policy.
Description: There are several policies that relate to matters of personnel. While these policies cannot be enforced through technology, nevertheless they are important for creating security "resiliency." One policy is a clean desk space policy. A clean desk space policy is designed to ensure that all confidential or sensitive materials, either in paper or electronic form, are removed from a user's workspace and secured when the items are not in use or an employee leaves the workspace. This not only reduces the risk of theft or "prying eyes" reading confidential information, but it can also increase the employee's awareness about the need to protect sensitive information. A clean desk space policy may include such statements as:

- Computer workstations must be locked when the workspace is unoccupied and turned off at the end of the business day.
- Confidential or sensitive information must be removed from the desk and locked in a drawer or safe when the desk is unoccupied and at the end of the work day.
- File cabinets must be kept closed and locked when not in use or not attended, and keys may not be left at an unattended desk.
- Laptops must be either locked with a locking cable or locked in a drawer or filing cabinet.
- Mass storage devices such as USB flash drives or portable external hard drives must be locked in a drawer or filing cabinet.
- Paper documents no longer needed must be shredded using the official shredder bins.
- Printouts should be immediately removed from the printer.
- Whiteboards containing confidential or sensitive information should be erased.

Use the Internet to locate three clean desk space policies from different organizations. Grade each policy on how thorough it is. Are any of the policies too restrictive so that they would interfere with an employee's work? Next, use this information to create your own clean desk space policy. How is it similar to these policies? How is it different?

Case Project 14-6: Right to be Forgotten

Estimated Time: 25 minutes

Objective: Research the EU "right to be forgotten" protection.

Description: Use the Internet to research the EU right to be forgotten principle. Read through the policy and note its strengths and weaknesses. Do you support this protection? Currently Internet tech platforms use data collected on users for advertising and thus do not charge for these services, such as searching, using social media sites, etc. Would you support paying a monthly subscription to these services if you erased your data? How could these tech platforms earn revenue in other ways? Write a one-page paper on your research.

Case Project 14-7: Security Operations Centers (SOCs)

Estimated Time: 25 minutes

Objective: Research SOCs.

Description: SOCs are vital functions in organizations today. Use the Internet to research SOCs. What do SOC team members do? What are the job roles at a SOC? What takes place in a SOC? What skills are needed to work there? Write a one-page paper on your research.

Case Project 14-8: Your Data Protections

Estimated Time: 25 minutes

Objective: Review personal data protections.

Description: How well protected is your personal data? What safeguards do you have in place to protect it? Research data protections and how you can use them to keep your data secure. Write a one-page paper on your research.

Case Project 14-9: Current State of Privacy

Estimated Time: 25 minutes

Objective: Research privacy regulations and laws.

Description: Regulators and government entities continue to pressure Apple and Google to make changes to their smartphones and to user data. Use the Internet to research current laws and regulations that address privacy. Are these adequate? Should more be done to protect users? What would you recommend? Write a one-page paper on your research.

Case Project 14-10: History of Apple Privacy Protections

Estimated Time: 25 minutes

Objective: Research Apple privacy protections.

Description: Research how Apple has changed the ways in which it protects user privacy on smartphones since 2010. Why have they made changes? Are these sufficient? Do Apple iPhones provide better privacy than Google Android devices? Why or why not? Write a one-page paper on your research.

Case Project 14-11: Artificial Intelligence Risks

Estimated Time: 25 minutes

Objective: Research risks associated with artificial intelligence.

Description: What are the risks associated with using artificial intelligence (AI)? What are the advantages of using AI? Should AI be regulated? If so, what regulations should be in place? Why? Use the Internet to research the risks associated with AI and write a one-page paper on your research.

Case Project 14-12: Bay Point Ridge Security

Estimated Time: 45 minutes

Objective: Research information security AI.

Description: Bay Point Ridge Security (BPRS) is a managed service provider (MSP) that manages networks, computers, cloud resources, and information security for small-to-medium enterprises (SMEs) in the region. BPRS provides internships to students who are in their final year of the security degree program at the local college and has recently hired you.

A new client has been reading about AI and has become very excited about using it in their SOC. However, they may not have a thorough understanding of how it can be used and the benefits and risks associated with it. You have been asked to lead a short session on AI for them.

1. Create a PowerPoint presentation about AI. Begin with what it is, how it can be used in information security, and what its disadvantages are. Your presentation should contain at least 10–12 slides.

2. After the presentation, the senior management is concerned that they may be moving too quickly. They have asked your opinion on when they should implement AI: now, in six months, or one year from now. Write a memo about your opinion for AI implementation.

Two Rights & A Wrong: Answers

Administration

1. Governance refers to the structures, systems, and practices an organization has in place to assign, oversee, and report.

2. A custodian is a proxy who acts on behalf of a data controller.

3. A procedure provides detailed mandatory steps that a user needs to follow in order to comply with a policy.

Answer: The wrong answer is #2.

Explanation: A processor is a proxy who acts on behalf of a data controller.

Security Operations

1. Complexity, ongoing support, cost, technical debt, and single point of failure are all risks of using automation in information security.

2. Security guardrails are automations that constantly watch cloud deployments, find deviations from desired baselines, and can even automatically remediate issues.

3. Threat hunting is an emergent activity that combines a reactive, repetitive (iterative), and predominantly human (instead of automated) identification of a cyber invasion to an IT network or endpoints.

Answer: The wrong answer is #3.

Explanation: Threat hunting is a proactive, not a reactive, event.

Module 15

Information Security Management

Module Objectives

After completing this module, you should be able to do the following:

1   Explain asset protections

2   Describe risk management

#TrendingCyber

Teaching security awareness to users with little background in technology, little understanding of cyber risks, and—far too often—little interest in protecting themselves or the organization for which they work is an ongoing challenge. And that challenge becomes exponentially more difficult when users hear misleading warnings from uninformed journalists on national news outlets, read erroneous warnings from misinformed bloggers who consider themselves to be tech experts, or see unsubstantiated advice distributed by federal authorities. This is the case with a recent dubious cyberattack warning again making the rounds.

"Juice jacking" is the name given for a proof-of-concept attack (a proof of concept is a demonstration of a product or service to determine if the idea can be turned into a reality). This proposed attack involves taking advantage of public recharging stations that allow users to recharge their mobile phones. In a typical scenario, a threat actor infects a public charging station or sets up their own equipment at an airport, shopping mall, hotel, or similar public area. This equipment looks identical to a regular charging station. However, once the user's mobile device is connected to the fake charging station, the station silently sends commands over the charging cord's cable back to the device to install malware or siphon data from the mobile phone.

This proof of concept (along with the name "juice jacking") first surfaced over 20 years ago in 2011 at Defcon, an annual conference in Las Vegas where participants are permitted and encouraged to demonstrate potential attacks (within reason) against fellow attendees. A demonstration of this concept was intended to bring awareness to a potential threat. In subsequent conferences, other researchers showed off similar techniques.

Since then, warnings about juice jacking have occasionally resurfaced in the popular media and on blogs. However, in 2023, the fears hit a new high when both the Federal Bureau of Investigation (FBI) and Federal Communications Commission (FCC) issued new warnings. An FBI field office issued a juice jacking alert, writing in part, "Bad actors have figured out ways to use public USB ports to introduce malware and monitoring software onto devices." Days later the FCC added a similar warning, stating, "In some cases, criminals may have intentionally left cables plugged in at charging stations. There have even been reports of infected cables being given away as promotional gifts."

These warnings then generated ominous news reports from hundreds of online sites and in print media. Statements about its serious dangers were common, such as juice jacking is a "significant privacy hazard" that can identify visited webpages in less than 10 seconds and by just plugging into a malicious charger "your device is now infected." It also prompted otherwise reputable print media to produce such headlines as "Don't Let a Free USB Charge Drain

Your Bank Account" and "Stop! Don't Charge Your Phone This Way." Worried users can even purchase a pluggable USB data blocker for $14.99 to "protect against juice jacking at public USB ports" and "defend against unwanted data transfers and hijacking."

But is juice jacking a viable threat?

Information security experts say that contrary to these reports, juice jacking is not a threat (unless you carry around government top-secret security documents on your mobile device and are targeted by deep-pocket nation-state attackers). There are several reasons why juice jacking is not something that users need to fear.

First, there are no documented cases of juice jacking ever taking place in the wild. To date, no users have claimed to be victims and no security experts have said they are aware of such an attack occurring. Even Apple representatives have stated that they are not aware of any such attacks ever taking place.

Second, public charging stations do not have USB *data ports* for recharging. Instead, they have USB *charging ports*, which are different. A charging port can only send power to the connected device but cannot send any data. Electrical wall outlets for consumers are available that have USB charging ports. Also, there are charging hubs that can be connected to a computer for recharging a mobile device. But these only send power and not data through the port. Connecting a device to a public charging station only sends power to the device without a data exchange taking place.

Third, Apple and Google have continued to harden their operating systems (OSs) against this type of (albeit remote) threat. Juice jacking can only be successful with the user's approval: modern Apple iPhones and Google Android devices require users to click through an explicit warning before they can exchange files with a device connected by a cable. Also, Apple iPhones require users to enter a password or provide a facial scan before an app can be installed.

Finally, unlike malware that can be universally written to infect large numbers of iOS or Windows devices, the OSs on mobile phones are much different. There is no single universal script for juice jacking that will work on the hundreds of different mobile devices; rather, it would require customized scripts for each type of connected mobile device. That puts juice jacking beyond the capabilities of most attackers. And because of the time required to write and troubleshoot so many different scripts (but not even knowing which type of mobile device will be connected), it is generally considered unlikely that a threat actor would make such a high investment for such a low rate of return.

What is interesting about these recent juice jacking alarms is that when those who sounded the warnings were asked for additional information or clarification, they could not produce any. A local district attorney's office published an alert warning users of juice jacking in which "criminals load malware onto charging stations or cables they leave plugged in at the stations so they may infect the phones and other electronic devices of unsuspecting users." When later asked by a reporter, the DA's office admitted that they have never been informed of a user who was a target of this attack, nor could they cite any other jurisdiction that had evidence of an attack. When an FBI spokesperson was asked about their warning, the response was that it was just a standard public service announcement post with "nothing new" to report, adding, "This was a general reminder for the American public to stay safe and diligent, especially while traveling." And when a security researcher pointed out to the FCC that there were no security experts on record ever verifying a juice jacking attack, the FCC glibly responded by asking the reporter if they had spoken to every living cyber expert.

Is it impossible for an attacker to build, program, and then install in a public facility a device with a USB data port to perform juice jacking? The answer is no. But is it so likely to occur that travelers who forget to bring their own charging cord should avoid all public chargers and let their mobile device go dead? The answer again is no.

So, what's the harm in bringing up these warnings to the general public?

The problem with the warnings coming out of the FCC, FBI, and media outlets is that they create a needless "echo chamber," in the words of security experts. The warnings divert needed attention away from bigger security threats, such as weak passwords and the failure to install security updates. These false warnings create unnecessary anxiety and inconvenience that run the risk of users simply giving up trying to be secure.

As one security professional said, if government officials are going to claim that criminals are carrying out juice jacking, the onus is on them to substantiate their claims by citing specific examples of attacks along with corroborating explanations and warnings from security experts. Absent that, they should stop repeating their unfounded claims.

Manage can be defined as using a degree of skill to direct a workflow or operation. There is perhaps no other entity that has a higher requirement for good management than information security. Due to the fact that security touches every employee at every level at all times, it is important for organizations to develop and utilize sound management across the entire company.

In this final module, you explore five key information security management processes: asset management, risk management, third-party risk management, change management, and awareness management. These are grouped into two major categories: asset protection and risk management.

Asset Protection

Protecting assets is at the core of information security. Asset protection involves asset management and change management.

Asset Management

It is important to know the definition of asset management and cybersecurity asset management along with the asset management lifecycle. There are tasks associated with managing selected assets.

What Is Asset Management?

An **asset** is any item that has a positive economic value. In an enterprise, assets have the following qualities: they provide value to the enterprise; they cannot easily be replaced without a significant investment in expense, time, worker skill, and/or resources; and they can form part of the enterprise's corporate identity.

Assets vary between different units of an enterprise; that is, not all units have the same assets. Enterprise assets range from people (employees, customers, business partners, contractors, and vendors) to physical assets (buildings, automobiles, and plant equipment). Information technology (IT) assets primarily include hardware, software, and data.

Obviously not all assets have the same value or worth. Some assets have a very high value while others do not. For example, a faulty laptop computer can easily be replaced and would not be considered an asset with a high value, yet the data contained on that computer may have a very high value. Table 15-1 describes the elements of an enterprise's IT infrastructure and whether these assets would normally be considered as having a high value.

Table 15-1   Typical IT assets

Asset	Description	Example	High value?
Data	Data that has been collected, classified, organized, and stored in various forms	Customer, personnel, production, sales, marketing, and finance databases	Yes: Extremely difficult to replace
Customized business software	Software that supports the business processes of the enterprise	Customized order transaction application	Yes: Unique and customized for the enterprise
System software	Software that provides the foundation for application software	Operating system	No: Can be easily replaced
Physical items	Computer equipment, communications equipment, storage media, furniture, and fixtures	Servers, routers, and power supplies	No: Can be easily replaced
Services	Outsourced computing services	Voice and data communications	No: Can be easily replaced

Asset management is the coordinated activity of an organization to realize value from its assets. To generate value from assets there must be a systematic approach to the governance of the assets and proper utilization of the assets in a cost-effective fashion. In short, asset management requires making the right decisions for optimizing the delivery of the value that assets can produce. While a common objective is to only minimize the cost of assets, this can be a short-sighted approach and in the long run harm the organization.

Note 1

The premiere document regarding asset management is ISO 55000:2014, which gives an overview of asset management, its principles and terminology, and the expected benefits from adopting asset management. It is 26 pages in length and can be purchased for $157.

Cybersecurity Asset Management (CAM)

Asset management requires having an accurate record of the assets that an organization holds. However, counting assets is a time-consuming process. By one estimate it takes on average 86 hours to generate a listing of assets by utilizing a combination of 8 to 10 different tools. Because of the complexity and expense, most organizations count assets in a "point-in-time" monthly or quarterly event. This leaves significant gaps between the acquisition of new assets and the counting and recording of those assets.

For information security, these gaps can be deadly. Without the knowledge that a new asset has been acquired, that asset may not be fully protected. In addition, an attack can occur that compromises data on a new but uncounted asset, leaving security operations center (SOC) personnel unable to identify the owner or custodian of the asset to provide an alert or request additional information. And if an attack compromises an unrecorded asset that then becomes the "beachhead" launching point for broader attacks on other assets, SOC personnel would be unable to identify the asset.

Note 2

As one information security professional noted, "You can't secure something if you don't know that it exists!"

Cybersecurity asset management (CAM) is a relatively new process that combines asset management with information security. CAM can identify assets on a continuous and real-time basis. These assets can include endpoints, servers, Internet of Things (IoT) devices, and even cloud-based resources. It can also identify the potential security risks or gaps that affect each asset through vulnerability scanners. In the event of an attack, CAM provides an up-to-date listing of assets that can immediately be referenced. This helps to answer questions such as which devices and users were associated with the alerts? Where are the devices located? What software is running on the device? Were the devices affected by known vulnerabilities?

Note 3

CAM has introduced a new metric in information security known as Mean Time to Inventory (MTTI). This metric helps determine when incident response is lagging as a result of missing inventory information.

Asset Management Lifecycle

Assets have a lifecycle. An asset's lifecycle begins when a need is first identified. From there, the asset is planned, created, or acquired. It is then operated and maintained, monitored, and ultimately replaced or upgraded when it reaches the end of its life. Figure 15-1 illustrates a typical asset lifecycle.

Figure 15-1   Asset lifecycle

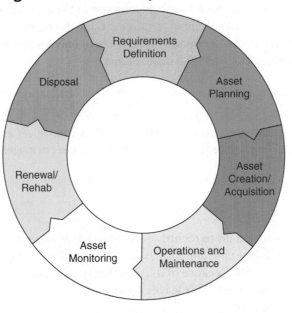

Costs associated with an asset are not just when the asset is first acquired. There are costs throughout its lifecycle, and these can vary depending on the current phase in the lifecycle of the asset. Figure 15-2 illustrates some of the costs associated with an asset through its lifecycle.

Figure 15-2   Asset costs

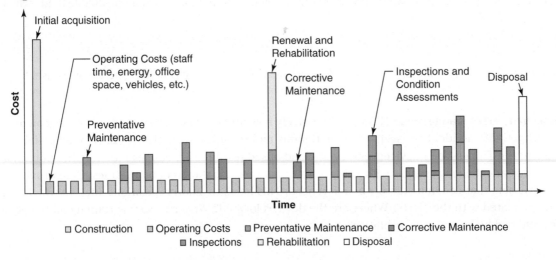

Selected Asset Management Tasks

There are specific management tasks associated with an asset as it moves through its lifecycle. These tasks include acquisition, assignment, tracking, and disposal.

Acquisition   Asset acquisition is the process of identifying and then securing an asset to support a business goal. Asset acquisition, also called asset procurement, can range from purchasing new hardware and software to procuring leases and contracts to acquiring real estate. Asset acquisition is an important part of business operations because it helps organizations acquire the resources that they need to achieve their goals.

Asset acquisition starts with the organization determining its overall current and future needs. This helps to determine if an additional asset is truly necessary; sometimes an internal change to a process can satisfy the need.

If a new asset is required, then the specifications of that asset are developed either by those who would be using the asset or through an internal unit that specializes in asset acquisition. After developing the specifications, then approval is granted and funding is secured.

Once the asset has been identified, approved, and funded, most businesses use a bidding process to ask vendors to submit a qualified bid. This helps ensure that the lowest price can be obtained for purchasing the asset. There are two types of bidding processes:

- **Standard bidding process.** In a standard bidding process, the organization solicits bids from qualified vendors before making a purchase decision. Vendors submit proposals that contain detailed information about the products they offer. After reviewing the proposals, the organization decides which vendor to buy from based on price, quality, availability, servicing, and other factors.
- **E-bidding process.** This process involves using electronic bidding platforms to find qualified vendors quickly and easily. Vendors can submit bids online without the need to provide any additional information aside from their pricing information. The organization then reviews the bids and makes a purchase decision based on price and other factors.

Assignment   Asset assignment/accounting is the process of determining and recording ownership (who owns the asset) and classification (into which category the asset belongs). Ownership of an asset is based on which entity purchased the asset (usually at the departmental level). Asset ownership can be transferred between departments when needed.

Assets are generally classified based on one of three factors:

- **How easy it is to turn the asset into cash.** The ease and speed with which an asset can be converted into cash is known as convertibility or liquidity. A **current asset** is one that can be used up or turned into cash within one fiscal year, while a **fixed asset** is a long-term asset that is kept for more than a year.
- **How the asset is used.** Another classification is how the asset is used. An **operating asset** is one needed for the primary business function of the enterprise, while **nonoperating assets** are those that are not used daily but nevertheless help keep the business financially stable.
- **If the asset physically exists.** Assets can be categorized based on whether they physically exist. A **tangible asset** is one that can be touched (hardware, cash, equipment, property, tools, etc.) whereas an **intangible asset** is one that has a monetary value but no physical form (software, data, patents, intellectual property, royalties, etc.).

Tracking   Asset tracking is tracing the location of tangible assets. It is important to have a detailed tracking process as part of an asset management system for all assets. This can help determine what assets add value and when they should be upgraded, replaced, or disposed of. There are three means for tracking tangible assets: through affixed barcode labels, radio-frequency identification (RFID) tags, or global positioning system (GPS) tracking sensors.

Note 4

RFID is covered in Module 10.

Asset tracking is often confused with related business "counting" activities. Counting assets is not the same as creating an inventory. Inventory is the raw materials, works in progress, and finished goods that are available for sale that a business owns. Also, counting assets is not the same as asset enumeration. Enumeration is a writing tool used to list items, events, ideas, or other parts of a story or setting. For example, "Today at the grocery store I bought apples, carrots, and green peppers." Asset enumeration is a listing of the assets by a seller of those assets.

Caution (!)

Asset enumeration should not be confused with information security enumeration, which creates an active connection to a target to uncover potential attack vectors by gathering information such as usernames, network services, routing tables, service settings, and audit configurations. It is an important tool for penetration testing, which is covered in Module 12.

Disposal   What happens when the asset has reached the end of its life and is no longer useful to the business? This typically involves a two-step process. First, the asset should be withdrawn from service (asset decommissioning). Second, it should be physically removed (asset disposal). In instances where the asset can still be used, it may be sold to another party. In instances in which this is not possible or desirable, the asset should to some degree be rendered unusable (destruction).

Assets that contain valuable data should first have that data transferred to a different device (data retention) before it is "scrubbed" clean of that data (sanitization). Because data itself is intangible, sanitization of data involves wiping clean or destroying the media on which the data is stored. Paper media is usually destroyed by shredding, which is cutting it into small strips or particles. There are different types of shredders. A strip-cut device shreds paper into long vertical strips, as seen in Figure 15-3. However, a determined threat actor could reconstruct these shredded documents.

Figure 15-3   Strip-cut shredding

Cheevarut/Shutterstock.com

Note 5

In 1979, student revolutionaries stormed the U.S. embassy in Tehran, Iran, taking 90 people hostage, including 66 Americans. In the chaos, embassy staffers raced to shred sensitive documents that contained highly confidential information using a strip-cut shredder. The strips, however, were left behind. Local Iranian carpet weavers used their skills to painstakingly reconstruct the documents, which resulted in U.S. government secrets being compromised and agents' lives put at risk. The Iranian government even released the information in a series of books called *Documents from the U.S. Espionage Den*.

A more secure means of shredding is to use a cross-cut shredder that adds horizontal cuts to make the shredded pieces even smaller. Newer micro-cut devices shred documents into tiny pieces. Micro-cut shredding is seen in Figure 15-4. Other options for destroying paper media are burning (lighting it on fire), pulping (breaking the paper back into wood cellulose fibers after the ink is removed), or pulverizing (hammering the paper into dust).

Figure 15-4   Micro-cut shredding

Sarah Biesinger/Shutterstock.com

If data is on electronic media, the data should never be erased using the OS "delete" command (purging). This is because the data could still be retrieved by using third-party forensic tools. Instead, data sanitation tools can be employed to securely remove data. One technique is called wiping (overwriting the disk space with zeros or random data). For a magnetic-based hard disk drive, degaussing will permanently destroy the entire drive by reducing or eliminating the magnetic field.

Caution !

There is no universal agreement on the differences between purging and wiping.

Consideration on which data destruction technique to use may hinge upon the need to verify the destruction for regulatory purposes (certification). Some techniques cannot provide this verification. For example, degaussing cannot provide verification that the drive was destroyed. In this instance, it may be necessary to first perform a wiping of the drive to verify that all data has been destroyed before then degaussing the drive to destroy it completely and permanently.

Change Management

Understanding change management requires knowing the need for it and the tools used for managing changes.

Need for Change Management

There are many normal day-by-day business processes that take place (standard operating procedures). These processes, although seemingly benign, can impact information security. Typical normal processes and their impact are listed in Table 15-2.

Table 15-2   Business processes and impact

Business process	Impact
Navigate multilayer **approval process**	An approval that must go through multiple layers of the organization in order to receive approval can dramatically slow the acquisition of needed appliances or software for information security.
Change in ownership or **stakeholders**	A change in the ownership of an asset can affect how that asset is used while a change in a stakeholder can impact the perception of the asset and if it should be used.
Implement **impact analysis** or **test results**	Reacting to a process for determining consequences of a decision or results of an information security test analysis can dramatically change how devices are used or configured.
Execute **backout plan** or **maintenance window**	A backout plan is the procedures needed if a "rollback" is required following a release of an asset into the production process while a maintenance window is a designated time in which systems are brought down for routine maintenance; both can significantly impact security.

In addition, there are routine technical processes that can likewise have an impact on security operations. These are listed in Table 15-3.

Table 15-3   Technology processes and impact

Technology process	Impact
Changing allow lists/deny lists	Modifying permissions of what is allowed or denied can significantly impact security.
Modifying restricted activities	Changing a restricted activity to a permitted activity can have unforeseen consequences.
Experiencing downtime	Downtime can result in a restart of one or more devices that may be out-of-sync with other devices.
Implementing service or application restarts	Starting a service or program that has been previously terminated can result in gaps in security coverage.
Using legacy applications	A legacy application is no longer in widespread use, often because it has been replaced by an updated version, and these programs may have unpatched vulnerabilities.
Adjusting dependencies	Changing the reliance between services can result in a security issue.

How can these organizational and technical processes continue without negatively impacting information security? The answer is through change management. As its name implies, change management is a systematic approach to dealing with transformations (adjustments, replacements, etc.) within an organization. While these transformations can include an organization's goals, most often they apply to work processes or technologies. The purpose of change management is to implement strategies that revolve around change: effecting change, controlling change, and adapting to change.

At a high level, change management should be a business strategy that takes into consideration how any transformations will impact processes, systems, and employees within the organization. It requires a verified process for planning and testing change, communicating change, scheduling and implementing change, and documenting change. Change management policies or formal statements that outline specific requirements or rules that must be met are important, as are the change management procedures (detailed mandatory steps needed to comply with a policy). Both policies and procedures for change management should be in place. Documentation is a particularly critical step, both to maintain an audit trail should a rollback become necessary and to ensure compliance with internal and external controls, especially regulatory compliance.

> ## Note 6
>
> Policies and procedures are covered in Module 14.

As with asset management, change management is particularly important to information security. While asset management monitors new assets that are added, change management watches for any adjustments or variations to assets that could impact security, such as making configuration changes to a router.

Change Management Tools

Effecting change management in an organization generally requires using a set of tools to assist in the process. These tools typically vary depending on the size of the organization. In a small company, the tools may simply consist of spreadsheets, flowcharts, and Gantt charts (a Gantt chart is a chart in which a series of horizontal lines shows the amount of work completed in certain periods of time in relation to the amount planned for those periods). There are also Microsoft Excel spreadsheet templates that can be used for tracking changes, as seen in Figure 15-5.

Figure 15-5   Change management template

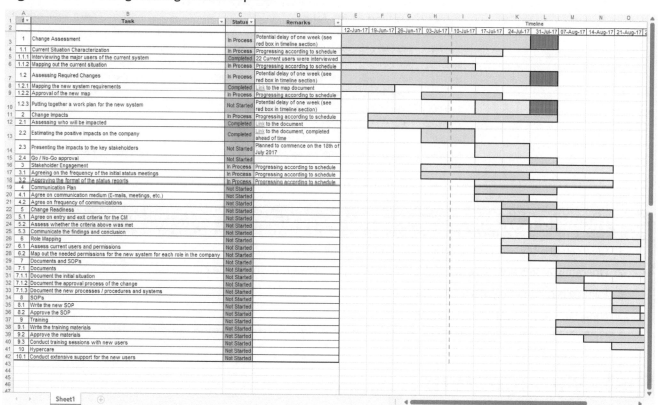

Source: ISO Docs

In larger organizations, specialized change management software suites are used to maintain change logs digitally. These can provide stakeholders with an integrated and more holistic view of changes and their impacts. Typically, software suites can automatically bring up to date new diagrams that illustrate the flow of the changes (updating diagrams). They also can indicate which organization policies or procedures need to be adjusted (updating policies/ procedures).

Another change management tool is frequently used in software development. Version control software tools assist with documentation and prevent more than one person from making changes to code at the same time. Such tools have capabilities to track changes and even back out of changes when necessary. Version control software is seen in Figure 15-6.

Figure 15-6   Version control software

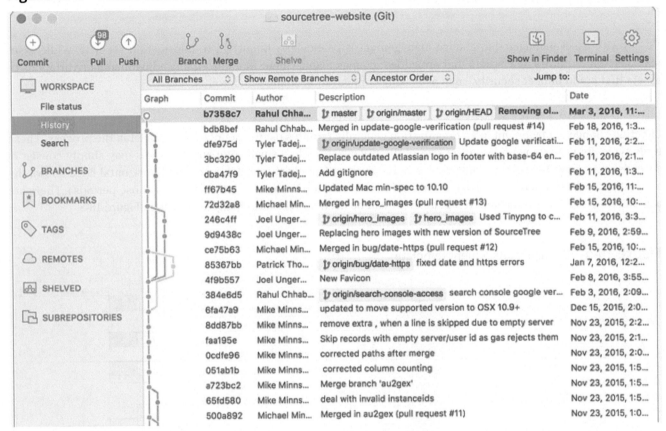

Source: Sourcetree

Two Rights & A Wrong

1. CAM can identify assets on a continuous and real-time basis.

2. Operating assets are those needed for the primary business function of the enterprise.

3. Pulping is hammering paper into dust.

See the answers at the end of the module.

Risk Management

Certification

5.2 Explain elements of the risk management process.

5.3 Explain the processes associated with third-party risk assessment and management.

5.6 Given a scenario, implement security awareness practices.

Another important information security management process is risk management. Managing risk involves defining what it is, knowing different methods of risk analysis, and understanding how to manage risk.

Defining Risk

Because an asset is any item that has a positive economic value, assets are continually under threat (a type of action that has the potential to cause harm). There are different classifications of threats against assets that are listed in Table 15-4.

Table 15-4   Threat classifications

Threat category	Description	Example
Strategic	Action that affects the long-term goals of the organization	Theft of intellectual property, not pursuing a new opportunity, loss of a major account, competitor entering the market
Compliance	Following (or not following) a regulation or standard	Breach of contract, not responding to the introduction of new laws
Financial	Impact of financial decisions or market factors	Increase in interest rates, global financial crisis
Operational	Events that impact the daily business of the organization	Fire, hazardous chemical spill, power blackout
Technical	Events that affect information technology systems	Denial of service attack, SQL injection attack, virus
Managerial	Actions related to the management of the organization	Long-term illness of company president, key employee resigning

Organizations must determine how realistic is the chance that a given threat will compromise an asset, called the **likelihood of occurrence**. This is stated in terms of risk. At a basic level, risk may be defined as a situation that involves exposure to some type of danger. At a more advanced level, risk can be described as a function of threats, the consequences of those threats, and the resulting vulnerabilities.

There are many different sources that can generate risk. These sources include:

- **Internal and external.** An **internal risk** comes from within an organization (such as employee theft), whereas an **external risk** is from the outside (like the actions of a hacktivist).
- **Legacy systems.** One type of platform that is well known for its risks is a legacy system. Although legacy hardware introduces some risks, more often risks result from legacy software, such as an OS or a program.
- **Multiparty.** Often overlooked in identifying risk types is the impact that vulnerabilities of one organization will have on other organizations that are connected to it. These are called **multiparty** risks that impact multiple "downstream" organizations.

Note 7

The results from the vulnerability of one organization rippling downstream are staggering. One study that examined over 90,000 cyber events found that multiparty risks that were exploited resulted in financial losses 13 times larger than single-party incidents. The number of organizations impacted by multiparty incidents outnumber primary victims by 850 percent, and these multiparty incidents will continue to increase at an average rate of 20 percent annually.

- **Software compliance and licensing.** Specialized software that is used by an enterprise is subject to licensing restrictions to protect the rights of the developer. An obvious violation would be for an organization to license software for a single manufacturing plant but then distribute that software to five other plants without paying for its usage. **Software compliance and licensing** risks are today considered a serious problem for organizations. It is recognized that most organizations unknowingly violate one or more licensing agreements. Several of the reasons for this are listed in Table 15-5.

Table 15-5   Reasons for software noncompliance

Reason	Example	Explanation
Software licensed for one reason but now used for a different reason	Limited-use license purchased only to be used in nonproduction development environment used in a production environment.	Organizations may purchase limited-use licenses rather than full-use licenses to obtain a pricing discount; a newly hired technician is not aware of the restriction and copies software into the production facility.
Product use rights changed	A third party accesses software purchased by the organization that is used in violation of new product use rights.	Although developers initially allowed third parties approved by the organization to use their software, now this "indirect access" is changed so a new license requires all users to have a purchased license.
Software installed on a virtual machine	Software migrated to a virtual machine and moved to multiple other machines in violation of license.	Some developers restrict software from being installed and then moved among multiple virtual machines without purchasing a new license.

Analyzing Risks

It is important for an organization to regularly perform a risk analysis. This is a process to identify and assess the factors that may place in jeopardy the success of a project or reaching a stated goal, often called risk identification. Following a methodology for performing risk identification analysis is important as is using tools for representing risk.

Methodology

How does an organization go about identifying its risks? It is important to approach this identification with sound methodologies. These include a risk control self-assessment and a risk assessment.

Risk Control Self-Assessment (RCSA)   Identifying risks can be a difficult process. This difficulty is due to two factors. First, risks can be elusive and often hard to identify. While obvious risks seem readily apparent (such as a firewall that is unplugged), not all risks are so clear to see (such as the danger of opening an email attachment that comes from a coworker's email account). Risks, by their very nature, are often hidden below the surface and are not apparent.

A second reason for the difficulty of identifying risks is due to human nature. One recognized reason for this difficulty is **unconscious human biases**.[1] Each of us has our own set of biases that we have developed through our own preferences, intuition, or past experiences. These biases influence our decision making and "vision." We may have a bias toward which foods to eat, what clothes to wear, or even the order of tasks to be tackled each day. Table 15-6 lists commonly recognized biases and effects.

Table 15-6   Decision-making biases and effects

Bias	Explanation
Aggregate bias	Inferring something about an individual by using data that actually describes trends for the broader population
Anchoring bias	Holding on to a specific feature or set of features of information early in the decision-making process
Availability bias	Perceiving how likely an event is to occur given how frequently the event is heard of
Confirmation bias	Making a decision before investigating and then only looking for data that supports the theory
Present bias	Tending to discount future risks and gains in favor of immediate gratification
Framing effect	Deciding on an option based on how the choices are worded
Fundamental attribution error	Viewing the failures or mistakes of others as part of their identity rather than attributing them to contextual or environmental influences

These unconscious biases and effects can impact identifying risks. For example, an anchoring bias may cause someone to focus on one of the first risks exposed and then marginalize other risks. Or a person with a confirmation bias could quickly decide that a risk is relatively unimportant—particularly on a system for which they are responsible—and then look for data to support the position. These biases could easily lead to focusing on the wrong individual as the source of a risk, making incorrect estimates about the potential impact of a risk, focusing on an unlikely risk, or even spending too much time on incorrect theories.[2]

Also, research into human behavior has revealed that most people have difficulties particularly with seeing risks and are prejudiced toward particular risks but minimize other risks. Generally, when dealing with risks, people tend to:

- Overreact to risks caused by intentional actions
- Underreact to risks associated with accidents, abstract events, and natural phenomena
- Overreact to risks that are considered insulting, disgusting, or offensive to our moral standards
- Overreact to immediate risks
- Underreact to long-term risks
- Underreact to risks and changes that occur slowly and over time

Due to the difficulty in identifying risks, a methodology has been developed that can be helpful in identifying risks. This methodology helps to minimize these human factors in identifying risk by not relying on just a few employees in an organization but instead involving a large number of individuals in the process. That is because as more employees are involved, biases and prejudices are minimized. An analysis of risk that involves a wide array of users is considered the most effective approach. **Risk control self-assessment (RCSA)** is an "empowering" methodology by which management and staff at all levels collectively work to identify and evaluate risks. The goal of RCSA is to not only minimize biases and prejudices but also to integrate risk management practices into the culture of the organization. As staff perform their normal activities and as business units work toward their objectives, the topic of risk permeates all these activities.

Risk Assessment   An organization that can accurately calculate risk is better prepared to address the risk. For example, if a customer database is determined to be of high value and to have a high risk, the necessary resources should be used to strengthen the defenses surrounding that database.

The frequency of conducting a risk assessment is debated. While some advocate for a scheduled assessment (one-time assessment), others state that it should be done whenever necessary (ad hoc assessment). Still others state that the assessment should be conducted on a calendar basis (recurring assessment), but there are those who claim that it should be conducted year-round (continuous assessment).

The answer to the frequency of conducting a risk assessment by an organization can be determined through the two risk assessment approaches. One approach is qualitative risk analysis. This approach uses an "educated guess" based on observation. For example, if it is observed that the customer database contains important information, it would be assigned a high asset value. Also, if it is observed that this database has frequently been the target of attacks, it would be assigned a high-risk value as well. Qualitative risk typically assigns a numeric value (*1–10*) or label (*High*, *Medium*, or *Low*) that represents the risk.

The second approach, quantitative risk analysis, is considered more formal and systematic. Instead of arbitrarily assigning a number or label based on observation, the quantitative risk calculation attempts to create "hard" numbers associated with the risk of an element in a system by using historical data. In the example, if the customer database has a higher risk calculation than a product database, more resources would be allocated to protecting it. Quantitative risk calculations can be divided into the likelihood of a cyber event occurring and the impact of the event if it is successful.

Risk Likelihood   Historical data is valuable in providing information on the likelihood (possibility) that a risk will become a reality within a specific period of time, also called the **risk probability**. For example, when considering the risk of equipment failure, several quantitative tools can be used to predict the likelihood of the risk, including:

- **Mean Time Between Failure (MTBF).** MTBF calculates the average (*mean*) amount of time until a component fails, cannot be repaired, and must be replaced. It is a reliability term used to provide the amount of failures. Calculating the MTBF involves dividing the total time measured by the total number of failures observed.

> **Caution !**
>
> Although MTBF is sometimes used to advertise the reliability of consumer hardware products like hard disk drives, the purchaser seldom considers this value. This is because most consumer purchases are simply price driven. MTBF is considered more important for industries than for consumers.

- **Mean Time to Recovery (MTTR).** MTTR is the average amount of time that it will take a device to recover from a failure that is not a terminal failure. Although MTTR is sometimes called *Mean Time to Repair* because in most systems this means replacing failed hardware instead of repairing it, the Mean Time to Recovery is considered a more accurate term.

> **Note 8**
>
> MTBF and MTTR are covered in Module 13.

- **Mean Time to Failure (MTTF).** MTTF is a basic measure of reliability for systems that cannot be repaired. It is the average amount of time expected until the first failure of a piece of equipment.
- **Failure in Time (FIT).** The FIT calculation is another way of reporting MTBF. FIT can report the number of expected failures per one billion hours of operation for a device. This term is used particularly by the semiconductor industry. FIT can be stated as *devices for 1 billion hours*, *1 billion devices for 1000 hours each*, or in other combinations.

Other historical data for calculating the likelihood of risk can be acquired through a variety of sources. These are summarized in Table 15-7.

Table 15-7 Historical data sources

Source	Explanation
Law enforcement agencies	Crime statistics on the area of facilities to determine the probability of vandalism, break-ins, or dangers potentially encountered by personnel
Insurance companies	Risks faced by other companies and the amounts paid out when these risks became reality
Computer incident monitoring organizations	Data regarding a variety of technology-related risks, failures, and attacks

Once historical data is compiled, it can be used to determine the likelihood of a risk occurring within a year. This is known as the Annualized Rate of Occurrence (ARO).

Risk Impact   Once historical data is gathered so that the ARO can be calculated, the next step is to determine the impact of that risk (risk impact). This can be done by comparing it to the monetary loss associated with an asset to determine how much money would be lost if the risk occurred.

> **Caution !**
>
> When calculating loss, it is important to consider all costs. For example, if a network firewall failed, the costs would include the amount needed to purchase a replacement, the hourly wage of the person replacing the equipment, and the pay for employees who could not perform their job functions because they could not use the network while the firewall was not functioning.

Three risk calculation formulas are commonly used to calculate expected losses. The Single Loss Expectancy (SLE) is the expected monetary loss every time a risk occurs. The SLE is computed by multiplying the Asset Value (AV) by the Exposure Factor (EF), which is the proportion of an asset's value that is likely to be destroyed by a particular risk (expressed as a percentage). The SLE formula is:

$$SLE = AV \times EF$$

For example, consider a building with a value of \$10,000,000 (AV) of which 75 percent of it is likely to be destroyed by a tornado (EF). The SLE would be calculated as follows:

$$7,500,000 = \$10,000,000 \times 0.75$$

The Annualized Loss Expectancy (ALE) is the anticipated monetary loss that can be expected for an asset due to a risk over a one-year period. It is calculated by multiplying the SLE by the ARO, which is the probability that a risk will occur in a particular year (in mathematics the probability is the extent to which an event is likely to occur, measured by the ratio of the favorable cases to the whole number of cases possible). The ALE formula is:

$$ALE = SLE \times ARO$$

In this example, if flood insurance data suggests that a serious flood is likely to occur once in 100 years, then the ARO is 1/100 or 0.01. The ALE would be calculated as follows:

$$75,000 = 0.01 \times \$7,500,000$$

The risk exposure factor is the probability of the risk occurring multiplied by the total loss on the occurrence of the risk. In other words, the risk exposure factor is the potential for a financial loss.

Representing Risks

There are different tools that can be used to represent risks identified through a risk assessment, called risk reporting. A risk register is a list of potential threats and associated risks. Often shown as a table, a risk register can help provide a clear snapshot of vulnerabilities and risks. Risk registers may include key risk indicators (the primary risk factors), risk owners (those responsible for the asset), and the risk threshold (the maximum amount of risk that can be tolerated). A sample risk register is shown in Figure 15-7.

Figure 15-7   Risk register

Risk Id	Risks	Current risk			Status	Owner	Raised	Mitigation Strategies	Residual risk		
		Likelihood	Impact	Severity					Likelihood	Impact	Severity
Category 1: Project selection and project finance											
RP-01	Financial attraction of project to investors	4	4	15	Open		01-march	• Data collection • Information of financial capability of investor • Giving them assurance of tremendous future return	4	3	12
RP-02	Availability of finance	3	4	12	Open		03-march	• Own resources • Commitment with financial institution • Exclusive management of investor	3	3	9
RP-03	Level of demand for project	3	3	9	Open		08-march	• Making possibility and identification of low cost and best quality material • Eradication of extra expenses from petty balance	2	3	6
RP-04	Land acquisition (site availability)	3	3	9	Open		13-march	• Making feasibilities • Analysis and interpretation of feasibilities • Possession and legal obligation of land	2	2	4
RP-05	High finance costs	2	2	4	Open		15-march	• Lowering operational expenses and transportation expenses • Proper management of current expenses	1	2	2

Another tool is called a **risk matrix/heatmap**. This is a visual color-coded tool that lists the impact and likelihood of risks. Figure 15-8 illustrates a risk matrix/heatmap.

Figure 15-8 Risk matrix/heatmap

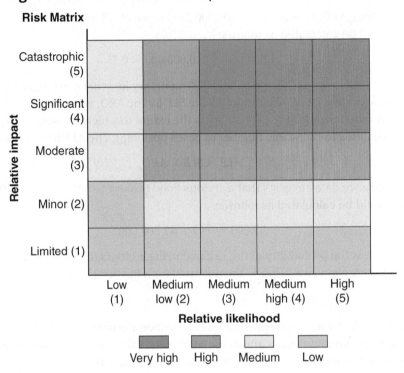

Managing Risks

The objective of managing risk is to create a level of protection that mitigates the vulnerabilities to the threats and reduces the potential consequences. This level is determined by that which the organization feels comfortable accepting. Risk tolerance is the level of risk that an organization can accept per individual risk. Risk appetite is the total risk that the organization can bear in a given risk profile. Risk tolerance is related to the acceptance of the outcomes of a risk should it occur and having the right resources in place to absorb it. It is usually expressed in qualitative and/or quantitative risk criteria. Risk appetite is related to the longer-term strategy of what needs to be achieved and the resources available to achieve it, expressed in quantitative criteria. The risk appetite of an organization can be conservative (little tolerance for risk), expansionary (high tolerance for risk), or neutral (neither low nor high tolerance for risk).

Managing risk involves using specific strategies, addressing third-party risk, and applying awareness management.

Determine a Strategy

There are four different strategies for dealing with risks. These can be illustrated through the following scenario. Suppose that Ellie wants to purchase a new motorized Italian scooter to ride from her apartment to school and work. However, because several scooters have been stolen near her apartment, she is concerned about its protection. Although she parks the scooter in the gated parking lot in front of her apartment, a hole in the fence surrounding the apartment complex makes it possible for someone to access the parking lot without restriction.

There are different options available to Ellie when dealing with the risk of her scooter being stolen, and these are the same that can be used by an organization:

- **Accept.** To accept a risk simply means that the risk is acknowledged but no steps are taken to address it. In Ellie's case, she could accept the risk and buy the new scooter, knowing there is the chance of it being stolen by a thief entering through a hole in the fence. In a similar fashion, an organization may decide to accept the risk that a flood will engulf its manufacturing plant if that flood is estimated to occur only once every 50 years. There may be instances in which a risk is accepted but there is an exception in that the security requirement cannot be fully implemented or there is an exemption from a regulating body so that the organization does not have to protect against the risk.

- **Transfer.** Ellie could transfer the risk to a third party. She can do this by purchasing insurance so that the insurance company absorbs the loss and pays if the scooter is stolen. This is known as a risk transfer. An organization may elect to purchase cybersecurity insurance as an example of transference so that in exchange for paying premiums to the insurance company, the organization is compensated in the event of a successful attack.

- **Avoid.** To avoid a risk involves identifying the risk but making the decision not to engage in the activity. Ellie could decide based on the risk of the scooter being stolen that she will not purchase the new scooter. Likewise, an organization may decide that after an analysis, building a new plant in another location is not feasible.

- **Mitigate.** To mitigate a risk is the attempt to address risk by making the risk less serious. Ellie could complain to the apartment manager about the hole in the fence to have it repaired, and an organization could erect a fence around a plant to deter thieves.

Implement Third-Party Risk Management

Another important process for managing risks is to implement third-party risk management. This involves identifying third-party risks, assessing and selecting third-party vendors, and using vendor agreement instruments.

Third-Party Risks   SolarWinds is a software company that sells network and computer management tools to over 33,000 customers. In early December 2020, it was discovered that threat actors had infected the SolarWinds distribution platform that sends out regular software updates to all clients. Malicious code was injected into a software update that was then widely distributed. And because the update had a digital certificate by SolarWinds to ensure that it came from a trusted source, it was readily accepted. The result was a massive infection of all SolarWinds customers. Not only the high number but also the scope of the victims was significant: as many as 400 of the top *Fortune* 500 companies were compromised along with government agencies like the Department of Homeland Security, the Treasury and Commerce Departments, national security agencies, and defense contractors.

Virtually all businesses today use external entities known as third parties. These include vendors (those from whom an organization purchases goods and services), business partners (a commercial entity with whom an organization has an alliance), and those as part of a supply chain (a network that moves a product from the supplier to the customer).

As the SolarWinds case illustrates, there are several risks associated with using third parties. First, with the sheer number of third parties used, it can be difficult to coordinate their diverse activities with the organization. Second, almost all third parties today require access to the organization's computer network to provide these external entities the ability to perform their IT-related functions (such as outsourced code development) and even do basic tasks such as submitting online invoices. Yet one of the major risks of this third-party system integration involves the principle of the weakest link: if the security of the third party has a vulnerability, it can provide an opening for attackers to infiltrate the organization's computer network (called a supply chain infection). Third, the difficulties associated with third-party integration, or combining systems and data with outside entities, are significant. The risks associated with this integration include:

- **On-boarding and off-boarding.** Partner on-boarding refers to the start-up relationship between partners, while partner off-boarding is the termination of such an agreement. Significant consideration must be given to how the entities will combine their services without compromising their existing security defenses. Also, when the relationship ends, particularly if it has been in effect for a significant length of time, work must be done to ensure that as the parties and their IT systems separate, no gaping holes are left open for attackers to exploit.

- **Application and social media network sharing.** How will different applications be shared between the partners? Who will be responsible for support and vulnerability assessments? And as social media becomes more critical for organizations in their interaction with customers, which partner will be responsible for sharing social media information?

- **Privacy and risk awareness.** What happens if the privacy policy of one of the partners is less restrictive than that of the other partner? And how will risk assessment be performed on the combined systems?
- **Data considerations.** All parties must have a clear understanding of who owns data that is generated through the partnership and how that data will be backed up. Restrictions on unauthorized data sharing must also be reached.

Assessing and Selecting Third Parties   It is important for organizations to reduce the risks associated with third parties, known as third-party risk management. Reducing risks can be accomplished through requiring a close oversight of a vendor (vendor monitoring) and may include:

- Requiring third parties to complete annual questionnaires about their supply-chain security protections in force.
- Demanding that third parties perform regular **penetration testing** and have a right-to-audit clause as part of an agreement so that the results can be vetted.
- Requiring evidence of internal audits and an independent assessment of the audits.
- Conducting regular evaluations of the steps in the supply chain (supply-chain analysis).
- Creating a model that defines expectations around how parties interact at all times in the relationship, such as how much information is shared and when it is shared (rules of engagement).
- Demand that third parties follow due diligence (reasonable steps to satisfy legal agreements) and have no conflict of interests (outside personal or financial interests that could impact an agreement).

Caution

Supply-chain analysis is difficult. Ultimately the purchaser has to trust somebody—the supplier, the manufacturer, the DevSecOps team, and so on—but it is increasingly complicated to know who can be trusted.

Vendor Agreement Instruments   Another means by which parties can reduce risk is to reach an understanding of their relationships and responsibilities is through interoperability agreements, or formal contractual relationships, particularly as they relate to security policies and procedures. These agreements, which should be regularly reviewed to verify compliance and performance standards, include:

- A service-level agreement (SLA) is a service contract between a vendor and a client that specifies what services will be provided, the responsibilities of each party, and any guarantees of service.
- A business partnership agreement (BPA) is a contract between two or more business partners that is used to establish the rules and responsibilities of each partner, including withdrawals, capital contributions to the partnership, and financial reporting.
- A memorandum of understanding (MOU) describes an agreement between two or more parties. It demonstrates a "convergence of will" between the parties for simple "common cause" agreements. An MOU is generally not a legally enforceable agreement but is more formal than an unwritten agreement.
- A nondisclosure agreement (NDA) is a legal contract between parties that specifies how confidential material will be shared between the parties but restricted to others. An NDA creates a confidential relationship between the parties to protect any type of confidential and proprietary information.
- A measurement system analysis (MSA) uses scientific tools to determine the amount of variation that is added to a process by a measurement system. For example, a third party who manufactures a product for an organization would need to demonstrate that how it measures the size, weight, dimensions, etc., of the product is both valid and does not contribute to any variation of the product.

- A memorandum of agreement (MOA) establishes common legal terms that create a "conditional agreement" where the transfer of funds for services is anticipated.
- A work order (WO)/statement of work (SOW) is a document within a contract that describes the work requirements for a specific project along with its performance and design expectations. The main purpose of the WO/SOW is to define the liabilities, responsibilities, and work agreements between two parties, usually clients and service providers.

Administer Security Awareness Management

An often-overlooked consideration in risk management is the importance of providing security awareness training to users. Known as **security awareness management** or **risk awareness**, it is the raising of understanding to all employees of what risks exist, their potential impacts, and how they are managed. Training helps make users aware of common risks and how they can become a "human firewall" to help mitigate these risks.

The goal of security awareness training is to help users achieve anomalous behavior recognition or be able to distinguish between what is normal and what is not normal. Training should also help users be able to determine that which is unexpected (not anticipated) and unintentional (not done on purpose) and as such it becomes risky (carries a high risk). This is also known as situation awareness.

One of the challenges of organizational education and training is to understand the traits of learners. Table 15-8 lists general traits of individuals born in the United States since 1946.

Table 15-8   Traits of learners

Year born	Traits	Number in U.S. population
Prior to 1946	Patriotic, loyal, have faith in institutions	75 million
1946–1964	Idealistic, competitive, question authority	80 million
1965–1981	Self-reliant, distrustful of institutions, adaptive to technology	46 million
1982–2000	Pragmatic, globally concerned, computer literate, media savvy	76 million

In addition to the traits of learners, training style also impacts how people learn. The way that one person was taught may not be the best way to teach all others. Most people are taught using a *pedagogical* approach (from a Greek word meaning "to lead a child"). For adult learners, however, an *andragogical* approach (the art of helping an adult learn) is often preferred. Some of the differences between pedagogical and andragogical approaches are summarized in Table 15-9.

Table 15-9   Approaches to training

Subject	Pedagogical approach	Andragogical approach
Desire	Motivated by external pressures to get good grades or pass on to next grade	Motivated by higher self-esteem, more recognition, desire for better quality of life
Student	Dependent on teacher for all learning	Self-directed and responsible for own learning
Subject matter	Defined by what the teacher wants to give	Learning is organized around situations in life or at work
Willingness to learn	Students are informed about what they must learn	A change triggers a readiness to learn or students perceive a gap between where they are and where they want to be

In addition to training styles, there are different learning styles. Visual learners learn through taking notes, being at the front of the class, and watching presentations. Auditory learners tend to sit in the middle of the class and learn best through lectures and discussions. The third style is kinesthetic, which many information technology professionals tend to have. These students learn through a lab environment or other hands-on approaches. Most people use a combination of learning styles, with one style being dominant. To aid in knowledge retention, trainers should incorporate all three learning styles and present the same information using different techniques. For example, a course could include a lecture, PowerPoint slides, and an opportunity to work directly with software and replicate what is being taught.

There are different techniques that are used for user training:

- **Computer-based training (CBT).** CBT uses a computer to deliver the instruction. It is frequently used for user training due to its flexibility (training can be done from any location and at any time) and ability to provide feedback about the progress of the learner. However, CBT is not always considered the best means of training. Instead, a variety of other modalities, such as specialized face-to-face instruction or informal "lunch-and-learn" sessions, may provide better overall learning results.

- **Role-based awareness training.** Many organizations use role-based awareness training. This involves specialized training that is customized to the specific role that an employee holds in the organization. An office associate, for example, should be provided security training that is different from that provided to an upper-level manager because the duties and tasks of these two employees are significantly different.

- **Gamification.** The fast-growing field of digital gaming is generally divided into two distinct markets: recreational gaming for entertainment and instructional gaming for training and education. Gamification is using game-based scenarios for instruction. User training can often include gamification in an attempt to heighten the interest and retention of the learner.

- **Phishing simulations.** Because phishing is the primary means by which threat actors initially launch an attack, many organizations use phishing simulations to help employees to recognize phishing attempts so that they will not be guilty of responding to reported suspicious messages. Measurements should be developed so that increases from initial training (the start of training) to recurring training (ongoing training) can be tracked, and there can be adequate reporting and monitoring so that training can continually be improved. These tools can be highly customized and provide detailed feedback on a dashboard, as seen in Figure 15-9. Phishing simulators can be one part of an entire phishing campaign that uses a variety of other tools (email reminders, printed posters, points earned to be redeemed for prizes, etc.) to counteract phishing attacks.

Figure 15-9 Phishing simulation dashboard

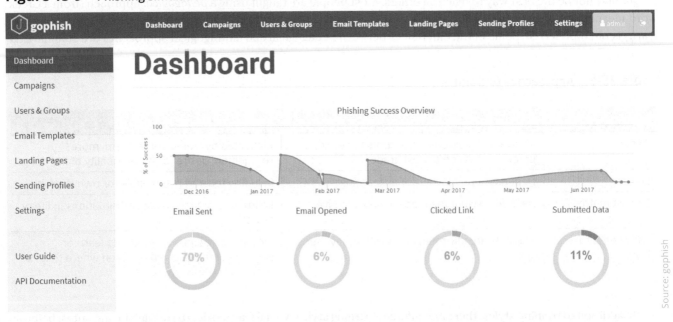

The content of user awareness training should be such that it provides practical guidance to the users. However, first and foremost, training should clearly emphasize that all computer users in an organization have a shared responsibility to protect the assets of the organization. It cannot be assumed that all users have the knowledge and skills to protect these assets. Instead, users need training in the importance of securing information, the roles that they play in security, and the steps they need to take to prevent attacks. And because new attacks appear regularly and new security vulnerabilities are continuously being exposed, user awareness and training must be ongoing. User training is an essential element of information security.

Note 9

Education in an enterprise is not limited to only certain employees. Human resource personnel need to keep abreast of security issues because in many organizations it is their role to train new employees on all aspects of the organization, including security. Even upper management needs to be aware of the security threats and attacks that the organization faces, if only to acknowledge the necessity of security in planning, staffing, and budgeting.

In addition, an awareness program should include the following:

- Recognition of insider threats
- Understanding of operational security
- Attacks through social engineering
- Instruction on password management
- Risks associated with removable media and cables
- Security difference between office work and hybrid/remote work environments
- Security material found in policies and handbooks
- Environmental physical attacks

Creating (development) of an awareness training is not an easy task and requires careful planning. Carrying out the training (**execution**) likewise should be carefully thought out.

Two Rights & A Wrong

1. Qualitative risk analysis is considered more formal and systematic.
2. A risk register is a list of potential threats and associated risks.
3. SLE is the expected monetary loss every time a risk occurs.

See the answers at the end of the module.

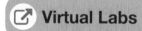 **Virtual Labs**   You're now ready to complete the simulations and live virtual machine labs for this module. The labs can be found in each module in MindTap.

Summary

- An asset is any item that has a positive economic value. Asset management is the coordinated activity of an organization to realize value from its assets. Cybersecurity asset management (CAM) combines asset management with information security to identify assets on a continuous and real-time basis and also identify the potential security risks or gaps that affect each asset. There are specific management tasks associated with an asset as it moves through its lifecycle. Asset acquisition is the process of identifying

and then securing an asset to support a business goal. Asset assignment/accounting is the process of determining and recording who owns the asset and into which category the asset belongs. Asset tracking is tracing the location of tangible assets. It is important to have a detailed tracking process as part of an asset management system for all assets. When the asset has reached the end of its life and is no longer useful to the business, the asset should be withdrawn from service and be physically removed.

- Once data is no longer useful, it should be properly destroyed. Because data itself is intangible, destroying data that is no longer needed involves destroying the media on which the data is stored. If any data other than data labeled public is on paper, that media should never be thrown away in a dumpster, recycle bin, or trash receptacle. Paper media can be destroyed by burning (lighting it on fire), shredding (cutting it into small strips or particles), pulping (breaking the paper back into wood cellulose fibers after the ink is removed), or pulverizing ("hammering" the paper into dust). If data is on electronic media, the data should never be erased using the operating system "delete" command (purging). This is because the data could still be retrieved by using third-party forensic tools. Instead, data sanitation tools can be employed to securely remove data. One technique is called wiping (overwriting the disk space with zeros or random data). For a magnetic-based hard disk drive, degaussing will permanently destroy the entire drive by reducing or eliminating the magnetic field.

- Change management is a systematic approach to dealing with adjustments and replacements within an organization. While these transformations can include an organization's goals, most often they apply to work processes or technologies. Change management policies are formal statements that outline specific requirements or rules that must be met. Effecting change management in an organization generally requires using a set of tools to assist in the process. These tools typically vary depending on the size of the organization.

- A risk is a situation that involves exposure to some type of danger. There are many different types of risk. An internal risk comes from within an organization while an external risk is from the outside. One type of platform that is well known for its risks is a legacy system. Often overlooked in identifying risk types is the impact that vulnerabilities of one organization will have on other organizations that are connected to it. Specialized software that is used by an enterprise is subject to licensing restrictions in order to protect the rights of the developer. Software compliance and licensing risks are today considered serious risks for organizations.

- It is important for an organization to regularly perform risk identification, or a process to identify and assess the factors that may jeopardize the success of a project or reaching a stated goal. Identifying risks can be difficult due to the elusive nature of risks, unconscious human biases, and prejudices toward certain types of risks. Risk Control Self-Assessment (RCSA) is an "empowering" methodology by which management and staff at all levels collectively work to identify and evaluate risks. The goal of RCSA is to not only minimize biases and prejudices but also to integrate risk management practices into the culture of the organization.

- There are two approaches to risk calculation: qualitative risk calculation, which uses an "educated guess" based on observation; and quantitative risk calculation, which is considered more scientific. Quantitative risk calculations can be divided into the likelihood of a risk and the impact of a risk being successful. The tools used for calculating risk likelihood include Mean Time Between Failure (MTBF), Mean Time to Recovery (MTTR), Mean Time to Failure (MTTF), Failure in Time (FIT), and the Annualized Rate of Occurrence (ARO). Risk impact calculation tools include Single Loss Expectancy (SLE), Annual Loss Expectancy (ALE), and risk exposure factor.

- Different tools can be used to represent risks identified through a risk assessment, called risk reporting. A risk register is a list of potential threats and associated risks. Often shown as a table, a risk register can help provide a clear snapshot of vulnerabilities and risks. Risk registers may include key risk indicators (the primary risk factors), risk owners (those responsible for the asset), and the risk threshold (the maximum amount of risk that can be tolerated). Another tool is called a risk matrix/heatmap. This is a visual color-coded tool that lists the impact and likelihood of risks.

- Several approaches are used to reduce risk. The level is determined by that which the organization feels comfortable accepting. Risk tolerance is the level of risk that an organization can accept per individual risk. Risk appetite is the total risk that the organization can bear in a given risk profile. An organization can accept, transfer, avoid, or mitigate risks.

- Several risks are associated with using third parties. It is important for organizations to reduce the risks associated with third parties, known as third-party risk management. One of the means by which the parties can reduce risk is to reach an understanding of their relationships and responsibilities through interoperability agreements, or formal contractual relationships, particularly as they relate to security policy and procedures. These agreements should be regularly reviewed to verify compliance and performance standards.

- An often-overlooked consideration in risk management is the importance of providing training to users. Training results in risk awareness, which is the raising of understanding of what risks exist, their potential impacts, and how they are managed. One of the challenges of organizational education and training is to understand the traits of learners. Different techniques are used for user training, such as computer-based training (CBT), which uses a computer to deliver the instruction. It is frequently used for user training due to its flexibility (training can be done from any location and at any time) and ability to provide feedback about the progress of the learner. Role-based training involves specialized training that is customized to the specific role that an employee holds in the organization. Gamification is using game-based scenarios for instruction. User training can often include gamification in an attempt to heighten the interest and retention of the learner. Because phishing is the primary means by which threat actors initially launch an attack, many organizations use phishing simulations to help employees recognize phishing emails.

Key Terms

accept
ad hoc assessment
adjusting dependencies
Annualized Loss Expectancy (ALE)
Annualized Rate of Occurrence (ARO)
anomalous behavior recognition
approval process
asset acquisition
asset assignment/accounting
asset decommissioning
asset disposal
asset enumeration
asset management
asset procurement
asset tracking
avoid
backout plan
business partnership agreement (BPA)
certification
change management
change management policies
change management procedures
changing allow lists/deny lists
classification
conflict of interests
conservative
continuous assessment
data retention
destruction
due diligence
evidence of internal audits
exception

exemption
expansionary
experiencing downtime
impact analysis
implementing service or application restarts
independent assessment
initial training
inventory
key risk indicators
likelihood
maintenance window
measurement system analysis (MSA)
memorandum of agreement (MOA)
memorandum of understanding (MOU)
mitigate
modifying restricted activities
neutral
nondisclosure agreement (NDA)
one-time assessment
ownership
phishing campaign
probability
qualitative risk analysis
quantitative risk analysis
questionnaires
recognize phishing attempts
recurring assessment
recurring training
reporting and monitoring
responding to reported suspicious messages

right-to-audit clause
risk
risk appetite
risk exposure factor
risk identification
risk impact
risk owners
risk register
risk reporting
risk threshold
risk tolerance
risky
rules of engagement
sanitization
service-level agreement
Single Loss Expectancy (SLE)
situation awareness
stakeholders
standard operating procedures
supply-chain analysis
test results
third-party risk management
transfer
unexpected
unintentional
updating diagrams
updating policies/procedures
using legacy applications
vendor monitoring
version control
vulnerability scanner
work order (WO)/statement of work (SOW)

Review Questions

1. Which of the following threats would be classified as the actions of a hacktivist?

   a. External threat
   b. Internal threat
   c. Environmental threat
   d. Compliance threat

2. Which of these is NOT a response to risk?

   a. Mitigate
   b. Accept
   c. Resist
   d. Avoid

3. Which of the following is NOT a threat classification category?

   a. Compliance
   b. Financial
   c. Tactical
   d. Strategic

4. In which of the following threat classifications would a power blackout be classified?

   a. Operational
   b. Managerial
   c. Technical
   d. Strategic

5. Which of the following approaches to risk calculation typically assigns a numeric value (*1–10*) or label (*High*, *Medium*, or *Low*) to represent a risk?

   a. Quantitative
   b. Qualitative
   c. Rule based
   d. Policy based

6. What is a list of potential threats and associated risks called?

   a. Risk assessment
   b. Risk matrix
   c. Risk register
   d. Risk portfolio

7. Giovanni is completing a report on risks. To which risk option would he classify the action that the organization has decided not to construct a new data center because it would be located in an earthquake zone?

   a. Transfer
   b. Avoid
   c. Reject
   d. Prevent

8. Aristide is explaining to a coworker the new cybersecurity asset management (CAM) system. Which of the following would he NOT say about a CAM?

   a. It is a relatively new process that combines asset management with information security.
   b. It can identify assets on a continuous and real-time basis.
   c. It can use vulnerability scanners.
   d. It is designed to replace asset management.

9. Emiliano needs to determine the expected monetary loss every time a risk occurs. Which formula will he use?

   a. AV
   b. SLE
   c. ARO
   d. ALE

10. Enzo is reviewing asset tracking for a certification exam. Which of the following is NOT true about asset tracking?

    a. Asset tracking can be used to determine when assets should be upgraded, replaced, or disposed.
    b. Asset tracking can help determine what assets add value.
    c. Asset tracking is part of an asset management system.
    d. Asset tracking traces the location of intangible assets.

11. Which of the following is a listing of assets by a seller of those assets?

    a. Asset enumeration
    b. Asset inventory
    c. Asset counting
    d. Asset verification

12. Which of the following is NOT a legally enforceable agreement but is still more formal than an unwritten agreement?

    a. BPA
    b. SLA
    c. MOU
    d. AMS

13. Angelo has received a document that is part of a contract that describes the work requirements for a specific project. What type of document is this?

    a. EOA
    b. BPP
    c. SOW
    d. EOS

14. Which of the following uses scientific tools to determine the amount of variation that is added to a process?

  a. XRS

  b. MSA

  c. RAR

  d. PDP

15. Which of the following risk management strategies utilizes cybersecurity insurance?

  a. Accept

  b. Transfer

  c. Mitigate

  d. Change

16. Which of the following is NOT a third-party risk?

  a. On-boarding

  b. Social media network sharing

  c. Risk awareness

  d. Network assignment

17. Sergio has been asked to provide historical data for calculating the likelihood of a risk. Which of the following data sets would he NOT submit?

  a. Network packet analysis

  b. Law enforcement data

  c. Insurance company data

  d. Data from computer incident monitoring organizations

18. Which of the following is used to minimize biases and prejudices regarding analyzing risks?

  a. RCSA

  b. RCA

  c. SCRA

  d. DOS

19. Which of the following is NOT a standard operating procedure that can impact information security?

  a. Change in ownership or stakeholders

  b. Implement impact analysis or test results

  c. Execute backout plan or maintenance window

  d. Change allow lists/deny lists

20. Gabe is creating a report for his supervisor Cora that outlines the total risk that the organization can bear in a given risk profile. Which of the following terms would Gabe be using?

  a. Risk tolerance

  b. Risk appetite

  c. Risk expansion

  d. Risk acceptance

Caution !

If you are concerned about installing any of the software in these projects on your regular computer, you can instead use the Windows Sandbox in the Module 1 Hands-On Projects. Software installed within the virtual machine will not impact the host computer.

Hands-On Projects

Project 15-1: Managing Risk Through Copying Data—Backups

Estimated Time: 25 minutes

Objective: Copy user data to the cloud using backups.

Description: For users who want to manage their risks from a cyber incident, arguably the most important first step is to make a copy of their data. Once a copy of data is safely in place, additional steps can and should be taken. For home users, the best data copy approach is a cloud-based journaling solution. All data is stored online in the cloud for quick and easy retrieval. In this project, you create an iDrive account and create an online backup as a scheduled event.

Note 10

Types of data copies are covered in Module 13.

1. Use your web browser to go to **www.idrive.com**.

2. Scroll down and click the **Mini** category. Note that iDrive offers a free tier and you do not need a credit card or make any payments for this tier.

3. Click the **Free 10 GB** tab.

4. Enter the requested information to create an iDrive account.

5. Read the information about encryption. If necessary, select **Default encryption key**, although for more security, you can use the **Private encryption key** instead. Click **Continue**.

6. Wait for the iDrive file application to download, launch that file, and then click **Accept and Install**.

7. Select one or more folders for online backup (to select multiple folders, hold down the CTRL key and click the folders). Click **Backup Now**.

8. Click **View Log** to see the information about the backup and click **Close** when finished.

9. In the left pane, click **Restore**. You can restore the backup by selecting one or more of the files or folders.

10. Click the **Scheduler** button in the left pane.

11. Select the backup start time and start days for the backup.

12. If necessary, click **Email notification** to receive verification of the backup.

13. Click the question mark next to **Notify on failure** and read through this information. Is "5%" an appropriate setting? When would you adjust it higher or lower?

14. If necessary, click **Notify me on desktop** to receive a notification through the iDrive application about the backup.

15. Click the check box next to **Start the missed scheduled backup when the computer is turned on** to launch the backup if your device was off when the backup had been scheduled to begin.

16. Click **Save Changes**.

17. Remain in iDrive for Project 15-2.

Project 15-2: Managing Risk Through Copying Data—Journaling

Estimated Time: 25 minutes
Objective: Copy user data to the cloud using journaling.
Description: While a scheduled event backup is important, even more important is having the flexibility to copy data between these scheduled events. This provides the best of all worlds: a backup can be scheduled to run daily at a specific time, but users can also designate specific data for immediate copying. In addition, software can monitor what files have changed and then automatically update the copies of the files with the most recent versions (replication). In this project, you explore these two additional data copy solutions using iDrive.

1. Another means of backing up files is to select files or folders to be copied immediately to iDrive. Click **Cloud Drive** in the left pane.

2. Click **Enable Sync**.

3. Open **File Explorer** on your computer.

4. Note that there is now a **WDAGUtilityAccount** folder. Open this folder.

5. Open the **Cloud-Drive** folder.

6. Read the **ReadMe** file.

7. Any file or folder that is dragged into the Cloud-Drive folder is immediately copied to iDrive. Select a file or folder and drag it into the **Cloud-Drive** folder.

8. A final means of copying data is to have any file that is changed to be immediately copied to iDrive. Create a folder named **Test** in one of the folders that you have previously selected to be copied to iDrive.

9. Create a document using Microsoft Word that contains your name and save the file as **Replicate1.docx** in that folder.

10. Click **Backup** in the left pane.

11. Click **Change**.

12. Browse through the computer folders that you designated to be copied to iDrive. Locate the **Test** folder and note that it now is included as a folder to be copied. Any subfolder that is created under a folder designated to be copied will automatically be included in future copies unless it is unchecked here. Click **Cancel**.

13. Immediate replication is turned on by default so that any file that is changed will be immediately copied to iDrive. Click **Settings** in the left pane.

14. Under **General Settings**, note that **Continuous Data Protection** is on and the **Frequency** is set to **Real-time**.

> **Caution** !
>
> Although several cloud data copy solutions advertise real-time continuous data protection, research has shown that these products take 15 minutes or longer to copy any changes to the cloud. iDrive is one of the few products that performs actual real-time updates.

15. If immediate (real-time) continuous data protection is not necessary, it can be changed to a lower time interval. Turn off **Continuous Data Protection**.

16. Click the down arrow next to **Frequency**. Note the options that are less than real-time protection. When would you choose one of these options instead of real-time protection?

17. Turn on **Continuous Data Protection**. Click **Save Settings**.

18. Navigate to the file **Replicate1.docx** on your computer using File Explorer.

19. Change the filename from **Replication1.docx** to **Replication2.docx**.

20. Click **Backup** in the left pane.

21. Click **Change**.

22. Navigate to the **Test** folder and locate the file stored in that folder. How quickly did iCloud change **Replication1.docx** to **Replication2.docx**?

23. How flexible is iDrive for users? Would you recommend it?

24. Close all windows.

Case Projects

Case Project 15-1: #TrendingCyber

Estimated Time: 15 minutes
Objective: Summarize your thoughts on the #TrendingCyber opener.
Description: Read again the opening #TrendingCyber in this module. Should government agencies be more respon-sible regarding distributing information security information to the public? Should security professionals first vet these? What could online and print media sources do to ensure that their distributed information is indeed accurate? Write a one-paragraph summary of your thoughts.

Case Project 15-2: Third-Party Risks

Estimated Time: 25 minutes
Objective: Research third-party risks.
Description: Until recently, third-party risks have not been considered as serious, but today they are a serious weak-ness for organizations. Use the Internet to research third-party risks. Why is there now a heightened emphasis on these risks? What are three examples of security incidents that were the result of a vulnerability in one organization affecting multiple other organizations? What were the outcomes of each of these? Should an organization that allows other organizations to be compromised through a third-party risk be held liable? What should be the penalty? How can these be mitigated? Write a one-page paper on your findings.

Case Project 15-3: Intellectual Property (IP) Theft

Estimated Time: 20 minutes
Objective: Research intellectual property thefts.
Description: Another type of risk over an asset is intellectual property (IP) theft. IP is an invention or a work that is the result of creativity. The owner of IP can apply for protection from others who attempt to duplicate it; these protections over IP or its expression are patent, trademark, copyright, and trade secret. Threat actors attempt to steal IP (IP theft) that may include research on a new product from an enterprise so that they can sell it to an unscrupulous foreign supplier who will then build an imitation model of the product to sell worldwide. This deprives the legitimate business of profits after investing hundreds of millions of dollars in product development and, because these foreign suppli-ers may be in a different country, they are beyond the reach of domestic enforcement agencies and courts. Use the Internet to find details on four recent incidents of IP theft from an organization. What was stolen? What vulnerability did the threat actors exploit? How valuable was the IP? What did the threat actors do with it? What loss did it create for the organization? How could it have been prevented? Write a one-page paper on your findings.

Case Project 15-4: Unconscious Biases in Security

Estimated Time: 25 minutes
Objective: Research unconscious biases.
Description: How could unconscious biases impact security? Review the information in Table 15-6 and select four of the biases. Then create a practical example of how each bias or effect could impact security. Now return to the table and list in order what you consider your own biases from most prevalent to least. What can be done to minimize the impact of these biases?

Case Project 15-5: Reacting to Risks

Estimated Time: 20 minutes
Objective: Research different ways to react to risks.
Description: Using the four options to risks (accept, transfer, avoid, and mitigate), identify a specific risk that you would place in each category. This risk should be something that involves you by identifying intentional actions,

accidents, etc. Evaluate your reaction to these risks. Could these play a part in how you might evaluate cybersecurity risks in an organization? How could they be addressed? Write a one-page paper on your analysis.

Case Project 15-6: User Awareness and Training—Part 1

Estimated Time: 20 minutes
Objective: Research user awareness and training.
Description: What user security awareness and training is available at your school or place of business? How frequently is it performed? Is it available online or in person? Is it required? Are the topics up to date? On a scale of 1–10, how would you rate the training? How could it be improved? Write a one-page summary.

Case Project 15-7: User Awareness and Training—Part 2

Estimated Time: 20 minutes
Objective: Research online user awareness and training.
Description: Use the Internet to research user awareness and training that is conducted by an organization other than your school or place of business. How frequently is it performed? Is it available online or in person? Is it required? Are the topics up to date? On a scale of 1–10, how would you rate the training? How could it be improved? Write a one-page summary.

Case Project 15-8: Cybersecurity Asset Management Products

Estimated Time: 20 minutes
Objective: Research cybersecurity asset management products.
Description: Cybersecurity asset management (CAM) is a relatively new process that combines asset management with information security. CAM can identify assets on a continuous and real-time basis, like endpoints, servers, Internet of Things (IoT) devices, and cloud-based resources. It can also identify the potential security risks or gaps that affect each asset through vulnerability scanners so that in the event of an attack CAM provides an up-to-date listing of assets that can immediately be referenced. Research CAM products. Identify three products and create a table that compares their features. Which of these would you recommend? Why?

Case Project 15-9: Version Control Products

Estimated Time: 20 minutes
Objective: Research version control products.
Description: Use the Internet to research version control products. Identify three products and analyze the strengths and weaknesses of each product. If you were a programmer, which would you choose? Why?

Case Project 15-10: Cybersecurity Insurance for Organizations

Estimated Time: 25 minutes
Objective: Research cybersecurity insurance for organizations.
Description: Purchasing cybersecurity insurance has been considered a panacea for large organizations, in that it allows them to perform a risk transfer so that in exchange for paying premiums to the insurance company, the organization is compensated in the event of a successful attack. However, the cybersecurity insurance market has been in a state of turbulence recently. First, the price of cyber insurance has fluctuated dramatically due to a rise particularly in ransomware hacks. This has caused insurers to take a harder line before renewing or granting new or additional coverage. Insurance companies are now asking for more in-depth information about companies' cyber policies and procedures. Organizations that cannot satisfy this greater level of scrutiny face higher premiums, are offered limited coverage, or are refused coverage entirely. Almost one out of every three businesses were denied cyber insurance coverage after failing to meet the insurers' criteria for endpoint protection and having the right response tools. Second, some insurers no longer cover attacks that can be traced back to nation-state actors. Research the current state

of cybersecurity insurance. Identify four products and evaluate their strengths and weaknesses. Should an enterprise invest in paying for cyber insurance? What is your opinion?

Case Project 15-11: Cybersecurity Insurance for Users

Estimated Time: 25 minutes
Objective: Research cybersecurity insurance for users.
Description: Over the past five years, the FBI's Internet Crime Complaint Center has received over 3.26 million complaints about personal cyberattacks, with estimated losses of $27.6 billion. In 2022 alone, the center received almost 810,000 complaints with losses totaling over $10 billion. As cyberattacks spread to more users, insurers are now expanding beyond offering cyber insurance to only businesses. Many insurers are offering personal cyber insurance policies to users as well.

Personal cyber insurance plans come in two forms. Many insurance carriers offer cyber protection as an add-on rider to an existing homeowner's or renter's insurance policy. Other carriers offer a separate stand-alone policy. Coverages vary and may differ based on the user's home state, but generally these products include the same coverage that is traditionally found in a commercial cyber insurance policy. Personal cyber policies most often cover money lost to social engineering attacks, remediation from ransomware attacks, payments for data restoration, and even reputational damage from a cyberbullying incident. Some policies also offer around-the-clock access to experts to help policyholders recover quickly in the event of a cyber incident, legal advice, and even psychological counseling to help with cyberbullying.

Costs for personal cyber insurance vary widely depending on the carrier, policy limits selected (most policy maximum coverage ranges from $10,000 to $100,000), and what cyber events are covered by the policy. Riders to an existing policy usually cost an additional $20 to $300 a year. A stand-alone policy may cost $5.25 a month for a limit of up to $10,000 and about $18.50 a month for a limit of $100,000.

Should users purchase personal cyber insurance? Should all users purchase this insurance or only those who regularly use online banking and investment accounts and have children who could be vulnerable to cyberbullying? Write a paper that argues the pros and cons of purchasing personal cyber insurance. Would you recommend purchasing it? Would you purchase this type of insurance? Why or why not?

Case Project 15-12: You Know More Than You Think

Estimated Time: 25 minutes
Objective: Review cybersecurity topics.
Description: Many learners first exposed to information security find the topic to be overwhelming due to the large number of different attacks and defenses. However, learners often underestimate what they have learned and really know more than they think they do. Access the Cybersecurity & Infrastructure Security Agency (CISA) guide on stopping ransomware (https://www.cisa.gov/sites/default/files/2023-06/StopRansomware_Guide_508c.pdf). Read through this document and put an **R** (remember) beside each topic that you remember learning from this study on information security. Use the table of contents of this book to look up any topics with an **R** and change the **R** to an **F** (forgot) to those topics that were covered but you did not initially remember. Finally, put a **U** (unknown) to any advanced information security topics that were not covered and that you are not familiar with. Does it surprise you how much you remembered? Are there specific topics that you forgot that you should remember? Are there unknown topics that you now want to explore to learn more about? Write a one-page paper on your analysis.

Case Project 15-13: Overview of Information Security

Estimated Time: 30 minutes
Objective: Record impressions of information security.
Description: Summarize what you have learned about information security. What were three items that most surprised you? How easy or difficult is information security to you? Would you recommend this as a career choice to someone else? What are its advantages and disadvantages? Write a one-page paper on your overview.

Case Project 15-14: Bay Point Ridge Security

Estimated Time: 45 minutes

Objective: Research risk assessment.

Description: Bay Point Ridge Security (BPRS) is a managed service provider (MSP) that manages networks, computers, cloud resources, and information security for small-to-medium enterprises (SMEs) in the region. BPRS provides internships to students who are in their final year of the security degree program at the local college and has recently hired you.

BPRS has identified a new client who has never conducted a detailed risk assessment and BPRS is recommending they undertake one immediately. However, this client is resisting investing the time to perform the assessment and thinks that because they have not been the target of a recent attack then their security is good. You have been asked to lead an informational session on risk assessment for them.

1. Create a PowerPoint presentation about risk assessment. Begin with what it is, how it can be used in information security, and what its advantages are. Your presentation should contain at least 10–12 slides.

2. After the presentation, the chief technology officer is concerned about whether they will be able to find all vulnerabilities and, if they are not able to, then why do a risk assessment? Write a memo that answers this concern.

Two Rights & A Wrong: Answers

Asset Protection

1. CAM can identify assets on a continuous and real-time basis.
2. Operating assets are those needed for the primary business function of the enterprise.
3. Pulping is hammering paper into dust.

Answer: The wrong statement is #3.

Explanation: Pulping is breaking the paper back into wood cellulose fibers.

Risk Management

1. Qualitative risk analysis is considered more formal and systematic.
2. A risk register is a list of potential threats and associated risks.
3. SLE is the expected monetary loss every time a risk occurs.

Answer: The wrong statement is #1.

Explanation: Quantitative risk analysis is more formal and systematic.

References

1. Cunningham, Margaret, "'Thinking about thinking' is critical to cybersecurity," *Forcepoint*, June 10, 2019, accessed June 1, 2023, www.forcepoint.com/blog/insights/thinking-about-thinking-critical-cybersecurity.
2. Zorz, Zeljka, "How human bias impacts cybersecurity decision making," *HelpNetSecurity*, June 10, 2019, accessed June 1, 2023, www.helpnetsecurity.com/2019/06/10/cybersecurity-decision-making/.

Appendix A

CompTIA Security+ SYO-701 Certification Exam Objectives

Bloom's Taxonomy is an industry-standard classification system used to help identify the level of ability that learners need to demonstrate proficiency. It is often used to classify educational learning objectives into different levels of complexity. The Bloom's Taxonomy column in the following table reflects the level of coverage for the respective SY0-701 objective domains. In all instances, the level of coverage in *CompTIA Security+ Guide to Network Security Fundamentals, 8th Edition* meets or exceeds that indicated by CompTIA for that objective. See the Introduction of this book for more information.

Security+ Exam Objective Domain/Objectives	Module	Section	Bloom's Taxonomy
1.0 General Security Concepts			
1.1 Compare and contrast various types of security controls.			
• Categories	1	How Attacks Occur	Remembering
○ Technical			
○ Managerial			
○ Operational			
○ Physical		What Is Information Security?	Understanding
• Control types			
○ Preventive			
○ Deterrent			
○ Detective			
○ Corrective			
○ Compensating			
○ Directive			
1.2 Summarize fundamental security concepts.			
• Confidentiality, Integrity, and Availability (CIA)	1	What Is Information Security?	Applying
• Non-repudiation			
• Authentication, Authorization, and Accounting (AAA)			
○ Authenticating people			
○ Authenticating systems			
○ Authorization models			
• Gap analysis	9	Security Appliances	Understanding

Security+ Exam Objective Domain/Objectives	Module	Section	Bloom's Taxonomy
• Zero trust	9	Secure Infrastructure Design	Applying
○ Control plane			
■ Adaptive identity			
■ Threat scope reduction			
■ Policy-driven access control			
■ Secured zones			
○ Data plane			
■ Subject/system			
■ Policy engine			
■ Policy automation			
■ Policy enforcement point			
• Physical security	2	Physical Security Controls	Applying
○ Bollards			
○ Access control vestibule			
○ Fencing			
○ Video surveillance			
○ Security guard			
○ Access badge			
○ Lighting			
○ Sensors			
■ Infrared			
■ Pressure			
■ Microwave			
■ Ultrasonic			
• Deception and disruption technology	9	Infrastructure Security Hardware	Understanding
○ Honeypot			
○ Honeynet			
○ Honeyfile			
○ Honeytoken			
1.3 Explain the importance of change management processes and the impact to security.			
• Business processes impacting security operation	15	Asset Protection	Analyzing
○ Approval process			
○ Ownership			
○ Stakeholders			
○ Impact analysis			
○ Test results			
○ Backout plan			
○ Maintenance window			
○ Standard operating procedure			
• Technical implications			
○ Allow lists/deny lists			
○ Restricted activities			
○ Downtime			
○ Service restart			
○ Application restart			
○ Legacy applications			
○ Dependencies			

(continues)

Security+ Exam Objective Domain/Objectives	Module	Section	Bloom's Taxonomy

• Documentation
   ○ Updating diagrams
   ○ Updating policies/procedures
• Version control			

1.4 Explain the importance of using appropriate cryptographic solutions.			

• Public key infrastructure (PKI)
   ○ Public key
   ○ Private key
   ○ Key escrow
	4	Public Key Infrastructure (PKI)	Applying

• Encryption
   ○ Level
      ■ Full-disk
      ■ Partition
      ■ File
      ■ Volume
      ■ Database
      ■ Record
   ○ Transport/communication
   ○ Asymmetric
   ○ Symmetric
   ○ Key exchange
   ○ Algorithms
   ○ Key length
	3	Defining Cryptography	Evaluating

• Tools
   ○ Trusted Platform Module (TPM)
   ○ Hardware security module (HSM)
   ○ Key management system
   ○ Secure enclave
	3	Using Cryptography	Applying

• Obfuscation
   ○ Steganography
   ○ Tokenization
   ○ Data masking
	3	Defining Cryptography	Analyzing

• Hashing	3	Cryptographic Algorithms	Understanding
• Salting	7	Authentication Best Practices	Evaluating
• Digital signatures	3	Using Cryptography	Creating
• Key stretching • Blockchain • Open public ledger			

• Certificates
   ○ Certificate authorities
   ○ Certificate revocation lists (CRLs)
   ○ Online Certificate Status Protocol (OCSP)
   ○ Self-signed
   ○ Third-party
   ○ Root of trust
   ○ Certificate signing request (CSR) generation
   ○ Wildcard
	4	Digital Certificates	Applying

Security+ Exam Objective Domain/Objectives	Module	Section	Bloom's Taxonomy
2.0 Threats, Vulnerabilities, and Mitigations			
2.1 Compare and contrast common threat actors and motivations.			
• Threat actors ○ Nation-state ○ Unskilled attacker ○ Hacktivist ○ Insider threat ○ Organized crime ○ Shadow IT • Attributes of actors ○ Internal/external ○ Resources/funding ○ Level of sophistication/capability • Motivations ○ Data exfiltration ○ Espionage ○ Service disruption ○ Blackmail ○ Financial gain ○ Philosophical/political beliefs ○ Ethical ○ Revenge ○ Disruption/chaos ○ War	1	Threat Actors and Their Motivations	Understanding
2.2 Explain common threat vectors and attack surfaces.			
• Message-based ○ Email ○ Short Message Service (SMS) ○ Instant messaging (IM) • Image-based • File-based • Voice call • Removable device • Vulnerable software ○ Client-based vs. agentless • Unsupported systems and applications	1	How Attacks Occur	Applying
• Unsecure networks ○ Wireless ○ Wired	10	Wireless Attacks	Analyzing
○ Bluetooth	1	How Attacks Occur	Understanding
• Open service ports • Default credentials • Supply chain ○ Managed service providers (MSPs) ○ Vendors ○ Suppliers			

Security+ Exam Objective Domain/Objectives	Module	Section	Bloom's Taxonomy

• Human vectors/social engineering
  ○ Phishing
  ○ Vishing
  ○ Smishing
  ○ Misinformation/disinformation
  ○ Impersonation
  ○ Business email compromise
  ○ Pretexting
  ○ Watering hole
  ○ Brand impersonation
  ○ Typo squatting
	2	Social Engineering Attacks	Creating

2.3 Explain various types of vulnerabilities.
 	
• Application
  ○ Memory injection
  ○ Buffer overflow
  ○ Race conditions
    ▪ Time-of-check (TOC)
    ▪ Target of evaluation (TOE)
    ▪ Time-of-use (TOU)
  ○ Malicious update
	5	Application Vulnerabilities and Attacks	Understanding

• Operating system (OS)–based	1	How Attacks Occur	Remembering

• Web-based
  ○ Structured Query Language injection (SQLi)
  ○ Cross-site scripting (XSS)
	5	Application Vulnerabilities and Attacks	Applying

• Hardware
  ○ Firmware
  ○ End-of-life
  ○ Legacy
	1	How Attacks Occur	Applying

• Virtualization
  ○ Virtual machine (VM) escape
  ○ Resource reuse
	11	Virtualization Security	Remembering

• Cloud-specific	11	Cloud Computing Security	Understanding

• Supply chain
  ○ Service provider
  ○ Hardware provider
  ○ Software provider
	1	How Attacks Occur	

• Cryptographic	3	Fundamentals of Cryptography	Remembering
• Misconfiguration			
• Mobile device	6	Mobile Device Risks	Understanding
○ Side loading ○ Jailbreaking	1	How Attacks Occur	Applying
• Zero-day			

Security+ Exam Objective Domain/Objectives	Module	Section	Bloom's Taxonomy
2.4 Given a scenario, analyze indicators of malicious activity.			

• Malware attacks
  ○ Ransomware
  ○ Trojan
  ○ Worm
  ○ Spyware
  ○ Bloatware
  ○ Virus
  ○ Keylogger
  ○ Logic bomb
  ○ Rootkit
	5	Malware Attacks	Evaluating

• Physical attacks
  ○ Brute force
  ○ Radio frequency identification (RFID) cloning
  ○ Environmental
	10	Wireless Attacks	Analyzing

• Network attacks
  ○ Distributed denial-of-service (DDoS)
    ▪ Amplified
    ▪ Reflected
  ○ Domain Name System (DNS) attacks
  ○ Wireless
  ○ On-path
  ○ Credential relay
  ○ Malicious code
	8	Attacks on Networks	Evaluating

• Application attacks
  ○ Injection
  ○ Buffer overflow
  ○ Replay
  ○ Privilege escalation
  ○ Forgery
  ○ Directory traversal
	5	Application Vulnerabilities and Attacks	Analyzing

• Cryptographic attacks
  ○ Downgrade
  ○ Collision
  ○ Birthday
	3	Cryptographic Limitations and Attacks	Analyzing

• Password attacks
  ○ Spraying
  ○ Brute force
	7	Types of Authentication Credentials	Applying

• Indicators
  ○ Account lockout
  ○ Concurrent session usage
  ○ Blocked content
  ○ Impossible travel
  ○ Resource consumption
  ○ Resource inaccessibility
  ○ Out-of-cycle logging
  ○ Published/documented
  ○ Missing logs
	5	Malware Attacks	Analyzing

(continues)

Security+ Exam Objective Domain/Objectives	Module	Section	Bloom's Taxonomy
2.5 Explain the purpose of mitigation techniques used to secure the enterprise.			
• Segmentation	9	Security Appliances	Applying
• Access control	7	Access Controls	Understanding
○ Access control list (ACL)			
○ Permissions			
• Application allow list	5	Securing Endpoint Devices	Applying
• Isolation	9	Security Appliances	Evaluating
• Patching	5	Hardening Endpoints	Applying
• Encryption	3	Using Cryptography	Analyzing
• Monitoring			
• Least privilege	9	Security Appliances	Applying
• Configuration enforcement			
• Decommissioning			
• Hardening techniques	5	Securing Endpoint Devices	Applying
○ Encryption			
○ Installation of endpoint protection			
○ Host-based firewall			
○ Host-based intrusion prevention system (HIPS)			
○ Disabling ports/protocols			
○ Default password changes			
○ Removal of unnecessary software			
3.0 Security Architecture			
3.1 Compare and contrast security implications of different architecture models.			
• Architecture and infrastructure concepts	11	Cloud Computing Security	Applying
○ Cloud			
■ Responsibility matrix			
■ Hybrid considerations			
■ Third-party vendors			
○ Infrastructure as code			
○ Serverless			
○ Microservices			
○ Network infrastructure	9	Secure Infrastructure Design	Understanding
■ Physical isolation			
□ Air-gapped			
■ Logical segmentation			
■ Software-defined networking (SDN)	11	Virtualization Security	Applying
○ On-premises			
○ Centralized/decentralized			
○ Containerization	6	Embedded Systems and Specialized Devices	Applying
○ Virtualization			
○ IoT			
○ Industrial control systems (ICS)/supervisory control and data acquisition (SCADA)			
○ Real-time operating system (RTOS)			
○ Embedded systems			
○ High availability			

Security+ Exam Objective Domain/Objectives	Module	Section	Bloom's Taxonomy

• Considerations
  ○ Availability
  ○ Resilience
  ○ Cost
  ○ Responsiveness
  ○ Scalability
  ○ Ease of deployment
  ○ Risk transference
  ○ Ease of recovery
  ○ Patch availability
  ○ Inability to patch
  ○ Power
  ○ Compute			

3.2 Given a scenario, apply security principles to secure enterprise infrastructure.			

• Infrastructure considerations
  ○ Device placement
  ○ Security zones
  ○ Attack surface
  ○ Connectivity
  ○ Inline
  ○ Failure modes
    ■ Fail-open
    ■ Fail-closed
  ○ Device attribute
    ■ Active vs. passive
  ○ Network appliances
    ■ Jump server
    ■ Proxy server
    ■ Intrusion protection system (IPS)/intrusion detection system (IDS)
    ■ Load balancer
    ■ Sensors
  ○ Port security
  ○ Firewall types
    ■ Web application firewall (WAF)
    ■ Unified threat management (UTM)
    ■ Next-generation firewall (NGFW)
    ■ Layer 4/Layer 7
	9	Security Appliances	Evaluating

• Secure communication
  ○ Virtual private network (VPN)
  ○ Remote access
	4	Secure Communication and Transport	Understanding

○ Tunneling
    ■ Transport Layer Security (TLS)
    ■ Internet protocol security (IPSec)
  ○ Software-defined wide area network (SD-WAN)
  ○ Secure access service edge (SASE)
• Selection of effective controls
	11	Virtualization Security	Applying

(continues)

Security+ Exam Objective Domain/Objectives	Module	Section	Bloom's Taxonomy

3.3 Compare and contrast concepts and strategies to protect data.
 	
• Data types
  ○ Regulated
  ○ Trade secret
  ○ Intellectual property
  ○ Legal information
  ○ Financial information
  ○ Human- and non-human-readable
• Data classifications
  ○ Sensitive
  ○ Confidential
  ○ Public
  ○ Restricted
  ○ Private
  ○ Critical
• General data considerations
  ○ Data states
    ■ Data at rest
    ■ Data in transit
    ■ Data in use
  ○ Data sovereignty
  ○ Geolocation
• Methods to secure data
  ○ Geographic restrictions
  ○ Encryption
  ○ Hashing
  ○ Masking
  ○ Tokenization
  ○ Obfuscation
  ○ Segmentation
  ○ Permission restrictions
	3	Data Controls	Analyzing

3.4 Explain the importance of resilience and recovery in security architecture.
 	
• High availability
  ○ Load balancing vs. clustering
• Site considerations
  ○ Hot
  ○ Cold
  ○ Warm
  ○ Geographic dispersion
	13	Preparatory Plans	Analyzing

• Platform diversity • Multi-cloud systems • Continuity of operations	13	Resilience Through Redundancy	Applying

Security+ Exam Objective Domain/Objectives	Module	Section	Bloom's Taxonomy

• Capacity planning
   ○ People
   ○ Technology
   ○ Infrastructure
• Testing
   ○ Tabletop exercises
   ○ Fail over
   ○ Simulation
   ○ Parallel processing
• Backups
   ○ Onsite/offsite
   ○ Frequency
   ○ Encryption
   ○ Snapshots
   ○ Recovery
   ○ Replication
   ○ Journaling
• Power
   ○ Generators
   ○ Uninterruptible power supply (UPS)			

4.0 Security Operations			
4.1 Given a scenario, apply common security techniques to computing resources.			

• Secure baselines
   ○ Establish
   ○ Deploy
   ○ Maintain
	8	Security Monitoring and Alerting	Applying

• Hardening targets	5	Securing Endpoint Devices	Understanding
○ Mobile devices	6	Protecting Mobile Devices	Understanding
○ Workstations ○ Switches	9	Security Appliances	Applying

○ Routers
   ○ Cloud infrastructure
   ○ Servers
   ○ ICS/SCADA
   ○ Embedded systems
   ○ RTOS
   ○ IoT devices			

• Wireless devices
   ○ Cryptographic protocols
   ○ Authentication protocols
   ○ Installation considerations
      ■ Site surveys
      ■ Heat maps
	10	Wireless Security Solutions	Analyzing

(continues)

Security+ Exam Objective Domain/Objectives	Module	Section	Bloom's Taxonomy

• Mobile solutions
  ○ Mobile device management (MDM)
  ○ Deployment models
    ▪ Bring your own device (BYOD)
    ▪ Corporate-owned, personally enabled (COPE)
    ▪ Choose your own device (CYOD)
  ○ Connections methods
    ▪ Cellular
    ▪ Wi-Fi
    ▪ Bluetooth
	6	Protecting Mobile Devices	Understanding

• Application security
  ○ Input validation
  ○ Secure cookies
  ○ Static code analysis
  ○ Code signing
• Sandboxing
• Monitoring
	6	Application Security	Applying

4.2 Explain the security implications of proper hardware, software, and data asset management.
 	
• Acquisition/procurement process
• Assignment/accounting
  ○ Ownership
  ○ Classification
• Monitoring/asset tracking
  ○ Inventory
  ○ Enumeration
• Disposal/decommissioning
  ○ Sanitization
  ○ Destruction
  ○ Certification
  ○ Data retention
	15	Asset Protection	Applying

4.3 Explain various activities associated with vulnerability management.
 	
• Identification methods
  ○ Vulnerability scan
  ○ Application security
    ▪ Static analysis
    ▪ Dynamic analysis
    ▪ Package monitoring
  ○ Threat feed
    ▪ Open-source intelligence (OSINT)
    ▪ Proprietary/third-party
    ▪ Information-sharing organization
    ▪ Dark web
	12	Vulnerability Scanning	Analyzing

Security+ Exam Objective Domain/Objectives	Module	Section	Bloom's Taxonomy

○ Penetration testing
   ○ Responsible disclosure program
     ■ Bug bounty program
   ○ System/process audit
• Analysis
   ○ Confirmation
     ■ False positive
     ■ False negative
   ○ Prioritize
   ○ Common Vulnerability Scoring System (CVSS)
   ○ Common Vulnerability Enumeration (CVE)
   ○ Vulnerability classification
   ○ Exposure factor
   ○ Environmental variables
   ○ Industry/organizational impact
   ○ Risk tolerance
• Vulnerability response and remediation
   ○ Patching
   ○ Insurance
   ○ Segmentation
   ○ Compensating controls
   ○ Exceptions and exemptions
• Validation of remediation
   ○ Rescanning
   ○ Audit
   ○ Verification
• Reporting			

4.4 Explain security alerting and monitoring concepts and tools.
• Monitoring computing resources
   ○ Systems
   ○ Applications
   ○ Infrastructure
• Activities
   ○ Log aggregation
   ○ Alerting
   ○ Scanning
   ○ Reporting
   ○ Archiving
   ○ Alert response and remediation/validation
     ■ Quarantine
     ■ Alert tuning
• Tools
   ○ Security Content Automation Protocol (SCAP)
   ○ Benchmarks
	8	Security Monitoring and Alerting	Analyzing

(continues)

Security+ Exam Objective Domain/Objectives	Module	Section	Bloom's Taxonomy
○ Agents/agentless 　■ Security information and event management (SIEM) 　■ Antivirus 　■ Data loss prevention (DLP) ○ Simple Network Management Protocol (SNMP) traps ○ NetFlow ○ Vulnerability scanners			
4.5 Given a scenario, modify enterprise capabilities to enhance security. • Firewall ○ Rules ○ Access lists ○ Ports/protocols ○ Screened subnets • IDS/IPS ○ Trends ○ Signatures • Web filter ○ Agent-based ○ Centralized proxy ○ Universal Resource Locator (URL) scanning ○ Content categorization ○ Block rules ○ Reputation • Operating system security ○ Group Policy ○ SELinux • Implementation of secure protocols ○ Protocol selection	9	Security Appliances	Analyzing
○ Port selection ○ Transport method • DNS filtering • Email security ○ Domain-based Message Authentication Reporting and Conformance (DMARC) ○ DomainKeys Identified Mail (DKIM) ○ Sender Policy Framework (SPF) ○ Gateway • File integrity monitoring • DLP • Network access control (NAC) • Endpoint detection and response (EDR)/extended detection and response (XDR) • User behavior analytics	8	Email Monitoring and Security	Applying

Security+ Exam Objective Domain/Objectives	Module	Section	Bloom's Taxonomy
4.6 Given a scenario, implement and maintain identity and access management.			
• Provisioning/de-provisioning user accounts	7	Types of Authentication Credentials	Analyzing
• Permission assignments and implications			
• Identity proofing	7	Authentication Best Practices	Applying
• Federation			
• Single sign-on (SSO)			
○ Lightweight Directory Access Protocol (LDAP)			
○ Open authorization (OAuth)			
○ Security Assertions Markup Language (SAML)			
• Interoperability			
• Attestation			
• Access controls			
○ Mandatory			
○ Discretionary			
○ Role-based			
○ Rule-based			
○ Attribute-based			
○ Time-of-day restrictions			
○ Least privilege			
• Multifactor authentication			
○ Implementations			
▪ Biometrics			
▪ Hard/soft authentication tokens			
▪ Security keys			
○ Factors			
▪ Something you know			
▪ Something you have			
▪ Something you are			
▪ Somewhere you are			
• Password concepts			
○ Password best practices			
▪ Length			
▪ Complexity			
▪ Reuse			
▪ Expiration			
▪ Age			
○ Password managers			
○ Passwordless			
• Privileged access management tools			
○ Just-in-time permissions			
○ Password vaulting			
○ Temporal accounts			

(continues)

Security+ Exam Objective Domain/Objectives	Module	Section	Bloom's Taxonomy
4.7 Explain the importance of automation and orchestration related to secure operations.			
• Use cases of automation and scripting	14	Security Operations	Understanding
○ User provisioning			
○ Resource provisioning			
○ Guard rails			
○ Security groups			
○ Ticket creation			
○ Escalation			
○ Enabling/disabling services and access			
○ Continuous integration and testing			
○ Integrations and Application programming interfaces (APIs)			
• Benefits			
○ Efficiency/time saving			
○ Enforcing baselines			
○ Standard infrastructure configurations			
○ Scaling in a secure manner			
○ Staff retention			
○ Reaction time			
○ Workforce multiplier			
• Other considerations			
○ Complexity			
○ Cost			
○ Single point of failure			
○ Technical debt			
○ Ongoing support			
4.8 Explain appropriate incident response activities.			
• Process	13	Incident Investigation	Applying
○ Preparation			
○ Detection			
○ Analysis			
○ Containment			
○ Eradication			
○ Recovery			
○ Lessons learned			
• Training	13	Preparatory Plans	Applying
• Testing			
○ Tabletop exercise			
○ Simulation			
• Root cause analysis			
• Threat hunting			
• Digital forensics			
○ Legal hold			
○ Chain of custody			
○ Acquisition			

Security+ Exam Objective Domain/Objectives	Module	Section	Bloom's Taxonomy
○ Reporting ○ Preservation ○ E-discovery			
4.9 Given a scenario, use data sources to support an investigation. • Log data 　○ Firewall logs 　○ Application logs 　○ Endpoint logs 　○ OS-specific security logs 　○ IPS/IDS logs 　○ Network logs 　○ Metadata • Data sources 　○ Vulnerability scans 　○ Automated reports 　○ Dashboards 　○ Packet captures	13	Incident Investigation	Analyzing
5.0 Security Program Management and Oversight			
5.1 Summarize elements of effective security governance. • Guidelines • Policies 　○ Acceptable use policy (AUP) 　○ Information security policies 　○ Business continuity 　○ Disaster recovery 　○ Incident response 　○ Software development lifecycle (SDLC) 　○ Change management • Standards 　○ Password 　○ Access control 　○ Physical security 　○ Encryption • Procedures 　○ Change management 　○ Onboarding/offboarding 　○ Playbooks • External considerations 　○ Regulatory 　○ Legal 　○ Industry 　○ Local/regional 　○ National 　○ Global • Monitoring and revision	14	Administration	Applying

(continues)

Security+ Exam Objective Domain/Objectives	Module	Section	Bloom's Taxonomy

• Types of governance structures
  ○ Boards
  ○ Committees
  ○ Government entities
  ○ Centralized/decentralized
• Roles and responsibilities for systems and data
  ○ Owners
  ○ Controllers
  ○ Processors
  ○ Custodians/stewards			

5.2 Explain elements of the risk management process.
• Risk identification
• Risk assessment
  ○ Ad hoc
  ○ Recurring
  ○ One-time
  ○ Continuous
• Risk analysis
  ○ Qualitative
  ○ Quantitative
  ○ Single loss expectancy (SLE)
  ○ Annualized loss expectancy (ALE)
  ○ Annualized rate of occurrence (ARO)
  ○ Probability
  ○ Likelihood
  ○ Exposure factor
  ○ Impact
• Risk register
  ○ Key risk indicators
  ○ Risk owners
  ○ Risk threshold
• Risk tolerance
• Risk appetite
  ○ Expansionary
  ○ Conservative
  ○ Neutral
• Risk management strategies
  ○ Transfer
  ○ Accept
    ▪ Exemption
    ▪ Exception
  ○ Avoid
  ○ Mitigate
• Risk reporting
• Business impact analysis
  ○ Recovery time objective (RTO)
  ○ Recovery point objective (RPO)
  ○ Mean time to repair (MTTR)
  ○ Mean time between failures (MTBF)
	15	Risk Management	Analyzing

Security+ Exam Objective Domain/Objectives	Module	Section	Bloom's Taxonomy
5.3 Explain the processes associated with third-party risk assessment and management.			
• Vendor assessment	15	Risk Management	Applying
○ Penetration testing			
○ Right-to-audit clause			
○ Evidence of internal audits			
○ Independent assessments			
○ Supply chain analysis			
• Vendor selection			
○ Due diligence			
○ Conflict of interest			
• Agreement types			Remembering
○ Service-level agreement (SLA)			
○ Memorandum of agreement (MOA)			
○ Memorandum of understanding (MOU)			
○ Master service agreement (MSA)			
○ Work order (WO)/statement of work (SOW)			
○ Non-disclosure agreement (NDA)			
○ Business partners agreement (BPA)			
• Vendor monitoring			
• Questionnaires			
• Rules of engagement			
5.4 Summarize elements of effective security compliance.			
• Compliance reporting	14	Administration	Understanding
○ Internal			
○ External			
• Consequences of non-compliance			
○ Fines			
○ Sanctions			
○ Reputational damage			
○ Loss of license			
○ Contractual impacts			
• Compliance monitoring			
○ Due diligence/care			
○ Attestation and acknowledgement			
○ Internal and external			
○ Automation			
• Privacy			
○ Legal implications			
▪ Local/regional			
▪ National			
▪ Global			
○ Data subject			
○ Controller vs. processor			
○ Ownership			
○ Data inventory and retention			
○ Right to be forgotten			

(continues)

Security+ Exam Objective Domain/Objectives	Module	Section	Bloom's Taxonomy

5.5 Explain types and purposes of audits and assessments.
 	
• Attestation
• Internal
  ○ Compliance
  ○ Audit committee
  ○ Self-assessments
• External
  ○ Regulatory
  ○ Examinations
  ○ Assessment
  ○ Independent third-party audit
• Penetration testing
  ○ Physical
  ○ Offensive
  ○ Defensive
  ○ Integrated
  ○ Known environment
  ○ Partially known environment
  ○ Unknown environment
  ○ Reconnaissance
    ▪ Passive
    ▪ Active
	12	Audits and Assessments	Applying

5.6 Given a scenario, implement security awareness practices.
 	
• Phishing
  ○ Campaigns
  ○ Recognizing a phishing attempt
  ○ Responding to reported suspicious messages
• Anomalous behavior recognition
  ○ Risky
  ○ Unexpected
  ○ Unintentional
• User guidance and training
  ○ Policy/handbooks
  ○ Situational awareness
  ○ Insider threat
  ○ Password management
  ○ Removable media and cables
  ○ Social engineering
  ○ Operational security
  ○ Hybrid/remote work environments
• Reporting and monitoring
  ○ Initial
  ○ Recurring
• Development
• Execution
	15	Risk Management	Understanding

Glossary

A

accept Acknowledging a risk but taking no steps to address it.

acceptable-use policy (AUP) A policy that defines the actions users may perform while accessing systems and networking equipment.

access badge A credential that indicates the user has been preapproved.

access control Granting or denying approval to use specific resources once authenticated.

access control list (ACL) A set of permissions that is attached to an object.

access control vestibule A buffer area that separates a nonsecure area from a secure area using two interlocking doors.

account lockout An indicator of attack in which a user account that is inaccessible through a normal login attempt.

accounting To create and preserve a record of who accessed the enterprise network, what resources they accessed, and when they disconnected from the network.

acknowledgment A statement of the organization's responsibility for establishing and maintaining effective internal controls as they relate to compliance.

acquisition Gathering evidence from a device.

active device attribute Automatically blocking an attack when it occurs.

active reconnaissance Directly probing for vulnerabilities and useful information.

ad hoc assessment A risk assessment that is done whenever necessary.

adaptive identity Verification of a user in a zero-trust architecture.

adjusting dependencies Changing the reliance between services.

age The period of time that a password must be used before a user can change it.

agent-based web filtering Web filtering software that resides on an endpoint device.

agentless Collecting data without the need of monitoring agents.

agentless software Software in which no additional processes are required to run in the background.

agents Software monitoring applications that are installed on devices.

air-gapped network A physically separated network.

alert tuning A monitoring activity that modifies the alerting function to weed out false positives.

alerting Detecting and notifying operators about meaningful events that may denote an attack.

algorithm A set of procedures based on a mathematical formula used to encrypt and decrypt the data. Also called a *cipher*.

amplified attacks A DDoS attack method to increase the deluge of data.

analysis An incident response process step of collecting data from tools and systems for further identification to identify indicators of compromise.

Annualized Loss Expectancy (ALE) The expected monetary loss for an asset due to a risk over a one-year period.

Annualized Rate of Occurrence (ARO) A calculation for determining the likelihood of a risk occurring within a year.

anomalous behavior recognition Being able to distinguish between what is normal and what is not normal.

antivirus (AV) Software that examines a computer for file-based virus infections as well as monitors computer activity and scans new documents that might contain a virus.

application allow listing Approving in advance only specific applications to run.

application logs Logs that can give information about attacks focused on different applications.

applications Software programs.

approval process An agreement that can slow the acquisition of needed appliances or software for information security.

archiving A monitoring activity that retains historical documents and records of monitoring.

assessment A judgment made about the results of an audit.

asset acquisition Process of identifying and then securing an asset to support a business goal.

asset assignment/accounting Process of determining and recording ownership and asset classification.

asset decommissioning   Withdrawing an asset from service.

asset disposal   Physically removing an asset.

asset enumeration   A listing of the assets by a seller of those assets.

asset management   Coordinated activity of an organization to realize value from its assets.

asset procurement   Process of identifying and then securing an asset to support a business goal.

asset tracking   Tracing the location of tangible assets.

asymmetric cryptographic algorithm   Cryptography that uses two mathematically related keys.

attack surface (threat vector)   Digital platform that threat actors target for their exploits.

attestation (compliance monitoring)   Verification of truth or authenticity.

attestation (internal audits)   Verifying that the organization is in compliance with required standards.

attestation (security keys)   A key pair "burned" into a security key during manufacturing and is specific to a device model.

Attribute-Based Access Control (ABAC)   An access control scheme that uses flexible policies that can combine attributes.

attributes of actors   Characteristic features of the different groups of threat actors.

audit   An examination of results to verify their accuracy performed by someone other than the person responsible for producing the results.

audit committee   A group that oversees the organization's financial statements and reporting.

authentication   Act of verifying that credentials are authentic and not fabricated.

authentication, authorization, and accounting (AAA)   Providing a framework to control access to computer resources.

authorization   Granting permission to take an action.

automated provisioning   Creating and setting up an IT infrastructure automatically.

automated reports   Reports from data collected by IP software monitors that are generated without the need for a user to manually analyze the data.

automation compliance tools   Tools that categorize and then collect and analyze data at various points in its lifecycle.

availability   A security constraint in which ensuring timely and reliable access to devices can be hampered by the constraints.

availability   Procedures that ensure data is accessible to only authorized users and not to unapproved individuals.

avoid   Identifying a risk but making the decision to not engage in the activity.

B

backout plan   Procedures needed if a "rollback" is required following a release of an asset into the production process.

backup   A single scheduled event for copying data.

benchmark   A standard or point of reference against which something may be compared or assessed.

biometrics   A category of authentication credentials that rests on the features and characteristics of the individual.

birthday attack   A statistical phenomenon that makes finding collisions easier.

blackmail   Threat actor's motivation of extortion or coercion by threat.

bloatware   Software installed on a device without the user requesting it.

block rules   Criteria for which a website is inaccessible to users.

blockchain   A shared, immutable ledger that facilitates the process of recording transactions and tracking assets in a business network.

blocked content   An indicator of attack in which data is no longer accessible.

bluejacking   An attack that sends unsolicited messages to Bluetooth-enabled devices.

bluesnarfing   An attack that accesses unauthorized information from a wireless device through a Bluetooth connection.

Bluetooth   A wireless technology that uses short-range radio frequency (RF) transmissions and provides rapid ad hoc device pairings.

board   An entity composed of internal directors who approve strategic organizational goals and policies.

bollard   A short but sturdy vertical post used as a vehicular traffic barricade.

brand impersonation   A social engineering attack by which a threat actor uses highly recognizable and well-known products or services to build immediate recognition and trust.

bring your own device (BYOD)   Allows users to use their own personal mobile devices for business purposes.

brute force attack An attack in which every possible combination of letters, numbers, and characters is combined to attempt to determine the user's password.

buffer overflow attack An attack in which a process attempts to store data in RAM beyond the boundaries of a fixed-length storage buffer so an attacker can overflow the buffer with a new address pointing to the attacker's malware code.

bug bounty program A practice of large enterprises to pay security researchers who uncover security bugs in their products and then privately report them.

business continuity The ability of an organization to maintain its operations and services in the face of a disruptive event or a major disaster.

business continuity plan (BCP) A strategic document that provides alternative modes of operation for business activities that, if interrupted, could result in a significant loss to the enterprise.

business email compromise (BEC) A type of phishing attack that takes advantage of the practice by businesses and organizations of electronically making payments or transferring funds.

business impact analysis (BIA) A process that identifies the business functions and quantifies the impact a loss of these functions may have on business operations.

business partnership agreement (BPA) A contract between two or more business partners that is used to establish the rules and responsibilities of each partner.

C

capacity planning The process of forecasting the need for future resources.

cellular A communications network in which the coverage area is divided into hexagon-shaped cells.

centralized (architecture and infrastructure) A model in which equipment and personnel are located locally at an organization's campus computing.

centralized (security governance) A governance body in which all authority is vested into a single group.

centralized proxy scanning Performing web filtering on a proxy appliance through which all requests are funneled.

certificate authority (CA) The entity that is responsible for digital certificates.

certificate revocation list (CRL) A list of certificate serial numbers that have been revoked.

certificate signing request (CSR) generation The process for requesting a digital certificate.

certification Verifying for regulatory purposes.

chain of custody Verifying that evidence was always under strict control and no unauthorized person was given the opportunity to corrupt the evidence.

change management A systematic approach to dealing with transformations within an organization.

change management policies Formal statement that outlines specific requirements or rules that must be met.

change management procedures Detailed mandatory steps needed to comply with a change management policy.

changing allow lists/deny lists Modifying permissions of what is allowed or denied.

choose your own device (CYOD) Employees choose from a limited selection of approved devices but the employee pays the upfront cost of the device while the business owns the contract.

Cipher Block Chaining Message Authentication Code (CBC-MAC) A component of CCMP that provides data integrity and authentication.

classification The category in which an asset belongs.

client-based software Software applications installed on a computer connected to a network.

cloud computing An on-demand infrastructure to a shared pool of configurable computing resources that can be rapidly provisioned and released.

cloud-specific vulnerabilities Unique challenges to securing the use of the cloud.

clustering Combining two or more devices to appear as a single unit.

code signing A process by which software developers digitally sign a program to prove that the software comes from the entity that signed it and that no unauthorized third party has altered it.

cold site A remote site that provides office space; the customer must provide and install all the equipment needed to continue operations.

collision When two files have the same hash.

committee An entity that is a subset of the board of directors that manages governance issues.

Common Vulnerability Scoring System (CVSS) Numeric scores on a vulnerability scan that are generated using a complex formula.

Common Weakness Enumeration (CWE) A categorical system for hardware and software weaknesses and vulnerabilities.

compensating controls Controls that provide an alternative to normal controls that for some reason cannot be used.

complexity A disadvantage of automation that introduces complications. Also, the variation of a password's composition.

compliance The process of ensuring that an organization adheres to mandated standards, laws and regulations related to information security, and user data privacy.

compliance monitoring The quality assurance tests that organizations perform to determine how well their business operations meet security regulations and standards.

compute A security constraint in which a device's small size results in low processing capabilities to incorporate comprehensive security measures.

concurrent session usage An indicator of attack in which both a legitimate user and an attacker are logged into the same account.

confidential The highest level of data sensitivity.

confidentiality Procedures that ensure only authorized parties can view the information.

confidentiality, integrity, and availability (CIA) Three basic security protections that must be extended over the information.

configuration enforcement Applying security measures to reduce unnecessary vulnerabilities.

conflict of interests Outside personal or financial interests.

connectivity The interconnection points between an IDS/IPS and other devices.

conservative Having little tolerance for risk.

containerization A reduced instance of virtualization.

containment An incident response process step of limiting the damage of the incident and isolating those systems that are impacted to prevent further damage.

content categorization Blocking websites based on the category of the site.

continuity of operations Ensuring that an organization can continue to function in the event of an environmental disaster or human-made disaster.

continuous assessment A risk assessment that is conducted year-round.

continuous integration and testing Continually adding and testing new appliances.

contractual impacts Suspending or terminating a contract as the result of not following compliance standards.

control Safeguard employed within an enterprise to protect the CIA of information. Also called a *countermeasure*.

control plane The means for communication in a zero-trust architecture.

controller The principal party for collecting data.

corporate-owned, personally enabled (COPE) Employees choose from a selection of company-approved devices.

corrective controls Controls intended to mitigate or lessen the damage caused by the incident.

cost A security constraint in which making products as inexpensive as possible results in leaving out security protections. Also, a disadvantage of automation is that it is more expensive.

Counter Mode with Cipher Block Chaining Message Authentication Code Protocol (CCMP) The encryption protocol used for WPA2 that specifies the use of a general-purpose cipher mode algorithm providing data privacy with AES.

credential relay attack An attack that attempts to steal authentication credentials and then use them to access a system.

critical Data classified according to availability needs so that the function and mission would be severely impacted if compromised.

cross-site scripting (XSS) An attack in which a website accepts user input without validating it so it can be exploited.

cryptography The practice of transforming information so that it is secure and cannot be understood by unauthorized persons.

custodian/steward An individual to whom day-to-day data actions have been assigned by the owner.

D

dark web Part of the web that is the domain of threat actors.

dashboard A SIEM visualization that can provide information collected from its sensors.

data at rest Data that is stored on electronic media.

data classifications Groupings of data categories.

data exfiltration Threat actor's motivation of unauthorized copying of data.

data in transit Data that is transmitted across a network.

data in use Data on which actions are being performed by devices.

data inventory Collected data.

data loss prevention (DLP) A system of security tools used to recognize and identify data that is critical to the organization and ensure it is protected.

data plane The means for the transfer of resources in a zero-trust architecture.

data retention Transferring data to a different device.

data sanitization The process of cleaning data to provide privacy.

data sovereignty The country-specific requirements that apply to data.

data state The condition of data.

data subjects Any living individual whose personal data is collected and stored by an organization.

database-level encryption Applying cryptography to a database.

decentralized A governance body in which planning and decision making are distributed to smaller groups within it. Also, a model in which equipment and personnel are in several different locations.

decommissioning Removing or dismantling a technology or service from a live production environment.

decryption The process of changing encrypted text into the original text.

default credentials Preselected options for authentication.

default passwords Standard preconfigured passwords.

defensive An assessment that only looks at the protections of a system.

deploy baselines Distributing a reference set of data.

de-provisioning Removing user accounts.

destruction Rendering an asset unusable.

detection An incident response process step of determining whether an event is actually a security incident.

detective controls Controls designed to identify any threat that has reached the system.

deterrent controls Controls that attempt to discourage security violations before they occur.

device placement Physically locating important devices in secure locations.

digital certificate A technology used to associate a user's identity to a public key and that has been "digitally signed" by a trusted third party.

digital forensics The retrieval of difficult-to-obtain data, which is usually hidden, altered, or even deleted by the perpetrator.

digital signature An electronic verification of the sender.

directive controls Controls designed to ensure that a particular outcome is achieved.

directory traversal An attack in which a threat actor takes advantage of a vulnerability to move from the root directory to other restricted directories.

disabling ports/protocols Closing unused ports and disabling unnecessary protocols.

disabling services and access Denying ingress traffic from threat actors.

disassociation attack A wireless attack in which false deauthentication or disassociation frames are sent to an AP that appear to come from another client device, causing the client to disconnect.

disaster recovery plan (DRP) A written document that details the process for restoring IT resources following an event that causes a significant disruption in service.

Discretionary Access Control (DAC) An access control scheme that is the least restrictive, giving an owner total control over objects.

disinformation False or inaccurate misinformation that comes from a malicious intent.

disruption/chaos Threat actor's motivation to produce extreme confusion.

distribute standard infrastructure configurations A benefit of automation is that it distributes infrastructure configurations to all devices.

distributed denial of service (DDoS) Attacks in which multiple devices make bogus requests to overwhelm the recipient.

DNS filtering Using DNS to block harmful or inappropriate content by filtering entire domains.

Domain Keys Identified Mail (DKIM) An email authentication technique that validates the content of the email message.

Domain Name System (DNS) attacks Attacks that substitute a DNS address so that the computer is silently redirected to a different device.

Domain-based Message Authentication, Reporting, and Conformance (DMARC) An email security protection that allows the administrative owner of a domain to publish a policy in their DNS records to specify which mechanism is used when sending email.

downgrade attack An attack in which the system is forced to abandon the current higher security mode of operation and "fall back" to implementing an older and less secure mode.

due care Taking reasonable steps to secure and protect an organization's assets, reputation, and finances.

due diligence Reasonable steps to satisfy legal agreements. Also, identifying and mitigating risks brought on by a third party.

duration field values attack A wireless attack designed to prevent access to a client through manipulating duration field values.

dynamic code analysis Examining code after the source code is compiled and when all components are integrated and running.

E

EAP-FAST An Extensible Authentication Protocol that securely tunnels any credential form for authentication (such as a password or a token) using TLS.

EAP-TLS An Extensible Authentication Protocol that uses digital certificates for authentication.

EAP-TTLS An Extensible Authentication Protocol that securely tunnels client password authentication within Transport Layer Security (TLS) records.

ease of deployment A security constraint in which an accelerated rollout of devices at a faster pace prevents them from being secured.

ease of recovery A security constraint in which a compromised sensor may have difficulty recovering to its normal state following an attack.

e-discovery Searching through electronic documents that have been uploaded to an e-discovery platform.

embedded system Computer hardware and software contained within a larger system that is designed for a specific function.

enabling services and access Providing access based on users' positions and permission levels.

encryption The process of changing plaintext into ciphertext.

end-of-life (EOL) End of a product's manufacturing lifespan.

endpoint detection and response (EDR) Tools that are more robust than HIDS and HIPS.

endpoint logs Logs that can provide a wide range of reports and alerts with events classified by their severity level.

enforce baselines A benefit of automation that can ensure that required baselines are imposed.

environmental variables Variables whose values are set outside the program, typically through functionality built into the OS or a microservice.

eradication An incident response process step of finding the cause of the incident and temporarily removing any systems that may be causing damage.

escalation The rapid detection of a threat incident so that its importance can immediately be elevated.

espionage Threat actor's motivation of spying.

establish baselines Creating a reference set of data against which operational data is compared.

ethical Threat actor's motivation of sound moral principles.

evidence of internal audits Verification that an audit occurred.

evil twin An AP set up by an attacker to mimic an authorized AP and capture transmissions, so a user's device will unknowingly connect to this evil twin instead of the authorized AP.

examinations Assessments by independent third-party auditors.

exception A security requirement that cannot be fully implemented.

exceptions and exemptions Declaring that certain vulnerabilities fall outside the bounds of what the organization will address.

exemption   An excuse from a regulating body.

expansionary   Having a high tolerance for risk.

experiencing downtime   Encountering a loss of availability of one or more devices.

expiration   The point in time when a password is no longer valid.

exposure factor   A subjective estimate of the loss to an asset if the specific threat occurs.

extended detection and response (XDR)   A technology that collects and correlates data across various network appliances, including servers, email systems, cloud repositories, and endpoints.

Extensible Authentication Protocol (EAP)   A framework for transporting authentication protocols that defines the format of the messages.

external assessments   Evaluations that are performed by professionals from outside the organization.

external compliance monitoring and reporting   Compliance monitoring that is performed by a professional third party.

F

fail closed   A failure mode in which the device shuts down when failure is detected.

fail open   A failure mode in which the device remains open and operations continue as normal.

fail over   An incident response testing exercise that is testing the process of temporarily switching to backup procedures after an attack.

failure mode   A predefined set of actions based on a failure of a network component.

false negative   The failure to raise an alarm when there is an issue.

false positive   An alarm that is raised when there is no problem.

federation   Single sign-on for networks owned by different organizations, also called federated identity management (FIM).

fencing   A tall, permanent structure to keep out unauthorized personnel.

file integrity monitoring (FIM)   A technology designed to watch files to detect any changes within the files that may indicate a cyberattack.

file-based   Attacks that focus on infecting individual files on a computer.

file-level encryption   To encrypt or decrypt files individually.

financial gain   Threat actor's motivation of earning revenue.

financial information   Data about the monetary transactions of the enterprise.

fines   Monetary penalties for not following compliance standards.

firewall   Hardware or software that is designed to limit the spread of malware.

firewall logs   Logs from a firewall that can be used to determine whether new IP addresses are attempting to probe the network and if stronger firewall rules are necessary to block them.

firewall port filtering   Restricting packets based on the source or destination port.

firewall protocol filtering   Restricting packets based on the protocol being used.

firmware   Software embedded into hardware.

forgery   A request that has been fabricated.

frequency   Determining how often copying data should be performed.

full-disk encryption (FDE)   A technology to protect the entire hard drive using cryptography including the installed OS.

G

gap analysis   A comparison of the organization's current state of information security with recommended controls.

generate workforce multiplier   A benefit of automation that gives staff the ability to be more productive.

generator   A device powered by diesel, natural gas, or propane gas to generate electricity.

geographic dispersal   Sites distributed across a larger area to mitigate the impact of environmental disasters and human-made disasters.

geographic restrictions   Limiting access to data to specific locations.

geolocation   Identifying data's location.

global body   A governance body that is worldwide in scope.

global data protections   Universal protections of user privacy data to which all nations adhere.

governance   The structures, systems, and practices an organization has in place to assign, oversee, and report.

government entity   An entity that is used by national governments to direct organizations through governance directives.

guardrails   Automations that constantly watch cloud deployments, find deviations from desired baselines, and automatically remediate issues.

guideline A document that provides general guidance and support for policies, standards, or procedures.

H

hacktivists Threat actors who are strongly motivated by philosophical or political beliefs.

hard/soft authentication tokens Hardware and software-based authentication tokens.

hardening cloud infrastructure Cloud security controls that can mitigate vulnerabilities.

hardening mobile devices Steps that can be taken to make mobile devices more resilient to attacks.

hardening RTOS Steps that can be taken to make a real-time operating system more resilient to attacks.

hardening targets Configuring and securing devices for resisting attacks.

hardware provider Type of supply chain for distributing computer hardware.

hardware security module (HSM) A removable external cryptographic device.

hashing The process of creating a digital fingerprint.

heat map A software tool that provides a visual representation of the wireless signal coverage and strength.

high availability An RTOS that is tuned to accommodate very high volumes of data that must be immediately processed for critical decision making. Also, making servers always accessible.

honeyfiles Software and data files on a honeypot that appear to be authentic but are actually imitations of real data files.

honeynet A network set up with intentional vulnerabilities.

honeypot A computer located in an area with limited security that serves as "bait" to threat actors and is intentionally configured with security vulnerabilities.

honeytoken Fake data that has been added to live production systems.

host intrusion prevention system (HIPS) Software that monitors endpoint activity to immediately block a malicious attack by following specific rules.

host-based firewall A software firewall that runs as a program on the local device to block or filter traffic coming into and out of the computer.

hot site A duplicate of the production site that has all the equipment needed for an organization to continue running, including office space and furniture, telephone jacks, computer equipment, and a live telecommunications link.

human vectors The attack surface of social engineering.

human-readable data Data that a person can read and interpret.

hybrid cloud considerations Special security challenges unique to hybrid clouds due to the nature of spanning both public and private spaces.

I

identity and access management (IAM) Technologies that provide control over user validation and the resources that may be accessed.

identity proofing Requiring the user to provide proof that they are the unique user.

image-based Attacks that focus on an image or copy of all a computer's contents.

impact analysis Reacting to a process for determining consequences of a decision.

impersonation Masquerading as a real or fictitious character and then playing out the role of that person on a victim.

implementing service or application restarts Starting a service or program that has been previously terminated.

impossible travel An indicator of attack in which a resource is accessed that is not possible due to geography.

improve staff retention A benefit of automation to reduce the stress and fatigue of workers.

inability to patch A security constraint in which the capacity is absent for updating to address exposed security vulnerabilities.

incident response process Action steps to be taken when an incident occurs.

independent assessment Verification by an outside third party.

independent third-party audit An audit performed by individuals outside the organization.

indicator of attack (IoA) A sign an attack is currently underway.

industrial control systems (ICS) Systems that control locally or at remote locations by collecting, monitoring, and processing real-time data to control machines.

industry A group that creates and audits governance policies for organizations that make up that industry.

industry/organizational impact A determination of the result an attack will have.

information sharing organizations Entities that gather, collate, analyze, and then distribute threat intelligence.

infrared (IR) sensor An electronic device that can measure and detect IR in the surrounding area.

infrastructure as code Instances of virtualization.

infrastructure capacity planning Capacity planning for predicting the future size of the network.

initial training The start of training.

injection An attack in which threat actors introduce something into RAM.

inline A system that is connected directly to the network and monitors the flow of data as it occurs.

input validation A coding technique for accounting for errors.

insider threat Employees, contractors, and business partners who pose a threat from the position of a trusted entity.

Instant messaging (IM) Technology that allows users to send real-time messages through a software application over the Internet and is not restricted to a cell phone.

insurance Payment to a third party for assuming risks and then being compensated for an attack.

integrated penetration tests A penetration test that probes for both technical and physical weaknesses.

integrations and application programming interfaces (API) A set of automated tools for connecting software applications that are deployed in different environments.

integrity Procedures that ensure that the information is correct and no unauthorized person or malicious software has altered the data.

intellectual property (IP) data An invention or a work that is the result of creativity.

internal audits Audits performed by company employees.

internal compliance monitoring Compliance monitoring performed by the organization itself.

internal compliance report A document to be provided to an auditor that verifies compliance.

internal/external Attribute of threat actors of origination from within the enterprise or outside it.

Internet of Things (IoT) Connecting any device to the Internet for the purpose of sending and receiving data to be acted upon.

Internet Protocol Security (IPSec) A protocol suite for securing IP communications.

interoperability The ability of systems to exchange information.

intrusion detection system (IDS) A device that can detect an attack as it occurs and sound an alarm for security personnel to investigate to determine if further action is needed.

intrusion detection systems (IDS)/intrusion prevention systems (IPS) logs Logs that record detailed security log information on suspicious behavior as well as any attacks that are detected.

intrusion prevention system (IPS) A device that attempts to automatically block an attack as it occurs.

inventory Raw materials, works in progress, and finished goods that are available for sale that a business owns.

isolation Keeping multiple instances of an attack surface separate so that each instance can only see and can affect itself.

J

jailbreaking Circumventing the installed built-in limitations on Apple iOS devices.

jamming Intentionally flooding the radio frequency (RF) spectrum with extraneous RF signal "noise" that creates interference and prevents communications from occurring.

journaling Making a copy of data whenever a change to the data occurs.

jump server A minimally configured administrator server (either physical or virtual) within the DMZ that is used to connect two dissimilar security zones while providing tightly restricted access between them.

just-in-time permissions Access control permissions that are immediately elevated to higher-level permissions to perform a specific function before dropping back to normal levels.

K

key escrow A process in which keys are managed by a third party, such as a trusted CA.

key exchange The process of sending and receiving secure cryptographic keys.

key length The number of bits in a key.

key management system A method of controlling public keys, private keys, and digital certificates.

key risk indicators Primary risk factors.

key stretching A password hashing algorithm that requires significantly more time than standard hashing algorithms to create the digest.

keylogger Software or hardware that silently captures and stores each keystroke that a user types on the computer's keyboard.

known environment A penetration test in which the testers have been given full knowledge of the network and the source code of applications.

L

Layer 4 firewall A stateful packet-filtering firewall that can allow or deny traffic based on the state of the session.

Layer 7 firewall A firewall that can look into the contents of the packets to determine whether they contain malware.

least privilege Granting access that is limited to what is only necessary for a user to complete their work.

legacy platform Older hardware platform for which there is a more modern version available but for a variety of reasons has not been updated or replaced.

legal An internal corporate department that interprets internal and external governance policies.

legal hold A demand from a court that data cannot be modified, deleted, erased, or otherwise destroyed.

legal implications Legal ramifications if protections of privacy of user data are violated.

legal information General factual information about the law and the legal process.

length The number of characters that make up a password.

lessons learned An incident response process step of completing incident documentation and performing detailed analysis to increase security and improve future response efforts.

level of sophistication/capability Attribute of threat actors of a high level of power and complexity.

lighting Lamps that illuminate an area so that it can be monitored after dark.

Lightweight Directory Access Protocol (LDAP) A protocol or communication process that enables users to access a network resource through a directory service.

likelihood The state or fact of something being likely or possible.

load balancer A device that distributes work across a network.

local/regional body A governance body in which the scope is limited to the immediate geographical area.

local/regional data protections Protections of user data limited to local or regional areas.

log A record of events that occur.

log aggregation Consolidating multiple logs together for analysis.

logic bomb Computer code that is typically added to a legitimate program but lies dormant and evades detection until a specific logical event triggers it.

logical segmentation Creating subnets through virtual networks or network addressing schemes.

loss of license The withdrawal of a permit to function as the result of not following compliance standards.

M

maintain baselines Updating a reference set of data.

maintenance window A designated time in which systems are brought down for routine maintenance.

malicious code attacks Network attacks that are the result of malicious software code and scripts.

malicious update Attack in which a software update is infected with malware and distributed.

malware Malicious software designed to interfere with a computer's normal functions and can be used to commit an unwanted and harmful action.

managed service providers (MSPs) IT service providers who manage networks, computers, cloud resources, and information security for small-to-medium enterprises.

managerial controls Controls that use administrative methods.

Mandatory Access Control (MAC) An access control scheme that is the most restrictive by assigning users' access controls strictly according to the custodian's desires.

masking Creating a copy of original data to make it unintelligible.

mean time between failures (MTBF) A statistical value that is the average time until a component fails, cannot be repaired, and must be replaced.

mean time to repair (MTTR) The average time needed to restore to working order a failed component or device and return it to production status.

measurement system analysis (MSA) Using scientific tools to determine the amount of variation that is added to a process by a measurement system.

memorandum of agreement (MOA) An agreement that establishes common legal terms.

memorandum of understanding (MOU) A document that describes an agreement between two or more parties that is not legally enforceable.

memory injection An attack in which threat actors introduce something into RAM.

message-based Communication tools that are popular threat vectors by attackers.

metadata logs Logs that contain data that describes information about other data.

microservices The process of dividing application development into smaller entities.

microwave sensor An electronic device that uses high-frequency radio waves and functions similarly to radar.

misconfigurations Erroneous technology settings.

misinformation False or inaccurate information, regardless of the intent to mislead.

missing logs An indicator of attack in which log files have mysteriously been deleted.

mitigate Addressing a risk by making the risk less serious.

mobile device management (MDM) Tools that allow a device to be managed remotely by an organization.

modifying restricted activities Changing a restricted activity to a permitted activity.

monitoring and revising Reporting on performance toward achieving intended results and then using that performance information to drive ongoing improvements and corrective actions.

monitoring applications Continually observing programs for evidence of an attack.

monitoring infrastructures Continually observing networks for evidence of an attack.

monitoring systems Continually observing devices for evidence of an attack.

multi-cloud systems Spreading cloud computing across multiple cloud providers.

multifactor authentication (MFA) Using more than one type of authentication credential.

N

national body A governance body that covers an entire nation.

nation-state actors Threat actors who are employed by their own government to carry out attacks.

NetFlow A session sampling protocol feature on Cisco routers that collects IP network traffic as it enters or exits an interface.

national data protections User privacy data protections that apply to a country or group of countries.

network access control (NAC) A security method that examines the current state of an endpoint before it can connect to a network and then restricts unauthorized users and devices from gaining access.

network logs Logs from different appliances, such as router and switch logs that provide general information about network traffic.

neutral Having neither low nor high tolerance for risk.

next generation firewall (NGFW) A firewall that has additional functionality beyond a traditional firewall such as the ability to filter packets based on applications.

NIDS sensors Devices that monitor the traffic entering and leaving a firewall and report back to the central device for analysis.

noncompliance Not following compliance standards.

nondisclosure agreement (NDA) A legal contract between parties that specifies how confidential material will be shared between the parties but restricted to others.

non-human-readable data Data that a device can interpret.

nonrepudiation The process of proving that a user performed an action.

O

OAuth (Open Authorization) An open-source federation framework.

obfuscation Making something unintelligible.

offboarding The actions to be taken when an employee leaves an enterprise.

offensive An assessment that probes a system for weaknesses.

offsite Storing copied data away from the production facility.

onboarding The tasks associated with hiring a new employee.

one-time assessment A risk assessment that is scheduled.

ongoing support A disadvantage of automation that requires continual monitoring.

Online Certificate Status Protocol (OCSP) A process that performs a real-time lookup of a certificate's status.

on-path attack An attack that occurs when a threat actor positions themself in the middle between two communicating users or devices.

on-premises Computing resources located on the campus of an organization.

onsite Storing copied data where the data is actually being used.

open public ledger A public blockchain in which anyone can join the blockchain network and become part of it.

open service ports Unnecessary ports that are not disabled.

Open-Source Intelligence (OSINT) Threat intelligence data that has been legally gathered from free and public sources.

operational controls Controls that are implemented and executed by people.

orchestration Automation used for entire processes instead of for a single task.

organized crime Close-knit group of highly centralized enterprises set up for the purpose of engaging in illegal activities.

OS-based vulnerabilities Vulnerabilities found within operating systems.

OS-specific security logs Logs that record system events that are operational actions performed by OS components and audit records that contain security event information.

out-of-cycle logging An indicator of attack in which log records do not correspond to actual events that have occurred.

owner A person responsible for information.

ownership (asset management) The entity that owns an asset.

ownership (compliance) Legal possession and control of data.

P

package monitoring Vulnerability scan tools that continuously analyze apps for vulnerabilities.

packet capture Information that is based on capturing packets.

parallel processing An incident response testing exercise that conducts the same tests simultaneously in multiple environments.

partially known environment A penetration test in which the testers have been given limited knowledge of the network and some elevated privileges.

partition-level encryption Applying cryptography to a partition of a hard drive.

passive device attribute Alerting security personnel to investigate an attack.

passive reconnaissance Using tools in a penetration test that do not raise any alarms.

password A secret combination of letters, numbers, and/or characters that only the user should have knowledge of.

password manager A software application or online website that stores user passwords along with login information.

password spraying An attack that uses one or a small number of commonly used passwords when trying to log in to several different user accounts.

password vaulting An enterprise-level system for storing user password credentials in a highly protected database on the organization's network.

passwordless A new technique for accessing a system without using passwords.

patch availability A security constraint in which manufacturers do not produce patches for devices.

patching Installing software security updates.

penetration testing A specific type of audit and assessment that attempts to uncover vulnerabilities and then exploit them, just as a threat actor would.

people capacity planning Capacity planning that involves calculating future human resources.

permission assignments and implications Determining why permissions are given, to whom, and what the impact may be.

permission restrictions Limiting individuals and devices to only those that have a legitimate business need to access the data.

permissions Authorizations for access control.

philosophical/political beliefs Threat actor's motivation of ideology for the sake of principles.

phishing Sending an email or displaying a web announcement that falsely claims to be from a legitimate source in an attempt to trick the user into taking an action.

phishing campaign A broad initiative that uses a variety of tools to train users to resist phishing attacks.

physical controls Controls that implement security in a defined structure and location.

physical isolation Separating a network from all other networks or the Internet.

physical penetration testing A penetration test that examines the physical environment.

platform diversity Using multiple different devices to host or serve an application or a service.

playbook A list of specific actions to take for threats.

policy A formal statement that outlines specific requirements or rules that must be met based on a decision by a governing body.

policy automation An automated process for referring to policies for approval.

policy engine A component of a zero-trust architecture that provides input to make the decision whether to grant access for a request.

policy-driven access control Preventing unauthorized access to data and services by making access control enforcement as precise and granular as possible.

port security Configuring switches to limit the number of MAC addresses that can be learned on ports, preventing the MAC address table from being overwhelmed.

port selection Opening the correct ports on devices for remote access.

power A security constraint in which a system lacks sufficient power to perform strong security measures.

preparation An incident response process step of equipping IT staff, management, and users to handle potential incidents when they arise.

preservation of evidence Ensuring that important proof is not corrupted or even destroyed.

pressure sensor An electronic device that is used to detect if a person or object has entered a restricted area.

pretexting Obtaining private information through social engineering.

preventive controls Controls used to prevent the threat from coming in contact with the vulnerability.

prioritize To treat one item as more important than another.

private Restricted data with a medium level of confidentiality.

privilege escalation An attack in which the threat actor gains illicit access of elevated rights or privileges beyond what is entitled for a user.

probability The extent to which an event is likely to occur.

procedure A document that provides detailed mandatory steps that a user needs to follow in order to comply with a policy.

processor A proxy who acts on behalf of a data controller.

produce time efficiency A benefit of automation that can improve productivity by reducing the needed time to complete a task.

proprietary Relating to ownership.

Protected EAP (PEAP) An EAP method designed to simplify the deployment of 802.1x by using Microsoft Windows logins and passwords.

protocol selection Selecting the best networking protocol to use for remote access.

provisioning Initially setting up user accounts.

proxy servers Network devices that act as substitutes on behalf of another device.

public Data for which there is no risk of release.

public key infrastructure (PKI) The underlying infrastructure for the management of keys and digital certificates at scale.

published/documented An indicator of attack in which evidence from external sources can be used to identify an attack.

Q

qualitative risk analysis An approach that uses an "educated guess" based on observation.

quantitative risk analysis An approach that attempts to create "hard" numbers associated with the risk of an element in a system by using historical data.

quarantine Isolating systems that have been compromised.

questionnaires Annual surveys about supply-chain security protections in force.

R

race condition Two concurrent threads of execution access a shared resource simultaneously, resulting in unintended consequences.

radio frequency identification (RFID) A wireless set of standards used to transmit information from paper-based tags to a proximity reader.

ransomware Malicious software designed to extort money from victims in exchange for their endpoint device to be restored to its normal working state.

real-time operating system (RTOS) An operating system that is specifically designed for an SoC in an embedded system.

recognize phishing attempts A goal of awareness training to identify phishing.

record-level encryption Applying cryptography to database records.

recovery An incident response process step of ensuring no threat remains, permitting affected systems to return to normal operation; also, restoring copied data.

recovery point objective (RPO) The maximum length of time that an organization can tolerate between backups.

recovery time objective (RTO) The length of time it will take to recover data that has been backed up.

recurring assessment A risk assessment that is done on a calendar basis.

recurring training Continued training.

reduce reaction time A benefit of automation that can dramatically decrease the time needed to react to an attack.

reflection attacks A type of DDoS attack in which data is first directed at other devices or services.

regulated data Data in which external stipulations are placed on it.

regulatory (audits) Requirements set forth by outside bodies.

regulatory (governance) An agency responsible for distributing and enforcing government directives.

remote access Accessing a network infrastructure from a location other than the campus on which the organization is located.

removable devices Media devices like a USB flash drive.

removal of unnecessary software Deleting software that is not essential to an operation in order to eliminate an attack vector.

replay An attack that copies data and then uses it.

replication Continuously copying data.

reporting (digital forensics) A detailed written description of the acquisition and analysis of evidence.

reporting (security monitoring) Generating documentation based on the results of monitoring activities.

reporting (vulnerability scanning) Distributing the results of a vulnerability scan to the appropriate parties.

reporting and monitoring Evaluation and analysis of training.

reputation score A score assigned to a website that reflects its relative safety.

reputational damage Negative perceptions that are the result of not following compliance standards.

rescanning Performing another vulnerability scan as validation of remediation.

resilience The ability to resist attacks.

resource automation provisioning Creating and setting up an IT infrastructure automatically for systems.

resource consumption An indicator of attack in which system resources such as memory or processing capabilities are suddenly depleted.

resource inaccessibility An indicator of attack in which a large-scale attack can block system resources from being accessed.

resource reuse A virtualization vulnerability in which physical resources that are not properly emptied could expose sensitive data to another VM.

resources/funding Attribute of threat actors of an extensive network of resources.

responding to reported suspicious messages A goal of awareness training to encourage users to resist phishing attacks.

responsibility matrix A table that lists the various security duties of the user and the cloud provider.

responsible disclosure program A practice of large enterprises to pay security researchers who uncover security bugs in their products and then privately report them.

responsiveness A security constraint in which IoT devices that require immediate responsiveness to inputs are crippled by adding security features.

restricted Data that is not available to the general public.

retention The length of time that data should be kept.

reuse Using the same password on multiple accounts.

revenge Threat actor's motivation of avenging by retaliation.

RFID cloning Capturing data through RFID and then transferring the data to another RFID tag.

right to be forgotten The legal right to have user private data erased.

right-to-audit clause Part of a third-party agreement to verify results of an audit.

risk A situation that involves exposure to some type of danger.

risk appetite The total risk that the organization can bear in a given risk profile.

risk exposure factor The probability of the risk occurring multiplied by the total loss on the occurrence of the risk.

risk identification A process to identify and assess the factors that may place in jeopardy the success of a project or reaching a stated goal.

risk impact Determining the impact of a risk.

risk owners Those responsible for an asset.

risk register A list of potential threats and associated risks.

risk reporting Representing risks identified through a risk assessment.

risk threshold The maximum amount of risk that can be tolerated.

risk tolerance The level of risk that an organization can accept per individual risk to achieve a result.

risk transference A security constraint in which shifting risk and responsibility from one area of oversight to another results in security vulnerabilities.

risky Behavior that carries a high risk.

rogue AP An unauthorized AP that allows an attacker to bypass many of the network security configurations and opens the network and its users to attacks.

Role-Based Access Control (RBAC) An access control scheme that is considered a more "real-world" access control that is based on a user's job function within an organization.

root cause analysis (RCA) The process of discovering the origin cause of a security event.

root of trust Tracing a certificate back to the highest level of a CA.

rootkit Malware that can hide its presence and the presence of other malware on the device.

router A network device that can forward frames across different computer networks.

Rule-Based Access Control An access control scheme that can dynamically assign roles to subjects based on a set of rules defined by a custodian.

rules Specific criteria to accept or deny packets.

rules of engagement Expectations around how parties interact at all times in a relationship.

S

salting Adding a random string to a hash algorithm for enhanced security.

sanctions A penalty such as withholding payments for not following compliance standards.

sandbox A container in which an application can be run so that it does not impact the underlying OS.

sanitization Cleaning a device of its data.

scalability A security constraint in which increasing the size and scope of an IoT device introduces new vulnerabilities.

scanning A monitoring activity that is a frequent and ongoing process, often automated, for continuously searching for evidence of an attack.

screened subnet Using a device to limit the protected internal network from the open external network.

secure access service edge (SASE) The convergence of several security services into a single, cloud-delivered service model.

secure baseline A standard of normal activities.

secure communication Protected remote access communication.

secure cookie A cookie that is only sent to the server with an encrypted request over the secure HTTPS protocol.

secure email gateway (SEG) A device through which incoming email is filtered.

secure enclave A technology for Apple and Android devices similar to TPM for PCs.

secured zone A secure location in a zero-trust architecture.

securely scale A benefit of automation of adding additional appliances to scale operations.

Security Assertion Markup Language (SAML) An Extensible Markup Language (XML) standard that allows secure web domains to exchange user authentication and authorization data.

Security Content Automation Protocols (SCAP) Open security standards that can help automate vulnerability management and determine whether the enterprise is compliant with required policies.

security groups A function that allows control over all inbound and outbound traffic to a particular cloud resource.

security guards Humans who patrol and monitor restricted areas.

Security Information and Event Management (SIEM) A product that consolidates real-time security monitoring and management of security information with analysis and reporting of security events.

security key A dongle inserted into a USB port (Windows and Apple) or Lightning port (Apple) or held near the device (such as a smartphone using near-field communication [NFC]). The key contains all the necessary cryptographic information to authenticate the user.

security zones Separate subnets for enhancing security.

Security-Enhanced Linux (SELinux) A security architecture for Linux systems that allows administrators to have more control over who can access the system.

segmentation Dividing a network into multiple subnets or segments with each acting as its own small network to improve monitoring and enhance security. Also, separating the most sensitive data.

selection of effective controls Choosing productive safeguards or countermeasures to limit the exposure of an asset to a danger.

self-assessments Inwardly focused audits on an organization.

self-signed A signed digital certificate that does not depend on any higher-level authority for authentication.

Sender Policy Framework (SPF) An email authentication method that identifies the MTA email servers that have been authorized to send email for a domain.

sensitive Data that could cause catastrophic harm to the company if disclosed, such as technical specifications for a new product.

sensor A device that detects or measures a physical property and responds to it.

server A device that distributes resources and services to devices connected to the network.

serverless A cloud infrastructure in which the capacity planning, installation, setup, and management are all invisible to the user because the cloud provider handles them.

service disruption Threat actor's motivation of obstructing the normal business electronic processes.

service providers Businesses that furnish solutions or services to users and organizations.

service-level agreement A service contract between a vendor and a client that specifies what services will be provided, the responsibilities of each party, and any guarantees of service.

shadow IT Process of bypassing corporate approval for technology purchases.

Short Message Service (SMS) Messaging that uses a cellular network and is typically sent by a cell phone.

sideloading Downloading unofficial and unapproved apps.

signatures Known attack patterns.

Simple Network Management Protocol (SNMP) trap An unsolicited message or notification sent about critical events in the managed device.

simulation An incident response testing exercise that is a hands-on simulation exercise using a realistic scenario to thoroughly test each step of the plan.

Single Loss Expectancy (SLE) The expected monetary loss every time a risk occurs.

single point of failure A disadvantage of automation that is an overreliance so that an issue could cause the entire process to abruptly cease.

single sign-on (SSO) Using one authentication credential to access multiple accounts or applications.

site survey An in-depth examination and analysis of a WLAN site.

situation awareness Determining what is so unexpected or unintentional it becomes risky behavior.

smishing A social engineering attack that uses SMS to send fraudulent text messages.

snapshot Taking a "picture" of the state of the data repeatedly.

social engineering A means of eliciting information or convincing a user to take action.

software development lifecycle (SDLC) policy A policy that outlines how applications should be developed.

software provider Type of supply chain for distributing computer software.

software-defined network (SDN) A network that virtualizes parts of the physical network so that it can be more quickly and easily reconfigured.

software-defined wide area network (SD-WAN) A virtualized service that connects and extends enterprise WAN networks over large geographical distances.

something you are An authentication method based on the features and characteristics of an individual.

something you have A type of authentication credential based on the approved user having a specific item in their possession.

something you know Authentication based on something the user knows but no one else knows.

somewhere you are Authentication based on where the user is located.

spyware Tracking software that is deployed without the consent or control of the user.

SQL injection (SQLi) An attack that inserts statements to manipulate a database server.

stakeholders Individuals who can impact the perception of an asset and if it should be used.

standard A document that specifies the uniform uses of specific technologies or settings for secure configurations.

standard operating procedures Normal day-by-day business processes.

static code analysis Analyzing and testing software from a security perspective before the source code is compiled.

steganography Hiding the existence of data within another type of file, such as an image file.

subject A user in a zero-trust architecture.

supervisory control and data acquisition (SCADA) A system that controls multiple industrial control systems (ICS).

suppliers First step in a supply chain that provides raw materials.

supply chain Network that moves a product from its creation to the end-user.

supply-chain analysis An evaluation of the steps in a supply chain.

switch A device that connects network devices and has a degree of intelligence.

symmetric cryptographic algorithm Encryption that uses a single key to encrypt and decrypt a message.

system A device in a zero-trust architecture.

system/process audit An evaluation of both the devices that are used and the processes to protect those devices.

T

tabletop An incident response testing exercise that is a monthly 30-minute discussion of a scenario conducted in an informal and stress-free environment.

target of evaluation (TOE) A system, product, and its documentation that is the subject of a security evaluation.

technical controls Controls that are incorporated as part of hardware, software, or firmware.

technical debt A disadvantage of automation that is a result of a problem not being immediately addressed.

technology capacity planning Capacity planning for predicting the future number of devices needed.

temporal accounts   One-time access to an account.

test results   An evaluation of information security.

testing   Conducting simulated exercises to make necessary adjustments.

third party   An entity that is trusted by others.

third-party risk management   Risks associated with third parties outside the organization.

third-party sources   Entities that offer their own threat intelligence as a paid subscription service.

third-party vendors   External sources that provide cloud security controls.

threat actor   Individual or entity who is responsible for attacks.

threat feeds   Input into the scanning software to be used in comparison with the enterprise's security defenses.

threat hunting   An emergent activity that combines a proactive, repetitive, and predominantly human identification of a cyber invasion to an IT network or endpoints.

threat scope reduction   Minimizes threats against assets.

ticket creation   Generating a special document or record.

time of check (TOC) to time of use (TOU)   A race condition in which a threat actor can influence the state of the resource between a check.

time-of-day restrictions   Access levels that are bound to a specific window of time.

tokenization   Obfuscation of sensitive data elements into a random string of characters.

trade secret data   Enterprise data that is undisclosed.

transfer   Transferring the responsibility of a risk to a third party.

Transport Layer Security (TLS)   A widespread cryptographic transport algorithm that replaces SSL.

transport method   The means through which remote access occurs.

transport/communication encryption   Cryptographic algorithms that are used to protect data in transit.

trends   New attacks for which there is no existing signature.

Trojan   An executable program that masquerades as performing a benign activity but also does something malicious.

Trusted Platform Module (TPM)   An international standard for cryptoprocessors.

tunneling   Data that is encapsulated within a secure outer shell.

typo squatting   Registering the domain names of sites that are spelled similarly to actual sites.

U

ultrasonic sensor   An electronic device that uses sound to measure how far away a target object is located.

unexpected   Not anticipated.

unified threat management (UTM)   An integrated device that combines several security functions.

unintentional   Not done on purpose.

uninterruptible power supply (UPS)   A device that maintains power to equipment in case of an interruption in the primary electrical power source.

Universal Resource Locator (URL) scanning   Scanning the web for malicious websites and then creating a database of URLs to be blocked.

unknown environment   A penetration test in which the testers have no knowledge of the network and no special privileges.

unsecure networks   Wired and wireless networks that lack security.

unskilled attackers   Individuals who want to perform attacks yet lack the technical knowledge to carry them out.

unsupported systems and applications   Computer systems and applications no longer supported by the organization that are often ignored and do not receive security updates.

updating diagrams   New diagrams that illustrate the flow of changes.

updating policies/procedures   Indicating which organization policies or procedures need to be adjusted.

user automation provisioning   Creating and setting up an IT infrastructure automatically for individuals.

user behavior analytics   Gathering data for monitoring user behavior.

using legacy applications   Accessing applications that are no longer in widespread use.

V

validation of remediation Corroborate that the vulnerabilities have indeed been properly addressed.

vendor monitoring Oversight of a vendor.

vendors Entities in a supply chain who purchase products for resale.

verification Analyzing a vulnerability scan for validation of its accuracy.

version control Software tools that assist with documentation and prevent more than one person from making changes to code at the same time.

video surveillance Monitoring activity captured by cameras that transmit a signal to a specific and limited set of receivers.

virtual private network (VPN) A security technology that enables authorized users to use an unsecured public network in a secure fashion.

virtualization A means of managing and presenting computer resources by function without regard to their physical layout or location.

virus Software that infects a computer with malware.

vishing Voice phishing that uses a telephone call to contact the victim.

VM escape The ability of a VM to break out from the contained environment and directly interact with the host OS.

volume-level encryption Applying cryptography to a volume of a hard drive.

vulnerability classification A system of categories for similar vulnerabilities.

vulnerability scan An ongoing automated process used to identify weaknesses and monitor information security progress.

vulnerability scanner Automated tool that identifies all IT assets and security risks.

vulnerable software Software that contains one or more security vulnerabilities.

W

walkthrough A review by IT personnel of the steps in an incident response plan.

war Threat actor's motivation of armed hostile combat.

warm site A remote site that contains computer equipment but does not have active Internet or telecommunication facilities and does not have backups of data.

watering hole attack An attack directed toward a small group of specific individuals.

web application firewall (WAF) A firewall that filters by examining the applications using HTTP.

web filtering Software that monitors the websites users are browsing.

web-based attacks Application attacks directed at programs running on Internet web servers.

wildcard digital certificate A certificate used to validate a main domain along with all subdomains.

wireless local area network (WLAN) A network designed to replace or supplement a wired local area network (LAN).

work order (WO)/statement of work (SOW) A document within a contract that describes the work requirements for a specific project along with its performance and design expectations.

workstation A special computer designed for scientific or highly technical applications.

worm A malicious program that uses a computer network to replicate.

Z

zero trust A strategic initiative about networks that is designed to prevent successful attacks by threat actors who are already within a network.

zero-day Vulnerability for which there are no days of advanced warning.

Index